INTERNATIONAL INVESTMENT LAW IN THE COMMONWEALTH CARIBBEAN

This textbook provides the first comprehensive pedagogical treatment of international investment law from a Caribbean perspective, addressing a critical gap in legal education resources.

International Investment Law in the Commonwealth Caribbean employs rigorous doctrinal analysis that places Caribbean experiences at its centre, while also building readers' analytical capabilities for engaging with complex issues in international economic law. The book is unique in showing how investment law operates in the context of small island developing states, making abstract legal concepts accessible through analysis of Caribbean case law, while also developing critical thinking skills. Each chapter integrates traditional black-letter law instruction with critical analysis, drawing on Third World Approaches to International Law (TWAIL) and post-colonial theory, thereby preparing readers to evaluate competing perspectives on investor protection, state sovereignty, and developmental needs.

Unlike existing investment law textbooks that marginalize developing country experiences, this textbook examines Caribbean states' encounters with international investment arbitration. The book analyses landmark cases including *RSM Production v Grenada*, *Peter Allard v Barbados*, and *Michael Lee-Chin v Dominican Republic*, illustrating fundamental legal principles while exposing structural inequalities in contemporary investment governance.

International Investment Law in the Commonwealth Caribbean is an essential reading for all students of Caribbean law and international economic law.

Jason Haynes is Associate Professor of Law at the University of Birmingham, UK

Commonwealth Caribbean Law

The Commonwealth Caribbean Law Series is the only series of law books that covers the jurisdiction of the English speaking Caribbean nations. The first titles in the series were published in 1995 to acclaim from academics, practitioners and the judiciary in the region. Several editions followed, and they have now become essential reading for those learning and practising Caribbean law.

This must have series is required holdings for any law library specialising in Caribbean legal information.

Titles in this series include:

Commonwealth Caribbean Tort Law
Gilbert Kodilinye

Commonwealth Caribbean Business Law
Natalie Persadie and Rajendra Ramlogan

Commonwealth Caribbean Corporate Governance
Edited by Suzanne Ffolkes-Goldson

Commonwealth Caribbean Family Law

Husband, Wife and Cohabitant
Karen Nunez-Tesheira

Commonwealth Caribbean Civil Procedure (Fourth Edition)
Gilbert Kodilinye and Vanessa Kodilinye

Commonwealth Caribbean Company Law
Andrew Burgess

Commonwealth Caribbean Sports Law
Jason Haynes and J. Tyrone Marcus

Commonwealth Caribbean Criminal Practice and Procedure (Fifth Edition)
Dana Seetahal, with updates from Roger Ramgoolam

Commonwealth Caribbean Insurance Law
Lesley Walcott

Commonwealth Caribbean Property Law (Fifth Edition)
Gilbert Kodilinye

Commonwealth Caribbean Tort Law (Sixth Edition)
Gilbert Kodilinye and Natalie Corthésy

International Investment Law in the Commonwealth Caribbean
Jason Haynes

For more information about this series please visit: https://www.routledge.com/Commonwealth-Caribbean-Law/book-series/CAV8

INTERNATIONAL INVESTMENT LAW IN THE COMMONWEALTH CARIBBEAN

Jason Haynes

Routledge
Taylor & Francis Group
LONDON AND NEW YORK

First edition published 2026
by Routledge
4 Park Square, Milton Park, Abingdon, Oxon, OX14 4RN

and by Routledge
605 Third Avenue, New York, NY 10158

Routledge is an imprint of the Taylor & Francis Group, an informa business

British Library Cataloguing-in-Publication Data
A catalogue record for this book is available from the British Library

Library of Congress Cataloging-in-Publication Data
Names: Haynes, Jason author
Title: International investment law in the commonwealth caribbean / Jason Haynes.
Description: 1. | New York : Routledge, 2026. | Series: Commonwealth caribbean law | Includes bibliographical references and index.
Identifiers: LCCN 2025049987 | ISBN 9781041228349 hardback | ISBN 9781041229254 paperback | ISBN 9781003734185 ebook
Subjects: LCSH: Investments, Foreign—Law and legislation—Caribbean Area | Arbitration (International law) | International commercial arbitration
Classification: LCC KGJ101.B87 H39 2026
LC record available at https://lccn.loc.gov/2025049987

ISBN: 978-1-041-22834-9 (hbk)
ISBN: 978-1-041-22925-4 (pbk)
ISBN: 978-1-003-73418-5 (ebk)

DOI: 10.4324/9781003734185

Typeset in Times New Roman
by Apex CoVantage, LLC

Access the Instructor Resources: www.routledge.com/9781041229254

CONTENTS

ACKNOWLEDGEMENTS

The completion of this book would not have been possible without the support and sacrifice of my lovely wife, Dr Chloe Walker. I am also immensely grateful to Dr Szilárd Gáspár-Szilágyi for his humour and thoughtful insights on the subject of international investment law on which we mutually share a profound interest. I am also especially grateful to my outstanding former students – Carissa Rodulfo (who not only greatly assisted with the research but also editing of the manuscript), Jamoy Morrison, Reyhan Jean, Sarah Baksh, Kara John, and Ivana Javis for their sterling contribution to this book through their incisive research. I am indebted.

Most of all, I wish to thank God for his great providence, and for giving me the strength to see this work through to completion, notwithstanding a great number of disappointments and frustrations along the way.

PREFACE

The Commonwealth Caribbean presents one of the most compelling yet under-researched case studies in contemporary international investment law. Despite collectively negotiating over seventy-five international investment agreements over four decades and being subject to numerous high-profile investor-state arbitral awards, the region has remained largely peripheral to mainstream investment law scholarship. This book addresses this critical gap by providing the first comprehensive analysis of international investment law from a distinctly Caribbean perspective.

The inspiration for this work emerged from a recognition that existing scholarship, while extensive in scope, has systematically overlooked the unique experiences, challenges, and perspectives of small island developing states, particularly those in the Caribbean region. Despite the fact that the region's integration into the international investment regime during the 1980s and 1990s occurred under circumstances of profound asymmetry – what scholars have termed 'imposed bilateralism', the implications of this coercive process for contemporary investment governance have received insufficient scholarly attention. From the extraordinary one-hour negotiation of the Grenada-USA BIT following the 1983 invasion to the recent proliferation of investor-state disputes challenging fundamental regulatory measures, Caribbean states have increasingly found themselves at the intersection of powerful global economic forces and their own developmental imperatives.

This book emerges from five years of intensive research involving extensive analysis of Caribbean international investment agreements, arbitral awards, domestic legislation, and sustained engagement with practitioners, policymakers, and students throughout the region. The research revealed not only the remarkable extent of the Caribbean's integration into global investment governance structures but also the profound tensions between investor protection and the regulatory autonomy essential for sustainable development in small island states facing climate change, economic vulnerability, and limited fiscal resources.

The central argument advanced throughout these pages is that the current international investment law regime, while ostensibly neutral in its application, systematically disadvantages developing states through structural asymmetries that constrain policy space, impose substantial litigation costs, and perpetuate colonial-era patterns of economic subordination. Drawing on decolonial scholarship and empirical evidence from Caribbean experiences, the book demonstrates how investment treaties function not merely as technical legal instruments but as mechanisms that can limit democratic governance and sustainable development.

Yet, the work is not merely a critique. It is intended to be constructive contribution to the ongoing global conversation about investment law reform, offering concrete recommendations for rebalancing the investor-state relationship to better serve developmental objectives while maintaining meaningful protections for foreign capital. The book's examination of the UNCITRAL Working Group III reform process, innovative treaty models like the Guyana-Brazil BIT, and emerging approaches to sustainable development integration provides a roadmap for transforming international investment law into a more equitable framework.

This book is written for students, practitioners, academics, and policymakers seeking to understand how international investment law operates in practice within small developing economies. It is my hope that by centring Caribbean experiences and perspectives, this work will contribute to the decolonisation of international investment law scholarship while providing essential guidance for navigating the evolving landscape of global investment governance.

Dr Jason Haynes
September 2025

TABLE OF CASES

TABLE OF LEGISLATION

CHAPTER 1

INTRODUCTION: UNDERSTANDING INTERNATIONAL INVESTMENT LAW IN THE CARIBBEAN

The English-speaking Caribbean[1] presents a compelling case study for understanding the complexities and contradictions of contemporary international investment law. Foreign direct investment patterns in the region in 2023 revealed significant variation across territories, with offshore financial centres continuing to dominate flows – the British Virgin Islands attracted $39.9 billion while the Cayman Islands received $28.1 billion, reflecting their roles as major international financial centres.[2] Among independent English-speaking Caribbean countries, the picture was more modest: Jamaica recorded $376.5 million in FDI inflows, Antigua and Barbuda received $327.9 million, and Barbados attracted $224.9 million, while Trinidad and Tobago experienced net outflows of $1.6 billion.[3] Guyana stands as a notable outlier, with foreign direct investments experiencing 47% growth in the first six months of 2022 to nearly $2 billion, driven primarily by transformative offshore oil development.[4] FDI inflows to the English-speaking Caribbean are primarily concentrated in critical minerals and commodities for clean energy technologies, renewable energy projects, including green hydrogen and green ammonia production, services (particularly information and communication technology), basic metals and metal products, and infrastructure development. The primary capital-exporting countries are the Caribbean's traditional partners: the United States, Spain, the Kingdom of the Netherlands, and Luxembourg. That said, despite broader regional growth of 6% in 2023 and flows to the Caribbean Community tripling since 2018,[5] the stagnation of greenfield projects, the economic uncertainty occasioned by the Covid-19 pandemic, and the ever-present threat of investor-state arbitration claims highlight the complexities facing these small island developing states.[6]

1 The primary focus of this book is on the independent islands of the English-speaking Caribbean, though it has broader relevance to the Spanish, French, and Dutch Caribbean, and, indeed, small island developing states. The independent English-speaking Caribbean islands include Antigua and Barbuda, The Bahamas, Barbados, Dominica, Grenada, Jamaica, Saint Kitts and Nevis, Saint Lucia, Saint Vincent and the Grenadines, and Trinidad and Tobago. These nations gained independence from the United Kingdom primarily between the 1960s and 1980s.

2 UN Conference on Trade and Development, 'World Investment Report: Regional Trends – Latin America and the Caribbean' (UNCTAD 2024) https://unctad.org/system/files/non-official-document/wir2024-regional_trends_lac_en.pdf.

3 UN Conference on Trade and Development, 'World Investment Report: Fact Sheet' (UNCTAD 2024) <https://unctad.org/system/files/non-official-document/wir2024_factsheet_lac.pdf>.

4 US Department of State, 'Investment Climate Statement for Guyana' (2024) <https://www.state.gov/reports/2024-investment-climate-statements/guyana/#:~:text=Guyana's%20industrial%20policy%20is%20rooted,and%20diversify%20its%20economic%20base>.

5 World Bank, 'Foreign Direct Investment Database' (2023) <https://data.worldbank.org/indicator/BX.KLT.DINV.CD.WD?locations=ZJ>

6 United Nations Economic Commission for Latin America and the Caribbean, 'Foreign Direct Investment in Latin America and the Caribbean Fell by 9.9% in 2023, but Amount Received is Above the Average in the Last Decade' (ECLAC 1 August 2024) <https://www.cepal.org/en/pressreleases/eclac-foreign-direct-investment-latin-america-and-caribbean-fell-99–2023-amount>.

DOI: 10.4324/9781003734185-1

This book addresses a critical gap in international investment law scholarship by providing the first comprehensive analysis of the field from a distinctly Caribbean perspective. While the region has collectively negotiated over seventy international investment agreements (IIAs) spanning four decades, no previous work has systematically examined the international investment architecture from a Caribbean perspective. In this context, employing a primarily doctrinal approach that draws on regional IIAs, arbitral awards, and domestic legislation, this book aims to critically assess how international investment law operates within the Commonwealth Caribbean, while identifying reform pathways that better align the fragile investment framework with regional development imperatives. Through systematic analysis of substantive and procedural standards of protection as applied in the Caribbean context, the book seeks to contribute to the decolonisation of international investment law scholarship by centring the Caribbean, while providing essential guidance for students, practitioners, academics, and policymakers navigating the evolving landscape of investment governance in small island developing states.

I. THE EVOLUTION OF THE INTERNATIONAL INVESTMENT REGIME

The contemporary international investment architecture represents the culmination of centuries of evolution in the protection of foreign capital, with roots extending deep into the medieval period, and later into the colonial period.[7] Consonant with the development of international law, international investment law gained momentum with the emergence of European empires extending their reach to the Third World, in so doing exploiting lands, racialised peoples and their resources,[8] while developing European markets. The colonial period was characterised by extra-territorial legal protection offered to foreign investors through the mechanism of Friendship, Commerce and Navigation treaties (FCNs),[9] which entitled them to more favourable treatment than locals.

The first modern BIT was concluded between Germany and Pakistan in 1959, entering into force in 1962.[10] This agreement established the template for subsequent investment treaties,[11] including many of the Caribbean BITs that will be discussed in this book, providing comprehensive protections for foreign investors while imposing minimal corresponding obligations on them. Other European powers quickly followed this model, which was no doubt hastened by the mid-1970s oil crisis and widespread expropriations in developing

7 Jeanrique Fahner, 'The Contested History of International Investment Law: From a Problematic Past to Current Controversies' (2015) 17(3) *International Community Law Review* 373.

8 Antony Anghie, 'The Evolution of International Law: Colonial and Postcolonial Realities' (2006) 27(5) *Third World Quarterly* 739.

9 Wolfgang Alschner, 'Americanization of the BIT BIT Universe: The Influence of Friendship, Commerce and Navigation (FCN) Treaties on Modern Investment Treaty Law' (2013) 5 *Goettingen Journal of International Law* 455.

10 Ingo Venzke and Philipp Günther, 'International Investment Protection Made in Germany? On the Domestic and Foreign Policy Dynamics Behind the first BITs' (2022) 33(4) *European Journal of International Law* 1183.

11 Jeswald Salacuse, 'BIT by BIT: The Growth of Bilateral Investment Treaties and Their Impact on Foreign Investment in Developing Countries' (1990) *The International Lawyer* 655.

states, especially Venezuela.[12] The United States, by contrast, initially preferred free trade arrangements with investment chapters, such as the North American Free Trade Area (NAFTA),[13] but later became a more active participant in the bilateral investment treaty system.

The post-colonial period witnessed significant efforts by newly independent states to assert control over their natural resources and foreign investment, leading to tensions that would ultimately catalyse their adoption, albeit reluctantly, of BITs. While the Declaration of Permanent Sovereignty over Natural Resources (PSNR) granted host states rights of ownership over natural resources found in their territories and urged that the international minimum standard should not be used to undermine the self-regulatory capacity of newly independent countries,[14] the subsequent New International Economic Order (NIEO),[15] which asserted that developing countries were entitled to regulate and control the activities of multinational enterprises operating within their territories, ultimately failed.[16]

The integration of Caribbean countries into the international investment law system occurred primarily during the 1980s and 1990s, a period characterised by significant external pressures and asymmetric power relations. Indeed, most of the 70 BITs concluded by Commonwealth Caribbean countries to date are older generation BITs, which were negotiated either as part of UNCTAD's mass 'BITs facilitation events',[17] or at the behest of Western countries, particularly the United States. For Schneiderman, the 'negotiations' that led to the conclusion of these BITs reflect 'an inequality in bargaining power, conjoined with an institutional incapacity to be heard in international arenas', which 'rendered the voices of poorer States barely heard by wealthier ones'.[18] In short, Caribbean countries and their Third World counterparts were subject to 'imposed bilateralism'.[19] In this regard, the BITs entered into by Caribbean states, 'though premised on a semblance of equality of bargaining power, barely hid the flagrant inequalities of the relationships expressed in these leonine treaties.'[20]

The coercive nature of this process is perhaps most starkly illustrated by the circumstances surrounding the negotiation of the Grenada-USA BIT. In this connection, Vandevelde recalls that discussions leading to the conclusion of the Grenada BIT had commenced two years after the August 1983 invasion of Grenada and the restoration of democracy. Remarkably, he recalls, the Grenada BIT was concluded in a 'single, hour-long negotiating session that

12 Wojciech Ostrowski, 'Oil Nationalism, Decolonization and Fragmentation' in Roland Dannreuther (ed), *Handbook on Oil and International Relations* (Edward Elgar Publishing 2022) 192.

13 David Gantz, 'Resolution of Investment Disputes Under the North American Free Trade Agreement' (1993) 10 *Arizona Journal of International and Comparative Law* 335.

14 Karol Gess, 'Permanent Sovereignty Over Natural Resources: An Analytical Review of the United Nations Declaration and Its Genesis' (1964) 13(2) *International & Comparative Law Quarterly* 398.

15 Antony Anghie, 'Legal Aspects of the New International Economic Order' (2015) 6(1) *Humanity: An International Journal of Human Rights, Humanitarianism, and Development* 145.

16 Eric Allen Engle, 'The Failure of the Nation State and the New International Economic Order: Multiple Converging Crises Present Opportunity to Elaborate a New *Jus Gentium*' (2003) 16 *Thomas Law Review* 187.

17 Olof Karsegard, Pedro Bravo and Hubert Blom, *UNCTAD Work Programme on Capacity Building in Developing Countries on Issues in International Investment Agreements: Final in-depth Evaluation Report* (United Nations 2006) Annex 5.

18 ibid.

19 ibid.

20 ibid. 'Leonine treaties' is a term borrowed from Bedjaoui.

resulted in a treaty identical to the 1984 model negotiating text'.[21] This extraordinarily truncated negotiation process reveals the extent to which Caribbean states were expected to accept predetermined terms rather than engage in meaningful bilateral negotiation.

The broader context of Caribbean BIT negotiations during this period was shaped by structural adjustment programmes and conditionality imposed by international financial institutions. Alvarez, building on Vandevelde's scholarship, argues that the circumstances surrounding the signing of BITs by Latin American and Caribbean countries, especially in the 1980s and 1990s, were coercive in nature.[22] He observes in this connection:

> for many, a BIT relationship is hardly a voluntary, uncoerced transaction. They feel that they must enter into the arrangement, or that they would be foolish not to, since they have already made the internal adjustments required for BIT participation in order to comply with demands made by, for example, the IMF.[23]

The result has been a systematic erosion of regulatory space that has gone far beyond Caribbean states could have imagined. Indeed, as will be demonstrated later in this chapter, the older generation BITs concluded by Caribbean states typically provide extensive protections for foreign investors while imposing minimal obligations and offering limited policy space for host state regulation. These agreements often include broad definitions of 'investment', expansive fair and equitable treatment obligations, comprehensive protection against expropriation, and asymmetrical investor-state dispute settlement mechanisms that generally allow only foreign investors to initiate arbitration against host states. In this connection, Caribbean states have increasingly found themselves as defendants in investor-state arbitration, often facing claims that challenge fundamental aspects of regulatory sovereignty. The cases involving telecommunications regulation in Belize,[24] renewable energy policy in Grenada,[25] and various other regulatory measures in other countries[26] demonstrate how investment treaties can constrain policy autonomy in ways that were likely not fully appreciated during the original negotiation process.

II. LEGAL FRAMEWORK ON FDI IN THE COMMONWEALTH CARIBBEAN

The Commonwealth Caribbean's approach to foreign investment protection has been crystallised into a multi-layered legal framework comprising BITs, free trade agreements (RTAs) with investment chapters, and domestic investment legislation. This framework reflects the region's strategic positioning as small island developing states hoping to use international investment agreements to incentivise foreign investors.

21 Kenneth Vandevelde, 'US Bilateral Investment Treaties: The Second Wave' (1992) 14 *Michigan Journal of International Law* 621, 635.

22 José Enrique Alvarez, 'Remarks by José E. Alvarez' (Proceedings of the ASIL Annual Meeting, vol 82, CUP 1988).

23 ibid 552.

24 *Dunkeld International Investment Ltd. v Government of Belize* (I), PCA Case No. 2010–13, Award, 28 June 2016.

25 *Grenada Private Power Limited and WRB Enterprises, Inc. v Grenada*, ICSID Case No. ARB/17/13, Award, 29 March 2020.

26 For example, *Peter Allard v The Government of Barbados*, PCA Case No. 2012–06, Award, 27 June 2016.

A. Bilateral Investment Treaties

The Commonwealth Caribbean has in place an extensive network of BITs; 70 BITs have been concluded over the space of four decades.[27] Of these treaties, 47 are currently in force (67%), 21 remain signed but not yet operative (30%), and two have been terminated (3%).[28] This high ratification rate arguably demonstrates the region's commitment to institutionalising investment protection through binding international law.

The Caribbean's engagement with BITs commenced with the Belize-United Kingdom agreement of April 30, 1982, which notably entered into force on the same day of signature. The temporal span extends to the most recent Ghana-Trinidad and Tobago BIT signed in September 2024, illustrating sustained engagement across 42 years. The chronological distribution reveals distinct phases: early agreements primarily with former colonial powers (1980s–1990s), followed by diversification toward European Union members and emerging economies (2000s–2010s), and recent engagement with Gulf states and Asian economies (2010s–2020s).

Interestingly, Germany is the most active developed country partner with 9 BITs concluded with Caribbean countries,[29] followed by the United Kingdom with eight agreements.[30] This pattern reflects both historical colonial relationships (UK) and contemporary economic partnerships (Germany's role as a major European home state for foreign investors). Other significant developed country partners include Switzerland (4 BITs), South Korea (3 BITs), and various European Union members, including France, Italy, Spain, the Netherlands, Austria, and BLEU (Belgium-Luxembourg Economic Union).

Among developing countries, China leads the way with 6 BITs concluded with Caribbean countries,[31] reflecting Beijing's Belt and Road Initiative and broader economic and diplomatic engagement.[32] Cuba has concluded 6 BITs with its English-speaking Caribbean neighbours, demonstrating pragmatic regional economic cooperation despite distinct political systems. The United Arab Emirates has also emerged as a significant partner with 5 BITs,[33] indicating growing Gulf investment interest in the Caribbean region. Despite geographic proximity and substantial economic ties, the United States has concluded only 3 BITs with Caribbean countries.[34] This limited engagement likely reflects the US preference for comprehensive free trade agreements over standalone investment treaties.

Caribbean BITs generally follow standard international templates incorporating the national treatment (NT) and most-favoured-nation (MFN) standards; fair and equitable treatment (FET) standard; full protection and security (FPS) standard; the guarantee against expropriation; free transfer of funds provisions; and investor-state dispute settlement

27 See 'International Investment Agreements Navigator' (UNCTAD).

28 These are: Barbados-Italy BIT (1995); India-Trinidad and Tobago BIT (2007).

29 Germany: 9 BITs (Antigua and Barbuda, Barbados, Dominica, Guyana, Jamaica, Saint Lucia, Saint Vincent and Grenadines, Trinidad and Tobago, and Belize).

30 United Kingdom: 8 BITs (Antigua and Barbuda, Barbados, Belize, Dominica, Grenada, Guyana, Jamaica, Saint Lucia, Trinidad and Tobago).

31 China: 6 BITs (Bahamas, Barbados, Guyana, Jamaica, Trinidad and Tobago).

32 Richard Bernal, 'The Growing Economic Presence of China in the Caribbean' (2015) 38(9) *The World Economy* 1409.

33 United Arab Emirates: 5 BITs (Antigua and Barbuda, Barbados, Belize, Dominica, Saint Kitts and Nevis, Saint Vincent and Grenadines).

34 Grenada, Jamaica, and Trinidad and Tobago.

mechanisms. In respect of the latter, most Caribbean BITs incorporate investor-state arbitration clauses, typically referencing ICSID, UNCITRAL, or other international arbitration forums, representing a significant commitment to binding third-party adjudication while effectively limiting sovereign immunity in investment matters.

The 21 signed but not-yet-in-force agreements indicate ongoing domestic ratification processes or pending fulfilment of entry-into-force conditions, suggesting expansion of the operational treaty network is possible and likely in future. The two terminated BITs (Barbados-Italy and India-Trinidad and Tobago) demonstrate that Caribbean states retain ultimate sovereignty over their investment treaty commitments despite the typically long-term nature of such agreements.

Recent BITs, including Guyana's BIT which it signed with Brazil, increasingly incorporate sustainable development considerations, environmental protections, and social responsibility provisions, reflecting evolving international standards and Caribbean priorities regarding climate change and sustainable development. Regrettably, CARICOM's Draft Template for Investment Chapters in External Trade Agreements, which contains many of these contemporary considerations, has not generated much interest among Caribbean states in terms of its adoption.

B. Free Trade Agreements with Investment Chapters

The Caribbean's engagement with Free Trade Agreements with Investment Chapters[35] has been far less pervasive, at least when compared to its engagement with BITs. The Agreement on Trade, Economic and Technical Cooperation between CARICOM and Venezuela (1992) represents an early regional approach to investment liberalisation and protection, providing in Article 9 that:

1. The Parties undertake to encourage the promotion and protection of investments by their nationals through the conclusion of bilateral investment treaties between the individual Member States of CARICOM and Venezuela, in accordance with national laws and legislation.

In the years that followed, the CARICOM-Dominican Republic FTA (1998) was adopted, which materialised this ambition, albeit in the context of another Contracting State, creating investment protections within a comprehensive trade agreement covering goods, services, and investment flows between CARICOM member states and the Dominican Republic. Meanwhile, the Agreement between CARICOM and Costa Rica (2004) further demonstrates the region's strategy of negotiating investment provisions within broader trade frameworks, extending Caribbean investment protection networks beyond immediate geographic neighbours. Separately, while technically a bilateral agreement, the Barbados-BLEU (Belgium

35 Examples of these at the international level include: North American Free Trade Agreement (NAFTA) (signed 1992, entered into force 1994) [replaced by the United States-Mexico-Canada Agreement (USMCA) in 2020]; Central America-Dominican Republic-United States Free Trade Agreement (CAFTA-DR) (signed 2004–2005); Energy Charter Treaty (ECT) (signed 1994, entered into force 1998); ASEAN Comprehensive Investment Agreement (ACIA) (signed 2009); Pacific Agreement on Closer Economic Relations Plus (PACER Plus) (signed 2017); Transatlantic Trade and Investment Partnership (TTIP) (negotiations suspended in 2016).

and Luxembourg) BIT (2009) reflects the complex interplay between bilateral and regional approaches, given BLEU's status as a customs union between Belgium and Luxembourg, illustrating how regional economic integration in Europe interfaces with Caribbean bilateral investment diplomacy.

C. National Investment Laws

Most Caribbean jurisdictions maintain dedicated investment promotion agencies with statutory authority to facilitate foreign investment.[36] These agencies typically operate under specific legislative mandates that provide streamlined approval processes for qualifying foreign investments; one-stop-shop services for investment applications and permits; and monitoring and aftercare services for established foreign investors. National investment laws typically maintain restrictions on foreign investment in sensitive sectors including telecommunications, utilities, strategic natural resources, and sometimes media and financial services. These restrictions often reflect similar restrictions found in IIAs.

Significantly, Caribbean National Investment Laws[37] offer a significant number of concessions, including tax holidays for qualifying investments, often ranging from 5–15 years; duty exemptions on imported equipment and raw materials; accelerated depreciation allowances; special economic zone provisions with enhanced incentive packages; and export processing zone arrangements with streamlined regulatory framework. These are aimed at enhancing the perceived attractiveness of the states in question.

III. SOURCES OF INTERNATIONAL INVESTMENT LAW

The sources of international investment law derive from the broader framework established under Article 38(1) of the Statute of the International Court of Justice (ICJ),[38] which identifies the fundamental sources of international law as treaties, international custom, general principles of law, and, subsidiarily, judicial decisions and the writings of the most highly qualified publicists. In practice, treaties (BITs/RTAs) are by far the most important source of international law relating to foreign investment.[39] That said, while treaties dominate contemporary investment law, customary international law continues to provide foundational principles, particularly the hotly contested 'international minimum standard' which has in some cases been collapsed into the fair and equitable treatment.[40] Meanwhile, general principles of international law, though less frequently invoked in investment disputes, provide additional sources of legal authority, particularly concepts such as good faith, proportionality,

36 Christian Volpe Martincus and Monika Sztajerowska, *How to Solve the Investment Promotion Puzzle: A Mapping of Investment Promotion Agencies in Latin America and the Caribbean and OECD Countries* (Vol. 735, Inter-American Development Bank 2019).

37 Guyana Investment Act 2004, Act No. 1 of 2004, Grenada Investment Promotion Act, Chapter 131B; Trinidad and Tobago Foreign Investment Act, Act No. 16 of 1990; The Investment Authority Act, 2006. No. 15 of 2006.

38 Statute of the International Court of Justice, 18th April 1946, 33 UNTS 993.

39 Moshe Hirsch, 'Sources of International Investment Law' in Andrea K. Bjorklund and August Reinisch (eds), *International Investment Law and Soft Law* (Edward Elgar Publishing 2012).

40 Hussein Haeri, 'A Tale of Two Standards: "Fair and Equitable Treatment" and the Minimum Standard in International Law' (2011) 27(1) *Arbitration International* 27.

and due process.[41] These principles often inform tribunals' interpretations of treaty provisions and fill gaps where treaty language may be ambiguous.[42]

Investment arbitration awards constitute an increasingly significant source of international investment law through the development of jurisprudential precedents,[43] despite the absence of a formal system of *stare decisis* in international arbitration.[44] Tribunals regularly cite previous awards as persuasive authority, creating *de facto* precedential effects (*jurisprudence constante*) that shape the interpretation and application of investment law principles.[45] The ICSID Convention provides the institutional framework for much of this jurisprudential development, as tribunals have jurisdiction over disputes 'arising directly out of an investment, between a Contracting State . . . and a national of another Contracting State'. The four prerequisites for ICSID jurisdiction include the existence of a legal dispute, an investment meeting the *Salini* test[46] (substantial commitment, significant duration, profit and risk elements, and contribution to host state development), disputing parties from different Contracting States, and written consent to ICSID jurisdiction. It is important to note, however, that not all disputes are resolved via ICSID arbitration; many, including a few from the Caribbean to date, are resolved by the Permanent Court of Arbitration, and, to a less extent ad hoc tribunals, through the application of the UNCITRAL Arbitration Rules.[47]

Beyond international investment agreements, investment contracts also serve as important sources of investor protection, sometimes referred to as 'concession agreements' or 'Build Operate and Transfer (BOT) agreements'.[48] As will be discussed further in the next chapter, these contracts often contain 'stabilisation clauses'[49] that promise that host states will not change their legal framework to the disadvantage of foreign investors over the duration of the investment project, creating contractual rights that may complement or supplement treaty-based protections. It is noteworthy that while investment contracts are generally governed by domestic law, their significance in international investment law derives from choice of forum clauses often included in such contracts that enable arbitration tribunals' jurisdiction over disputes,[50] effectively internationalizing what would otherwise be purely

41 Stephan Schill and Tarcisio Gazzini, 'General Principles of Law and International Investment Law' in Tarcisio Gazzini and Eric De Brabandere (eds), *International Investment Law: The Sources of Rights and Obligations* (Brill 2012) 133.

42 Tarcisio Gazzini, 'General Principles of Law in the Field of Foreign Investment' (2009) 10(1) *The Journal of World Investment & Trade* 103.

43 Zachary Douglas, 'Can a Doctrine of Precedent Be Justified in Investment Treaty Arbitration?' (2010) 25(1) *ICSID Review* 104.

44 Patrick Norton, 'The Role of Precedent in the Development of International Investment Law' (2018) 33(1) *ICSID Review-Foreign Investment Law Journal* 280.

45 Richard Chen, 'Precedent and Dialogue in Investment Treaty Arbitration' (2019) 60 *Harvard International Law Journal* 47.

46 Markus Petsche, 'The Application of the Salini Test Beyond Article 25 of the ICSID Convention: Analysis of Recent Trends in Treaty and Arbitral Practice' (2023) 24(6) *The Journal of World Investment & Trade* 879.

47 Norbert Horn, 'Current use of the UNCITRAL Arbitration Rules in the Context of Investment Arbitration' (2008) 24(4) *Arbitration International* 587.

48 Ivar Alvik, 'Concessions in International Law' (2022) 91(4) *Nordic Journal of International Law* 568.

49 Patrick Ng'ambi, Sangwani, 'The Effect of Stabilsation Clauses in Concession Agreements' (2012) 43 *Zambia Law Journal* 57.

50 Roland Brown, 'Choice of Law Provisions in Concession and Related Contracts' (1976) 39(6) *The Modern Law Review* 625.

domestic legal relationships. Umbrella clauses in investment treaties may also raise a breach of a concession contract to the level of a breach of international law, thereby incurring the state's international responsibility.[51]

IV. THE PURPORTED ADVANTAGES OF FOREIGN DIRECT INVESTMENT

The conventional wisdom surrounding FDI rests on a foundational premise that foreign capital inflows provide an unqualified benefit for host states.[52] According to this orthodox narrative, FDI serves as a catalyst for economic transformation, technological advancement, and social progress in recipient countries.

The preamble to bilateral investment treaties, exemplified, for example, by the Grenada-USA BIT, reflects this optimistic framing. The treaty expresses the parties' desire 'to promote greater economic cooperation between them, particularly with respect to investment by nationals and companies of one Party in the territory of the other Party', while 'recognizing that agreement upon the treatment to be accorded such investment will stimulate the flow of private capital and the economic development of the Parties'. This language embodies the fundamental assumption that FDI flows and economic development are inextricably linked, with the former serving as a necessary precondition for the latter.

A core part of the argument advanced by proponents of FDI liberalisation is that the more revenue an investor earns, the more revenue a host state can generate through the imposition of taxes.[53] The argument continues that the generation of revenue is occasioned by the fact that foreign corporations are often subject to more stringent reporting requirements and compliance mechanisms that facilitate revenue collection. The Caribbean's experience provides instructive examples of this dynamic. FDI data over the last few decades demonstrates substantial investment inflows across the region, with countries such as Jamaica and Trinidad and Tobago, and more recently Guyana, experiencing significant FDI inflows.[54] This suggests the significant scale of foreign investment activity in the region and its potential contribution to government revenues through corporate taxation, withholding taxes, and other fiscal mechanisms.[55]

A. Technology Transfer and Knowledge Spillovers

The purported technology transfer occasioned by FDI represents another compelling advantage of FDI.[56] This argument essentially rests on the assumption that foreign investors

51 Stephan Schill, 'Enabling Private Ordering: Function, Scope and Effect of Umbrella Clauses in International Investment Treaties' (2009) 18 *Minnesota Journal of International Law* 1.

52 Selma Kurtishi-Kastrati, 'The Effects of Foreign Direct Investments for Host Country's Economy' (2013) 5(1) *European Journal of Interdisciplinary Studies* 1.

53 David Hartman, 'Tax Policy and Foreign Direct Investment' (1985) 26(1) *Journal of Public Economics* 107.

54 Preeya Mohan, Patrick Kent Watson, and Patick Watson, 'CARICOM foreign direct investment flows' (2014) *Social and Economic Studies* 281.

55 Sandra Sookram et al., 'Determining Factors of FDI Flows to Selected Caribbean Countries' (2022) 15(2) *Journal of Risk and Financial Management* 48.

56 Kamal Saggi, 'Trade, Foreign Direct Investment, and International Technology Transfer: A Survey' (2002) 17(1) *The World Bank Research Observer* 191.

serve as conduits for the diffusion of advanced technologies, management practices, and specialised knowledge from developed to developing economies.[57] In the Caribbean context, this argument finds particular resonance in sectors such as telecommunications, tourism, and financial services, where foreign investors have introduced cutting-edge technologies and service delivery models.[58] The telecommunications sector, in particular, provides a compelling illustration, with foreign investors (for example, Cable and Wireless, as it then was, and later Digicel) bringing advanced infrastructure, digital platforms, and service capabilities that have transformed connectivity throughout the region.[59] Similarly, international hotel chains, like the Marriott, have introduced sophisticated reservation systems, customer relationship management technologies, and operational efficiencies that have enhanced the region's competitive position in the global tourism market. The knowledge spillover effects extend beyond technological hardware to encompass management techniques, quality control systems, marketing strategies, and advanced organisational practices.[60] Foreign-owned enterprises often implement international best practices in areas such as environmental management, workplace safety, and corporate governance, creating benchmarks that influence standards in host countries.[61] The training provided to local employees in foreign-owned enterprises often generates human capital that subsequently benefits the broader economy as workers move between employers or establish their own businesses.

B. Employment Creation and Skills Development

Employment generation represents another pillar of the pro-FDI argument.[62] Employment creation in the region typically operates through both direct hiring within foreign-owned enterprises and indirect employment generation through supply chain relationships, service providers, and the broader multiplier effects of increased economic activity. The direct employment effects of FDI are often immediately visible and politically significant. Foreign investors frequently establish operations that provide formal sector employment with regular wages, benefits, and working conditions that may exceed local standards. This is particularly important in Caribbean economies where informal employment and underemployment represent persistent challenges.[63] The establishment of foreign-owned enterprises can provide employment opportunities for educated workers, particularly those employed in management positions, who might otherwise emigrate in search of better opportunities, contributing to the retention of human capital within the region. Furthermore, foreign investors

57 Ronald Findlay, 'Some Aspects of Technology Transfer and Direct Foreign Investment' (1978) 68(2) *The American Economic Review* 275.

58 Esperanza Lasagabaster and Rekha Reddy, 'Supporting Innovation in Latin America and the Caribbean: Successful Examples of Technology Transfer Promotion' (2010) 39 *Review of Economic and Statistics* 312.

59 Carlos Miranda Levy, *Information Society and Public ICT Policies in the Caribbean: A Review of Advances and Challenges, Policy Instruments and Country Experiences* (ECLAC 2007).

60 Te Velde and Dirk Willem, *Policies Towards Foreign Direct Investment in Developing Countries: Emerging Best-Practices and Outstanding Issues* (Overseas Development Institute 2001).

61 Ann. Harrison, 'The Role of Multinationals in Economic Development: The Benefits of FDI' (1994) 29(4) *The Columbia Journal of World Business* 6.

62 Diego Vacaflores, John Mogab and Ruby Kishan, 'Does FDI Really Affect Employment in Host Countries? Subsidiary Level Evidence' (2017) 51(2) *The Journal of Developing Areas* 205.

63 Roland Craigwell and Allan Wright, 'Explaining Unemployment in the Caribbean Again' (2012) 4(9) *International Journal of Business and Social Science* 263.

often provide specialised training in technical skills, language proficiency, computer literacy, and industry-specific competencies that increase worker productivity and earning potential.[64] These skills are often transferable across employers and sectors, creating positive externalities that benefit the broader economy. Additionally, exposure to international business practices, quality standards, and customer service protocols can enhance the overall skill level of the domestic workforce. The indirect employment effects operate through backward and forward linkages with domestic enterprises.[65] Foreign investors, particularly those operating in the hotel industry in the region, often source inputs locally (e.g. fruits and vegetables), utilise domestic service providers, and create market opportunities for domestic suppliers, thereby generating employment throughout the value chain.

C. Infrastructure Development and Capital Formation

Proponents of FDI emphasise its role in infrastructure development, particularly in rural communities.[66] More particularly, foreign investors often require infrastructure standards that exceed existing capabilities in host countries, creating incentives for infrastructure upgrading that benefits the broader economy. This can include investments in transportation networks, telecommunications systems, power generation and distribution, water and sanitation services, and educational facilities.[67] The Caribbean region has benefitted from foreign investment in tourism infrastructure, including airports, ports, hotels, and recreational facilities that have enhanced the region's attractiveness as a destination while providing infrastructure that serves broader economic and social needs.[68] The influx of FDI may also incentivise states to undertake regulatory reforms that improve the business environment, support the development of capital markets and financial institutions, and contribute to the establishment of industry standards and professional practices that benefit the entire economy.

D. Productivity Enhancement and Competitive Dynamics

Proponents of FDI suggest that foreign investment enhances productivity through competitive pressures and knowledge spillovers.[69] The central argument here is that domestic firms' productivity increases through competition as foreign enterprises introduce more efficient production methods, higher quality standards, and innovative business models that compel domestic firms to improve their performance. Foreign enterprises may offer superior products or services that force domestic competitors to upgrade their offerings, improve

64 Mahnaz Muhammad Ali, Ishtiaq Ahmad, and Kiran Khalil, 'Role of Foreign Direct Investment in Employment Generation: Evidence from FDI Recipient Economies' (2022) 6(3) *Pakistan Languages and Humanities Review* 94.

65 Nigel Driffield, 'Indirect Employment Effects of Foreign Direct Investment into the UK' (1999) 51(3) *Bulletin of Economic Research* 207.

66 Frank Sader, *Attracting Foreign Direct Investment into Infrastructure: Why Is It So Difficult?* (Vol. 12, World Bank Publications 2000).

67 Mo Yamin and Rudolf Sinkovics, 'Infrastructure or Foreign Direct Investment? An Examination of the Implications of MNE Strategy for Economic Development' (2009) 44(2) *Journal of World Business* 144.

68 DeLisle Worrell, 'Investment in the Caribbean' (1993) *Social and Economic Studies* 243.

69 Erol Taymaz and Şule Özler, 'Foreign Ownership, Competition, and Survival Dynamics' (2007) 31 *Review of Industrial Organization* 23.

efficiency, or develop new capabilities.[70] The presence of foreign competitors can also reveal market opportunities and business models that domestic entrepreneurs can adapt and implement. Additionally, the mobility of workers between foreign and domestic enterprises facilitates the transfer of knowledge, skills, and best practices throughout the economy. The productivity enhancement effects can extend beyond direct competitors to encompass suppliers, customers, and service providers who must meet the standards and requirements of foreign-owned enterprises. This can drive improvements in quality, reliability, and efficiency throughout supply chains and business networks, creating economy-wide productivity gains that enhance competitiveness and living standards.

E. Balance of Payments and Financial Integration

FDI is often touted for its positive impact on balance of payments equilibrium.[71] More particularly, FDI provides a stable source of foreign currency that can help address current account deficits and support exchange rate stability.[72] Indeed, unlike portfolio investment or short-term capital flows, FDI is generally viewed as a more stable form of foreign financing that is less susceptible to sudden reversals or speculative attacks.[73] This stability derives from the long-term nature of direct investment commitments, which involve substantial sunk costs and operational complexity that discourage rapid capital flight. For small island developing states in the Caribbean, this stability can be particularly valuable given their vulnerability to external shocks and limited access to international capital markets.[74]

F. Market Expansion and Export Development

FDI can serve as a catalyst for market expansion and export development,[75] particularly in small economies like those found in the Caribbean region. Foreign investors often bring established international market relationships, distribution networks, and brand recognition that can facilitate access to global markets for host country products and services. This market access dimension is particularly relevant for Caribbean economies that face the challenge of small domestic markets and high transportation costs for accessing international markets.[76] Foreign investors in tourism, for example, bring established marketing networks,

70 Philippe Gugler and Serge Brunner, 'FDI Effects on National Competitiveness: A Cluster Approach' (2007) 13 *International Advances in Economic Research* 268.

71 Jeffrey Green, 'The Foreign Direct Investment Regulation-A Solution to the United States Balance of Payments Crisis' (1972) 55 *Marquette Law Review* 553.

72 Andrew Abbott, David Cushman, and Glauco De Vita, 'Exchange Rate Regimes and Foreign Direct Investment Flows to Developing Countries' (2012) 20(1) *Review of International Economics* 95.

73 Joseph Abodakpi, Gorm Jacobson, and Konrad Stelmach, 'Reserve Accumulation and Sudden Stops: Evidence from Foreign Direct Investment Dynamics in Selected Emerging Economies' (2024) 14(3) *Theoretical Economics Letters* 1347.

74 John Gafar, 'Macroeconomic Performance and External Shocks on Small, Open Economies: The Caribbean Experience' (1996) 30(3) *The Journal of Developing Areas* 341.

75 James Markusen and Anthony Venables, 'Foreign Direct Investment as a Catalyst for Industrial Development' (1999) 43(2) *European Economic Review* 335.

76 Cecilia Briceno-Garmendia et al. 'Connectivity for Caribbean Countries: An Initial Assessment' (World Bank Policy Research Working Paper 7169, 2015).

reservation systems, and customer relationships that enable Caribbean destinations to reach international travellers more effectively than might be possible through purely domestic marketing efforts. Similarly, foreign investment in export-oriented manufacturing or services can provide access to international value chains and supply networks that would be difficult for domestic enterprises to access independently.[77]

V. DISADVANTAGES OF FDI

While the purported advantages of foreign direct investment described above appear compelling, the empirical evidence regarding their realisation in practice presents a more complex picture. The Caribbean's experience suggests that the benefits of FDI are neither automatic nor uniformly distributed, and that their realisation depends critically on the specific terms under which foreign investors are admitted and regulated.

A. Excessive Investment Incentives

The Economic Commission for Latin America and the Caribbean (ECLAC) has documented the 'very generous' nature of investment concessions offered to foreign investors throughout the region, noting that 'many Caribbean countries provide complete tax holiday for investors in export-oriented activities.'[78] The scope of these incentives is breathtaking in both their comprehensiveness and their potential for abuse. In this connection, ECLAC observes that 'the BPO industry is practically exempted from any income tax' and that 'even the extractive industries, which in most other countries are subject to stricter tax regulations often including royalties, are benefiting from incentives in the Caribbean'.[79]

The legislative framework facilitating these concessions demonstrates the extent to which host states have subordinated their fiscal sovereignty to foreign capital. Antigua and Barbuda's Investment Authority Act, for example, exemplifies this problematic approach, offering standing concessionary benefits to foreign investors who meet minimal investment thresholds. These benefits include comprehensive exemptions from customs duties, sales taxes, income taxes, and stamp duties – concessions that ECLAC describes as contributing to 'a race-to-the-bottom, in which tax advantages offered by one jurisdiction are matched by other ones, in order to continue to be equally competitive'.[80] Significantly, ECLAC notes that 'conditions for qualifying for these incentives are often not strict'[81] and that 'many governments do state their "preferences" with regards to foreign investment, but these are not necessarily hard requirements'.[82] This laxity in conditionality ensures that the purported developmental benefits of FDI remain largely theoretical while the costs to host states remain painfully real.

77 Aleksandra Kordalska et al., 'Decoding Specialisation Patterns in Global Value Chains: The Role of Multinationals and Domestic Firms' (2025) 20(1) *International Journal of Emerging Markets* 313.

78 O De Groot and M Pérez Ludeña, 'Foreign Direct Investment in the Caribbean: Trends, Determinants and Policies' (ECLAC – Studies and Perspectives Series – The Caribbean – No. 35, 2014) 33.

79 ibid.

80 ibid 35.

81 ibid 33.

82 ibid.

B. Profit Expatriation and the Illusion of Development

The fundamental flaw in the prevailing FDI paradigm lies in its failure, in many cases, to ensure that investment generates sustainable local development. As Schneiderman observes, citing Memmi, the 'astounding privileges' and 'host of advantages' afforded to foreign investors primarily serve to 'boost the profits of investors, who seldom allow such profit to find its dynamic in local economies as investors generally expatriate such profits back to their home country or to some offshore jurisdiction with an even looser tax regime.'[83] This dynamic was clearly illustrated in the case of *Grenada Private Power Limited and WRB Enterprises Inc. v Grenada*,[84] where despite receiving significant import duty and tax concessions ostensibly to incentivise the development of Grenada's renewable energy sector, the investor instead paid significant sums in special dividends to its shareholders. When challenged, the ICSID tribunal remarkably endorsed this approach, finding that the investment 'was intended to make money for the shareholders or investors and they acted accordingly',[85] and ruling that the dividend policy, though admittedly not in keeping with their corporate social responsibility, was nonetheless lawful.

C. The Myth of Inevitable Improvement

The prevailing discourse surrounding FDI rests on the assumption that foreign investment inevitably results in sustained improvements in host states. However, empirical evidence challenges this fundamental premise. ECLAC, in particular, has commented upon the 'doubtful success' of FDI on economic development in the Caribbean region, noting that 'there is little hard evidence about the impact of the generous incentives given by Caribbean governments on FDI and economic growth'.[86] In the same vein, Goyal and Chai, in the context of the incentive regime in the Organisation of Eastern Caribbean States (OECS), found that these countries 'forgo some 9½ to 16 per cent of annual GDP in tax incentives, without much noticeable impact'.[87] Critically, these researchers concluded that 'investors are in fact not very price sensitive at all, and that the removal of generous financial subsidies yields a potential revenue of 7–13 per cent of GDP'.[88] In this connection, ECLAC concludes:

> At a time when many Caribbean countries are reducing fiscal deficits, the incentives awarded to foreign investors have to come from higher taxes to other constituencies. These raise costs of doing business in the economy and may even push many local companies into the informal economy.[89]

D. Environmental Degradation and Resource Extraction

The environmental consequences of FDI, particularly in the extractive industries, represent another significant disadvantage that challenges the narrative of inevitable improvement.

83 David Schneiderman, *Investment Law's Alibis: Colonialism, Imperialism, Debt and Development* (CUP 2022) 24.

84 ICSID Case No. ARB/17/13 (Award).

85 ibid 159.

86 O Ludeña, 'Foreign Direct Investment in the Caribbean: Trends, Determinants and Policies' (ECLAC – Studies and Perspectives Series – The Caribbean – No. 35, 2014) 34.

87 ibid.

88 ibid.

89 ibid 35.

Jamaica's experience with bauxite mining, in particular, provides an instructive case study.[90] As McCarthy documents, following independence in 1962, Jamaica allowed five major multinational corporations to invest in Jamaica's bauxite resources, thereby enabling Jamaica to become the world's largest supplier of the ore.[91] However, this apparent success came at enormous environmental cost. McCarthy notes that 'bauxite mining was hugely degrading for inland Jamaica, particularly in the eastern mountains', with 'clear-cutting a patch of forest and tearing up the earth beneath' completely destroying 'whatever ecosystem once existed'.[92] Beyond deforestation, the processing of the bauxite ore has produced pollution, creating long-term environmental liabilities that far exceed any short-term economic gains.

E. The Usurpation of Sovereign Functions

Perhaps most troubling is the extent to which certain foreign investors have sought to usurp fundamental sovereign functions of host states. The case of *RSM v Grenada*[93] provides a stark illustration of this phenomenon. The tribunal found that RSM's approach to maritime boundary negotiations was a 'secretive, unilateral, unauthorised, crude "horse-trading" approach, backed up with wild threats and vexatious litigation if unsuccessful',[94] which contradicted the essential principles of maritime boundary negotiations between Grenada's neighbours. The tribunal noted that RSM's actions had a significant damaging impact on Grenada's diplomatic relations with its neighbours, with both Venezuela and Trinidad and Tobago expressly requesting that the investor's representative not be involved in further inter-state negotiations. As the tribunal observed, 'any involvement by RSM in such processes, as a private party pursuing its own commercial interests, must be regarded as highly unusual by any ordinary State practice in boundary delimitation negotiations'.[95] The *RSM* case demonstrates how foreign investors may not merely seek economic concessions but may actually attempt to co-opt core sovereign functions, with potentially devastating consequences for host state diplomacy and international relations.

VI. STRUCTURAL DEFECTS OF INTERNATIONAL INVESTMENT LAW

Not only have the foundational assumptions regarding FDI been challenged in recent years, but so too the structural defects inherent in international investment law. International investment law, which is a core feature of international economic law and therefore the neoliberal economic order, has been variously described as asymmetrical[96] and colonial.[97]

90 Noel Cowell, 'The Impact of Bauxite Mining on Peasant and Community Relations in Jamaica' (1987) *Social and Economic Studies* 171.

91 T McCarthy, 'Extraction, Exploitation and Degradation: A Brief Environmental History of Western Investment in Jamaica' (2013) 3 *Caribbean Quilt* 171, 179.

92 ibid.

93 ICSID Case No. ARB/05/14, Award, 13 March 2009.

94 ibid 327.

95 ibid 287.

96 Alessandra Arcuri, 'The Great Asymmetry and the Rule of Law in International Investment Arbitration' (2018) *Yearbook on International Investment Law and Policy* 394.

97 Jason Haynes and Antonius Hippolyte, 'The Coloniality of International Investment Law in the Commonwealth Caribbean' (2023) 72(1) *International & Comparative Law Quarterly* 105.

A. The Myth of Investment Treaty Efficacy

One of the most enduring assumptions in contemporary international economic law is the proposition that BITs unequivocally serve as effective instruments for attracting foreign direct investment.[98] This assumption, despite its widespread acceptance among policy-makers and international organisations,[99] lacks robust empirical foundation and has been systematically challenged by scholarly research.[100] Indeed, there is much contestation over whether and the extent to which there is a clear correlation between signing BITs and attracting new FDI – a position that finds particular resonance in the Caribbean context.[101]

The Caribbean experience provides compelling evidence against the treaty-investment nexus. St Kitts and Nevis, which has notably signed only one BIT to date, stands as one of the region's fastest growing economies, with growth fuelled by investments made principally in the hospitality and tourism industry by foreign investors, and, indeed, citizenship by investment.[102] Similarly, Antigua and Barbuda, Barbados, Grenada, Saint Lucia and Saint Vincent, and the Grenadines – islands that have collectively signed no more than fifteen BITs – continue to experience significant foreign investment inflows.

This empirical reality should not surprise informed observers.[103] Contrary to the ongoing, unchallenged mantra that the means to achieving improved foreign direct investment is through signing BITs, empirical research demonstrates that this correlation is tenuous at best. Research surveying a sample of twelve states found that BITs do not attract 'development-enhancing FDI',[104] while a comprehensive meta-analysis of existing empirical evidence concluded that the correlation between BIT ratification and attracting foreign direct investment is 'economically negligible'.[105] The Organisation for Economic Co-operation and Development (OECD) has acknowledged this empirical weakness, confirming that 'the vast majority of the existing studies do not offer a satisfying answer to the question whether IIAs

98 Jennifer Tobin and Susan Rose-Ackerman, 'When BITs Have Some Bite: The Political-economic Environment for Bilateral Investment Treaties' (2011) 6 *The Review of International Organizations* 1.

99 Eric Neumayer and Laura Spess, 'Do Bilateral Investment Treaties Increase Foreign Direct Investment to Developing Countries?' (2005) 33 *World Development* 1567:

> The message to developing countries therefore is that succumbing to the obligations of BITs does have the desired payoff of higher FDI inflows . . . BITs fulfil their purpose, and those developing countries that have signed more BITs with major capital exporting developed countries are likely to have received more FDI in return.

100 Jason Yackee, 'Do Bilateral Investment Treaties Promote Foreign Direct Investment-Some Hints from Alternative Evidence' (2010) 51 *Virginia Journal of International Law* 397.

101 Mary Hallward-Driemeier, 'Do Bilateral Investment Treaties Attract Foreign Direct Investment? Only a Bit and They Could Bite' in *Only a Bit and They Could Bite* (World Bank, June 2003).

102 Imran Williams and Roger Hosein, 'Citizenship by Investment Program in the OECS, A Necessary Lifeline?' (2019) 44(1) *Journal of Eastern Caribbean Studies* 1.

103 Lauge Poulsen, 'The Importance of BITs for Foreign Direct Investment and Political Risk Insurance: Revisiting the Evidence' in K Sauvant (ed), *Yearbook on International Investment Law & Policy* (OUP 2010) 539–74.

104 Nicolás Perrone and David Schneiderman, 'International Economic Law's Wreckage: Depoliticization, Inequality, Precarity' in E Christodoulidis, R Dukes and M Goldoni (eds), *Research Handbook on Critical Legal Theory* (Edward Elgar 2019)

105 Julien Chaisse and Christian Bellak, 'Navigating the Expanding Universe of International Treaties on Foreign Investment: Creation and Use of a Critical Index' (2015) 18(1) *Journal of International Economic Law* 79.

influence capital allocation in treaty partners.'[106] More recently, a comprehensive analysis by Bonnitcha, Poulsen and Waibel concluded that 'the literature suggests that investment treaties do have some impact on some investment decisions in some circumstances, but they are unlikely to have a large effect on the majority of investment decisions.'[107]

B. The Asymmetrical Nature of Investor-State Dispute Settlement

The structural defects in international investment law become most apparent in the design of the investor-state dispute settlement (ISDS) regime, which embodies a profound asymmetry that systematically favours private investors over sovereign states. This asymmetry was explicitly acknowledged by the tribunal in *Michael Lee-Chin v The Dominican Republic*,[108] which noted the one-sided nature of arbitration initiation:

> there is only one way to institute investor-State arbitration. Specifically, States have offered their consent in Article XIII, and that consent is perfected when an investor accepts the offer by instituting an arbitration proceeding. This is widely known as anticipated consent or offer of consent to arbitrate. The opposite way is not possible – at least, regarding arbitration – as the investor is clearly not a Contracting Party to the Treaty.[109]

This structural asymmetry creates what can only be characterised as a 'one-way street' in international dispute resolution, with profound implications for state sovereignty and regulatory autonomy. One of these implications is that in circumstances where the language used in the BIT in question does not allow for counterclaims, a respondent state may not sue a foreign investor that has committed breaches of environmental and other core regulations in its territory.[110]

Orford's incisive analysis in *International Law and the Politics of History* exposes the systematic wealth transfer effects embedded within the ISDS regime.[111] She observes that

> part of the investment law regime's legitimacy crisis flowed from the asymmetrical nature of the system, in which only investors could trigger the dispute settlement process while the costs of the resulting arbitration were borne by both parties.[112]

This structure ensures that even when states successfully defend against investor claims, they face substantial financial penalties. The implications of this design are stark:

> the best outcome for a State sued by an investor would be that the government would be held not to have breached its investment protection obligations but still find itself paying millions of dollars to cover the costs of the arbitration.[113]

106 Joachim Pohl, *Societal Benefits and Costs of International Investment Agreements: A Critical Review of Aspects and Available Empirical Evidence* (OECD 2018) 19.

107 Jonathan Bonnitcha, Lauge Poulsen and Michael Waibel, *The Political Economy of The Investment Treaty Regime* (OUP 2017) 166.

108 ICSID Case No. UNCT/18/3 Partial Award on Jurisdiction.

109 ibid 125.

110 Andrea Bjorklund, 'The Role of Counterclaims in Rebalancing Investment Law' (2013) 17 *Lewis & Clark Law Review* 461.

111 Anne Orford, *International Law and the Politics of History* (CUP 2021).

112 ibid 313.

113 ibid.

This creates a perverse incentive structure where the mere threat of arbitration can induce regulatory compliance, regardless of the merits of potential investor claims.

Orford astutely identifies the distributional consequences of this arrangement. She argues:

> While many States have been willing to gamble on the resulting system, perhaps in the hope that their investors would win against other States often enough to make the overall deal worthwhile, the payoff is less clear for those whose citizens are largely not in the foreign investing class. The result is that the net effect of the system is to transfer wealth from States to private actors as the price of regulating in a broad range of areas.[114]

The investment law regime's structural biases have also inevitably drawn international tribunals into ideological controversies that should properly remain within domestic political processes. As Orford notes in this context,

> the privileging of international adjudication over domestic political processes for resolving conflicts between the protection of property rights and competing values of public health, environmental protection, or survival has inevitably embroiled judges and arbitrators in ideological controversies and political struggles.[115]

C. Treaty Shopping and the Abuse of Corporate Nationality

The international investment regime has facilitated sophisticated forms of treaty shopping that fundamentally undermine the integrity of the bilateral treaty system. The tribunal in *Gambrinus Corporation v Venezuela*,[116] for example, explicitly endorsed this practice, ruling that it is not wrong for a prudent investor (in this case a mailbox company incorporated in Barbados but having no business activities there) 'to organise its investment in a way that affords maximum protection under existing treaties, usually by establishing a company in a State that . . . accepts incorporation as a basis for corporate nationality'.[117] This judicial endorsement of treaty shopping is also evident in tribunals allowing investors to rely upon the most-favoured national treatment (MFN) clause found in a base treaty to import more favourable dispute settlement mechanisms from treaties concluded by host states and other third countries. In this context, it can be argued that the international investment regime caters to and protects the interests of the 'prudent investor' even when their goal is to tacitly circumvent the treaty system to gain 'maximum protection', even though their relationship to the host State is nothing more than tenuous.

D. The Absence of Investor Obligations

The contemporary international investment law regime demonstrates a troubling disregard for the developmental purpose that ostensibly justifies investor protections. The seemingly pervasive approach in arbitral practice of ignoring investors' contribution to the host State's

114 ibid.
115 ibid.
116 ICSID Case No. ARB/11/31, Award, 15 June 2015.
117 ibid 142.

economic development as a qualifying element of the criteria for establishing 'investment'[118] i.e. *ratione materiae* is of special concern to Caribbean States, in particular, who are heavily reliant on foreign direct investment for development purposes. Similarly, the general absence of binding positive human rights and environmental obligations on foreign investors is deeply problematic.[119] These deficits are compounded by the weakness of existing accountability mechanisms. More pointedly, very few Caribbean BITs impose corporate social responsibilities on investors,[120] while the national investment laws that do address such responsibilities typically use hortatory language and have weak enforcement capabilities.[121] The result is a regime that provides extensive protections to investors while imposing minimal corresponding obligations.

E. Institutionalised Unpredictability

The Fair and Equitable Treatment (FET) standard, in particular, best exemplifies the institutionalised unpredictability of international investment law.[122] Indeed, as Schneiderman argues, the regime embodies a presumption that 'policy measures, no matter how beneficial or desirable, are not to be tolerated if they depart from "normal" state behaviour'.[123] This presumption finds its clearest expression in the vague and ubiquitous FET standard, which has become perhaps the most controversial of investor protection standards in international law.[124] The application of the FET standard creates particular challenges for Caribbean states due to the absence of certainty and predictability about the standard of review applicable to the FET clause, as well as uncertainty regarding whether the controversial concepts of stability and predictability and legitimate expectations form part of the content of the FET standard.[125] The doctrine of legitimate expectations, in particular, which Linarelli, Salomon

118 Souvik Mukherjee and Nirmal Kanti Chakrabarti, 'Is "Contribution to the Host States Development" an Essential Criterion to Define Investment Under International Investment Law? A Search Through the Lens of Arbitral Awards' (2021) 42(3) *Liverpool Law Review* 429.

119 Barnali Choudhury, 'Investor Obligations for Human Rights' (2020) 35(1) *ICSID Review-Foreign Investment Law Journal* 82.

120 The Guyana-Brazil BIT (2018) is the only publicly available instrument that mentions corporate social responsibility.

121 One exception to this general trend is Schedule 4 of Antigua and Barbuda's Investment Authority Act (2006) which provides:

> Investors will be required to recognise the economic and social objectives and the policies and priorities of the Government as well as the goals of the CARICOM Single Market and Economy (CSME); observe workers' rights relating to collective bargaining; and safeguard the environment. They will not be permitted to engage in unethical practices or corrupt activities. It should particularly be noted that the Government will not waive or otherwise derogate from its domestic environment laws, nor will it waive or otherwise derogate from its domestic labour laws in order to encourage the establishment, acquisition, expansion or retention of an investment in its territory.

122 Jason Haynes, 'The Evolving Nature of the Fair and Equitable Treatment (FET) Standard. Challenging its Increasing Pervasiveness in Light of Developing Countries' Concerns – The Case for Regulatory Rebalancing' (2013) 14(1) *The Journal of World Investment & Trade* 114.

123 Schneiderman, *Investment Law's Alibis* (n 83) 30.

124 Rumana Islam, Ghosh Islam, and Ghosh, *Fair and Equitable Treatment (FET) Standard in International Investment Arbitration* (Springer 2018).

125 Julian Arato, Chester Brown, and Federico Ortino, 'Parsing and Managing Inconsistency in Investor-State Dispute Settlement' (2020) 21(3) *The Journal of World Investment & Trade* 336.

and Sornarajah argue was 'plucked out of thin air [and which has become] the staple of many arbitral awards',[126] exemplifies the problematic expansion of investor protections. This doctrine was accepted without dispute by the Tribunal in *Peter Allard v Barbados*,[127] despite uncertainties surrounding its scope after *Tecmed v Mexico*,[128] demonstrating the extent to which arbitral tribunals have been willing to expand investor protections without adequate doctrinal foundation. Similar issues of incoherence and unpredictability arise in connection with other standards of protection, including indirect expropriation, largely on account of inconsistent arbitral awards.[129] This has given rise to claims that international investment law suffers from a legitimacy crisis.[130]

F. Regulatory Chill and Democratic Deficit

The cumulative effect of these structural defects is the creation of what scholars' term 'regulatory chill'.[131] Scholars observe that violation of investment protection rules gives rise to state liability and that 'often, the damages that are imposed are staggering'.[132] Consequently, 'states become constrained by the rules. They act in accordance with the neoliberal prescriptions even where such restraint is not in the public interest'.[133] Regulatory chill creates a particularly pernicious form of policy paralysis. In particular, the national treatment standard and similar investment protections prevent host states from responding to competitive disadvantages faced by domestic firms, proverbially tying the host State's hands by preventing it, on the pain of penalty, from responding in ways that could offer a lifeline to these struggling domestic firms. The result is an investment regime that systematically favours foreign capital over domestic enterprise and public policy flexibility. Perhaps most troubling is the regime's systematic disregard for legitimate public policy considerations. In many cases, even 'where State action has a reasonable basis in public policy, tribunals nonetheless apply investor protection standards in an inflexible manner thereby disabling a balancing of competing interests'.[134] This approach effectively subordinates democratic governance and public welfare to investor profit maximisation.

Despite the foregoing, however, it is important to note that the regulatory chill hypothesis faces significant empirical challenges and scholarly scepticism. Critics argue that demonstrating regulatory chill 'conclusively requires counterfactual evidence about the regulations

126 John Linarelli, Margot Salomon and Muthucumaraswamy Sornarajah, *The Misery of International Law: Confrontations with Injustice in the Global Economy* (OUP 2018) 167.

127 PCA Case No. 2012–06 (Award).

128 *Tecmed, S.A. v The United Mexican States*, ICSID Case No. ARB (AF)/00/2, Award, 29 May 2003.

129 Mojtaba Dani, and Afshin Akhtar-Khavari, 'The Uncertainty of Legal Doctrine in Indirect Expropriation Cases and the Legitimacy Problems of Investment Arbitration' (2016) 22 *Widener Law Review* 1.

130 Susan Franck, 'The Legitimacy Crisis in Investment Treaty Arbitration: Privatizing Public International Law through Inconsistent Decisions' (2004) 73 *Fordham Law Review* 1521.

131 Ashley Schram et al., 'Internalisation of International Investment Agreements in Public Policymaking: Developing a Conceptual Framework of Regulatory Chill' (2018) 9(2) *Global Policy* 193.

132 John Linarelli, Margot Salomon, and Muthucumaraswamy Sornarajah, *The Misery of International Law: Confrontations with Injustice in the Global Economy* (OUP 2018) 161

133 ibid.

134 David Schneiderman, *Investment Law's Alibis* (Vol. 168, CUP 2022) 32.

that would have existed in the absence of the purported chilling.'[135] Indeed, as Bonnitcha observes, policy chill is especially challenging to identify in cases where policymakers have internalised investment treaty standards since it is difficult to disentangle policy preferences from the effects of the agreements.[136] Moreover, empirical studies reveal mixed findings regarding the prevalence and scope of regulatory chill. Williams, for example, demonstrates that states are still choosing to defend their actions in investment arbitration at the behest of domestic interests, and thus the regulatory chill hypothesis does not hold across the board.[137] Similarly, research in developed countries with high regulatory capacity suggests that regulatory chill is limited in scope and time,[138] while some studies take the form of a single case study and cover a relatively short period, revealing important snapshots of country experiences, but telling us little about how the impacts of IIAs vary across contexts and the conditions under which policy chill takes hold.[139]

The debate over regulatory chill ultimately reflects deeper tensions between competing theoretical frameworks and empirical methodologies. Together, the case studies suggest that IIAs can have a chilling effect on domestic regulation, but this effect is not linked to infringement costs alone.[140] Pro-market domestic actors, declining FDI, and poor economic performance can reinforce the authority IIAs have in policy circles and generate a chilling effect on domestic regulation.[141] Conversely, policy chill also depends on the programmatic beliefs that policymakers hold: a government that prefers the kinds of policies available under an IIA will seek alignment even when conditions are conducive to infringement.[142] This suggests that regulatory chill may be better understood as a contextual phenomenon that varies significantly across different political, economic, and institutional settings rather than as a universal consequence of investment treaty regimes.

G. Colonial Continuities

Among the countries which have recently joined their counterparts in giving serious contemplation to the coloniality of the international investment regime are Caribbean countries, most of whom, though relatively new to this regime, nonetheless have over the last 40 years collectively negotiated and concluded over 70 IIAs. This proliferation of investment agreements reflects not merely a technical evolution in international economic law, but rather what leading scholars increasingly recognise as the continuation of colonial power structures through legal mechanisms rather than direct political control.[143] Sornarajah, one of the foremost critics of the contemporary investment regime, identifies a clear 'continuity

135 Jonathan Bonnitcha, *Substantive Protection under Investment Treaties: A Legal and Economic Analysis* (CUP 2014) 115.

136 ibid.

137 Zoe Williams, *The Political Economy of Investment Arbitration* (OUP 2022) 29.

138 Dafina Atanasova, 'The Impact of Investment Treaties on the Rule of Law in Singapore' in Jansen Calamita and Ayelet Berman (eds), *Investment Treaties and the Rule of Law Promise: The Internalisation of International Commitments in Asia* (CUP 2022) 184.

139 Julia Calvert, *The Politics of Investment Treaties in Latin America* (OUP 2022) 211.

140 ibid 212.

141 ibid.

142 ibid.

143 José Alvarez, 'Contemporary Foreign Investment Law: An Empire of Law or the Law of Empire' (2008) 60 *Alabama Law Review* 943.

from the decolonization period through contract-based protection and then to treaty-based investment arbitration.'[144] His incisive analysis reveals that although the use of force and gunboat diplomacy, which were characteristic of the colonial period, are no longer resorted to in contemporary societies, investor-state arbitration has become 'a substitute for the use of force'.[145] Colonial power relations are, therefore, reified through an apparently neutral legal framework that achieves the same subordination of developing states to the economic interests of capital-exporting nations.

Miles provides a complementary and equally damning analysis, endorsing the sentiments expressed by Anghie[146] regarding the discursive threads between colonialism and contemporary international investment law. She argues that the substantive principles and institutional frameworks that underpin international investment law are, in essence, drawn from the colonial period, and continue to this day to reflect those origins.[147] In her view, because the colonial origins of international investment law continue to be manifested in the 'modern principles, structures, agreements, and dispute resolution systems,'[148] host states are placed in a 'permanent condition of otherness.'[149] This otherness is not merely rhetorical but constitutive of the entire legal framework, which systematically privileges the interests of foreign capital over the legitimate regulatory autonomy and development aspirations of host states. Miles further argues that this colonial continuity is best illustrated by reference to the law's:

> sole focus on investor protection, its lack of responsiveness to the impact of investor activity on the local communities and environment of the host state, the alignment of home state interests with those of the investor, the categorisation of public welfare regulation as a treaty violation, and the commodification of the environment in host states for the use of foreign entities.[150]

Like Schneiderman, who challenges the coloniality of international investment law, Miles identifies unequal treaties, extensive concessions, and regulatory chill as key challenges confronting the international investment regime, which necessarily require recalibration.[151] For Caribbean states, these colonial continuities are particularly acute given their historical experience of extraction-based colonialism and their continued vulnerability to external economic pressures that limit their capacity to pursue independent development strategies.

H. Racial Capitalism

The concept of racial capitalism is insightful in unpacking how international investment law perpetuates historical patterns of exploitation and subordination in the Caribbean region and broader Latin American region. Racial capitalism describes the process by which perceived

144 Muthucumaraswamy Sornarajah, *Resistance and Change in the International Law on Foreign Investment* (CUP 2015) 86.
145 ibid 82.
146 Antony Anghie, *Imperialism, Sovereignty and the Making of International Law* (Vol. 37, CUP 2007).
147 Kate Miles, *The Origins of International Investment Law: Empire, Environment and the Safeguarding of Capital* (CUP 2013) 1.
148 ibid 3.
149 ibid.
150 ibid.
151 ibid.

racial differences between white/European people and non-white/non-European people become socially constructed and re-inscribed as being natural and necessary through social, economic, political, and legal structures that serve to extract social and economic value from the latter.[152] This process is particularly evident in the extractives industry, where Burden-Stelly observes that racialisation 'justifies inequitable distribution of resources, destabilisation of local self-sustaining economies, and the conscription of entire populations into global labour regimes',[153] creating a system where 'whiteness and Blackness become metonyms for progress and stagnation, expropriator and expropriated, and exploiter and exploited, [such] that perpetual accumulation is possible'.[154] The fundamental premise underlying this system is that 'racialised people are deserving of exploitation because they are inherently inferior to the economically dominant group'.[155]

This racial capitalist framework manifests through international investment law's systematic privileging of foreign investors over racialised communities, as demonstrated in cases like *South American Silver v Bolivia*,[156] where Canadian mining company's aggressive tactics divided Indigenous communities through selective employment offers and donations while ignoring established consensus-based decision-making processes. In this connection, Gathii and Tzouvala have argued, 'the international investment law regime is deeply implicated in racial/racialised capitalism',[157] while Tzouvala specifically notes that the full protection and security standard 'demands that the host state represses violently those who refuse to participate in or worse disrupt processes of cross-border capitalist accumulation',[158] effectively ensuring 'that foreign investors will benefit from the cheap labour and land of racialised peoples while being shielded from the social unrest that tends to come about when land and labour are cheapened'.[159] This dynamic is further reinforced by what Perrone describes as the investment treaty regime's role in 'rendering invisible these local entitlements and community values',[160] as evidenced in cases like *Bear Creek Mining v Peru*.[161] In that case, the tribunal privileged investor rights over Indigenous communities' rights to consultation

152 Jason Haynes, 'Racialised Extractivism: A Tale of Fetishism, Narcissism, Primitive Accumulation and Expropriation' in Mohsen al Attar and Claire Smith (eds), *Emancipating International Law: Confronting the Violence of Racialised Boundaries* (OUP 2025).

153 Charisse Burden-Stelly, 'The Capitalist Foundations of Racialization' (National African-American Reparations Commission, 5 November 2021) <https://reparationscomm.org/reparations-news/the-capitalist-foundations-of-racialization/> accessed 4 March 2024.

154 ibid.

155 Tendayi Achiume, *Global Extractivism and Racial Equality: Report of the Special Rapporteur on Contemporary Forms of Racism, Racial Discrimination, Xenophobia and Related Intolerance* (UN Human Rights Council, May 2019) 42.

156 PCA Case No. 2013–15 (Award).

157 James Gathii and Ntina Tzouvala, 'Racial Capitalism and International Economic Law: Introduction' (2022) 25(2) *Journal of International Economic Law* 199.

158 Ntina Tzouvala, 'Full Protection and Security (for Racial Capitalism)' (2022) 25(2) *Journal of International Economic Law* 224.

159 ibid.

160 Nicolás Perrone, 'The "Invisible" Local Communities: Foreign Investor Obligations, Inclusiveness, and the International Investment Regime Part of: Investor Responsibility' (2019) *American Journal of International Law Unbound* 16.

161 *Bear Creek Mining Corporation v Republic of Peru*, ICSID Case No. ARB/14/21 (Award).

and environmental protection, perpetuating what Fraser characterises as the 'violence and theft concealed behind the orderly facade of contractual relations and market exchanges.'[162]

VII. THE IMPERATIVE FOR REFORM

The discussion presented above demonstrates that the current international investment law regime suffers from fundamental structural defects that undermine both its stated developmental objectives and basic principles of democratic governance. The regime's failure to generate demonstrable increases in development-enhancing investment, combined with its systematic transfer of wealth from public to private actors and its constraining effects on regulatory autonomy, calls into question its continued legitimacy. Indeed, the asymmetrical nature of ISDS, the facilitation of treaty shopping, the expansion of investor protections through vague doctrinal concepts, and the resulting regulatory chill occasioned by the threat of arbitration collectively create a system that serves primarily to protect and enhance investor returns rather than promote sustainable development or respect for democratic governance. For Caribbean states and other developing economies that remain heavily reliant on foreign direct investment for development purposes, the current regime represents not an unequivocal opportunity for development but at times a constraint on the policy flexibility necessary to achieve genuine developmental objectives. Fundamental reform of the international investment law regime, such as those proposed by UNCITRAL[163] and UNCTAD,[164] is therefore not merely desirable but essential. Such reform must address the structural asymmetries that characterise the current system, establish meaningful obligations for investors that correspond to their extensive protections, and restore the policy space necessary for democratic governments to pursue legitimate public policy objectives without fear of crippling liability to foreign investors.

VIII. PRINCIPLES OF TREATY INTERPRETATION

In interpreting bilateral investment treaties and other international investment agreements, arbitral tribunals consistently apply the interpretive framework established by Articles 31 and 32 of the Vienna Convention on the Law of Treaties (VCLT).[165] These provisions have achieved particular significance in investment arbitration because they reflect customary international law and are therefore binding even on states that have not formally ratified the Vienna Convention. The ICJ's application of these articles in cases involving non-parties, such as *Sovereignty Over Pulau Litigan and Pulau Sipidan* (*Indonesia v Malaysia*)[166] and

162 Nancy Fraser, 'Expropriation and Exploitation in Racialized Capitalism: A Reply to Michael Dawson' (2016) 3(1) *Critical Historical Studies* 163, 168.

163 United Nations Commission on International Trade Law. See Malcolm Langford et al., 'UNCITRAL and Investment Arbitration Reform: Matching Concerns and Solutions: An Introduction' (2020) 21(3) *The Journal of World Investment & Trade* 167.

164 UN Trade and Development. See Elisabeth Tuerk and Diana Rosert, 'The Road Towards Reform of the International Investment Agreement Regime: A Perspective from UNCTAD' (2016) *European Yearbook of International Economic Law* 769.

165 United Nations, *Vienna Convention on the Law of Treaties*, Treaty Series, vol. 1155, 331 (United Nations, 23 May 1969).

166 Judgment, ICJ Reports 2002, 653, para. 53.

Kasikili/Sedudu Island (Botswana/Namibia),[167] demonstrates their universal applicability as expressions of fundamental interpretive principles.

A. Ordinary and Natural Meaning

The cornerstone of treaty interpretation in investment arbitration is the primacy accorded to the text itself. As the tribunal in *Wintershall v Argentina*[168] explained,

> the carefully-worded formulation in Article 31 is based on the view that the text must be presumed to be the authentic expression of the intention of the parties. The starting point of all treaty interpretation is the elucidation of the meaning of the text, not an independent investigation into the intention of the parties from other sources.[169]

This textual emphasis reflects a fundamental principle that tribunals must begin with what the parties wrote rather than attempting to divine unexpressed intentions. The ICJ has consistently reinforced this approach, establishing in its Advisory Opinion on *Admission of a State to Membership in the United Nations*[170] that courts should not resort to preparatory work if the text of a convention is sufficiently clear in itself. This principle was further elaborated in the *case concerning the Arbitral Award of 31 July 1989* (*Guinea-Bissau v Senegal*),[171] where the ICJ articulated the fundamental rule that 'the first duty of a tribunal which is called upon to interpret and apply the provisions of a treaty, is to endeavour to give effect to them in their natural and ordinary meaning in the context in which they occur. If the relevant words in their natural and ordinary meaning make sense in their context, that is an end of the matter.'[172]

Investment tribunals have embraced the Vienna Convention's emphasis on 'ordinary meaning' while recognising that this concept extends beyond mere literalism. The determination of ordinary meaning requires careful consideration of context and purpose. Indeed, tribunals have consistently recognised that treaty terms 'are obviously not drafted in isolation, and their meaning can only be determined by considering the entire treaty text'.[173] This contextual analysis encompasses not only the immediate textual environment, including the remaining terms of the sentence and of the paragraph; the entire article at issue, but also the remainder of the treaty, i.e. its text including its preamble and annexes. This approach has been consistently applied in investment arbitration, where tribunals such as those in *Austrian Airlines v Slovak Republic*[174] and *Mondev International Ltd. v United States of America*[175] emphasised that interpretation should follow an 'ex ante neutral approach' that avoids predetermined notions of restrictive or extensive interpretation. The *Daimler v Argentina*[176] award exemplified this balanced approach, noting that interpretation requires

167 1999 ICJ Reports, 1045 (13 December 1999), para. 325.
168 ICSID Case No. ARB/04/14, Award, 8 December 2008.
169 ibid 78.
170 ICJ Reports, 1948, 63.
171 Judgment of November 12, 1991, *ICJ Reports*, 1991, 69.
172 ibid 48.
173 Ian Sinclair, *The Vienna Convention on the Law of Treaties* (2nd edn Manchester University Press Manchester 1984) 121.
174 UNCITRAL Case, Award, 20 October 2009, paras. 119–121.
175 ICSID Case No. ARB(AF)/99/2, Award, 11 October 2001, para. 43.
176 ICSID Case No. ARB/05/1, 22 August 2012.

careful attention to textual meaning while avoiding the temptation to read into treaties what they do not contain. Sir Ian Sinclair's has, however, warned about 'the risk that the placing of undue emphasis on the 'object and purpose' of a treaty will encourage teleological methods of interpretation [which], in some of its more extreme forms, will even deny the relevance of the intentions of the parties.'[177]

B. Supplementary Means of Interpretation

When primary interpretive methods under Article 31 prove insufficient, investment tribunals may resort to supplementary means of interpretation under Article 32 of the Vienna Convention.[178] As established in ICJ jurisprudence and confirmed by investment tribunals, recourse to supplementary means is appropriate when 'the meaning remains ambiguous or obscure, or leads to a result which is manifestly absurd or unreasonable'.[179] These supplementary means include preparatory work and the circumstances of treaty conclusion, though they may only be used to confirm interpretations reached under Article 31 or to resolve ambiguities that cannot be resolved through primary interpretive methods. In practice, investment tribunals have consistently applied this hierarchical approach, ensuring that supplementary means do not override clear textual meaning but serve only to clarify genuine uncertainties or confirm interpretations reached through primary methods.[180] This reflects the broader principle that the text remains the primary expression of state intent, with external materials serving only a subsidiary role.

C. Systemic Integration

Investment tribunals face particular challenges in applying interpretive principles due to the fragmented nature of international investment law, which consists of thousands of bilateral and regional agreements with varying textual formulations. The principle of systemic integration, reflected in Article 31(3)(c) of the Vienna Convention, requires tribunals to consider any relevant rules of international law applicable in the relations between the parties. Systemic integration requires tribunals to balance treaty-specific interpretation with broader consistency across the international investment law system.[181]

177 Ian Sinclair, *The Vienna Convention on the law of treaties* (Manchester University Press 1984) 130.

178 Mahmoud Hajjar and Seyed Ahmad Tabatabaei, 'The Role of Supplementary Means of Interpretation in the Interpretation of Treaties' (2025) 55(1) *Public Law Studies Quarterly* 621.

179 Competence of the General Assembly for the Admission of a State to the United Nations, Advisory Opinion, ICJ Reports 1950, 8, 19.

180 Duncan French, 'Treaty Interpretation and the Incorporation of Extraneous Legal Rules' (2006) 55(2) *International & Comparative Law Quarterly* 281.

181 Daniel Rosentreter, *Article 31 (3)(c) of the Vienna Convention on the Law of Treaties and the Principle of Systemic Integration in International Investment Law and Arbitration* (Vol. 4, Nomos Verlag 2015.)

D. The Principle of Effectiveness

The principle of effectiveness (*effet utile*) is one of the most significant interpretive principles in investment arbitration.[182] It requires tribunals to interpret treaties in a manner that gives meaning to all provisions. Investment tribunals have consistently applied this principle as a cardinal rule of the interpretation of treaties that each and every operative clause of a treaty is to be interpreted as meaningful rather than meaningless. In *Eureko BV v Republic of Poland*,[183] the tribunal noted in this connection that treaty clauses are to be interpreted so as to render them effective rather than ineffective. This principle has been consistently applied in a number of other investment arbitral awards.[184] In short, in accordance with the principle of effectiveness, rules are given their fullest weight and effect consistent with the normal sense of the words and with other parts of the text and in such a way that a reason and a meaning can be attributed to every part of the text. In this context, no provision becomes mere surplusage.

IX. CHAPTER OUTLINE

Chapter 2 examines the fundamental principles governing jurisdiction and admissibility in Commonwealth Caribbean investment arbitration, analysing the jurisdictional requirements under Article 25 of the ICSID Convention and regional IIAs across the four criteria: *ratione materiae* (qualifying investments), *ratione personae* (eligible investors), *ratione temporis* (temporal scope), and *ratione voluntatis* (consent to arbitration). The chapter demonstrates how Caribbean tribunals have interpreted these requirements through case law, particularly emphasising the broad permissive approach to investment definitions in regional BITs while highlighting ongoing tensions between investor protection and state sovereignty. It concludes by addressing key admissibility considerations, including the legality requirement for investments and the abuse of process doctrine, that may bar claims despite established jurisdiction, providing essential guidance for understanding when and how investment disputes in the Caribbean context proceed to arbitration.

Chapter 3 provides a comprehensive examination of the principle of non-discrimination in international investment law, with particular emphasis on the national treatment (NT) and most-favoured-nation (MFN) standards and their application to Caribbean states. The chapter explores the contested interpretative approaches tribunals have adopted regarding key concepts such as 'like circumstances' and 'less favourable treatment' under national treatment provisions, while demonstrating how inconsistent jurisprudential methodologies create regulatory uncertainty for host states. The chapter also critically examines the highly controversial procedural use of MFN clauses to import more favourable dispute settlement mechanisms, highlighting the jurisprudential

182 Tomoko Ishikawa, 'The Principle of Effective Interpretation in the World Trade Organization and Investment Arbitration: Difference in Parameters' (2015) 8 *Contemporary Asia Arbitration Journal* 267
183 Partial Award (Ad hoc, 19 August 2005), para. 248.
184 *Noble Ventures v Romania*, ICSID Case No. ARB/01/11, Award, 12 October 2005, para. 50; *Pan American Energy LLC and BP Argentina Exploration Co. v Argentina*, ICSID Case No. ARB/03/13, Decision on Preliminary Objections, 27 July 2006, para. 132; *Cemex Caracas Investments B.V. and Cemex Caracas II Investments B.V. v Bolivarian Republic of Venezuela*, ICSID Case No. ARB/08/15, Decision on Jurisdiction, December 30 2010, para. 104; *Tidewater Inc. and others v The Bolivarian Republic of Venezuela*, ICSID Case No. ARB/10/5, Decision on Jurisdiction, 8 February 2013.

schism between the liberal *Maffezini* line of cases and the restrictive *Plama* approach. It argues that this uncertainty particularly disadvantages Caribbean states by transforming carefully negotiated arbitration provisions into unpredictable investor-selected options through treaty shopping.

Chapter 4 examines the guarantee against expropriation, analysing the distinction between direct and indirect expropriation and the conditions under which states may lawfully expropriate foreign property. The chapter critically addresses the evolving jurisprudential approaches to determining when regulatory measures cross the line from legitimate state action to compensable indirect expropriation, advocating for a framework that focuses on substantial deprivation of the incidents of ownership rather than mere diminution in investment value. The chapter also explores the police powers doctrine as a defence to expropriation claims, examining how states can balance their sovereign regulatory authority with investor protection obligations under international investment agreements.

Chapter 5 provides a comprehensive analysis of the Fair and Equitable Treatment (FET) standard in international investment law from a distinctly Caribbean perspective, examining its various formulations – from clauses linked to customary international law to autonomous FET standards – and their differing thresholds for liability. The central argument advanced is that while the FET standard represents one of the most important investor protection mechanisms in contemporary investment agreements, its broad and evolving interpretation by arbitral tribunals makes it arguably the most invasive standard that may unduly constrain Caribbean states' regulatory autonomy. The chapter critically assesses the constituent elements of FET (including legitimate expectations, transparency, denial of justice, and prohibitions against arbitrary and discriminatory treatment) while advocating for more balanced interpretations that account for developing states' need to preserve policy space for legitimate public interest measures.

Chapter 6 examines four critical but often underexplored standards of protection in international investment law: full protection and security (FPS), free transfer provisions, umbrella clauses, and performance requirements. The chapter reveals how these provisions have evolved from relatively straightforward guarantees into complex legal instruments that blur traditional boundaries between contractual and treaty obligations, with tribunals reaching divergent interpretations that create significant uncertainty for both investors and host states. The chapter argues that while these standards serve essential protective functions, their inconsistent application – particularly regarding whether FPS extends beyond physical to legal security, how umbrella clauses can transform contractual breaches into treaty violations, and the scope of permissible performance requirements – reflects the ongoing tension between investor protection and state sovereignty in the modern global economy.

Chapter 7 examines the merits-related aspects of investment arbitration after jurisdictional requirements are satisfied, focusing on how tribunals determine treaty breaches and craft appropriate remedies. It analyses the range of available remedies – particularly compensation using contested valuation methodologies like discounted cash flow – and explores state defences including *force majeure*, contributory fault, and essential security exceptions that can excuse non-performance of treaty obligations. The chapter also addresses the growing tension between investment protection and public interest considerations such as human rights and environmental protection, demonstrating how tribunals balance investor rights against broader societal concerns in the evolving landscape of investor-state dispute settlement.

Chapter 8 examines the ongoing UNCITRAL Working Group III reform process from the perspective of Caribbean small island developing states, analysing how proposed reforms to both procedural and substantive aspects of investor-state dispute settlement could address the structural asymmetries that have rendered these nations particularly vulnerable to costly arbitral awards. The chapter argues that while Caribbean states have been largely disengaged from the reform process despite their acute exposure to regulatory chill, the proposed Advisory Centre, Multilateral Instrument, Standing Mechanism, and procedural reforms offer critical opportunities to rebalance the investor-state relationship in favour of legitimate regulatory objectives. Drawing on recent Caribbean arbitration cases and innovative treaty models like the Guyana-Brazil BIT, the analysis contends that comprehensive reform of both procedural frameworks and substantive investment standards is essential to transform international investment law from a colonial-era system that constrains regulatory autonomy into a balanced framework that protects both investor rights and state sovereignty.

The book thereafter concludes, summarising some of the key claims and arguments raised by each of the chapters.

CHAPTER 2

JURISDICTION AND ADMISSIBILITY

INTRODUCTION

The resolution of investment disputes has evolved considerably over the last few decades, from its origins in diplomatic protection[1] to a now complex system of state-state and investor-state dispute settlement (ISDS). This evolution represents a deliberate move toward depoliticisation through arbitration,[2] creating alternative pathways for resolving conflicts between foreign investors and host states, without having to resort to municipal courts.[3] While these mechanisms – including state-state dispute settlement, investor-state arbitration, mediation,[4] and conciliation – offer important benefits, they also entail significant costs and procedural complexities for all parties involved.[5]

This chapter examines the fundamental principles and requirements of jurisdiction and admissibility in investment arbitration, with particular emphasis on Caribbean international investment agreements (IIAs) and relevant case law. It begins by exploring state-state dispute settlement mechanisms before moving on to analyse contract-based dispute resolution through concession agreements. The chapter then turns to its primary focus – investor-state dispute settlement – examining in detail the jurisdictional requirements under Article 25 of the ICSID Convention and Caribbean IIAs, including *ratione materiae* (qualifying investments), *ratione personae* (eligible investors), *ratione temporis* (temporal scope), and *ratione*

1 *Plama Consortium Limited v Republic of Bulgaria*, ICSID Case No. ARB/03/24, Decision on Jurisdiction, 8 February 2005, para. 198:

> With the advent of bilateral and multilateral investment treaties since the 1980s (today estimated to be more than 1,500), the traditional diplomatic protection mechanism by home states for their nationals investing abroad has been largely replaced by direct access by investors to arbitration against host states. Nowadays, arbitration is the generally accepted avenue for resolving disputes between investors and states.

2 Ursula Kriebaum, 'Evaluating Social Benefits and Costs of Investment Treaties: Depoliticization of Investment Disputes' (2018) 33(1) *ICSID Review-Foreign Investment Law Journal* 14.

3 The creation of ICSID and the adoption of bilateral investment treaties offered to investors assures that disputes that might flow from their investments would not be subject to the perceived hazards of delays and political pressures of adjudication in national courts. See Andreas Lowenfeld, *International Economic Law* (OUP 2002) Ch 15, 456–61, 473–88. See, also, Rudolf Dolzer and Margrete Stevens, *Bilateral Investment Treaties* (Martinus Njihoff Publishers 1995); Teresa McGhie, 'Bilateral and Multilateral Investment Treaties' in Daniel Bradlow and Alfed Escher (eds), *Legal Aspects of Foreign Direct Investment* (Kluwer Law International 1999) 107–35.

4 Edna Sussman, 'Investor-State Dispute Mediation: The Benefits and Obstacles' in Arthur W. Rovine (ed), *Contemporary Issues in International Arbitration and Mediation: The Fordham Papers (2009)* (Brill Nijhoff 2010) 321–38.

5 United Nations Conference on Trade and Development, 'Dispute Settlement: Investor-State' (2003) UNCTAD/ITE/IIT/30; Sussman (n 4); Matthew H. Kirtland, 'Mediation and Conciliation' in Arthur E. Appleton and Patrick F.J. Macrory (eds), *Business Guide to Trade and Investment – Volume 2: International Investment* (Marat Umerov, Borzu Sabahi and Ian Laird (eds), International Chamber of Commerce 2018) 146–48.

DOI: 10.4324/9781003734185-2

voluntatis (consent). The final section addresses admissibility considerations, particularly the legality requirement and the abuse of process doctrine, which may bar claims despite jurisdiction having been established. Ultimately, the chapter highlights how tribunals have interpreted these requirements, providing essential guidance for understanding when and how investment disputes are resolved by arbitration.

I. STATE–STATE DISPUTE SETTLEMENT

Several Caribbean IIAs provide for the possibility of state-to-state investment arbitration.[6] Failing the resolution of a dispute concerning the interpretation or application of the IIA in question as between the state parties, these clauses allow either party to initiate arbitral proceedings. By way of example, Article 9 of the Trinidad and Tobago-Switzerland BIT provides:

(1) Disputes between the Contracting Parties regarding the interpretation or application of the provisions of this Agreement shall if possible be settled through diplomatic Channels.
(2) If the dispute between the Contracting Parties cannot be settled within a period of six months from the date at which the issue was raised in writing by one of the Contracting Parties, it shall upon request of either Party to the dispute be submitted to an arbitral tribunal.
(3) Such an arbitral tribunal shall be constituted for each individual case in the following way. Within two months of the receipt of the request for arbitration, each Contracting Party shall appoint one member of the tribunal. Those two members shall then within two months select a national of a third State who shall be the Chairman of the tribunal.
(4) If within the periods specified in paragraph (3) of this Article the necessary appointments have not been made, either Contracting Party may, in the absence of any other arrangement, invite the President of the International Court of Justice to make any necessary appointments. If the President is a national of either Contracting Party or if

6 Antigua-Germany BIT: Article 10; Antigua-UK BIT: Article 9; Belgium-Luxembourg-Barbados BIT: Article 9; Barbados-Canada BIT: Article XV; Barbados-China BIT: Article 8; Barbados-Cuba BIT: Article 9; Barbados-Germany BIT: Article 10; Barbados-Mauritius BIT: Article 9; Barbados-Switzerland BIT: Article 10; Barbados-UK BIT: Article 9; Barbados-Venezuela BIT: Article 9; Belize-China BIT: Article 8; Belize-Cuba BIT: Article 9; Belize-El Salvador BIT: Article 8; Belize-Netherlands BIT: Article 12; Belize-UK BIT: Article 9; Dominica-Germany BIT: Article 10; Dominica-UK BIT: Article 9; Grenada-UK BIT: Article 9; Grenada-US BIT: Article VII; Guyana-Brazil BIT: Article 25; Guyana-China BIT: Article 8; Guyana-Germany BIT: Article 10; Guyana-South Korea BIT: Article 9; Guyana-Switzerland BIT: Article 9; Guyana-UK BIT: Article 9; Jamaica-US BIT: Article VII Jamaica-China BIT: Article 7; Jamaica-Egypt BIT: Article 9; Jamaica-Germany BIT: Article 10; Jamaica-Indonesia BIT: Article VIII; Jamaica-South Korea BIT: Article 9; Jamaica-Switzerland BIT: Article 10; Jamaica-Netherlands BIT: Article 12; Jamaica-UK BIT: Article 10; St Lucia-Germany BIT: Article 11; St Lucia-UK BIT: Article 9; SVG-Germany BIT: Article 10; SVG-Taiwan BIT: Article XIV; Trinidad and Tobago-Canada BIT: Article XV; Trinidad and Tobago-China BIT: Article 11; Trinidad and Tobago-Cuba BIT: Article 11; Trinidad and Tobago-France BIT: Article 9; Trinidad and Tobago-Germany BIT: Article 12; Trinidad and Tobago-India BIT: Article 10 (terminated); Trinidad and Tobago-South Korea BIT: Article 9; Trinidad and Tobago-Switzerland BIT: Article 9; Trinidad and Tobago-UK BIT: Article 11; Trinidad and Tobago-USA BIT: Article X.

he is otherwise prevented from discharging the said function, the Vice-President shall be invited to make the necessary appointments. If the Vice-President is a national of either Contracting Party or if he is also otherwise prevented from discharging the said function, the Member of the International Court next in seniority who is not a national of either Contracting Party shall be invited to make the necessary appointments

(5) The arbitral tribunal shall determine its own procedures. Unless otherwise agreed by the Contracting Parties, all submissions shall be made and all hearings shall be completed within six months of the date of selection of the Chairman. The tribunal shall reach its decisions by a majority of votes, and it shall render its award within two months of the date of final submissions or date of the closing of the hearings, whichever is later.

(6) The decisions by the tribunal shall be final and binding upon both Contracting Parties. Each Contracting Party shall bear the cost of its own member of the tribunal and of its representation in the arbitral proceedings. The cost of the Chairman and the remaining costs shall be borne in equal parts by the Contracting Parties, unless the arbitral tribunal decides otherwise.

To date, there has not been any Caribbean state-to-state arbitration, and, more generally, there have been very few cases globally in this area.[7] That said, the value of such a provision, in the absence of an agreed joint interpretation between the parties, cannot be understated, as it can provide clarity to states, and, ultimately investors, on the nature and extent of obligations arising from a particular IIA,[8] thereby leading to stability, and thus improving the legitimacy of the IIA regime.

II. CONTRACT-BASED DISPUTE SETTLEMENT

While the vast majority of investment-related disputes are treaty-based, that is, they arise out of an alleged breach of a BIT or Free Trade Agreement with an investment chapter, there are comparatively fewer disputes that are contract-based.[9] These disputes arise from a breach of a Concession Contract[10] entered into by the host state with the investor, and are typically found in the context of infrastructure projects (such as building and operating

7 See e.g. *Empresas Lucchetti SA and Lucchetti Peru SA v Peru*, ARB/03/4, Award on Jurisdiction (7 February 2005), paras. 7, 9.

8 Murilo Otávio Lubamdo de Melo, 'Host-States and State-State Investment Arbitration' (2017) 14(2) *Brazilian Journal of International Law* 81.

9 International Centre for Settlement of Investment Disputes, 'The ICSID Caseload – Statistics (Issue 2025–2)' (*International Centre for Settlement of Investment Disputes*, 27 August 2025) <https://icsid.worldbank.org/resources/publications/icsid-caseloadstatistics> accessed 24 August 2025.

10 See *Togo Terminal v Republic of Togo*, ICSID Case No. ARB/18/16; *Autopista del Norte S.A.C. v Republic of Peru*, ICSID Case No. ARB/18/17; *La Camerounaise des Eaux (CDE) v Republic of Cameroon and Cameroon Water Utilities Cooperation (CAMWATER)*, ICSID Case No. CONC/19/1; *Contour Global Kosovo LLC v Republic of Kosovo and others*, ICSID Case No. ARB/20/50; *Mauritanian Copper Mines S.A. v Islamic Republic of Mauritania*, ICSID Case No. ARB/21/9; *AGEM Ltd v Republic of Mali*, ICSID Case No. ARB/21/62; *Digicel (Singapore) Private Limited v Independent State of Papua New Guinea*, ICSID Case No. ARB/22/18; *Upland Oil and Gas LLC (USA) and Upland Oil and Gas LLC (Perú) v PeruPetro S.A.*, ICSID Case No. ARB/22/19; *Palmerola International Airport, S.A. de C.V. v Republic of Honduras*, ICSID Case No. ARB/23/42.

roads, bridges, airports and other infrastructure); utilities (such as power plants, water distribution systems, or other public utilities); and resource extraction (such as exploiting natural resources like oil, gas, or minerals).

Concession contracts are usually of a relatively lengthy duration (typically 20–30 years). They are intended to provide a stable legal framework that protects the investor's investment, while affording the investor recourse to dispute settlement in the event of a breach of one or more of its provisions. Among other things, these agreements are notorious for providing a range of concessions to foreign investors, including a reduction in, or the non-imposition of, income, import, or property tax.[11] They typically also contain a stabilisation clause, which effectively precludes a host state from making changes to the investment landscape, legislative or otherwise, that may adversely affect the investment.[12] In other words, the state effectively agrees to freeze its legal framework, particularly taxes, for the life of the contract. A typical stabilisation clause may preclude the following:

> 'Change in Law' means any of the following events after the Signing Date:
>
> (a) a change in, modification to or amendment, repeal, revocation or expiration of any Applicable Law;
> (b) the enactment, adoption or promulgation of any new Applicable Law;
> (c) a change in application, interpretation or enforcement of any Applicable Law;
> (d) the imposition of any material condition not required as of the Signing Date in connection with the issuance, renewal or modification of any Consent by any Governmental Authority or the imposition of any new Consent;
> (e) the change or modification of any Consent by a Governmental Authority or the imposition of other obligations imposing a cost on the Concessionaire or any Contractor; or
> (f) a Change in Tax.

A stabilisation clause of this nature gave rise to a legal dispute in *Alcoa Minerals of Jamaica Inc. v Jamaica*.[13] Here, a US company entered a 25-year concession contract with the Government of Jamaica for the construction of a bauxite refining plant in Jamaica. In turn, Jamaica agreed to grant various tax concessions and long-term mining leases to Alcoa. The contract contained a 'no further tax' clause – essentially a stabilisation clause – which provided:

> No further taxes (including any income tax or withholding tax in circumstances in which none is now payable under the Income Tax Law and the disallowance of any expense as a deduction in circumstances in which it is now allowable under the Income Tax Law), burdens, levies, excises, customs or imposts will be imposed on bauxite, bauxite reserves, or bauxite operations or on alumina or the production of alumina or any operations carried on in relation to or incidental thereto or on any raw materials, supplies, property or other assets used in connection

11 George Lent, 'Tax Incentives for Investment in Developing Countries' (1967) 14(2) *IMF Staff Papers* 249; Jingqing Chai and Rishi Goyal, 'Tax Concessions and Foreign Direct Investment in the Eastern Caribbean Currency Union' (2008) IMF Working Paper WP/08/257 <https://www.imf.org/external/pubs/ft/wp/2008/wp08257.pdf> accessed 23 August 2025, Olaf De Groot and Miguel Pérez Ludeña, 'Foreign Direct Investment in the Caribbean: Trends, Determinants and Policies' (2014) 35 *ECLAC – Studies and Perspectives Series – The Caribbean*.

12 Suzy H. Nikièma and others, 'Stabilization Clauses: The Hidden Provisions That Can Hinder Tax and Investment Policy Reform' (*International Institute for Sustainable Development*, 22 November 2024) <https://www.iisd.org/articles/insight/hidden-clauses-tax-investment-policy-reform> accessed 23 August 2025.

13 ICSID Case No. ARB/74/2, Decision on Jurisdiction and Competence, 6 July 1975.

> therewith in Jamaica or its territorial waters or any mortgage, lien or charge on such assets or on any dividends or other distributions of profit arising from bauxite or alumina operations, including but not limited to any additional royalty under the Mining Law, any other royalty whatsoever, any tax, burden or manufacture, processing, transportation, storage, handling, export, employment, sales, shipping, capital or reserves, or any personal property tax, enforced investments or savings, or prepayment of taxes or any other impost EXCEPT as specifically provided elsewhere in this agreement and except normal license duties of general application, such as licenses on motor vehicles, harbour and light dues and customs and excise duties all of general application but not any duty which would be a tax, burden or impost of the nature of any of those enumerated above.

Alcoa constructed the plant and began mining bauxite. Pursuant to the contract, Alcoa paid Jamaica income tax on the alumina operation and taxes and royalties on the extraction of bauxite at the stipulated rate. Six years later, however, Jamaica announced that the government was increasing the taxes charged on the extraction of bauxite ninefold. Failing mutual agreement following negotiations, the new tax was imposed, pursuant to the Bauxite (Production Levy) Act. Alcoa, considering Jamaica's actions to be a breach of the agreement, initiated ICSID proceedings, in accordance with the dispute resolution provisions of the applicable agreement. The tribunal ultimately found that the dispute was within its jurisdiction. Although the formal case report has not been made public, Schmidt notes that the tribunal granted the relief requested by Alcoa in the light of Jamaica's non-compliance with the stabilisation clause, namely restitution of taxes paid under protest, and a declaration that collection of the tax imposed by the Bauxite (Production Levy) Act was in violation of the 1968 Agreement.[14]

Although Schmidt, commenting on the case, contends that the 'probable effect of the ICSID Convention will be to better secure the good faith performance of investment agreements',[15] stabilisation clauses of this nature are concerning.[16] More pointedly, such clauses effectively freeze the regulatory environment, thereby preventing the enactment and enforcement of much-needed statutory and/or regulatory measures in future which could improve the state's regulatory prospectus. This includes not only beneficial tax-related measures, but also, depending on how broadly drafted the stabilisation clause is, human rights and/or environmental measures which may destabilise the investment. Because stabilisation clauses bind states to commitments entered into by previous governments even when priorities subsequently change, it effectively prevents later governments from making necessary changes in their public interest due to the potential exposure to arbitral proceedings – a phenomenon generally referred to as 'regulatory chill'.[17]

14 John Schmidt, 'Arbitration under the Auspices of the International Centre for Settlement of Investment Disputes (ICSID): Implications of the Decision on Jurisdiction in *Alcoa Minerals of Jamaica, Inc. v Government of Jamaica*' (1976) 17(1) *Harvard International Law Journal* 90.

15 ibid 108.

16 Divine Shuemenang, 'Understanding the Ramifications of Stabilisation Clauses in Investment Contracts: A Developing Economy's Perspective' (2021) 4(2) *International Journal of Law, Management & Humanities* 805; Athina Fouchard Papaefstratiou, 'Stabilisation Clauses in Long-Term Investment Contracts' in Elena Cima and Makane Moïse Mbengue (eds), *A Multifaceted Approach to Trade Liberalisation and Investment Protection in the Energy Sector* (Brill Nijhoff 2021) 43–69.

17 John Linarelli, Margot E. Salomon, M. Sornarajah, *The Misery of International Law: Confrontations with Injustice in the Global Economy* (OUP 2018) 161.

Suffice it to say, concession contracts also generally contain applicable law clauses, which specifically provide which law should govern the proceedings were a dispute to arise.[18] For example, in *Grenada Private Power Limited and WRB Enterprises, Inc. v Grenada*,[19] Section 11(1) of the Concession Contract provided that the agreement was to be governed by and construed in accordance with the law of Grenada, including the 'the Constitution of Grenada' and 'the common law of Grenada'.

Relatedly, concession contracts provide for dispute resolution in the event a conflict about legal rights and obligations arises between the parties. The parties may select the Permanent Court of Arbitration (PCA), in accordance with the UNCITRAL Rules, or the International Centre for the Settlement of Investment Disputes (ICSID) as the dispute settlement mechanism in such circumstances, or another ad hoc mechanism. For example, in *Grenada Private Power Limited and WRB Enterprises, Inc. v Grenada,* the parties agreed in Section 11.2(a) of the Concession Contract to submit any dispute 'arising out of or in connection with' the agreement to ICSID. The circumstances of that case were that the Government of Grenada was, in 1992, advised by the World Bank and others to privatise electricity in that country. The then party in power, the National Democratic Congress (NDC), embraced the recommendation. The main party then in opposition, the New National Party (NNP), opposed it. Two years later, the NDC government sold a controlling interest in the local electricity company (GRENLEC) to Grenada Private Power Ltd. (GPP), a Grenadian company in which WRB Enterprises Inc., a closely held private company based in Tampa, Florida, United States of America, indirectly held 75% of the shares. The privatisation package included a share purchase agreement that was made conditional upon the Government of Grenada enacting a favourable regulatory structure in the 1994 Energy Supply Act (ESA) and the 1994 Public Utilities Commission Act (PUCA). The SPA specifically provided that upon the occurrence of any one of fifteen 'Repurchase Events', the investor would have the right to 'put' their shares to the Government of Grenada, and the Government of Grenada would be obliged to repurchase them at a price calculated in accordance with the Second Schedule of the 1994 ESA.

Twenty-two years thereafter, the incoming NNP Government decided to restructure the electricity sector through sweeping changes to its regulation, production, and distribution. More pointedly, the Senate of Grenada passed the Electricity Supply Act and Public Utilities Regulatory Commission Act (respectively, the '2016 ESA' and the '2016 PURCA'). These pieces of legislation were part of a restructuring of the electricity sector promised by the NNP Government, consistent with its long-standing view that privatisation of GRENLEC had been a mistake and its implementation bungled. The 2016 Acts shortened and narrowed GRENLEC's exclusive licence on the generation of electricity and cut short any future licence, cancelled its monopoly on permitting or refusing self-generators, abolished the statutory rate-setting mechanism, and replaced it with a more discretionary procedure, as well as eliminated GRENLEC's import duty and tax concessions. In this connection, GRENLEC no longer had authorisation to harness potential wind and waterpower without making payment to the Government, and the guarantee of compensation for revocation of the licence contained in Section 28, 29, and the Second Schedule to the 1994 ESA was removed.

18 Roland Brown, 'Choice of Law Provisions in Concession and Related Contracts' (1976) 39(6) *The Modern Law Review* 625; Sangwani Patrick Ng'ambi, 'The Effect of Stabilsation Clauses in Concession Agreements' (2012) 43 *Zambian Law Journal* 57.

19 ICSID Case No. ARB/17/13, Award, 29 March 2020.

Consequent upon the passage of these Acts, the investors wrote to the Government stating that the 2016 Acts gave rise to several 'Repurchase Events' and demanded the purchase price according to the Second Schedule, which the investors calculated at US$65,428,963, payable within 30 days. Following unsuccessful attempts to negotiate a solution, the government of Grenada declared its rejection of any obligation to repurchase the shares and refused to pay the amount claimed. This set in train ICSID arbitration proceedings.

At the hearing, the government of Grenada argued that its repurchase obligation was void and unenforceable under Grenadian law; that the SPA repurchase obligation constituted a penalty under Grenadian law, which rendered it unenforceable, and, in any event, the repurchase provisions were void as unconstitutional because their effect was to fetter the authority of the government to regulate the electricity sector in the public interest. The respondent also argued that the investors committed wilful malfeasance in their management of GRENLEC which (under the express terms of the SPA) disentitled them from insisting on the government's repurchase of the shares. Moreover, the respondent argued that the investors were poor corporate citizens in that they sought at all times to maximise their return on investment with little regard for meeting GRENLEC's capital investment needs or the well-being of the island's economy, including, in particular, the investors' persistent failure to develop Grenada's ample renewable energy resources. The investors responded, arguing that the repurchase obligation was neither a penalty nor unconstitutional. They argued that it was a straightforward commercial investment whose terms were fairly negotiated and which they were entitled to enforce. Their view was that 'a deal is a deal'.[20]

Interestingly, the tribunal considered that it had no authority to judge whether or not in the period 1994 to 2016 the investors were not a good corporate citizen of Grenada.[21] It noted that its task was simply to determine whether the complex contractual arrangements between the parties were complied with and, if not, what remedy should be awarded. Ultimately, the tribunal ruled in favour of the investors, finding that the agreement was valid in that its terms were not contrary to the Constitution of Grenada. In addition, the tribunal noted that the respondent had not established either the procedural condition precedent or the substantive factual prerequisites to deny the investors compensation on the basis of wilful malfeasance. Having established a 'repurchase' event which required the respondent to pay compensation at the level agreed to in the Second Schedule, the tribunal felt constrained to award the investors Second Schedule compensation.

One of the arguments made by Grenada, but which was rejected by the tribunal, was that the formula in the Second Schedule of the 1994 ESA contained 'a bizarre formula inherited from the colonial past' whose application produced compensation 'extravagantly disproportionate to the actual fair market value of the shares',[22] and that, in any event, the investors' monopoly, which allowed it to dish out dividends to its shareholders, was an anomalous 'colonial-era' monopoly.[23] On the latter point, the tribunal considered that the special dividend paid by the investors simply reflected the role of the investor's investment in GRENLEC. In other words, while the government of Grenada saw the investors as a key player in the economic development of the island and believed that the investors should share that vision by, for example, making significant investment in renewable energy, the

20 ibid 7.
21 ibid 8.
22 ibid 113.
23 ibid 47.

investors saw their investment as a profit-making enterprise which was 'rightly managed to maximise shareholder value.'[24] In light of the fact that there was no provision under Grenadian law which was violated by the payment of the special dividend, the tribunal felt that the investors were under no legal obligation to share the Grenadian government's view regarding the best interest of Grenada.[25]

In so far as the agreement as a whole was concerned, the tribunal rejected the respondent's general challenge to the 1994 package of laws and agreements made by the prior (and rival) NDC government. More specifically, the tribunal refused to countenance the argument that the investors performed their obligations badly; that they reaped unconscionable benefits while hindering progress and, in particular, obstructed the development of 'utility scale' renewable energy; and that it would be oppressive and unfair to reward the investors for their mismanagement with a grossly excessive award of compensation calculated under the Second Schedule. In this connection, although the tribunal recognised that the terms of the agreement did not 'look as attractive to the present NNP Government as they did to the 1994 NDC Government',[26] it nonetheless felt that this was no basis for concluding that the government was the victim of a lopsided or unfair negotiation.

Another interesting argument advanced by the respondent was that the 2016 restructuring laws were in the national interest because the claimants were squandering Grenada's renewable energy potential. It pointed out that Grenada is blessed with much sun for solar energy, much wind for industrial turbines, and much potential for the generation of geo-thermal energy, but that the investors' investment in renewable energy was a pittance. It referred, in particular, to a report from the Inter-American Development Bank which observed that development of energy resources in Grenada was hampered by the regime created by the 1994 ESA since that regime enabled a monopolistic, fossil fuel-biased development of the electricity sector, severely impeding the development of renewable energy technologies. The tribunal, however, felt unimpressed by this argument, holding that Grenada was unable to identify any statutory or contractual obligation on the part of the investors to develop renewable energy.

Ultimately, the tribunal accepted that the investors 'may have fallen short of what might be expected of a good corporate citizen',[27] but nonetheless then went on to blame the 1994 NDC Government for creating a regulatory framework which was toothless and for failing to set performance standards for renewable energy which, with the benefit of hindsight, would have promoted Grenada's development. It is submitted that this decision clearly reinforces Professor Schneiderman's contention that foreign investors investing in developing countries are generally unwilling to see themselves as constrained by principles of corporate social responsibility, a reality which is exacerbated by Concession agreements which are typically asymmetrical in nature.[28]

The question of asymmetry has become a talking point in recent years in the light of the 2016 Petroleum Agreement Between Guyana and ExxonMobil et al., which expressly

24 ibid 96.
25 ibid.
26 ibid 119.
27 ibid 140.
28 Jason Haynes and Antonius Hippolyte, 'The Coloniality of International Investment Law in The Commonwealth Caribbean' (2023) 72(1) *International and Comparative Law Quarterly* 105.

permits the latter to exploit Guyana's newly discovered gas reserves.[29] Though Guyana stands to benefit (and is already benefiting from revenue derived from the permit), the Agreement has been met with heavy criticism by a range of stakeholders.[30] Sanzillo, for example, argues that the Agreement is one-sided and unfavourable to the host country for a number of reasons.[31] First, ExxonMobil and partners received approximately G$752.4 billion (US$3.6 billion) while Guyana received only G$127 billion (US$607 million) through 2021 – an 85.5% to 14.5% split favouring the companies. Second, by 2027, Guyana may carry a hidden liability of more than G$6.27 trillion (US$34 billion) owed to the oil companies for development costs, decommissioning, and tax giveaways.[32] Third, Guyana pays the oil companies' income taxes (approximately G$335.3 billion or US$1.7 billion over five years).[33] Fourth, Guyana is required to advance G$666.1 billion (US$3.2 billion) for future decommissioning costs with no requirement for the companies to set aside these funds. Fifth, ExxonMobil was able to weaken environmental protections, changing from a 'zero routine flaring' standard to allowing 'incremental non-routine' flaring. Finally, since oil production began in December 2019, Guyana's public debt has increased.[34] In short, Sanzillo argues that the agreement's structure creates an inherent conflict: Guyana benefits from minimal recoverable costs, while the oil companies benefit from maximising them. The lack of ring-fencing provisions in the Concession Contract allows revenues from operational wells to fund development of new wells, further delaying Guyana's access to its fair share of revenues.[35]

The foregoing discussion illustrates how concession contracts, particularly in the area of resource extraction, can create long-term financial implications for host countries, especially when there are asymmetries in negotiating power and technical expertise. In particular, the Guyana-ExxonMobil case demonstrates the critical importance of initial contract terms, transparency provisions, and environmental safeguards in determining the long-term distribution of benefits from natural resource extraction in the context of Concession contracts.

III. INVESTOR-STATE DISPUTE SETTLEMENT

Investor-state arbitration involves an investor relying upon the provisions of a BIT or RTA with an investment chapter to bring arbitral proceedings against a host state on account of some action or omission that is alleged to be inconsistent with one or more of the standards

29 Petroleum Agreement between the Government of the Cooperative Republic of Guyana and Esso Exploration and Production Guyana Limited, CNOOC Nexen Petroleum Guyana Limited and Hess Guyana Exploration Limited dated 27 June 2016.

30 See Kiana Wilburg, 'Extensive Review of 130 Oil Contracts Exposes Inferiority of Guyana and ExxonMobil's PSA' (*Kaieteur News*, 21 July 2019) <https://kaieteurnewsonline.com/2019/07/21/extensive-review-of-130-oil-contracts-exposes-inferiority-of-guyana-exxonmobil-psa/> accessed 24 August 2025; Tom Sanzillo, 'IEEFA Report Findings: 2016 Petroleum Agreement between Guyana, ExxonMobil, et al.' (*Institute for Energy Economics and Financial Analysis*, 23 May 2022) <https://ieefa.org/resources/ieefa-report-findings-2016-petroleum-agreement-between-guyana-exxonmobil-et-al> accessed 24 August 2025.

31 Sanzillo (n 30).

32 ibid 2.

33 ibid.

34 ibid 7.

35 ibid 3.

of protection provided for in the treaty.[36] The offer to arbitrate is a standing one[37] contained in the treaty in question,[38] usually couched in terms such as Article 8 of the Grenada-UK BIT:

> (I) Disputes between a national or company of one Contracting Party and the other Contracting Party concerning an obligation of the latter under this Agreement in relation to an investment of the former which have not been amicably settled shall, after a period of three months from written notification of a claim, be submitted to international arbitration if either party to the dispute so wishes.
>
> (2) Where the dispute is referred to international arbitration, the investor and the Contracting Party concerned in the dispute may agree to refer the dispute either to:
>
> (a) the International Centre for the Settlement of Investment Disputes (having regard to the provisions, where applicable, of the Convention on the Settlement of Investment Disputes between States and Nationals of other States, opened for signature at Washington DC on 18 March 1965 and the Additional Facility for the Administration of Conciliation, Arbitration and Fact-Finding Proceedings); or
>
> (b) the Court of Arbitration of the International Chamber of Commerce; or
>
> (c) an international arbitrator or ad hoc arbitration tribunal to be appointed by a special agreement or established under the Arbitration Rules of the United Nations Commission on International Trade Law.

In accordance with this provision, if, after three months (the consultation period)[39] from written notification of the claim, there is no agreement to an alternative procedure, either

36 Michael Waibel, 'Investment Arbitration: Jurisdiction and Admissibility' in Marc Bungenberg and others (eds), *International Investment Law* (Nomos 2015) 1261–336.

37 Stanley Nweke-Eze, 'Jurisdiction: Main Elements' (*Global Arbitration Review*, 21 December 2023) <https://globalarbitrationreview.com/guide/the-guide-investment-treaty-protection-and-enforcement/second-edition/article/jurisdiction-main-elements> accessed 24 August 2025.

38 The investor-state dispute resolution clause can be found in the following Caribbean BITs: Antigua-Germany BIT Article 11; Antigua-UK BIT Article 8; Belgium-Luxembourg-Barbados BIT Article 8; Barbados-Canada BIT Article XIII; Barbados-China BIT Article 9; Barbados-Cuba BIT Article 8; Barbados-Germany BIT Article 11; Barbados-Mauritius BIT Article 10; Barbados-Switzerland BIT Article 9; Barbados-UK BIT Article 8; Barbados-Venezuela BIT Article 8; Belize-China BIT Article 7; Belize-Cuba BIT Article 8; Belize-El Salvador BIT Article 7; Belize-Netherlands BIT Article 9; Belize-UK BIT Article 8; Dominica-UK BIT Article 8; Grenada-UK BIT Article 8; Grenada-US BIT Article VI; Guyana-Brazil BIT Article 25; Guyana-China BIT Article 9; Guyana-Germany BIT Article 11; Guyana-South Korea BIT Article 8; Guyana-Switzerland BIT Article 8; Guyana-UK BIT Article 8; Jamaica-US BIT Article VI; Jamaica-China BIT Article 8; Jamaica-Egypt BIT Article 8; Jamaica-Germany BIT Article 11; Jamaica-Indonesia BIT Article IX; Jamaica-South Korea BIT Article 8; Jamaica-Switzerland BIT Article 9; Jamaica-Netherlands BIT Article 9; Jamaica-UK BIT Article 9; St Lucia-Germany BIT Article 10; St Lucia-UK BIT Article 8; SVG-Taiwan BIT Article XI and XII; Trinidad and Tobago-Canada BIT Article XIII; Trinidad and Tobago-China BIT Article 10; Trinidad and Tobago-Cuba BIT Article 10; Trinidad and Tobago-France BIT Article 8; Trinidad and Tobago-Germany BIT Article 13; Trinidad and Tobago-Guatemala BIT Article 10 and 11; Trinidad and Tobago-India BIT Article 9; Trinidad and Tobago-South Korea BIT Article 8; Trinidad and Tobago-Switzerland BIT Article 8; Trinidad and Tobago-UK BIT Article 10; Trinidad and Tobago-USA BIT Article IX.

39 The consultation period varies across jurisdictions. 3 months: Antigua-UK BIT (Article 8): 3 months; Barbados-Cuba BIT (Article 8): 3 months; Belgium-Luxembourg-Barbados BIT (Article 8(3)): 3 months; Belize-China BIT (Article 7): 3 months; Belize-Cuba BIT (Article 8): 3 months; Belize-El Salvador BIT (Article 7): 3 months; Belize-UK BIT (Article 8): 3 months; Dominica-UK BIT (Article 8): 3 months; Grenada-UK BIT (Article 8): 3 months; Jamaica-US BIT (Article VI(3)(a)): 3 months minimum; St Lucia-UK

party may decide to submit the claim to arbitration. In other words, an investor perfects the standing offer to arbitrate by accepting this offer[40] – that is, through the initiation of proceedings before one of the specified dispute resolution mechanisms.

After the arbitrator or arbitrators are appointed in accordance with the procedure laid down by the treaty,[41] the proceedings formally begin with considerations of the tribunal's jurisdiction, admissibility issues, and ultimately consideration of the merits, provided that the tribunal decides that it has jurisdiction. Reinisch asserts in this connection that, whereas jurisdiction is concerned with the consent of the state to arbitrate (who, against whom, based on what agreement, pursuant to what dispute, when?), admissibility is concerned with issues that relate to the nature of the claim once the tribunal confirms jurisdiction (fraudulent investment, bribery, corruption, etc).[42]

A. Fork-in-the-Road

If the relevant treaty contains a fork-in-the-road provision,[43] and the investor chooses to pursue domestic litigation, they effectively waive their right to engage in international arbitration.[44] Article IX(4) of the Jamaica-Indonesia BIT is instructive in this regard:

> Pursuant to Paragraph 2 and 3, where an investor or a Contracting Party has submitted a dispute to the aforementioned competent Tribunal of the contracting party where the investment has been made or to international arbitration, this decision shall be final.[45]

BIT (Article 8): 3 months; Trinidad and Tobago-USA BIT (Article IX(3)(a)): 3 months; Barbados-Canada BIT (Article XIII(2)): 6 months Barbados-China BIT (Article 9(2)): 6 months Barbados-Germany BIT (Article 11(2)): 6 months; Barbados-Mauritius BIT (Article 10(2)): 6 months; Other periods: Grenada-US BIT (Article VI(3)(a)): 6 months minimum; Guyana-China BIT (Article 9(3)): 6 months; Guyana-South Korea BIT (Article 8(3)): 6 months; Guyana-Switzerland BIT (Article 8(2)): 6 months; Jamaica-China BIT (Article 8(2)): 6 months; Jamaica-Egypt BIT (Article 8(2)): 6 months; Jamaica-Indonesia BIT (Article IX(2)): 6 months; SVG-Taiwan BIT (Article XI(2)): 6 months; Trinidad and Tobago-Canada BIT (Article XIII(2)): 6 months; Trinidad and Tobago-China BIT (Article 10(2)): 6 months; Trinidad and Tobago-Cuba BIT (Article 10(2)): 6 months; Trinidad and Tobago-Germany BIT (Article 13(2)(a)): 6 months; Trinidad and Tobago-Guatemala BIT (Article 10(3)): 6 months; Trinidad and Tobago-India BIT (Article 9(2)): 6 months; Trinidad and Tobago-South Korea BIT (Article 8(3)): 6 months; Trinidad and Tobago-Switzerland BIT (Article 8(2)): 6 months Trinidad and Tobago-UK BIT (Article 10(1)): 6 months; Jamaica-South Korea BIT (Article 8(3)): 9 months; 12 months; Barbados-Switzerland BIT (Article 9(2)): 12 months; Jamaica-Switzerland BIT (Article 9(2)): 12 months.

40 Nweke-Eze (n 37).

41 In respect of a three-member arbitration panel, each party appoints one member of the tribunal. Those two members then jointly appoint an arbitrator of a non-disputing state who serves as chair or president of the tribunal.

42 August Reinisch, 'Jurisdiction and Admissibility in International Investment Law' (2017) 16 *The Law and Practice of International Courts and Tribunals* 21.

43 Rudolf Dolzer, Ursula Kriebaum and Christoph Schreuer, *Principles of International Investment Law* (3rd edn, OUP 2012) 384.

44 Johan Billiet, *International Investment Arbitration: A Practical Handbook* (Maklu 2016) 187–88.

45 See, also, Jamaica-US BIT (Article VI(2)); Trinidad and Tobago-Germany BIT (Article 13(2)(b)); Guatemala BIT (Article 10(4)); SVG-Taiwan BIT (Article XI(3)(b)); Barbados-Canada BIT (Article XIII(3)(b)); Trinidad and Tobago-Canada BIT (Article XIII(3)(b)).

A similar provision can be found in Article 9 of The Bahamas-China BIT:

> Once the investor has decided to submit the dispute to the competent court of the relevant Contracting Party or the ICSID, the choice of one of the above two procedures shall be final.

The interpretation and application of fork-in-the-road provisions have generated significant jurisprudence, with tribunals adopting different approaches on the question of when these provisions preclude investors from pursuing international arbitration. Some tribunals adopt the 'fundamental basis' test, while others adopt the 'triple identity' test.[46] The former test was applied in *H&H v Egypt*[47] in a dispute concerning a management and operation contract regarding a resort in Egypt. Following commercial arbitration and court proceedings in Egypt, the claimant brought ICSID proceedings pursuant to the Egypt-United States BIT (1986) claiming, *inter alia*, that the respondent state's eviction of the investor from the resort and its refusal to recognise the investor's option to buy the resort breached the BIT. The tribunal held that the bulk of the claims were barred as a result of the prior arbitral and judicial proceedings in Egypt, and thus the application of the BIT's fork-in-the-road provision. In reaching its conclusion, the tribunal rejected the claimant's argument that claims are only barred by a fork-in-the-road clause when the claims in the domestic proceedings and the claims in the international proceedings meet the so-called 'triple identity test'; that is, claims involving the same parties, same object, and same cause of action. Rather than relying on interpretations developed by other tribunals in the context of other investment treaties, the tribunal focused on the BIT before it, concluding that the purpose of the fork-in-the-road clause was 'to ensure that the same dispute is not litigated before different fora'.[48] As a result, the tribunal held that instead of requiring specifically that the parties be the same or focusing on whether the causes of actions relied upon in the claims brought to the local courts and the arbitration are identical, it would look to determine whether the treaty claims had the same fundamental basis as the claims submitted before the local fora. On the facts, the tribunal concluded that the fork-in-the-road provision had been triggered and that it was without jurisdiction to decide on the claimant's BIT claims.

In contrast, the tribunal in *Charanne and Construction Investments v Spain*[49] dismissed the respondent state's objection that the claimants, by bringing local administrative proceedings and a proceeding before the European Court of Human Rights (ECtHR), triggered the fork-in-the-road provision of the Energy Charter Treaty (ECT) and were therefore precluded from bringing the case before an ISDS tribunal. The tribunal considered, in particular, that there were no identical parties in the local or the ECtHR proceedings as required under a 'triple identity test' (same parties, same object, and same cause of action), and that the ECtHR did not constitute a court or administrative tribunal of a Contracting Party to the ECT. Meanwhile, in *Toto Costruzioni v Lebanon*,[50] the tribunal applied the triple identity test and found that the contractual claims previously submitted to Lebanese courts were

46 Markus Petsche, 'The Fork in the Road Revisited: An Attempt to Overcome the Clash Between Formalistic and Pragmatic Approaches' (2019) 18 *Washington University Global Studies Law Review* 391.

47 ICSID Case No. ARB 09/15, Award, 6 May 2014.

48 ibid 367.

49 SCC Case No. 062/2012, Award, 21 January 2016, para. 398.

50 ICSID Case No. ARB/07/12, Decision on Jurisdiction, 11 September 2009, paras. 211–217.

distinct from the treaty claims later brought to arbitration, allowing the investment arbitration to proceed despite the fork-in-the-road provision.

The application of fork-in-the-road provisions has evolved as states have adjusted their treaty language in response to tribunal interpretations. In *Supervision y Control v Costa Rica*,[51] for example, the tribunal noted that the Spain-Costa Rica BIT contained an unusually worded fork-in-the-road provision that specifically precluded investors from submitting to international arbitration 'the same dispute' that had been submitted to domestic courts. The tribunal interpreted this language as requiring a stricter identity between domestic and international proceedings than provisions in other treaties. Against this backdrop, more recent treaties have begun to clarify the scope of fork-in-the-road provisions. For example, the Comprehensive and Progressive Agreement for Trans-Pacific Partnership (CPTPP) (Annex 9-J) specifies that a claimant may not submit a claim to arbitration if it has initiated a proceeding seeking resolution of 'the same alleged breach' before a domestic court or administrative tribunal, adopting a more specific test than either the fundamental basis or triple identity approaches.

In the final analysis, the application of fork-in-the-road provisions ultimately depends on the specific wording of the relevant treaty provision and the factual relationship between domestic and international proceedings. While many tribunals have applied the triple identity test as a safeguard for investors' rights to pursue distinct treaty and contract claims in different forums, others have adopted the more holistic 'fundamental basis' approach that may bar claims with substantive overlap regardless of their formal characterisation. This divergence in approaches highlights the importance for Caribbean host states to carefully consider their dispute resolution strategy from the outset of any investment dispute.

B. Local Remedies Requirement

Where a treaty mandates that an investor pursues domestic remedies, and specifies a timeframe in this connection (say 18 months before arbitration can be commenced), this requirement must be honoured, unless pursuing these remedies will be futile (because, for example, the legal system is heavily stacked against the investor due to there being a pattern of unfair treatment of foreign investors by domestic tribunals amounting to a denial of justice).[52] Investment treaties differ significantly in how they structure the relationship between domestic remedies and international arbitration. Some BITs contain mandatory provisions requiring investors to pursue local remedies for a specified period before initiating arbitration, while others make this optional. In respect of the latter, a useful example is Article 9(2) of the Jamaica-UK BIT, which provides that parties may proceed to arbitration:

51 ICSID Case No. ARB/12/4, Award, 18 January 2017, para. 296.

52 Note, however, *Kiliç İnşaat İthalat İhracat Sanayi Ve Ticaret Anonim Şirketi v Turkmenistan*, ICSID Case No. ARB/10/1, Award, 2 July 2013, para. 8.1.4

> A tribunal cannot properly come to a conclusion that an investor is not required to comply with mandatory prior recourse to a state's courts unless a clear case has been made out, based on sufficient and 'best' evidence, that recourse is not available to the state's court or, if available, the investor would not have been treated fairly before those courts.

The tribunal went on to note that:

> [8.1.10] . . . . if a party to proceedings such as these is to make a futility argument, it has the onus of showing that recourse to the Contracting State's courts would be futile or ineffective, and that requires the tendering of probative evidence that goes to the specificity of the issue in dispute. It is not enough to make generalised allegations about the insufficiency of a state's legal system.

> If any such dispute should arise and agreement cannot be reached between the parties to the dispute through pursuit of local remedies in accordance with international law then, if the national or company affected also consents in writing to submit the dispute to the Centre for settlement by conciliation or arbitration under the Convention, either party may institute proceedings by addressing a request to that effect to the Secretary-General of the Centre as provided in Articles 28 and 36 of the Convention.[53]

Meanwhile, some provisions are couched in discretionary language, such as Article 9(4) of the Guyana-China BIT, which provides:

> . . . the Contracting Party involved in the dispute *may* require the investor concerned to exhaust the domestic administrative review procedures specified by the laws and regulations of that Contracting Party.[54]

In *ICS Inspection v Argentina*,[55] the tribunal found that it lacked jurisdiction due to the claimant's failure to comply with the mandatory 18-month recourse-to-local-courts requirement set forth in Article 8 of the Argentina-UK BIT. The tribunal emphasised that the 18-month recourse-to-local-courts requirement constituted a condition to the respondent state's consent to arbitration. Notably, the tribunal refused to ignore this requirement even when faced with arguments about inefficiency, stating that it could not

> create exceptions to treaty rules where these are merely based upon an assessment of the wisdom of the policy in question, having no basis in either the treaty text or in any supplementary interpretive source, however desirable such policy considerations might be seen to be in the abstract.[56]

Similarly, in *Daimler v Argentina*,[57] the tribunal held that since the 18-month domestic litigation requirement constitutes a treaty-based precondition to the host state's consent to arbitrate, it could not be bypassed or otherwise waived by the tribunal as a mere 'procedural' or 'admissibility-related' matter.

Meanwhile, in *Enron Corporation and Ponderosa Assets, L.P. v Argentine Republic*,[58] the tribunal declared that the six-month negotiation period was 'very much a jurisdictional one. A failure to comply with that requirement would result in a determination of lack of jurisdiction'.[59] In the same vein, the tribunal in *Burlington Resources Inc. v Republic of Ecuador*[60] was clear that the six-month negotiation requirement was a jurisdictional one:

> . . . by imposing upon investors an obligation to voice their disagreement at least six months prior to the submission of an investment dispute to arbitration, the Treaty effectively accords host States the right to be informed about the dispute at least six months before it is submitted

53 See, also, 3 months mandatory: Barbados-UK BIT (Article 8(3)); Guyana-UK BIT (Article 8(3)) Jamaica-UK BIT (Article 9(1)); 18 months mandatory: Jamaica-Netherlands BIT (Article 9(3)); 24 months mandatory: Jamaica-Germany BIT (Article 11(2)).

54 See, also, Barbados-China BIT (Article 9(3)); Trinidad and Tobago-China BIT (Article 10 2(b)); Guyana-China BIT (Article 9(4)); Jamaica-Switzerland BIT Article 9(4) provides: 'the Contracting Party may require the exhaustion of local administrative or judicial remedies as a condition of its agreement to arbitration'.

55 UNCITRAL, PCA Case No. 2010–9, Award on Jurisdiction, 10 February 2012, para. 273.

56 ibid 267.

57 ICSID Case No. ARB/05/1, Award, 22 August 2012, para. 194.

58 ICSID Case No. ARB/01/3, Decision on Jurisdiction, 14 January 2004, para. 88.

59 ibid.

60 ICSID Case No. ARB/08/5, Decision on Jurisdiction, 2 June 2010, para. 315.

> to arbitration. The purpose of this right is to grant the host State an opportunity to redress the problem before the investor submits the dispute to arbitration. In this case, Claimant has deprived the host State of that opportunity. That suffices to defeat jurisdiction.[61]

Further, the tribunal in *Wintershall*[62] noted:

> And the eighteen-month requirement of a proceeding before local courts (stipulated in Article 10(2)) is an essential preliminary step to the institution of ICSID Arbitration, under the Argentina-Germany BIT; it constitutes an integral part of the 'standing offer' ('consent') of the Host State, which must be accepted on the same terms by every individual investor who seeks recourse (ultimately) to ICSID arbitration for resolving its dispute with the Host State under the concerned BIT . . . . The requirement of recourse to local courts for an eighteen-month period in Article 10(2) is fundamentally a jurisdictional clause, not a mere procedural provision.[63]

Separately, in *Murphy v Ecuador*,[64] the tribunal considered that the waiting period was a jurisdictional requirement, and that non-respect for such waiting period had as its consequence the lack of jurisdiction of the tribunal.[65]

By contrast, in *Muhammet Çap v Turkmenistan*,[66] the tribunal assessed whether Article VII.2 of the Turkey-Turkmenistan BIT imposed a mandatory one-year local litigation requirement. The claimants contended that the treaty provided merely for an option to submit the dispute to domestic courts, without requiring it. The tribunal agreed with the claimants that Article VII.2 allowed the investor to choose between three arbitration venues or local courts. In the tribunal's view, the fact that the claimants had not submitted the dispute to the courts of Turkmenistan prior to arbitration was no impediment to the investor bringing the proceedings.

From a Caribbean perspective, it is submitted that the former approach is more defensible as a matter of principle. More particularly, because the dispute resolution clause specifies the conditions under which the Contracting Parties give their consent to arbitration, these conditions should not be easily dispensed with, unless the pursuit of local remedies will be futile.[67] For example, in *SGS v Pakistan*,[68] the respondent government had shown no interest in entering into negotiations with the claimant during the long period that had elapsed prior to the registration of the BIT claim. Moreover, the Government of Pakistan had no incentive to do so, since the Supreme Court of Pakistan had already issued a binding decision

61 ibid.

62 *Wintershall v Argentine Republic*, ICSID Case No. ARB/04/14, Award, 8 December 2008.

63 ibid 160, 172.

64 ICSID Case No. ARB/08/4, Decision on Jurisdiction, 15 December 2010.

65 ibid 140–57. cf *Ronald Lauder v The Czech Republic*, UNCITRAL, IIC 205 (2001), Final Award, 3 September 2001, para. 187.

66 ICSID Case No. ARB/12/6, Decision on Respondent's Objection to Jurisdiction under Article VII(2) of the Turkey-Turkmenistan Bilateral Investment Treaty, 13 February 2015.

67 cf The tribunal in *İçkale İnşaat Limited Şirketi v Turkmenistan*, ICSID Case No. ARB/10/24, para. 260: the BIT does not provide for any 'futility exception' to the local litigation requirement in Article VII(2) of the BIT. Any claim arising out of the alleged inadequacy of the local legal system would have to be pursued as a denial of justice claim, which does allow a party to dispense with the requirement to exhaust local remedies in circumstances in which recourse to such remedies would be demonstrably futile. However, the Claimant has not even attempted to submit the dispute to local courts. There can be no denial of justice where there has been no legal process in the first place.

68 ICSID Case No. ARB/01/13.

adverse to the claimant's position. The tribunal was therefore of the opinion that requiring the claimant to observe any further negotiation period would have been futile in the circumstances. Meanwhile, in *Giovanni Alemanni v Argentina,*[69] the tribunal confirmed the existence of a 'futility exception' to the applicable treaty's requirement to have recourse to local courts for a certain minimum length of time. While it noted that the legal effect of the host state's offer to arbitrate 'can only be produced if the investor accepts the offer on the terms specified by the host State'[70] (including the 18-month domestic court requirement), it found that that requirement 'shows unambiguously . . . that the Contracting States had in view as the intervening step a process that would be potentially effective to settle the issue in dispute'.[71] The *Alemanni* tribunal determined that in the circumstances it was shown that Argentina's judicial system was not reasonably capable of providing effective relief, and that therefore the claimants' failure to comply with the BIT's preconditions to arbitration did not act as a jurisdictional bar to their commencing ICSID arbitration. Similar observations were made in *Ambiente Ufficio v Argentina*[72] and *Philip Morris v Uruguay,*[73] where the tribunals acknowledged that while the domestic litigation requirement was a jurisdictional condition, the futility exception could apply where the claimant could demonstrate that pursuing local remedies would be ineffective or meaningless. The standard for establishing futility, however, is high. Indeed, as noted in *Kiliç İnşaat v Turkmenistan,*[74] an investor claiming futility must show more than mere likelihood of failure on the merits; rather, the investor must demonstrate systemic deficiencies in the judicial system that would make pursuing local remedies meaningless or ineffective.

C. The International Centre for Settlement of Investment Disputes (ICSID)

ICSID functions not as a court but as an administrative body that manages various services, with the administration of investor-state arbitration being its primary service.[75] The rules governing ICSID proceedings depend on the Contracting Parties' relationship to ICSID. When both Contracting States are ICSID members, the ICSID Convention and Arbitration Rules (2022) apply.[76] However, if only one party is an ICSID member,[77]

69 ICSID Case No. ARB/07/8, Decision on Jurisdiction and Admissibility, 17 November 2014, para. 310.
70 ibid 305.
71 ibid 311.
72 ICSID Case No. ARB/08/9, Decision on Jurisdiction and Admissibility, 8 February 2013, para. 628.
73 ICSID Case No. ARB/10/7, Decision of Jurisdiction, 2 July 2013, para. 234.
74 ICSID Case No. ARB/10/1, Award, 2 July 2013, para. 8.1.15.
75 International Centre for Settlement of Investment Disputes, 'About ICSID' (*International Centre for Settlement of Investment Disputes*) <https://icsid.worldbank.org/About/ICSID> accessed 1 September 2025.
76 International Centre for Settlement of Investment Disputes, 'Procedures' (*International Centre for Settlement of Investment Disputes*) <https://icsid.worldbank.org/procedures/arbitration/convention/overview/2022> accessed 1 September 2025.
77 Some dispute resolution clauses provide for ICSID proceedings only: Jamaica-South Korea BIT (Article 8); Barbados-Venezuela BIT (Article 8); (with Additional Facility if Venezuela not ICSID member); Barbados-Switzerland BIT (Article 9); Barbados-UK BIT (Article 8); Guyana-UK BIT (Article 8); Jamaica-UK BIT (Article 9); Jamaica-Netherlands BIT (Article 9). On the other hand, most provide for multiple arbitration options, including both ICSID and UNCITRAL: Antigua-UK BIT (Article 8): ICSID, ICC, UNCITRAL;

the ICSID Additional Facility Rules govern the proceedings, as exemplified in cases such as *Besserglik v Mozambique*.[78]

An ICSID arbitration begins when a party submits a request for arbitration to the ICSID Secretary-General, in accordance with the requirements of Article 36 of the ICSID Convention, the ICSID Institution Rules, and Administrative and Financial Regulation 18. This request must fulfil several specific conditions under Institution Rule 2: it must be written in an official ICSID language (English, French, or Spanish), identify all parties with their contact details, provide evidence of consent to arbitration, and demonstrate compliance with the jurisdictional requirements outlined in Article 25 of the ICSID Convention. The request must also include evidence of the party's nationality, details of the investment, a summary of relevant facts and claims, and documentation proving consent to ICSID arbitration. For cases involving juridical persons who are nationals of the host state, the request must include an agreement that the entity should be treated as a national of another member state, consistent with Article 25(2)(b) of the Convention. After receiving the request and the non-refundable lodging fee of US$25,000, the Secretary-General screens it to determine whether the dispute falls manifestly outside ICSID's jurisdiction, in accordance with Article 36(3) of the Convention. If the Secretary-General concludes that the jurisdictional requirements of Article 25 are not manifestly lacking, the request is registered, thus initiating time limits for constituting the tribunal.

Following registration, the parties must agree on the number of arbitrators and the method of their appointment. According to Article 37 of the ICSID Convention and Arbitration Rules 15 and 16, if the parties fail to reach an agreement within 45 days after registration, a default mechanism applies: a three-member tribunal is formed where each party appoints one arbitrator, and together they appoint the President of the tribunal. The appointment of arbitrators must comply with nationality requirements specified in Article 39 of the Convention and

Belgium-Luxembourg-Barbados BIT (Article 8): UNCITRAL, ICSID, ICC/LCIA; Barbados-Canada BIT (Article XIII): ICSID, Additional Facility, UNCITRAL; Barbados-China BIT (Article 9): ICSID, UNCITRAL; Barbados-Cuba BIT (Article 8): ICC, UNCITRAL; Barbados-Germany BIT (Article 11): ICSID (if both parties are members); Barbados-Mauritius BIT (Article 10): ICSID, UNCITRAL; Belize-China BIT (Article 7): ICC, UNCITRAL; Belize-Cuba BIT (Article 8): ICC, UNCITRAL; Belize-El Salvador BIT (Article 7): ICC, UNCITRAL; Belize-UK BIT (Article 8): ICSID, ICC, UNCITRAL; Dominica-UK BIT (Article 8): ICSID, ICC, UNCITRAL; Grenada-UK BIT (Article 8): ICSID, ICC, UNCITRAL Grenada-US BIT (Article VI): ICSID, Additional Facility; Guyana-Brazil BIT (Article 25): Ad hoc or permanent arbitration; Guyana-China BIT (Article 9): ICSID, ad hoc; Guyana-South Korea BIT (Article 8): ICSID, ICC, UNCITRAL; Jamaica-US BIT (Article VI): ICSID, UNCITRAL; Jamaica-China BIT (Article 8): Ad hoc arbitration for expropriation disputes; Jamaica-Egypt BIT (Article 8): ICSID, UNCITRAL; Jamaica-Indonesia BIT (Article IX): ICSID, UNCITRAL; St Lucia-UK BIT (Article 8): ICSID, ICC, UNCITRAL; SVG-Taiwan BIT (Article XII): ICSID, Additional Facility, UNCITRAL; Trinidad and Tobago-Canada BIT (Article XIII): ICSID, Additional Facility, UNCITRAL; Trinidad and Tobago-China BIT (Article 10): ICSID, UNCITRAL; Trinidad and Tobago-Cuba BIT (Article 10): ICC, UNCITRAL; Trinidad and Tobago-France BIT (Article 8): ICSID, ICC, UNCITRAL; Trinidad and Tobago-Germany BIT (Article 13): ICSID, ICC, UNCITRAL; Trinidad and Tobago-Guatemala BIT (Article 10): ICSID, Additional Facility, UNCITRAL; Trinidad and Tobago-India BIT (Article 9): ICSID, Additional Facility, UNCITRAL; Trinidad and Tobago-South Korea BIT (Article 8): ICSID, ICC, UNCITRAL; Trinidad and Tobago-Switzerland BIT (Article 8): ICSID, UNCITRAL, ICC; Trinidad and Tobago-UK BIT (Article 10): ICSID, ICC, UNCITRAL; Trinidad and Tobago-USA BIT (Article IX): ICSID, Additional Facility, UNCITRAL.

78 ICSID Case No. ARB(AF)/14/2.

Arbitration Rule 13, which require that a majority of arbitrators must be nationals of states other than the parties to the dispute. All arbitrators must meet the qualifications listed in Article 14(1) of the Convention: high moral character, recognised competence in relevant fields, and independence of judgment. A tribunal is officially constituted on the date the Secretary-General notifies the parties that all arbitrators have accepted their appointments and signed their declarations, as required by Arbitration Rule 21. This constitution triggers several procedural steps, including designation of the Tribunal Secretary, scheduling of the first session, and the request for advance payment of costs.

The first session of the tribunal must be held within 60 days after its constitution, as required by Arbitration Rule 29(3). During this session, the tribunal establishes procedural rules for the case, including the language(s) to be used, place of proceedings, and the procedural calendar. These decisions are formalised in Procedural Order No. 1, which must be issued within 15 days after the first session, according to Arbitration Rule 29(5). The tribunal must also conduct case management conferences with the parties to ensure an expeditious and cost-effective process, as stipulated in Arbitration Rule 31. These conferences help identify uncontested facts, narrow the issues in dispute, and address procedural or substantive questions.

The written procedure typically follows a structure of two rounds of submissions, as outlined in Arbitration Rule 30: a Memorial by the requesting party, followed by a Counter-Memorial from the opposing party, then a Reply and Rejoinder. Each party bears the burden of proving the facts they rely upon to support their claims or defences, in accordance with Arbitration Rule 36(2). Evidence may include exhibits, witness statements, expert reports, and other documentary materials. The production of documents is governed by Arbitration Rule 37, which requires the tribunal to consider several factors: the scope and timeliness of requests, the relevance and materiality of the documents sought, the burden of production, and any objections raised.

Hearings follow the written phase unless the parties agree otherwise, as per Arbitration Rule 32(1). If the parties cannot agree on the location for a hearing, it must be held at ICSID's seat in Washington, D.C., as noted by Article 62 of the Convention and Arbitration Rule 32(3). Witnesses and experts who have filed written statements may be called for examination according to Arbitration Rule 38(2), and the tribunal may pose questions directly to counsel, witnesses, and experts as allowed by Arbitration Rule 32(4).

The ICSID Rules provide several specific procedural mechanisms. Under Arbitration Rule 41, a party may object that a claim manifestly lacks legal merit within 45 days after the tribunal's constitution, with the tribunal being required to issue a decision within 60 days after the last submission. Parties may raise preliminary objections to jurisdiction or admissibility under Arbitration Rules 43–45. If bifurcation is requested under Arbitration Rule 44, the tribunal decides whether to separate these objections from the merits and must decide on bifurcated objections within 180 days after the last submission. The tribunal may recommend provisional measures to preserve parties' rights under Article 47 of the Convention and Arbitration Rule 47, with decisions typically issued within 30 days after the last submission.

Arbitration Rule 53 allows a party to request security for costs, which the tribunal must decide upon within 30 days after the last submission, considering the requesting party's ability and willingness to comply with an adverse decision on costs. For parties seeking a faster resolution, Arbitration Rules 75–86 provide for expedited arbitration, which with the consent of all parties, compresses timelines and modifies certain procedural rules to conclude the arbitration within 470–530 days after registration.

As the proceedings conclude, the tribunal must render its Award within specific timeframes: 60 days for decisions on objections that claims manifestly lack legal merit (Arbitration Rule 41(2)(e)), 180 days for decisions declining jurisdiction in bifurcated proceedings (Arbitration Rule 44(3)), and 240 days in all other cases (Arbitration Rule 58(1)). The Award must be reasoned, signed by tribunal members, and comply with formal requirements under Article 48 of the Convention and Arbitration Rule 59. It becomes binding when ICSID dispatches certified copies to the parties, as specified in Arbitration Rule 60(2).

The ICSID Convention provides specific post-award remedies. Parties may request a supplementary decision or rectification under Article 49(2) of the Convention and Arbitration Rule 61 within 45 days after the Award to address omitted questions or correct clerical errors. If parties dispute the meaning or scope of the Award, they may request an interpretation at any time under Article 50 of the Convention and Arbitration Rules 69, 70, 72, and 73. A party may apply for revision within 90 days after discovering a decisive new fact that was unknown when the Award was rendered, provided this application is made within three years after the Award, as governed by Article 51 of the Convention and Arbitration Rules 69, 70, 72, and 73.

There is some dispute as to whether ICSID is a more advantageous system compared to UNCITRAL, for example. On the one hand, it could be argued that ICSID arbitration is more favourable to investors than UNCITRAL arbitration, because ICSID arbitration is institutional arbitration; ICSID is specialised in investor-state disputes; ICSID arbitration is insulated from interference by courts at the seat of the arbitration; a decision in favour of jurisdiction may not be challenged until after the final award; local courts are not involved in enforcement or review of ICSID awards; and there is no uncertainty about the seat of arbitration, as there is in UNCITRAL arbitration. On the other hand, it could be argued that ICSID arbitration is not objectively more favourable than UNCITRAL arbitration, in the light of the risk of annulment of awards in ICSID arbitration and the availability of the New York Convention to enforce UNCITRAL awards. More generally, however, several scholars point to the fact that neither system is inherently better than the other.[79] This view was taken by the majority in *Garanti Koza LLP v Turkmenistan*,[80] when they held:

> The Tribunal finds itself in agreement with the Respondent that ICSID Arbitration cannot be described as objectively more favorable to investors than UNCITRAL Arbitration. Each system has its advantages and disadvantages, as the comparisons made by both parties illustrate. ICSID does indeed offer the advantages of administration by experienced professionals on behalf of a specialized institution. It also offers the considerable advantage of freedom from interference by courts at the seat of the arbitration, the perils of which are illustrated by the recent decision of the United States Court of Appeals for the District of Columbia Circuit

79 See Freya Baetens, 'Enforcement of Arbitral Awards: "To ICSID or Not to ICSID" Is Not the Question' in Ian Laird and Todd Weiler (eds), *Investment Treaty Arbitration and International Law* (Vol. 5 Juris 2012) 212; Gaetan Verhoosel, 'Annulment and Enforcement Review of Treaty Awards: To ICSID or Not to ICSID' in Albert Jan van den Berg (ed), *50 Years of the New York Convention: ICCA International Arbitration Conference*, ICCA Congress Series, 2009 Dublin (Vol. 14 Kluwer Law International 2009); Stephen Jagusch and Jeffrey Sullivan, 'A Comparison of ICSID and UNCITRAL Arbitration: Areas of Divergence and Concern' in Michael Waibel, Asha Kaushal, Kyo-Hwa Chung and Claire Balchin (eds), *The Backlash Against Investment Arbitration* (Kluwer Law International 2010) 109 ('These systems are similar on many levels, but they also diverge in certain fundamental areas. Neither system is perfect, particularly in relation to transparency and the review of awards.').

80 ICSID Case No. ARB/11/20, 3 July 2013, para. 89.

> in *The Republic of Argentina v BG Group plc.*[81] But at least one learned commentator has applauded the role of national courts 'in annulment proceedings where indeed they have come to provide, with few exceptions, a guarantee of stability and legal certainty not always found in some recent decisions of ICSID annulment committees'.[82] ICSID Arbitration has also been criticized for the overuse by unsuccessful parties of the annulment procedure provided by Chapter VII of the ICSID Rules,[83] and some parties favor the greater flexibility offered by the UNCITRAL Rules.[84]

Though there is no clear agreement that ICSID is a better mechanism than other modes of dispute resolution, the high number of Caribbean ISDS cases resolved through ICSID arbitration, even in circumstances where other methods were available, suggest that parties have generally had a strong affinity for ICSID arbitration.

D. Jurisdiction

Article 25(1) of the ICSID Convention provides the threshold requirements for establishing jurisdiction in the context of ICSID proceedings. It provides:

> The jurisdiction of the Centre shall extend to any legal dispute arising directly out of an investment, between a Contracting State (or any constituent subdivision or agency of a Contracting State designated to the Centre by that State) and a national of another Contracting State, which the parties to the dispute consent in writing to submit to the Centre.

Each of the key cumulative elements of this important provision is described further below.

(i) A Legal Dispute

A legal dispute is not simply a disagreement between the parties in question. Rather, as noted by the tribunal in *Alcoa Minerals v Jamaica*,[85] a legal dispute concerns the legal rights and obligations of the parties, in that case, rights and obligations under their 1968 agreement, specifically whether Jamaica's imposition of the new bauxite tax violated the 'no further tax' clause.

(ii) Ratione Materiae ('Qualifying Investment')

Jurisdiction *ratione materiae* is concerned with the question of whether the putative investor has invested a particular asset in the territory of the host state[86] that is recognised by the relevant treaty in question (and in ICSID proceedings, the implicit requirements of a

81 Citing 665 F.3d 1363 (D.C. Cir. 2012). The United States Supreme Court granted BG Group's petition for a writ of certiorari to review that decision on June 10, 2013.

82 Citing Francisco Orrego Vicuña, 'Reports of [Maffezini's] Demise Have Been Greatly Exaggerated' (2012) 3(2) *Journal of International Dispute Settlement* 308.

83 Citing Stephen Jagusch and Jeffrey Sullivan, 'A Comparison of ICSID and UNCITRAL Arbitration. Areas of Divergence and Concern' in Michael Waibel and others (eds), *The Backlash Against Investment Arbitration. Perceptions and Reality* (Kluwer 2010) 79–109.

84 ICSID Case No. ARB/11/20 (n 80) 89.

85 Schmidt (n 14).

86 Simon Weber, 'Jurisdiction Ratione Materiae' (*Jus Mundi*, 17 September 2025) <https://jusmundi.com/en/document/publication/en-jurisdiction-ratione-materiae> accessed 19 September 2025.

qualifying 'investment', discussed below). Caribbean IIAs[87] typically adopt a broadly permissive approach in this regard, generally defining an 'investment' as 'every kind of asset'. For example, Article 1(a) of the Trinidad and Tobago-France BIT provides:

For the purposes of this Agreement:

(a) 'investment' means every kind of asset and in particular, though not exclusively, includes:
   (i) movable and immovable property and any other property rights such as mortgages, liens or pledges;
   (li) shares in and stock and debentures of a company and any other form of participation in a company;
   (iii) claims to money or to any performance under contract having a financial value;
   (iv) intellectual property rights, goodwill, technical processes and know-how;
   (v) business concessions conferred by law or under contract, including concessions to search for, cultivate, extract or exploit natural resources.

This non-exhaustive language, which can be found in the vast majority of IIAs globally, has been interpreted to cover a range of assets, including infrastructure;[88] real estate;[89] financing and pledge agreements;[90] bank guarantees;[91] lease agreements;[92] and, quite controversially, even promissory notes.[93]

87 See, also: Antigua and Barbuda-Germany BIT: Article 1(1); Barbados-China BIT: Article 1(1); Barbados-Cuba BIT: Article 1(a); Barbados-Germany BIT: Article 1(1); Barbados-Mauritius BIT: Article 1(1)(a); Barbados-Switzerland BIT: Article 1(2); Barbados-Venezuela BIT: Article I(a); Belize-China BIT: Article 1(a); Belize-Cuba BIT: Article 1(a); Belize-El Salvador BIT: Article I(a); Belize-UK BIT: Article 1(1)(a); Dominica-UK BIT: Article 1(a); Dominica-Germany BIT: Article 1(1); Grenada-UK BIT: Article I(i); Guyana-China BIT: Article 1(1); Guyana-Germany BIT: Article 1(1); Guyana-South Korea BIT: Article 1(1); Guyana-Switzerland BIT: Article 1(2); Guyana-UK BIT: Article I(a); Haiti-Germany BIT: Article 8(1); Haiti-UK BIT: Article I(a); Jamaica-China BIT: Article 1(1); Jamaica-Egypt BIT: Article 1(1); Jamaica-Germany BIT: Article 1(1); Jamaica-Indonesia BIT: Article I(1); Jamaica-South Korea BIT: Article 1(1); Jamaica-Switzerland BIT: Article 1(c); Jamaica-Netherlands BIT: Article 1(a); Jamaica-UK BIT: Article 1(a); St. Lucia-Germany BIT: Article 1(1); St. Lucia-UK BIT: Article 1(a); Suriname-Netherlands BIT: Article I(a); SVG-Germany BIT: Article 1(1); SVG-Taiwan BIT: Article 1(1); Trinidad and Tobago-Canada BIT: Article I(f); Trinidad and Tobago-China BIT: Article 1(1); Trinidad and Tobago-Cuba BIT: Article 1(a); Trinidad and Tobago-France BIT: Article 1(a); Trinidad and Tobago-India BIT: Article 1(b); Trinidad and Tobago-South Korea BIT: Article 1(1); Trinidad and Tobago-Switzerland BIT: Article 1(2); Trinidad and Tobago-Germany BIT: Article 1(1)(a); Trinidad and Tobago-UK BIT: Article 1(a). Slightly different phrasing can be found in some regional IIAs: 'every kind of investment': Grenada-USA BIT: Article 1(b); Jamaica-USA BIT: Article 1(a); Trinidad and Tobago-USA BIT: Article I(d). 'Any kind of asset': Barbados-Canada BIT: Article I(f); Jamaica-Argentina BIT: Article I(1).

88 *Bayindir v Pakistan*, ICSID Case No. ARB/03/29 Decision on Jurisdiction, 14 November 2005 (a six-lane highway); *Michael Lee-Chin v Dominican Republic*, ICSID Case No. UNCT/18/3 Partial Award on Jurisdiction, 15 July 2020 (a landfill); *Hassan Awdi v Romania*, ICSID Case No. ARB/10/13, Award, 2 March 2015 (a private building).

89 *Peter Allard v Government of Barbados*, PCA Case No. 2012–06, Award on Jurisdiction, 13 June 2014 (a nature reserve sanctuary).

90 *Burimi v Albania*, ICSID Case No. ARB/11/18, Award, 29 May 2013.

91 *Joy Mining v Egypt*, ICSID Case No. ARB/03/11, Award on Jurisdiction, 6 August 2004

92 *Al Tamimi v Oman*, ICSID Case No. ARB/11/33, Award, 3 November 2015 found that the lease agreements related to the development and operation of a limestone quarry constituted investments qualified as 'other tangible and intangible movable or immovable property' as mentioned in the treaty's definition of investment).

93 *Fedax v Venezuela*, 37 ILM (1988) 137, Decision of the Tribunal on Objections to Jurisdiction, 11 July 1997 (promissory notes issued by Venezuela were considered to be an 'investment' because the acquisition of these notes was not a short-term arrangement; the notes were acquired for the purpose of providing for the orderly development of public finances). By contrast, in *Lion Mexico Consolidated LP v Mexico*,

In *Michael Lee-Chin v Dominican Republic*,[94] while the tribunal was prepared to find that the Lajun landfill satisfied the requirement of the BIT in question, it ruled differently in respect of the potential Waste-to-Energy (WTE) plant. While acknowledging that the Concession Agreement contained references to a potential WTE plant, the tribunal concluded that it did not constitute a protected investment. The tribunal determined that though the construction of a WTE plant was envisaged by the Agreement, it was not guaranteed or assured by the state, even subtly or indirectly. It considered that the claimant could not invoke an exclusive right and assurance to build the WTE plant because he had failed to demonstrate he had taken any concrete actions to materialise this potential undertaking. The tribunal noted that the claimant had not purchased the additional land that would have been needed for the plant, had not initiated any procedures to obtain necessary permits, and had not taken any steps toward transforming this potentiality into a tangible reality. Furthermore, the tribunal emphasised that construction of a WTE plant would have required satisfaction of additional formal requirements, including specific concessions from the central government that were beyond the authority of the municipality. The tribunal thus rejected Lee-Chin's claims for damages based on the hypothetical future operation of a WTE plant, finding it to be purely speculative.

Some BITs are more restrictive than the Trinidad and Tobago-France BIT. For example, the Guyana-Brazil BIT (Article 1(3)) explicitly excludes several types of investments, including 'portfolio investments'; that is, those that do not allow the investor to exert a significant degree of influence in the management of the enterprise or in another enterprise:

> 1.3. Investment means any kind of asset invested by investors of one Party, established or acquired in the territory of the latter Party, that allows, directly or indirectly, the investor to exercise control of the shareholding, or with a significant degree of influence over the management of the production of goods or provision of services in the territory of the other Party in accordance with the laws and regulations of each Party, including but not limited to:
>
> a) shares, stocks, participations and other equity types in an enterprise;
> b) movable or immovable property and other property rights such as mortgages, bens, pledges, encumbrances or similar rights and obligations;
> c) the rights of exploration, exploitation and use conferred by a license, permit or concession granted and governed by the legislation of the host Party and/or by a contract;
> d) intra-company loans and instruments of debt between a company and its subsidiary;
> e) intellectual property rights as defined or referenced to in the WTO TRIPS Agreement.
>
> For the purposes of this Agreement and for greater certainty, 'investment' does not include:
>
> i) an order or judgment issued as a result of a lawsuit or an administrative process;
> ii) debt securities issued by a Party or loans granted from a Party to the other Party, bonds, debentures, loans or other debt instruments of a State-owned enterprise of a Party that is considered to be public debt under the legislation of that Party;
> iii) portfolio investments i.e. those that do not allow the investor to exert a significant degree of influence in the management of the enterprise or in another enterprise;
> iv) claims to money that arise solely from commercial contracts for the sale of goods or services by an investor in the territory of a Party to a national or an enterprise in

ICSID Case No. ARB(AF)/15/2, Decision on Jurisdiction, 30 July 2018 (the promissory notes in issue did not qualify as investments since there was no contribution of capital. In contrast, the mortgages met both requirements set up by Article 1139(h) of NAFTA to be qualified as protected investments: they fell within the provided category of assets in the form of 'intangible real estate' and were used for economic benefit or another business purpose).

94 *Michael Lee-Chin* (n 88).

the territory of another Party, or the extension of credit in connection with a commercial transaction, or any other claims to money that do not involve the kind of interests set out in sub-paragraphs (a)–(e) above; and

v) claims deriving from any expenses or other financial obligations incurred by the investor prior to the establishment of the investment, including in order to comply with the regulations for the admission of foreign capital or other specific limits or conditions, according to the legislation on the admission of investments of the Host Party.

Meanwhile, the Barbados-Canada BIT (Article 1(f)) defines 'investment' in a manner which excludes property not acquired in the expectation of or used for the purpose of economic benefit or other business purposes:

For the purpose of this Agreement:

f. 'investment' means any kind of asset owned or controlled either directly, or indirectly through an investor of a third State, by an investor of one Contracting Party in the territory of the other Contracting Party in accordance with the latter's laws and, in particular, though not exclusively, includes:
i. movable and immovable property and any related property rights, such as mortgages, liens or pledges;
ii. shares, stock, bonds and debentures or any other form of participation in a company, business enterprise or joint venture;
iii. money, claims to money, and claims to performance under contract having a financial value;
iv. goodwill;
v. intellectual property rights;
vi. rights, conferred by law or under contract, to undertake any economic and commercial activity, including any rights to search for, cultivate, extract or exploit natural resources,
but does not mean real estate or other property, tangible or intangible, not acquired in the expectation or used for the purpose of economic benefit or other business purposes.

In *Peter Allard v Barbados*,[95] the tribunal had to interpret the peculiar phrase, 'real estate or other property, tangible or intangible, not acquired in the expectation or used for the purpose of economic benefit or other business purposes'. It considered that the exception in Article 1(f) would not apply if the assets were 'acquired in the expectation . . . of economic benefit'. The tribunal clarified that this was a subjective test focused on the investor's actual expectations at the time of acquisition, not whether a rational investor would have had the same expectations. Despite the fact that Allard and his staff had made public statements emphasising philanthropic and environmental motivations for acquiring 34.24 acres of wetlands to establish a bird sanctuary and nature reserve within some 240 acres of wetlands and open space that comprised the former Graeme Hall Plantation on the south coast of Barbados, the tribunal found sufficient evidence that Allard had an expectation of eventual profit or return on investment. In this connection, the tribunal noted that 'the BIT does not require any quantification of economic benefit' and it was enough that Allard expected 'in the long run the Sanctuary would pay a return on, or even eventually repay, the monies committed for the Sanctuary project'.[96]

95 *Peter Allard* (n 89).
96 ibid 52.

Separately, the Trinidad and Tobago-Guatemala BIT (Article 1(b)) has a unique definition focused on 'assets established or acquired by an investor that involve the contribution of capital, the expectation of profit or the assumption of risk':

For the purpose of this Agreement:

(b) 'investment' means the assets established or acquired by an investor that involve the contribution of capital, the expectation of profit or the assumption of risk, including in particular though not exclusively:
(i) movable or immovable property and any other property rights such as mortgages, liens and pledges;
(ii) shares, stocks, debentures and any other form of participation in the capital of a company;
(iii) claims to money or any performance under contract having an economic value, directly related to an investment;
(iv) debt instruments of a company when the company is a subsidiary of the investor, or if the original due term of the debt instrument is at least three years;
(v) intellectual property rights including copyrights, patents, industrial designs, trademarks, trade names, geographical indications, technical processes, and know-how; and
(vi) concessions conferred by law or under contract to undertake any economic and or commercial activity, including concessions to explore, develop, extract or exploit natural resources;

but does not include:

1) a debt instrument of a Contracting Party, regardless of due term;
2) claims to money that arise solely from:
(i) commercial contracts for the sale of goods and services by an of one Contracting Party, in the territory of the other Contracting Party;
(ii) the granting of credit in connection with a commercial transaction; and
3) any tangible asset or other claims to money, that do not involve at least one of the types of investment as set out in paragraph (b) (i) to (vi) above.

Reference to 'contribution of capital, the expectation of profit or the assumption of risk' is highly reminiscent of extant jurisprudence which suggests that it is not merely sufficient for an asset to meet the BIT's definition, but that it must also possess the aforementioned inherent characteristics of a foreign direct investment. Indeed, it is now widely accepted that for an investor's asset to gain protection, it must satisfy the definition of an 'investment' as contained in the relevant BIT, as well as Article 25(1) of the ICSID Convention, at least in ICSID proceedings.[97] It is to be noted, however, that Article 25 of the ICSID Convention, in imposing jurisdictional requirements, does not specifically define an 'investment'. For this reason, tribunals have, over the years, sought to rely upon certain criteria or benchmarks, as espoused in *Salini v Morocco*,[98] to identify a lawful investment, and distinguish said foreign direct investments from portfolio investments.

Because of the all-encompassing definition of 'investment', almost any subject matter can constitute an 'investment' under regional BITs. However, the *Salini* test attempts to

97 *CSOB v Slovakia*, ICSID Case No. ARB/97/4, Award, 29 December 2004.

98 *Salini Costruttori S.p.A. and Italstrade S.p.A. v Kingdom of Morocco*, ICSID Case No. ARB/00/4, Decision on Jurisdiction, 31 July 2001.

narrow what can qualify as an investment for the purposes of international arbitration proceedings, requiring that the subject matter represents:

(a) *a contribution of capital*;[99]
(b) *a certain* duration;[100]
(c) *a regularity of return of profit*;[101]
(d) *an element of risk*;[102] and
(e) *a contribution to the economic development of the host state*.[103]

99 *Deutsche Bank AG v Sri Lanka*, ICSID Case No. ARB/09/02 (the Hedging Agreement was held to be an 'investment' as it was a legal property with economic value for Deutsche Bank. It was a claim to money which had been used to create economic value. More particularly, Deutsche Bank was held to have contributed by the resources and time it had devoted to negotiating the agreement, and by its commitment to pay US$2.5 million if the costs of importing oil arose above US$112.50 over the following 12 months. Deutsche Bank also made payments of US$35 523.81 to the costs).

100 *Global Trading v Ukraine* ICSID Case No. ARB/09/11, Award, 1 December 2010 (a series of individual contracts of limited duration were purely commercial transactions and not an 'investment'); *Nova Scotia Power Incorporated v Venezuela*, ICSID Case No. ARB(AF)/11/1, Award, 30 April 2014 (with respect to an ordinary commercial contract, the tribunal found that this commercial operation did not deserve the protection of the BIT as an investment because it was *not sufficiently long term*); cf. *Deutsche Bank v Sri Lanka*, ICSID Case No. ARB/09/2 (the tribunal found that the investment was of a certain duration, even if the commitment was originally for twelve months and despite the fact that it was terminated after 125 days. It noted that short-term projects are not deprived of 'investment' status solely by virtue of their limited duration and that duration is to be analysed in light of all the circumstances and of the investor's overall commitment).

101 *Caratube International Oil Company (CIOC) v Kazakhstan (I)*, ICSID Case No. ARB/08/12, Award, 5 June 2012 (the 'investment' was understood by the tribunal as 'an economic arrangement requiring a contribution to make profit and thus involving some degree of risk').

102 Most tribunals require evidence of an investment, as opposed to mere, commercial risk, e.g. *Romak S.A v Uzbekistan*, PCA Case No. AA280, Award, 26 November 2009 (the supply of up to 50,000 tonnes of wheat was Romak's first and last economic transaction in relation to Uzbekistan. This was a one-off transaction, and not an 'investment'. cf. *RREEF v Spain*, ICSID Case No. ARB/13/30, Decision on Jurisdiction, 6 June 2016 (with respect to the respondent's argument that the assumption of risk was an intrinsic characteristic of 'investment', the tribunal held that it would be 'improper' to read this or criteria such as the contribution of economic resources and duration into the ECT or the ICSID Convention).

103 Some tribunals have insisted on contribution to host state development. See, for example, *Bayindir v Pakistan*, ICSID Case No. ARB/03/29. cf. *Romak S.A v Uzbekistan*, PCA Case No. AA280, Award, 26 November 2009; *Nova Scotia Power v Venezuela*, ICSID Case No. ARB(AF)/11/1, Award (excerpts), 30 April 2014, para. 130 (*obiter dictum*) (the tribunal explained that the test is 'whether the host State received a benefit'. The tribunal recognised that economic development might indicate a benefit to the host State; however, the tribunal went on to caution that the benefit 'does not necessarily have to be economic development, [as this is] a highly subjective element' that can only be assessed in hindsight. Instead, 'it is the alleged investment at the time of its inception that should be considered, not the impact that the investment has ultimately had'. See, also, the tribunal in *Electrabel v Hungary*, ICSID Case No. ARB/07/19, Award, 25 November 2015, para. 5.43 noted that

> [w]hile there is incomplete unanimity between tribunals regarding the elements of an investment, there is a general consensus that the three objective criteria of (i) a contribution, (ii) a certain duration, and (iii) an element of risk are necessary elements of an investment. The tribunal also noted that, while the economic development of the host state was one of the objectives of the ICSID Convention (and a desirable consequence of the investment), it was 'not necessarily an element of an investment'.

The tribunal in *Quiborax v Bolivia*, ICSID Case No. ARB/06/2, Decision on Jurisdiction, 27 September 2012, para. 219 noted that the commitment of resources, risk and duration are all part of the ordinary definition of

Arbitral awards involving Caribbean parties (whether as investors or respondent states) have countenanced the 'double key-hole' approach referred to in *Salini v Morocco*,[104] *CSOB v Slovakia*[105] and *Malaysian Historical Salvors v Malaysia*.[106] The Trinidadian case of *F-W Oil Interests, Inc. v The Republic of Trinidad and Tobago*[107] is instructive in this regard. Here, F-WO Oil, a United States registered Energy Company which engaged in offshore exploration, development and production of oil and natural gas, entered into a confidentiality agreement with the respondent which enabled its engineers to review data concerning the Soldado Oil Field in Trinidad. It thereafter made a proposal for assuming control over the Field, but the proposal was not adopted, resulting in the commencement of a public tender process. F-WO was one of those responding with a tender. Trinmar originally contemplated awarding the project to F-WO, but its minority shareholder, Textrin, felt that this invitation was improper. The bidding process ultimately led to the selection of F-WO as the preferred bidder, which was approved by the Board of Trinmar. F-WO was formally notified that it had been awarded the tender, but with the caveat that this was 'subject to the negotiation and execution of a mutually agreeable operating agreement'.

F-WO thereafter wrote two letters to Trinmar. The first sought a guarantee or other form of security to secure payment to F-WO under the anticipated contract on the ground that F-WO's outside interests who were intended to finance F-WO's share in the project required security as a prerequisite for participation. Meanwhile, the second letter asked for assurances that F-WO would be compensated for work done in anticipation of an agreement to carry out the project, in the event such an agreement was not concluded. Neither letter received a positive response from the respondent. As to the former, Trinmar did not agree or promise that any such guarantee would be provided, while in relation to the latter, Trinmar simply replied that it did not hold itself liable for any costs or expenditure incurred by F-WO prior to the execution of a contract. Effectively, the award was subject to the negotiation and execution of a mutually agreed contract.

Five months later, Trinmar notified F-W Oil that it had withdrawn from the negotiations. Following intensive consultation with Petrotrin and with the responsible Government Minister, Trinmar set in train instead an alternative bidding process in which F-WO declined to take part. F-WO thereafter brought arbitration proceedings. The key issues for determination were whether F-WO had the benefit of a binding pre-contractual agreement, which constituted an investment in Trinidad and Tobago, and, if so, whether the State unfairly infringed, either by using its powers to ensure that Trinmar did not take the bidding process to a conclusion, or by itself failing to perform the agreement. The essence of the complaint of F-WO in this case was not that something had gone wrong with the bidding, but that the award had not been followed up by a binding final contract.

The tribunal held that no 'investment', in accordance with the applicable BIT, was discernible in this case. It considered that the equivocal pre-contractual arrangements in question did not give rise to proprietary nor contractual rights, and were, therefore, outside of the ambit of protection afforded by the BIT. In the tribunal's view:

> Although the language of the BIT suggested that the definition given in Article I(d) was on its own terms not exhaustive (because it was expressed merely to 'include' the forms of investment itemised on the list), the common thread is nevertheless so strong that the Tribunal is

---

an investment, while a contribution to the development of the host state, conformity with the laws of the host State and respect of good faith are not.

104 ICSID Case No. ARB/00/4, Decision on Jurisdiction, 31 July 2001.

105 *CSOB v Slovakia* (n 97).

106 ICSID Case No. ARB/05/10, Award, 17 May 2007.

107 ICSID Case No. ARB/01/14, Award, 3 March 2006.

> unable to conclude that the intention can have been to bring within the scope of the term claims other than those based on proprietary or contractual rights, which, in the Tribunal's view, corresponds in any event to the whole underlying notion of an 'investment'.[108]

The tribunal noted that no final, binding contract had come into existence which would have otherwise been categorised as an 'investment' for the purposes of the BIT in question. The pre-contractual agreement was akin to a common law agreement to contract, which, even under municipal law, was not generally enforceable. The tribunal further considered that the respondent's request for proposals expressly stated that the respondent would not be responsible for any costs and expenses incurred by any bidder in connection with the preparation, submission, and presentation of bid proposals; that, upon evaluation, bidders were required to present their proposals to Trinmar, after which the 'successful bidder shall be notified in writing of acceptance of its bid'; and that 'the formal contract shall be executed thereafter'.[109] Furthermore, in its Technical and Financial Proposals, F-WO had made it clear that its 'Tender [was] made on the condition that if accepted F-WO shall be obligated to Trinmar only upon the entry into force of a definitive written agreement between F-WO and Trinmar'.[110] In addition, the respondent's letter to F-W Oil clearly stated:

> [T]his award is made subject to the negotiation and execution of a mutually agreeable operating agreement for the provision of facilities and services in Trinmar Limited's West and Southwest Soldado Fields . . . we intend to negotiate in good faith and in an expeditious manner towards the execution of such agreement between Trinmar Limited and F-W Oil Trinidad, L.L.C. The operating agreement will incorporate the contractual terms generally set forth in the attached 'Heads of Agreement' together with other terms and conditions mutually acceptable to the parties found in transactions of this nature'. More than this, the subsequent letter to F-W Oil following its request for a guarantee read, 'Trinmar makes no guarantee as to the provision of this security, and awaits a decision of its Shareholders. Please note further that Trinmar does not hold itself liable for any costs or expenditure incurred by F-W Oil Interests prior to the execution of a contract on this tender'.[111]

F-W Oil v Trinidad and Tobago reaffirms the importance of satisfying the definition of 'investment' contained in the BIT in question. It is also an important decision because it makes clear that, notwithstanding the broad and seemingly all-inclusive definition of 'investment' contained in BITs, there is a limit to the types of alleged subject matter that may be protected, seemingly to the exclusion of pre-contractual agreements which have no proprietary or contractual underpinnings. More than this, the tribunal in *F-WO Oil* is to be commended for aligning its ruling with previously decided cases which adopted the defensible position that pre-contractual arrangements are generally not considered 'investments' under international investment law. Indeed, the *F-WO* award shares striking similarities with the ruling in *SGS v Philippines*[112] that 'ICSID Tribunals have been very reluctant to acknowledge that an investment has actually been made until the contract has been signed or at least approved and acted on',[113] as well as *Mihaly v Sri Lanka,*[114] which considered

108 ibid 125.
109 ibid 65.
110 ibid 68.
111 ibid 90.
112 ICSID Case No. ARB/02/6, Decision on Jurisdiction, 29 January 2004.
113 ibid 132(d).
114 ICSID Case No. ARB/00/2, Award, 15 March 2002.

that the expenditures made by the claimant in that case in the expectation of the award of the contract for power generation in Sri Lanka did not in the circumstances amount to an 'investment' for the purposes of the relevant BIT.

Caribbean ISDS case law has also brought clarity to the question of whether indirect investments are protected by international investment law. This is an area of significant contestation,[115] and can aptly be described as being in a state of flux.[116] The question of whether protection should be afforded to indirect investors and indirect investments by parity of reasoning arose for consideration in the Caribbean case of *Michael Anthony Lee-Chin v The Dominican Republic*.[117] Here, the claimant, a Jamaican national, was the sole owner of shares, stocks and interests in two Panamanian companies (Lution Investment SA and Kigman Del Sur SA), which, in turn, held shares, stocks and interests in a Panamanian company (Nagelo Enterprises SA) and in a Dominican company (Wilkison Company SRL), which, in turn, held shares, stocks, and interests in Lajun Corporation SRL in the Dominican Republic. The claimant brought a claim under the CARICOM-Dominican Republic Free Trade Agreement, alleging that his investment in the Duquesa Landfill (through Lajun) had been subject to unlawful expropriation at the hands of the Dominican Republic.

The main question for determination by the tribunal was whether the claimant held a valid 'investment' in the Dominican Republic, given the indirect nature of the arrangements in question. The claimant argued that, by means of the complicated structure described above, he owned (albeit indirectly) 90% of Lajun and the land, whereas the remaining 10% was owned by a Dominican entrepreneur. He contended that the extremely broad terms used in the Treaty to define both 'investor' and 'investment' qualified him as well as his investment as an 'indirect investor' and 'indirect investment' under the treaty in question. By contrast, the respondent argued that the absence of an express reference to indirect investments and indirect investors meant that the Treaty only applied to investors who made direct investments.

The tribunal agreed with the claimant, finding that, given that Lee-Chin, a Jamaican national, owned virtually all of Lajun, the subject matter in issue was a lawful indirect investment. It carefully examined Article I(1) of the Treaty in question which defined the term 'investment' as 'every kind of asset and, in particular, though not exclusively, includes: . . . (b) shares, stocks and debentures of companies or interests in the property of such companies . . .' ultimately finding that:

> the text cited in the foregoing paragraph shows the Treaty drafters' intention to adopt an open definition of the investments covered thereby. In general, it is worth pointing out that the drafters were free to reduce the scope of protected investments. The Tribunal finds no sign of a restrictive legislative policy option to such effect in this text. On the contrary, in light of the language of the provision under analysis, the Tribunal cannot but conclude that the intention of the Contracting Parties to the Treaty was the exact opposite. The Tribunal is aware of the general maxim of interpretation whereby where the text makes no distinction, the interpreter should

115 Gabriel Bottini, 'Indirect Claims under the ICSID Convention' (2007) 29 *University of Pennsylvania Journal of International Law* 563; Inna Uchkunova, 'Indirect Investments Through Chain of Intermediary Companies: A Philosopher's Stone or not Any More?' (*Kluwer Arbitration Blog*, 3 July 2013) <https://legalblogs.wolterskluwer.com/arbitration-blog/indirect-investments-through-chain-of-intermediary-companies-a-philosophers-stone-or-not-any-more/> accessed 23 August 2025.

116 Jason Haynes, 'The Contribution of Caribbean ISDS Jurisprudence to International Investment Law's Ongoing Legitimacy Project' (2021) 18(2) *Manchester Journal of International Economic Law* 205.

117 ICSID Case No. UNCT/18/3, Partial Award on Jurisdiction, 15 July 2020.

> make no distinction as well. The Tribunal could adopt similar maxims such as *expressio unius est exclusio alterius* as bases, although with some differences, to reach the same conclusion.[118]

In circumstances where the text of the treaty made no specific reference to direct or indirect investments, but rather used the formula 'though not exclusively, includes', the tribunal considered that an expansive reading of the provision was desirable. In this connection, although Professor Marcelo Kohen issued an interesting, albeit unconvincing, dissenting opinion[119] in this case rejecting the inference of indirect investments, it is submitted that the approach of the majority was both rational and coherent, having regard to a textual approach to treaty interpretation, as well as a number of previously decided cases which ruled in a similar manner. For example, the tribunal in *Cemex v Venezuela*[120] concluded that indirect investments were not excluded because they were not specifically mentioned in the BIT in question. Similar sentiments were countenanced by the tribunal in *Anglo American PLC v Venezuela*,[121] which proffered:

> A literal interpretation of Article 1(a) of the Treaty handed down by the Arbitral Tribunal, in addition to being in accordance with the rules of interpretation of the Vienna Convention, is not affected by the mere fact that, in other treaties, the Contracting States have chosen to specify that indirect investments were protected. No interpretative conclusion can be inferred from this circumstance for purposes of this case.[122]

Having regard to the foregoing, it is submitted that the approach of the majority in *Michael Lee-Chin* is to be preferred, over the contrasting approach adopted in *Berschader v Russia*[123] that 'it would seem likely that if the Contracting Parties had so intended, they would have expressly provided protection for such indirect investments in the terms of the Treaty, as in the case of the other relevant BITs concluded by Belgium and Luxembourg.'[124]

Caribbean ISDS jurisprudence has also provided insights into the characteristics establishing the existence of an 'investment' for the purpose of Article 25 of the ICSID Convention. The case of *RSM Production Corporation v Grenada*[125] is instructive in this regard. Here, the claimant, a company organised under the laws of Texas, USA, entered into a written agreement with Grenada whereby RSM could apply for an 'Exploration Licence' from Grenada for oil and gas. As a term of the agreement, in the event of commercial discovery of oil and gas, RSM was to apply for one or more 'Development Licences'. RSM notified the Government of Grenada (on 18 July 1996) of the occurrence of a *force majeure* event; that is, a dispute as to the Government of Grenada's ownership of or control over the petroleum in a portion of the Agreement area. RSM's letter of 18 July 1996 concerning *force majeure* had the effect of suspending the time within which RSM had to apply for an exploration licence. In other words, RSM, because of the *force majeure* event, was excused from the performance of all of its obligations under the Agreement.

118 ibid 211.
119 *Michael Anthony Lee-Chin v The Dominican Republic*, ICSID Case No. UNCT/18/3, Dissenting Opinion of Professor Marcelo G. Kohen, 6 October 2023.
120 ICSID Case No. ARB/08/15, Decision on Jurisdiction, 30 December 2010.
121 ICSID Case No. ARB(AF)/14/1, Final Award, 18 January 2019.
122 ibid 197.
123 SCC Case No. 080/2004, Award, 21 April 2006.
124 ibid 147.
125 ICSID Case No. ARB/05/14, Final Award, 13 March 2009.

Eight years later, on 12 January 2004, RSM wrote to the Prime Minister of Grenada stating that 'because we are now confident that we can proceed with our licence offshore Grenada we are revoking the *force majeure*'. Thereafter, on 14 April 2004, RSM applied for an exploration licence, but the Government of Grenada, on 5 July 2005, formally notified RSM that it was terminating the Agreement because, under clause 3.1 of the agreement between the parties, the 90-day period for applying for the exploration licence expired on 28 March 2004, and RSM did not apply for an exploration licence within this timeframe. In Grenada's view, RSM failed to comply with the strict time limit imposed by clause 3.1, which it viewed as a fundamental term of the contract, breach of which warranted Grenada's uniliteral termination of said agreement. Unsurprisingly, RSM brought a claim before ICSID against Grenada.

The first issue for the tribunal's consideration was whether RSM had a valid 'investment' for the purposes of the BIT in question, as well as Article 25 of the ICSID Convention. The tribunal began its incisive assessment by acknowledging the 'soundness of [the] general characteristics'[126] of an investment, as articulated in *Salini v Morocco*.[127] While noting that these general characteristics do not constitute 'jurisdictional criteria' under Article 25(1) of the ICSID Convention nor 'the Article 25(1) test',[128] the tribunal nonetheless countenanced the view that 'they are . . . benchmarks or yardsticks to help a tribunal in assessing the existence of an investment, and their proponents or users rightly insist on the flexibility with which they should be used by a tribunal'.[129]

Having regard to the facts of the case in issue, the tribunal found that the Agreement between RSM and Grenada did in fact include commitments undertaken by the claimant relating to the exploration period that qualified as an 'investment' for the purpose of Article 25 of the ICSID Convention. It noted that there was no formal separation in the Agreement between the terms relating, respectively, to the pre-exploration period, the exploration period, and the development period; they all formed a single and overall agreement. That said, even if the Agreement's provisions relating to the grant of an exploration licence were to constitute only a preliminary agreement within the Agreement, the tribunal considered that they were a fundamental part of an overall project, having regard to the ruling in *CSOB v Slovakia*,[130] which considered:

> An investment is frequently a rather complex operation, composed of various interrelated transactions, each element of which, standing alone, might not in all cases qualify as an investment. Hence, a dispute that is brought before the Centre must be deemed to arise directly out of an investment even when it is based on a transaction which, standing alone, would not qualify as an investment under the Convention, provided that the particular transaction forms an integral part of an overall operation that qualifies as an investment.[131]

The *RSM* tribunal adopted the general approach countenanced by other arbitral tribunals[132] when assessing the essential characteristics of the alleged 'investment' in question. First, in

126 ibid 241.
127 *Salini Costruttori* (n 98).
128 ibid.
129 ibid.
130 *CSOB v Slovakia* (n 97).
131 ICSID Case No. (n 125) 255.
132 *Mihaly International Corporation v Democratic Socialist Republic of Sri Lanka*, ICSID Case No. ARB/00/2, Award, 15 March 2002, 17 *ICSID Rev – FILJ* 142 (2002), 41 *ILM* 867 (2002), 6 ICSID Rep

terms of commitment, the tribunal, relying on *Mihaly v Sri Lanka*,[133] accepted that although RSM expended just US $400,000 during the initial exploration period, 'the idea that the existence of an investment as a requirement for jurisdiction is not dependent on the amounts actually spent by the alleged investor.'[134] It further accepted, having relied upon *Salini v Morocco*,[135] *Bayindir v Pakistan*[136] and *Mitchell v Democratic Republic of Congo*,[137] that an investment may be financial or through work, including know-how or industry. On the facts, given that RSM's know-how and industry were ostensibly dedicated to the project as soon as the Agreement was signed by the parties, and both could have been put to use had the exploration licence been issued by Grenada (in addition to the necessary contribution of capital), an appropriate commitment in accordance with Article 25 ICSID was found to have been made. In any event, the tribunal was inclined to note that there was no need for actual expenses to have been incurred by the investor, since the relevant criterion was the *commitment* to bring in resources toward the performance of such exploration. The tribunal further noted that had the exploration licence been issued, RSM would have been irrevocably committed to bringing in, directly or indirectly by turning to other sources, the necessary capital.

In addressing the duration criterion, the *RSM* tribunal considered that, although, because of the *force majeure* event, the project was suspended after only fourteen days, one had to look prospectively at the likely duration of the agreement (over 50 years) if the venture had been successful. In this connection, the claimant could not be unduly penalised for the short period that was occasioned by the *force majeure* event, which, in any event, was contemplated by the parties' agreement.

In terms of regularity of return of profit, the tribunal considered that this element had to be interpreted flexibly, having regard to the facts of the case in issue. More pointedly, it noted that if the exploration had proved successful, it was clear that RSM would be in receipt of profits associated with its exploration of oil in Grenada. As such, this criterion was held to have been satisfied.

On the question of risk, the tribunal considered that the commercial risk for the claimant was that its application for a development licence might be turned down by the Government as not meeting the requirements enumerated in the agreement between the parties. Having also noted the 'magnitude of the commercial risk involved',[138] the tribunal felt constrained

---

310 (2004); *Joy Mining Machinery Limited v Arab Republic of Egypt*, ICSID Case No. ARB/03/11, Award, 6 August 2004, 19 *ICSID Rev – FILJ* 486 (2004), 13 ICSID Rep 123; *Liberian Eastern Timber Corporation v Republic of Liberia*, ICSID Case No. ARB/83/2, Award, 31 March 1986, 26 *ILM* 647 (1987), 2 ICSID Rep 346 (1994); *Consortium Groupement L.E.S.I. – DIPENTA v People's Democratic Republic of Algeria*, ICSID Case No. ARB/03/8, Award, 10 January 2005 [French original] 19 *ICSID Rev – FILJ* 426 (2004); *Patrick Mitchell v Democratic Republic of the Congo*, ICSID Case No. ARB/99/7, Decision on the Application for the Annulment, 1 November 2006; *Bayindir Insaat Turizm Ticaret Ve Sanayi A.S. v Islamic Republic of Pakistan*, ICSID Case No. ARB/03/29, Decision on Jurisdiction, 14 November 2005; *Jan de Nul N.V. and Dredging International N.V. v Arab Republic of Egypt*, ICSID Case No. ARB/04/13, Award, 6 November 2008; *Autopista Concesionada de Venezuela, C.A. v Bolivarian Republic of Venezuela*, ICSID Case No. ARB/00/5, Decision on Jurisdiction, 27 September 2001; *Nagel v Czech Republic* (2004) *Stockholm Arb Rep* 141.

133 *Mihaly* (n 132).

134 ibid 51.

135 *Salini Costruttori* (n 98) 53.

136 *Mihaly* (n 132) 31.

137 ibid 27.

138 ICSID Case No. (n 125) 243.

to rule that exploration for oil in maritime areas required the commitment of a significant amount of capital, and that if oil was not found, or was not found in sufficient quantities, or was found to lie in locations that did not make exploitation economically viable, capital would have been spent in vain. As such, this criterion was held to have been satisfied on the facts of the case.

Perhaps the most contentious aspect of the *RSM* decision was the tribunal's treatment of the fifth criterion, namely contribution to the host state's development. In this connection, the tribunal considered that there was no doubt that if the project had reached the 'development stage' (following the 'exploration stage'), there would have been a significant contribution to Grenada's development, since 'oil concession granted by a State to a foreign private party is indeed the quintessential investment operation.'[139]

While the ruling is, on the facts of the case in question, understandable, it is the broader view expressed by the tribunal that the criterion with respect to investors' contribution to the host state's development is not in all cases a necessary requirement that is cause for concern. This is concerning because the preamble and/or objectives of the ICSID Convention and most BITs concluded by Caribbean Contracting Parties speak to reciprocal protection of investments and improving the economic development of the states parties in question. In this context, to adopt an approach, as the tribunal did in *RSM,* where the criterion of substantial contribution to the host state's development is dispensable is arguably inconsistent with the tenor of the ICSID Convention and regional BITs, as well as a growing corpus of extant case law.[140] More fundamentally, the *RSM* approach reinforces the asymmetrical nature of the extant international investment regime, and provides very little by way of incentives for foreign investors to meaningfully contribute to the host state's development. Indeed, in dispensing with the criterion that the investment contributes to the host state development betrays the trust and confidence that small island developing host states have reposed in the perceived legitimacy of international investment law. It is submitted that the better approach therefore appears to be *Bridgestone v Panama*[141] in which the tribunal considered that the *Salini* criteria should not be inflexibly applied, but then went on to note that a trademark, where it is not exploited, does not qualify as an 'investment' because it will not, *inter alia*, have contributed to the host state's development.

(iii) Ratione Personae *(Qualifying Investor)*

An important jurisdictional requirement that must be satisfied by persons wishing to rely on an IIA to pursue investment arbitration proceedings against a host state is that of jurisdiction *ratione personae.*[142]

139 ibid 242

140 Alex Grabowski, 'The Definition of Investment under The ICSID Convention: A Defense of Salini' (2014) 15 *Chicago Journal of International Law* 287.

141 *Bridgestone Americas, Inc. and Bridgestone Licensing Services, Inc. v Republic of Panama*, ICSID Case No. ARB/16/34, Decision on Expedited Objections, 13 December 2017, para. 164.

142 Chou Sean Yu and others, 'Accessing Investment Treaty Protection: The Investor's Perspective' (*Global Arbitration Review*, 21 December 2023) <https://globalarbitrationreview.com/guide/the-guide-investment-treaty-protection-and-enforcement/second-edition/article/accessing-investment-treaty-protection-the-investors-perspective> accessed 24 August 2025.

(A) Natural Persons

In ICSID proceedings, a natural person must establish that they are a citizen or national of their home state. Article 25(2) of the ICSID Convention provides:

> (2) 'National of another Contracting State' means:
>
> (a) any natural person who had the nationality of a Contracting State other than the State party to the dispute on the date on which the parties consented to submit such dispute to conciliation or arbitration as well as on the date on which the request was registered pursuant to paragraph (3) of Article 28 or paragraph (3) of Article 36, but does not include any person who on either date also had the nationality of the Contracting State party to the dispute.

ICSID specifically excludes dual nationals from instituting arbitration proceedings.[143] However, in UNCITRAL proceedings, no such presumption exists, such that the terms of the relevant BIT would prevail. This principle was demonstrated in *García Armas v Venezuela*,[144] where the tribunal upheld jurisdiction in a dispute brought by Spanish nationals who also held Venezuelan nationality. The tribunal held that, first, some Venezuelan IIAs explicitly excluded dual nationals while others, including the applicable BIT, did not contain such exclusions. Second, it recognised that the ICSID Convention's Article 25(2) exclusion of dual nationals did not apply to UNCITRAL proceedings. Third, applying the VCLT and having regard to previous tribunal decisions, it concluded that if a treaty does not expressly limit its application to dual nationals, it is not possible to devoid of effect the nationality granted freely by a state and accepted as valid by the other. Notably, the tribunal rejected applying the 'dominant and effective nationality' test, considering it part of diplomatic protection law rather than applicable to investment treaty contexts.

Caribbean IIAs adopt various positions on the question of who is a qualifying 'investor' with respect to natural persons. Some regional IIAs are permissive, providing that the natural person in question need only be a national of their home state (i.e. a nationality requirement).[145] For example, Article 1(b)(i) Barbados-Mauritius BIT provides:

> (b) 'investor' means in respect of either Contracting Party:
>
> (i) a natural person who has the nationality of the Contracting Party in accordance with its applicable law.

143 August Reinisch, 'Jurisdiction and Admissibility in International Investment Law' (2017) 16(1) *The Law & Practice of International Courts and Tribunals* 21.

144 ICSID Case No. ARB(AF)/16/1.

145 Antigua and Barbuda-Germany BIT Article 1(3)(a)(i); Barbados-China BIT Article 1(2)(a)(i); Barbados-Mauritius BIT Article 1(b)(i); Barbados-Switzerland BIT Article 1(a); Belize-China BIT Article 1(c); Belize-El Salvador BIT Article 1(c)(i); Belize-UK BIT Article 1(c)(i); Grenada-USA BIT Article 1(c); Guyana-China BIT Article 1(2)(a); Guyana-South Korea BIT Article 1(3)(a); Jamaica-Argentina BIT Article 1(2)(a); Jamaica-China BIT Article 1(2)(a); Jamaica-Egypt BIT Article 1(2)(a); Jamaica-Germany BIT Article 1(3)(a); Jamaica-South Korea BIT Article 1(2)(a); Jamaica-Switzerland BIT Article 1(a); Jamaica-The Netherlands BIT Article 1(b)(i); Jamaica-UK BIT Article 1(c)(ii); Jamaica-USA BIT Article 1(c); Trinidad and Tobago-China BIT Article 2(a); Trinidad and Tobago-France BIT Article 1(2); Trinidad and Tobago-Guatemala BIT Article 1(c)(i); Trinidad and Tobago-India BIT Article 1(e); Trinidad and Tobago-South Korea BIT Article 1(3)(a); Trinidad and Tobago-Switzerland BIT Article 1(a); Trinidad and Tobago-UK BIT Article 1(c)(i); Trinidad and Tobago-USA BIT Article 1(c).

By contrast, other IIAs[146] take a more restrictive approach requiring citizenship. For example, Article 1(2)(I) Jamaica-Indonesia BIT provides:

> 2. The term 'investor' means:
>   (i) any natural person possessing citizenship of a Contracting Party who invests in the territory of the other Contracting Party in accordance with the laws and regulations of that Contracting Party.

Yet, still, some regional IIAs are equally permissive of persons holding relevant citizenship *or* nationality.[147] For example, Article 1(g) of the Trinidad and Tobago-Canada BIT provides:

> g. 'investor' means
> in the case of Canada:
> i. any natural person possessing the citizenship of or permanently residing in Canada in accordance with its laws; or
> in the case of the Republic of Trinidad and Tobago:
> . . .
> iii. any natural person possessing the citizenship of or permanently residing in the Republic of Trinidad and Tobago in accordance with its laws.

The Belize-Cuba BIT (Article 1(c)(ii)) is most restrictive, requiring both citizenship and permanent residence in the home state:

> (c) 'nationals' means:
>   (i) in respect of Belize: any person who holds citizenship as defined by the Constitution and laws of Belize.
>   (ii) in respect of Cuba: natural persons who have the citizenship of that State in accordance with its laws and who reside permanently in the national territory.

A citizenship requirement is more demanding than a nationality requirement,[148] as it assumes that the person has an unequivocal link to the state, which is attended by a bundle of full rights and obligations, such rights being generally significantly curtailed in connection with mere nationals. In other words, a lesser degree of protection is afforded to foreign investors where a 'citizenship' requirement is imposed, whereas a greater degree of protection is afforded where a nationality requirement is imposed.

Of the arbitral awards that have been rendered to date involving Caribbean countries, only two – *Peter Allard v Barbados*[149] and *Michael Lee-Chin v Dominican Republic*[150] – have been concerned with natural persons. In the former case, a dispute arose between Allard, a Canadian businessman, and the Government of Barbados under the Canada-Barbados

146 Barbados-Cuba BIT Article 1(c); Belize-Cuba BIT Article 1(c)(i); Dominica-UK BIT Article 1(ii); Grenada-UK BIT Article 1(ii); Guyana-Germany BIT Article 1(3)(b); Guyana-UK BIT Article 1(c)(ii); Jamaica-Indonesia BIT Article 2(i); St. Lucia-Germany BIT Article 1(3)(b); St. Lucia-UK BIT Article 1(c)(ii); SVG-Germany BIT Article 1(3)(b); SVG-Taiwan BIT Article 1(2)(a); Trinidad and Tobago-Cuba BIT Article 1(c)(i).

147 Barbados-Canada BIT Article 1(g)(i); Trinidad and Tobago-Canada BIT Article 1(g)(i); Trinidad and Tobago-Germany BIT Article 1(3)(a)(i); Jamaica-South Korea BIT Article 1(2)(a).

148 Dolzer et al. (n 43) Chapter III.

149 *Peter Allard* (n 89).

150 *Michael Lee-Chin* (n 88).

BIT. Allard invested approximately C$18.8 million to develop an eco-tourism site called the Graeme Hall Nature Sanctuary in Barbados. He claimed that Barbados failed to take necessary environmental protection measures and directly contributed to contaminating his investment, thereby destroying its value. The tribunal was asked, *inter alia*, to assess whether Allard qualified as an 'investor' under the BIT in respect of his alleged ownership or control of the Sanctuary. The tribunal concluded that despite some inconsistencies in the corporate documentation and record-keeping, Allard indirectly owned the Sanctuary through a corporate chain. He owned GHBVI (a British Virgin Islands company), which in turn owned GHNSI (a Barbadian company that owned the Sanctuary lands). Additionally, Allard directly made loans to fund the Sanctuary's operations. Accordingly, the tribunal rejected Barbados's objection to jurisdiction *ratione personae*, finding that Allard did qualify as an investor under the BIT.

The latter case concerned a dispute arising from the Dominican Republic's alleged interference with Lee-Chin's investment in the Duquesa Landfill operation. Lee-Chin claimed to have acquired an indirect 90% ownership interest in Lajun Corporation (the Dominican company operating the landfill) through a multi-layered corporate structure involving Panamanian intermediary companies. The Dominican Republic challenged the Tribunal's jurisdiction ratione personae, arguing that the Treaty did not protect 'indirect investors' – those who hold investments through intermediary companies rather than directly. The core question was whether Lee-Chin, as an individual who owned shares in Panamanian companies (Lution Investments and Kigman Del Sur) that in turn owned interests in other companies (Nagelo Enterprises and Wilkison Company) which finally owned Lajun Corporation, qualified as an 'investor' entitled to protection under the Treaty. A majority of the tribunal rejected the Dominican Republic's objection, finding that the Treaty protected indirect investors even though it made no explicit reference to them. The majority concluded that the Treaty's definition of 'investor' was broad and unrestricted. The absence of express language limiting protection to 'direct' investors indicated no intention to exclude indirect investors. The broad definition and open-ended formula chosen by the drafters supported including indirect investors within the Treaty's protection. The majority accordingly determined that Lee-Chin qualified as an investor under the Treaty, despite the fact that his ownership interest in Lajun Corporation flowed through multiple corporate entities.

In his dissenting opinion, Professor Kohen argued that Lee-Chin did not qualify as an 'investor' under the Treaty's terms. He emphasised that Lee-Chin's investment constituted a 'fourth-degree indirect investment' through four different companies at different levels. He considered that under the Treaty, the actual holders of rights granted to 'investors' were the immediate shareholders of Lajun (Nagelo Enterprises and Wilkison Company), not Lee-Chin personally. He further noted that the CARICOM-Dominican Republic Treaty did not apply to Panamanian companies or Dominican companies with investments in the Dominican Republic. Professor Kohen accordingly concluded that the tribunal lacked *ratione personae* jurisdiction. He maintained that Lee-Chin's decision to structure his investment through multiple Panamanian companies was a matter of choice, the consequences of which should not be circumvented through an expansive interpretation of the Treaty. While acknowledging that other tribunals had accepted protection for indirect investors in different treaty contexts, Professor Kohen argued that the specific corporate structure used by Lee-Chin placed him outside the scope of protection as an 'investor' under this particular Treaty.

(B) Legal Persons

Article 25(2)(b) of the ICSID Convention provides:

> (b) any juridical person which had the nationality of a Contracting State other than the State party to the dispute on the date on which the parties consented to submit such dispute to conciliation or arbitration and any juridical person which had the nationality of the Contracting State party to the dispute on that date and which, because of foreign control, the parties have agreed should be treated as a national of another Contracting State for the purposes of this Convention.

The first part of the provision establishes the basic nationality requirement: a juridical person must have the nationality of a Contracting State other than the host state on the date when both parties consented to ICSID arbitration. This implements the fundamental principle that ICSID arbitration is designed for international disputes between a foreign investor and a host state. The second part creates an important exception to this rule, often called the 'foreign control exception.'[151] It allows a company that has the nationality of the host state to nevertheless access ICSID arbitration if:

1. It is under 'foreign control' (by nationals of another Contracting State), and
2. The parties have agreed to treat it as a national of that other Contracting State.

This exception recognises the reality that many investments are structured through locally incorporated companies, as host states often require or prefer foreign investors to operate through domestic entities. Without this provision, such locally incorporated subsidiaries would be excluded from ICSID jurisdiction despite their foreign ownership. The provision also requires explicit agreement between the parties to treat the local company as a foreign national, which can be established through investment treaties, investment contracts, or other means of consent. The determination of 'foreign control' is fact-specific, as demonstrated in *National Gas v Egypt*,[152] where the tribunal looked beyond formal ownership to determine that ultimate control rested with an Egyptian national, thus defeating jurisdiction.

(i) 'Incorporation' Test

Most Caribbean IIAs[153] impose a simple test of incorporation or constitution under the laws of the home state without adding substantive requirements like territorial seat, business

151 *Waibel* (n 36).

152 ICSID Case No. ARB/11/7, Award, 3 April 2014.

153 Antigua and Barbuda-UK BIT Article 1; Barbados-Canada BIT Article 1(g)(ii); Barbados-Cuba BIT Article 1(d)(i); Barbados-Venezuela BIT Article 1(d); Belize-China BIT Article 1(c); Belize-Cuba BIT Article 1(d); Belize-El Salvador BIT Article 1(c)(ii); Belize-UK BIT Article 1(d)(i); Dominica-UK BIT Article 1; Grenada-UK BIT Article 1(ii); Grenada-USA BIT Article 1(a); Guyana-China BIT Article 1(2)(b); Guyana-Germany BIT Article 1(4)(b); Guyana-South Korea BIT Article 1(3)(b); Guyana-UK BIT Article 1(d)(ii); Haiti-USA BIT Article 1(a); Jamaica-China BIT Article 2(b); Jamaica-Egypt BIT Article 1(2)(b); Jamaica-Indonesia BIT Article 1(2)(ii); Jamaica-South Korea BIT Article 1(2)(b); Jamaica-UK BIT Article 1(d)(ii); Jamaica-USA BIT Article 1(b); St. Lucia-UK BIT Article 1; Suriname-The Netherlands BIT Article 1(b)(ii); Trinidad and Tobago-Canada BIT Article 1(g)(ii); Trinidad and Tobago-China Article 1(2)(b); Trinidad and Tobago-Cuba BIT Article 1(d)(i); Trinidad and Tobago-India BIT Article 1(a); Trinidad and Tobago-South Korea BIT Article 1(3)(b); Trinidad and Tobago-UK BIT Article 1(d)(i); Trinidad and Tobago-USA BIT Article 1(b).

activities, or management control as the basis for determining whether the legal person in question is an investor. For example, Article 1 Grenada-UK BIT provides:

(i) in respect of the United Kingdom: corporations, firms and associations, incorporated or constituted under the law in force in any part of the United Kingdom or in any territory to which this Agreement is extended in accordance with the provisions of Article II;
(ii) in respect of Grenada: corporations, firms and associations incorporated or constituted, under the law in force in any part of Grenada.

The question of whether companies which are incorporated in the home state but which do not actually carry out substantial business activities there ('shell companies') could still benefit from the protections afforded by IIAs has been one of the most contentious issues in international investment law for quite a number of years.[154] On the one hand, there is an argument that, similar to principles of diplomatic protection as espoused in the *Barcelona Traction* case,[155] the mere incorporation of a juridical entity in a jurisdiction does not *per se* entitle that entity to benefit from the nationality of the jurisdiction in question, unless this is coupled with 'a permanent and close connection' between the home state and the relevant entity.[156] On the other hand, there is a body of authority that strongly suggests that, on a natural and ordinary meaning of the provisions of IIAs, if a requirement of incorporation alone is provided for, then this is necessarily what must be complied with by the juridical entity.[157] In short, the argument advanced by this camp is that diplomatic protection is not applicable in circumstances where IIAs expressly address the question of nationality, and that one should not read into the provisions of IIAs the requirement of substantial business activity;[158] if the parties to the IIA in question intended for this to be the case, they would have included a denial of benefits provision.

An increasing number of arbitral tribunals are adopting a simple incorporation test where this is permissible, even if not expressly, under the IIA in question. Several cases illustrate this position, including *Yukos v Russia*,[159] *ADC v Hungary*,[160] *Tokios Tokelès v Lithuania*,[161] *Aucoven v Venezuela*,[162] *Rompetrol v Romania*[163] and *Saluka v Czech Republic*.[164] In the latter case, in particular, the Czech-Dutch BIT defined, in Article 1(b)(ii)), 'investors' as 'legal persons constituted under the laws of [the Netherlands]'. In circumstances where the

154 Paul Blyschak, '*Yukos Universal v Russia*: Shell Companies and Treaty Shopping in International Energy Disputes' (2010) 10 *Richmond Journal of Global Law and Business* 179; Utku Topcan, 'Abuse of the Right to Access ICSID Arbitration' (2014) 29(3) *ICSID Review-Foreign Investment Law Journal* 627.
155 *Barcelona Traction, Light and Power Company, Limited (Belgium v Spain) (New Application: 1962)* [1970] ICJ 1.
156 ibid 71.
157 See *Tokios Tokelės v Ukraine*, Decision on Jurisdiction, 29 April 2004; *Wena Hotels v Egypt*, Decision on Jurisdiction, 29 June 1999, 6 ICSID Rep 74, 79–84; *Saluka v Czech Republic*, Partial Award, 17 March 2006.
158 ibid *Tokios Tokelės v Ukraine* [36].
159 PCA Case No. AA 227, Interim Award on Jurisdiction and Admissibility (UNCITRAL), 30 November 2009.
160 ICSID Case No. ARB/03/16, Award, 2 October 2006.
161 ICSID Case No. ARB/02/18, Decision on Jurisdiction, 29 April 2004.
162 ICSID Case No. ARB/00/5, Decision on Jurisdiction, 27 September 2001.
163 ICSID Case No. ARB/06/3, Decision on Jurisdiction and Admissibility, 18 April 2008.
164 UNCITRAL, Partial Award, 17 March 2006.

claimant alleged, *inter alia*, a breach of the fair and equitable treatment standard on account of the host state's privatisation of its bank, the claimant brought arbitration proceedings against the Czech Republic. In response, the Czech Republic argued that Saluka was not an investor for the purposes of the relevant BIT because it was not a national of the Netherlands, since, in its view, it was owned and controlled by Normura Europe, a UK entity. In effect, then, the Czech Republic was contending that Saluka was a UK company, and since the BIT only afforded protection to home country, i.e. Dutch investors, the claimant could not benefit from arbitration proceedings under the Czech-Dutch BIT. The tribunal, however, held that the language of the BIT introduced a simple test of incorporation, making irrelevant the question of who owned or controlled Saluka. In the tribunal's view, if the parties to the BIT had intended for a narrower test to be applied, they should have specifically indicated that ownership and control must rest with nationals of the home state, but, in the absence of such express indication, the plain language of the BIT should take effect.[165]

The second argument raised by the Czech Republic was that Saluka should not qualify as an investor because it lacked real, factual, social, or economic links to the Netherlands. Essentially, the respondent's contention was that the BIT was meant to afford protection to investors who had business operations in the home state, and not mere shell companies that were simply incorporated in the home state. Although showing 'some sympathy' for the respondent's argument in this context, the tribunal nonetheless held that it could not 'in effect impose upon the parties a definition of "investor" other than that which they themselves agreed',[166] given that they had complete 'freedom of choice in this matter.'[167] While recognising Saluka as a Dutch company, it is instructive to note, however, that the tribunal was nonetheless very concerned that juridical entities which do not have substantial business activities but which claim protection under the relevant home state – host state BIT arguably abuse the arbitral procedure in a manner akin to 'treaty shopping' or 'forum shopping'.

In *Gabrinus,*[168] the tribunal endorsed the liberal approach countenanced in *Yukos, ADC, Tokios, Aucoven, Rompetrol,* and *Saluka.* In that case, four companies concluded a Fertilizer Development Agreement, setting forth the framework for the creation of a joint venture for the construction and operation of a fertilizer production facility called 'Fertinitro' in Venezuela. One of the companies, Polar, owned 10% of the interest in this facility. Polar, as part of its restructuring exercise, concluded a share purchase agreement with Gambrinus through which, in exchange for the payment of US$80,000,100.00, Polar sought to transfer its 10% equity interest in Fertinitro.

At this time, Venezuela began restructuring its food and agriculture industry aimed at achieving food security by way of increasing its agriculture productivity. Against this backdrop, Venezuela sought, in 2010, to ensure adequate fertilizer supply by enacting a decree which provided for the expropriation of companies involved in the fertilizer industry. This resulted in the forced acquisition of Fertinitro, albeit that Gambrinus did not receive compensation from Venezuela in this connection. Accordingly, Gambrinus filed its request for arbitration against Venezuela before ICSID on the basis of the BIT between the Government of Barbados and the Government of the Republic of Venezuela.

165 ibid 241.
166 ibid.
167 ibid.
168 ICSID Case No. ARB/11/31, Award, 15 June 2015.

Venezuela objected to the tribunal's jurisdiction on the basis that Gambrinus did not, in its view, qualify as an 'investor' under the BIT because it was an empty offshore entity with no operations in Barbados. Venezuela considered that Gambrinus was owned, controlled, and run by Polar, a Venezuelan company, in Venezuela, and that, having regard to Gambrinus' economic reality, it should not be considered a foreign investor under the BIT. Venezuela outrightly rejected the simple test of incorporation for determining whether Gambrinus should benefit from protection under the BIT, arguing that, even if the tribunal was inclined to consider that only the incorporation criterion should be followed, Gambrinus' corporate veil should have been pierced on the basis of an occurrence of abuse of process and *fraude de ley*.

The tribunal, relying on *Tokios, Aucoven, Rompetrol,* and *Saluka*, emphatically found in favour of Grambinus on this jurisdictional question. It noted that the jurisdiction of ICSID depends on the consent of the Contracting Parties, who enjoy broad discretion to choose the disputes that they will submit to ICSID. Applying the natural and ordinary meaning of the provisions of the relevant BIT in question, the tribunal found that mere incorporation in Barbados was sufficient to establish the nationality of the company:

> In the exercise of its functions, the Tribunal is guided by the terms in which the Contracting Parties to the BIT have agreed to establish its jurisdiction. According to the Tribunal's interpretation, the BIT only requires that Claimant be constituted under the laws of one of the Contracting Parties. As a company incorporated or constituted in Barbados, one of the BIT's Contracting Parties, Gambrinus satisfies the jurisdiction *ratione personae*.[169]

Another matter which arose for consideration in the *Gambrinus* case was whether the corporate veil should be pierced on account of the company's alleged abuse of process by engaging in corporate restructuring in an effort to benefit from the relevant BIT. The tribunal, having considered the relevant timelines wherein which Gambrinus' restructuring activities occurred relative to the passage of the Expropriation Decree, found no evidence that the company engaged in corporate restructuring at a time when the dispute had already arisen, or was at the very least reasonably foreseeable. Rather, Gambrinus's Share Transfer with Polar responded to business considerations; at the time of the purported Share Transfer to Gambrinus, the expropriation of Fertinitro was not only far from being in existence but was also not reasonably foreseeable nor highly probable. In short, at the time when Gambrinus' restructuring took place, there was no 'disagreement' or 'conflict of legal opinions or of interests'.[170]

The tribunal in *Gambrinus* then went on to emphatically reject Venezuela's reliance on *Barcelona Traction* which it argued empowers tribunals to pierce the corporate veil so as to prevent the misuse of the privilege of legal personality. It considered that *Barcelona Traction* was decided in the context of diplomatic proceedings, 'a context which is not the one of investment protection regulated by the ICSID Convention and the BIT'.[171] Given that there was no evidence that Gambrinus had used its status as a Barbadian entity to perpetrate fraud or engage in malfeasance:

> [T]here [was] nothing wrong for a prudent investor to organise its investment in a way that affords maximum protection under existing treaties, usually by establishing a company in a State that . . . accepts incorporation as a basis for corporate nationality.[172]

169 ibid 144.
170 ibid 198.
171 ibid 142.
172 ibid.

The tribunal's decision in this case appears reasonable. First, the reasoning of the tribunal on the question of the relevant test for the determination of an investor's nationality is congruent with the previously decided leading cases of *Tokios, Aucoven, Rompetrol,* and *Saluka,* thereby demonstrating consistency and predictability, key tenets of legitimacy. Second, the tribunal's reasoning in *Gambrinus* is fully consistent with Article 31 of the VCLT, which mandates that tribunals give consideration to the natural and ordinary meaning of words as their first point of reference; clearly, if the parties, through their BITs, make reference to a simple test of incorporation, a tribunal should not take it upon itself to introduce new requirements not expressly considered by the parties. Third, the tribunal's rejection of *Barcelona Traction* in the context of ICSID proceedings is fully consistent with the approach countenanced by leading academics in the field,[173] as well as other tribunals which have arrived at a similar conclusion. In fact, the International Court of Justice (ICJ) in *Ahmadou Sadio Diallo (Republic of Guinea v Democratic Republic of the Congo)*[174] has itself pronounced:

> . . . in contemporary international law, the protection of the rights of companies and the rights of their shareholders, and the settlement of the associated disputes, are essentially governed by bilateral or multilateral agreements for the protection of foreign investments, such as the treaties for the promotion and protection of foreign investments, and the Washington Convention of 18 March 1965 on the Settlement of Investment Disputes between States and Nationals of Other States, which created an International Centre for Settlement of Investment Disputes (ICSID), and also by contracts between States and foreign investors. In that context, the role of diplomatic protection somewhat faded, as in practice recourse is only made to it in rare cases where treaty regimes do not exist or have proved inoperative.[175]

Finally, the *Gambrinus* tribunal was correct in its articulation of the principles relating to abuse of process on account of corporate restructuring. Indeed, the tribunal's marshalling of the evidence relative to the timing of the share transfer agreement cannot be faulted, nor its reasoning that a dispute was not highly foreseeable at the relevant time. Its statement of principle that investors are free to structure their investments in a manner that best fits their need for international protection, provided that they do not modify their investment after a dispute has already arisen or is highly probable, is also fully consistent with a number of arbitral awards, including *Phoenix v Czech Republic*,[176] *Mobil v Venezuela*,[177] and *Renee Rose v Peru*.[178]

Notwithstanding the foregoing, that an arbitral tribunal would countenance an approach which effectively allows a company that has not tangibly contributed to the development of the host state nor maintained any economic linkage to the host state to benefit from the protections conferred by the BIT in question raises important questions regarding the

173 See, e.g. Katia Yannaca-Small, 'Who is entitled to Claim: The Definition of Nationality in Investment Arbitration' in Katia Yannaca-Small (ed), *Arbitration under international investment agreements: A Guide to the Key Issues* (OUP 2018) 10.28.

174 Preliminary Objections, Judgment, ICJ Reports 2007.

175 ibid 88.

176 ICSID Case No. ARB/06/5, Award, 15 April 2009:

> [t]he tribunal has to ensure that the ICSID mechanism does not protect investments that it was not designed for to protect, because they are in essence domestic investments disguised as international investments for the sole purpose of access to this mechanism.

177 ICSID Case No. ARB/07/27, Decision on Jurisdiction, 10 June 2010.

178 ICSID Case No. ARB/11/17, Award, 9 January 2015.

asymmetrical nature of the international investment regime,[179] and the seemingly subservient place of host states in the context of this regime. The effect of the ruling is to somewhat legitimize the practice of investors treaty shopping; that is, setting up shell companies in foreign jurisdictions only to benefit from investor protection standards contained in BITs between their home state and the other Contracting Party. It may very well be that the time has therefore come for the older generation Caribbean BITs to be reconceptualised such that they adopt the *siège social* approach to corporate nationality. Under this approach, the paper nationality (i.e. where the company has been incorporated) is not the imperative consideration, but the investor's effective nationality which contemplates its engagement in actual business activity in the host state – its principal place of establishment.

Interestingly, in *Blue Bank International & Trust (Barbados) Ltd. v Venezuela*,[180] the arbitral tribunal refused to accept a simple test of incorporation as the basis for establishing corporate nationality. Here, Blue Bank, a trust company incorporated under the laws of Barbados, alleged expropriation and other violations of obligations under the BIT in relation to its tourism and hospitality business in Venezuela. Venezuela, however, objected to the jurisdiction of ICSID and the competence of the tribunal, arguing that the real investors, if any, were Venezuelan nationals, and, as such, they were not protected under the Convention or the BIT. By contrast, Blue Bank contended that there was no basis under the BIT or the Convention to look to anything other than Blue Bank's place of incorporation to determine its nationality as an investor as the BIT did not require that an investor hold a beneficial interest in the investment.

The tribunal held that, notwithstanding Blue Bank's incorporation under the laws of Barbados, it was not the owner of the investment in question. It construed Article 1 of the BIT, which provides that the assets comprising the investment must be 'invested' by the investor, to mean that the claimant had to own the assets in question. In this connection, it noted that the party that came closest to satisfying the requirement of 'ownership' with regard to the assets of the Trust was a person called 'Hampton', who enjoyed ultimate control over the Trust assets. Blue Bank, as a trustee holding the assets of the Trust, did not, in the tribunal's view, own the assets of the Trust, and therefore could not be said to have invested these assets for its own account.

While the *Blue Bank* decision rightly expresses concerns about the usefulness of the simple test of incorporation, the tribunal seemed to have shifted the pendulum too far in favour of the host state when it equated the term 'invested' with 'ownership'. More pointedly, although the BIT in question simply required that the company in question be constituted under the laws of the home state (which it was), and that the company must have invested in the host state, the tribunal did not consider this to be sufficient bases for establishing jurisdiction since the company did not have beneficial ownership of the Trust assets in question. This cannot, from a principled perspective, be correct, as the tribunal's approach in ignoring legal ownership and simultaneously placing great emphasis on beneficial ownership, as opposed to place of incorporation, arguably ignores the textual parameters of the BIT in question. The tribunal's wild goose chase in trying to determine who were the beneficial owners of the Trust is also inconsistent with *Cortec v Kenya*,[181] which held that

179 Rachel Anderson, 'Toward Global Corporate Citizenship: Reframing Foreign Direct Investment Law' (2009) 18 *Michigan State University College Law Journal of International Law* 1.

180 ICSID Case No. ARB 12/20, Award, 26 April 2017.

181 ICSID Case No. ARB/15/29, Award, 22 October 2018.

a tribunal should not deny jurisdiction simply because an investor's shareholders are from jurisdiction(s) other than the Contracting Parties to the BIT in question.

(ii) 'Ownership/Control'

Some regional IIAs[182] require proof of ownership or control (disjunctively). For example, Article 1(2)(b) of the SVG-Taiwan BIT provides:

> 2. the term 'investor' shall mean in the case of the Republic of China (Taiwan);
>
> b) any enterprise that is owned or controlled by citizens of the Republic of China (Taiwan) and incorporated or duly constituted in accordance with applicable laws of the Republic of China (Taiwan), and who makes the investment in the territory of Saint Vincent and The Grenadines and who does not possess the citizenship of Saint Vincent and The Grenadines.

Other IIAs[183] impose only a condition of control (without mentioning ownership). For example, Article 1(c) of the Barbados-Switzerland BIT provides:

> legal entities established under the law of any country which are, directly or indirectly, controlled by natural persons within the meaning of (a) above or by legal entities within the meaning of (b) above.

At least one BIT is very restrictive in that it requires proof of both control and ownership: Article 1(b)(i) of the Jamaica-Switzerland BIT:

> juridical persons or business associations which are effectively controlled by Swiss nationals having a substantial part in the ownership.

In arbitral practice, tribunals have developed nuanced approaches to interpreting ownership and control requirements, as illustrated by several key cases. In *Standard Chartered Bank v Tanzania*,[184] the dispute concerned loans originally made by Malaysian financial institutions to Tanzanian borrowers that were subsequently acquired by a Hong Kong company in which the British claimant owned equity interest. The tribunal determined that this indirect chain of ownership was insufficient to qualify the loans as investments of the claimant under the UK-Tanzania BIT. The tribunal established a higher threshold requiring that an investment be made 'at the claimant's direction, that the claimant funded the investment or that the claimant controlled the investment in an active and direct manner'.[185] This stricter approach emphasised active involvement beyond mere ownership in the investment chain.

Meanwhile, *Occidental v Ecuador (II)*[186] was an ICSID annulment proceeding that partially reduced an original \$1.77 billion award to \$1.06 billion. The underlying dispute concerned oil exploitation rights in Ecuador to a so-called 'Block 15'. While Occidental formally held 100% of the interest, it had transferred beneficial ownership of 40% to Alberta Energy Corporation through a 'farmout' arrangement, retaining only nominal ownership of that portion. The ad hoc committee determined that the original tribunal had committed a

182 SVG-Taiwan Article 1(2)(b); Trinidad and Tobago-Switzerland Article 1(1)(c); Trinidad and Tobago-France Article 1(3); Guyana-Brazil Article 1.4.

183 See, also, Jamaica-The Netherlands BIT Article 1(b)(iii).

184 ICSID Case No. ARB/10/12, Award, 2 November 2012.

185 ibid 230.

186 ICSID Case No. ARB/06/11, Decision on Annulment of the Award, 2 November 2015.

manifest excess of powers by assuming jurisdiction over and awarding compensation for the 40% interest that Occidental no longer effectively owned, emphasising substance over form in ownership determinations.

Separately, *Guardian Fiduciary Trust v Macedonia*[187] addressed whether a New Zealand company could claim protection under the Macedonia-Netherlands BIT by virtue of being 'controlled directly or indirectly' by Dutch nationals. The ownership structure involved an intermediate company with split ownership between a Dutch entity (legal owner) and a Marshall Islands company (beneficial owner). Despite formal legal ownership by the Dutch entity, the tribunal conducted a detailed factual analysis of actual control, noting that the director of the Marshall Islands company had authorised the arbitration request. Finding insufficient evidence of actual Dutch control, the tribunal declined jurisdiction, demonstrating that formal ownership may not be determinative.

Finally, in *National Gas v Egypt*,[188] the tribunal examined whether an Egyptian-incorporated company could be considered a foreign investor under the Egypt-UAE BIT through the 'foreign control' exception in Article 25(2)(b) of the ICSID Convention. Although National Gas was formally owned by UAE companies, the factual evidence revealed it was ultimately controlled by an Egyptian national, Mr. Reda Ginena. The tribunal therefore concluded that the company failed to meet the 'foreign control' requirement necessary for ICSID jurisdiction. From this case, it would seem that tribunals may pierce through multiple corporate layers to identify ultimate controllers when determining jurisdiction.

(iii) The 'seat' Test

Finally, a clear pattern emerges that German BITs consistently include the 'seat' requirement for juridical persons. For example, Article 1(4) of the St Lucia-Germany BIT provides:

> The term 'companies' shall mean:
>
> (a) In respect of the Federal Republic of Germany: any juridical person as well as any commercial or other company or association with or without legal personality having its seat in the German area of application of the present.[189]

This approach reflects the German legal tradition, which often emphasises the real seat theory (*Sitztheorie*) of corporate nationality,[190] as opposed to the incorporation theory more typical in common law jurisdictions. In arbitral practice, tribunals have interpreted this 'seat' requirement substantively. In *Tenaris and Talta v Venezuela (II)*,[191] for example the tribunal determined that 'seat' meant effective seat rather than merely statutory seat – the place where actual management activities occurred. The tribunal evaluated three criteria: (i) where shareholder and board meetings took place, (ii) where management activities like client contacts and major contract conclusions occurred, and (iii) where books and accounts

187 ICSID Case No. ARB/12/31, Award, 22 September 2015.

188 ICSID Case No. ARB/11/7 (n 152).

189 See, also, Antigua and Barbuda-Germany BIT Article 1(3)(a)(ii); Barbados-Germany BIT Article 1(4)(a); Dominica-Germany Article 1(4)(a); Haiti-Germany BIT Article 1(4)(a); Guyana-Germany BIT Article 1(4)(a); Guyana-Switzerland BIT Article 1(b); Jamaica-Germany BIT Article 1(4)(a); St. Lucia-Germany BIT Article 1(4)(a); Trinidad and Tobago-Germany BIT Article 1(4)(b).

190 Christoph Benedict, 'The Determination of the Nationality of Investors under Investment Protection Treaties' (2011) 106(3) *Beiträge zum Transnationalen Wirtschaftsrecht* 26.

191 ICSID Case No. ARB/12/23, Award, 12 November 2016.

were located. Similarly, in *Tenaris and Talta v Venezuela (I)*,[192] a different tribunal interpreted 'seat' to mean 'the place of actual or effective management'[193] while acknowledging that the standard must be applied contextually. For holding companies with limited day-to-day operations, the tribunal recognised that maintaining extensive offices or workforce would be unreasonable. Instead, the tribunal found that having premises in the home state, holding annual meetings there, and maintaining certain documented ties was sufficient to satisfy the 'actual or effective management' test.

(iv) Denial of Benefits

Some BITs[194] impose a requirement that the putative investor must be carrying on business/economic activities in the home state. For example, Article 1(c) Trinidad and Tobago-Guatemala BIT provides:

> c) 'investor' of a Contracting Party means any natural or legal person of a Contracting Party that invests in the territory of the other Contracting Party and which has substantive business operations in the territory of that Contracting Party.

Meanwhile, some BITs expressly allow for the host state to deny benefits ('denial of benefits' clause) in circumstances where the putative investor does not conduct substantial business activities in the home state. In other words, this clause allows denial of benefits to shell companies without substantial business activities. For example, Article 1(2) Jamaica-USA BIT provides:

> 2. Each Party reserves the right to deny to any company the advantages of this Treaty if nationals of any third country control such company and, in the case of a company of the other Party, that company has no substantial business activities in the territory of the other Party or is controlled by nationals of a third country with which the denying Party does not maintain normal economic relations.

Tribunals have reached divergent conclusions regarding when states may invoke denial of benefits clauses. In *Pac Rim Cayman v El Salvador*,[195] for example, the tribunal determined that the time limit for denying benefits is governed by ICSID Arbitration Rule 41, which requires jurisdictional objections to be made as early as possible and no later than the expiration of the time limit fixed for the filing of the Counter-Memorial. This represents a departure from earlier decisions like *Plama v Bulgaria*,[196] which held that a state may not deny benefits of the treaty to the investor after the claim was brought. In *Khan Resources v Mongolia*,[197] the tribunal ruled that a state could not exercise this right toward an investor after the latter commenced ISDS proceedings against it, reasoning that the treaty's purpose was 'to create a predictable legal framework for investments' which requires investors to 'know in advance whether they are entitled to the protections of the Treaty'.[198] Conversely,

192 ICSID Case No. ARB/11/26, Award, 29 January 2016.

193 ibid 154.

194 Barbados-Switzerland BIT Article 1(b); Grenada-USA BIT Article 1(2); Guyana-Switzerland BIT Article 1(b); Trinidad and Tobago-USA BIT Article 12.

195 ICSID Case No. ARB/09/12, Award, 14 October 2016, para. 5.42.

196 ICSID Case No. ARB/03/24, Decision on Jurisdiction, 8 February 2005.

197 UNCITRAL, Decision of Jurisdiction, 25 July 2012.

198 ibid 426.

in *Guaracachi America v Bolivia*,[199] the tribunal accepted the denial of benefits invoked in the respondent's statement of defence, holding that 'the denial can and usually will be used whenever an investor decides to invoke one of the benefits of the BIT'.[200]

Meanwhile, regarding the 'substantial business activities' requirement, the *Pac Rim*[201] tribunal held that this requirement relates not to the collective activities of a group of companies, but to activities attributable to the 'enterprise' itself. While acknowledging a holding company could potentially carry substantial business activities, the tribunal concluded that the claimant did not meet this threshold when its activities were merely holding assets (shares of subsidiaries). A more flexible approach to the 'substantial business activities' test appeared in *Bridgestone v Panama*.[202] The tribunal there held that 'benefits should not be denied to firms that . . . have a real and continuous link with, the country where they are established'.[203] Notably, the tribunal found that a trademark management company had substantial business activities in the United States despite sharing its address with another group company and having no employees of its own.

In short, tribunals remain divided on when states can invoke denial of benefits clauses – some allowing invocation as late as the statement of defence (*Pac Rim, Guaracachi America*), while others require invocation before arbitration begins (*Khan Resources*). The divergent approaches highlight that this area of investment law continues to develop, with no firm consensus yet established on either timing requirements or the substantive threshold for 'substantial business activities'.

(v) Profitability

Interestingly, while most IIAs are silent on whether the enterprise set up by the allege investor must be for profit, some BITs[204] are specific in offering protection to investors, even where the enterprise is not set up for profit. For example, Article 1(a)(1) of the Barbados-Canada BIT provides:

> a. 'enterprise' means:
>   i. any entity constituted or organized under applicable law, whether or not for profit, whether privately-owned or governmentally-owned, including any corporation, trust, partnership, sole proprietorship, joint venture or other association.

Given that one of the hallmarks of foreign direct investment is that of the regularity of return of profits, it would appear that the approach of the aforementioned BITs in not mandating the profitability of enterprises is conceptually incongruent. However, it is submitted that, as a matter of principle, in accordance with Article 31 VCLT, such clear wording of said BITs must be respected as it expresses the will of the parties.

199 UNCITRAL, PCA Case No. 2011–17, Award, 31 January 2014.

200 ibid 378.

201 ICSID Case No. ARB/09/12 (n 194), para. 4.66.

202 ICSID Case No. ARB/16/34, Decision on Expedited Objections, 13 December 2017.

203 ibid 302.

204 Antigua and Barbuda-Germany BIT Article 1(3)(a)(ii); Jamaica-Argentina BIT Article 1(2)(b); Jamaica-South Korea BIT Article 1(2)(b); Trinidad and Tobago-Guatemala BIT Article 1(a); Trinidad and Tobago-USA BIT Article 1(a).

(vi) State Owned Corporations

Some Caribbean IIAs[205] specify clearly that state/government owned corporations can qualify as investors. For example, Article 1(2) Jamaica-Egypt BIT provides:

> (2) The term 'investor' shall mean any natural or juridical person, including the Government of a Contracting Party who invests in the territory of the other Contracting Party.

There is significant contestation over whether state-owned entities (SOEs) (i.e. companies owned or controlled by the home state) when operating in their sovereign capacity or commercial capacity are excluded from protection under IIAs.[206] Nonetheless, Article 1(2) Jamaica-Egypt BIT expressly affords protection to these entities once they invest in the host state. As a matter of principle, in accordance with Article 31 VCLT, such clear wording of said BITs must be respected as it expresses the will of the parties. This inclusive approach has been tested in several cases to date. In *Beijing Urban Construction v Yemen*,[207] for example, while the tribunal acknowledged that ICSID dispute resolution is not available to state-owned companies acting as state agents or performing governmental functions, it found that the claimant was engaged in commercial activities (an airport project) sufficiently removed from Chinese governmental functions. Similarly, in *China Heilongjiang v Mongolia*,[208] Mongolia's argument that the Chinese state-owned claimants were not legitimate investors because they lacked profit motivation and independence was rejected. The UNCITRAL tribunal found no basis in the China-Mongolia BIT to restrict investors based on their organisation, purpose, ownership, or control. The tribunal determined that state ownership was irrelevant to qualification as 'economic entities' under the treaty and found no evidence the claimants were acting as instruments of Chinese government policy.

(vii) Against Whom?

Under Article 25(1) ICSID Convention, jurisdiction *ratione personae* extends to legal disputes arising between a Contracting State (or any constituent subdivision or agency of a Contracting State designated to the Centre by that state) and the foreign investors of another Contacting Party. Relatedly, under paragraph (3) of this provision, consent by a constituent subdivision or agency of a Contracting State requires the approval of that state unless that State notifies the Centre that no such approval is required. In *Cable Television of Nevis Ltd. and Cable Television of Nevis Holdings Ltd. v The Federation of St. Christopher (St. Kitts) and Nevis*,[209] the tribunal dismissed the arbitration request due to lack of jurisdiction on several grounds, including the fact that the proper party to the investment agreement was the Nevis Island Administration (NIA), and not the Federation of St. Kitts and Nevis. Even though the NIA was a constituent subdivision of the Federation, it had not been designated to ICSID as required by Article 25(1) of the ICSID Convention. In this context, Cable Television

205 Belize Cuba Article 1(d); Guyana-South Korea Article 1(3)(b); Jamaica-Egypt Article 1(2)(b); Trinidad and Tobago-USA Article 1(a).

206 Paul Blyschak, 'State-owned Enterprises and International Investment Treaties: When Are State-Owned Entities and Their Investments Protected?' (2011) 6(2) *Journal of International Law & International Relations* 27–52.

207 ICSID Case No. ARB/14/30, Decision of Jurisdiction, 31 May 2017.

208 PCA Case No. 2010–20, Award, 15 June 2015.

209 ICSID Case No. ARB/95/2, Award of the Tribunal, 13 January 1997.

had incorrectly named the Federation as respondent when it should have been NIA, thereby prompting the tribunal to reject the attempted substitution of the Federation for NIA.

IV. RATIONE TEMPORIS

Caribbean IIAs typically provide that while they apply to investments that are made in the host state(s) prior to and after the coming into force of said agreements, they do not, however, apply to claims which are initiated prior to the entry into force of the relevant IIA. This is the essence of jurisdiction *temporis*, which refers to whether the dispute falls within the timeframe covered by the applicable treaty.[210]

> For example, Article 25 of the Austria-Belize BIT provides:
>
> This Agreement shall apply to investments made in the territory of either Contracting Party in accordance with its legislation by investors of the other Contracting Party *prior as well as after* the entry into force of this Agreement.
>
> (2) This Agreement shall not apply to claims which have been settled or procedures which have been initiated prior to its entry into force.[211]

In circumstances where no such explicit provision is found in the relevant IIA, tribunals will apply general principles of international law and will likely find against the retroactive application of the treaty to disputes arising before it came into effect.[212]

If the relevant IIA contains an express provision that requires a claim to be initiated within a particular period of time (say three years) after the investor becomes aware of it, or could reasonably have become aware of it, a failure to comply with this requirement may mean that the case is time-barred for failing jurisdiction *ratione temporis*. In several notable cases, tribunals have strictly enforced these limitation periods, rejecting various attempts by investors to circumvent them. In *Ansung Housing v China*,[213] for example, the tribunal dismissed the investor's claims as being 'manifestly without legal merit' under ICSID Arbitration Rule 41(5) on the ground that the investor had failed to bring its claim within the three-year limitation period set forth in the China-Republic of Korea BIT (2007). The claimant argued that because China's conduct (failure to provide the additional land for the project) was of a 'continuing' nature, it was entitled to claim damages from a date later than its first knowledge of China's continuing breach. The tribunal rejected this argument and dismissed the claims:

210 *Chevron Corporation and Texaco Petroleum Company v The Republic of Ecuador (I)*, PCA Case No. 2007–02/AA277, Partial Award on the Merits, 30 March 2010.

211 See, also, Barbados-Belgium-Luxembourg Agreement Article 14; Barbados-Canada BIT Article XVII(1); Barbados-China BIT Article 11; Barbados-Mauritius BIT Article 2; Belize-China BIT Article 11; Belize-El Salvador BIT Article 11; Guyana-Brazil BIT Article 2(1); Guyana-China BIT Article 11; Jamaica-Argentina BIT Article 1(1); Jamaica-China BIT Article 10; SVG-Taiwan BIT Article XVI(1); Trinidad and Tobago-Canada BIT Article XVII(1); Trinidad and Tobago-China BIT Article 2; Trinidad and Tobago-Cuba BIT Article 2; Trinidad and Tobago-Guatemala BIT Article 2(1); Trinidad and Tobago-India BIT Article 2; Trinidad and Tobago-UK BIT Article 2.

212 Armand Terrien, 'Jurisdiction Ratione Temporis' (*Jus Mundi*, 11 August 2025) <https://jusmundi.com/en/document/publication/en-jurisdiction-ratione-temporis> accessed 28 August 2025.

213 ICSID Case No. ARB/14/25, Award, 9 March 2017.

> To allow [the] Claimant to adjust that date of first knowledge by selecting the date from which it wants to claim damages for continuing breach would be . . . to allow an 'endless parsing up of a claim into ever finer sub-components of breach over time in an attempt to come within the limitation period'.[214]

Meanwhile, in *Rusoro Mining v Venezuela*,[215] the tribunal applied a similar time bar found in the Canada-Venezuela BIT (1996). Under the relevant provision, the cut-off date for claims was three years before the claimant's July 2012 request for arbitration. The tribunal's task was therefore to determine which claims met this cut-off date by identifying the dates when the alleged breaches to the BIT occurred. Reviewing the measures on which the claims were based, the tribunal found that the claimant was aware of certain measures taking place before the cut-off date and that, accordingly, claims based upon those measures were barred. The tribunal rejected the claimant's argument that these earlier measures should be treated as intrinsically linked to later measures, and instead decided to '[break] down each alleged composite claim into individual breaches, each referring to a certain governmental measure, and to apply the time bar to each of such breaches separately.'[216] Similarly, in *Corona Materials v Dominican Republic*,[217] the tribunal declined jurisdiction over the claimant's entire case because the investor had failed to comply with the three-year limitation period in the CAFTA-DR. The tribunal determined that the claimant had actual knowledge of the alleged breach and knowledge of the resulting loss more than three years before submitting its arbitration request. Despite the claimant's attempts to characterise the government's failure to respond to its motion for reconsideration as a separate, later breach, the tribunal found that the limitation period had begun to run from the original denial of the environmental permit.

Finally, it is worth noting that the MFN clause cannot be used to modify the condition *ratione temporis* for the existence of the treaty rights.[218] This has been acknowledged, for example, in *Tecmed v Mexico*.[219] In that case, the Mexico-Spain BIT provided that it was only applicable to investments made after its entry into force. The tribunal accordingly refused to utilise the MFN clause to introduce a provision of the Mexico-Austria BIT according to which investments made before the entry into force of the BIT were also be protected:

> . . . matters relating to the application over time of the Agreement, which involve more the time dimension of application of its substantive provisions rather than matters of procedure or jurisdiction, due to their significance and importance, go to the core of matters that must be deemed to be specifically negotiated by the Contracting Parties. These are determining factors for their acceptance of the Agreement, as they are directly linked to the identification of the substantive protection regime applicable to the foreign investor and, particularly, to the general (national or international) legal context within which such regime operates, as well as to the access of foreign investor to the substantive provisions of such regime. Their application cannot therefore be impaired by the principle contained in the most favored nation clause.[220]

214 ibid 113.
215 ICSID Case No. ARB(AF)/12/5, Award, 22 August 2016.
216 ibid 231.
217 ICSID Case No. ARB(AF)/14/3, Award, 31 May 2016.
218 Suzy Nikièma, 'The Most-Favoured-Nation Clause in Investment Treaties' (IISD Best Practices Series – February 2017) <https://www.iisd.org/system/files/publications/mfn-most-favoured-nation-clause-best-practices-en.pdf> accessed 1 September 2025, para. 4.2.4.
219 ICSID Case No. ARB (AF)/00/2, Award, 29 May 2003.
220 ibid 69.

V. RATIONE VOLUNTIS

Because arbitration is based on the consent on the parties,[221] a tribunal may only assume jurisdiction over an investment claim if such consent has been clearly and unambiguously expressed.[222] Typically, this consent is expressed in the dispute settlement clause of the relevant BIT,[223] such as Article 8 of the Guyana-South Korea BIT, which provides:

221 The importance of the state's consent has been underscored in numerous decisions of international jurisdictions, among which the PCIJ and the ICJ. For example, the ICJ noted in the *Armed Activities* case [88]:

> [The Court's] jurisdiction is based on the consent of the parties and is confined to the extent accepted by them . . . . When that consent is expressed in a compromissory clause in an international agreement, any conditions to which such consent is subject must be regarded as constituting the limits thereon.

Meanwhile, *In the Phosphates in Morocco* case (*Italy v France*) PCIJ Reports, Ser. A/B No. 74, 1938, 141938, the PCIJ observed that it was advisable, in case of doubt, to give a restrictive interpretation of a clause in a treaty because such a clause 'must on no account be interpreted in such a way as to exceed the intention of the States that subscribed to it'. See, also, *Armed Activities on the Territory of the Congo* (New Application: 2002) (*Democratic Republic of the Congo v Rwanda*), Jurisdiction and Admissibility, Judgment of 3 February 2006, ICJ Reports 2006.

222 In *Plama v Bulgaria*, ICSID Case No. ARB/03/24, Decision on Jurisdiction, 8 February 2005, paras. 198, 199, the tribunal emphasised the importance of clear an unambiguous consent:

> Nowadays, arbitration is the generally accepted avenue for resolving disputes between investors and states. Yet, that phenomenon does not take away the basic prerequisite for arbitration: an agreement of the parties to arbitrate. It is a well-established principle, both in domestic and international law, that such an agreement should be clear and unambiguous. In the framework of a BIT, the agreement to arbitrate is arrived at by the consent to arbitration that a state gives in advance in respect of investment disputes falling under the BIT, and the acceptance thereof by an investor if the latter so desires.

The decision in *Wintershall* [116] also insisted that the state must have given its consent and that this consent is a condition for access to international arbitration:

> In the present case, therefore the BIT between Argentine/and Germany is a treaty undoubtedly providing for a right of access to international arbitration (ICSID) for foreign investors, who are German nationals – but this right of access to ICSID arbitration is not provided for unreservedly, but upon condition of first approaching competent Courts in Argentina . . . a local-remedies rule may be lawfully provided for in the BIT – under the first part of Article 26; once so provided, as in Article 10(2), it becomes a condition of Argentina's 'consent' – which is, in effect, Argentina's 'offer' to arbitrate disputes under the BIT, but only upon acceptance and compliance by an investor of the provisions *inter alia* of Article 10(2); an investor (like the Claimant) can accept the 'offer' only as so conditioned.

Meanwhile, the ICC Award in *SPP v Egypt* ICC Award No. 3493, 16 February 1983, Yearbook Com. Arb. 1984, vol. IX, fifteen considered that consent to arbitration must be clear and certain: 'We accept the principle that acceptance of an arbitration clause should be clear and unequivocal'. The award was annulled by the French courts, precisely because, on the facts of the case, the consent of Egypt was not clear and unequivocal.

223 Antigua-Germany BIT Article 11; Antigua-UK BIT Article 8; Belgium-Luxembourg-Barbados Agreement Article 8; Barbados-Canada BIT Article 13; Barbados-China BIT Article 9; Barbados-Cuba BIT Article 8; Barbados-Germany BIT Article 11; Barbados-Mauritius BIT Article 10; Barbados-Switzerland BIT Article 9; Barbados-UK BIT Article 8; Barbados-Venezuela BIT Article 8; Belize-China BIT Article 7; Belize-Cuba BIT Article 8; Belize-El Salvador BIT Article 7; Belize-Netherlands BIT Article 9; Belize-UK

1. Any dispute between a Contracting Party and an investor of the other Contracting Party derived from an alleged breach of an obligation under this Agreement including expropriation or nationalisation of investments shall, as far as possible, be settled by the parties to the dispute in an amicable way.
2. The local remedies under the laws and regulations of one Contracting Party in the territory of which the investment has been made shall be available for investors of the other Contracting Party on the basis of treatment no less favourable than that which would be accorded to investments of its own investors or investors of any third State, whichever is more favourable to investors.
3. If the dispute cannot be settled within six (6) months from the date on which the dispute has been raised by either party, and if the investor waives the rights to initiate any dispute under paragraph 2 of this Article, with respect to the same dispute, the dispute shall be submitted upon the request of the investor of the Contracting Party to:
   a) the International Center for Settlement of Investment Disputes (ICSID) established by the Washington Convention of 18 March 1965 on the Settlement of Investment Disputes between States and Nationals of other States;
   (b) the Court of Arbitration of the International Chamber of Commerce; or (c) an international arbitrator or ad hoc arbitral tribunal to be appointed by a special agreement or established under the Arbitration Rules of the United Nations Commission on International Trade Law.
4. The investor, notwithstanding that it may have submitted the dispute to the international arbitration under paragraph 3, may seek interim injunctive relief, not involving the payment of damages, before the judicial or administrative tribunals of the Contracting Party that is a party to the dispute for the preservation of its rights and interests.
5. Each Contracting Party hereby consents to the submission of a dispute to arbitration in accordance with the procedures set out in this Agreement.
6. The award made by the international arbitration shall be final and binding on the parties to the dispute. Each Contracting Party shall ensure the recognition and enforcement of the award in accordance with its relevant laws and regulations.

While a provision of this nature is fairly straightforward in that it is represents a standing offer to arbitrate,[224] which the investor accepts by initiating proceedings against the host

BIT Article 8; Dominica-UK BIT Article 8; Grenada-UK BIT Article 8; Grenada-USA BIT Article 6; Guyana-Brazil BIT Article 25; Guyana-China BIT Article 9; Guyana-Germany BIT Article 11; Guyana-South Korea BIT Article 8; Guyana-Switzerland BIT Article 8; Guyana-UK BIT Article 8; Jamaica-USA BIT Article 6; Jamaica-China BIT Article 8; Jamaica-Egypt BIT Article 8; Jamaica-Germany BIT Article 11; Jamaica-Indonesia Article 9; Jamaica-South Korea Article 8; Jamaica-Switzerland Article 9; Jamaica-Netherlands BIT Article 9; Jamaica-UK BIT Article 9; St Lucia-Germany BIT Article 10; St Lucia-UK BIT Article 8; SVG-Taiwan BIT Article 11 and 12; Trinidad and Tobago-Canada BIT Article 13; Trinidad and Tobago-China BIT Article 10; Trinidad and Tobago-Cuba BIT Article 10; Trinidad and Tobago-France BIT Article 8; Trinidad and Tobago-Germany BIT Article 13; Trinidad and Tobago-Guatemala BIT Article 10 and 11; Trinidad and Tobago-India BIT Article 9; Trinidad and Tobago-South Korea BIT Article 8; Trinidad and Tobago-Switzerland BIT Article 8; Trinidad and Tobago-UK BIT Article 10; Trinidad and Tobago-USA BIT Article 9.

224 *Hochtief AG v Argentine Republic*, ICSID Case No. ARB/07/31, para. 27: The 'acceptance' is contained in the request for arbitration.

state,[225] there have been disputes over whether the state can carve out an exception to certain disputes being submitted for arbitration after the ICSID Convention has been ratified by that state party in circumstances where it has not made such a reservation at the time of its deposit of the instrument. This was the issue that arose for consideration in *Alcoa Minerals of Jamaica, Inc. v Government of Jamaica.*[226] Here, in 1968, Alcoa Minerals (an American corporation) entered into a 25-year investment agreement with the Government of Jamaica. Alcoa agreed to construct an alumina refining plant in Jamaica in exchange for tax concessions

225 Professor Schreuer's view is that the investor may accept or not accept the offer as it stands in the BIT, but it cannot alter it unilaterally. He argues

> where ICSID's jurisdiction is based on an offer made by one party, subsequently accepted by the other, the party's consent is only to the extent that offer and acceptance coincide. . . . It is evident that the investor's acceptance may not validly go beyond the limits of the host State's offer. Therefore, any limitation contained in the legislation or treaty would apply irrespective of the terms of the investor's acceptance. If the terms of acceptance do not correspond with the terms of the offer there is no perfected consent

see Christoph Schreuer, 'Consent to Arbitration, *Course on Dispute Settlement, International Centre for the Settlement of Investment Disputes*, (UNCTAD) Module 2.3, 30. See, also, Noureddine Gara, 'Les nouveaux instruments du consentement à l'arbitrage CIRDI' in *Ou Va Le Droit De L'investissement? Desordre Normatif Et Recherche D'equilibre – Actes Du Colloque Organise a Tunis Les* (Pédone 2007) 50:

> (If the State's consent to arbitration is included in the treaty, the investor's consent must be expressed subsequently, after the dispute against the State has arisen. It is only at this time that the investor expresses its acceptance of the arbitration offer made by the State. Such acceptance can materialise and be effective only if it complies with the requirements of the treaty that serves as a support thereto.)

See, also, *Republic of Ecuador v Chevron Corporation, Texaco Petroleum Company* (US Court of Appeals for the Second Circuit, 17 March 2011) 12–13

> . . . the BIT merely creates a framework through which foreign investors, such as Chevron, can initiate arbitration against parties to the Treaty. In the end, however, this proves to be a distinction without difference, since Ecuador, by signing the BIT, and Chevron, by consenting to arbitration, have created a separate binding agreement to arbitrate. . . . All that is necessary to form an agreement to arbitrate is for one party to be a BIT signatory and the other to consent to arbitration of an investment dispute in accordance with the Treaty's terms. In effect, Ecuador's accession to the Treaty constitutes a standing offer to arbitrate disputes covered by the Treaty; a foreign investor's written demand for arbitration completes the 'agreement in writing' to submit the dispute to arbitration.

Paul Szasz, 'The Investment Disputes Convention – Opportunities and Pitfalls (How to Submit Disputes to ICSID)' (1970) 5 *Journal of Law and Economic Development* 23, 29 ('The related point to be observed when consent is expressed in diverse instruments, is the extent to which these overlap – for it is only in the area of coincidence that the consent is both effective and irrevocable.'). Christopher Dugan, Don Wallace, Noah Rubins, and Borzu Sabahi, *Investor-state Arbitration* (OUP 2008) 220–21

> Today, states typically provide their consent to submit future investment disputes to arbitration through bilateral investment treaties (BITs), multilateral treaties, or the state's own domestic legislation. Expression of consent by a state, however, is insufficient to bestow jurisdiction on a tribunal; 'the investor must perform some reciprocal act to perfect the consent'. Consent of a government in a law or a treaty is merely an offer to agree to arbitration, rather than a full contractual compromise as one would find in an investment contract. The government's unilateral offer is consummated as a binding obligation to arbitrate only with the investor's acceptance of that offer.

226 Schmidt (n 14).

and long-term bauxite mining leases. The agreement contained a 'no further tax' clause limiting what taxes Jamaica could impose on Alcoa's operations. The agreement included an arbitration clause providing for ICSID arbitration for any disputes. In 1974, Jamaica imposed a new tax through the Bauxite (Production Levy) Act, which resulted in a ninefold increase in taxes on Alcoa's mining operations. Alcoa considered this to be a violation of the 'no further tax' clause and initiated ICSID arbitration. Shortly before enacting the new tax, Jamaica had notified ICSID that disputes involving natural resources would not be submitted to ICSID arbitration. Jamaica accordingly refused to participate in the arbitration proceedings, claiming ICSID lacked jurisdiction. The main question before the tribunal was: could Jamaica's notification effectively withdraw its prior consent to arbitrate disputes with Alcoa?

The tribunal focused on Article 25(1) of the ICSID Convention, which contains the critical provision: 'when the parties have given their consent, no party may withdraw its consent unilaterally'. The tribunal applied this language without limitation, finding that it created an irrevocable international legal obligation. The tribunal ruled that Jamaica's notification under Article 25(4) could only operate prospectively – informing potential future investors of Jamaica's position on natural resources disputes. It could not retroactively to invalidate consent already given in existing agreements. In this connection, the tribunal stated that 'this consent having been given could not be withdrawn. The notification under Article 25 only operates for the future by way of information to the Centre and potential future investors.'[227] The tribunal emphasised that ruling otherwise would essentially render the Convention meaningless, as host states could simply withdraw consent whenever faced with an unwelcome arbitration. More pointedly, it cautioned that this interpretation would 'very largely, if not wholly, deprive the Convention of any practical value'.[228] The ruling established a fundamental principle in international investment law: once a state has consented to ICSID arbitration in an investment agreement, that consent becomes binding and irrevocable. States cannot escape their arbitration commitments through subsequent unilateral actions, even through formal notifications to ICSID itself.

Separately, albeit in respect of a contract claim (as opposed to a treaty claim), the question arose in *Cable Television of Nevis Ltd. and Cable Television of Nevis Holdings Ltd. v St Christopher and Nevis*[229] as to whether, in accordance with Article 25(1) of the ICSID Convention, the tribunal could exercise jurisdiction in circumstances where Nevis was not designated to ICSID as a subdivision of the Federation for the purposes of ICSID proceedings. The facts were that in 1986, Cable Television of Nevis Ltd. and Cable Television of Nevis Holdings Ltd. entered into a Concession Agreement with the Government of Nevis to establish and operate a cable television system on the island of Nevis. The agreement included a clause (Clause 16) that provided for ICSID arbitration. A dispute arose when the claimant attempted to increase its rates, which the Nevis Island Administration (NIA) opposed. The NIA obtained a court injunction preventing the claimant from raising rates until arbitration was completed. The claimant then filed a request for ICSID arbitration in October 1995, naming the Federation of St. Kitts and Nevis as the respondent, rather than the NIA or Government of Nevis who had signed the Agreement.

The Nevis Island Administration (NIA) was determined to be a constituent subdivision of the Federation but had never been formally designated to ICSID by the Federation as

227 ibid 10–11.
228 ibid 11.
229 ICSID Case No. ARB/95/2 (n 208).

required by Article 25(1). Meanwhile, although Article 25(3) provided, 'consent by a constituent subdivision or agency of a Contracting State shall require the approval of that State unless that State notifies the Centre that no such approval is required', no such approval or notification had been provided by the Federation. The Tribunal therefore concluded that while NIA had some autonomy and juridical personality, it remained a constituent subdivision requiring proper designation. The failure to make such designation meant that the requirement of consent for jurisdictional purposes was not satisfied. The ruling underscores that ICSID jurisdiction is strictly consent-based, and that consent must satisfy the specific technical requirements of Article 25. Even where economic realities might suggest an investment dispute appropriate for ICSID, the formal jurisdictional requirements cannot be bypassed or loosely interpreted.

The question of whether investors can rely on the MFN clause to invoke more favourable procedural provisions from third-country treaties is considered in chapter 3.

VI. ADMISSIBILITY

Although the line between jurisdiction and admissibility has in some cases been blurred, there is jurisprudence to suggest that whereas the former is concerned with the tribunal's competence over a particular dispute, the latter is concerned with the nature of the claim that has been brought.[230] The tribunal in *Hochtief Aktiengesellschaft v Argentine Republic*,[231] for example, noted that 'jurisdiction is an attribute of a tribunal and not of a claim, whereas admissibility is an attribute of a claim but not of a tribunal.'[232] This distinction is not only necessary, but appropriate, as noted by the tribunal in *Abaclat v Argentina*.[233] In other words, because admissibility assumes that the tribunal has jurisdiction,[234] an objection on admissibility grounds brings into question the varied reasons that a tribunal, although it has jurisdiction, may decline to hear a particular case.[235] In the discussion that follows below, two of the main admissibility requirements are examined in detail: the legality requirement and abuse of process.

A. The Legality Requirement

Caribbean BITs typically contain a provision that investments are to be admitted 'in accordance with the [law] of the host state.'[236] The effect of this provision is to introduce a 'legal-

230 Dr Ranjah Zia Ullah, 'Jurisdiction of Arbitral Tribunals' (*Jus Mundi*, 6 August 2025) <https://jusmundi.com/en/document/publication/en-jurisdiction-ratione-materiae> accessed 4 September 2025.

231 ICSID Case No. ARB/07/31, Decision on Jurisdiction, 24 October 2011.

232 ibid 90.

233 ICSID Case No. ARB/07/5, Decision on Jurisdiction and Admissibility, 4 August 2011, para. 248.

234 *Micula v Romania*, ICSID Case No. ARB/05/20, Decision on Jurisdiction and Admissibility, 24 September 2008, para. 63: 'an objection to jurisdiction goes to the ability of a tribunal to hear a case while an objection to admissibility aims at the claim itself and presupposes that the tribunal has jurisdiction'.

235 *Erhas Dis Ticaret Ltd. Sti, et al. v Republic of Turkmenistan*, PCA Case No. 2013–27, Separate Declaration of Stanimir A. Alexandrov, 19 May 2015, para. 5.

236 Antigua-Germany BIT Article 2(1); Barbados-Belgium-Luxembourg Agreement Article 2(1); Barbados-China BIT Article 1(1); Barbados-Germany BIT Article 2(1); Barbados-Cuba BIT Article 2(1); Belize-China BIT Article 1(a); Belize-Cuba BIT Article 2(1); Belize-El Salvador BIT Article 2(1);

ity' requirement. This requirement effectively means that, in appropriate circumstances, where an investor engages in unlawful conduct that breaches an admission requirement, the tribunal may either deny jurisdiction or find the claim inadmissible. These admission requirements[237] may be contained in BITs, National Investment Laws, and other sources of domestic law. The requirements typically include licensing requirements, which serve as preconditions for the investment being lawfully recognised as such by the host state.

Over the last decade or so, there have been repeated instances of investors not acting in accordance with host states' laws, thereby resulting in tribunals, in some cases, finding claims inadmissible or denying jurisdiction to hear the matter. While some tribunals have articulated that fundamental breaches of international law by an investor at the admission phase may result in them denying jurisdiction or finding claims inadmissible, other tribunals have grappled with the difficult question as to what exactly will constitute a sufficiently egregious form of illegality that would necessitate such outcomes. Regrettably, because of the absence of a *de jure* system of precedent in international investment arbitration, apart from the axiomatic cases of breaches of fundamental public policy by investors, there is growing uncertainty as to what types of conduct constitute an egregious enough illegality to result in the dismissal of claims.[238] This lack of certainty is a constant complaint of host states, in particular, who in practice have argued that they simply are not able to predict what is an appropriate response to an investor who has breached an admission requirement.

An elementary area of uncertainty which has arisen in the context of admission requirements is whether there is a need for an express clause in the IIA requiring investments to be 'in accordance with the laws of the host state' before a respondent state can raise objections based on investor illegality. Interestingly, on the one hand, in *Bear Creek Mining v Peru*,[239] the tribunal considered that, in the context of the Canada-Peru FTA (2008), there was no express jurisdictional requirement to the effect that the investment had to be lawfully constituted under the laws of Peru, and that, for this reason, the tribunal could properly refuse to import a requirement that the claim should only be admissible in circumstances where the investor complied with the host state's laws which touch and concern admission

---

Belize-Netherlands BIT Article 2; Dominica-Germany BIT Article 2; Guyana-Brazil BIT Article 2; Guyana-China BIT Article 2(1); Guyana-Germany BIT Article 2(1); Guyana-South Korea BIT Article 2(1); Guyana-Switzerland BIT Article 2; Jamaica-Argentina BIT Article 1(1); Jamaica-China BIT Article 1(1); Jamaica-Egypt BIT Article 1(1); Jamaica-Germany BIT Article 2(1); Jamaica-Indonesia BIT Article 2(1); Jamaica-South Korea BIT Article 2(2); Jamaica-Netherlands BIT Article 2(1); St Lucia-Germany BIT Article 2; SVG-Germany BIT Article 2; SVG-Taiwan BIT Article 2(1); Trinidad and Tobago-China BIT Article 1(1); Trinidad and Tobago-France BIT Article 1(1); Trinidad and Tobago-Germany BIT Article 2; Trinidad and Tobago-Guatemala BIT Article 2; Trinidad and Tobago-India BIT Article 2; Trinidad and Tobago-Korea BIT Article 2(1); Trinidad and Tobago-Switzerland BIT Article 2; Trinidad and Tobago-USA BIT Article 14(2).

237 Admission requirements in investment law refer to the conditions, restrictions, and procedural obligations that a host state imposes on foreign investors seeking to establish or acquire investments within its territory, typically including sectoral limitations, ownership caps, screening procedures, performance requirements, and regulatory compliance obligations.

238 Rob Howse, 'International Investment Law and Arbitration: A Conceptual Framework' (2019) *International Law and Litigation* 363; Juan Garcia Blesa, 'Indeterminacy, Ideology and Legitimacy in International Investment Arbitration: Controlling International Private Networks of Legal Governance?' (2021) 35 *International Journal for the Semiotics of Law* 1967.

239 ICSID Case No. ARB/14/21, Award, 30 November 2017.

requirements. On the other hand, however, the tribunal in *Cortec v Kenya*[240] found that it was inconsequential that the relevant BIT did not include an express reference to the investment being made in accordance with the host state's laws, as the very nature of an 'investment' presupposes its legal validity. It is submitted that the latter approach is consistent with general principles of international law, namely that, to benefit from investor protection standards, an investor must act in accordance with the host state's laws.[241]

The second elementary matter that must be noted is that there is a distinction between a breach of an admission requirement committed at the admission phase by an investor, which may have the effect of the tribunal finding the claim inadmissible or denying jurisdiction, and a breach committed after the investor has entered the jurisdiction. The tribunal in *Bear Creek Mining v Peru*[242] felt that both matters are distinct considerations, and that even though a tribunal does not find the alleged illegality sufficient to dismiss the claim at the preliminary phase, this does not preclude the possible relevance of illegality or lack of good faith with respect to the merits of the case. A similar approach was countenanced in *South American Silver Limited (Bermuda) v Bolivia.*[243] Here, the investor incorporated a company in Bolivia to explore and develop a mining project, and had, in fact, acquired ten mining concessions. Because the area within which the concessions were located was principally inhabited by Indigenous communities, a dispute arose, whereby members of the Indigenous communities accused the investor of polluting sacred spaces, abusing its authority, deceiving and threatening community members, and condoning the rape of women from the community. After a decree was issued by the Bolivian government reversing the ownership of the mining concessions, the investor claimed that the Reversion constituted expropriation under Article 5 of the Bolivia-United Kingdom BIT. The central issue for the tribunal was whether the alleged illegalities related to the investment affected its ability to hear the claim. The tribunal refused to dismiss the claim on these grounds, finding that there was no evidence of a causal link between the alleged illegalities and the investment itself. In other words, Bolivia had not shown that the alleged violations went to the essence of the investment such that it must be considered illegal. Importantly, for the purpose of this discussion, the tribunal noted that even if the allegations were true, it could not take them into account at the jurisdiction phase since they allegedly occurred in the post-admission (i.e. the establishment) phase of the investment cycle. That said, the tribunal nonetheless acknowledged that the allegations of illegality could be taken into account at the merits phase.

(i) Denial of Jurisdiction

Although there is, at present, no precise configuration of scenarios where a tribunal would deny jurisdiction because of an investor's breach of admission requirements, extant awards give some indication as to the types of conduct that are considered dispositive of the matter. What is clear from the awards to date is that the investor's impugned conduct must be egregious to necessitate a tribunal denying jurisdiction.

240 ICSID Case No. ARB/15/29 (n 180).

241 Rahim Moloo and Alex Khachaturian, 'The Compliance with the Law Requirement in International Investment Law' (2011) 34(6) *Fordham International Law Journal* 1473.

242 ICSID Case No. ARB/14/21 (n 238).

243 PCA Case No. 2013–15, Award, 22 November 2018.

Perhaps the most straightforward of these cases is where corruption is alleged to have occurred in the investor's dealings at the admission phase. In such a case, tribunals will be quick to deny jurisdiction on the basis that corruption, like fraud, is inimical to international public policy, as well as domestic law, and is so adverse to the interests of the host state that to allow jurisdiction would be an abuse of the arbitral system of dispute settlement. This view was countenanced in *Metal-Tech Ltd. v Uzbekistan.*[244] Here, Metal-Tech entered into a joint venture with two Uzbek state-owned enterprises to build and operate a modern plant to produce molybdenum (a silvery-white metal) in Uzbekistan. Metal-Tech concluded three consulting agreements having a total value of US$4.4 million with individuals that were closely connected to the Uzbek government. Thereafter, Uzmetal was ordered to distribute the unpaid dividends, but did not do so, such that bankruptcy proceedings against Uzmetal were thereafter initiated. Upon a claim by Metal-Tech that the host state had breached the fair and equitable treatment standard, the full protection and security standard, and the guarantee against expropriation as contained in the Israel-Uzbekistan BIT, the tribunal denied its jurisdiction on the basis that there were 'suspicions of corruption' on the evidence presented, namely the payment of a sum of more than US$4 million to the applicant's consultants. Having raised a *prima facie* case of corruption, the tribunal then reversed the burden of proof on the applicant to disprove the allegations of corruption, but they were unable to do so. Quite instructively, and, indeed, pragmatically, the tribunal considered that it was clear that no services or at least no legitimate services were performed at the time of the establishment of the investment by the investor. The tribunal applied Transparency International's 'red flags' analysis, ultimately finding that the amount of payments made to the applicant; the fact that there was no proof of services; the lack of qualification of the consultants; the sham consulting contracts; the lack of transparency of the payee; and the connections of the consultants with public officials in charge of Metal-Tech's investment, all demonstrated a strong circumstantial case of corruption sufficient for the tribunal to deny jurisdiction. Because the investor's conduct was a non-trivial violation of the host state's admission requirements, the tribunal considered that the investment was not 'implemented in accordance' with the laws of Uzbekistan, and that, therefore, Uzbekistan's consent to ICSID arbitration, as expressed in Article 8(1) of the BIT, was vitiated.

Another case in which a tribunal denied jurisdiction was *Anderson et al. v Republic of Costa Rica,*[245] where one hundred and thirty-seven (137) individual nationals of Canada brought ICSID proceedings against Costa Rica pursuant to the Canada-Costa Rica BIT. The circumstances of the case were that Costa Rican nationals, the Villalobos brothers, had, at the time of the incidents giving rise to this case, been engaged in various business activities in Costa Rica. One of their businesses was a currency exchange, which the Central Bank of Costa Rica licensed. The brothers, however, surreptitiously developed a scheme whereby individuals and companies would place funds with the brothers in return for a high interest rate on their deposits, as well as the repayment of the principal amount under stipulated conditions, contrary to Costa Rican law. More than 6,200 persons deposited a total of approximately US$405 million with the Villalobos brothers, albeit that the brothers provided minimal documentation to the persons depositing funds with them. As a result of the Villalobos brothers making no reports to the tax or other governmental authorities of Costa Rica or any other government on their operations or on the income earned by depositors in

244 ICSID Case No. ARB/10/3, Award, 4 October 2013.
245 ICSID Case No. ARB(AF)/07/3, Award, 19 May 2010.

the scheme, a domestic court sentenced one of the brothers to a period of imprisonment for his criminal conduct. In light of this, the claimants, Canadian nationals, who had effectively lost their deposits with the Villalbos brothers, commenced arbitration proceedings against the Costa Rican government for compensation for the loss sustained on the ground that such loss had been caused by various actions or omissions of the government of Costa Rica in violation of the Canada-Costa Rica BIT. The tribunal, however, held that in actively seeking and accepting deposits from the claimants, the Villalobos brothers were engaged in financial intermediation without authorisation by the Central Bank or any other government body as required by law. Given that they were clearly not acting in accordance with the laws of Costa Rica, the entire transaction between the Villalobos brothers and each claimant was illegal because it violated the Organic Law of the Central Bank. Because the transaction by which the Villalobos acquired the deposit was illegal, it followed that the acquisition by each claimant of the asset resulting from that transaction was also not valid in accordance with the law of Costa Rica. In short, their deposits and resulting relationships with Villalobos did not constitute an 'investment' under the BIT. The tribunal then went on to note, with concern, that:

> prudent investment practice requires that any investor exercise due diligence before committing funds to any particular investment proposal. An important element of such due diligence is for investors to assure themselves that their investments comply with the law. Such due diligence obligation is neither overly onerous nor unreasonable.[246]

In short, the tribunal denied jurisdiction because the claimants did not exercise the kind of due diligence that reasonable investors would have undertaken to assure themselves that their deposits with the Villalobos scheme were in accordance with the laws of Costa Rica. This was a true jurisdictional issue as it concerned whether there was a qualifying investment under the treaty (*ratione materiae*).

A contrasting outcome was arrived at in *Plama v Bulgaria.*[247] Here, the Bulgarian Privatisation Agency, before giving permission for the share purchase by the claimant, required certain disclosures to be made regarding the persons behind the purchase of the shares. However, Bulgaria argued that Plama had obtained its investment through misrepresentation by misleading Bulgaria into believing the investment consortium consisted of Norwegian Oil Company and André & Cie, and in never revealing that these companies had withdrawn and that Mr. Vautrin (a French national) had become the actual owner. Bulgaria contended that this misrepresentation violated Bulgarian law and vitiated Bulgaria's consent, making the investment invalid. The tribunal, however, *rejected* this illegality-based jurisdictional challenge on several grounds, including the fact that Bulgaria's jurisdictional challenge had not been advanced before the hearing. Crucially, the tribunal held that the dispute settlement provisions of the ECT, including Article 26, were autonomous and separable from Part III of that Treaty. In its view, they were independent of the entire Nova Plama transaction so that even if the parties' agreement regarding the purchase of Nova Plama was arguably invalid because of misrepresentation by the claimant, the agreement to arbitrate remained effective. In short, rather than denying jurisdiction, the tribunal acknowledged these were 'serious charges which, the Tribunal will have to examine on the merits' and 'join[ed] the issue of misrepresentation to the consideration of the merits of the case.'[248]

246 ibid 58.
247 ICSID Case No. ARB/03/24 (n 195).
248 ICSID Case No. ARB/03/24, Decision on Jurisdiction, paras. 229, 230.

(ii) Claims Rendered Inadmissible

Whereas jurisdictional issues concern the tribunal's power to hear a dispute, admissibility issues relate to whether a specific claim, though falling within that power, should be heard on its merits. *Cortec v Kenya*[249] provides a useful example of the latter. Here, a British investor, Cortec Mining Kenya Limited (CMK), invested in a mining project at Mrima Hill. They obtained a special prospecting licence and a special mining licence. However, upon the election of a new Kenyan government, a decision was taken to investigate and suspend the claimant's licence on the basis that the investor had breached an important admission requirement related to environmental protection. More specifically, the Kenyan Mining Act and Environmental Impact (Assessment and Audit) Regulations required that the claimant conduct an Environmental Impact Assessment (EIA) before obtaining a licence. However, it appeared that the claimant hurriedly conducted a mine feasibility report which failed to fulfil standard industry practices. In addition, the investor failed to undertake an EIA that might have allowed them to obtain a valid mining licence. As a result of their failure to comply with Kenyan law (which was a condition precedent to the issuance of a special mining licence), the tribunal found that the state had acted proportionately in revoking the investor's licence.

The tribunal engaged in an analysis of the methodology that should assist tribunals in the determination, on a case-by-case basis, as to when illegality should operate deny a treaty's protection. Three factors the tribunal noted should be taken into account: first, there must be an assessment of the significance of the obligation allegedly breached by the investor; second, the seriousness of the investor's conduct; and third, whether the legal consequences of such violation are proportional to the harshness of denying access to the protections of the BIT. On the facts, because non-compliance with the legal regulatory framework was a serious breach, Kenya had acted proportionately in revoking the licenses, and the tribunal felt convinced that it should accordingly dismiss the claim.

Kim et al. v Uzbekistan[250] is also instructive on the question of admissibility. Here, the claimants, Kazakhstan investors, invested in two cement plants in Uzbekistan. Their business interests were subject to a campaign of harassment by the respondent, involving criminal and regulatory investigations, the arrest and detention of employees, disruption of business activities, the confiscation of company property, and court-sanctioned expropriation of shares. When the investors alleged a breach of investor protection standards, the respondent, in response, challenged the admissibility of the claim on the basis that the investment was not made in accordance with Uzbek securities law, as required by the Kazakhstan-Uzbekistan BIT. The tribunal held that to successfully invoke the legality principle to render a claim inadmissible, there must be breach of a significant obligation. On the facts, the tribunal did not consider the breaches to be sufficiently egregious as to render the claim inadmissible. In arriving at this conclusion, the tribunal had regard to a number of pertinent facts, including the claimants' deliberate entry of incorrect price which it held did not itself demonstrate intent to defraud other market participants or manipulate the market; and the claimants' non-registration of the companies on the stock exchange (TSE) which it held was not an egregious breach, as the law did not clearly require for registration of private contracts for the purchase of share. In the tribunal's estimation, the claimants' violation of

249 ICSID Case No. ARB/15/29 (n 180).
250 ICSID Case No. ARB/13/6, Decision on Jurisdiction, 8 March 2017.

the various domestic laws generally did not lead to a nullity (but in most cases a fine), and there was no evidence that the claimants induced third parties or other market participants to purchase shares from them. Further, there was nothing immoral and anti-social about the claimants' behaviour.

Moreover, the tribunal considered that the conduct of the claimants was not egregious because Uzbekistan had an uncertain legal environment at the time of them making the investment, making compliance difficult; the claimant had acted on the advice of its brokers for the purposes of complying with Uzbek Law; the claimants were purchasers in good faith and had made substantial subsequent investments; the rules of Stock Exchange (TSE) were difficult to ascertain; and there was lack of evidence of governmental prosecution of Uzbek security laws. More pointedly, the tribunal reasoned that a finding of inadmissibility would have far-reaching consequences; that is, a finding of inadmissibility would mean not only that the tribunal could not hear the claim, but also that the BIT protections would not apply:

> 20. In the Tribunal's view, the interpretive task is guided by the principle of proportionality. The Tribunal must balance the object of promoting economic relations by providing a stable investment framework with the harsh consequence of entirely denying the application of the BIT when the investment is not made in compliance with legislation. The denial of the protections of the BIT is a harsh consequence that is a proportional response only when its application is triggered by noncompliance with a law that results in a compromise of a correspondingly significant interest of the Host State.[251]

In this respect, therefore, the tribunal cautioned about finding too quickly that investors' breach of admission requirements give rise to the conclusion that claims should be deemed inadmissible. Like the tribunal in *Cortec v Kenya*, the tribunal in *Kim* expressed that the significance of the obligation breached, and the seriousness of the investor's conduct are key considerations which should inform a tribunal as to whether to find a claim inadmissible where illegality on the part of an investor is alleged.

One of the most recent cases on the issue of legality, and certainly the only from the Caribbean to date, is *Peter Allard v Government of Barbados*.[252] Here, the claimant, a retired Canadian attorney and businessman, incorporated a Barbadian company, the Graeme Hall Bird Sanctuary Inc (GHNSI), in Barbados, to acquire 34.24 acres of wetlands to establish a bird sanctuary and nature reserve, within some 240 acres of wetlands and open space. He also incorporated another company, GHNBVI, for tax purposes, in the British Virgin Islands (BVI). His Barbadian company (GHNSI) issued shares to his BVI company (GHBVI), without prior approval of the Exchange Control Authority. After he made an investment of C$18.8 million in the acquisition and development of the eco-tourism site in Barbados, the project failed on account of alleged environmental drainage issues arising from the inappropriate operation of a sluice gate to discharge of raw sewage that seriously contaminated the Sanctuary. He sued for damages, alleging a breach of the fair and equitable treatment standard, full protection and security standard, and the guarantee against expropriation. One of the issues that arose for consideration at the preliminary phase was what was the effect of GHNSI's issuance of securities to GHBVI without the Exchange Control Authority's permission. To this, the tribunal held that while Barbados had a legitimate interest in tracking and regulating monies being remitted into its territory, there was no basis for finding that GHNSI's issuance of shares to GHBVI was offensive to public policy or

251 ibid 20.
252 *Peter Allard v Government of Barbados* (n 89).

tainted with criminality. It explained that the Exchange Control Act allowed the Authority to grant an approval with retrospective effect; Allard had made an investment in good faith in the Sanctuary; there was no evidence of any misconduct by the claimant in making the investment; and he did not attempt to conceal his investment in the Sanctuary. Accordingly, non-compliance with the Exchange Control Act was an inadvertent and technical breach of local law that did not render the claim inadmissible.[253] In other words, the non-compliance did not involve 'the breach of fundamental legal principles of Barbados.'[254]

In short, then, a respondent would only likely succeed in invoking the illegality ground if the investor did not act in compliance with the act(s) of non-compliance with local law results in a compromise of a significant interest that justifies, as a proportionate response, the harshness of denying application of the BIT.

(iii) Waiver by the Host State

If a host state allows or overlooks, as a matter of practice, an activity by a foreign investor which is, in principle, illegal, it may not later seek to rely on the illegal activity as a basis for arguing that the claim is inadmissible because the investment has not acted 'in accordance with its laws'. This is because the state, by its conduct, might be said to have waived its right to enforce the non-compliance by the investor with its admission requirements. This issue arose for consideration in *David Aven and Others v Republic of Costa Rica*.[255] Here, the claimant bought shares in several special purpose vehicle companies (SPVs) incorporated under the laws of Costa Rica in an effort to develop a real estate comprising a land plot of 37 hectares. They received all required permits and approvals, including the Environmental Viability Permit (EV), but because potential wetlands on the project site were identified, Costa Rican authorities later issued a series of injunctions prohibiting the works at the project. Criminal proceedings were thereafter initiated against the claimant for allegedly violating local laws on forestry and wildlife conservation. Although the Maritime Terrestrial Zone Law required that a Costa Rican national hold, at all times, at least 51% of the shares of said company, the investor in this case did not comply with this requirement. Interestingly, though, for a number of years, no action was taken by the state against this investor, nor, indeed, other investors who routinely ignored the requirement without being sanctioned. In addition, the investor had, for over 14 years, not paid taxes to the municipality, although this was a legal requirement. However, no tax was ever demanded by the municipality, and other investors did not pay tax also.

On the question of whether the claim was admissible in light of the alleged breaches by the claimant, the panel considered that the customary arrangements where local owned 51% of the shares, though really and truly the company was controlled by the foreign investor, appeared to be common throughout Costa Rica, and the government of Costa Rica had elected not to enforce the laws that could void such structures. Because the state had, for a long time, been tolerant of such conduct on the part of investors, it could not now rely upon that conduct before the arbitral tribunal to advance an argument that the claim was inadmissible. Similarly, with respect to the claim that the claimants had failed to pay municipal taxes for several years, this too was dismissed by the tribunal because neither the Municipality

253 ibid, Award on Jurisdiction, 13 June 2014, para. 94.
254 ibid.
255 ICSID Case No. UNCT/15/3, Award, 18 September 2018.

nor the State took any action prior to the filing by the claimants of the Notice of Arbitration. Against this backdrop, the tribunal found the claim admissible, and the matter proceeded to the merits phase.

(iv) Reflections

The cases discussed above, most of which have been decided upon in the last five years, demonstrate that, although there was, before *Kim et al.* and *Cortec*, a patchwork of approaches to determining what factors a tribunal should take into account before deciding to deny jurisdiction or find a claim inadmissible, this is no longer the case, as tribunals now principally consider, among other things, the seriousness of the obligation allegedly breached, the likely consequences of said breach, and the proportionality of the host state's response to said breach. This, it is submitted, is an excellent guide for future tribunals which may be confronted by difficult sets of facts wherein which two outcomes on the question of admissibility might be equally plausible.

That said, while it is commendable that tribunals are attempting to narrow down the circumstances in which claims may be found inadmissible for reasons of illegality, namely where fraud, corruption, and misrepresentation are in issue, the *Kim* and *Allard* case are difficult to reconcile. In both of these cases, notwithstanding the *Anderson* tribunal's sentiments that investors must act conscientiously and with due diligence when making an investment, the respective tribunals seem to have given little weight to the investor's fulsome reliance on the broker's flawed advice in *Kim*, and the investor's constructive knowledge of the requirements of Barbadian law in *Allard*. More than this, the tribunal in *Allard*, in particular, seems to have only cursorily dealt with the seriousness of the obligation breached, merely finding it to be 'trivial', but without fully engaging in the type of robust analysis that we saw in *Cortec*. In describing the requisite obligation as trivial, the *Allard* tribunal seems to have adopted an approach that completely ignores that, in different states, different obligations, for reasons of legal history and tradition, may be significant, such that if a subjectively serious obligation is breached, the tribunal should be inclined to find the claim inadmissible. Indeed, it would seem that the tribunal in *Cortec* took into account the subjective views of Kenya as to the significance of the obligation breached, here, environmental laws, whereas in *Allard*, such as analysis from the tribunal was sparse.

Having said that, it would seem, from the preponderance of authority discussed above, that the more serious the admission requirement breached, the more willing a tribunal will be to find claims inadmissible or deny jurisdiction, as appropriate. That said, it might be argued that a tribunal will not, as a matter of practice, easily dismiss claims, as to do so in cases where trivial breaches are alleged may have a chilling effect on foreign investors. However, even accepting that tribunals would be minded to find claims inadmissible in cases wherein serious obligations are breached, namely those related to fraud, corruption, misrepresentation and even the environment, in future, it is very likely that tribunals, based on *Aven*, would be increasingly minded to use evidence of a state's failure to enforce the obligations owed by investors as a basis for finding claims admissible.

B. Abuse of Process

International investment tribunals have developed a robust corpus of jurisprudence addressing abuse of process claims in various contexts. This doctrine serves as an important limitation on investors' ability to manipulate treaty protections through strategic corporate restructuring, nationality changes, or the pursuit of multiple proceedings for the same dispute.

The timing and purpose of corporate restructuring has been a central focus of abuse of process analysis. In *Pac Rim Cayman v El Salvador*,[256] for example, the tribunal noted that the dividing line in determining whether a change of nationality constitutes an abuse of process occurs 'when the relevant party can see an actual dispute or can foresee a specific future dispute as a very high probability and not merely as a possible controversy.'[257] Applying this test, the tribunal found no abuse where the corporate restructuring (changing the claimant's nationality from the Cayman Islands to the USA) occurred before the basis of the claim (El Salvador's *de facto* mining ban) materialised. The tribunal in *Levy and Gremcitel v Peru*[258] refined this approach, distinguishing abuse of process from jurisdiction *ratione temporis*. While acknowledging that 'the threshold for a finding of abuse of process is high',[259] the tribunal found abuse where shares were transferred to a protected investor just one day before the challenged measure was issued. The tribunal determined this 'striking proximity of events' was not coincidental, concluding that 'the only purpose of the transfer was to obtain access to ICSID/BIT arbitration, which was otherwise precluded.'[260] This timing analysis was developed even further in *Philip Morris v Australia*,[261] where the tribunal examined a corporate restructuring undertaken shortly before Australia enacted 'plain packaging' legislation affecting tobacco companies. While acknowledging that the mere fact of restructuring an investment to obtain BIT benefits is not *per se* illegitimate, the tribunal found abuse where a dispute was 'foreseeable' at the time of restructuring, defining foreseeability as 'a reasonable prospect that a measure which may give rise to a treaty claim will materialise'.[262] Finding that Philip Morris had failed to demonstrate legitimate business reasons for the restructuring beyond gaining treaty protection, the tribunal considered the claim to be inadmissible.

By contrast, in *Lao Holding v Laos*,[263] the tribunal found no abuse of process. The tribunal rejected the argument that the claimant was incorporated in Aruba (the Netherlands) as an 'opportunistic device' after the dispute (over the new tax code) arose, with the aim of gaining access to the rights and remedies afforded by the Laos-Netherlands BIT. In the tribunal's view, the investment restructuring had been made some time before the dispute actually materialised. The tribunal emphasised that the dispute must be 'highly probable' at the time of restructuring to constitute abuse. Notably, the tribunal distinguished between abuse of process and *ratione temporis* objections, focusing its analysis on when the dispute crystallised rather than whether it was foreseeable. Similarly, in *Transglobal v Panama*,[264] the tribunal examined multiple factors including 'the timing of the purported investment, the timing of the claim, the substance of the transaction, the true nature of the operation, and the degree of foreseeability of the governmental action at the time of restructuring.'[265] Finding that the transfer of interests was clearly undertaken to create artificial international

256 ICSID Case No. ARB/09/12, Decision on the Respondent's Jurisdictional Objections, 1 June 2012.
257 ibid 2.99.
258 ICSID Case No. ARB/11/17, Award, 9 January 2015.
259 ibid 186.
260 ibid 191.
261 UNCITRAL, PCA Case No. 2012–12, Award on Jurisdiction and Admissibility, 17 December 2015.
262 ibid 554.
263 ICSID Case No. ARB(AF)/12/6, Decision on Jurisdiction, 21 February 2014.
264 ICSID Case No. ARB/13/28, Award, 2 June 2016.
265 ibid 103.

jurisdiction over a pre-existing domestic dispute, the tribunal upheld the respondent's objection of abuse of process.

The abuse of process doctrine sometimes intersects with questions of corporate nationality. For example, in *Capital Financial Holdings v Cameroon*,[266] the majority declined jurisdiction after determining the claimant lacked genuine connections to Luxembourg despite being formally incorporated there. Analysing various 'real seat' indicators (including the location of shareholder and board meetings, financial record-keeping, and physical office presence), the tribunal found the claimant had no substantive presence in Luxembourg at the time the dispute arose. The majority considered it particularly abusive that the company had been inactive for several years and was suddenly 'revived' after the treaty dispute was notified, with corporate formalities retroactively completed.

The pursuit of multiple claims based on the same underlying dispute has also triggered abuse of process concerns. In *Orascom v Algeria*,[267] for example, the tribunal confronted three arbitrations initiated under different investment treaties by companies in the same corporate chain, all concerning essentially identical measures and seeking recovery for the same economic harm. While acknowledging that structuring an investment through several layers of corporate entities in different states is not illegitimate, the tribunal found that initiating multiple proceedings to recover for the same economic harm constituted an exercise of rights for purposes that are alien to those for which these rights were established, rendering the claims inadmissible. A more nuanced approach to overlapping claims emerged in *Ampal-American and others v Egypt*,[268] where the tribunal faced four parallel arbitrations concerning the same factual matrix. The tribunal distinguished between contract and treaty claims, finding no inherent abuse in their parallel pursuit. However, the tribunal did identify a problematic overlap between claims in the ICSID proceeding and a parallel UNCITRAL arbitration under another BIT. Rather than dismissing the overlapping claim outright, however, the tribunal invited the claimant to elect which forum would hear the claim, indicating it would 'revisit the question of abuse of process' based on the claimant's response.[269] By contrast, in *Sanum v Laos*,[270] the tribunal rejected the respondent's claim that pursuit of overlapping claims in two different arbitral tribunals under different BITs by related parties constituted an abuse of process. The tribunal found it significant that the respondent had refused to consolidate the proceedings, effectively precluding the abuse of process claim.

The jurisprudence on abuse of process reveals that while tribunals have consistently emphasised that restructuring to gain treaty benefits is not inherently improper, they have drawn the line at corporate manoeuvres designed to create artificial jurisdiction over disputes that were foreseeable or had already crystallised. Similarly, tribunals have recognised that while investors may legitimately pursue different legal theories in different forums, pursuing multiple claims for the same economic harm may constitute an abuse of the arbitral process.

266 ICSID Case No. ARB/15/18, Award, 22 June 2017.
267 ICSID Case No. ARB/12/35, Award, 31 May 2017.
268 ICSID Case No. ARB/12/11, Decision on Jurisdiction, 1 February 2016.
269 ibid 339.
270 UNCITRAL, PCA Case No. 2013–13, Award on Jurisdiction, 13 December 2013.

CONCLUSION

Jurisdictional requirements under Article 25 of the ICSID Convention and relevant IIAs establish clear parameters for qualifying investments and eligible investors, though tribunals have adopted varying approaches to questions such as indirect investments, corporate nationality, and the application of the *Salini* criteria. The incorporation test remains dominant in determining corporate nationality, despite concerns about 'treaty shopping' through shell companies. Meanwhile, *ratione temporis* and *ratione voluntatis* requirements provide further constraints, ensuring that disputes fall within the temporal scope of treaties and that state consent to arbitration is properly established.

Admissibility considerations serve as additional filters, with the legality requirement and abuse of process doctrine allowing tribunals to decline otherwise jurisdictionally sound claims. Recent cases like *Cortec v Kenya* and *Kim v Uzbekistan* have clarified the framework for assessing investor illegality, focusing on the significance of the obligation breached, the seriousness of the investor's conduct, and the proportionality of consequences. Similarly, the jurisprudence on abuse of process has developed nuanced approaches to corporate restructuring and multiple proceedings, balancing investors' legitimate interests against the integrity of the arbitral system.

These developments reflect the system's ongoing effort to balance investor protection with state sovereignty concerns. While the diverse approaches taken by tribunals to date sometimes lead to inconsistent outcomes, the extant jurisprudence provides some guidance for both investors and states navigating ISDS. As investment treaty practice continues to evolve, particularly through new generation IIAs with more precise definitions and requirements, the parameters of jurisdiction and admissibility will likely become more clearly defined while remaining adaptable to the diverse contexts in which investment disputes arise.

CHAPTER 3

NON-DISCRIMINATION IN INTERNATIONAL INVESTMENT LAW

INTRODUCTION

Non-discrimination represents one of the fundamental pillars of international investment law, serving as a mechanism against protectionism, thereby ensuring that foreign investors are not subjected to prejudicial treatment based on their nationality.[1] In contemporary investment treaty practice, the principle of non-discrimination manifests primarily through two complementary yet distinct standards: the national treatment (NT) obligation, which guarantees that foreign investors receive treatment no less favourable than that accorded to domestic investors in like circumstances,[2] and the most-favoured-nation (MFN) standard, which ensures that investors from different foreign countries are treated equally by requiring that no foreign investor receive less favourable treatment than investors from any third state.[3]

For Caribbean states, these non-discrimination standards assume particular significance given the region's heavy reliance on foreign investment to drive economic development. The Caribbean's extant network of IIAs incorporates both national treatment and MFN clauses, reflecting the region's commitment to creating a predictable and fair investment climate. Yet, the practical application of these standards has generated considerable jurisprudential complexity, with arbitral tribunals adopting varying approaches to fundamental interpretative questions that potentially impact how Caribbean states regulate foreign investment within their territories.

This chapter provides a comprehensive examination of the non-discrimination principle in international investment law, with particular attention to its application and implications for Caribbean states. The analysis proceeds in three parts. First, the chapter examines the national treatment standard, exploring the essential elements required to establish a violation, including the contested concepts of 'like circumstances' and 'less favourable treatment', while analysing how tribunals have approached justifications and reservations that have been raised by host states. Second, the chapter turns to the MFN standard, exploring both its substantive application – through which investors can import more favourable standards of protection from third-party treaties – and its highly controversial procedural use for accessing more advantageous dispute settlement mechanisms. Third, the chapter addresses the various reservations and exceptions that Caribbean IIAs carve out to preserve policy space for legitimate governmental objectives, examining how arbitral tribunals interpret these provisions and their practical implications for Caribbean states' regulatory autonomy.

1 Marcos Orellana, 'Investment Agreements and Sustainable Development: The Non-discrimination Standards' (2011) 11(3) *Sustainable Development Law & Policy* 4.

2 Manini Brar, 'The National Treatment Obligation: Law and Practice of Investment Treaties' in Julien Chaisse, Sufian Jusoh, and Leïla Choukroune (eds), *Handbook of International Investment Law and Policy* (Springer 2019).

3 Tony Cole, 'The Boundaries of Most Favored Nation Treatment in International Investment Law' (2011) 33 *Michigan Journal of International Law* 537.

DOI: 10.4324/9781003734185-3

I. THE NATIONAL TREATMENT STANDARD

The national treatment standard represents one of the fundamental pillars of international investment law, serving as a relative standard of protection that ensures foreign investors receive treatment no less favourable than that accorded to domestic investors in like circumstances.[4] A typical national treatment clause may read like Article 5 of the Trinidad and Tobago-Guatemala BIT:

1. Each Contracting Party shall accord to investors of the other Contracting Party treatment no less favourable than that which it accords in like circumstances, to *its own investors* with respect to the management, maintenance, use, enjoyment or disposition of investments.
2. Each Contracting Party shall accord to investments of investors of the other Contracting Party treatment no less favourable than that which it accords in like circumstances, to *investments* of its own investors with respect to the management, maintenance, use, enjoyment or disposition of investments.

As noted in *Apotex Holdings Inc. and Apotex Inc. v United States of America*,[5] proving a violation of the national treatment obligation requires a fact-specific analysis encompassing three essential elements: first, that the foreign investor or investment received treatment by the host state with respect to establishment, acquisition, expansion, management, conduct, operation, and sale or other disposition of investments; second, that the foreign investor was in like circumstances with identified domestic investors or investments; and third, that the treatment received was less favourable than that accorded to the comparable domestic investors or investments. The legal burden of establishing these elements rests squarely on the claimant.

While the question as to whether a foreign investor has been subject to 'treatment' is generally not in issue, as will be demonstrated below, there is often significant contestation over whether the parties in question are in 'like circumstances' and whether, indeed, the foreign investor has been subject to less favourable treatment.[6]

A. 'In like Circumstances/Situations'

An elementary requirement for establishing a breach of the national treatment standard is that the foreign and domestic investors are in like circumstances. The language of 'like circumstances' or 'like situations' is found in several Caribbean IIAs,[7] including Article 5 of the Guyana-Brazil BIT:

4 David Collins, 'National Treatment in Emerging Market Investment Treaties' in Anselm Kamperman Sanders (ed), *The Principle of National Treatment in International Economic Law* (Edward Elgar Publishing 2014) 161.

5 ICSID Case No. ARB(AF)/12/1.

6 Wenhua Shan, Norah Gallagher and Sheng Zhang, 'National Treatment for Foreign Investment in China: A Changing Landscape' (2012) 27(1) *ICSID Review* 120.

7 Barbados-Canada BIT Article 3; Grenada-USA BIT Article 2; Guyana-Brazil BIT Article 6; Haiti-USA BIT Article 2; Jamaica-USA BIT Article 2; Suriname-Brazil BIT Article 6; Trinidad and Tobago-Canada BIT Article 3; Trinidad and Tobago-Guatemala BIT Article 6; Trinidad and Tobago-USA BIT Article 2.

1. Without prejudice to the measures in force under its legislation on the date of entry into force of this Agreement, each Party shall accord to investors of the other Party treatment no less favourable than that it accords, in like circumstances, to its own investors with respect to the establishment, acquisition, expansion, management, conduct, operation, and sale or other disposition of investments in its territory.
2. Without prejudice to the measures in force under its legislation on the date of entry into force of this Agreement, each Party shall accord to investments of investors of the other Party treatment no less favourable than that it accords, in like circumstances, to investments in its territory of its own investors with respect to the establishment, acquisition, expansion, management, conduct, operation, and sale or other disposition of investments.
3. Nothing in this Agreement shall be construed as to prevent a Party from amending any measure referred to in paragraphs 1 and 2 of this Article, to the extent that the amendment does not make the measure more discriminatory than it was immediately before the amendment.
4. For greater certainty, whether treatment is accorded in 'like circumstances' depends on the totality of the circumstances, including whether the relevant treatment distinguishes between investors or investments on the basis of legitimate public interest objectives.
5. For greater certainty, this Article shall not be construed to require any Party to compensate for any inherent competitive disadvantages which result from the foreign character of the investor or investments.

The tribunal in *Clayton and Bilcon v Canada*[8] cautioned that language of this nature is not restricted as it is in some other trade-liberalising agreements, such as those that refer to 'like products' under the GATT. More particularly, the national treatment standard in international investment law refers to the way in which either the investor or investment is treated, rather than being confined to concerns over discrimination to comparisons between similar articles of trade. It is also instructive to note that the operative word in most Caribbean IIAs is 'similar', not 'identical'.

There is no fixed methodology for determining 'like circumstances',[9] though the tribunal in *Apotex Holdings Inc. and Apotex Inc. v United States of America*[10] suggested that a range of approaches may be taken, including assessing whether those which are said to be comparators:

(i) are in the same economic of business sector;
(ii) have invested in, or are businesses that compete with the investor or its investments in terms of goods or services; or
(iii) are subject to a comparable legal regime or regulatory requirements, as the Claimants and their investments.[11]

8 Award on Jurisdiction and Liability, 17 March 2015.
9 *Vento Motorcycles, Inc. v United Mexican States*, ICSID Case No. ARB(AF)/17/3, Award, 6 July 2020, para. 240:

> given that national treatment and most favoured nation treatment are relative standards that compare the conduct of the host State toward certain investors or their investments with respect to the host-State's conduct toward other investors or their investments, there is no precise methodology to perform the analysis. These are necessarily fact-specific enquiries and what may be an appropriate starting point in one case may not be so in another.

10 ICSID Case No. ARB(AF)/12/1, Award, 25 August 2014.
11 ibid 8.15.

As will be seen below, no one methodology has gained traction with tribunals to date. Different tribunals have to date placed different emphases on different approaches depending on the facts in question, and the general affinity of the arbitrator towards a narrow or broad construction of what it means by like circumstances.

(i) Same Sector

In *S.D. Myers, Inc. v Government of Canada*,[12] the claimant contended that Article 1102 NAFTA was breached by a ban imposed by the respondent on the export of PCB waste from Canada to the US where it operated a facility. It argued that such less favourable treatment was not justified by *bona fide* health or environmental concerns but had the aim and effect of protecting and promoting the market share of producers who were Canadians and who performed the work in Canada. The tribunal found that the claimant was in 'like circumstances' with Canadian operators, such as Chem-Security and Cintec. They all were engaged in providing PCB waste remediation services, and the claimant was in a position to attract customers that might otherwise have gone to the Canadian operators because it could offer more favourable prices and because it had extensive experience and credibility. Indeed, it was precisely because the claimant was in a position to take business away from its Canadian competitors that Chem-Security and Cintec lobbied the Minister of the Environment to ban exports when the US authorities opened the border. On the question of the scope of 'like circumstances' or 'like situations', the tribunal explained that the requisite comparison is between domestic and foreign-controlled enterprises operating in the same sector:

> The concept of 'like circumstances' invites an examination of whether a non-national investor complaining of less favourable treatment is in the same 'sector' as the national investor. The Tribunal takes the view that the word 'sector' has a wide connotation that includes the concepts of 'economic sector' and 'business sector'.[13]

Ultimately, although the tribunal considered that Canada's desire to maintain the ability to process PCBs within Canada in the future was a legitimate goal consistent with the policy objectives of the Basel Convention, there were several legitimate ways by which Canada could have achieved this without preventing the claimant from exporting PCBs for processing in the USA. In other words, the method chosen – the Interim Order and the Final Order – contravened Canada's international commitments under Article 1102 NAFTA.

Outside of NAFTA, tribunals charged with interpreting BITs have equally been keen to adopt the 'same sector' test for determining whether domestic and foreign investors are in 'like circumstances'. By way of example, in *Olin Holdings Ltd v Libya*,[14] two of the claimant's domestic competitors in the dairy and juice industry which were physically located in the same Fallah industrial area were exempted from an expropriation order, whereas the state refused to extend this treatment to Olin. The tribunal held that, given that Olin, OKBA, and Al-Aseel operated in the same business sector, namely the dairy and juice market in Libya, and they were also very closely situated on the map of Tripoli in the same industrial zone, they were similarly situated. While acknowledging that mere differences of treatment

12 UNCITRAL, Partial Award, 13 November 2000.
13 ibid 250.
14 ICC Case No. 20355/MCP, Award, 25 May 2018.

do not necessarily constitute discrimination,[15] on the facts, the tribunal was convinced that OKBA and Al-Aseel were formally exempted from demolition pursuant to the expropriation order and were in fact allowed to remain on site permanently. By contrast, Olin did not receive a formal expropriation exemption. In these circumstances, the tribunal held that Olin was clearly operating in less favourable circumstances than its competitors and given that the respondent had failed to prove that the difference between the treatment accorded to Olin and the treatment accorded to its national competitors was justified, there was a breach of Article 3 of the Cyprus-Libya BIT.

Separately, some tribunals, however, take a broad view of 'like circumstances' or 'like situations', thereby not requiring evidence that the domestic and foreign investors are in the same sector of activity. For example, the claimant, an oil producer, in *Occidental Exploration and Production Company v The Republic of Ecuador*[16] argued that Ecuador breached the national treatment obligation because several companies involved in the export of other goods, particularly flowers, mining, and seafood products, were entitled to receive VAT refund and continuously enjoyed this benefit. The claimant contended that the meaning of 'in like situations' did not refer to those industries or companies involved in the same sector of activity, such as oil producers, but to companies that were engaged generally in exports, even if encompassing different sectors. Interestingly, the tribunal agreed, finding the claimants' arguments in this regard 'convincing':

> 'in like situations' cannot be interpreted in the narrow sense advanced by Ecuador as the purpose of national treatment is to protect investors as compared to local producers, and this cannot be done by addressing exclusively the sector in which that particular activity is undertaken.[17]

The tribunal rejected a narrow reading of the 'in like situation' test proffered by the respondent, and in so doing also rejected the 'like products' test that has been countenanced by GATT/WTO jurisprudence.[18] In this connection, it noted that whereas in the trade context 'like products' are related to the narrow concept of directly competitive or substitutable products, the opposite is true in the international investment law context, since in the former context, the aim of the national treatment standard is to avoid exporters being placed at a disadvantage in foreign markets because of the indirect taxes paid in the country of origin.[19] Ultimately, the tribunal concluded that, on the facts, the claimant had received treatment less favourable than that accorded national companies, even though this was not done with the intent of discriminating against foreign-owned companies. The fact of less favourable treatment was itself sufficient to ground a finding of a breach of Article II (I) of the Ecuador-United States BIT.

The approach countenanced by the tribunal in *Occidental* is, from a Caribbean perspective, problematic because it fundamentally undermines states' ability to implement sector-specific regulatory measures tailored to their distinct economic, social, and environmental

15 Relying on Robert Jennings and Arthur Watts (eds), *Oppenheim's International Law* (9th edn, Longman 1992) 378.

16 LCIA Case No. UN3467, Award, 1 July 2004.

17 ibid 173.

18 See generally Won-Mog Choi, *'Like Products' in International Trade Law: Towards a Consistent GATT/WTO Jurisprudence* (OUP 2003).

19 In *Occidental*, the tribunal asserted that in GATT/WTO, the purpose of the 'like products' test is to avoid imported products being affected by a distortion of competition with similar domestic products because of taxes and other regulations in the country of destination.

realities. More particularly, the tribunal's cross-sectoral interpretation of 'like circumstances' creates an untenable regulatory straitjacket for Caribbean governments seeking to implement targeted economic policies. Caribbean states frequently employ differentiated treatment across sectors to achieve legitimate policy objectives, such as promoting tourism over extractive industries for environmental sustainability or providing enhanced incentives to manufacturing over services to diversify their economies away from traditional commodity dependence. Under the *Occidental* reasoning, any preferential treatment accorded to domestic arrowroot exporters, for instance, could potentially be claimed by foreign oil companies on the basis that both are 'generally engaged in exports', despite the vastly different economic, environmental, and social dimensions of these sectors. Further, the tribunal's rejection of competitive relationship requirements creates particular difficulties for Caribbean states' efforts to promote economic diversification. Many Caribbean nations are actively seeking to transition from mono-crop or extractive economies toward more sustainable, knowledge-based sectors. This transition necessarily involves providing differential treatment to emerging sectors (such as renewable energy or information technology) compared to traditional sectors (such as sugar or petroleum). The *Occidental* reasoning would effectively prohibit such developmental policies by requiring identical treatment across all export sectors, regardless of their contribution to long-term economic sustainability. Ultimately, the *Occidental* reasoning regarding uniform treatment across all export sectors would force states to either extend preferential treatment to all foreign investors (creating unsustainable fiscal burdens) or eliminate sector-specific incentives entirely (undermining targeted development strategies).

(ii) Comparable Legal and Regulatory Regime

Several investment arbitration awards do not merely focus on the sector within which foreign and domestic investors operate, but the legal and regulatory regime applicable to the parties in question.[20] Perhaps the leading case on this subject is *Pope & Talbot Inc. v The Government of Canada.*[21] Here, a US investor in Canada, which was obliged to pay export fees on soft lumber, alleged that it was in like circumstances with Canadian producers in other provinces that were not subject to export fees. The tribunal, however, rejected the claim, holding that there were more than 500 Canadian producers in other provinces which were subject to the fees. The tribunal selected the entities that were in the most 'like circumstances' who were subjected to the same restrictive legal regime as the claimant and not comparators that were in less 'like circumstances'. Ultimately, the tribunal found that given that the fees affected over 500 Canadian owned producers in the non-covered provinces

20 For example, *Archer Daniels v Mexico*, ICSID Case No. ARB (AF)/04/5, Award, 21 November 2007, para. 197; *Grand River Enterprises Six Nations, Ltd., et al. v United States of America*, UNCITRAL, Award, 12 January 2011, para. 166. NAFTA tribunals have given significant weight to the legal regimes applicable to particular entities in assessing whether they are in 'like circumstances' under Article 1102. While each case involved its own facts, tribunals have assigned important weight to 'like legal requirements' in determining whether there were 'like circumstances'. See, also, *Methanex v USA* UNCITRAL (Final Award of the Tribunal on Jurisdiction and Merits), 3 August 2005, the tribunal (citing *Pope & Talbot,* Decision by Tribunal, 6 September 2000) emphasised the importance of assuring that purported comparators face similar regulatory requirements.

21 UNCITRAL, Award on the Merits of Phase 2, 10 April 2001.

precisely as it affected the investor, it could not reasonably be said to be discriminatory and in breach of Article 1102 NAFTA. In other words, producers in the non-covered provinces (both foreign and domestic investors who did not have to pay fees) were not in like circumstances with those in the covered provinces (both foreign and domestic investors who had to pay fees) because the legal regime applicable to the respective provinces was different.

Meanwhile, in *Apotex Holdings Inc. and Apotex Inc. v United States of America*,[22] the claimants contended that the FDA's placement of an Import Alert on Apotex Inc.'s two Canadian manufacturing facilities, Etobicoke and Signet, constituted a breach by the respondent of NAFTA Article 1102's national treatment standard. According to the claimants, the Import Alert had the effect of detaining, without physical examination or prior notice, new solid dose generic drugs manufactured at the Etobicoke and Signet facilities.

In the tribunal's view, even though the three domestic comparators proposed by the claimants were in the same sector as the claimants, sold like drug products to those sold by Apotex Inc., and were direct competitors in the US market, the question of whether the claimants and their investments were subject to the same legal regime or regulatory requirements (to those to which the identified US-comparators were subject) was an important differentiator. More particularly, drug manufacturers located in the USA were directly subject to the jurisdiction of the FDA, whereas those located abroad were not. In other words, while, in respect of domestic manufacturers, the FDA had authority to enter US drug manufacturing facilities, at reasonable times, without the need for agreeing and scheduling such an inspection in advance, the FDA, being a US regulator, had no unilateral authority to enter and carry out an inspection of premises located on foreign territory in respect of foreign investors. Another important difference in the legal and regulatory regime that governed foreign products manufactured outside the USA and those that were manufactured at USA-based facilities was that Section 801(a) of the Federal Food, Drug, and Cosmetic Act, which authorised the FDA district offices to detain products at the US border, without physical examination, did not apply to domestic products that were manufactured in the USA, regardless of whether the manufacturing facilities are US-owned or foreign-owned. In other words, the differences in the FDA's ability to deny access to the US market as between foreign and domestically manufactured drugs were substantial, and these constituted a material distinction between the legal and regulatory regimes applicable to foreign and domestic manufacturing facilities. In the tribunal's view, these differences went to 'like circumstances'. The tribunal concluded that when, as here, the only domestic comparators proposed by the claimants could never have been subject to any similar measure, it was impermissible to contend that such comparators were in 'like circumstances' to the claimants and their investments.

A similar application of the comparable 'legal and regulatory regime' test was evident in *Vento Motorcycles, Inc. v United Mexican States*.[23] Here, the claimant, a US company, argued that it was subjected to disparate treatment in respect of the importation into Mexico of disassembled motorcycles. It contended that the respondent did not apply a 30% import duty in respect of its domestic companies, and further that it allowed these companies to label their motorcycles as 'Made in Mexico' and to use corresponding vehicle identification numbers, while Vento branded motorcycles were required to be labelled as 'Made in China' which placed them at a reputational disadvantage. The tribunal, however, rejected the claim of breach of national treatment under Article 1102 NAFTA on the basis that the

22 ICSID Case No. ARB(AF)/12/1, Award, 25 August 2014.
23 ICSID Case No. ARB(AF)/17/3, Award, 6 July 2020.

comparators in question were not in like circumstances. More particularly, the tribunal found that the claimant did not specifically identify whom or to what Vento should be compared *qua* investor. In fact, although the purported comparators that the claimant identified were corporations operating in Mexico, they were either state-owned or Japanese-owned. In this connection, because the claimant could not identify any of the Mexican owners of such corporations as appropriate comparators, the claim of less favourable treatment could not succeed.

(iii) Businesses/Products that are in Competition/Substitutable

Some national treatment clauses make no reference at all to 'like circumstances' or 'like situations'. For example, Article 3 of the St Vincent and the Grenadines-Germany BIT of provides:

(1) Neither Contracting Party shall subject investments in its territory owned or controlled by nationals or companies of the other Contracting Party to treatment less favourable than it accords to investments of its own nationals or companies or to investments of nationals or companies of any third Slate.
(2) Neither Contracting Party shall subject nationals or companies of the other Contracting Party as regards their activity in connexion with investments in its territory to treatment less favourable than it accords to its own nationals or companies or to nationals of companies of any third State.[24]

Where there is no reference to 'like circumstances' or 'like situations' in the relevant national treatment clause, at least one tribunal – *Sergei v Mongolia*[25] – has suggested that regard may be had to the approach countenanced by GATT jurisprudence. Here, the claimants alleged that, by adopting a different taxation regime for copper in contrast to gold, the respondent breached the national treatment standard in the Mongolia-Russia BIT. It contended that although both gold and copper were subject to significant tax increases, it was wiser if the state had adopted similar legislation for both products. The tribunal took the view that

24 Antigua and Barbuda-Germany BIT Article 3; Antigua and Barbuda-UK BIT Article 3; Barbados-Belgium-Luxembourg Agreement Article 3; Barbados-China BIT Article 3; Barbados-Cuba BIT Article 3; Barbados-Germany BIT Article 3; Barbados-Mauritius BIT Article 4; Barbados-Switzerland BIT Article 3; Barbados-UK BIT Article 3; Barbados-Venezuela BIT Article 3; Belize-China BIT Article 3; Belize-Cuba BIT Article 3; Belize-El Salvador BIT Article 3; Belize-The Netherlands BIT Article 3; Belize-UK BIT Article 3; Dominica-Germany BIT Article 3; Dominica-UK BIT Article 3; Haiti-Germany BIT Article 2; Grenada-UK BIT Article 3; Guyana-China BIT Article 3; Guyana-Germany BIT Article 3; Guyana-South Korea BIT Article 3; Guyana-Switzerland BIT Article 4; Guyana-UK BIT Article 3; Haiti-UK BIT Article 3; Jamaica-Argentina BIT Article 3; Jamaica-China BIT Article 3; Jamaica-Egypt BIT Article 3; Jamaica-Indonesia BIT Article 3; Jamaica-South Korea BIT Article 3; Jamaica-Switzerland BIT Article 3; Jamaica-The Netherlands BIT Article 3; Jamaica-UK BIT Article 3; St Lucia-Germany Article 3; St Lucia-UK BIT Article 3; Suriname-The Netherlands BIT Article 3; SVG-Germany BIT Article 3; Trinidad and Tobago-China BIT Article 4; Trinidad and Tobago-Cuba BIT Article 5; Trinidad and Tobago-France BIT Article 4; Trinidad and Tobago-India BIT Article 4; Trinidad and Tobago-South Korea BIT Article 3; Trinidad and Tobago-Switzerland BIT Article 4; Trinidad and Tobago-Germany BIT Article 4; Trinidad and Tobago-UK BIT Article 5.

25 UNCITRAL, Award on Jurisdiction and Liability, 28 April 2011.

the sectors covered should relate to competitive and substitutable products, an expression regularly used in WTO/GATT cases. In this regard, the tribunal refused to conduct a cross-industry (e.g. the petroleum industry) or a gold-copper comparison, finding instead that there were important differences between the two affected sectors which justified different solutions. More particularly, the different treatment meted out in this case to gold and copper was on account of the greater opportunities for tax evasion existing in the gold mining industry and a desire to see the proceeds from copper exports used for the building of a copper-processing plant in Mongolia thereby adding value to Mongolian copper production. Against this backdrop, the tribunal did not consider gold and copper to be competitive and substitutable products, such that the claim of a breach of national treatment failed.

It is submitted that while the 'like products' analysis (competitive and substitutable products) might have been appropriate in this case, there is nothing to suggest that a national treatment clause which does not explicitly refer to 'like circumstances' should be narrowly construed. Indeed, one might very well argue that, depending on the particular facts of a case, a broad cross-sector analysis (similar to the *Occidental* analysis) might even be possible, given the absence of express reference to investors having to be in 'identical' or 'like' circumstances.

B. 'Less Favourable' Treatment

In *SD Myers v Canada*,[26] the tribunal explained that in assessing whether a foreign investor has been subject to less favourable treatment, consideration must be given to whether the practical effect of the measure is to create a disproportionate benefit for nationals over non-nationals, and whether the measure, on its face, appears to favour nationals over non-nationals who are protected by the relevant treaty.[27] Similar sentiments were expressed by the tribunal in *Apotex Holdings v United States of America*,[28] when it considered that less favourable treatment equates to 'non-insignificant practical negative impact',[29] that is, worse *de jure* or *de facto* treatment, compared to compactors in like circumstances.

Several cases illustrate tribunals' approach to the determination of less favourable treatment. In *Clayton and Bilcon v Government of Canada*,[30] for example, the claimants contended that unlike a number of domestic investor projects involving quarries and marine terminals in ecologically sensitive zones which were evaluated in accordance with the standard of likely significant adverse effects after mitigation, their project was evaluated less favourably treatment by the state's employment of a Joint Review Panel (JRP). The tribunal held that the fact that similarly placed domestic investors were assessed in a more lenient manner than the claimants meant that the latter received less favourable treatment. In particular, the claimants were not able to benefit from the identification of mitigation measures in contrast to similarly placed domestic investors. In this connection, the tribunal queried: 'had the investor been local, for example, would the JRP have considered the impact on "community core values" to be decisive, without examining mitigating effects'?[31] It went on to conclude that:

26 Partial Award, 13 November 2000.
27 ibid 252.
28 ICSID Case No. ARB(AF)/12/1, Award, 25 August 2014.
29 ibid 8.21.
30 PCA Case No. 2009–04, Award on Jurisdiction and Liability, 17 March 2015.
31 ibid 715.

> it is a real point of departure from the standard of host state conduct required by Article 1102 if a foreign investor is treated less favorably than domestic investors in like circumstances for the purposes of the laws of its central government.[32]
>
> . . . When a quarry project is combined with a marine terminal, and one or both components are assessed under the laws of federal Canada or Nova Scotia, it can be a denial of national treatment to apply a harsher standard to the non-Canadian project in like circumstances.[33]

A similar finding of less favourable treatment, though in circumstances giving rise to *de facto* discrimination, was arrived at in *Feldman v Mexico*.[34] Here, Mexico enacted a law that made it a condition of obtaining tax rebates upon export of cigarettes that the applicant be a taxpayer who possessed invoices showing the tax amount stated separately. The claimant argued that it had been denied national treatment in circumstances where the state permitted at least three resellers of cigarettes to export cigarettes and to receive rebates, notwithstanding the fact that, like the claimant, they purchased their goods from retailers, were not formally taxpayers and thus could not have invoices stating the tax amounts separately. In their view, even though the law was non-discriminatory on its face, it was applied in a discriminatory manner.

After finding that the claimant was in like 'like circumstances' with Mexican owned resellers of cigarettes for export,[35] the tribunal concluded that the claimant was subject to *de facto* discrimination by the state, inconsistent with Mexico's obligations under Article 1102 NAFTA. More pointedly, the invoice requirement was ignored or waived for domestic cigarette reseller/exporters, but not for foreign-owned cigarette reseller/exporters, and domestically owned cigarette exporters were granted rebates while such treatment was denied to a foreign reseller, the claimant. Although it noted that it need not be proved that the claimant was discriminated against on the ground of his nationality, the evidence nonetheless clearly showed that there was a nexus between the discrimination and the claimant's status as a foreign investor. In particular, the claimant appeared to have been subject to more prejudicial treatment because his company, CEMSA, was owned by a very outspoken foreigner, who had, prior to the initiation of the audit, filed a NAFTA Chapter 11 claim against the Government of Mexico. In short, the claimant's demonstration of a pattern of official action (or inaction) over several years, as well as *de facto* discrimination, was sufficient to ground an actionable breach under Article 1102.

Without a showing of less favourable treatment, a claim for breach of national treatment will not succeed. For example, in *Methanex v USA*,[36] the claimant alleged that California, and thereby the USA, denied foreign methanol producers, including Methanex, the more favourable treatment it accorded to domestic ethanol investors, thus violating Article 1102 NAFTA. The tribunal, however, rejected the claimant's argument, finding that, first, because Methanex produced methanol as a feedstock for MTBE and not as a gasoline additive, ethanol and methanol products could not be said to be in competition. Second, on the question of less favourable treatment, the tribunal held that the California ban did not differentiate between foreign investors or investments and various MTBE producers in California. The

32 ibid 702.

33 ibid 705.

34 ICSID Case No. ARB(AF)/99/1, Award, 16 December 2002.

35 ibid 171:

> The 'universe' of firms in like circumstances are those foreign-owned and domestic-owned firms that are in the business of reselling/exporting cigarettes. Other Mexican firms that may also export cigarettes, such as Mexican cigarette producers, are not in like circumstances.

36 UNCITRAL, Final Award of the Tribunal on Jurisdiction and Merits Details, 3 August 2005.

treatment meted out was uniform, as the ban applied to all MTBE manufacturers, both domestic and foreign. Accordingly, Methanex's claim under Article 1102 failed.

A similar negative outcome was arrived at in the case of *Grand River Enterprises Six Nations, Ltd., et al. v United States of America,*[37] which concerned a Canadian corporation, and Indigenous peoples, who imported cigarettes manufactured by Grand River and distributed to wholesalers and retail outlets on Indian reservations in the United States. The dispute arose from the implementation of the 1998 Master Settlement Agreement (MSA), which was concluded between US state attorneys general and major tobacco producers to settle litigation over states' costs of treating tobacco-related illnesses. The MSA required participating manufacturers to restrict advertising and fund smoking prevention programmes, while non-participating manufacturers (NPMs), like the claimants, were required by state escrow laws to place funds in escrow approximating what they would have paid under the MSA. Grand River strategically concentrated its off-reservation marketing of Seneca® brand cigarettes in a limited number of states to take advantage of 'allocable share provisions' that allowed substantial rebates of escrowed funds, which initially proved successful and significantly increased their market share. However, as NPMs collectively grew to capture 8.1% of the US market by 2003, threatening states' MSA revenues, the states responded by intensifying enforcement of escrow laws, enacting 'complementary legislation' that prohibited tax stamps on non-complying manufacturers' cigarettes and ultimately repealing the allocable share provisions in 38 states by September 2004, which the claimants argued violated the national treatment standard under Article 1102 of NAFTA.

In the tribunal's view, the comparable investments for the purposes of Article 1102 NAFTA were other firms engaged in the wholesale distribution of cigarettes in the United States and potentially subject to enforcement actions under the states' complementary legislation. On the facts, however, the tribunal was not convinced that the claimants were subjected to enforcement measures that were not applied to other similarly situated domestic businesses, or that other similarly situated investments received better treatment. As there was no showing that the disputed enforcement measures to which the claimants were subjected amounted to treatment less favourable than that accorded the appropriate domestic comparator, the claim under NAFTA Article 1102 failed.

Finally, in *ADF Group Inc. v United States of America,*[38] the tribunal addressed a national treatment challenge to the United States' 'Buy America' provisions, which required that steel materials used in federally funded highway construction projects be 100% produced and fabricated domestically. The Canadian investor argued that these measures were inherently discriminatory, claiming they were designed to favour US steel manufacturers and fabricators over foreign competitors, and therefore violated NAFTA Article 1102's national treatment obligation. However, the tribunal rejected this claim after conducting a detailed comparative analysis of the treatment meted out in like circumstances, finding that both Canadian and US steel faced identical restrictions when fabricated outside the United States. More specifically, steel from any source, regardless of the investor's nationality, was equally excluded from the Springfield Interchange Project if fabricated in Canada or elsewhere outside the US. The tribunal emphasised that ADF had failed to present any evidence of a similarly situated US steel manufacturer or fabricator that had been exempted from the Buy

37 UNCITRAL, Award, 12 January 2011.

38 ICSID Case No. ARB (AF)/00/1, Award, 9 January 2003.

America requirements or accorded more favourable treatment, noting that US companies faced the same three options as the Canadian investor: expand fabrication facilities within the US, subcontract to domestic fabricators, or forgo bidding on federal highway projects. Consequently, the tribunal concluded that the US measures were facially neutral in their application and dismissed the national treatment claim.

C. Intent

Several arbitral tribunals[39] and legal scholarship[40] have affirmed that there is no requirement for a host state to have intended to treat a foreign investor less favourable on the basis of their nationality. Indeed, as noted by the tribunal in *Feldman v Mexico*:[41]

> . . . requiring a foreign investor to prove that discrimination is based on his nationality could be an insurmountable burden to the Claimant, as that information may only be available to the government. It would be virtually impossible for any claimant to meet the burden of demonstrating that a government's motivation for discrimination is nationality rather than some other reason. Also, as the Respondent argues, if the motives for a government's actions should not be examined, there is effectively no way for the Claimant or this Tribunal to make the subjective determination that the discriminatory action of the government is a result of the Claimant's nationality, again in the absence of credible evidence from the Respondent of a different motivation. If Article 1102 violations are limited to those where there is explicit (presumably *de jure*) discrimination against foreigners, e.g., through a law that treats foreign investors and domestic investors differently, it would greatly limit the effectiveness of the national treatment concept in protecting foreign investors.[42]

Similar sentiments were expressed by the tribunal in *SD Myers v Canada*[43] when it noted:

> Intent is important, but protectionist intent is not necessarily decisive on its own. The existence of an intent to favour nationals over non-nationals would not give rise to a breach of Chapter 1102 of the NAFTA if the measure in question were to produced no adverse effect on the non-national complainant. The word 'treatment' suggests that practical impact is required to produce a breach of Article 1102, not merely a motive or intent that is in violation of Chapter 11.[44]

In short, then, although discriminatory intent alongside less favourable treatment of similarly placed investors may make it easier, at least from an evidential perspective, for a

39 *Siemens v Argentina*, ICSID Case No. ARB/02/8, Award, 6 February 2008, para. 321: 'The Tribunal concurs that intent is not decisive or essential for a finding of discrimination, and that the impact of the measure on the investment would be the determining factor to ascertain whether it had resulted in non-discriminatory treatment'. *Clayton and Bilcon v Canada,* PCA Case No. 2009–04, Award on Jurisdiction and Liability, 17 March 2015, para. 719:

> it is not self-evident, as the Respondent argues that any departure from national treatment must be explicitly shown to be a result of the investor's nationality. There is no such language in Article 1102. Rather, Article 1102 by its terms suggests that it is sufficient to show less favorable treatment for the foreign investor than for domestic investors in like circumstances.

40 August Reinisch, 'National Treatment' in *International Investment Law* (Nomos 2015).

41 ICSID Case No. ARB(AF)/99/1, Award, 16 December 2002.

42 ibid 183.

43 UNCITRAL, Partial Award, 13 November 2000.

44 ibid 254.

foreign investor to successfully establish a claim of breach of the national treatment standard, the existence of such intent is neither necessary nor decisive.[45]

D. Justification

If the claimant can prove that it was treated less favourably than a domestic investor who is similarly situated, there would be discriminatory treatment, unless the respondent can prove that such different treatment was justified. While reservations which are expressly carved out in IIAs do not raise particular issues as a matter of principle (though factual issues regarding their application often arise), the question as to whether a justification for differential treatment which is not expressly provided for can nonetheless be implied into the national standard is rife with controversy.[46] At least one tribunal – *Clayton and Bilcon v Canada*[47] – has, however, suggested that this might be possible in some circumstances:

> The approach taken in *Pope & Talbot* would seem to provide legally appropriate latitude for host states, even in the absence of an equivalent of Article XX of the GATT, to pursue reasonable and non-discriminatory domestic policy objectives through appropriate measures even when there is an incidental and reasonably unavoidable burden on foreign enterprises. Consistently with the approach taken in the *Feldman* case, however, the present Tribunal is also of the view that once a prima facie case is made out under the three-part UPS test, the onus is on the host state to show that a measure is still sustainable within the terms of Article 1102. It is the host state that is in a position to identify and substantiate the case, in terms of its own laws, policies and circumstances, that an apparently discriminatory measure is in fact compliant with the 'national treatment' norm set out in Article 1102.[48]

On the facts of *Clayton and Bilcon*, the tribunal held that it was unable to discern any justification for the differential and adverse treatment accorded to the claimants that would satisfy the *Pope & Talbot* test with respect to the standard of evaluation under the laws of federal Canada. In its view, the 'community core values' approach adopted by the JRP was not a rational government policy; it was at odds with law and policy and was not consistent with the investment liberalising objectives of NAFTA.

In the final analysis, it might be argued that although the tribunals in *Clayton and Bilcon, Pope & Talbot* and *Feldman* have broadly expressed that, as a matter of principle, a state may raise justifications in respect less favourable treatment, the law in this area is in a state of flux, as at least two of these tribunals seemed to have expressed these sentiments on an *obiter* basis. In any event, other tribunals have not appeared to suggest that, outside of express reservations, discussed below, other justifications are possible.

Notwithstanding, Article 5 of the Guyana-Brazil BIT appears to introduce legitimate public interest justifications for differential treatment of domestic and foreign investors:

45 *Thunderbird Gaming Corporation v United Mexican States*, UNCITRAL, Award, 26 January 2006 176–77

> . . . Thunderbird must show that its investment received treatment less favourable than Mexico has accorded, in like circumstances, to investments of Mexican nationals. It is not expected from Thunderbird that it shows separately that the less favourable treatment was motivated because of nationality.

46 Andrea Bjorklund, 'The National Treatment Obligation' in Arrow Katia Yannaca-Small (ed), *Arbitration Under International Investment Agreements: A Guide to the Key Issues* (OUP 2018).

47 PCA Case No. 2009–04, Award on Jurisdiction and Liability, 17 March 2015.

48 ibid 723.

4. For greater certainty, whether treatment is accorded in 'like circumstances' depends on the totality of the circumstances, including whether the relevant treatment distinguishes between investors or investments on the basis of legitimate public interest objectives.

While tribunals do not appear to have interpreted a provision of this nature to date, it would seem that the question of justification is to be considered when tribunals are assessing whether treatment is accorded in 'like circumstances' rather than justification arising as a separate consideration.

E. Treaty-based Reservations

Some Caribbean IIAs expressly provide for reservations[49] in respect of which a host state may not be held liable for violating the national treatment standard in circumstances where the less favourable treatment meted out to the foreign investor falls into one of the carve outs. If the tribunal upholds the objection, it will not consider the claimant's national treatment claim any further. An example of such a provision is Article IV of the Trinidad and Tobago-Canada BIT, which provides:

1. Each Contracting Party shall grant to investments or returns of investors of the other Contracting Party treatment no less favourable than that which, in like circumstances, it grants to investments or returns of its own investors with respect to the expansion, management, conduct, operation and sale or disposition of investments.
2. Subparagraph (3)(a) of Article II, paragraph (1) of this Article, and paragraphs (1) and (2) of Article V do not apply to:
   a.
      i. any existing non-conforming measures maintained within the territory of a Contracting Party; and
      ii. any measure maintained or adopted after the date of entry into force of this Agreement that, at the time of sale or other disposition of a government's equity interests in, or the assets of, an existing state enterprise or an existing governmental entity, prohibits or imposes limitations on the ownership of equity interests or assets or imposes nationality requirements relating to senior management or members of the board of directors;
   b. the continuation or prompt renewal of any non-conforming measure referred to in subparagraph (a);
   c. an amendment to any non-conforming measure referred to in subparagraph (a), to the extent that the amendment does not decrease the conformity of the measure, as it existed immediately before the amendment, with those obligations;
   d. the right of each Contracting Party to make or maintain exceptions within the sectors or matters listed in the Annex to this Agreement.

ANNEX

1. In accordance with Article IV, subparagraph 2(d), Canada reserves the right to make and maintain exceptions in the sectors or matters listed below:
   - social services (i.e. public law enforcement; correctional services; income security or insurance; social security or insurance; social welfare; public education; public training; health and child care);

49 Barbados-Canada BIT Article 4; Grenada-USA BIT Article 2; Guyana-Brazil BIT Article 5; Haiti-USA BIT Article 2; Jamaica-USA BIT Article 2; Suriname-Brazil BIT Article 5; Trinidad and Tobago-Guatemala BIT Article 5; Trinidad and Tobago-USA BIT Article 2.

- services in any other sector;
- government securities – as described in SIC 8152;
- residency requirements for ownership of oceanfront land;
- measures implementing the Northwest Territories and the Yukon Oil and Gas Accords.

2. In accordance with Article IV, subparagraph 2(d), the Republic of Trinidad and Tobago reserves the right to make and maintain exceptions in the sectors or matters listed below: civil aviation; real property; customs brokers and customs clerks; gambling, betting and lotteries.
3. For the purpose of this Annex, 'SIC' means, with respect to Canada, Standard Industrial Classification numbers as set out in Statistics Canada, Standard Industrial Classification, fourth edition, 1980.

A provision of this nature was subject to arbitral proceedings *in Global Telecom Holding S.A.E. v Canada.*[50] Here, an Egyptian telecommunications investor, sought to exercise its option to gain voting control in a joint venture after Canada relaxed its ownership and control rules. In turn, Canada denied the claimant the exercise of their right on account of the share conversion constituting an 'acquisition' under the Investment Canada Act, and thereby subject to a security review. The claimant argued that the state, in so doing, breached the national treatment clause of the Egypt-Canada BIT, while Canada retorted that the claim was precluded by the reservation it made pursuant to Article IV(2)(d) of the BIT, and the tribunal therefore lacked jurisdiction *ratione materiae* over the claim. The claimant's main contentions were Canada never exercised its right to make or maintain an exception under Article IV(2)(d), and, in any event, Canada did not reserve the right to maintain exceptions with respect to investments made in the telecommunications sector. The relevant provision of the BIT, *inter alia*, excepted:

- social services (i.e. public law enforcement; correctional services; income security or insurance; social security or insurance; social welfare; public education; public training; health and child care);
- services in any other sector.

. . .

The majority considered that this language left no room for doubt that Canada had the right to make exceptions to the national treatment obligation with respect to 'services', which included telecommunications services. In their view, to adopt a different approach, for example, a procedural requirement of prior notification to trigger the exception, would amount to a rewriting the BIT. If the Contracting Parties had intended for the exception to be subject to any notification requirement beyond listing the relevant sector or matter in the Annex, they would have included it in the text of the BIT, the majority noted. In this connection, the majority compared the BIT here to the one in *Lemir v Ukraine*,[51] a case in which the relevant treaty expressly provided for a prior notification requirement as a condition

50 ICSID Case No. ARB/16/16, Award, 27 March 2020.

51 The *Lemire*, ICSID Case No. ARB/06/18, Decision on Liability, 14 January 2010, tribunal ruled that the state's right to make or maintain exceptions to the national treatment in protected sectors was not unlimited, but subject to specific notification requirements, namely Article II.1 of the BIT which provided:

> Each Party agrees to notify the other Party before or on the date of entry into force of this Treaty of all such laws and regulations of which it is aware concerning the sectors or matters listed in the Annex.

for triggering the exception. Ultimately, the tribunal dismissed the claim, concluding that under Article IV(2)(d) and the Annex, Canada was entitled to adopt or apply measures with respect to 'services in any other sector', including telecommunication services, that were not in conformity with its national treatment obligation.

In a powerful dissenting opinion, Gary Born rejected the majority's view, instead concluding that:

> The Tribunal's analysis produces what, in my view, is a very remarkable result – namely, that the vast bulk of Canada's obligation to provide non-discriminatory national treatment under the BIT is almost entirely without any substance or effect. Under the Tribunal's analysis, Canada is free, at any time and in any manner, to impose blatantly discriminatory measures favoring Canadian nationals, in broad sectors of its economy, without any prior notice to Egypt or Egyptian investors and without any other requirement or limitation. That result makes the Treaty's basic promise of non-discriminatory, transparent treatment of foreign businesses, pursuant to the rule of law, largely illusory. That is a deeply unattractive result, which contradicts the basic objectives of both the Treaty and international law more generally.[52]

In his view, the reservation of a right, as permitted by Article IV(2)(d) and the Annex, was not the actual exercise of that right. In other words, the right to make or maintain an exception was fundamentally different from the right to impose the measures. On the related issue of whether the exceptions to national treatment protection contained in Article IV(2)(d) and the related Annex encompassed the telecommunications sector, Born argued that the natural reading of the Annex was that services in 'any other sector' was a limited a reference to other 'social services' in sectors not already specified in the parenthetical quoted text of the Annex. His view was because the Annex did not say 'any services' or 'any sector in which services are provided', the language 'any other sector' had to be narrowly construed as excluding the telecommunications sector.

The issues raised by Born not only highlight the often open-textured nature of treaty interpretation but also emphasises the need for drafters of IIAs to carefully structure the language of these agreements so as to avoid interpretative misgivings. That said, from a Caribbean perspective, it is arguable that implying into the text of a BIT prior notification requirement as a precondition for invoking exceptions to the national treatment standard, as Born suggests, not only substantially re-writes the agreement, but places an additional burden on the host state which may inadvertently reinforce the asymmetrical nature of the international investment regime.

Other cases have, however, proven to be far more straightforward to decide upon. In *Mesa Power Group, LLC v Government of Canada*,[53] for example, the tribunal addressed a national treatment claim arising from Ontario's Green Energy and Green Economy Act (GEGEA)

> Moreover, each Party agrees to notify the other of any future exception . . . and to limit such exceptions to a minimum.

In the tribunal's view, the prior notification requirement was not simply a formality: it was a fundamental requirement in order to guarantee that investors enjoy legal certainty, and that the state could therefore not invoke the exception *ex post facto*, surprising the investor's good faith. Given that Ukraine did not notify the US of any laws or regulations concerning the radio sector, it could not subsequently rely on the exception.

52 *Global Telecom Holding S.A.E. v Canada*, ICSID Case No. ARB/16/16, Award, 27 March 2020. Dissenting Opinion of Gary Born), para. 16.

53 UNCITRAL, PCA Case No. 2012–17, Award, 24 March 2016.

and its Feed-in Tariff (FIT) Programme, which was enacted to build a green economy and procure energy from renewable sources through standardised contracts offering guaranteed pricing for twenty years. The claimant argued that the programme's domestic content requirements violated the national treatment obligation under NAFTA Article 1102. However, the tribunal rejected the claimant's allegation, finding that the FIT Programme constituted 'procurement' by the respondent's state enterprise (the Ontario Power Authority), thereby triggering the Article 1108(7)(a) exception that explicitly excluded procurement activities from the national treatment obligation under Article 1102. Consequently, the tribunal dismissed Mesa's national treatment claims entirely, finding that Ontario's acts in implementing the renewable energy procurement programme could not be challenged, regardless of any discriminatory effects on foreign investors.

II. THE MOST-FAVOURED NATION TREATMENT STANDARD

The MFN standard is an important, albeit relative (as opposed to absolute), standard of treatment in international investment law. It aims to ensure that foreign investors from different countries who invest in the host state are subject to the same treatment, thereby levelling the playing field as between investors[54] in so far as their protection in circumstances giving rise to substantive and (arguably) procedural breaches of investment treaties by the host state. The nature of the MFN standard has been summed up by tribunal in *Mesa Power Group, LLC v Government of Canada*[55] when it explained:

> For an MFN clause in a base treaty to allow the importation of a more favorable standard of protection from a third-party treaty, the applicability of the MFN clause in the base treaty must first be established. Put differently, one must first be under the treaty to claim through the treaty. Thus, the Claimant must first establish that the MFN provision of the base treaty

54 Schreuer in his Commentary on the ICSID Convention notes: . . .

> an MFN clause . . . is intended to endow its beneficiary with rights that are additional to the rights contained in the basic treaty. The meaning of an MFN clause is that whoever is entitled to rely on it be granted rights accruing from a third-party treaty even if these rights clearly go beyond the basic treaty.

See Chistopher Schreuer, Loretta Malintoppi, August Reinisch, and Anthony Sinclair, *The ICSID Convention: A Commentary* (CUP 2009) 577. See, also, United Nations Conference on Trade and Development, 'Most-Favored-Nation Treatment' in UNCTAD Series on Issues in International Investment Agreements II (2010) 45 ('in most MFN treatment claims, tribunals have been directly applying the allegedly better treatment as opposed to finding a violation and compensating for the damage created by its violation'). Gaillard, 'Establishing Jurisdiction Through a Most-Favored-Nation Clause' (2005) 233(105) *New York Law Journal* 1

> (Under an MFN clause, the beneficiary of the clause is entitled to a more favorable treatment that is accorded by the state parties to the treaty to the nationals of a third country. The clause contained in what is defined as the 'basic treaty', which governs the rights of the beneficiary of the MFN clause. The more favorable treatment is found in 'third-party treaty').

Stephan Schill, 'Multilateralizing Investment Treaties Through Most-Favored-Nation Clauses' (2009) 27(2) *Berkeley Journal of International Law* 504 ('An investor covered by a BIT with an MFN clause can . . . invoke the benefits granted to third-party nationals by another BIT of the host State and import them into its relationship with the host State').

55 UNCITRAL, PCA Case No. 2012–17, Award, 24 March 2016.

applies. Then, relying on that provision, it may be able to import a more favorable standard of protection from a third-party treaty.[56]

Simply put, to establish a breach of the MFN standard, an investor needs to prove, on a balance of probabilities, that they have been treated less favourably than a foreign investor from a third state.[57] For example, while Article 3 of the Barbados-Cuba BIT requires less favourable treatment, it does not expressly state that the foreign investors in question must be in 'like circumstances':

(1) Neither Contracting Party shall in its territory subject investments or returns of national or companies of be other Contracting Party to treatment less favourable than that which it accords to investments or returns of its own nationals or companies or to investments or returns of nationals or companies of *any third State.*
(2) Neither Contracting company shall in its territory subject nationals or companies of the other Contracting Party as regards their management, maintenance, use, enjoyment or disposal of their investments, to treatment less favourable than that which it accords to its own nationals or companies or to nationals or companies of any *third State.*[58]

By contrast, other Caribbean BITs expressly provide that the foreign investors must be in like circumstances.[59] For example, Article 6 of the Trinidad and Tobago-Guatemala BIT provides:

1. Each Contracting Party shall accord to investors of the other Contracting Party treatment no less favourable than that which it accords, *in like circumstances*, to investors of any third State with respect to the management, maintenance, use enjoyment or disposition of investments.

56 ibid 401.

57 Rudolf Dolzer and Christoph Schreuer, *Principles of International Investment Law* (OUP 2008) 186:

> The [MFN] clause may not have any practical significance if the state concerned fails to grant any relevant benefit to a third party. However, as soon as the state does confer a relevant benefit, it is automatically extended to the state that benefits from the MFN clause.

58 See, also, Antigua and Barbuda-Germany BIT Article 3; Antigua and Barbuda-UK BIT Article 3; Barbados-Belgium-Luxembourg Agreement Article 3; Barbados-China BIT Article 3; Barbados-Cuba BIT Article 3; Barbados-Germany BIT Article 3; Barbados-Mauritius BIT Article 4; Barbados-Switzerland BIT Article 3; Barbados-UK BIT Article 3; Barbados-Venezuela BIT Article 3; Belize-China BIT Article 3; Belize-Cuba BIT Article 3; Belize-El Salvador BIT Article 3; Belize-The Netherlands BIT Article 3; Belize-UK BIT Article 3; Dominica-Germany BIT Article 3; Dominica-UK BIT Article 3; Haiti-Germany BIT Article 2; Grenada-UK BIT Article 3; Guyana-China BIT Article 3; Guyana-Germany BIT Article 3; Guyana-South Korea BIT Article 3; Guyana-Switzerland BIT Article 4; Guyana-UK BIT Article 3; Haiti-UK BIT Article 3; Jamaica-Argentina BIT Article 3; Jamaica-China BIT Article 3; Jamaica-Egypt BIT Article 3; Jamaica-Indonesia BIT Article 3; Jamaica-South Korea BIT Article 3; Jamaica-Switzerland BIT Article 3; Jamaica-The Netherlands BIT Article 3; Jamaica-UK BIT Article 3; St Lucia-Germany BIT Article 3; St Lucia-UK BIT Article 3; Suriname-The Netherlands BIT Article 3; SVG-Germany BIT Article 3; Trinidad and Tobago-China BIT Article 4; Trinidad and Tobago-Cuba BIT Article 5; Trinidad and Tobago-France BIT Article 4; Trinidad and Tobago-India BIT Article 4; Trinidad and Tobago-South Korea BIT Article 3; Trinidad and Tobago-Switzerland BIT Article 4; Trinidad and Tobago-Germany BIT Article 4; Trinidad and Tobago-UK BIT Article 5.

59 Barbados-Canada BIT Article 3; Grenada-USA BIT Article 2; Guyana-Brazil BIT Article 6; Haiti-USA BIT Article 2; Jamaica-USA BIT Article 2; Suriname-Brazil BIT Article 6; Trinidad and Tobago-Canada BIT Article 3; Trinidad and Tobago-Guatemala BIT Article 6; Trinidad and Tobago-USA BIT Article 2.

2. Each Contracting Party shall accord to investments of investors of the other Contracting Party treatment no less favourable than that which it accords, in like circumstances, to investments of any third State with respect to the management, maintenance, use, enjoyment or disposition of investments.

Yet, still, some Caribbean BITs are more restrictive, requiring that the foreign investors are not merely in like circumstances, but rather in the 'same' or 'equivalent' circumstances. For example, Article 3 of the Belize-UK BIT provides:

(1) Neither Contracting Party shall in its territory subject investments or returns of nationals or companies of the other Contracting Party to treatment less favourable than that which it accords in the *same circumstances* to investments or returns of its own nationals or companies or to investments or returns of nationals or companies of any third State.
(2) Neither Contracting Party shall in its territory subject nationals or companies of the other Contracting Party, as regards their management, use, enjoyment or disposal of their investments, to treatment less favourable than that which it accords in the *same circumstances* to its own nationals or companies or to nationals or companies of any third State.

Meanwhile, Article 3 of the Barbados-Germany BIT provides:

1. Neither Contracting Party shall subject investments in its territory owned or controlled by nationals or companies of the other Contracting Party to treatment less favourable than it accords in *equivalent circumstances* to investments of its own nationals or companies or to investments of nationals or companies of any third State.
2. Neither Contracting Party shall subject nationals or companies of the other Contracting Party, as regards their activity in connection with investments in its territory, to treatment less favourable than it accords in *equivalent circumstances* to its own nationals or companies or to nationals or companies of any third State.

Unlike the extensive jurisprudence on the national treatment standard, judicial pronouncements on the meaning of 'like circumstances' in respect of the MFN standard have been quite sparse. One instructive case in this connection, however, is *İçkale İnşaat Limited Şirketi v Turkmenistan*,[60] a case in which the tribunal explained that:

> The terms 'treatment accorded in similar situations' therefore suggest that the MFN treatment obligation requires a comparison of the factual situation of the investments of the investors of the home State and that of the investments of the investors of third States, for the purpose of determining whether the treatment accorded to investors of the home State can be said to be less favorable than that accorded to investments of the investors of any third State. . . . Investors cannot be said to be in a 'similar situation' merely because they have invested in a particular State.[61]

In other words, investors must be in factually similar circumstances. This might mean having similar investments in terms of their nature, size, and scope, being in a competitive

60 ICSID Case No. ARB/10/24, Award, 8 March 2016.
61 ibid 329.

relationship, operating in the same sector, facing similar regulatory frameworks, or being subject to comparable business risks and operational challenges. The determination of whether investors are in 'like circumstances' or 'similar situations' requires a facts-specific analysis.

Meanwhile, with regard to 'less favourable treatment', the award in *Daimler Financial Services AG v Argentine Republic*[62] is instructive. Here, the tribunal noted that the words 'less' and 'more' are, by their nature, relative terms,[63] necessitating a comparison between the two types of treatment invoked.[64] In its view, 'different treatment' does not automatically mean 'less favourable' treatment.[65] A qualitative and quantitative assessment of the relative burdens, disadvantages, benefits, and practical impacts of different treatment is required. On the facts of that case, the tribunal held that the MFN guarantee did not apply because the claimant had not shown that the dispute resolution process (an 18-month domestic procedure before resorting to international arbitration) prescribed by Article 10 of the German-Argentine BIT was objectively less favourable to the claimant than that afforded by comparator treaties.[66]

A. By Agreement

In some cases, the parties to a dispute, during the course of arbitral proceedings, may agree that the MFN clause applies to allow for the invocation of substantive standard(s) of protection. In such circumstances, the tribunal will, of course, determine the scope of the MFN clause, and assess, based on the evidence tendered, the extent to which the claimant establishes that, being similarly placed to another foreign investor from a third country, it has been subject to less favourable treatment. By way of example, in *Rumeli Telekom A.S. and Telsim Mobil Telekomunikasyon Hizmetleri A.S. v Republic of Kazakhstan*,[67] the parties agreed that the MFN clause contained in the relevant BIT could be relied upon to invoke more favourable treatment from another BIT concluded with Kazakhstan, including the obligation to ensure the fair and equitable treatment and the obligation to accord full protection and security. Having done so, the tribunal proceeded to satisfy itself that the terms of the MFN clause permitted the use of the provisions of the Denmark BIT and Croatia BIT as a basis for the claims that the obligation to award permits subsequent to approval of an investment and to fulfilment of contractual obligations, respectively, could be considered to be part of fair and equitable treatment.

B. Substantive use of the MFN Clause

The MFN clause serves as a mechanism for importing more favourable substantive protections from third-party treaties into the base treaty. This substantive application of the MFN

62 ICSID Case No. ARB/05/1, Award, 22 August 2012.

63 ibid 241.

64 ibid.

65 ibid 242.

66 In particular, Article X of the Chilean-Argentine BIT (the comparator treaty) contained a fork-in-the-road clause, whereas Article 10 of the German-Argentine BIT (the base treaty) did not.

67 ICSID Case No. ARB/05/16 (Award).

clause has generated significant jurisprudence regarding its scope and limitations, particularly concerning whether investors can invoke certain standards of protection – such as fair and equitable treatment, full protection and security, or umbrella clauses – that are absent from their base treaty but present in the host state's agreements with other countries.[68] As will be explained below, the key interpretive question addressed by tribunals in this context centres on the precise wording of the MFN clause and whether it extends beyond treatment standards to encompass the importation of entirely new rights or obligations.[69] Tribunals adopt varying approaches to balance the protective purpose of MFN clauses against the principle that parties should be bound only by the specific commitments they have carefully negotiated.

In *Bayindir v Islamic Republic of Pakistan* (I),[70] the claimant argued that, despite the absence of a specific clause in the Turkey-Pakistan BIT providing for fair and equitable treatment, an FET obligation could be derived from the operation of the MFN clause in Article II(2) of the Treaty. In other words, the claimant sought to import through Article II(2) of the Treaty the provisions on FET from the bilateral investment treaties concluded by Pakistan with France, the Netherlands, China, Australia, Switzerland, and the United Kingdom. By contrast, the respondent argued that the Contracting Parties' intention had clearly been to exclude the FET standard to the extent that Turkey and Pakistan deliberately decided not to include an FET clause in the Treaty. The tribunal held that, on an ordinary reading of Article II(2), the parties did not intend to exclude the importation of a more favourable substantive standard of treatment accorded to investors of third countries. In the tribunal's view, the issue was therefore not whether the claimant could invoke the FET obligation, but rather which one. In this case, a self-standing treaty obligation, as opposed to the customary international minimum standard, was imported from Article 4 of the Pakistan-Switzerland BIT. That said, the tribunal ultimately found that the respondent had not breached the FET standard applicable through the operation of the MFN clause.

Some Caribbean IIAs specifically delimit the application of the MFN clause to fair and equitable treatment.[71] For example, Article 3 of the Barbados-Switzerland BIT provides:

> (2) Each Contracting Party shall ensure fair and equitable treatment within its territory of the investments of the investors of the other Contracting Party. This treatment shall not be less favourable than that granted by each Contracting Party to investments made within its territory by its own investors, or than that granted by each Contracting Party to the investments made within its territory by investors of the most favoured nation, if this latter treatment is more favourable.

The question arises in this connection as to whether an MFN clause of this nature should be strictly applied *only* to the importation of a more favourable FET standard from treaties with third countries, or can be used to import other, more favourable substantive standards

68 Martins Paparinskis, 'MFN Clauses and Substantive Treatment: A Law of Treaties Perspective of the "Conventional Wisdom"' (2018) *AJIL Unbound* 49.

69 Facundo Pérez-Aznar, 'The Use of Most-Favoured-Nation Clauses to Import Substantive Treaty Provisions in International Investment Agreements' (2017) 20(4) *Journal of International Economic Law* 777. See, also, Tanjina Sharmin, 'Application of MFN to the Substantive Standards: Why Should We Re-Investigate the Uncontested' (2018) 15 *Manchester Journal of International Economic Law* 85.

70 ICSID Case No. ARB/03/29, Award, 27 August 2009.

71 Barbados-China BIT Article 3; Barbados-Mauritius BIT Article 4; Belize-China BIT Article 3; Jamaica-China BIT Article 3; Jamaica-Egypt BIT Article 3; Jamaica-Indonesia Article 3; Jamaica-South Korea BIT Article 3.

absent from the base treaty in question. Although the relevant MFN clause in *Teinver v The Argentine Republic*[72] was worded slightly different from the aforementioned provision, the analysis offered by the tribunal in this case is particularly instructive. Here, the claimants invoked the MFN clause contained in Article IV(2) of the Argentina-Spain BIT to incorporate provisions from the US-Argentina BIT in support of claims that the respondent failed to accord them full protection and security and failed to observe obligations with respect to their investments. Article IV of the Treaty provided:

1. Each Party shall guarantee in its territory *fair and equitable treatment* of investments made by investors of the other Party.
2. *In all matters governed by this Agreement*, such treatment shall be no less favourable than that accorded by each Party to investments made in its territory by investors of a third country.

The claimant sought to invoke Article II(2)(a) and (c) of the US-Argentina BIT which provided:

a) Investment shall at all times be accorded fair and equitable treatment, shall enjoy full protection and security and shall in no case be accorded treatment less than that required by international law.
c) Each Party shall observe any obligation it may have entered into with regard to investments.

The respondent submitted that the scope of the MFN clause contained in Article IV(2) of the Treaty was restricted to fair and equitable treatment since it followed Article IV(1) which provided for fair and equitable treatment of investments. In its view, Article IV(2) of the Treaty was limited because it referred to 'such treatment', as opposed to 'all treatments'. The tribunal, however, rejected the respondent's argument, finding that:

> Article IV(2) of the Treaty expressly refers to 'all matters governed by this Agreement', which the Tribunal has found to be unambiguously inclusive. This broad language is inconsistent with the notion that only fair and equitable treatment was intended to be the subject of the most favorable nation treatment. *If such were the case, then the MFN Clause would apply only to more favorable FET provisions contained in other BITs.* In the Tribunal's view, the plain or ordinary meaning of the language does not sustain this interpretation. Rather, reading Articles IV(1) and (2) together, a more harmonious and logical interpretation is that the parties to the Treaty are required to accord fair and equitable treatment of investments made by investors of a Party and that in all matters governed by the Treaty, the treatment accorded to investments (which must be fair and equitable treatment pursuant Article IV(1)) shall be no less favorable than the treatment accorded to investments made by investors of a third country.[73]

In other words, the MFN clause contained in Article IV(2) of the Treaty extended to matters other than fair and equitable treatment; that is, all matters governed by the Treaty, thereby incorporating more favourable provisions from other BITs concluded by Argentina. However, although the MFN clause referenced 'all matters', this was subject to the caveat 'governed by this agreement', whose plain and ordinary meaning was that of the various

72 ICSID Case No. ARB/09/1, Award, 21 July 2017.
73 ibid 880.

rights or forms of protection contained in the individual provisions of the Treaty. In this context, the tribunal found that use of the MFN clause to incorporate an umbrella clause into the Treaty would have resulted in the incorporation of a new right or standard of treatment not provided for in the Treaty. In other words, while the MFN clause could 'improve' the standards of protection contained in the Treaty by incorporating more favourable standards from another treaty (for example, more favourable provisions on discriminatory or unjustified measures, fair and equitable treatment, expropriation and transfers of income or earnings), the claimants could not use the MFN clause to invoke an umbrella clause in circumstances where there was no umbrella clause in the Treaty in the first place.

The take-away from this decision, then, is that if the MFN provision does not refer to 'all matters', but only to fair and equitable treatment, 'then the MFN clause would apply only to more favourable FET provisions contained in other BITs',[74] and not other substantive standards of protection.

Meanwhile, with respect to the use of the MFN clause to import the full protection and security obligation, the case of *Micula and others v Romania* [II][75] is instructive. Here, the claimants argued that although the Sweden-Romania BIT did not specifically provide for full protection and security of investments made by investors of Contracting Parties, the MFN clause in Article 3(1) of the BIT allowed investors to invoke a more favourable substantive standard of protection contained in another investment treaty entered into by the host state with a third party. They sought to invoke Article 4(1) of the Romania-Albania BIT, which provides that 'investments by investors of either Contracting Party shall enjoy full protection and security'. On this basis, the claimants contended that the respondent's failure to properly enforce its alcohol tax laws and prevent the growth of the illegal spirits market constituted a failure to respect the full protection and security obligation. While the tribunal accepted that the MFN provision in Article 3(1) of the Sweden-Romania BIT could bring into the relations between the parties an obligation of full protection and security, the claim that the respondent failed to enforce its tax laws was not substantiated on the facts. Accordingly, the claim that there had been a violation of the obligation of full protection and security was rejected.

The MFN clause has also been used to an import umbrella clause into a base treaty from a treaty with a third country even where the base treaty does not contain an umbrella clause. Indeed, in *Consutel Group S.p.A. in liquidazione v People's Democratic Republic of Algeria*,[76] the tribunal held that the MFN clause of Article 3 of the Italy-Algeria BIT allowed the claimant to invoke the umbrella clause contained in Article 10(2) of the BIT concluded between Algeria and Switzerland. However, on the facts, the umbrella clause was not applicable to the contractual obligations entered into by Algérie Télécom under the Partnership Agreement and its amendments as Algérie Télécom had not acted on behalf of the state. In arriving at this decision, the tribunal reaffirmed the general principle stated in *Arif v Moldova* that:

> umbrella clauses are substantive in nature. A breach of specific undertakings covered by an 'umbrella' clause will give rise to a substantive breach of the BIT. In this sense, the Tribunal rejects Respondent's argument that 'umbrella' clauses are procedural in nature and cannot be imported through an MFN clause because they give a means of protection for contractual and other undertakings, rather than a unique standard of behavior.[77]

74 ibid.

75 ICSID Case No. ARB/14/29, Award, 5 March 2020.

76 PCA No. 2017–33, Award, 3 February 2020.

77 ibid 358.

Separately, in *EDFI et al. v Argentina*,[78] the claimants argued that by virtue of the MFN clause they were entitled to any substantive protections which were more favourable than those contained in Article 4 of the Argentina-France BIT which were found in third-party investment treaties (including the Article 10(2) of the Argentina-Luxembourg BIT), such as the umbrella clause. The tribunal held that the MFN clause of the base treaty, which provided for treatment no less favourable in respect of 'investments and the activities connected therewith', did in fact permit recourse to the umbrella clauses of third-country treaties. In its view, given the fact that the MFN clause was loosely worded, 'to ignore the MFN clause in this case would permit more favourable treatment to investors protected under third countries, which is exactly what the MFN Clause is intended to prevent'.[79] On the facts, the tribunal held that the pesification and freezing of tariffs pursuant to the emergency measures breached the respondent's obligation to respect its contractual commitments contained in Concession agreements granted to foreign investors for specific investments. More particularly, the serious repudiation of concessions obligations implicated by failure to respect the currency clause was a violation of the umbrella clause imported from Article 10(2) Argentina-Luxembourg BIT.

Finally, on the question of whether the MFN clause can be used to expand the definition of 'investment', that is, the tribunal's jurisdiction *rationae materiae*, the tribunal in *Société Générale v Dominican Republic*[80] made it clear that because the MFN clause typically refers to '*treatment* accorded to investments', as opposed to the definition of 'investment' itself, it cannot be used to enlarge the scope of the base treaty's definition of 'investment'.

The take-away, then, is that the MFN clause can be used to import more favourable substantive protections from third-party treaties, but their scope of application depends heavily on their specific wording. Broadly worded MFN clauses (referring to 'all matters') allow investors to import various standards like fair and equitable treatment, full protection and security, or even umbrella clauses from other treaties. However, more narrowly worded clauses may be limited to specific protections like fair and equitable treatment only. Crucially, MFN clauses can enhance existing standards of protection but generally cannot create entirely new rights or obligations that do not exist in some form in the base treaty, and they cannot expand the definition of 'investment' itself to broaden tribunals' jurisdiction.

C. Procedural Use of MFN

The procedural use of the MFN clause has, relatively speaking, been far more controversial than the MFN clause's application to substantive standards.[81] The procedural use of the MFN clause enables a foreign investor to import more favourable dispute settlement provisions contained in other IIAs into the base treaty. While some tribunals have endorsed such

78 ICSID Case No. ARB/03/23, Award, 11 June 2012.

79 ibid 932.

80 UNCITRAL, LCIA Case No. UN 7927, Award on Preliminary Objections to Jurisdiction, 19 September 2008.

81 See generally Jürgen Kurtz, 'The MFN Standard and Foreign Investment: An Uneasy Fit?' (2004) 5(6) *The Journal of World Investment & Trade* 861. Tony Cole, 'The Boundaries of Most Favored Nation Treatment in International Investment Law' (2011) 33 *Michigan Journal of International Law* 537. Tanjina Sharmin and Emmanuel Laryea, 'Application of MFN to Investment Dispute Settlement: Rule of Law Issues' (2021) 20(1) *Journal of International Trade Law and Policy* 21.

a use of the MFN clause,[82] others have staunchly maintained their opposition to such use, arguing that it subverts the consent to arbitration carefully negotiated by states parties to IIAs. The tribunal in *Impregilo S.p.A. v Argentine Republic*[83] summed up the current state of affairs in the following terms:

> It appears from these awards that some tribunals have had rather strong reservations about the general development of the case law in this area. It is therefore clear that these issues remain controversial and that the predominating jurisprudence which has developed is in no way universally accepted.
>
> Nevertheless, the Arbitral Tribunal finds it unfortunate if the assessment of these issues would in each case be dependent on the personal opinions of individual arbitrators. The best way to avoid such a result is to make the determination on the basis of case law whenever a clear case law can be discerned. It is true that, as stated above, the jurisprudence regarding the application of MFN clauses to settlement of disputes provisions is not fully consistent. Nevertheless, in cases where the MFN clause has referred to 'all matters' or 'any matter' regulated in the BIT, there has been near unanimity in finding that the clause covered the dispute settlement rules.[84]

Similar sentiments were expressed in *Wintershall Aktiengesellschaft v Argentine Republic*[85] when the tribunal noted:

> In a wide variety of cases, arbitral tribunals (ICSID and other) have been called upon to interpret an MFN Clause in a BIT to determine whether or not it extends to dispute resolution, (a jurisdiction clause). Their decisions have been neither uniform nor consistent; different tribunals faced with differently worded treaties (sometimes even similarly worded treaties) have reached different, if not conflicting, conclusions. In the sphere of MFN Clauses (in BITs) and their reach, adjudications by ad hoc tribunals have proved to be an obstacle to the development of a jurisprudence *constante*. Under the ICSID system, there is no mechanism for promoting certainty and predictability. But this does not mean that decisions of tribunals (ICSID or other) are not cited by parties before an arbitration tribunal in a particular case. As a matter of fact, in this very case each side has relied on a plethora of decisions – of course, none of them binding, on the Tribunal.[86]

82 Guido Tawil, 'Most Favoured Nation Clauses and Jurisdictional Clauses in Investment Treaty Arbitration' in Christina Binder, Ursula Kriebaum, August Reinisch, and Stephan Wittich (eds), *International Investment Law for the 21st Century, Essays in Honour of Christoph Schreuer* (OUP 2009) 13: 'the prevailing view seems to be the one that allows the investor to by-pass . . . [the] procedural requirement'. See, also, Ronald Dolzer and Christoph Schreuer, *Principles of International Investment Law* (OUP 2008) 254–55; Martins Paparinskis, 'MFN Clauses and International Dispute Settlement: Moving beyond *Maffezini* and *Plama*?' (2011) 26 *ICSID Review-Foreign Investment Law Journal* 28.

83 ICSID Case No. ARB/07/17, Award, 21 June 2011.

84 ibid 107. See, also, *Vladimir Berschader v Russian Federation* SCC Case No. 080/2004, Award, April 21, 2006, 61–62:

> while it is universally agreed that the very essence of an MFN provision in a BIT is to afford to investors all material protection provided by subsequent treaties, it is much more uncertain whether such provisions should be understood to extend to dispute resolution clauses. It is so uncertain, in fact, that the issue has given rise to different outcomes in a number of cases and to extensive jurisprudence on the subject . . . .

85 ICSID Case No. ARB/04/14, Award, 8 December 2008.

86 ibid 178.

The disparity in jurisprudence between the liberal and restrictive approaches with respect to the procedural use of the MFN clause is discussed in further detail later in this chapter.

D. Explicit Inclusion/Exclusion of Dispute Settlement Provisions in IIAs

Some Caribbean IIAs[87] expressly provide that the MFN clause is applicable with respect to particular articles, including the dispute settlement clause. For example, Article 3(3) of the Barbados-Belgium-Luxembourg Economic Cooperation Agreement provides that:

> For the avoidance of doubt, it is confirmed that the treatment provided for in paragraphs (1) and (2) above *shall apply to the provisions of Articles 1 to 15 of this Agreement.*

As noted by the tribunal in *Ansung Housing Co., Ltd. v People's Republic of China*,[88] 'the ambit of an MFN clause is dependent on its wording'.[89] As such, in circumstances like these, in accordance with the ordinary meaning of the relevant MFN clause, tribunals will respect the expressed will of the Contracting Parties for the MFN treatment to be applied to more favourable dispute resolution mechanism contained in treaties with third countries. This point was noted in *Garanti Koza LLP v Turkmenistan*,[90] a case in which the tribunal interpreted the MFN clause contained in Article 3(3) of the UK-Turkmenistan BIT, which applied 'to the provisions of Articles 1 to 11 of this Agreement', as expressly permitting the invocation of more favourable dispute resolution clauses in other treaties than that of Article 8 (investor-state dispute resolution provision) of the BIT in question.

The need for tribunals to respect the ordinary meaning of a treaty's explicit provisions was also noted in *Anglia Auto Accessories Ltd. v Czech Republic*,[91] a case in which the tribunal (majority) considered as determinative the fact that the MFN clause in Article 3 of the relevant BIT was excluded from the scope of Article 8(1) (investor-state dispute resolution provision). In the majority's view, it followed from this specific exclusion that an investor, such as the claimant in this case, could not rely on Article 3 of the BIT to import more favourable dispute resolution provisions found in another investment treaty. In this connection, the tribunal considered that the tough questions confronting other tribunals, such as the scope of the MFN clause (the meaning of 'treatment' as regards 'management, maintenance, use, enjoyment or disposal') were moot. It accordingly concluded:

> the Tribunal is bound by the express language of the BIT, which reflects a choice made by its drafters, and cannot rewrite Article 8(1) or substitute provisions taken from other investment treaties for those that have expressly been included by the drafters of the BIT. In the majority's view, this ends this Tribunal's inquiry.[92]

87 See, also, Barbados-Cuba BIT Article 3; Barbados-UK BIT Article 3; Barbados-Venezuela BIT Article 3; Belize-Cuba BIT Article 3; Trinidad and Tobago-Cuba BIT Article 5; Trinidad and Tobago-UK BIT Article 5.

88 ICSID Case No. ARB/14/25, Award, 9 March 2017.

89 ibid 137. See, also, Dolzer and Schreuer who argue that 'much will depend on the wording of the particular MFN clause' Ronald Dolzer and Christoph Schreuer, *Principles of International Investment Law* (OUP 2008) 257.

90 ICSID Case No. ARB/11/20, Decision on Jurisdiction, 3 July 2013.

91 SCC Case No. V 2014/181, Award, 10 March 2017.

92 ibid 192.

Interestingly, Article 6(3) of the Guyana-Brazil BIT expressly excludes the procedural use of the MFN clause:

> This Article shall not be construed to require a Party to grant to an investor of another Party or their investments the benefit of any treatment, preference or privilege arising from:
>
> i) provisions relating to investment dispute settlement contained in an investment agreement or an investment chapter of any commercial agreement.

Again, given the clear and unambiguous language used by this provision, on the basis of *Itisaluna Iraq LLC and others v Republic of Iraq*[93] which addressed a similar provision, tribunals ought to refuse any attempt by investors to rely on the MFN clause to invoke more favourable dispute settlement provisions in treaties concluded by Guyana with third countries.

E. Pro-Procedural use of the MFN Treatment: Jurisprudence

Maffezini v Kingdom of Spain[94] is a foundational, albeit highly controversial, case on the procedural use of the MFN clause. Here, Article IV of the Argentina-Spain BIT provided that '*in all matters subject to this Agreement*, this treatment shall not be less favourable than that extended by each Party to the investments made in its territory by investors of a third country'. The claimant contended that Article IV embraced not only substantive investment rights but also dispute resolution procedures, so that it was entitled to invoke the dispute resolution clause in Article 10(2) of the Chile-Spain BIT, which provided merely that the investor could opt for arbitration after a six-month period of negotiations had expired, with no other preconditions. The respondent, however, argued that Article IV was confined to material economic treatment and did not extend to procedural matters. Ultimately, the tribunal upheld the claimant's submission and ruled that, given that international arbitration and other dispute resolution provisions were essential to the protection of the rights envisaged under the pertinent BITs, the MFN clause contained in Article IV could be interpreted as giving the claimant the benefit of any wider dispute resolution clause contained in any other BIT between Spain and a third state, in the instant case the Chile-Spain BIT. In reaching its decision, the tribunal placed particular emphasis on the precise terms of the MFN clause which spoke to 'all matters subject to this Agreement'. In the tribunal's view, the phrase 'all matters' (as opposed merely to 'treatment', which was used in other Spanish treaties) was intended to cover not only substantive standards of protection, but also dispute resolution.

The tribunal, aware of the danger of disruptive treaty shopping, proffered some important qualifications based on public policy, though the source of these remains unclear:

> . . . there are good reasons to conclude that today dispute settlement arrangements are inextricably related to the protection of foreign investors . . . .[95]
>
> . . . the beneficiary of the clause should not be able to override public policy considerations that the contracting parties might have envisaged as fundamental conditions for their acceptance of the agreement in question, particularly if the beneficiary is a private investor, as will often be the case.[96]

93 ICSID Case No. ARB/17/10, Award, 3 April 2020.

94 ICSID Case No. ARB/97/7, Decision of the Tribunal on Objections to Jurisdiction, 25 January 2000.

95 ibid 54.

96 ibid 56.

> . . . First, if one contracting party has conditioned its consent to arbitration on the exhaustion of local remedies, which the ICSID Convention allows, this requirement could not be bypassed by invoking the most favored nation clause in relation to a third-party agreement that does not contain this element since the stipulated condition reflects a fundamental rule of international law. Second, if the parties have agreed to a dispute settlement arrangement which includes the so-called fork in the road, that is, a choice between submission to domestic courts or to international arbitration, and where the choice once made becomes final and irreversible, this stipulation cannot be bypassed by invoking the clause. This conclusion is compelled by the consideration that it would upset the finality of arrangements that many countries deem important as a matter of public policy. Third, if the agreement provides for a particular arbitration forum, such as ICSID, for example, this option cannot be changed by invoking the clause, in order to refer the dispute to a different system of arbitration. Finally, if the parties have agreed to a highly institutionalized system of arbitration that incorporates precise rules of procedure, which is the case, for example, with regard to the North America Free Trade Agreement and similar arrangements, it is clear that neither of these mechanisms could be altered by the operation of the clause because these very specific provisions reflect the precise will of the contracting parties. Other elements of public policy limiting the operation of the clause will no doubt be identified by the parties or tribunals. It is clear, in any event, that a distinction has to be made between the legitimate extension of rights and benefits by means of the operation of the clause, on the one hand, and disruptive treaty-shopping that would play havoc with the policy objectives of underlying specific treaty provisions, on the other hand.[97]

The implications of these qualifications will be explored in greater detail later in this chapter. It suffices here, however, to note that *Maffezini* has provoked significant contestation both among arbitral tribunals as well as scholars.[98] For example, McLachlan, Shore, and Weiniger[99] have argued that the *Maffezini* award is problematic because it compromises the principle that the jurisdiction of a tribunal depends solely upon consent, and that where states parties carefully select particular modes of dispute settlement, ‘it is not to be presumed that this can be disrupted by an investor selecting at will from an assorted menu of other options provided in other treaties, negotiated with other State Parties and in other circumstances’.[100] Against this backdrop, in their view, the MFN ‘clause should not apply to investment treaties’ dispute settlement provisions, save where the States expressly so provide’.[101]

Similarly, Fietta has argued that in allowing claimants the possibility of importing more favourable dispute settlement provisions, the *Maffezini* tribunal ‘opened the door to a

97 ibid 63.

98 See generally, Stephen Sutton, ‘*Emilio Augustin Maffezini v Kingdom of Spain* and the ICSID Secretary-General’s Screening Power’ (2005) 21 *Arbitration International* 113; Kara Smith, ‘The Jurisdiction-Limiting MFN Clause’ (2024) 99 *New York University Law Review* 1139; Ruth Teitelbaum, ‘Who’s Afraid of Maffezini-Recent Developments in the Interpretation of Most Favored Nation Clauses’ (2005) 22 *Journal of International Arbitration* 225; İnci Ataman Figanmeşe, ‘The Impact of the Maffezini Decision on the Interpretation of MFN Clauses in Investment Treaties’ (2011) 8 *Ankara Law Review* 221; Stephan Schill, ‘Most-Favored-Nation Clauses as a Basis of Jurisdiction in Investment Treaty Arbitration: Arbitral Jurisprudence at a Crossroads’ (2009) 10 *The Journal of World Investment & Trade* 225; Martins Paparinskis, ‘MFN Clauses and International Dispute Settlement: Moving Beyond Maffezini and Plama?’ (2011) 26 *ICSID Review* 14; Pavel Šturma, ‘Goodbye, Maffezini? On the Recent Developments of Most-Favoured-Nation Clause Interpretation in International Investment Law’ (2016) 15 *The Law & Practice of International Courts and Tribunals* 81.

99 Campbell McLachlan, Laurence Shore, and Matthew Weiniger, *International Investment Arbitration: Substantive Principles* (OUP 2007).

100 ibid 263.

101 ibid 264.

potentially infinite variety of dispute resolution permutations and combinations that different investors might rely upon so as best to meet their individual circumstances.'[102] In other words, there is a real danger that the 'heretical decision' of *Maffezini* on the procedural use of the MFN clause will fundamentally subvert the carefully negotiated balance of BITs, thereby leading to chaos.[103]

Despite these criticisms, however, *Maffezini* continues to be relied upon by tribunals to support the use of the MFN clause to import more favourable dispute resolution processes. In *Gas Natural SDG, SA v Argentine Republic*,[104] the claimant contended that it was not bound by the requirement of prior resort to national courts contained in Article X of the Argentina-Spain BIT by virtue of Article IV(2) of the BIT – the MFN clause – which provided that '*in all matters governed by the present Agreement*, such treatment shall not be less favorable than that accorded by each Party to investments made in its territory by investors of Third States'. The claimant asserted that of the more than fifty bilateral investment treaties entered into by Argentina, only ten contained a requirement of prior resort to national courts. It accordingly sought to rely on the BIT between the United States of America and the Argentine Republic which did not contain any requirement of prior resort to the national courts of the host country. Argentina, however, argued that the MFN clause related to substantive standards of protection, and that accordingly the requirement of prior resort to national courts, being a procedural matter concerning dispute settlement, could not be displaced by reliance on the more favourable dispute resolution clause contained in the Argentina-United States BIT. In any event, Argentina contended that, on the basis of *Maffezini's obiter*, to require it to engage in an arbitration with a national of Spain under conditions to which it did not consent (i.e. to arbitration without prior resort to its courts) would be against the public policy of Argentina.

The tribunal, however, ruled in favour of the claimant, finding that the introductory phrase in Article IV(2) of the BIT – 'all matters governed by the present Agreement. . .' was inclusive and broad enough to allow resort to more favourable dispute resolution mechanisms. In its view, provision for international investor-state arbitration is intended to ensure protection for foreign investors, and that accordingly access to arbitration only after resort to national courts and an eighteen-month waiting period was a less favourable degree of protection than access to arbitration immediately upon expiration of the negotiation period. Accordingly, the claimant was entitled to avail itself of the dispute settlement provision in the United States-Argentina BIT in accordance with Article IV(2) of the Spain and Argentina BIT. The tribunal further held that it did not find the public policy argument raised by Argentina to be persuasive, particularly in view of the fact that many of the BITs concluded by Argentina (in addition to the United States-Argentina BIT) did not require resort to national jurisdiction prior to access to international arbitration.

Similarly, in *Impregilo S.p.A. v Argentine Republic*,[105] the claimant sought to rely upon the MFN clause in Article 3(1) of the Argentina-Italy BIT for the purposes of avoiding the obligation to resort to the local courts for 18 months. More pointedly, the claimant sought to rely on the more favourable treatment contained in the Argentina-US BIT, which

102 Stephen Fietta, 'Most Favoured Nation Treatment and Dispute Resolution under Bilateral Investment Treaties: A Turning Point?' (2005) 2(3) *TDM* 131.

103 Campbell McLachlan, Laurence Shore, and Matthew Weiniger, *International Investment Arbitration: Substantive Principles* (OUP 2007) 254, 257.

104 ICSID Case No. ARB/03/10, Decision on Jurisdiction, 17 June 2005.

105 ICSID Case No. ARB/07/17, Award, 21 June 2011.

provides only for a six-month period of consultations to try to amicably resolve the dispute. Article 3 of Argentina-Italy BIT provided that in respect of income and activities related to investments and *all other matters regulated by this Agreement*, foreign investors should be afforded treatment no less favourable than that accorded investors from third-party countries. On this basis, the tribunal ruled that the term 'treatment' was in itself wide enough to be applicable also to procedural matters such as dispute settlement, and that, in any event, the wording 'all other matters regulated by this Agreement' was also wide enough to cover the dispute settlement rules. In its view, the treatment afforded in the Argentina-Italy BIT offered greater choice to the investor and was therefore more favourable, and so, by virtue of the MFN clause in Article 3(1) of the Argentina-Italy BIT, could be invoked by the claimant in this case.

Other tribunals have shown great affinity to *Maffezini* even in circumstances where the relevant MFN clause is more restrictively worded. For example, in *Siemens A.G. v Argentine Republic*,[106] the MFN clause contained in Article 3 of the Argentina-Spain BIT prohibited 'less favorable treatment of activities related to investments'. This language is similar to that contained in a number of Caribbean IIAs,[107] including Article II(1) of the Grenada-USA BIT, which provides:

> Each Party shall permit and *treat investment*, and *activities associated therewith*, on a basis no less favorable than that accorded in like situations to investment or associated activities of its own nationals or companies, or of nationals or companies of any third country, whichever is the most favorable . . .

In this connection, the claimant in *Siemens* sought to invoke Article 3 of the Argentina-Spain BIT to avoid prior submission of the dispute to the local courts (an 18-month period) on the basis of a more favourable dispute settlement clause contained in the BIT between Argentina and Chile. In the tribunal's view, if it were the parties' intention to limit Article 3, then the terms 'treatment' or 'activities' would have been qualified. The fact that these terms were not qualified, in the tribunal's assessment, indicated a wide scope, including the MFN clause's application to more favourable dispute resolution mechanisms. The tribunal considered that because access to dispute resolution is part of the protection offered by BITs, even though the BIT here did not refer to 'all matters subject to this Agreement', but rather simply to 'treatment' and 'activities related to the investments' (an admittedly narrower formulation than the one in *Maffezini*), it was not precluded from finding that the MFN clause was applicable to dispute settlement. As such, the investor was entitled to invoke against Argentina the wider dispute resolution clause contained in the Chile-Argentina BIT.

Not only have tribunals construed the words 'all matters', and 'treatment' and 'activities related to the investments' as sufficient to ground the application of the MFN clause to more favourable dispute settlement mechanisms contained in BITs concluded with third countries, but also language such as 'the management, utilization, use and enjoyment of an investment'. Such language is found in, for example, Article 3(2) of the Dominica-UK BIT:

> Neither Contracting Party shall in its territory subject nationals or companies of the other Contracting Party, as regards their management, use, enjoyment or use of investments, to

106 ICSID Case No. ARB/02/8, Decision on Jurisdiction, 3 August 2004.

107 Jamaica-USA BIT Article 2; Barbados-China BIT Article 3; Barbados-Mauritius BIT Article 4; Jamaica-China BIT Article 3; Guyana-China BIT Article 3; Trinidad and Tobago-China BIT Article 4; Trinidad and Tobago-France BIT Article 4.

> treatment less favourable than that which it accords to its own or companies or to nationals or companies of any third State.[108]

In *Hochtief AG v Argentine Republic*,[109] the respondent submitted that the MFN provision in Article 3 of the Argentina-Germany BIT applied only to substantive protections under the BIT, which did not include the clause on dispute resolution in Article 10. In any event, Article 10 of the Argentina-Germany BIT imposed a mandatory 18-month submission to the national courts as a precondition of unilateral recourse to arbitration under the BIT. The issue for the tribunal was whether the MFN provision in Article 3 was in principle capable of applying to dispute settlement provisions so as to modify Article 10 of the BIT in accordance with the Argentina-Chile BIT which permitted unilateral reference of a dispute to arbitration six months after the dispute has been raised. The tribunal considered that the phrase used in the MFN clause 'the management, utilization, use and enjoyment of an investment' included recourse to dispute settlement as an aspect of the 'management' of the investment. In any event, the tribunal found that even if there were doubts as to whether the pursuit of dispute settlement procedures fell within the scope of 'management', there was no doubt that the settlement of disputes was an 'activity in connection with investments', to use the language of Article 3 of the BIT itself. Accordingly, the tribunal allowed the claimant to use the MFN provision in Article 3 of the Argentina-Germany BIT to import a more favourable dispute settlement precondition into Article 10 of that BIT, thereby ensuring that they reached the position it would have reached quicker and more cheaply without first pursuing litigation in the courts of Argentina for 18 months. The tribunal went on to note that the 18-month litigation period gave no inherent benefit, other than the interposition of a period in which the parties could refine and reflect upon their respective positions, to the other party.

However, on the facts, the tribunal ultimately ruled that the claimant in this case could not rely upon the lack of an 18-month litigation period in the Argentina-Chile BIT and ignore the fact that Article 10(2) of the Argentina-Chile BIT imposed a 'fork-in-the-road' provision; it had to rely upon the whole scheme as set out in either Article 10 of the Argentina-Chile BIT or Article 10 of the Argentina-Germany BIT. This conclusion, however, appears to be inconsistent with the conclusion arrived at in *Siemens A.G. v Argentine Republic*[110] that:

> . . . as a general matter, claiming a benefit by the operation of an MFN clause does not carry with it the acceptance of all the terms of the treaty which provides for such benefit whether or not they are considered beneficial to the party making the claim; neither does it entail that the claiming party has access to all benefits under such treaty. This will depend on the terms of the MFN clause and other terms of the treaties involved.[111]

108 See, also, Antigua and Barbuda-UK BIT Article 3; Barbados-Belgium-Luxembourg Agreement Article 3; Barbados-Canada BIT Article 3; Barbados-Cuba BIT Article 3; Barbados-UK BIT Article 3; Barbados-Venezuela BIT Article 3; Belize-Cuba BIT Article 3; Belize-UK BIT Article 3; Grenada-UK BIT Article 3; Guyana-South Korea BIT Article 3; Guyana-Switzerland BIT Article 4; Guyana-UK BIT Article 3; Haiti-UK BIT Article 3; Jamaica-Egypt BIT Article 3; Jamaica-South Korea BIT Article 3; Jamaica-UK BIT Article 3; St Lucia-UK BIT Article 3; Trinidad and Tobago-Canada BIT Article 3; Trinidad and Tobago-Cuba BIT Article 5; Trinidad and Tobago-Guatemala BIT Article 5; Trinidad and Tobago-Guatemala BIT Article 6; Trinidad and Tobago-India BIT Article 4; Trinidad and Tobago-South Korea BIT Article 3; Trinidad and Tobago-Switzerland BIT Article 4; Trinidad and Tobago-Germany BIT Article 4; Trinidad and Tobago-UK BIT Article 5.

109 ICSID Case No. ARB/07/31, Decision on Jurisdiction, 24 October 2011.

110 ICSID Case No. ARB/02/8, Decision on Jurisdiction, 3 August 2004.

111 ibid 109.

From a Caribbean perspective, given the significant encroachment on the consent of states of parties resorting to the MFN clause to import a more favourable dispute settlement mechanism is it is preferable that limits be imposed, one such being, as noted by the *Hochtief* tribunal, that if the MFN clause applies to procedural issues, the investor should bear the risk of accepting the full dispute settlement clause, including all aspects of such clause, such as the folk-in-the-road provision, which may delimit its unlimited access to dispute settlement.

F. Non-Application of MFN Treatment to Dispute Settlement: Jurisprudence

Other tribunals have adopted a more restrictive approach to the procedural use of the MFN clause.[112] The leading case in this connection is *Plama Consortium Limited v Republic of Bulgaria*.[113] Here, the claimant sought to rely on the MFN provision contained in Article 3(1) of the Bulgaria-Cyprus BIT, which provided that Contracting States shall apply to investments in its territory treatment not less favourable than that accorded to investments made by investors of third states, to import more favourable dispute settlement provisions from the Bulgaria-Finland BIT. The tribunal held that Article 3(1) could not be interpreted as providing consent to submit a dispute under the Bulgaria-Cyprus BIT to ICSID arbitration. Unlike previous tribunals, the tribunal here did not attach particular significance to the words 'treatment . . . accorded to investments'. In its view, the extension of the MFN clause to dispute settlement provisions must be clearly and unambiguously expressed, which was not the case here:

> . . . dispute resolution provisions in a specific treaty have been negotiated with a view to resolving disputes under that treaty. Contracting States cannot be presumed to have agreed that those provisions can be enlarged by incorporating dispute resolution provisions from other treaties negotiated in an entirely different context.[114]
>
> the principle with multiple exceptions as stated by the tribunal in the *Maffezini* case should instead be a different principle with one, single exception: an MFN provision in a basic treaty does not incorporate by reference dispute settlement provisions in whole or in part set forth in another treaty, unless the MFN provision in the basic treaty leaves no doubt that the Contracting Parties intended to incorporate them.[115]

112 Zachary Douglas, 'The MFN Clause in Investment Arbitration: Treaty Interpretation off the Rails' (2011) 2(1) *Journal of International Dispute Settlement* 97, 107. Douglas makes the case for a negative answer to the question of whether an MFN clause in a basic treaty ('basic treaty') can be relied upon by an investor to expand the jurisdiction of an international tribunal established in accordance with the jurisdiction provisions in the basic treaty by incorporating the more favourable 'treatment' reflected in the jurisdictional provisions in a third treaty ('comparator treaty'). Douglas considers that for an investor to assert a claim for MFN treatment, it must first accept the state's standing offer to arbitrate in accordance with the terms of the basic treaty. Douglas points out that for a claimant to assert a right to more favourable treatment by claiming through the MFN clause in the basic treaty:

> It can only do so by instituting arbitration proceedings and thus by accepting the terms of the standing offer of arbitration in the basic treaty. At that point an arbitration agreement between the claimant and the host state comes into existence. And the existence of that arbitration agreement is critical to the viability of the arbitration regime envisaged by the investment treaty.

113 ICSID Case No. ARB/03/24, Decision on Jurisdiction, 8 February 2005.

114 ibid 207.

115 ibid 223.

On the facts, it was not evident that when parties agreed to ad hoc arbitration in the Bulgaria-Cyprus BIT they intended that, by operation of the MFN clause, their specific agreement on such a dispute settlement mechanism could be replaced by a totally different dispute resolution mechanism (ICSID arbitration):

> It is one thing to add to the treatment provided in one treaty more favorable treatment provided elsewhere. It is quite another thing to replace a procedure specifically negotiated by parties with an entirely different mechanism.[116]

Against this backdrop, the tribunal was emphatic in its conclusion that:

> When concluding a multilateral or bilateral investment treaty with specific dispute resolution provisions, states cannot be expected to leave those provisions to future (partial) replacement by different dispute resolution provisions through the operation of an MFN provision, unless the States have explicitly agreed thereto (as in the case of BITs based on the UK Model BIT).[117]

The tribunal was also highly critical of the *Maffezini* award, in particular rejecting that tribunal's contention that the application of the MFN clause to dispute settlement might result in the harmonisation of investment agreements:

> The present Tribunal fails to see how harmonization of dispute settlement provisions can be achieved by reliance on the MFN provision. Rather, the 'basket of treatment' and 'self-adaptation of an MFN provision' in relation to dispute settlement provisions (as alleged by the Claimant) has as effect that an investor has the option to pick and choose provisions from the various BITs. If that were true, a host state which has not specifically agreed thereto can be confronted with a large number of permutations of dispute settlement provisions from the various BITs which it has concluded. Such a chaotic situation – actually counterproductive to harmonization – cannot be the presumed intent of Contracting parties.[118]

Ultimately, the *Plama* tribunal found that the MFN provision in the Bulgaria-Cyprus BIT could not be interpreted as providing consent to submit a dispute under the Bulgaria-Cyprus BIT to ICSID arbitration and that the claimant accordingly could not rely on dispute settlement provisions in other BITs to which Bulgaria was a Contracting Party.

The *Kiliç İnşaat İthalat İhracat Sanayi Ve Ticaret Anonim Şirketi v Turkmenistan*[119] award was also concerned with the interpretation of an MFN clause (Article II(2) of the Turkey-Turkmenistan BIT) whose terms provided for 'treatment' accorded 'in its territory' to 'investments and activities associated therewith'. The same BIT (Article VII(2)) imposed a requirement for prior recourse to the courts of Turkmenistan a condition of Turkmenistan's consent to ICSID arbitration. In these circumstances, the question for the tribunal was whether the MFN clause encompassed the BIT's dispute resolution provision so as to permit the claimant to rely on a more favourable dispute resolution provision in the Switzerland-Turkmenistan BIT. The majority held that the series of steps set out in Article VII(2) of the Turkey-Turkmenistan BIT provided for a right to arbitrate, provided that prior recourse to the courts of Turkmenistan had been complied with. In finding that this step was a condition precedent of the state's consent, and therefore a fundamental jurisdictional (as opposed to

116 ibid 209.
117 ibid 212.
118 ibid 219.
119 ICSID Case No. ARB/10/1, Award, 2 July 2013.

mere admissibility) requirement, the tribunal noted that it could only be dispensed with if it were shown that the respondent's domestic court had decided unfairly against the claimant, albeit within one year, provided that the other conditions had been met. It then interpreted the reference to 'treatment' (as opposed to 'all matters') in Article II(2) of the BIT as indicating that, at the time of the signature of the BIT, Turkey and Turkmenistan did not intend that Article VII.2's mandatory requirement for prior submission of disputes to the local courts of the host state should be over-ridden by the operation of Article II(2) MFN clause. Nor was the tribunal convinced that it would have been ineffective or futile for the claimant to have sought to comply with Article VII.2's requirement for prior recourse to the courts of Turkmenistan.

Meanwhile, *Daimler Financial Services AG v Argentine Republic*[120] was also concerned with the interpretation of an MFN clause in the Germany-Argentina BIT that applied to 'activities in connection with investments in its territory'. In response to the claimant's request that the tribunal use this MFN clause to import a more favourable dispute settlement provision from the Chile-Argentina BIT (one that did not require that the claimant wait a period of 18 months of the initiation of domestic judicial proceedings before proceeding to arbitration), the tribunal refused to do so, finding that arbitrators could not presume or artificially construct states' will as expressed in the BIT. In its view, the Contracting Parties, in the context of the applicable dispute settlement clause, sought to make each step in the dispute settlement process contingent upon the fulfilment of prior steps. In short, the requirement of judicial resolution for a period of at least 18 months constituted a treaty-based precondition to the host state's consent to arbitrate, such that it could not be bypassed or otherwise waived as a mere procedural or admissibility-related matter.

With respect to the ordinary meaning of the term 'treatment' as contained in the relevant BIT's MFN clause, the tribunal considered that this was likely meant by the Contracting Parties, at the time of the conclusion of the BIT, to refer to the host state's direct treatment of the investment and not to the conduct of international arbitration arising out of that treatment. Moreover, the words 'in its territory' as used in the MFN clause territorially limited its scope; treatment (extra-territorial dispute resolution provisions) outside the territory of the host state did not, in the tribunal's view, fall within the scope of the clause. In other words, the arguably open-textured nature of the word 'treatment' was necessarily limited by the words 'in its territory'. Even further, the failure of the MFN clause to refer to 'all matters' subject to the treaty was held to be a salient omission, which provided an indication that Germany and Argentina, at the time of the conclusion of the BIT, maintained a distinction between the host state's direct treatment of investments (substantive standards) within its territory and the international settlement of investor-state disputes (procedural standards).

A similar process of reasoning was employed by the tribunal in *ICS Inspection and Control Services Limited (United Kingdom) v The Republic of Argentina* (I),[121] a case in which the question of whether the MFN clause permitted the claimant to circumvent the required 18-month period of recourse to local courts before resorting to international arbitration by reference to other BITs that did not impose such a requirement arose for consideration. The relevant MFN clause in that case prohibited less favourable 'treatment' of third-country investors as 'regards their management, maintenance, use, enjoyment or disposal of their investments' 'in its territory'. Like the *Daimler* award, the tribunal here

120 ICSID Case No. ARB/05/1, Award, 22 August 2012.
121 UNCITRAL, PCA Case No. 2010–9, Award on Jurisdiction, 10 February 2012.

considered that the term 'treatment' did not encompass jurisdictional treatment. In its view, the term was

> most likely meant by the two Contracting Parties to refer only to the legal regime to be respected by the host State in conformity with its international obligations, conventional or customary. The settlement of disputes meanwhile remained an entirely distinct issue, covered by a separate and specific treaty provision.[122]

Meanwhile, with regard to the meaning of treatment by the host state 'in its territory', the tribunal here, like the *Daimler* award, found the MFN guarantee to be territorially limited. According to the tribunal, because international dispute resolution is non-territorial in nature (that is, not an activity inherently linked to the territory of the respondent state), treatment outside the territory of the host state could not fall within the scope of the MFN clause. As such, the claimant was unable to use the MFN clause to avoid the 18-month period of recourse to local courts before resorting to international arbitration.

The tribunal in *Beijing Urban Construction Group Co. Ltd. v Republic of Yemen*[123] was similarly asked to consider the interpretation to be ascribed to Article 3(1) of the China-Yemen BIT which prohibited less favourable 'treatment' 'in its territory with respect to the activities of their investments'. Like the awards in *Daimler* and *ICS Inspection,* the tribunal here ruled that the words 'in the territory' tied the MFN clause to activities that take place 'in the territory' associated geographically with the investment. In this connection, according to the tribunal, this geographical limitation was not consistent with the Contracting Parties giving their consent to the use of the MFN clause to expand the scope of international arbitration beyond the provisions of Article 10. In other words, the claimant could not rely on the MFN clause to import a more favourable dispute resolution mechanism because international arbitration is not itself an activity inherently linked to the territory of the respondent.

Finally, the language 'treatment' of 'capital investments' as contained in the MFN clause (Article 3) of the Argentina-Germany BIT was subject to interpretation in *Wintershall Aktiengesellschaft v Argentine Republic*.[124] The respondent's contention was that Wintershall could not rely on this provision in order to avoid compliance with the requirements set out in Article 10(2) of the Argentina-Germany BIT; that is, an eighteen-month requirement of a proceeding before local courts. The tribunal ruled that the claimant could not avoid prior compliance with Article 10(2) of the Argentina-Germany BIT before initiating arbitration proceedings. Interestingly, unlike other tribunals that placed considerable emphasis on the word 'treatment' in the MFN clause as indicative of the substantive limits of MFN treatment, the tribunal here emphasised the

> particular significance that has been attached by the Contracting States to the eighteen-month requirement in Article 10(2): it is part and parcel of Argentina's integrated 'offer' for ICSID arbitration; this 'offer' must be accepted by the investor on the same terms.[125]

In its view, the Contracting Parties could have expressly provided that they intended the MFN clause to apply to dispute settlement, but the mere fact that they did not do so meant that the ordinary presumption that the MFN clause would not operate so as to replace one

122 ibid 296.

123 ICSID Case No. ARB/14/30, Decision on Jurisdiction, 31 May 2017.

124 ICSID Case No. ARB/04/14, Award, 8 December 2008.

125 ibid 162.

means of dispute settlement with another applied. This tribunal contrasted such a finding with the UK Model BIT which expressly provides (in Article 3(3)) that 'for avoidance of doubt MFN treatment shall apply to certain specified provisions of the BIT including the dispute settlement provision':

> Because, ordinarily and without more, the prospect of an investor selecting at will from an assorted variety of options provided in other treaties negotiated with other parties under different circumstances, dislodges the dispute resolution provision in the basic treaty itself – unless of course the MFN Clause in the basic treaty clearly and unambiguously indicates that it should be so interpreted: which is not so in the present case.[126]

In short, on the facts, in the absence of language or context to suggest the contrary, the tribunal considered that the ordinary meaning of 'investments shall be accorded treatment no less favourable than that accorded to investments made by investors of any third State' referred to the investor's substantive rights with respect to the investments are to be treated no less favourable than under a BIT between the host state and a third state:

> It is one thing to stipulate that the investor is to have the benefit of MFN treatment but quite another to use an MFN clause in a BIT to bypass a limitation in the settlement resolution clause of the very same BIT when the Parties have not chosen language in the MFN clause showing an intention to do this.[127]

In any event, the MFN clause in this case did not refer to 'treatment' with respect to '*all matters* covered by this treaty' (in contrast to *Maffezini*), which the tribunal here found to also be instructive in support of its finding that the claimant could not rely on the MFN clause in Article 3 of the Argentine-Germany BIT in order to avoid compliance with the requirements set forth in Article 10(2) of the BIT.

G. Using MFN to Import Consent to ICSID

Although the tribunal in *Maffezini* considered that the MFN clause can be used to import more favourable dispute settlement provisions, it made it clear that this is not an unlimited proposition:

> the beneficiary of the clause should not be able to override public policy considerations that the contracting parties might have envisaged as fundamental conditions for their acceptance of the agreement in question, particularly if the beneficiary is a private investor, as will often be the case.[128]

One of these conditions that was identified by the tribunal in *Maffezini* was this: 'if the agreement provides for a particular arbitration forum, such as ICSID, for example, this option cannot be changed by invoking the clause, in order to refer the dispute to a different system of arbitration'.[129]

126 ibid 167.
127 ibid 168.
128 *Emilio Agustín Maffezini v The Kingdom of Spain*, ICSID Case No. ARB/97/7, Decision on Jurisdiction, 25 January 2000.
129 ibid 63.

This precaution has, however, proved difficult to apply in practice, as evidenced by the divergent jurisprudential approaches countenanced by arbitral tribunals to date. On one end of the spectrum, the decision in *Itisaluna Iraq LLC and others v Republic of Iraq*,[130] stands for the proposition that, by reason of public policy considerations, the MFN clause may not be relied upon to import consent to ICSID arbitration where no such consent exists in the base treaty. Here, the claimants' case was that Article 17 of the OIC Agreement constituted the respondent's consent in writing to submit a dispute to arbitration in general terms and that, by operation of Article 8(1) of the OIC Agreement (the MFN clause), the respondent's consent in writing to submit the dispute to ICSID arbitration in Article 17(4)(a) of the Iraq-Japan BIT could be read into the OIC Agreement. Article 4 of the OIC Agreement provided:

> 1. Each Contracting Party shall in its Area accord to investors of the other Contracting Party and to their investments treatment no less favourable than the treatment it accords in like circumstances to investors of a non-Contracting Party and to their investments with respect to investment activities.
>
> . . .
>
> 3. It is understood that *the treatment referred to in paragraph 1 does not include treatment accorded to investors of a non-Contracting Party and their investments by provisions concerning the settlement of investment disputes such as the mechanism set out in Article 17*, that are provided for in other international agreements between a Contracting Party and a non-Contracting Party.

In the tribunal's view, the effect of Article 8(1) of the OIC Agreement was to preclude a foreign investor from relying on the MFN clause to invoke the dispute settlement provisions in some other investment treaty. It noted that the express wording of the provision had to be respected so as to guard 'against the risks of overreach.'[131] Commenting on *Maffezini*, a case in which the tribunal there explained that the operation of the MFN clause has some important limits arising from public policy considerations, the tribunal in *Itisaluna Iraq LLC* emphatically ruled that:

> These are wise words that should be well heeded in the sometimes headlong rush to push the boundaries of investor-State dispute settlement and broaden the reach of the MFN principle as an instrument to this end. The Tribunal considers them a touchstone in the context of the present case. As will be readily apparent, three of the situations expressly envisaged in abstract terms by the Maffezini tribunal 20 years ago as limiting the application of the MFN principle to dispute settlement arrangements on grounds of public policy either address or approach the situation with which the Tribunal is faced in the circumstances of the present case.[132]

The tribunal further ruled that:

> . . . there are manifest public policy considerations going to issues of systemic overreach that compel a conclusion that the MFN clause in the OIC Agreement cannot be relied upon to incorporate into the OIC Agreement an ICSID consent to arbitration clause from an unrelated bilateral investment treaty concluded by one of the OIC Contracting Parties alone. In the words of the *Maffezini* tribunal, with which this Tribunal is happy to agree, 'a distinction has to be made between the legitimate extension of rights and benefits by means of the operation of the clause, on the one hand, and disruptive treaty-shopping that would play havoc with the policy objectives of underlying specific treaty provisions, on the other hand'.[133]

130 ICSID Case No. ARB/17/10, Award, 3 April 2020.
131 ibid 208.
132 ibid 212.
133 ibid 220.

On the facts, the tribunal found it instructive that nowhere in the OIC Agreement was ICSID arbitration provided for, although the parties could very easily have done so. The necessary implication from this, according to the tribunal, was that this omission was a conscious decision to prevent the MFN clause from being used to import consent to ICSID arbitration where it did not exist in the base treaty:

> While, for example, it may be said (as in Le Chèque Déjeuner) that the MFN principle is capable of enlarging the reach of ICSID arbitration to which consent has already been given in the principal treaty, the Tribunal does not consider that the MFN principle can properly be used to derive from another treaty consent to ICSID arbitration that is not only absent from the principal treaty but evidently intentionally so, given the bespoke nature of the dispute settlement arrangements in the principal treaty.[134]

Despite this pragmatic and policy-oriented approach, which arguably respects the will of states parties and gives premium to the importance of as a consent to a arbitration as jurisdictional threshold, at least one other tribunal – in *Garanti Koza LLP v Turkmenistan*[135] – has adopted the position that consent to ICSID arbitration can be imported via an MFN clause. In this case, the question arose as to whether the MFN clause contained in Article 3 of the UK-Turkmenistan BIT should be applied to the investor-state arbitration provision contained in Article 8, given the specific language of Article 3(3) of the UK-Turkmenistan BIT, which provided:

> (3) For the avoidance of doubt, it is confirmed that the treatment provided for in paragraphs (1) and (2) above *shall apply to the provisions of Articles 1 to 11 of this Agreement.*

Article 8(2), meanwhile, provided that the fall-back option, failing a case-specific agreement to use ICSID arbitration or arbitration before the Court of Arbitration of the International Chamber of Commerce, was UNCITRAL arbitration.

While the majority accepted that, strictly speaking, Turkmenistan had consented to international arbitration with UK investors, but not to ICSID Arbitration, they held that great weight had to be given the parties' express agreement for the MFN clause to apply to Articles 1 to 11 (which included Article 8 on dispute resolution). In their view, refusing to apply the MFN clause in these circumstances would deprive it of *effet utile*.[136] Having not found it 'conceptually difficult'[137] for the claimant to import a provision for ICSID arbitration from one treaty to another by operation of the MFN clause of a treaty, the majority held that the MFN provision in the UK-Turkmenistan BIT effectively replaced Article 8(2) of the UK-Turkmenistan BIT with Article 8(2) of the Switzerland-Turkmenistan BIT, which required no case-specific consent. It accordingly concluded that:

> there is no reason why Turkmenistan's consent to ICSID Arbitration in its BIT with Switzerland may not be relied upon by a U.K. investor, if the provision for ICSID Arbitration or an unrestricted choice between ICSID Arbitration and UNCITRAL Arbitration provides treatment more favorable to the investor than the treatment provided by the base treaty.[138]

In short, the claimant here was able to use the MFN clause to avail itself of that more favourable treatment by commencing ICSID arbitration.

134 ibid 221.
135 ICSID Case No. ARB/11/20, Decision on the Objection to Jurisdiction for Lack of Consent, 3 July 2013.
136 ibid 54.
137 ibid 73.
138 ibid 79.

However, in a powerful dissent, arbitrator Laurence Boisson de Chazournes considered that neither the interpretation of the UK-Turkmenistan BIT nor investment law practice could lead to the conclusion that the MFN clause could replace consent to UNCITRAL arbitration with ICSID arbitration:

> . . . The role of the MFN clause is not to substitute for a lack of consent, but to ensure that the consent given is implemented in the most favourable manner to the individual investor entitled to protection, as compared to the treatment given to other such individuals in treaties with third countries. The *National Grid v Argentina* tribunal correctly noted that an MFN clause is not a basis for creating consent to ICSID arbitration when none exists.[139]

He went on to emphasise that, as a matter of policy:

> . . . If the requirement of consent to ICSID arbitration, as stipulated in Article 8 of the UK-Turkmenistan BIT, as well as in the ICSID Convention itself, could easily be put aside because of the interplay of MFN clauses, there would be a threat to the entire system of investor-state arbitration. BITs providing for ICSID jurisdiction should abide by the ICSID Convention.
>
> Granting Article 3(3) of the UK-Turkmenistan BIT such extensive effect as to allow for consent to ICSID through incorporation by reference in the frame of a treaty that does not allow this, would have the effect of 'replac[ing] a procedure specifically negotiated by parties with an entirely different mechanism' or 'system of arbitration'. It would involve a forum-shopping attitude that bypasses the consent requirement of the Respondent while running against the fundamental principles of international adjudication.[140]
>
> No attempt to establish consent to ICSID arbitration under an MFN clause is possible, since it will have the perverse effect of replacing actual non-consent by virtual consent. That would go against the fundamental pillars of the law of treaties (principle of consent, *pacta sunt servanda*, etc.) as well as against the pillars of the ICSID system.[141]

While the arguments advanced by the dissenting arbitrator are compelling, it is arguable that the majority's ruling is equally compelling given that the relevant MFN clause was worded in a manner indicative of its explicit application to dispute settlement. Had this not been the case, the policy-related arguments advanced by the dissenting arbitrator relating to the unmalleable nature of consent to arbitration would have been even stronger.

H. Reflections

The foregoing discussion aptly demonstrates that the law in this area is in a regrettable state of flux.[142] Indeed, the approach countenanced by the *Maffezini* line of cases raises

139 ibid (dissenting opinion) 61.

140 ibid 62–63.

141 ibid 64.

142 Douglas has observed that '[t]he *Maffezini* decision represents a point of departure from the existing conception of the function of MFN clauses in international law', and that investment treaty tribunals which have followed this approach

> have attempted to convert the fiction of automatic incorporation into a reality by pretending that the terms of their own jurisdiction in the basic treaty are rewritten before the commencement of proceedings by reference to the provisions of a third treaty. The claimant/investor is not making a claim for MFN treatment but is rather being permitted to enforce this fiction. This is contrary to general principle and authority . . . .

real concerns, as noted by the tribunal in *Salini Costruttori S.p.A. and Italstrade S.p.A. v Hashemite Kingdom of Jordan,*[143] when it expressed the view that:

> the precautions [relating to public policy limitations on the use of MFN to import more favourable dispute settlement provision] taken by the authors of the award [in *Maffezini*] may in practice prove difficult to apply, thereby adding more uncertainties to the risk of 'treaty shopping'.[144]

Similar concerns were expressed in *Sanum Investments Limited v Lao People's Democratic Republic,*[145] a case in which the tribunal emphatically rejected the pro-procedural line of MFN jurisprudence on the basis that:

> Read[ing] into that clause a dispute settlement provision to cover all protections under the Treaty when the Treaty itself provides for very limited access to international arbitration would result in a substantial re-write of the Treaty and an extension of the States Parties' consent to arbitration beyond what may be assumed to have been their intention, given the limited reach of the Treaty protection and dispute settlement clauses.[146]

Perhaps the most incisive critique of *Maffezini* and, indeed, the pro-procedural line of MFN jurisprudence was proffered by Arbitrator Stern in her powerful dissenting opinion in *Impregilo S.p.A. v Argentine Republic*.147 Stern criticised *Maffezini* for opening the floodgates to the controversial procedural use of MFN clauses, noting that the approach countenanced in that case 'does not really make any sense'.148 In agreeing with the *Plama* award, Stern was strongly convinced that MFN clauses should not apply to dispute settlement mechanisms, thereby rejecting the presumption emanating from the *Maffezini* line of cases that dispute resolution provisions invariably fall within the scope of an MFN provision in a BIT, unless the contrary is plainly demonstrated.149 Instead, she expressed her support for the second line of cases on the reverse presumption that dispute resolution provisions would never fall within the scope of an MFN provision in a BIT, unless the contrary is plainly demonstrated. In her view, if there is an MFN clause expressly including the dispute settlement procedures or expressly excluding them, there is no need for an interpretation. However, where no such circumstances exist, it is in her view unprincipled to replace a procedure specifically negotiated by the parties with an entirely different mechanism.

In response to the cases discussed above that seemed to suggest the term 'treatment' as used in the MFN clause applies to dispute settlement provisions, Stern contended that

---

See Zachary Douglas, 'The MFN clause in investment arbitration: treaty interpretation off the rails' (2011) 2(1) *Journal of International Dispute Settlement* 97, 102.

143 ICSID Case No. ARB/02/13, Decision on Jurisdiction, 29 November 2004, para. 115.

144 ibid 115.

145 UNCITRAL, PCA Case No. 2013–13, Decision on Jurisdiction, 13 December 2013.

146 ibid 358.

147 ICSID Case No. ARB/07/17, Concurring and Dissenting Opinion of Professor Brigitte Stern), 21 June 2011.

148 ibid 102.

149 Stern worries that the international investment treaty arbitration stands likely to be converted from a scheme of bilateral relationships into a multilateral system nearing compulsory arbitral jurisdiction. See Brigitte Stern, 'ICSID Arbitration and the State's Increasingly Remote Consent: Apropos the *Maffezini* Case' in Steve Charnovitz, Debra Steger, and Peter Van den Bossche (eds), *Law in The Service of Human Dignity: Essays in Honour of Florentino Feliciano* (CUP 2009) 252–59.

'treatment' instead refers to the protection of substantive rights, and did not encompass any access to specific procedures of settlement of disputes concerning these rights, which are always an exception in international law.[150] In her view, even though, on a subjective plane, international arbitration, on which it is well-known that foreign investors rely heavily for their protection, is considered by those foreign investors as a significant and important aspect of the treatment their investments receive from a host state, such subjective perception could not be reconciled with legal analysis. More pointedly, she notes that substantive treatment and jurisdictional treatment are to be regarded differently under the *ejusdem generis* principle, precisely because the qualifying conditions in order to benefit from each type of treatment are not the same.

Meanwhile, with respect to the cases discussed above that seemed to suggest the term 'all matters covered by this treaty' as used in the MFN clause applies to dispute settlement provisions, Stern, relying on the award in *Berschader v Russia*,[151] contended that such language was not unambiguous. In her view, while such language applies to the substantive standards of protection an investor can enjoy, it cannot modify the fundamental conditions for the enjoyment of such rights, in other words, 'the insuperable conditions of access to the rights granted in the BIT'.[152] In other words, just as an MFN clause cannot be utilised, for example, to enlarge the scope of the definition of an 'investment' – although it is clearly a matter regulated by the treaty – and grant the rights under the treaty to companies that are established under the law of the state but do not have their seat in its territory, the conditions shaping the host state's consent to arbitration must be fulfilled before a right to arbitration can arise. In this connection, the reference to 'all matters' in the MFN clause could not, at least in her view, be taken literally, and, in any event, cannot change the conditions of access to arbitration:

> Just as an MFN clause cannot change the conditions *ratione personae, ratione materiae, and ratione temporis*, as has just been demonstrated, it must be equally true that an MFN clause cannot change the condition *ratione voluntatis*, which is a qualifying condition for the enjoyment of the jurisdictional rights open for the protection of substantial rights.[153]

Ultimately, Stern was convinced that despite a chorus of arbitral awards to the contrary in recent years, an MFN clause cannot enlarge the scope of the basic treaty's right to international arbitration. In her view, the MFN clause cannot be used to grant access to international arbitration when this is not possible under the conditions provided for in the basic treaty as if the qualifying conditions of access to a right could be modified this would completely change the scope of the BIT:

> If therefore all conditions shaping the State's consent are considered jurisdictional prerequisites to the existence of a right to international arbitration, it follows that an MFN clause will never be able to change the parameters of such consent to a mechanism of international arbitration. All the conditions – whether a waiting period or a condition of exhaustion of local remedies, whether a restriction of consent to a certain type of arbitration, whether a restriction

150 *Impregilo S.p.A. v Argentine Republic,* ICSID Case No. ARB/07/17, Concurring and Dissenting Opinion of Professor Brigitte Stern, 21 June 2011, para. 27.

151 SCC Case No. 080/2004, Award, 21 April 2006.

152 *Impregilo S.p.A. v Argentine Republic*, ICSID Case No. ARB/07/17, Concurring and Dissenting Opinion of Professor Brigitte Stern, 21 June 2011, para. 47.

153 ibid 78.

on the scope of the arbitration – are jurisdictional conditions to the State's consent to arbitration, that cannot be displaced by an MFN clause.[154]

If the offer to arbitrate under certain conditions, which is already made to a broad category of investors which are not known in advance by the State, could also be modified as far as the conditions shaping such consent are concerned, the 'cornerstone of ICSID arbitration' would look as a completely inchoate consent. A consent that is given by a State to a defined but undetermined category of investors, which would moreover also be undefined as far as the conditions under which it is given or its scope are concerned, and would depend on the vagaries of possible other treaties entered into by the State, would not be a clear consent at all, it would be a versatile consent, it could even be said that it would not be a consent at all.[155]

Unless specifically stated to the contrary, the qualifying conditions put by the State in order to accept to be sued directly on the international level by foreign investors cannot be displaced by an MFN clause, and a conditional right to ICSID cannot magically be transformed into an unconditional right by the grace of the MFN clause. The access to the right as provided in the basic treaty cannot be modified through an MFN clause. Any other solution comports in my view great dangers.[156]

Despite Arbitrator Stern's principled, compelling, and uncompromising comments, however, it must be remembered it is unlikely that an ICSID award countenancing a pro-procedural approach to the use of the MFN clause will be successfully annulled, if challenged on the basis of a manifest excess of powers, a serious departure from a fundamental rule of procedure or a failure to state reasons. Indeed, the committee in *Suez, Sociedad General de Aguas de Barcelona, S.A. and Vivendi Universal, S.A. v Argentine Republic*[157] made it clear that even if a respondent may not be satisfied with a tribunal's findings on the procedural use of the MFN clause, any such disagreement does not permit an annulment of the tribunal's decision in the light of the fact that:

The Committee is aware that, contrary to what a recital of the above suggests and as recognized by the tribunals in the above mentioned cases as well as by other tribunals dealing with the same question, ICSID jurisprudence is far from unanimous on the question whether MFN clauses can be invoked by investors to benefit from more favorable dispute settlement provisions in third-State treaties. However, while the MFN clause in Article IV(2) of the Treaty may well be susceptible to an interpretation that is different from that given by the Tribunal in the present case, it is not for this Committee to re-decide the case but rather to assess whether the Tribunal's decision fulfils any of the annulment grounds advanced by Respondent.[158]

A similar outcome was arrived at by the committee in *Impregilo v Argentina*,[159] which found that, as the application of an MFN clause to dispute settlement provisions is a complex and debated issue, '[n]either applying an MFN clause to jurisdictional issues nor refusing to apply it to assume jurisdiction may be considered, per se, as a manifest excess of powers.'[160]

154 ibid 88.
155 ibid 98.
156 ibid 99.
157 Formerly *Aguas Argentinas, S.A., Suez, Sociedad General de Aguas de Barcelona, S.A. and Vivendi Universal, S.A. v Argentine Re*, ICSID Case No. ARB/03/19, Annulment Decision, 5 May 2017.
158 ibid 252.
159 ICSID Case No. ARB/07/17, Decision of the ad hoc Committee on the Application for Annulment, 24 January 2014.
160 ibid 140.

In the same vein, the committee in *Daimler v Argentina*[161] observed that 'when more than one interpretation is possible, an award cannot be annulled on the ground that it suffers from an exercise of excess of powers, much less a manifest excess of powers.'[162]

I. Treaty-based Reservations

Some Caribbean IIAs expressly provide for reservations;[163] that is, situations in respect of which treatment that is less favourable to a similarly placed third-country investor will not be regarded as unlawful in breach of the MFN standard. By way of example, Article II(3) of the Barbados-Canada BIT provides:

> Each Contracting Party shall permit establishment of a new business enterprise or acquisition of an existing business enterprise or a share of such enterprise by investors or prospective investors of the other Contracting Party on a basis no less favourable than that which, in like circumstances, it permits such acquisition or establishment by:
>
> a. its own investors or prospective investors; or
> b. investors or prospective investors of any third state.
>
> **Establishment and Exceptions to MFN**
>
> 1. Each Contracting Party shall grant to investments, or returns of investors of the other Contracting Party, treatment no less favourable than that which, in like circumstances, it grants to investments or returns of investors of any third State.
> 2. Each Contracting Party shall grant investors of the other Contracting Party, as regards their management, use, enjoyment or disposal of their investments or returns, treatment no less favourable than that which, in like circumstances, it grants to investors of any third State.
> 3. Subparagraph (3) (b) of Article II and paragraphs (1) and (2) of this Article do not apply to treatment by a Contracting Party pursuant to any existing or future bilateral or multilateral agreement:
>   a. establishing, strengthening or expanding a free trade area, common market or customs union;
>   b. negotiated within the framework of the GATT or its successor organization and liberalizing trade in services; or

161 ICSID Case No. ARB/05/1, Decision on Annulment, 7 January 2015.

162 ibid 187.

163 Antigua and Barbuda-Germany BIT Article 3; Barbados-Canada BIT Article 3; Barbados-China BIT Article 3; Barbados-Germany BIT Article 3; Barbados-Mauritius BIT Article 4; Barbados-Switzerland BIT Article 3; Belize-China BIT Article 3; Belize-El Salvador BIT Article 3; Belize-The Netherlands BIT Article 3; Dominica-Germany BIT Article 3; Guyana-Brazil BIT Article 6; Guyana-China BIT Article 3; Guyana-Germany BIT Article 3; Guyana-South Korea BIT Article 3; Guyana-Switzerland BIT Article 4; Jamaica-Argentina BIT Article 3; Jamaica-China BIT Article 3; Jamaica-Indonesia BIT Article 3; Jamaica-South Korea BIT Article 3; Jamaica-The Netherlands BIT Article 3; St Lucia-Germany BIT Article 3; Suriname-Brazil BIT Article 6; Suriname-The Netherlands BIT Article 3; SVG-Germany BIT Article 3; Trinidad and Tobago-Canada BIT Article 3; Trinidad and Tobago-China BIT Article 4; Trinidad and Tobago-Cuba BIT Article 5; Trinidad and Tobago-France BIT Article 4; Trinidad and Tobago-Guatemala BIT Article 6; Trinidad and Tobago-India BIT Article 4; Trinidad and Tobago-South Korea BIT Article 3; Trinidad and Tobago-Switzerland BIT Article 4.

c. relating to:
   i. aviation;
   ii. telecommunications transport networks and telecommunications transport services;
   iii. fisheries;
   iv. maritime matters, including salvage; or
   v. financial services.

Where the treatment meted out against a similarly placed third-country investor falls within any of these reservations, such conduct would be exempted from being held to be inconsistent with the MFN standard. In this context, when interpreting reservations, arbitral tribunals do not countenance a restrictive interpretation; rather, as noted by the tribunal in *Mobil v Canada*:[164]

> the task of ascertaining the meaning of a reservation, like the task of interpreting any other treaty text, involves understanding the intention of the NAFTA Parties, and it is to be achieved by following the customary rules of interpretation of public international law, as reflected in Articles 31 and 32 of the VCLT.[165]

The case of *Mesa Power Group LLC v Government of Canada*[166] illustrates tribunals' approach to the interpretation of reservations in the context of the MFN standard. Here, the Government of Ontario enacted the Green Energy and Green Economy Act, 2009 to build a green economy. It authorised the Minister of Energy to direct the Ontario Power Authority (OPA) to establish a Feed-in Tariff Programme (FIT), which was described as a procurement programme, aimed at procuring energy from renewable energy sources under certain circumstances. By doing so, the Government not only attracted investors by somewhat mitigating the commercial risks associated with developing renewable energy, but also ensured that Ontario's renewable energy development would be sufficiently robust to meet its future energy needs. The claimant, a US company adversely affected by the measure, argued that the MFN provision (Article 1103 NAFTA), read together with the Canada-Czech FIPA or the Slovak Treaty, precluded the application of Article 1108 of NAFTA. The tribunal, however, held that the FIT Programme constituted 'procurement' by a Party or state enterprise under Article 1108 of NAFTA, and that, therefore, the MFN provision enshrined in Article 1103 could not apply. In other words, the claimant could not rely on that provision to import the allegedly more favourable provisions of the Canada-Czech FIPA or of the Slovak Treaty. In the tribunal's view, where an express reservation to MFN treatment exists in an IIA, an investor cannot rely on the MFN clause to avoid the obligation, as this would be contrary to the rule of *effet utile* in treaty interpretation. In short, once it is established that the reservation applies, in this case the 'procurement' exception, the MFN does not apply.

J. Justifications

Aside from the explicit and specific reservations that appear in Caribbean IIAs, only one Caribbean BIT provides for a general justification defence – namely, that, in exceptional circumstances where good reasons exist, a state may afford less favourable treatment to investments or returns of investors of third states: Article 3 of the Antigua and Barbuda-UK BIT:

164 ICSID Case No. ARB(AF)/07/4, Decision on Liability, 22 May 2012.
165 ibid 254.
166 UNCITRAL, PCA Case No. 2012–17, Award, 24 March 2016.

(1) Neither Contracting Party shall in its territory subject investments or returns nationals or companies of the other Contracting Party to treatment less favourable that which it accords to investments or returns of its own nationals or companies or investments or returns of nationals or companies of any third State.
(2) Neither Contracting Party shall in its territory subject nationals or companies of other Contracting Party, as regards their management, use, enjoyment or disposal of investments, to treatment less favourable than that which it accords to its own nationals or companies or to nationals or companies of any third State.
(3) Notwithstanding paragraphs (1) and (2) above, in exceptional circumstances Contracting Party is entitled *in specific cases and on special grounds to give treatment to the nationals or companies of a third State where there is good reason justify this.*

This provision not only requires the provision of the host state of 'good reasons', but also that the treatment meted out is limited to specific cases and special grounds. While there are no cases that have interpreted this particular provision to date, the case of *Apotex Holdings Inc. and Apotex Inc. v United States of America*[167] arguably offers some general insights. Although the tribunal accepted that two foreign companies, Teva and Sandoz, were treated more favourably than the claimants in that the relevant US legal and regulatory regime with respect to import alerts and detention (without physical examination) of certain products applied more preferentially to the former but not the latter, the Food and Drug Administration's (FDA) differential treatment was materially influenced by the FDA's *genuine concerns over shortages of essential drugs* manufactured at Teva's Jerusalem facility intended for shipment and sale in the USA. In the tribunal's view, there was no evidence that the FDA especially targeted or sought to discriminate against the claimants, based on the public speeches of its senior officers. The treatment meted out was done in good faith and in a non-arbitrary manner. In dismissing the claimants' claim, the tribunal considered that Teva and Sandoz were not in like circumstances to the claimants within the meaning of NAFTA Article 1103.

In short, then, it appears that a justification for a failure to afford MFN treatment may only be countenanced if the treaty allows for such a justification, the reason for the less favourable treatment is a good one (i.e. a genuine rationale), and such treatment is necessitated by special circumstances.

CONCLUSION

The jurisprudence surrounding non-discrimination standards in international investment law reveals a complex and often inconsistent landscape that poses challenges for Caribbean states as they navigate their obligations under IIAs. More pointedly, the national treatment standard, while appearing straightforward in principle, has proven difficult to apply in practice, with tribunals adopting varying methodologies for determining 'like circumstances' and 'less favourable treatment'. The fragmented approaches countenanced by extant jurisprudence – ranging from narrow same-sector analyses to broader cross-industry comparisons – create uncertainty for Caribbean states seeking to understand the boundaries of their regulatory space while fulfilling their international commitments. Meanwhile, the MFN

167 ICSID Case No. ARB(AF)/12/1, Award, 25 August 2014.

standard presents even greater complexity, particularly regarding its procedural application to more favourable dispute settlement mechanisms. The ongoing contestation between liberal *Maffezini* line of cases and the more restrictive *Plama* line of cases has created a jurisprudential schism that leaves Caribbean states uncertain about the scope of their consent to arbitration. This uncertainty is particularly problematic for these small island developing states with limited geopolitical power, as the procedural use of MFN clauses can effectively transform carefully negotiated dispute settlement arrangements into unpredictable 'menus' of arbitral options selected by investors through treaty shopping.

For Caribbean policymakers, the extant state of affairs relative to the application of the non-discrimination principle underscores the critical importance of precise treaty drafting. Indeed, this chapter has demonstrated that explicit language regarding the inclusion or exclusion of dispute settlement provisions from MFN clauses can provide much-needed certainty, as evidenced by provisions in agreements such as the Guyana-Brazil BIT. Similarly, carefully crafted reservations and exceptions offer essential policy space for legitimate regulatory objectives while maintaining investor protection.

CHAPTER 4

THE GUARANTEE AGAINST EXPROPRIATION

INTRODUCTION

Expropriation is arguably one of the most serious interferences with the property rights of foreign investors.[1] Whether it is a case in which the investor is deprived of the title of his or her asset or a case in which the foreign investor is substantially deprived of the economic value of his or her asset while retaining ownership, expropriation casts a negative light on the credibility of states that so engage in such conduct. That said, a finding of unlawful expropriation in international law is not automatic, as states do in fact have a sovereign right to 'take' property belonging to a foreign investor,[2] provided that certain conditions are satisfied – a public purpose, due process, non-discrimination, and the payment of compensation. States may also be exempt from liability in circumstances where they are able to invoke their 'police powers', otherwise known as the exercise of a 'legitimate taking'.[3] While there have not been a significant number of Caribbean cases in which expropriation has been alleged, much less proved, in the light of the fact that most regional IIAs provide for a guarantee against expropriation,[4] it is essential that researchers, students and practitioners appreciate the nature of an 'expropriatory act'; the distinction between direct and indirect expropriation; the conditions under which an expropriation may be deemed to be lawful; and the circumstances in which a state may exercise its police powers. This chapter critically addresses these issues.

1 Ursula Kriebaum and August Reinisch, *Property, Right to, International Protection* (Max Planck Encyclopedia of Public International Law 2009).

2 Gary Minda, 'The Dilemmas of Property and Sovereignty in the Postmodern Era: The Regulatory Takings Problem' (1991) 62 *University of Colorado Law Review* 599.

3 Noam Zamir, 'The Police Powers Doctrine in International Investment Law' (2017) 14 *Manchester Journal of International Economic Law* 318.

4 Article 4 Antigua and Barbuda-Germany BIT; Article 5 Antigua and Barbuda-UK BIT; Article VIII Barbados-Canada BIT; Article 4 Barbados-China BIT; Article 5 Barbados-Cuba BIT; Article 4 Barbados-Germany BIT; Article 5 Barbados-Mauritius BIT; Article 5 Barbados-Switzerland BIT; Article 5 Barbados-Venezuela BIT; Article 5 Belize-China BIT; Article 5 Belize-Cuba BIT; Article 5 Belize-El Salvador BIT; Article 5 Belize-UK BIT; Article 5 Dominica-UK BIT; Article 4 Dominica-Germany BIT; Article 3 Haiti-Germany BIT; Article 5 Grenada-UK BIT; Article III Grenada-USA BIT; Article 7 Guyana-Brazil BIT; Article 4 Guyana-China BIT; Article 4 Guyana-Germany BIT; Article 5 Guyana-South Korea BIT; Article 6 Guyana-Switzerland BIT; Article 5 Guyana-UK BIT; Article 5 Haiti-UK BIT; Article III Haiti-USA BIT; Article 4 Jamaica-Argentina BIT; Article 4 Jamaica-China BIT; Article 5 Jamaica-Egypt BIT; Article 4 Jamaica-Germany BIT; Article IV Jamaica-Indonesia BIT; Article 5 Jamaica-South Korea BIT; Article 5 Jamaica-Switzerland BIT; Article 6 Jamaica-The Netherlands BIT; Article III Jamaica-USA BIT; Article 4 St Lucia-Germany BIT; Article 5 St Lucia-UK BIT; Article 7 Suriname-Brazil BIT; Article 6 Suriname-Netherlands BIT; Article 4 St Vincent and the Grenadines-Germany BIT; Article VI St Vincent and the Grenadines-Taiwan BIT; Article VIII Trinidad and Tobago-Canada BIT; Article 6 Trinidad and Tobago-China BIT; Article 7 Trinidad and Tobago-Cuba BIT; Article 5 Trinidad and Tobago-France BIT; Article 8 Trinidad and Tobago-Guatemala BIT; Article 5 Trinidad and Tobago-India BIT; Article 5 Trinidad and Tobago-South Korea BIT; Article 6 Trinidad and Tobago-Switzerland BIT; Article 5 Trinidad and Tobago-Germany BIT; Article 7 Trinidad and Tobago-UK BIT; Article III Trinidad and Tobago-USA BIT.

DOI: 10.4324/9781003734185-4

BACKGROUND AND CONTEXT

The guarantee against expropriation is one of the oldest and foundational rules of international law.[5] Even before the normalization of Bilateral Investment Treaties (BITs), the guarantee against expropriation appeared in Friendship, Commerce and Navigation (FCN) Treaties.[6] While acknowledging that states have the sovereign right to regulate property located in their jurisdiction, the guarantee against expropriation seeks to protect investors against the whims and fancies of despotic and protectionist regimes that seek to take foreign-owned property without affording due process guarantees.[7] A typical expropriation clause reads as follows:

1. Investments of investors of either Party shall not be nationalised, expropriated or subjected to measures having effects equivalent to nationalisation or expropriation (hereafter referred to as 'expropriation') in the territory of the other Party except in the social interest or public purpose, under due process of law, on a nondiscriminatory basis and against prompt, adequate and effective compensation. Such compensation shall amount to the market value of the investment expropriated immediately before the expropriation or before the impending expropriation became public knowledge, whichever is earlier. It shall be made without delay and shall include interest at the normal banking rate until the date of payment, and shall be effectively realisable. Measures to settle and satisfy the compensation shall be taken at the latest at the moment of expropriation or nationalisation.
2. The investor affected thereby shall have a right, under the law of either Party making the expropriation, to prompt review, by judicial or other independent authorities of the Party in accordance with the procedures established by the law of that Party, of his or its case and of the valuation of his or its investment in accordance with the principles set out in this Article.[8]

Although FET is by far the most prominent ISDS standard of protection invoked in arbitration proceedings today, this was not always the case. In fact, in the 1960s–1980s, unlawful expropriation was alleged in significantly more cases than FET, particularly in the oil and gas sector.[9] Indeed, after the Declaration of Permanent Sovereignty of Natural Resources[10] was adopted, and in an attempt to resist neo-liberalisation, many oil-rich countries, including Kuwait, Saudi Arabia, and Venezuela, sought to take property belonging to foreign

5 Rudolf Dolzer, 'New Foundations of the Law of Expropriation of Alien Property' (1981) 75(3) *American Journal of International Law* 553.

6 Kenneth Vandevelde, *The First Bilateral Investment Treaties: US Postwar Friendship, Commerce and Navigation Treaties* (OUP 2017) 210.

7 Kevin Gray, 'Human Property Rights: The Politics of Expropriation' (2005) 16(3) *Stellenbosch Law Review* 398.

8 Article 5 Belize-El Salvador BIT.

9 George Joffé, et al., 'Expropriation of Oil and Gas Investments: Historical, Legal and Economic Perspectives in a New Age of Resource Nationalism' (2009) 2(1) *Journal of World Energy Law & Business* 3.

10 Permanent Sovereignty over Natural Resources General Assembly resolution 1803 (XVII) New York, 14 December 1962.

investors, whether through nationalisation or confiscation.[11] Nationalisation is the taking of investors' property by the state itself, while privatisation is arguably more egregious in that it involves the taking of investors' property and the vesting of said property in private, third parties.[12]

In more recent years, IIAs, and by extension arbitral tribunals, have added to the list of expropriatory conduct behaviour 'tantamount to expropriation',[13] and 'creeping expropriation'.[14] The former arises from conduct that, while not formally described as expropriatory, nonetheless has the effect of permanently and substantially depriving the investor of the value of its assets,[15] while the latter covers a series of offending behaviour which culminate in the substantial deprivation of the investor's assets, even though the individual acts themselves, taken in isolation, do not have this effect.[16] These types of conduct have, in a significant number of cases, been deemed to be compensable forms of expropriation, warranting the award of damages.[17] That said, the award of damages does not automatically follow from a taking; damages will only follow from a finding of an unlawful expropriation – that is, if one or more of the four conditions for legality of an expropriation is not satisfied – a public purpose, due process, non-discrimination, and the payment of compensation.[18] Damages will also not flow from an expropriation where there is no demonstrable economic loss resulting from same.[19]

In *Bayindir v Pakistan,*[20] the tribunal outlined the steps to be followed when assessing whether an allegation of expropriation has been made out. It noted that the first step is to identify the relevant assets allegedly expropriated. Having identified the assets, the next step is to identify the allegedly expropriatory conduct. The third step in this inquiry involves examining whether the alleged interference with the property or the rights of the investor has been made in the state's exercise of its sovereign powers. The fourth step involves an analysis of the conditions specified in the relevant Treaty, typically (i) the lack of a public purpose, (ii) discrimination, (iii) the absence of payment of prompt, adequate, and effective compensation, and (iv) a breach of 'due process of law'.[21] These steps are described in more detail in the ensuing sections.

11 Paasha Mahdavi, 'Why Do Leaders Nationalize the Oil Industry? The Politics of Resource Expropriation' (2014) 75 *Energy Policy* 228.
12 Piotr Kobielski, 'Forms of Direct Expropriation in Practice of States and International Tribunals' (2012) 54 *Studia Iuridica* 109.
13 Ursula Kriebaum, 'Partial Expropriation' (2007) 8 *Journal of World Investment and Trade* 69.
14 Cynthia Day Wallace, 'Control Through Indirect Taking: Creeping Expropriation' in *The Multinational Enterprise and Legal Control* (Brill Nijhoff 2002) 1009.
15 Jeffrey Turk, 'Compensation for Measures Tantamount to Expropriation Under NAFTA: What it Means and Why it Matters' (2005) 1 *International Law and Management Review* 41.
16 Sanja Djajic and Petar Djundic, 'Creeping Expropriation-In Search for a More Comprehensive Approach' (2012) 2 *Yearbook on International Arbitration* 239.
17 'Expropriation – A Sequel UNCTAD Series on Issues in International Investment Agreements II' (UNCTAD 2013).
18 Norah Gallagher and Wenhua Shan, *Chinese Investment Treaties: Policies and Practice* (OUP 2009) chapter 7.
19 *Biwater Gauff (Tanzania) Ltd. v United Republic of Tanzania*, ICSID Case No. ARB/05/22, Award, 24 July 2008.
20 ICSID Case No. ARB/03/29.
21 ibid 442–46.

It is worth noting that if breach of the guarantee against expropriation is alleged alongside breaches of other standards of protection, as noted by the tribunal in *El Paso Energy International Company v Argentina,*[22] a sequential order should be followed, 'proceeding from expropriation to violation of the FPS. In other words, the Tribunal will examine first whether there is an indirect expropriation, second whether there is arbitrary or discriminatory treatment, third whether there is a violation of the FET, and fourth whether there is a breach of the FPS'.[23]

I. IDENTIFYING THE RELEVANT ASSETS

In *Emmis International Holding et al. v Hungary,*[24] the tribunal noted that an elementary consideration in expropriation cases is the need for the investor to establish their ownership over a proprietary right capable of being expropriated. Similarly, in *AWG Group Ltd. v Argentina,*[25] it was considered that 'just as in a case of the expropriation of physical assets, a tribunal must first understand the nature of the rights allegedly expropriated before proceeding to determine whether they have been expropriated under international law. To assess the nature of these rights, in a case of alleged expropriation of contractual rights one must look to the domestic law under which the rights were created'.[26]

In keeping with the non-exhaustive definition of 'investment' contained in Caribbean IIAs, this proprietary right may exist in a wide range of assets, including:

(i) movable and immovable property as well as any other rights in rem in respect of every kind of asset;
(ii) rights derived from shares, bonds and other kinds of interests in companies and joint-ventures;
(iii) title to money or other assets or to any performance under contract or law having an economic value;
(iv) rights in the field of intellectual property, technical processes, goodwill and know-how;
(v) rights to conduct commercial activities including rights to prospect, explore, extract and win natural resources granted under contract or under the legislation of the Contracting Party in the territory of which such activities are undertaken.[27]

In extant arbitral jurisprudence, a wide variety of assets have been the subject of expropriation claims, including lands,[28] money,[29] shares,[30] licences,[31] intellectual property rights,[32]

22 ICSID Case No. ARB/03/15, Award, 27 August 2009.
23 ibid 231.
24 ICSID Case No. ARB/12/2, Award, 16 April 2014.
25 UNCITRAL Award, Decision on Liability, 30 July 2010.
26 ibid 151.
27 See for example, Article 1(a) Jamaica-The Netherlands BIT.
28 *Gavrilović v Croatia*, ICSID Case No. ARB/12/39, Award, 25 July 2018.
29 *von Pezold v Zimbabwe*, ICSID Case No. ARB/10/15, Award, 28 July 2015.
30 *GAMI v Mexico*, UNCITRAL Final Award, 15 November 2004.
31 *Ampal-American Israel Corp. and others v Egypt*, ICSID Case No. ARB/12/11, Decision on Liability and Heads of Loss, 21 February 2017.
32 *Phillip Morris v Uruguay*, ICSID Case No. ARB/10/7, Decision on Jurisdiction, 2 July 2013, para. 209 (provided that these rights are being exploited).

and even contractual rights.[33] Many of these claims have been successful, provided that the state, in relation to these rights, was acting in its sovereign, as opposed to mere contractual, capacity at the relevant time.[34] The mere taking of these assets is, however, not sufficient. The investor must establish that he or she at the relevant time owned some proprietary right in the asset that was expropriated.

II. EXPROPRIATORY ACTS

There are myriad ways in which states may breach the guarantee against expropriation. In this connection, the burden of proof is on the claimant to identify the 'expropriatory act' that is responsible for the transfer of title (in the case of direct expropriation) or the substantial deprivation of the use or enjoyment of the asset (in the case of indirect expropriation).

In *AWG Group Ltd. v Argentina,*[35] although the tribunal accepted that the BIT in question (as do most other IIAs) did not define the noun 'measure', it was useful to resort to the dictionary definition of the term: 'a plan or course of action taken to achieve a particular purpose'.[36] On the facts of the case, the tribunal considered that the various *legislative, regulatory, and administrative actions* taken by the Argentine authorities prior to, during, and following the country's financial crisis qualified as 'measures',[37] and that such measures undoubtedly had a negative impact on the claimants' concession.

Can a failure to take action, such as to revise a tariff, constitute a 'measure'? Interestingly, in *AWG Group Ltd. v Argentina,* the tribunal found that Argentina's refusal to revise the tariff was not merely an omission but the result of a carefully considered decision formally communicated to the claimant's subsidiary, and that this decision constituted a 'measure' within the meaning of BIT in question.[38] Interestingly, in *Olguín v Paraguay,*[39] the tribunal asserted that 'expropriation therefore requires a teleologically driven action for it to occur; omissions, however egregious they may be, are not sufficient for it to take place'.[40]

A. Tax Measures

States have considerable margin of discretion in enacting and enforcing tax measures. The rationale for this margin of appreciation lies in the fact that 'tax is the payment of a debt established by law in favour of the public treasury, the price we pay for civilization'.[41] In this regard, the presumption is that tax measures are bona fide, unless there is convincing evidence that, upon a true characterisation, they constitute a 'taking'.[42]

33 *Inmaris Perestroika Sailing Maritime Services GmbH and Others v Ukraine*, ICSID Case No. ARB/08/8, Decision on Jurisdiction, 8 March 2010.

34 *Vannessa Ventures Ltd v The Bolivarian Republic of Venezuela*, ICSID Case No. ARB(AF)04/6, Award, 16 January 2013.

35 UNCITRAL Award, Decision on Liability, 30 July 2010.

36 ibid 131.

37 ibid.

38 ibid 141.

39 *Eudoro Olguín v Republic of Paraguay*, ICSID Case No. ARB 96/5, Award, 26 January 2001.

40 ibid 84.

41 *Quasar de Valores SICAV S.A., Orgor de Valores SICAV S.A., GBI 9000 SICAV S.A. and ALOS 34 S.L. v The Russian Federation*, SCC Case No. 24/2007, para. 48.

42 Matthew Davie, 'Taxation-based Investment Treaty Claims' (2015) 6(1) *Journal of International Dispute Settlement* 202; Tracey Epps, 'Taxation and Expropriation' (2013) 13 *Otago Law Review* 145.

Over the years, arbitral tribunals have been generally slow to reach the conclusion that ostensible tax measures are compensable takings. One case in which such tax measures were, however, treated as an expropriatory act was *Renta 4 SVSA v The Russian Federation.*[43] Here, the tribunal agreed with the claimant that Russia's imposition of disproportionate tax assessments and tax levies, the seizure and transfer of Yukos' prime asset, Rosneft, a state-owned oil company, and the liquidation of the remainder of Yukos' assets in state-initiated bankruptcy proceedings were expropriatory conduct, warranting the award of damages. While accepting that, in the ordinary course of things, taxation measures will not be treated as expropriatory, the tribunal considered that the collection of taxes here was part of a series of measures designed to effect a dispossession outside the normative constraints and practices of the taxing powers. In this regard, it concluded that:

> . . . there is a world of difference between incidental detriment, even of a substantial nature, and purposeful dispossession. It is no answer for a state to say that its courts have used the word 'taxation'- any more than the word 'bankruptcy' – in describing judgments by which they effect the dispossession of foreign investors. If that were enough, investment protection through international law would likely become an illusion, as states would quickly learn to avoid responsibility by dressing up all adverse measures, perhaps expropriation first of all, as taxation.[44]

The question of whether taxation can amount to an expropriatory act was also considered in *Burlington Resources Inc. v Ecuador.*[45] Here, the tribunal affirmed that taxation is an essential prerogative of state sovereignty and that, accordingly, states may tax not only their own nationals but also aliens, including foreign investors. It is, by definition, non-compensable, as general taxation is the result of a state's permissible exercise of regulatory powers. It is thus, in principle, not an expropriation. However, there are limits to the state's power in this regard:

> Customary international law imposes two limitations on the power to tax. Taxes may not be discriminatory, and they may not be confiscatory. Confiscatory taxation essentially 'takes too much from the taxpayer'. The determination of how much is too much constitutes a fact specific inquiry. Among the factors to be considered one counts first and foremost the tax rate and the amount of payment required. If the amount required is so high that taxpayers are forced to abandon the property or sell it at a distress price, the tax is confiscatory.[46]

In the tribunal's estimation, the most important factor for distinguishing permissible from confiscatory taxation is the effect of the tax. If the tax results in a substantial deprivation of the value of the investment, then this would constitute an expropriation without compensation, and is unlawful.[47]

Meanwhile, in *El Paso Energy International Company v Argentina,*[48] the investor alleged that Argentina violated its right to freely export hydrocarbons by imposing a withholding tax. It argued that such a measure deprived it of a significant amount of revenue, and

43 SCC No. 24/2007.

44 ibid 179. For a critique of the decision, see Paul Stephan, 'Taxation and Expropriation-The destruction of the Yukos Oil Empire' (2013) 35 *Houston Journal of International Law* 1.

45 ICSID Case No. ARB/08/5, Decision on Liability, 14 December 2012.

46 ibid 393.

47 ibid 395. For critique of the case, see Arno Gildemeister, '*Burlington Resources, Inc v Republic of Ecuador*: How Much is Too Much: When is Taxation Tantamount to Expropriation?' (2014) 29(2) *ICSID Review* 315.

48 ICSID Case No. ARB/03/15, Award, 31 October 2011.

artificially depressed the domestic crude oil and LPG prices. In response, Argentina argued that its imposition of export duties on oil and gas within the context of the financial crisis was a reasonable, non-compensable governmental regulation. The tribunal considered that, as a matter of principle, tax policy involves the sovereign power of the state to impose taxes on its territory that it deems appropriate at any particular time. In this context, there is a presumption of validity in favour of legislative measures adopted by a state, and it is up to those who challenge such measures to demonstrate their invalidity. Accordingly, foreign investors have neither the right nor any legitimate expectation that the tax regime will not change during the period of the investment, even though this may reduce its economic benefits, except where a stabilisation of the tax regime (at least for certain taxes) was agreed on by the state. Absent such a regime, a state cannot be considered to have a duty to adapt its tax regime to the best interests of foreign investors, and an unfavourable calculation of taxes cannot be equated with an expropriation, especially where the claimant does not quantify its alleged losses.[49]

On the facts, the tribunal held that the imposition of the export duties on oil and gas was a reasonable governmental regulation within the context of the financial crisis. Because the crisis necessitated the devaluation of the peso and thus a significant reduction in revenues from the export sector, it was logical for Argentina to impose a tax on exports. In fact, during the crisis, the Argentine peso had lost 200% against the US dollar while the price of oil climbed, peaking over US$35/per barrel. Faced with this new economic situation, the export duties imposed on oil and gas of only between 4.76% and 16.67% were reasonable. In this regard, the tribunal relied on the decision in *Aminoil v Kuwait*,[50] where it was held that it was acceptable to impose taxes on the oil industry in connection with unexpected income attributable to the 'explosion' of oil prices. In any event, in *El Paso's* case, the tax measures in question had only a limited impact on the claimant's property rights. The export withholdings could not be said have caused a forced sale constituting an expropriation of El Paso's shares in the Argentinian companies subjected to these withholdings or constitute an expropriation by themselves. In short, the tax measures were reasonable and did not result in the neutralisation of the property rights of the claimant.

B. Breach of Contract

In investor-state arbitrations involving breaches of contracts concluded between a claimant and a host government, tribunals have made a distinction between *acta iure imperii* and *acta iure gestionis*, that is to say, actions by a state in exercise of its sovereign powers and actions of a state as a Contracting Party.[51] It is the use by a state of its sovereign powers that gives rise to treaty breaches, while actions as a Contracting Party merely give rise to contract claims not ordinarily covered by an investment treaty.[52] Breaches of contract by the state in its sovereign capacity giving rise to international state responsibility were found in

49 ibid 285.

50 Final Award, 24 March 1982, 21 ILM 976.

51 Marco Bollini and Virginie Colaiuta, 'Expropriation of Contractual Rights in Investment Treaty Arbitration' in Renato Nazzini (ed), *Transnational Construction Arbitration Key Themes in the Resolution of Construction Disputes* (Routledge 2018) 111.

52 Marianna Tsatsanifou, 'Contractors' Claims for Expropriation of Contractual Rights on the Basis of International Investment Treaties' (2021) 16 *Constitutional Law International* 30.

cases as early as the *Rudolff* case,[53] which held that the taking away or destruction of rights acquired, transmitted, and defined by contract, is as much a wrong entitling the sufferer to redress as the taking away or destruction of a tangible property. The 1922 Norwegian *Shipowners Claims case*,[54] and the 1927 *Chorzów Factory case*[55] came to a similar conclusion. Meanwhile, in the 1948 *Jalapa Railroad* case,[56] the tribunal held that international responsibility was triggered when the government of Veracruz stepped out of the role of Contracting Party and sought to escape vital obligations under the contract by exercising its sovereign power. Then, in 1989, the Iran-US Claims tribunal in *Phillips Petroleum*[57] considered whether the termination of an oil Concession Agreement constituted an expropriation of contract rights or alternatively, a breach and repudiation of the contract. The termination of the contract followed a series of actions by the Iranian Government that slowly eroded the claimant's rights under the contract. The Claims Tribunal held that

> expropriation by or attributable to a State of the property of an alien gives rise under international law to liability for compensation, and this is so whether the expropriation is formal or *de facto* and whether the property is tangible . . . or intangible, such as the contract rights involved in the present case.[58]

The tribunal considered that

> the acts complained of appear more closely suited to assessment of liability for the taking of foreign-owned property under international law than to assessment of the contractual aspects of the relationship, and so decided to consider the claim in this light.[59]

More recent arbitral jurisprudence supports the position that a state may be liable for expropriating contractual rights when acting in its sovereign capacity. In *Siemens v Argentina*,[60] for example, the tribunal considered that

> for the behaviour of the State as a party to a contract to be considered a breach of an investment treaty, such behaviour must be beyond that which an ordinary contracting party could adopt and involve State interference with the operation of the contract.[61]

In that case, the tribunal found that Argentina took a series of measures, based not on its contract with Siemens' subsidiary, but on the exercise of its public authority, one of which was a governmental decree which terminated the contract. It, therefore, found that Argentina

53 Rudloff Case (1903), US-Venezuelan Claims Commission, Interlocutory Decision 9 RIAA 2144, Reports of International Arbitral Awards, Volume 9, 250.
54 Norwegian Shipowners' Claims (*Nor v U.S.*), (Perm Ct Arb 1922) 1 RIAA 307.
55 Case Concerning the Factory at Chorzów (*FRG v Pol*) (1927) PCIJ Series A No 9.
56 Jalapa R.R. and Power Co. Claim (1948), (1976) Whitesman's Digest of International Law, Vol. 8, 908–9 (American Mexican Claims Commission under the Act of Congress Approved December 18, 1942, Report to the Secretary of State with Decisions Showing the Reasons for the Allowance or Disallowance of the Claims (Dept. of State Pub. No. 2859, Arbitration Series No. 9) (1948)).
57 *Phillips Petroleum Company Iran v the Islamic Republic of Iran and NIOC*, Award No. 425-39-2, Award of 29 June 1989, 21 Iran-U.S. C.T.R. 75, para. 79.
58 ibid 76.
59 ibid 75.
60 ICSID Case No. ARB/02/8, Award, 17 January 2007.
61 ibid 248.

had expropriated Siemens' contractual rights. A similar finding was reached in *Vivendi II*,[62] wherein the tribunal concluded that 'there can be no doubt that contractual rights are capable of being expropriated, and several treaty cases have arisen out of contractual disputes. The same act that may violate a treaty may also violate a contract, or both the treaty and the contract. The fact that there is overlap does not prevent a tribunal from considering the act as a possible treaty breach. Further, whether a given act was in breach, or was thought by one of the parties to be in breach of the contract, may well inform the tribunal's assessment of that act for purposes of a treaty claim.'[63] Similarly, the tribunal in *SPP v Egypt*[64] noted that contract rights are entitled to the protection of international law and the taking of such rights involves an obligation to make compensation.

Meanwhile, in *Inmaris Perestroika Sailing Maritime Services GmbH and Others v Ukraine,*[65] the Tribunal found that a telegram instructing a certain party not to let the claimant's ship leave the territorial waters of Ukraine, and the continuation of the travel ban for the ensuing year, was a sovereign act, and therefore an expropriatory act, taken by the respondent. In the tribunal's view, that act deprived the claimants of access to and control over the essential asset for its investment, i.e. the ship, and thus of the claimants' contractual rights to use that asset. Although the travel ban was lifted after one year, the damage to the investment had by that time been done; an entire sailing season was cancelled, and the claimants' business suffered substantial harm such that they could not reasonably have been expected to resume operations as if nothing had happened. Indeed, at that stage, two of the claimants' entities were in insolvency proceedings, and, even if those entities had remained solvent, it could not be assumed that customers would have been willing to work with them in light of these events. Against this backdrop, the tribunal concluded that, at a minimum, the travel ban amounted to an indirect expropriation (which was not accompanied by any compensation) in that it destroyed the value of the claimants' contractual rights. Such diminution in value (due to the lasting damage to the claimants' business) was, for all intents and purposes, permanent.

In *Crystallex v Venezuela,*[66] the claimant complained against the denial of their mining permit (for gold), as well as allegedly being subject to hostile statements from Venezuelan governmental officials resulting in a gradual devaluation of the investor's investment, and subject to the rejection of administrative remedies, and the ultimate recission of the mining operation concession (MOC). The tribunal considered that the decision at the highest level of the Venezuelan state had been taken to oust Crystallex from the mine, Las Cristinas, and to take the mine back in governmental hands, with a view to developing it in collaboration with new partners. In its view, the statements made by government officials effected an incremental encroachment of the claimant's contractual rights, resulting in a gradual, yet significant, decrease in the value of the claimant's investment. In short, the state's action, including the last measure – termination of the concession, taken together, constituted creeping expropriation.

62 ICSID Case No. ARB/03/19, Award, 9 April 2015.

63 ibid, para. 7.5.4.

64 *Southern Pacific Properties (Middle East) Limited v Arab Republic of Egypt* (ICSID Case No. ARB/84/3), Award on the Merits of May 20, 1992, 321.L.M. 937 (1993).

65 ICSID Case No. ARB/08/8, Excerpts of Award dated March 1, 2012, 1 March 2012.

66 ICSID Case No. ARB(AF)/11/2, Award, 4 April 2016.

The question also arose as to whether the tribunal could adjudicate on the alleged contract claim in the context of expropriation proceedings. For the tribunal, while it could not decide on whether the concession was duly performed, or whether it was rightly or wrongfully terminated, and what would be the consequences of any wrongful termination, it was not precluded from assessing whether the respondent, in terminating the contract, acted in the exercise of its sovereign powers (*puissance publique*) rather than as an ordinary Contracting Party. This assessment allowed the tribunal to distinguish between mere breaches of contracts (which would normally not give rise to international responsibility) and acts which, while expressed as contractual, were in reality sovereign acts which could implicate state responsibility. Differently put, the tribunal had to objectively determine whether the purported exercise of a contractual act evidenced the characteristics of the exercise of sovereign power and was thus to be characterised as a sovereign act.

Having reviewed the circumstances of the case, and, in particular, all of the acts which throughout the years implicated several governmental organs – the Ministry of Environment, the Ministry of Mines, the Venezuelan Presidency, and other agencies, the tribunal came to the conclusion that the true nature of the termination, though purported to be an alleged contractual ground, i.e. failure to perform for one year (as well as for reasons of opportunity and convenience), was one involving the exercise of sovereign authority. In short, the termination was not due to a bona fide dispute about the parties' obligations under the concession or its performance by Crystallex. It was devised to give effect to the respondent's unconcealed political agenda in respect of mining generally, and the Las Cristinas mine, in particular. The termination, for which the statements of Venezuela's President and Ministers provided the true rationale, was an attempt by Venezuela to 'recover the mine', without paying any compensation. It thus constituted the final sovereign act which completed the expropriatory process. In other words, the combination of acts performed by different governmental organs, starting from the actions surrounding the denial of the permit, continuing with the announcements that Venezuela would 'take back' Las Cristinas, and ending with the repudiation of the MOC, had the effect of substantially depriving Crystallex of the economic use and enjoyment of its investment, and ultimately rendered it entirely useless. The tribunal thus concluded that the cumulative and incremental effect of those measures was 'equivalent to . . . expropriation' under Article VII(1) of the Treaty.[67]

Meanwhile, in *Gold Reserve Inc. v Venezuela*,[68] while the tribunal accepted that actions of a purportedly contractual nature could constitute an expropriation if the true nature was the exercise of sovereign authority, it did not find that the respondent's termination of the mining concessions in this case was an expropriatory act. In fact, the tribunal found that the nature of the breach by the claimant (failure to exploit within the required timeframe) was such that termination on this ground could not be said to be merely 'pretextual', to use the language of the tribunal in *Malicorp v Egypt*.[69] Rather, this was an important provision in both concessions which the claimant had not complied with. As such, the *Gold Reserve* tribunal adopted a similar position to that taken by the *Malicorp* Tribunal that the reasons given by the respondent for terminating the concessions were sufficiently well founded that the terminations could therefore not be considered as a form of expropriation under international law. In other words, the respondent's acts were an exercise of regulatory powers

67 ibid 644.

68 ICSID Case No. ARB(AF)/09/1, Award, 22 September 2014.

69 ICSID Case No. ARB/08/18, Award, 7 February 2011.

under the 1999 Mining Law and the relevant Mining Titles, and therefore not acts of an expropriatory nature.

Separately, in *Vannessa Ventures Ltd v Venezuela,*[70] the tribunal found that the respondent's termination of the Concession Contract in respect of certain mining rights in the Las Cristinas region in South Easter Venezuela was not an expropriatory act because the state's termination was trigged by the claimant's illegal purchase of certain shares. The tribunal, in finding that the state did not step out of its role as a Contracting Party and interfere with the contract on the basis of its sovereign authority, considered that three contractual breaches were committed by the claimants warranting termination of the Concession contract: the violation of its obligation to submit detailed reports; the failure to resume work on the mine, after the expiration of the last extension on 15 July 2001; and the entry into a transaction with the claimant for the transfer of all of the shares of MINCA thus contravening express contractual provisions contained in clause 25 by virtue whereof it was bound to obtain due written authorisation by the state. In short, the tribunal did not consider that the termination of the contract rose above the 'high threshold that separates a contractual dispute from a violation of a treaty prohibition on expropriation'.[71] The allegation of expropriation was accordingly rejected on the basis that the conduct of the state did not go beyond that which an ordinary Contracting Party could adopt.

In *AWG v Argentina,*[72] the claimants alleged that measures taken by Argentina from the time the financial crisis began to emerge in 1999 until the concession was terminated in 2006 amounted to an indirect expropriation. The claimant complained against (i) acts of a general legal or regulatory nature, not directed specifically at them, enacted to cope with the financial crisis and its aftermath; (ii) the alleged failure of the Argentine Government to revise the tariff charged to users by the concession during and after the crisis; and (iii) the actions taken by the Argentine Government at the time of the termination of the concession.

On issue (i), namely the general regulatory measures taken by Argentina that limited the amounts of cash withdrawals by account holders, the imposition of new taxes, and the enactment of emergency law which abolished the currency board that had linked the Argentine peso to the US dollar, abolished the adjustment of public service contracts according to agreed upon indexations, and which authorised the Executive Branch of government to renegotiate all public service contracts, the tribunal found that although these measures made the operation of the concession more difficult and reduced its profitability significantly, they did not affect the claimants' control or possession of the concession. The claimants remained in possession of the concession and continued to provide water and sewage services to Buenos Aires and surrounding municipalities. Moreover, the claimants retained possession of their shares undisturbed. In other words, there was no substantial, permanent deprivation of the economic substance of the investment and thus no indirect expropriation. In any event, given the severe nature of the crisis facing the country, the general measures adopted by Argentina were within the state's general police powers.

Meanwhile, on issue (ii), namely Argentina's refusal to revise the tariff in the context of rising costs in respect of the payments that the claimants were to receive from consumers for water and sewage services, the tribunal held that there was no indirect expropriation because there was no substantial deprivation of the investment. Rather, the claimants

70 ICSID Case No. ARB(AF)04/6, Award, 16 January 2013.

71 ibid 214.

72 UNCITRAL Award, Decision on Liability, 30 July 2010.

remained in control of the concession and its authority to manage and direct the operation of the water and sewage system was undiminished.

Finally, in respect of issue (iii), namely Argentina's alleged termination of the concession, and taking back possession of the water distribution and wastewater systems that had been the subject of the Concession, the tribunal held that there had not been an indirect expropriation. More particularly, unlike the situation in the *Norwegian Shipowners Claims* case,[73] the *Chorzów Factory* case,[74] and *CME v Czech Republic*,[75] where the respondent states had respectively interfered with contracts between the claimants and third parties, in the present case, Argentina was taking action with respect to a contract to which it was a party and whose terms gave it a right to terminate under certain conditions. In other words, the claimants here did not own or have property rights in the physical assets of the water and sewage system of Buenos Aires. Had they owned the system, a seizure of that system by the Argentine Government would have constituted an expropriation. Instead, the claimants merely held contractual rights as a concessionaire to operate that system and to derive income from that operation. In any event, the Concession Contract had specifically granted the Argentine Government the right to terminate the concession due to the fault of the concessionaire and to retake possession of the water and sewage system.

More fundamentally, the tribunal considered that Argentina did not act in the exercise of its sovereign powers (*acta iure imperii*), but rather as an ordinary Contracting Party (*acta iure gestionis*) when it terminated the Concession Contract with the claimants. If Argentina had been acting in the former capacity, then Argentina may have expropriated the contractual rights of the claimants. But on the facts, it was acting in the latter capacity such that no expropriation took place; the claimants, like any other private Contracting Party, only had contractual claims in respect of the alleged termination of the Concession Contract.

Finally, it is worth noting that the mere fact that there is *some* government involvement in the events that lead to the termination of a contract does not necessarily mean that such termination is the result of an exercise of sovereign powers, as noted recently by the tribunal in *Bayindir v Pakistan*.[76] An assessment of all the circumstances of the case is apposite.

C. Judicial Acts

Generally speaking, actions by state courts to enforce contractual rights, including rights to terminate a contract, are not considered as expropriatory acts, unless there is an element of serious and fundamental impropriety about the legal process.[77] For example, in *Garanti*

73 (*Norway v United States*) (1921) 1 RIAA 307.

74 *Germany v Poland*, Jurisdiction, Judgment, PCIJ Series A No 9, ICGJ 247 (PCIJ 1927).

75 UNCITRAL Final Award, 14 March 2003.

76 *Bayindir Insaat Turizm Ticaret ve Sanayi A ù v Islamic Republic of Pakistan*, (ICSID Case No. ARB/03/29), Award, 27 August 2009, paras. 128, 129: . . .

> in assessing whether there has been a treaty breach a tribunal may review contract matters . . . . These considerations do not imply that the assessment of a treaty breach in the context of a contractual relationship requires a determination that the contract has been breached. Breach of contract and breach of treaty are separate questions giving rise to separate enquiries . . . . Because the enquiries are different, the fact that a State exercises a contract right or remedy does not in and of itself exclude the possibility of a treaty breach.

77 See generally, Vid Prislan, 'Judicial Expropriation in International Investment Law' (2021) 70(1) *International & Comparative Law Quarterly* 165; Sara Mansour, *Judicial Expropriations: Difficulties in Drawing the Line Between Adjudication and Expropriation* (Springer 2020).

Koza v Turkmenistan,[78] the seizure by the courts of the claimant's factory and equipment that remained in Turkmenistan after it defaulted on its work on a project to construct a bridge was not deemed to be an expropriatory act. The tribunal considered that the seizure of the property by the court was a result of a normal domestic legal process which was not tainted by serious impropriety, since the claimant had defaulted on the project. In other words, the reason (i.e. the claimant's default) for the termination constituted a legally valid ground for termination which did not incur the state's international responsibility.

That said, the interference by courts with an arbitration agreement with a foreign investor may constitute a violation of international law. The rationale for this approach, in the words of Judge Schwebel, is that 'the contractual right of an alien to arbitration of disputes arising under a contract to which it is party is a valuable right, which often is of importance to the very conclusion of the contract.'[79] In this regard, unless the IIA indicates otherwise, there is no reason in principle why a sufficiently egregious judicial act may not result in an expropriation. This may occur, for example, where the court's conduct is illegal to the extent that it eviscerates the investor's right to arbitrate, and the rights determined by any arbitral Award (that is, residual contract rights in the investment that are crystallised by the Award) that may have been rendered by an arbitral tribunal.

Saipem v Bangladesh[80] is instructive in this regard. Here, the Bangladesh Oil, Gas and Mineral Corporation (Petrobangla), a state entity, entered into an agreement with the claimant for the supply of condensate and gas across various locations in Bangladesh. The contract was governed by the laws of Bangladesh and contained an arbitration clause for referral to arbitration by an ICC Tribunal in the event of a dispute between the parties. When Petrobangla did not repay the second half of the retention money despite the issuance of the warranty bond by the claimant, the claimant attempted to invoke the arbitration clause, in relation to which the ICC Tribunal issued an award on jurisdiction dismissing Petrobangla's challenge to its jurisdiction. Following several adverse procedural decisions by the ICC Tribunal (e.g. refusal to hear evidence from a certain witness), Petrobangla sought the support of the local courts. Several local courts sought to revoke the ICC Tribunal's authority, and the Supreme Court of Bangladesh eventually issued an injunction restraining Saipem from proceeding with the ICC Arbitration. When the ICC Tribunal resumed proceedings, the High Court Division issued an injunction restraining Saipem from pursuing the ICC Arbitration. However, the ICC Tribunal proceeded to hear the matter and rendered an award holding that Petrobangla had breached its contractual obligations to compensate Saipem for the time extension and additional works and ordered Petrobangla to pay to Saipem damages (which included the retention money which remained unpaid) plus interest. It also ordered Petrobangla to return the warranty bond to Saipem. This award was not, however, enforced by the Bangladeshi courts, which prompted the claimant to institute ICSID proceedings. The claimant's case was based on local courts' alleged unlawful disruption of the ICC Arbitration, and their *de facto* annulment of the ICC Award. These acts were alleged to deprive Saipem of the sums awarded to it by the ICC Award and thus claimed to have amounted to an illegal expropriation in breach of Article 5 of the relevant BIT.

78 ICSID Case No. ARB/11/20, Award, 19 December 2016.

79 Stephen Schwebel, Luke Sobota and Ryan Manton, *International Arbitration: Three Salient Problems* (2nd edn, CUP 2020) 79.

80 ICSID Case No. ARB/05/07, Award, 30 June 2009.

The ICSID tribunal found that the ICC Award and/or the rights determined by the Award were capable of being expropriated, in accordance with principles of general international law that recognise that immaterial rights can be the subject of expropriation. Having found that rights under judicial decisions are protected property that can be the subject of an expropriation, the tribunal held that the local courts' conduct in this case were measures having similar effects to expropriation in that they substantially deprived Saipem of the benefit of the ICC Award. In its view, the taking of the residual contractual rights arising from the investments, as crystallised in the ICC Award, was an expropriatory act that amounted to not only a substantial deprivation, but also an illegal act. In this connection, it explained:

> . . . given the very peculiar circumstances of the present interference, the Tribunal agrees with the parties that the substantial deprivation of Saipem's ability to enjoy the benefits of the ICC Award is not sufficient to conclude that the Bangladeshi courts' intervention is tantamount to an expropriation.[81]
>
> . . . both parties consider that the actions of (or the actions attributable to) Bangladesh must be 'illegal' in order to give rise to a claim of expropriation.[82]

After cautioning that its analysis 'should not be understood as a departure from the "sole effects doctrine"',[83] the tribunal went on to consider whether there was any illegal act committed by the ICC Tribunal on the facts. In this regard, the tribunal found that the ICC Tribunal had not committed any misconduct such as to justify the revocation of the arbitrators. To this end, the Bangladeshi courts had abused their supervisory jurisdiction over the arbitration process by revoking the arbitrator's authority in the absence of misconduct. In addition, the tribunal also found that the conduct of the Bangladeshi courts amounted to a breach of Article II(1) of the New York Convention on the Recognition and Enforcement of Arbitral Awards which imposes an obligation to 'recognize' arbitration agreements. It concluded that although the courts of Bangladesh did not target the arbitration or the arbitration agreement in itself, but rather revoked the authority of the arbitrators, this still amounted to a violation of Article II of the New York Convention because it *de facto* prevented or immobilized the arbitration that sought to implement the arbitration agreement, thus completely frustrating, if not the wording, at least the spirit, of the Convention.

Finally, in *Karkey v Pakistan*,[84] the tribunal found that Pakistan had expropriated the claimant's investment through a judgment of the Supreme Court which incorrectly declared the contract in issue to be *void ab initio*.

The take-away from these cases, then, is that judicial conduct that is (i) illegal and (ii) have the effect of substantially depriving an investor of the use and enjoyment of their asset may be an expropriatory act.

III. TYPES OF EXPROPRIATION

While determining the existence of a direct expropriation is usually not difficult because of the usually obvious physical manifestations that come with depriving an investor of title

81 ibid 133.
82 ibid 134.
83 ibid.
84 ICSID Case No. ARB/13/1, Award, 22 August 2017.

and control, identifying an indirect expropriation is often a much more complicated matter which requires an inquiry into whether a regulatory measure has the effect of an expropriation on an investment or constitutes a valid exercise of a state's regulatory power. Indeed, as the tribunal in the NAFTA case of *Feldman v Mexico*[85] acknowledged, recognising a direct expropriation is not difficult, but

> it is much less clear when governmental action that interferes with broadly-defined property rights . . . crosses the line from valid regulation to a compensable taking, and it is fair to say that no one has come up with a fully satisfactory means of drawing this line.[86]

In the sections below, we seek to uncover the contours of direct and indirect expropriation.

A. Direct Expropriation

For a direct expropriation to be found to exist, there must be a deprivation of property which amounts to a transfer of title of the investment from the investor to the state,[87] and this transfer must be permanent in nature.[88]

While in the past direct expropriations occurred with disturbing frequency, in the last three decades or so, cases of direct expropriations have been relatively few and far between. That said, there are a couple of key cases which aptly illustrate the nature and operation of direct expropriations.

In *Flughafen Zürich and Gestión Engineering v Venezuela*,[89] the claimants, a consortium, had been offered a contract to manage the Isla Margarita Airport. Sometime later,

85 *Marvin Roy Feldman Karpa v United Mexican States*, (ICSID Case No. ARB(AF)/99/1); Award, 16 December 2002.

86 ibid 100.

87 *LG&E Energy Corp., LG&E Capital Corp. and LG&E International Inc. v Argentine Republic,* ICSID Case No. ARB/02/1, Decision on Liability of 3 October 2006, para. 187; *Enron Creditors Recovery Corporation (formerly Enron Corporation) and Ponderosa Assets, L.P. v Argentine Republic*, ICSID Case No. ARB/01/3, Award of 22 May 2007, para. 243; *Sempra Energy International v Argentine Republic*, ICSID Case No. ARB/02/16, Award of 28 September 2007, para. 280; *National Grid P.L.C. v Argentina Republic*, UNCITRAL, Award of 3 November 2008, para. 145; *El Paso Energy International Company v Argentine Republic*, ICSID Case No. ARB/03/15, Award of 31 October 2011, para. 265; *Spyridon Roussalis v Romania*, ICSID Case No. ARB/06/1, Award of 1 December 2011, para. 327. See, also, Ronald Dolzer and Christoph Schreuer, *Principles of International Investment Law* (OUP 2008) 92: 'The difference between a direct and formal expropriation and an indirect expropriation turns on whether the legal title of the owner is affected by the measure in question'.

88 Although the requirement of permanence has been addressed mostly in the context of indirect expropriations, its rationale also applies to direct expropriations. See, e.g. *LG&E v Argentina, Decision on Liability*, 3 October 2006, para. 193: 'Generally, the expropriation must be permanent, that is to say, it cannot have a temporary nature, unless the investment's successful development depends on the realization of certain activities at specific moments that may not endure variations'; *Fireman's Fund Insurance Company v United Mexican States*, ICSID Case No. ARB(AF)/02/01, Award of 17 July 2006, para. 176(d) (holding that one of the elements of an expropriation is that '[t]he taking must be permanent, and not ephemeral or temporary'). The approach of some tribunals to determining whether a taking is sufficiently long-lasting to amount to an expropriation is 'flexible'. See *S.D. Myers, Inc. v Government of Canada*, NAFTA/UNCITRAL, Partial Award, 13 November 2000, para. 283 (the tribunal noted that 'in some contexts and circumstances, it would be appropriate to view a deprivation as amounting to an expropriation, even if it were partial or temporary').

89 ICSID Case No. ARB/10/19, Award, 18 November 2014.

however, they were prevented from exercising the rights under the contract because the government annulled the contract and directed police officials to accompany senior officials from Daisy flower to take over the Airport. The Supreme Court thereafter handed over the administration of the Airport to National Power. The Consortium did not receive compensation in respect of the annulled contract, even though Decree 806 recognised this right. The claimants accordingly claimed that there had been an unlawful direct expropriation.

The tribunal agreed with the claimant, finding that the state had failed to comply with the guarantee against expropriation under the relevant BIT. The tribunal considered that given that the rights arising under the contract had passed from the claimants to the state, without the claimants retaining even a nominal right over the investment, there had been a direct expropriation. It noted that a direct expropriation may occur in an outright fashion or as a result of successive measures attributable to the state which ended with the dispossession of the investment.[90] In short, the conduct of the municipality, along with the Supreme Court, were acts of the sovereign, and not merely contractual in nature, and therefore attributable to the state. The interference did not satisfy the requirements of due process, and the claimants did not receive compensation. Hence, there was an unlawful direct expropriation.

Meanwhile, in *Gavrilović v Croatia*,[91] the claimants had invested in several business ventures in Croatia over many years, including several plots of land and apartments. A dispute arose regarding ownership over these investments in the context of bankruptcy proceedings, ultimately resulting in Croatia assigning the rights to 400 apartments whose ownership was in dispute to third parties. The claimants received no compensation for any of these properties. Unnervingly, the claimants were never notified of these sales until they requested excerpts from the land registry at which point they discovered that the plots of land had been registered in Croatia's name or were removed from the sheet altogether. To substantiate the transfer of the properties to Croatia, an agency known as the 'Croatian Privatisation Fund' was established, which issued an opinion which considered that it was not possible to determine which assets the claimants had purchased in the bankruptcy sale. The Croatian Fund concluded that, given the alleged impossibility of determining the assets purchased by the claimants, Article 362(3) of the Ownership Act gave Croatia ownership of property by default. Croatia, within two months of becoming owner of all the claimants' properties, granted to a purchaser of the property what the claimants were not able to achieve in 20 years, namely ownership of the properties purchased through bankruptcy.

The tribunal found that the registration under Article 362(3) of the Ownership Act was expropriatory. The practical effect of such registration was that the state claimed ownership for itself over the relevant properties, such ownership not being limited in time or in any other way. Because no compensation was paid, or offered, by the state, the tribunal concluded that there was a direct expropriation of the claimants' plots of land.

Separately, in *Quiborax and Non-Metallic Minerals v Bolivia*,[92] the first claimant was a shareholder in the second claimant's mining company in the largest dry salt lake in the world in Bolivia. The granting of the environmental licence, however, triggered strong protests from civic organisations. This 'war to death' included hunger strikes and the blockade of roads and railways. Consequently, the relevant Ministry first suspended all mining activities and subsequently revoked the second claimant's licence. Later, the President of

90 ibid 502.

91 ICSID Case No. ARB/12/39, Award, 25 July 2018.

92 ICSID Case No. ARB/06/2, Award, 16 September 2015.

Bolivia issued Decree 27, effectively revoking the claimants' mining concessions. He also issued, on the same day, Decree 27,590 banning the export of non-metallic minerals, such as unprocessed boron and unprocessed or partly processed ulexite. In compliance with the 30-day time limit fixed in the Revocation Decree, the second claimant handed over its eleven mining concessions to the Prefect of the Department of Potosí. Bolivia then annulled the revoked concessions through writs of annulment on the grounds that there had been errors in the requests for concessions. Bolivia argued that there had been a systematic refusal by the claimants to provide information to the National Tax Service and the National Customs Service, thus preventing the audits from being carried out, and that there were discrepancies in the amount of ulexite declared and actually transported in violation of the Tax Code.

The tribunal considered that the irregularities identified therein were minor breaches of law, and that these irregularities could not justify the termination of the contract. More pointedly, the claimants were not notified and thus could not participate in the audits mandated by the law before the revocation, and, in any event, none of the official reports by the Customs Service concluded that there were discrepancies in the amount of ulexite declared and exported. In other words, the revocation seemed to respond to pressure of the local community rather than breaches of the law by the claimants.

On the facts, there had been an unlawful direct expropriation. In the tribunal's view, the auditing procedures that formed the basis of the Revocation Decree failed to comply with minimum standards of due process: the second claimant was only notified of the initiation of the audit the day before the concessions were revoked, which did not allow the claimants to participate in the audit prior to the revocation of the concessions. Further, the revocation lacked valid reasons. On the latter point, the tribunal found that the Revocation Decree was not a legitimate exercise of Bolivia's police powers. In short, the Revocation Decree had the effect of transferring the title of the second claimants' mining concessions to the state. In particular, because the second claimant was required to physically hand over the concessions to the Prefecture of the Potosí Region within thirty days, this amounted to a permanent deprivation of its investments in Bolivia, and hence a direct expropriation.

Finally, in *von Pezold v Zimbabwe*,[93] in the context of Zimbabwe's land redistribution programme, the claimants alleged that their properties were directly expropriated by a Constitutional Amendment which vested in the State title to the 10 'Forrester Properties', 21 of the 28 'Border Properties', and six of the nine 'Makandi Properties'. The claimants argued that, without title, they were unable to sell or otherwise realise the properties, and that they faced criminal prosecution for continuing to occupy them.

The tribunal held that although the claimants remained in control or possession of parts of the properties, this did not mean that they had not been expropriated. In fact, the tribunal agreed with the claimants' contention that the transfer of legal title was sufficient here to establish direct expropriation. Because no compensation had been paid for the expropriated properties, the expropriation could not be said to have fulfilled the legality criteria. It further considered that the continued use of the properties by the claimants did not constitute prompt, adequate, and effective compensation for the expropriation, although it noted that such income would be a factor in assessing damages and loss. Moreover, it considered that the Constitutional Amendment expressly denied the claimants access to due process by removing the ability of landowners to challenge the acquisition of their land, as well as having criminalized the continued possession or occupation of agricultural land expropriated.

93 ICSID Case No. Arb/10/15, Award, 28 July 2015.

For the tribunal, these steps did not constitute a mere 'constraint' on due process, but rather its total elimination.[94]

Meanwhile, on the question of non-discrimination, the tribunal found evidence that the (Caucasian) claimants were targeted because of their skin colour and, hence, the taking was discriminatory in breach of the Swiss-Zimbabwe BIT. More pointedly, there was a policy towards black farmers (in contrast to that toward white farmers) which was not to expropriate their farms, and under the new Constitution, black Zimbabweans were compensated for land and improvements, whereas white Zimbabweans were only compensated for improvements. Finally, the state was also held to have failed to establish that there was a legitimate public purpose behind the expropriation. The tribunal, while noting the state's argument of 'righting of historical wrongs', refused to accept that a legitimate public purpose was pursued by the interference since large parts of the properties had not actually been re-distributed to a historically disadvantaged or otherwise landless population, but remained in the *de facto* possession of the claimants. In any event, with regard to the land that had been re-distributed, there appeared to be a clear trend towards politically motivated allocations of land.

Separately, the tribunal considered that there had also been a direct expropriation in relation to monies directly debited from the claimants' accounts by the state – namely, when the state took US dollars directly from the claimants' accounts. Finally, it found that a direct expropriation arose from the state's seizure of 4,500 tonnes of maize from the claimants' Forrester Estate. Such expropriation had taken place without due process.

B. Indirect Expropriation

As intimated earlier, indirect expropriations are far more prevalent today than direct expropriations. As such, it is perhaps unsurprising that it is a hotly contested area of legal practice and scholarly inquiry.[95] Indirect expropriation may take the form of measures equivalent

94 ibid 500.

95 See generally, Peter Isakoff, 'Defining the Scope of Indirect Expropriation for International Investments' (2012) 3 *Global Business Law Review* 189; Robert Sloane and Michael Reisman, 'Indirect Expropriation and its Valuation in the BIT Generation' (2004) 75 *British Yearbook of International Law* 115; Prabhash Ranjan and Pushkar Anand, *Determination of Indirect Expropriation and Doctrine of Police Power in International Investment Law: A Critical Appraisal* (Springer Singapore 2016); Yves Fortier and Stephen Drymer, 'Indirect Expropriation in the Law of International Investment: I Know it When I See It, or Caveat Investor' (2005) 13(1) *Asia Pacific Law Review* 79; Brigitte Stern, 'In Search of the Frontiers of Indirect Expropriation' in Arthur Rovine (ed), *Contemporary Issues in International Arbitration and Mediation: The Fordham Papers* (2007) (Brill Nijhoff 2008); Bjørn Kunoy, 'Developments in Indirect Expropriation Case Law in ICSID Transnational Arbitration' (2005) 6(3) *The Journal of World Investment & Trade* 467; Ivan Pupolizio, 'The Right to an Unchanging World–Indirect Expropriation in International Investment Agreements and State Sovereignty' (2016) 10(2) *ICL Journal* 143; Christoph Schreuer, 'The Concept of Expropriation under the ETC and Other Investment Protection Treaties' (2005) 2(3) *Transnational Dispute Management* 1; Ana Maria Daza-Clark, 'Indirect Expropriation and International Investment Law' in Ana Maria Daza-Clark (ed), *International Investment Law and Water Resources Management* (Brill Nijhoff 2017); Laura-Cristiana Spătaru-Negură, 'Special Considerations Regarding Indirect Expropriation in International Economic Law' (2017) 7(14) *Tribuna Juridică* 124; Ursula Kriebaum, 'Indirect Expropriation: A Comparative Approach' in *General Principles of Law and International Investment Arbitration* (Brill Nijhoff 2018); Mojtaba Dani and Afshin Akhtar-Khavari, 'The Uncertainty Of Legal Doctrine in Indirect Expropriation Cases and the Legitimacy Problems of Investment Arbitration' (2016) 22 *Widener Law*

to or tantamount to an outright taking,[96] or a series of measures (creeping expropriation) which, when assessed collectively, result in a permanent and substantial deprivation of the use and enjoyment of the investment in question.

Several early cases illustrate the historic contours of indirect expropriations. In *Starrett Housing v Iran*,[97] for example, Iran appointed its own 'temporary manager' of an Iranian firm in which the claimant owned a majority interest. The tribunal found that this interfered with the investor's ability to manage the company, thus rendering the investor's rights 'useless', and thereby constituting an indirect expropriation. By contrast, in *Foremost Tehran, Inc. v Iran*,[98] no indirect expropriation was found in circumstances where Foremost retained incidents of ownership (shares, two directors on the board, and limited shareholder rights). In that case, the claimant alleged that their 50% initial ownership interest in a joint venture ('Pak Dairy') had decreased to 31% at the time of the Islamic Revolution against the backdrop of the agents and instrumentalities of the government of Iran allegedly seizing control of the Board of Directors of Pak, and taking a series of other hostile actions, including allegedly blocking the claimant's receipt of dividend payments. The Iran-US Claims Tribunal held that Iran had not expropriated Foremost's investment in Pak Dairy, principally because the deprivation was not irreversible since Foremost retained its minority ownership. Similarly, in *International Systems & Controls v Iran*,[99] the Iran-US Claims Tribunal rejected the claim for indirect expropriation in circumstances where the claimant alleged that the Iranian Government deliberately interfered with its projects by requiring it to justify continuation of the projects in the context of the Revolution, and then by refusing to permit the projects to continue under the agreed arrangements. It reasoned as follows:

> the owner must at least be deprived of *some fundamental rights of ownership* and that the deprivation must be not merely ephemeral. The claim for destruction of a business must go beyond a showing of a classical breach of contract . . . The Respondents' failure to renew a contract or their failure to pay a debt cannot be said to amount to expropriation as in any event the Respondents have rights under the contracts to terminate them for cause or without cause upon making stipulated payments.[100]

In the ISDS context, there have been several important rulings on indirect expropriation in early cases. In *Marvin Feldman v Mexico*,[101] for example, the investor, a US citizen, operated a cigarette export business in Mexico, which benefitted from rebated production and sales taxes upon export. Two years later, however, Mexico changed the law to permit export

Review 1; Maurizio Brunetti, 'Introduction: Indirect Expropriation in International Law L'expropriation indirecte en droit international' (2003) 5(3) *International Law Forum du droit International* 150; Rudolf Dolzer and Felix Bloch, 'Indirect Expropriation: Conceptual Realignments?' (2003) 5 *International Law Forum du Droit International* 155.

96 In *Tecmed v Mexico*, ICSID Case No. ARB (AF)/00/2, para. 114, the tribunal recognised that, although terms such as 'equivalent to expropriation' or 'tantamount to expropriation' do not have a clear or unequivocal definition in international law, 'it is generally understood that they materialize through actions or conduct, which do not explicitly express the purpose of depriving one of rights or assets, but actually have that effect'. A similar pronouncement was articulated in *South American Silver Limited v Bolivia PCA* Case No. 2013–15.

97 No. 32-24-1, Award of December 19, 1983, Iran-U.S. C.T.R. 122, 1983.

98 No. 220–37/231-1, Award of April 11, 1986, 10 Iran-U.S. C.T.R. 228.

99 No. 256-439-2, Award of September 26, 1986, 10 Iran-U.S. C.T.R. 223.

100 ibid 98.

101 ICSID Case No. ARB(AF)/99/1, Award, 16 December 2002.

rebates only for cigarette producers. The ICSID tribunal found that there was no expropriation because Mexico had not interfered with the management or control of Feldman's business.

Meanwhile, in *Waste Management v Mexico*,[102] the tribunal rejected Waste Management's claim that its investment rights under the Concession Agreement were taken. Because the claimant at all times retained control and use of its property, and when the company ceased business, assets were sold off in an orderly way, the tribunal concluded that, although Mexican authorities may have breached the concession contract, 'absent arbitrary intervention by the State amounting to a virtual taking or sterilising of the enterprise,'[103] there was no expropriation.

The Appropriate Standard of Review for Establishing Indirect Expropriation

Several tests have been proffered over the years as the appropriate standard for reviewing whether an indirect expropriation has in fact occurred in an individual case. On the one hand, some tribunals ascribe to the so-called '*Pope & Talbot*' criteria, while, on the other hand, some tribunals have been concerned with the loss of expected benefits or value of the investment. In recent years, there is a growing trend among arbitral tribunals to subscribe to the *Pope & Talbot* criteria, but to treat these criteria as flexible, with the preponderance of authority requiring that investors show that the incidents of ownership (control, management, use, or enjoyment) have been eviscerated, sterilised, or neutralised.

(i) The *Pope & Talbot* 'Criteria'

In *Pope & Talbot*,[104] the tribunal asserted that in determining whether an indirect expropriation has taken place, several factors must be considered, including:

(i) whether the investor remained in control of its investment,
(ii) whether it directed its day-to-day operations,
(iii) whether its officers and employees were detained by the State,
(iv) whether the State supervised the work of the investor's officers and employees or not,
(v) whether the State had taken the proceeds of sales other than through taxation,
(vi) whether the State interfered with management or shareholders' activities,
(vii) whether the State prevented the distribution of dividends to shareholders,
(viii) whether the State interfered with the appointment of directors or management, and
(ix) whether the State had taken any other actions ousting the investor from full ownership and control of the investment.[105]

These criteria were applied in *Chemtura Corporation v Canada*.[106] Here, the claimant was one of four registrants in Canada of lindane-based pesticides. Lindane-based pesticide

102 ICSID Case No. ARB(AF)/00/3, Award, 30 April 2004.
103 ibid 160.
104 UNCITRAL Interim Award 26 Jun 2000.
105 ibid 100.
106 PCA Case No. 2008–01.

products, which were first registered on the Canadian market, were not approved for sale or distribution in the United States as a seed treatment for canola. The claimant confirmed its agreement to voluntarily remove canola from the product labels of its seed protectants that contained lindane insecticide, provided that it had suitable alternative products registered to replace them. The claimant then ceased to manufacture lindane products for canola use in Canada and canola use was removed from its labels. Later, however, it filed a request for reinstatement of canola use on its lindane labels. The regulatory authority, however, announced that it had completed a special review and that it had formed the view that the risk assessment findings warranted regulatory action by way of suspension or termination of lindane registrations. The authorities advised the claimant that its remaining registrations for lindane products were suspended. In this connection, the claimant argued that the suspension of the lindane product registrations was a measure tantamount to expropriation.

The tribunal held that the cancellation of Chemtura's lindane registrations did not amount to a 'substantial deprivation' of the claimant's investment. First, the sales from lindane products were a relatively small part of the claimant's overall sales at the relevant time. In these circumstances, the interference with the claimant's investment could not be deemed to be 'substantial'. Second, there was no interference with the claimant's management, daily operations, or the payment of dividends. In other words, the claimant remained at all relevant times in control of its investment. Finally, irrespective of the existence of a contractual deprivation, the tribunal considered that the measures challenged by the claimant constituted a valid exercise of the respondent's police powers; the authorities took measures within their mandate, in a non-discriminatory manner, and these measures were motivated by the increasing awareness of the dangers presented by lindane for human health and the environment. A measure adopted under such circumstances was a valid exercise of the state's police powers and, as a result, did not constitute an unlawful expropriation.

The tribunal ruled that the determination of whether there has been a substantial deprivation must be based on a fact-sensitive assessment, having regard to *Pope & Talbot* 'criteria'. In the tribunal's view, each criterion or at least some of them must be present for a deprivation to be 'substantial'. In its view, these criteria are intended to

> guide the inquiry of the Tribunal when it seeks to determine whether the effects of the measures challenged are to 'substantially' deprive the investor of the benefit of its investment. This is a matter of degree and not one of specific conditions.[107]

The tribunal further noted:

> One important feature of fact-sensitive assessments is that they cannot be conducted on the basis of rigid binary rules. It would make little sense to state a percentage or a threshold that would have to be met for a deprivation to be 'substantial' as such modus operandi may not always be appropriate. For instance, one could think of cases where one specific asset (a building, a piece of land, a line of business) which represents a part of the value of all the different assets held by a foreign investor in the host State has been entirely expropriated. In such case, applying a percentage or threshold approach to the overall assets held by the investor in the host State would preclude the deprivation from being 'substantial', whereas applying the same assessment to the specific asset in question would lead to the opposite conclusion. Given the diversity of situations that may arise in practice, it is preferable to examine each situation in the light of its own specific circumstances.[108]

107 ibid 247.
108 ibid 249.

A similar reliance on the *Pope & Talbot* 'criteria' can be seen in *Grand River Enterprises Six Nations, Ltd., et.al. v United States of America.*[109] Here, the claimants were a Canadian corporation owned by Indigenous peoples or First Nations peoples belonging to the Six Nations of the Iroquois Confederacy. They carried on a tobacco distribution business through a wholly owned company, Native Wholesale Supply Company ('NWS'). They created and carried on substantial business in the United States, importing cigarettes manufactured by Grand River and distributing them to wholesalers and retail outlets on Indian reservations in the United States.

The claim originated in litigation brought by more than 40 US state attorneys general against the major US tobacco producers in the 1990s, claiming compensation for the states' costs associated with treating tobacco-related illnesses. As part of an elaborate settlement of the states' lawsuits ('MSA'), each participating company, including the claimant's, agreed to extensive restrictions on advertising and other marketing practices, and to fund smoking prevention and cessation programmes. The MSA also required each company to make cash payments in perpetuity to a central account in respect of its sales. Meanwhile, each participating state received a share of the substantial amounts paid by companies in this regard, proportional to the total amount of cigarette sales subject to the MSA in that state. The amounts charged per cigarette increased each year in accordance with an agreed formula. Eventually, however, the authorities determined to limit the claimant's off-reservation cigarette sales. The claimants alleged that they suffered a decline in market share as a result. The respondent contended that considerations of public health were important motivating factors.

The tribunal held that the claimants were not deprived of ownership or control of an apparently prosperous and growing business importing and distributing Grand River's cigarettes. The claimant was free to pursue other continuing lines of export trading, such as exporting alcoholic beverages, photographic supplies, or other products, although they were effectively precluded from exporting cigarettes. In the tribunal's estimation, there was no indirect expropriation because the claimants' financial statements showed substantial growth in the firm's value, and the claimants ultimately remained in possession of its business activity. On the facts, the state action allegedly impairing only a limited portion of the value of an otherwise ongoing and profitable investment like Native Wholesale Supply could not give rise to a 'partial' expropriation under either NAFTA Article 1110 or general international law.

In the tribunal's view, for there to be an indirect expropriation, the measure in question must affect the totality of the investment. Expropriation, it recalled, involves the 'deprivation or impairment of all, or a very significant proportion of, an investor's interests.'[110] In other words, there must be a complete or very substantial deprivation of owners' rights in the totality of the investment, or a lasting removal of the ability of an owner to make use of its economic rights.

The tribunal, relying on *Glamis Gold*, *Feldman v Mexico*, and *Pope & Talbot*, considered that an indirect expropriation would only arise if the claimants had been radically deprived of the economical use and enjoyment of its investments, as if the rights related thereto had ceased to exist or the measures 'substantially impair[ed] the investor's economic rights, i.e. ownership, use, enjoyment or management of the business, by rendering them useless. Mere restrictions on the property rights do not constitute takings'.[111] In short,

109 UNCITRAL Award, 12 January 2011.
110 ibid 147.
111 ibid 150.

> expropriation requires very great loss or impairment of all of a claimant's investment' or significant diminution of the value of a claimant's property where the claimant nevertheless retained ownership and control . . . Interference with the investment's ability to carry on its business is not satisfied where the investment continues to operate, even if profits are diminished.[112]

While the *Chemtura* and *Grand River Enterprises* tribunals, respectively, treated the *Pope and Talbot* 'criteria' as a 'guide' in their assessment, other tribunals have treated these 'criteria' in a less flexible manner. For example, in *CMS Gas v Argentina*,[113] the claimant invested in the gas transportation sector allegedly in reliance on the Argentine Government's promises and guarantees, particularly those that offered a real return in US dollar terms (the Argentine peso was at par with the US dollar) and the adjustment of tariffs every six months in accordance with the United States Producer Price Index (US PPI). Towards the end of the 1990's, however, a serious economic crisis began to unfold in Argentina, which eventually had profound political and social ramifications for the country. Against this background, the Argentine Government called, in late 1999, a meeting with representatives of gas companies in order to discuss a temporary suspension of the US PPI adjustment of the gas tariffs. The companies agreed to temporarily defer the adjustment due for a period of six months. The agreement provided that the costs of the deferral would be subsequently recouped, and that resulting income losses would be indemnified.

Significant capital flight from Argentina followed. In this light, the Government introduced a decree that drastically limited the right of investors to withdraw deposits from bank accounts. Default was declared and several presidents succeeded one another in office within a matter of days. Emergency Law No. 25.561 was enacted declaring a public emergency. It reformed the foreign exchange system. More pointedly, the currency board which had pegged the peso to the dollar under the 1991 Convertibility Law was abolished, the peso was devalued, and different exchange rates were introduced for different transactions. The right of licensees of public utilities to adjust tariffs according to the US PPI was terminated, as was the calculation of tariffs in dollars. The respective tariffs were redenominated in pesos at the rate of one peso to the dollar. The same rate was applied to all private contracts denominated in dollars or other foreign currencies. The claimant alleged that, as a result of these developments, it lost income and, in part, its ability to pay its debt was reduced by a factor of more than three because the debt was denominated in US dollars and there had been an intervening devaluation of the peso. The claimant also asserted that the value of its shares in the domestic subsidiary, TNG, had dropped by 92%. In short, the claimant contended that the measures adopted by the Argentine Government during the period 2000–2002 resulted in indirect, and more specifically, creeping expropriation of its acquired rights.

Although the tribunal acknowledged that the measures had 'an important effect on the business of the Claimant',[114] it nonetheless concluded that there had not been an indirect expropriation. The tribunal applied the test in the *Lauder* case of whether it could be said that the state's actions 'effectively neutralised the enjoyment of the property.'[115] The tribunal also referenced the test from the *Iran-United States Claims* Tribunal that the deprivation must affect 'fundamental rights of ownership'.[116] Interestingly, the tribunal also applied the

112 ibid 151.
113 ICSID Case No. ARB/01/8, Award, 12 May 2005.
114 ibid 260.
115 ibid 261.
116 ibid 262.

'criteria' from the *Pope & Talbot* award, finding that 'the list of issues to be taken into account for reaching a determination of substantial deprivation, as discussed in that case, is not present in the instant dispute'.[117] More pointedly, it considered that the investor was still in control of the investment; the Government did not manage the day-to-day operations of the claimant; and the investor had full ownership and control over the investment.

Although an inflexible reading of the *Pope & Talbot* criteria is not endorsed by this book, it is submitted that, as a 'guide', they represent good law, as they focus the arbitrator's mind on the incidence of ownership, rather than just the loss of value, when determining whether the evidential threshold is met for establishing an indirect expropriation.

(ii) Loss of Utility and/or Benefit v Loss of the Incidents of Ownership

There is some jurisprudence to suggest that a loss of use and benefits or the loss of value of an investment can amount to an indirect expropriation. In *Middle East Cement v Egypt*,[118] for example, the ICSID tribunal found that Egypt had violated the provision on expropriation of the Egypt-Greece BIT. In that case, the Egyptian General Authority for Investment and Free Zones had granted a ten-year licence to a Greek bulk cement importer for the importation and storage of cement. Some years later, Egypt issued a decree prohibiting the importation of certain types of cement. This decree, which on its face did not purport to take the investor's property or affect the investor's import licence, nevertheless paralysed the investor's operations. In the ensuing arbitration proceedings, the investor argued that, although the licence technically remained in effect after the decree, the decree destroyed the economic benefit of the investment. The tribunal concluded that there had been an expropriation, although the decree remained in force for only four months. The tribunal concluded that

> when measures are taken by a State the effect of which is to deprive the investor of the *use and benefit* of its investment even though it may retain nominal ownership of the respective rights being the investment, the measures are often referred to as 'creeping' or as 'indirect' expropriation, or, as in the BIT, as measures the effect of which is tantamount to expropriation.[119]

Meanwhile, in *Goetz and Others v Burundi,*[120] the tribunal held that

> since . . . the revocation by the Minister for Industry and Commerce of the free zone certificate forced [the claimants] to halt all activities . . . which deprived their investments of *all utility and deprived the claimant investors of the benefit* which they could have expected from their investments, the disputed decision can be regarded as a 'measure having similar effect' to a measure depriving of or restricting property within the meaning of Article 4 of the Investment Treaty.[121]

Separately, in *Metalclad v Mexico*,[122] the municipality denied the investor the right to operate a landfill, notwithstanding the fact that the project was fully approved and endorsed by the federal government. The municipality allegedly denied the local construction permit

117 ibid 263.
118 ICSID Case No. ARB/99/6, Award, 12 April 2002.
119 ibid 107.
120 ICSID Case No. ARB/95/3, Award, 10 February 1999.
121 ibid 124.
122 ICSID Case No. ARB(AF)/97/1, Award, 30 August 2000.

in part because of its perception of the adverse environmental effects of the hazardous waste landfill and the geological unsuitability of the landfill site. The Governor of the Municipality also issued an Ecological Decree covering a large expanse of lands that included the landfill site. Because the Decree created an ecological reserve, the landfill was effectively barred from operating.

The tribunal held that there had been an indirect expropriation. By participating or acquiescing in the denial to Metalclad of the right to operate the landfill, the municipality was held to have acted outside its authority. The municipality had denied the construction permit in the absence of a timely, orderly, or substantive basis for such denial, which was an act tantamount to expropriation. A further ground for finding indirect expropriation was the fact that the Ecological Decree issued by the Governor had the effect of barring forever the operation of the landfill. The tribunal considered that it need not decide on the motivation or intent of the adoption of the Ecological Decree; the mere implementation of the Ecological Decree was, in and of itself, an act tantamount to expropriation in the absence of compensation. In the tribunal's view:

> expropriation under NAFTA includes . . . covert or incidental interference with the use of property which has the effect of depriving the owner, in whole or in significant part, of the use **or** *reasonably-to-be-expected economic benefit* of property even if not necessarily to the obvious benefit of the host State.[123]

The *Metalclad* Award is reminiscent of *Biloune et al. v Ghana Investment Centre*.[124] In that case, a private investor, on the basis of the representations of a government affiliated entity, began constructing a resort restaurant in Ghana before applying for a building permit. A stop work order was issued after a substantial amount of work had been completed. The order was based on the absence of a building permit. An application was submitted, but although it was not expressly denied, a permit was never issued. The tribunal held that an indirect expropriation had taken place because the totality of the circumstances had the effect of causing the irreparable cessation of work on the project. Because the investor had relied on the government's representations regarding the permit, the government authorities knew of the construction for more than one year before issuing the stop work order, the permits had not been required for other projects and no procedure was in place for dealing with building permit applications, an indirect expropriation had taken place.

Separately, in *Tecmed v Mexico*,[125] the claims concerned an investment in land, buildings, and other assets relating to a controlled landfill operation with hazardous industrial waste. A resolution cancelling the authorisation to run the waste landfill operation was adopted, *inter alia*, because of the strong opposition of the local population. The tribunal considered that to establish whether the Resolution was a measure equivalent to an expropriation under the terms of Section 5(1) of the Agreement, it had to, first, determine if the claimant, due to the Resolution, was radically deprived of the *economical use and enjoyment of its investments*, as if the rights related thereto – such as *the income or benefits* related to the landfill or to its exploitation – had ceased to exist. On the facts, due to the actions of the respondent, the investment had lost its value or economic use, hence there was an indirect expropriation.

123 ibid 103.
124 95 *ILR* 183, 207–10 (1993) (Judge Schwebel, President; Wallace and Leigh, Arbitrators).
125 ICSID Case No. ARB (AF)/00/2, 29 May 2003.

Finally, in *Consortium R.F.C.C. v Morocco,*[126] the tribunal explained that for an indirect expropriation to arise, the measures taken by the state must have 'substantial effects of a definite intensity that *decrease and/or make disappear the benefits* that can be legitimately expected from the exploitation of the rights that were the object of the measure to such an extent that they render the possession of those rights useless.'[127]

However, in the recent past, a growing number of arbitral tribunals have taken the general approach that loss of benefits/value is generally not sufficient to establish an indirect expropriation. Loss of control or another incident of ownership (management, use, control, or enjoyment) that results in a substantial evisceration of benefits, however, would be sufficient.

The leading case in this regard is *El Paso v Argentina.*[128] Here, the claimant argued that Argentina indirectly expropriated its investments by repudiating its contractual rights in its Argentinian subsidiaries; failing to abide by the requirement to collect payments as promised; pesification of capacity payments at an artificial exchange rate; and the alteration of the price-setting mechanism for electrical generators. It contended that, as a result of these measures, over 80% of the value of its equity value was destroyed, and it was 'forced' to sell its shares at a considerable loss (for less than 15% of what would have been their value in the absence of the impugned measures).

The tribunal held that the impugned measures adopted in connection with the oil and electric power generation industries did not substantially deprive the claimant of the use of and profits from its investment. On the contrary, the companies continued operating and earning profits, despite the crisis. On the question of whether the sale was the only and unavoidable consequence of the measures taken by the government, the tribunal disagreed. It considered that the sale was freely entered into by the claimant, and it was not effectively compelled to do so because of Argentina's measures. Only if the sale was the only possible consequence of the Argentinian measures could it have been concluded that these measures were expropriatory, in that they entailed a loss of control over the investment directly attributable to the state. In short, El Paso did not suffer any interference with its property, as shown by the fact that it could decide what to do with it, and chose to sell its shares. The sale was not an unavoidable and direct consequence of Argentina's measures.

The tribunal made some general pronouncements on the nature of indirect expropriation that are worth noting here:

1. Some general regulations can amount to indirect expropriation.
   a. As a matter of principle, general regulations do not amount to indirect expropriation.
   b. By exception, unreasonable general regulations can amount to indirect expropriation.
2. A necessary condition for expropriation is the *neutralisation of the use of the investment.*
   a. This means that at least one of the essential components of the property rights must have disappeared.
   b. This means also, a contrario, that *a mere loss in value of the investment, even an important one, is not an indirect expropriation.*[129]

126 ICSID Case No. ARB/00/6, Award, 22 December 2003.

127 ibid 69.

128 ICSID Case No. ARB/03/15, 31 October 2011.

129 ibid 233.

The *El Paso* tribunal relied on *S.D. Myers v Canada,*[130] *Pope and Talbot v Canada,*[131] *CMS v Argentina,*[132] and *Continental v Argentina*[133] to bolster its claim that there must be a substantial deprivation (i.e. disappearance, destruction, sterilisation, or neutralisation) of at least one of the essential aspects of ownership (i.e. use, management, enjoyment, or disposition/transferability); no lesser interference is sufficient. In its view, this usually implies a 'removal of the ability of an owner to make use of its economic rights' or, in other words, the 'loss of control' of the investment.[134] Fortified by the awards in *Enron v Argentina*[135] and *Sempra v Argentina,*[136] the tribunal in *El Paso* was emphatic in finding that 'if the measures do not interfere with the control of the property, there can be no expropriation'.[137]

The implication of the tribunal's ruling in *El Paso* is that 'a mere loss in value of the investment, even if important, is not an indirect expropriation'.[138] In other words, while the loss of benefits or expectations is necessary for a finding of an indirect expropriation, it is not sufficient. In this context, the tribunal in *El Paso* rejected a reading of *Middle East Cement v Egypt, Goetz and Others v Republic of Burundi, Metalclad, Tecmed* and *Consortium R.F.C.C. v Morocco,* discussed above, which suggested that dicta in these cases support the idea that a substantial deprivation of the value of, or the benefits to be deprived from, an investment can also be viewed as an indirect expropriation. In its view, these dicta have been misconstrued.

First, in response to the *Middle East Cement* award, the *El Paso* tribunal interpreted that ruling in the following manner:

> if indeed a reference is made to the deprivation of the benefit of the investment, the formula used by the tribunal in *Middle East Cement* refers more precisely to the deprivation of '*the use and benefit*'. The loss of benefit is a result of the impossibility to use the investment – equivalent to a loss of control over the investment – and not an expropriation *per se*.[139]

The *El Paso* tribunal then turned its attention to *Goetz and Others*, offering the following observations:

> there is a reference to the deprivation of the expected benefit [in the *Goetz* award], but this was a result of the cancellation by the State of a free-zone certificate which prevented the investor from continuing any economic activity, which is indeed a situation where it can be said that the investor was expropriated as it completely lost the use of its property.[140]

Meanwhile, in respect of the *Metalclad* award, the *El Paso* tribunal considered that:

> the loss of benefits is a result of a deprivation of the use of the investment. Second, considering the facts and not the mere broad language, it is evident that the tribunal in Metalclad did not hold that there was an expropriation because the benefits of the investor were not as expected,

130 UCITRAL Partial Award (Merits), 13 November 2000.
131 UNCITRAL Award, 30 December 2002.
132 ICSID Case No. ARB/01/8, Award, 12 May 2005.
133 ICSID Case No. ARB/03/9, Award, 5 September 2008.
134 *El Paso v Argentina*, ICSID Case No. ARB/03/15, Award, 31 October 2011, para. 245.
135 ICSID Case No. ARB/01/3, Award, 22 May 2007.
136 ICSID Case No. ARB/02/16, Award, 28 September 2007.
137 *El Paso v Argentina*, ICSID Case No. ARB/03/15, Award, 31 October 2011, para. 248.
138 ibid 249.
139 ibid 250.
140 ibid 251.

> but decided that there was an expropriation of the investment because, after the investor was granted the federal permit to exploit the landfill, and given assurances that it would receive the municipal permit to the same effect, the latter was not granted, rendering the whole project impossible to pursue: it was because there was a complete neutralisation of the investment project that an expropriation was found.[141]

Separately, in relation to *Tecmed*, the *El Paso* tribunal considered that:

> it was not just a loss of benefits that was considered to be expropriatory; it was the cancellation of the permit which neutralised the whole investment, as no other activity could be performed on the landfill. This was underscored by the tribunal, according to which there is an indirect expropriation when 'the economic value of the use, enjoyment or disposition of the assets or rights affected by the administrative action or decision have been neutralized or destroyed'.[142]

Finally, in respect of *Consortium R.F.C.C. v Morocco,* the *El Paso* tribunal explained that the *Consortium R.F.C.C* Tribunal had been quite clear that:

> the disappearance of benefits had to be the result of a loss of control or access to the property rather than of a change in the assets' value: 'The expropriation of an asset or a right is characterised by the disappearance, for the expropriated person, if not of the title to property at least of the enjoyment of the said property or of the access to it'.[143]

The *El Paso* tribunal then rallied support from the tribunals dealing with the Argentinean cases, most of which found that the loss in value of the investment was not a sufficient basis for a finding of indirect expropriation, even where the loss was quite significant. For example, in *LG&E v Argentina*,[144] although it was alleged that the value of LG&E's holdings in the licenses had been reduced by more than 90% as a result of respondent's abrogation of the principal guarantees of the tariff system, the tribunal there did not find an indirect expropriation, as the measures themselves did not interfere 'with the investment's ability to carry on its business,'[145] even though the profits were drastically diminished.

A similar rejection of mere loss of value in favour of the test of evisceration of the essence of ownership was countenanced in *Compañiá de Aguas del Aconquija and Vivendi Universal v Argentina*.[146] Here, the claimants argued that certain measures adopted by the Province of Tucumán had a significantly damaging impact on the economic viability of their concession. First, they alleged that the Provincial Government used its regulatory authority to compel a local subsidiary (CAA) to stop invoicing customers for certain fees, contrary to the Province's own prior instructions and to the express terms of the Concession Agreement. Second, it alleged that the Province used its authority over CAA to effectively deny a 10% tariff increase to which it was entitled in each of the second and third years of the concession. Against this backdrop, it considered that CAA had no choice but to agree to try to renegotiate the Agreement three times during the two-and-a-half-year effective life of the concession. Third, it argued that the Legislature unilaterally changed the legal framework that governed CAA, drastically altering the economic viability of the concession. In

141 ibid 252.
142 ibid 253.
143 ibid 254.
144 ICSID Case No. ARB/02/1 Decision on Liability, 3 October 2006.
145 ibid 191.
146 ICSID Case No. ARB/97/3, Award, 20 August 2007.

particular, Law 6826 purported to approve a new contract to govern the concession, but the version enacted contained approximately 70 economically significant changes to the terms earlier agreed upon by claimants and the Governor.

Beyond these measures, the claimants alleged that the municipalities demanded that they be given control over the water and sewerage services, followed quickly by public statements from the Governor, legislators, and the Attorney General condemning the concession. Then, the Legislature introduced a series of bills and other proposals demanding the nullification or renegotiation of the Concession Agreement. The Legislature also appointed an Investigative Commission to review the privatisation and analyse the options for renegotiating the tariff. It was also alleged that legislators handed out 3,000 applications in the public square to encourage people to submit claims against CAA and to block CAA's collection efforts. Similarly, the claimants contended that the Ombudsman established a claims procedure that would allow users to refuse to pay for CAA's services. It allegedly also issued a formal resolution which effectively prevented CAA from cutting the service to customers who refused to pay their bills and to provide a legal defence to customers if CAA challenged their refusal to pay. By the time the Concession Agreement was rescinded, CAA's recovery rate hovered around 20 percent, in stark contrast to the rate of 89–90% upon which the Concession Agreement was premised. In their view, this amounted to a clear deprivation of their property. Moreover, the claimants contended that even after the expropriation of the claimants' investment in the concession was complete (i.e. upon termination of the Concession Agreement), the Tucumán authorities effected a further taking by compelling CAA to continue to provide services to the Province outside the terms of any contractual arrangement. In effect, they argued, the Province appropriated for itself and its citizens the value of CAA's services for a period of over ten months, and yet paid no compensation to CAA for the services.

The tribunal considered that there was an indirect expropriation because the respondent's measures 'struck at the economic heart of, and crippled, the Claimants' investment'.[147] In the tribunal's view, the state's action had 'a devastating effect on the economic viability of the concession',[148] evidenced by the fact that CAA's recovery rate declined dramatically over the life of the concession. The tribunal was concerned that the measures in question, taken cumulatively, rendered the concession valueless and forced CAA and Vivendi to incur unsustainable losses. This was not a case where the value of the claimants' investment had simply been diminished. Rather, here, as in the *Tecmed* case, the claimants were 'radically deprived of the economic *use and enjoyment* of their concessionary rights.'[149] In other words, CAA's contractual rights under the Concession Agreement were rendered worthless by the Province's actions while its losses continued to mount. It was the neutralisation and rendering as useless the claimants' rights which constituted an indirect expropriation. Because the Province's conduct had the effect of putting an end to the investment, rescission of the Concession Agreement was the only rational alternative for the claimants.

Meanwhile, in *Glamis Gold, Ltd. v United States of America*,[150] the investor, a Canadian mining company, sought permission to develop a mine in California using open-pit techniques. The claimant alleged that the respondent breached the guarantee against expropriation

147 ibid 7.5.25.
148 ibid 7.5.26.
149 ibid 7.5.34.
150 UNCITRAL Award 8 Jun 2009.

in circumstances where the State of California adopted measures that strictly determined how mining was to be undertaken, requiring complete backfilling and restoration of the site. While other techniques to mine the property remained available, California banned open-pit mining in an effort to protect Native American cultural sites. Although the new regulations did not dispossess the investor of its property or preclude its development of other mining processes, their profits were nonetheless negatively impacted.

The tribunal noted that in determining whether there had been an indirect expropriation, consideration had to be given to whether the federal and California measures substantially impaired the investor's economic rights, i.e. ownership, use, enjoyment, or management of the business, by rendering them useless. In its view, mere restrictions on the property rights do not constitute takings. On the facts, the majority of the tribunal held that the California backfilling measures did not result in a radical diminution in the value of the Imperial Project, and therefore the claimant's claim of indirect expropriation failed.

Separately, in *Mamidoil v Albania*,[151] the claimant alleged that the respondent adopted a series of measures which curtailed the profitability of its investment. It contended that, first, the state unexpectedly enacted a new land use plan which banned petroleum products from the port of Durres, including the unloading of vessels. For this reason, their fuel tanks had to be abandoned, thereby making it impossible to earn profits. It further argued that the 'final blow' was the closing of the port of Durres for the discharging of petroleum tankers. It its view, this amounted to an indirect expropriation, as the operation of the tank farm had become completely uneconomical.

The tribunal held that, contrary to the claimant's assertion, there was no indirect expropriation. The claimant was not caught by surprise when the state enacted the new land use plan which banned petroleum products from the port. In fact, the claimant was aware that regulatory changes and a transformation of the port of Durres were imminent. In other words, before the claimant's construction of its tank farm even began, the claimant had been aware that regulatory changes were coming. Further, there was no evidence that the Albanian authorities put pressure on the claimant to relocate the tank farm.

The tribunal rejected the claimant's allegation that (the lack of) policy measures made it impossible to earn any profits. In fact, the claimant did earn profit before the port of Durres was closed. In any event, the impugned measure did not result in the claimant's loss of any of the attributes of its property. The claimant continued to use, possess, control, and dispose of the property. For this reason, no indirect expropriation was found on the facts.

Commenting on the nature of indirect expropriation, the tribunal considered that such expropriation arises where the state adopts 'measures that deprive an investor completely or in [significant] part of its property, or of its economic enjoyment'.[152] This means that the investor must have truly lost at least one of the essential components of their property rights. In other words, it is not sufficient that the investment must have lost its value or that the investor has been deprived of benefits, but that 'these effects resulted from a loss of one or several attributes of ownership'.[153] These attributes of ownership are use and enjoyment, control and possession, and disposal and alienation. If one or more of these attributes is affected, the resulting loss of value and/or benefit may lead to a successful claim of indirect expropriation. In other words, even if there is a loss of value or benefits suffered as a result

151 ICSID Case No. ARB/11/24, Award, 30 March 2015.
152 ibid 564.
153 ibid 568.

of the state's measure, if the substance and attributes of property are left intact, there will be no indirect expropriation. If, however, the essence or attributes of the property are adversely affected, and no compensation is paid, there will be an expropriation. The tribunal then cited with approval *El Paso v Argentina,* wherein the tribunal in that case considered that 'for an expropriation to exist, the investor should be substantially deprived not only of the benefits, but also of the use of its investment. A mere loss of value, which is not the result of an interference with the control or use of the investment, is not an indirect expropriation.'[154]

The case of *Unglaube v Costa Rica*[155] is also instructive. The case concerned certain properties which were owned by the claimants in the vicinity of Playa Grande, a picturesque beach on Costa Rica's Pacific coast, in the municipality of Santa Cruz. Given the endangered status of female Leatherback turtles in the area, and Costa Rica's well-known reputation as an eco-tourism destination, the Government took steps to protect their nesting habitat. These steps included the creation of a national park in the area. In this connection, the Government passed Resolution 375 which purported to expropriate 75-metre by 100-metre strip which was adjacent to the Park (the state essentially treated this strip as if it were inside the Park when in reality it belonged to the claimants). Thereafter, the Supreme Court ordered the state to either proceed with the expropriation of the claimants' property within the Park within a reasonable period of time, or if there were no funds available to do so, grant the permits or authorisations to them so that they could exercise their property rights once they obtained the necessary environmental impact study and the environmental permits that ruled out the possibility of further endangerment of the leatherbacks. More than three years after this ruling, the state still had not purchased the claimants' property nor granted them the necessary permits to allow them to exercise and enjoy their property rights.

The tribunal, relying on the *Santa Elena*[156] decision, found that the state had committed an act tantamount to expropriation when it enclosed the 75-metre strip within the Park without having made timely arrangements for payment of compensation to the claimants. Although the claimants remained in possession of their investment, the strip was negatively impacted in terms of saleability and use; in other words, there was an indirect expropriation because 'the rights of the owner of the 75-metre strip had been seriously and negatively impacted',[157] such that 'the practical and economic use of the Property by the Claimant was irretrievably lost'.[158]

A final case is worth noting – *Philip Morris v Uruguay.*[159] Here, the respondent adopted a Regulation whose effect was to restrict the sale of tobacco products. The claimants alleged that by effectively banning seven of its thirteen variants and substantially diminishing the value of the remaining ones, the respondent expropriated its brand assets, including the intellectual property and goodwill associated with each of the claimants' brand variants. The respondent, by contrast, argued that the Regulation could not be considered expropriatory since they were a legitimate exercise of the state's sovereign police power to protect public health. The respondent further contended that, in any event, even after the adoption of the measures, the claimants' investment continued to be profitable such as to negate a

154 ibid 570.
155 ICSID Case No. ARB/09/20, Award 16 May 2012.
156 ICSID Case No. ARB/96/1, Award, 17 February 2000.
157 *Unglaube v Republic of Costa Rica*, ICSID Case No. ARB/08/1, Award, 16 May 2012, para. 220.
158 ibid.
159 ICSID Case No. ARB/10/7, Award, 8 July 2016.

finding of a severe economic impact on the claimants' business that rendered it virtually without value.

The tribunal considered that 'in order to be considered an indirect expropriation, the government's interference with the investor's rights must have a major adverse impact on the Claimants' investments'.[160] In other words, the measures must amount to a 'substantial deprivation' of its value, use or enjoyment.[161] The 'determinative factors' in this connection are 'the intensity and duration of the economic deprivation suffered by the investor as a result of such measures'.[162] On the facts, although the claimants' trademarks were capable of being expropriated, there was no indirect expropriation occasioned by the 80/80 Regulation as the claimants' Marlboro brand and other distinctive elements continued to appear on cigarette packs in Uruguay. In other words, the effects of the Regulation were not such as to deprive the claimants of the value of its business or cause a substantial deprivation of the value, use, or enjoyment of the investment. In the tribunal's view, the state's limitation to 20% of the space available for the Marlboro brand and other distinctive elements for the purpose of promoting public health did not have a substantial effect on the claimants' business, and, in any event, the claimants continued earning profits, notwithstanding the application of the impugned measure:

> as long as sufficient value remains after the Challenged Measures are implemented, there is no expropriation. As confirmed by investment treaty decisions, a partial loss of the profits that the investment would have yielded absent the measure does not confer an expropriatory character on the measure.[163]

In other words, the interference with the claimant's investment is not expropriatory where the investment continues to operate, even if profits are diminished. Only if the impact is substantial, beyond profitability, in that one of the essential elements of ownership is rendered worthless, would there be an indirect expropriation.

A related issue which arose was whether indirect expropriation may relate to identifiable distinct assets comprising the investment or, rather, is to be determined considering the investment as a whole. In the tribunal's view, the answer to this question largely depends on the facts of the individual case, but as a general rule of thumb, even though a business may have several assets which are affected by a measure, the business is to be considered as a whole if the measure affects its activities in their entirety.[164] A Tribunal, in this connection, might, for example, look at whether any countermeasures taken to mitigate the effects of the measure involve the business as a whole or just aspects of the business.

In the final analysis, the Tribunal ultimately concluded that the measures adopted by Uruguay were a valid exercise of the State's police powers to regulate harmful products in order to protect public health.

From a Commonwealth Caribbean perspective, it is arguable that the high standard for a finding of indirect expropriation articulated by the *El Paso, Vivendi*, and *Mamidoil* tribunals is desirable in that it offers respondent states a reasonable degree of regulatory autonomy to adopt measures which, even if they result in a loss of value in an investment, will not be an

160 ibid 192.
161 ibid.
162 ibid.
163 ibid 286.
164 ibid 283.

expropriation once the incidents of ownership are not neutralised. In other words, regulations that reduce the profitability of an investment but do not shut it down completely and leave the investor in control should generally not qualify as an indirect expropriation even though they might give rise to liability for violation of other standards of treatment, such as the national treatment standard or fair and equitable treatment standard. Indeed, as repeatedly asserted above, for there to be an indirect expropriation, one or more of the incidents of ownership (use, enjoyment, management/control, and/or disposition) must be subject to a substantial deprivation, with the result being that a substantial loss of benefits/value of the asset has been sustained. A mere loss of value, on its own, which is not the result of an interference with the incidents of ownership, is not an indirect expropriation.

Finally, it is submitted that the criteria in *Pope & Talbot,* to the extent that they are not construed inflexibly, do not substantively conflict with the rulings in the *El Paso, Vivendi* and *Mamidoil* awards, and so these should remain highly persuasive in future assessments of indirect expropriation.

(iii) 'Dispossession': Loss of Value v Loss of Control?

It appears that if the relevant IIA[165] refers to 'dispossession' in its guarantee against expropriation, the appropriate test for indirect expropriation is loss of control of the investment. Loss of value is not sufficient, unless the investor is able to prove a *total loss of value*. That is, the property has been rendered worthless by the measure. This principle was articulated in *Total S.A. v Argentina,*[166] a case in which the tribunal examined the term 'dispossession' in Article 5(2) of the French-Argentina BIT, finding that such term is a civil law concept that requires a showing that the investor has lost *factual* control over the investment in question, irrespective of whether the title has been transferred. In its view, such an approach to expropriation differs from the parallel provisions contained in the lesser restrictive Argentina-US BIT ('tantamount to expropriation') and the Argentina-UK BIT which refers only to 'equivalent to nationalisation or expropriation'.

On the facts, since the claimant had not been dispossessed of TGN (its subsidiary holding) nor the management of its business, there had not been an indirect expropriation. Rather, the claimant remained in full control of its investment; its subsidiary operated under the management of its shareholders and carried on its daily activities; and it remained listed on the Buenos Aires Stock Exchange. Further, the trust fund instituted by the state did not

165 See for example, Article 5(2) French-Argentina BIT. The Contracting Parties shall not, directly or indirectly, measures of expropriation or nationalisation or any other similar measures having an effect equivalent dispossession, except for a public purpose and provided that they are neither discriminatory nor contrary to a specific engagement. The measures referred to above that could be taken shall be subject to the payment of prompt and adequate compensation in the amount calculated on the real value of the investment concerned must be assessed in relation to a normal economic situation and prior to any threat of dispossession. Such compensation, its amount and has no later than the date of dispossession. the compensation shall be paid without delay, and effectively realisable freely transferable. it produces until the date of payment, shall include interest at an appropriate rate of interest. For a slightly different wording, see Article 8(2) Trinidad and Tobago-Guatemala BIT: the compensation shall:

a. be equivalent to the fair market value of the expropriated investment immediately before the expropriation or impending expropriation became public knowledge, whichever is earlier.
b. include interest from the date of *dispossession* of the expropriated property until the date of payment.

166 ICSID Case No. ARB/04/01, Decision on Liability, 27 December 2010.

interfere with the ability of the claimant's shareholders to manage TGN. In short, the negative economic impact of the measures in question did not deprive the claimant's investment, on a permanent basis, of *all or substantially all its value.*[167]

The tribunal, however, clarified that it is possible in an appropriate case for there to be an indirect expropriation where control remains in the hands of the foreign investor but the *economic profitability* of the investment has been *totally destroyed* in some other way. In this connection, it cited with approval the decision of *Sempra Energy International v Argentina*, where the tribunal there stated that:

> a finding of indirect expropriation would require more than adverse effect. It would require that the investor no longer be in control of its business operation, or that the value of the business have been virtually annihilated.[168]

It also cited with approval *LG&E v Argentina*, a case in which the tribunal there found that:

> [i]nterference with the investment's ability to carry on its business is not satisfied where the investment continues to operate, even if profits are diminished. The impact must be substantial in order that compensation may be claimed for the expropriation.[169]

Returning to the facts, the tribunal in *Total* concluded that, first, regarding the pesification, this measure, in the absence of a stabilisation clause, was a bona fide regulatory measure of general application, which was reasonable in the light of Argentina's economic and monetary emergency and proportionate to the aim of facing such an emergency. Second, the pesification was not contrary to any specific undertaking given by Argentina to Total; the provision according to which the gas tariffs were calculated in US dollars and adjusted in accordance with US PPI variations could not be properly construed as 'promises' or 'specific undertakings' given by Argentina to Total since they were not addressed directly or indirectly to Total. And finally, the *de facto* freezing of the gas tariffs implied neither a deprivation of the investment nor a total loss of its value.

The take-away from the foregoing, then, is that where an IIA uses the term 'dispossession' in its guarantee against expropriation, such clause should be construed restrictively, requiring evidence that the investor has lost (*de facto*) control over its investment as a result of the impugned measure.

IV. PARTIAL DEPRIVATION

While it is reasonably well-settled that the full deprivation of the use of the relevant property rights would likely amount to an indirect expropriation,[170] tribunals have shown remarkable inconsistency on the question of whether the partial deprivation of use or benefit of an investment as a result of a state's measures are tantamount to expropriation. For example, in *S.D. Myers*,[171] the tribunal considered that 'it may be that, in some contexts and circumstances, it would be appropriate to view a deprivation as amounting to an expropriation,

167 ibid 196.
168 ibid fn 227.
169 ibid.
170 *Starrett Housing Corporation v Iran* 16 Iran-U.S. C.T.R. 112 referred to rights being rendered 'useless.'
171 UNCITRAL Partial Award (Merits), 13 November 2000.

even if it were *partial* or temporary'.[172] It did not, however, explain what those 'contexts and circumstances' might be. By contrast, the *Metalclad*[173] tribunal appears to suggest that for an indirect expropriation to arise, the state's measures must have substantially deprived the investor of at least a 'significant part' of the use or reasonably-to-be expected economic benefit of property. Meanwhile, in *GAMI v Mexico*,[174] after reviewing *Pope and Talbot*, *SD Myers*, and *Metalclad*, the tribunal seemed unable to come to a definitive position, ultimately concluding that it 'need not decide whether partial destruction of shareholding interests may be tantamount to expropriation'.[175] It, however, did suggest that the nature of the property in respect of which the investor has been allegedly partially deprived of is fundamental to its analysis. In its estimation, the taking of 50 acres of a farm is equally expropriatory whether that is the 'whole farm or just a fraction'.[176] By contrast, it noted that if only one of five equally valuable mills had been impaired, this would not be equivalent to a taking, unless that one mill was the only one having a positive value.

What, then, might we take away from these seemingly conflicting pronouncements? It is submitted that a partial deprivation of use or benefit should not normally amount to an expropriation, unless such deprivation is substantial enough to adversely affect (sterilise or neutralise) the incidents of ownership (use, enjoyment, or management or control) of the investment. Because this analysis seeks to assess whether the very essence of the investor's interests have been abrogated, it is submitted that tribunals must necessarily engage in both a qualitative and quantitative examination of the duration and impact/effect of the measure(s) on the investment in question.

V. TEMPORARY/PERMANENT NATURE OF THE EXPROPRIATORY MEASURE

There now appears to be consensus that for the impugned measure to be considered to reach the threshold of an indirect expropriation, the measure in question must not be merely transitory or ephemeral, but rather permanent in nature. In this connection, in *Tecmed v Mexico*,[177] the tribunal underscored that:

> measures adopted by a State, whether regulatory or not, are an indirect *de facto* expropriation if they are irreversible and *permanent* . . . . Under international law, the owner is also deprived of property where the use or enjoyment of benefits related thereto is exacted or interfered with to a similar extent, even where legal ownership over the assets in question is not affected, and so long as the deprivation is not temporary.[178]

Similarly, the *Santa Elena v Costa Rica*[179] tribunal considered that an indirect expropriation arises where 'events demonstrate that the owner was deprived of fundamental rights of ownership and it appears that this deprivation is not merely ephemeral.'[180]

172 ibid 283.
173 ICSID Case No. ARB(AF)/97/1, Award, 30 August 2000.
174 UNCITRAL Final Award, 15 November 2004.
175 ibid 132.
176 ibid 126.
177 ICSID Case No. ARB (AF)/00/2, Award, 29 May 2003.
178 ibid 116.
179 ICSID Case No. ARB/96/1, Award, 17 February 2000.
180 ibid 77.

There have been ISDS awards which, however, cast doubt on the general rule that impugned measures that are of a temporary nature will not give rise to an indirect expropriation. In *S.D. Myers v Canada*,[181] for example, the tribunal asserted that 'it may be that, in some contexts and circumstances, it would be appropriate to view a deprivation as amounting to an expropriation, even if it were partial or temporary'.[182] Interestingly, and perhaps regrettably, it did not explain what these 'contexts and circumstances' might be.

Meanwhile, in *Olin v Libya*,[183] in assessing the overall impact of the expropriation order on Olin's investment, the Tribunal considered that measures adopted by the state, 'even if temporary, can have an effect equivalent to expropriation if their length and impact on the investment are sufficiently important.'[184] In this case, the impugned Libyan measures considerably impaired Olin's investment between November 2006 and June 2011, which, according to the tribunal, was 'a significant period of time for a business that had just started its operations'.[185] These measures coincided with Olin accumulating a negative cash flow of LYD 18,8 million, largely due to delays in the launch of Olin's products and its inability to realise the benefits of its investment during the four years and a half of uncertainty that followed the application of the 2006 Expropriation Order. During this time, Olin was overtaken by its competitors on the Libyan market and had lost the advantage of being one of the first entrants as a local private producer.

What, then, can we take away from the disparate approaches adopted by tribunals in the foregoing cases? It is submitted that, as a matter of principle, temporary measures should not generally give rise to an indirect expropriation. However, there might be circumstances, as in *Olin*, where, having regard to the nature of the measures in question, their duration and impact, a tribunal might be tempted to find an indirect expropriation, notwithstanding the fact that the measures are temporary in nature. In other words, there is an argument to be made that a temporary measure which neutralises one or more incidents of ownership and which results in a significant loss of benefits in this connection should be compensable.

VI. CREEPING EXPROPRIATION

Creeping expropriation is a form of indirect expropriation. According to the tribunal in *Siemens A.G. v Argentina*,[186]

> By definition, creeping expropriation refers to a process, to steps that eventually have the effect of an expropriation. If the process stops before it reaches that point, then expropriation would not occur. This does not necessarily mean that no adverse effects would have occurred. Obviously, each step must have an adverse effect but by itself may not be significant or considered an illegal act. The last step in a creeping expropriation that tilts the balance is similar to the straw that breaks the camel's back. The preceding straws may not have had a perceptible effect but are part of the process that led to the break.[187]

181 UNCITRAL Partial Award, 13 November 2000.
182 ibid 283.
183 ICC Case No. 20355/MCP.
184 ibid 165.
185 ibid.
186 ICSID Case No. ARB/02/08, Award, 6 February 2007.
187 ibid 263.

A similar definition was proffered by the tribunal in *Generation Ukraine Inc. v Ukraine*:[188]

> Creeping expropriation is a form of indirect expropriation with a distinctive temporal quality in the sense that it encapsulates the situation whereby a series of acts attributable to the State over a period of time culminate in the expropriatory taking of such property.[189]

In *Siemens*, the claimant responded to Argentina's call for the submission of bids for the implementation of an immigration control, personal identification, and electoral information system, including the provision of all equipment necessary for data processing and the intercommunication of such equipment, start-up, technical support and maintenance services, and preparation, printing, and home delivery of national identity cards. Siemens ultimately won the bid, and was assured that, for its services, it was entitled to charge a fee for each national identity card issued, including home delivery and updates to the cards, fees for the immigration proceedings processed through the system and fees for printing the voting rolls.

Upon the commencement of the contract, first, Argentina requested that the claimant postpone production of the new identity cards. Second, after the elections and a new President was elected, the claimant's operations were halted on the basis that the system required governmental authorisation. Thereafter, Argentina suspended the production, printing, and distribution of all new identity cards apparently because, in the case of foreigners' identity cards, the system printed the left thumbprint at the place reserved for the right thumbprint. Argentina then prohibited the claimant from introducing any modification to the system to correct this problem. The Government then sought to renegotiate the claimant's fees for implementing the new system and correspondingly sought to increase the number of free-of-charge identity cards.

A commission to review the contract, with input from Siemens, made several proposals, which were sent to the Government for approval. However, at a meeting between Siemens' representatives and the President of Argentina, the President allegedly promised to issue a decree approving the negotiated terms of the Contract Restatement Proposal. However, the Decree was never issued. Siemens thereafter addressed several complaints to the Minister of Interior, but these were to no avail. Following the passage of the 2000 Emergency Law, the claimant received a new draft proposal from the Government which differed from the Contract Restatement Proposal, to which they expressed concerns. The Minister then informed Siemens that the new proposal was non-negotiable, and ultimately the Contract was terminated by Decree 669/01 under the terms of the 2000 Emergency Law.

In these circumstances, the tribunal held that the series of measures taken by Argentina amounted to a creeping expropriation. Here, the last straw – Decree 669/01 – proverbially broke the camel's back. Indeed, while the individual actions leading up to the Decree did not amount to an expropriation in and of themselves, when these measures were combined with the Decree, they had the effect of substantially depriving the investor of the use of its investment. In this regard, the tribunal considered the 'effect and permanence' of the measures in question, and considered that the gradual process, 'with the issuance of Decree 669/01, culminated in the expropriation of Siemens' investment'.[190]

Meanwhile, in *Azurix Corp. v Argentina*,[191] the tribunal considered the question of what the appropriate timeframe is, if any, over the course of which a creeping expropriation must be established. In this regard, it concluded that:

188 UNCITRAL Award, 15 September 2003.

189 ibid 20–22.

190 ibid 271.

191 ICSID Case No. ARB/01/12, Award, 14 July 2006.

> There is no specific time set under international law for measures constituting creeping expropriation to produce that effect. It will depend on the specific circumstances of the case. Arbitral tribunals have considered that a measure is not ephemeral if the property was out of the control of the investor for a year (*Wena*) or an export license was suspended for four months (*Middle East Cement*), or that the measure was ephemeral if it lasted for three months (*S.D. Myers*). These cases involved a single measure. When considering multiple measures, it will depend on the duration of their cumulative effect. Unfortunately, there is no mathematical formula to reach a mechanical result. How much time is needed must be judged by the specific circumstances of each case. As expressed by the tribunal in *Generation Ukraine*: 'The outcome is a judgment, i.e., the product of discernment, and not the printout of a computer program'.[192]

The tribunal went on to note that in assessing at which point a creeping expropriation has actually taken place, the arbitrator will bear in mind the date on which the governmental 'interference' has deprived the owner of his rights or has made those rights practically useless.[193]

In practice, there is often disagreement between the parties as to whether, in order to prove that a creeping expropriation has occurred, the final result of each individual measure must be an actual expropriation or deprivation of property rights. In this connection, in *Teinver S.A., v Argentina,*[194] the tribunal proffered:

> the relevant focus of the inquiry for this purpose is the effect or result of the measure, as opposed to the purpose for which each measure was undertaken. A creeping expropriation is a particular type of indirect expropriation, which requires an inquiry into the particular facts. The use of the term 'creeping' to describe this type of expropriation indicates that the entirety of the measures should be reviewed in the aggregate to determine their effect on the investment rather than each individual measure on its own.[195]

The case of *Crystallex v Venezuela*[196] concerned the issue of whether certain measures adopted by Venezuela over a certain period of time amounted to a creeping expropriation of the claimant's investment in the area called 'Las Cristinas'. Las Cristinas is reported to

192 ibid 313.

193 ibid 417.

194 ICSID Case No. ARB/09/1, Award, 21 July 2017.

195 The Tribunal cited W.M Reisman and R Sloane, 'Indirect Expropriation and its Valuation in the BIT Generation' (2004) 74 *British Yearbook of International Law* 115, 123–25:

> A creeping expropriation therefore denotes, in the paradigmatic case, an expropriation accomplished by a cumulative series of regulatory acts or omissions over a prolonged period of time, no one of which can necessarily be identified as the decisive event that deprived the foreign national of the value of its investment. Moreover, they may be interspersed with entirely lawful state regulatory actions. By definition, then, creeping expropriations lack the vividness and transparency not only of formal expropriations, but also of many regulatory or otherwise indirect expropriations, which may be identified more closely with a few discrete events. The gradual and sometimes furtive nature of the acts and omissions that culminate in a creeping expropriation tends to obscure what tribunals ordinarily denominate the 'moment of expropriation'.

At 128: The Tribunal also cited with approval Professors Reisman and Sloane who note that:

> Discrete acts, analyzed in isolation rather than in the context of the overall flow of events, may, whether legal or not in themselves, seem innocuous vis-à-vis a potential expropriation. Some may not be expropriatory in themselves. Only in retrospect will it become evident that those acts comprised part of an accretion of deleterious acts and omissions, which in the aggregate expropriated the foreign investor's property rights.

196 ICSID Case No. ARB(AF)/11/2, Award, 4 April 2016.

contain one of the largest undeveloped gold deposits in the world. The claimant contended that Venezuela's denial of a permit to Crystallex to exploit the gold deposits at Las Cristinas, and the rescission by a state-run corporation of the Mine Operation Contract (MOC), were a breach of the Venezuela-Canada BIT.

The tribunal, relying on *Siemens v Argentina*, found that Venezuela's actions amounted to a creeping expropriation. In the tribunal's view, there were three broad groups of actions that had been taken which, taken cumulatively, affirmed its finding that a creeping expropriation had occurred. First, the host state exhibited 'fundamental unfairness' in the manner in which it treated the claimant during the process leading to the denial of permit. Although it accepted that investors do not have an automatic entitlement to be granted a permit by states, on the facts, the denial of the permit here was the 'first tangible occurrence of the investor's rights and the value associated thereto being severely affected as a result of measures attributable to Venezuela'.[197] Second, following the denial of the permit, Venezuelan governmental officials of the highest level targeted Crystallex's investment with statements that resulted in a gradual devaluation of the investor's investment. More pointedly, then Venezuela's President Hugo Chávez announced in a public address that the intention of the Government was to take back 'big mines', including the Las Cristinas mine. This was followed by an official press release from the Ministry of Mines which announced the plan to seize Las Cristinas. In the Tribunal's estimation, these statements 'effected an incremental encroachment of the Claimant's contractual rights and resulted in a gradual yet significant decrease of the value of the Claimant's investment'.[198] Finally, the MOC was rescinded, which, in the tribunal's view, constituted 'the third and last of the measures or groups of measures, and which taken together constituted the creeping expropriation suffered by Crystallex'.[199] While the tribunal accepted that ordinarily the termination of a contract will be purely a matter of domestic law and not international law (since the state would typically be acting in its commercial capacity), on the facts, it considered that the recission was a matter of international law, since the state was acting in its sovereign capacity. In other words, the MOC was not terminated for an alleged contractual ground, e.g. failure to perform, but as was evident from the governmental statements and acts in question, it was terminated for policy reasons, i.e. to return the mine into Venezuelan hands, without payment of any compensation. In this regard, the termination of the MOC could not be viewed as anything other than a sovereign act.

The main Caribbean case that addresses the issue of creeping expropriation is *Michael Lee-Chin v Dominican Republic*.[200] The dispute concerned a Concession Agreement entered into between the claimant's (a Jamaican national) subsidiary, Lajun Corporation, and the Municipality of Santo Domingo, for the administration and operation of the Duquesa Landfill, in which final disposal of urban solid waste was carried out in the area of Gran Santo Domingo in the Dominican Republic. As consideration for the performance of services under the Concession Agreement, Lajun was authorised to charge the Municipalities of the Gran Santo Domingo area a tipping fee per tonne of waste. According to the claimant, 13 days following its acquisition of Lajun, under the pretext of Lajun's failure to comply with certain environmental regulations, the local authority notified Lajun of its decision to rescind

197 ibid 674.
198 ibid 683.
199 ibid 685.
200 ICSID Case No. UNCT/18/3, Award, 6 October 2023.

the Concession Agreement, ultimately taking possession of the landfill and ejecting Lajun and their employees from the property. The local authority and Lajun thereafter concluded a settlement agreement whereby the former returned the possession of the land and authorised Lajun to continue with the operation and administration of the landfill. Shortly thereafter, however, the Ministry of Environment imposed sanctions on Lajun for violations of its environmental permit and Law No. 64–00 of the Environment. The claimant contended that subsequently, following an alleged new interference by the respondent in the Duquesa Landfill's operation, the local authority and Lajun executed a second settlement agreement pursuant to which the claimant regained control of his property. In the months that followed, the Superior Administrative Court ordered the provisional intervention and administration of the Duquesa Landfill by a commission composed of the Minister of Environmental and Natural Resources, the Minister of Public Health, and the mayor. The following day, this commission took control of the Duquesa Landfill, which the claimant argued constituted an indirect expropriation under the CARICOM-Dominican Republic Free Trade Agreement (2002).

The respondent objected to the claimant's assertion. They contended that Lajun, in breach of the Concession Agreement, had considerably cut their operating hours, seriously affecting waste collection and leading to public health concerns. In addition, they argued that Lajun had announced that it would cease providing waste dumping services to three municipalities, and that for this reason, the local authority decided to exercise its unilateral right to terminate provided for under the Concession Agreement.

The tribunal considered that an indirect expropriation results from 'behaviour which substantially and permanently deprives an investor of the value of its investment.'[201] On the facts, the tribunal held that the termination of the Concession Agreement was part of a larger effort by the state to eject the claimant from the operation of the investment. More pointedly, the tribunal considered that after the state acknowledged the difficulties related to the operation of the investment, particularly low tipping fees, and genuinely offered prospects for future collaboration through the execution of several agreements, the investment was abruptly subjected to a series of actions on all fronts. These actions significantly affected the investment so much so that the claimant was deprived of its use and benefit. In short, the tribunal concluded that the respondent's actions constituted an indirect creeping expropriation.

By contrast, in *Teinver v Venezuela,*[202] the tribunal declined to find that there had been a creeping expropriation, though it ultimately held that there had been an unlawful indirect expropriation where the host state took over management of the claimants' airline. On the question of creeping expropriation, the tribunal found that, first, in respect of the alleged 'airfare squeeze', there was no evidence that the state did not grant appropriate increases; second, there was insufficient evidence of acts taken by the government-supported air transportation unions in striking; third, there was no evidence that the state coerced the claimant to obtain additional shares at no cost; fourth, there was no evidence of the alleged unilateral modification of the text of the Agreement between the parties or its breach by a failure to set compliant airfares; and fifth, there was no evidence that the state made a lowball purchase offer in an attempt to force out the claimants from management of the airline. In light of these findings, the tribunal concluded that a creeping expropriation of the claimants' investment had not occurred; the claimants could not demonstrate that there was a link between the individual measures and the ultimate taking.

201 ibid 343.
202 ICSID Case No. ARB/09/1, Award, 21 July 2017.

VII. LEGALITY OF EXPROPRIATION

Expropriations are not *per se* illegal in international law, as states retain their sovereign right to expropriate foreign property. That said, as noted by the tribunal in *ADC v Hungary*,[203]

> the legality of a measure of expropriation is conditioned on three (or four) requirements. These requirements are contained in most treaties. They are also seen to be part of customary international law. These requirements must be fulfilled cumulatively:
>
> The measure must serve a *public purpose*. Given the broad meaning of 'public purpose,' it is not surprising that this requirement has rarely been questioned by the foreign investor.
>
> The measure must *not be arbitrary and discriminatory* within the generally accepted meaning of the terms.
>
> Some treaties explicitly require that the procedure of expropriation must follow principles of *due process*. Due process is an expression of the minimum standard under customary international law and of the requirement of fair and equitable treatment. Therefore, it is not clear whether such a clause, in the context of the rule of expropriation, adds an independent requirement for the legality of the expropriation.
>
> The expropriatory measure must be accompanied by *prompt, adequate, and effective compensation*. Adequate compensation is generally understood today to be equivalent to the market value of the expropriated investment.[204]

Failure to fulfil any one of these conditions entails a breach of the expropriation provision.[205]

A. Public Purpose

States are permitted under international law to pursue a wide range of public purposes in the context of the expropriation of foreign investors' property. Indeed, it has been widely acknowledged that 'states are afforded a wide margin of appreciation in determining whether an expropriation serves a public purpose'.[206]

In *Teinver v Argentina*,[207] the tribunal held that the respondent's decision to expropriate the Airlines' shares and to continue operating the Airlines were steps taken in the bona fide public interest to preserve airline connectivity. More particularly, because a substantial proportion of the domestic market served was served by the Airlines, and their ongoing financial difficulties threatened to jeopardize this, it was reasonable for the respondent to expropriate both airlines to ensure that the public interest of connectivity continued to be served. Although, ultimately, an indirect expropriation was found because the state had failed to provide adequate compensation, the tribunal was emphatic in its observation that the state is afforded a wide margin of appreciation in respect of the public purposes it pursues:

> A State must be accorded a certain amount of deference in determining how to best advance its public interest once a public interest has been demonstrated as the reason for which an expropriation occurred. Further, there is no requirement at international law that expropriation, in order to be in the public interest, must be the only means available for the State to meet that interest.[208]

203 ICSID Case No. ARB/03/16, Award, 2 October 2006.
204 ibid 429–33.
205 *Reinhard Unglaube v Republic of Costa Rica*, ICSID Case No. ARB/09/20, Award, 16 May 2012.
206 *Crystallex v Venezuela*, ICSID Case No. ARB(AF)/11/2, Award 4 April 2016, para. 712.
207 ICSID Case No. ARB/09/1, Award, 21 July 2017.
208 ibid 985.

Although the state has a broad margin of appreciation in determining the requisite public interest pursued, said public interest must be a genuine one. In this connection, in *ADC v Hungary,*[209] a case in which it was alleged that the state expropriated the investor's management of an airport when it handed over the facility to a domestic agency, the tribunal opined that:

> a treaty requirement for 'public interest' requires some genuine interest of the public. If mere reference to 'public interest' can magically put such interest into existence and therefore satisfy this requirement, then this requirement would be rendered meaningless since the Tribunal can imagine no situation where this requirement would not have been met.[210]

On the facts, the tribunal could see no public interest being served by the respondent's act of depriving the claimants' investments in the Airport project, although the respondent repeatedly argued that its actions were important for the harmonisation of the Hungarian Government's transport strategy, laws, and regulations with EU law.

A genuine public interest was similarly not found to exist in *Valeri Belokon v Kyrgyz Republic,*[211] which concerned the imposition of an administrative and sequestration regime on Manas Bank for a period of at least four years. The taking was held not to have been for a public purpose, but rather served the narrower interests of the Government in clamping down on suspicions of wrongdoing on account of a connection between the claimant and the Bakiev political regime.

Similarly, in *von Pezold v Zimbabwe,*[212] the respondent contended that the purpose behind the 'Fast-Track Land Reform Programme' (FTLRP), which involved forcing predominantly white farm owners off their lands along with their workers without compensation and the seizure of said land, had been to right historical colonial wrongs (land grabbing by white settlers). The tribunal, however, rejected the legitimacy of this argument, finding that the measures taken were not directed at righting historical wrongs, but were politically motivated, and racially discriminatory. More pointedly, once taken, large parts of the properties had not actually been re-distributed to historically disadvantaged or otherwise landless groups but remained in the *de facto* possession of the claimants. Meanwhile, regarding the land that had been re-distributed, there appeared to be a trend towards politically motivated allocations of the land. By contrast, the tribunal did not question the legitimacy of the Lancaster House Agreement and its corresponding policy from 1979–2000 that expropriated land, with compensation, for redistribution. In its view, the discrimination under this regime in favour of Indigenous Zimbabweans was necessary in order to remedy the unconscionable anti-aboriginal policies implemented during the Rhodesian era.

Meanwhile, in *British Caribbean Bank Limited v Belize,*[213] the state compulsorily acquired the claimant's interest in certain loan and security agreements concluded with Belize Telemedia, a telecommunications company registered in Belize, and Sunshine Holdings Limited, a company that held shares in Telemedia. The claimant provided Sunshine with US$10,000,000; it also extended Sunshine a facility of US$1,000,000. However, before Sunshine and Belize Telemedia Limited repaid the claimant, the Minister responsible for telecommunications issued an order compulsorily taking control over the telecommunications

209 ICSID Case No. ARB/03/16, Award, 2 October 2006.
210 ibid 432.
211 UNCITRAL Award, 24 October 2014.
212 ICSID Case No. ARB/10/15, Award 28 July 2015.
213 PCA Case No. 2010–18, Award, 19 December 2014.

infrastructure, including Sunshine and Belize Telemedia Limited. The Order noted that the public purpose pursued was 'the stabilisation and improvement of the telecommunications industry and the provision of reliable telecommunications services to the public at affordable prices in a harmonious and non-contentious environment'.[214]

The claimant wrote to Telemedia and Sunshine repeatedly, indicating that it considered the loan facility to be in default, that no repayment had been received, and that if payment was not made in full, it would take appropriate steps pursuant to the Companies Act to recover the sums owed. Although a Notice of Acquisition was issued by the Ministry of Finance requesting that all interested persons who had claims to compensation for the acquisition of Telemedia and Sunshine to submit these claims to the Ministry of Finance, no compensation was provided, even after the claimant submitted claims for compensation to the Ministry of Finance.

The tribunal held that, in these circumstances, the state violated Article 5 of the BIT by expropriating the claimant's interest in the Loan and Security Agreements without complying with the public purpose and compensation requirements. In respect of the former, while the tribunal acknowledged that the state was entitled to broad latitude to devise its public policy as it saw fit, 'mere avoidance of payment of compensation to injured investors, without more, could not serve as a legitimate public policy objective for the expropriation of property'.[215] More generally, the tribunal considered that certain statements made by the then Prime Minister of Belize suggested that the purpose was political. He said, *inter alia*:

> there will thus be no more Telemedia awards against us; no more Telemedia court battles; no more debilitating waste of governments' energies and resources; and there will be no more suffering of this one man's campaign to subjugate an entire nation to his will.
>
> This is the people of Belize against the Ashcroft interests and I will never relent in the same way as he is indicating he will never relent.[216]

In the tribunal's estimation, these words suggested that the motivation for the Orders included a personal animus against Lord Michael Ashcroft (ultimate owner of the investment) that bore no reasonable relationship to the ostensible public purposes of stabilising and improving the telecommunications industry of Belize, or of providing reliable telecommunications services to the public. In short, the respondent did not convincingly show that the acquisition of the Loan and Security Agreements was undertaken for a public purpose.

Meanwhile, in *OI European Group B.V. v Venezuela*,[217] while the tribunal accepted that the state nationalised the claimant's investment to foster endogenous development, and that this was a valid public purpose, it rejected the respondent other argument that the alleged position of dominance of the claimant in the Venezuelan glass market could be considered a factor of public interest that justified the expropriation. In this connection, it noted that

> even if the Companies had a dominant position, this would never justify such an extreme measure as expropriation: experts for both Parties agree in that the expropriation could not be carried out exclusively to remedy an alleged position of dominance on the part of the Claimant.[218]

214 ibid 88.
215 ibid 236.
216 ibid 239.
217 ICSID Case No. ARB/11/25 Award, 10 March 2015.
218 ibid 381.

(a) A Nexus Between the Declared Purpose and the Actual Purpose

There appears to be growing consensus in arbitral practice that when assessing the legality of an expropriation, there must be a determination of whether the expropriatory measure adopted by the state had a reasonable nexus with the declared public purpose or was at least capable of furthering that purpose. By way of example, in *Vestey Group Limited v Venezuela*,[219] Vestey began its operations in Venezuela in 1909 and, by the end of the 20th century, it operated a cattle farming business extending to over more than 290,000 hectares of land with a herd exceeding 100,000 heads of livestock. In 1999, Venezuela adopted a new constitution mandating land reform. To implement its land reform agenda, Venezuela passed the 2001 Land Law which authorised the state to recover large idle estates for public utility purposes and social use. Between 2001 and 2006, the respondent served several recovery notices directed towards certain farms which Vestey operated. In this context, Vestey agreed to sell one of its farms and to donate another one to the state. After failed negotiations, the respondent ordered in 2011 the recovery of all the remaining farms operated by Vestey and took control over Vestey's movable and immovable property located on the farms. Vestey claimed that this amounted to an indirect expropriation. The tribunal agreed with Vestey, finding that Venezuela's takeover of the investment constituted an expropriation.

In examining whether a public purpose was served by the measures in question, the tribunal considered that such an assessment requires that the state be afforded 'broad deference'.[220] In this connection, it accepted that policies adopted by the state for the common good should generally be respected by tribunals, except in situations of blatant misuse of the power.[221]

While the tribunal, in principle, deferred to the state's policy determination – that is, the assertion that its measures were adopted to ensure the availability and timely access to food by its citizens as part of its national plan to ensure food self-sufficiency – the inquiry did not end there. It noted that beyond this, it must inquire into 'whether the impugned expropriatory measure was "for" the public purpose' proposed.[222] In this respect, all relevant circumstances were considered, including the state's post-expropriation conduct since 'the government's failure to advance a declared purpose may serve as evidence that the measure was not taken in furtherance of such purpose'.[223] While the declared purpose of the investment's take over was to secure the population's access to food, the tribunal held that, in reality, that purpose was not actually served by the expropriation. In fact, after the takeover, Agroflora's output did not increase, nor did the population gain wider or cheaper access to the beef produced by Agroflora. To the contrary, the government's management of Agroflora resulted in a decline in the production levels.

Another justification advanced by Venezuela for the takeover of Agroflora was the need to guarantee wider public access to Vestey's genetically superior cattle. In reality, however, after the expropriation, the government did not actually increase purebred cattle sales or decrease its sale price. On the contrary, under the government's control, Agroflora sold purebred cattle at higher than regulated prices. Finally, with regard to the respondent's

219 ICSID Case No. ARB/06/4, Award, 15 April 2016.
220 ibid 294.
221 ibid.
222 ibid 296.
223 ibid.

argument that its aim was to facilitate public access to food which in turn warranted the redistribution to the people of the large uncultivated land plots in private hands, the tribunal held that the Agroflora was a productive enterprise before expropriation. In any event, there was no evidence that the government distributed the ownership to the land to private persons or had any plans to this effect. In the final analysis, the tribunal concluded that the nexus between Venezuela's declared purpose to achieve wider public access to food and the expropriation of Agroflora was not obvious.[224]

There is no special formula that is required to be used when declaring a public purpose as the reason for an expropriatory act, so long as the nexus between the declared public purpose and the actual purpose served is obvious. This point was noted in *South American Silver v Bolivia*.[225] Here, the investor's mining concessions in certain Indigenous communities in Bolivia were revoked in circumstances where the investor, by its conduct, caused division among local communities, demonstrations, violence, and even deaths. Notwithstanding the fact that the investor was aware, from the very outset of making its investment, that the affected Indigenous groups made decisions by consensus, the investor engaged in an aggressive strategy to weaken opposition to its project by offering employment and donations to its supporters, while ignoring those who opposed the project. Although ultimately the tribunal found that there had been an unlawful expropriation to the extent that compensation did not attend the expropriatory measure, a public purpose was nonetheless served by the measure in question, even though the state did not use a 'sacramental formula'[226] when invoking human rights considerations:

> If the protection of life – the quintessential human right – and the need to return to normalcy in a region with an indigenous population that is affected and altered by the Project emerge clearly as motivations in the Reversion Decree, the Tribunal cannot understand that the mere absence of a sacramental formula to expressly refer to human rights or to the protection of the communities may lead to the conclusion that the Reversion was not conducted in a social benefit related to the internal needs of Bolivia. In other words, the premises mentioned in the Reversion Decree as causes for Reversion have been proven and such premises include the protection of human rights – the right to life and the right to peace, both expressly mentioned in the Reversion Decree – and the protection of the communities and the ayllus against the difficulties resulting from the Project.[227]

The tribunal rejected the claimant's assertion that the Reversion did not serve a social benefit related to the internal needs of Bolivia because the Project would have brought millions of dollars of investments to one of the poorest areas of Bolivia, and that neither the Government nor the local communities have any benefit ever since the Reversion, and that the Indigenous community representatives had requested that it come back to the area to continue with the Project. In this connection, it considered that:

> The Claimant cannot simply equate social benefit with purely economic benefit and expect the Tribunal to analyze compliance with this requirement from the point of view of the returns that the Project would have generated for the community, ignoring the social, cultural and political situation and the seriousness of the existing social conflict in the area.[228]

224 ibid 300.
225 PCA Case No. 2013–15, Award, 22 November 2018.
226 ibid 561.
227 ibid.
228 ibid 578.

Apart from food security and human rights considerations, there are a wide variety of public purposes that may be served by an expropriatory measure, including the protection of cultural heritage and environmental protection.

In *Southern Pacific Properties (SPP) Limited v Egypt*,[229] the investor was granted permission to engage in hotel development on the Giza Plateau in Egypt (the site of the Pyramids), but Egypt later issued a series of decrees which resulted in the project's cancellation. By that time, SPP had invested approximately US$ 5 million in the project after being unable to construct villas and multi-family accommodations on 286 lots. Overall, it suffered losses of around US$ 10 million. In respect of the claim of expropriation, the tribunal considered that the respondent was entitled to cancel the tourist development project for the purpose of preserving and protecting antiquities in the area. However, the state's defence against expropriation ultimately failed because it did not offer the claimant prompt, adequate, and effective compensation.

In so far as environmental protection is concerned, the case of *Eco Oro v Columbia*[230] recognises this as a legitimate public purpose. Here, the claimant argued that the state's delimitation of the Páramo deprived it of over 50% of the area of its mining concession which overlapped with the Preservation Zone carved out by the state to protect the environment. The tribunal, in finding that there had not been an indirect expropriation, considered that protection of the Páramo was in all respects a legitimate public purpose. In its view, the Páramos have significant environmental importance, such as supplying 70% of Colombia's water, and the regulation of the water cycle, and capturing large amounts of carbon from the atmosphere. Because the Páramos are under threat from both human intervention and climate change, the state was justified in adopting measures to protect the environment.

(b) *Proportionality when Assessing Public Purpose*

There is arbitral practice to suggest that there is a requirement for proportionality when assessing the public purpose of an expropriatory measure adopted by the state. In *Vestey Group Limited v Venezuela*,[231] for example, the tribunal considered that 'if the government indeed aimed at wider public access to Agroflora's purebred cattle, measures lighter than expropriation were available. The government could for instance have adopted a regulation obliging Agroflora to increase the sales of purebred cattle or semen and/or to lower the prices.'[232]

Similarly, in *Eco Oro v Columbia*,[233] the tribunal considered whether the manner in which the Páramo ecosystem was delimited was proportionate to its purpose. To this, the Tribunal held that the Páramo required protection and that once damaged, it is uncertain whether or not they can be restored and, if so, the length of time such restoration will take. Accordingly, the precautionary principle was clearly relevant when considering the proportionality of the measures in question. In short, because ensuring the Páramo was protected from potential

229 ICSID Case No. ARB/84/3, Award, 20 May 1992.

230 ICSID Case No. ARB/16/41, Decision on Jurisdiction, Liability and Directions on Quantum, 9 September 2021.

231 ICSID Case No. ARB/06/4, Award, 15 April 2016.

232 ibid 298.

233 ICSID Case No. ARB/16/41, Decision on Jurisdiction, Liability and Directions on Quantum, 9 September 2021.

adverse interaction animated the state's expropriatory measure, the measure could not be said to be disproportionate.

Meanwhile, in *Tecmed v Mexico,*[234] the state passed a resolution which effectively denied the investor authorisation to operate their landfill and ultimately ordered that it be closed. Among other things, the issue arose as to whether the state's actions were proportionate to the public interest. In the tribunal's view:

> Although the analysis starts at the due deference owing to the State when defining the issues that affect its public policy or the interests of society as a whole, as well as the actions that will be implemented to protect such values, such situation does not prevent the Arbitral Tribunal, without thereby questioning such due deference, from examining the actions of the State in light of Article 5(1) of the Agreement to determine whether such measures are reasonable with respect to their goals, the deprivation of economic rights and the legitimate expectations of who suffered such deprivation. *There must be a reasonable relationship of proportionality between the charge or weight imposed to the foreign investor and the aim sought to be realized by any expropriatory measure.* To value such charge or weight, it is very important to measure the size of the ownership deprivation caused by the actions of the state and whether such deprivation was compensated or not. On the basis of a number of legal and practical factors, it should be also considered that the foreign investor has a reduced or nil participation in the taking of the decisions that affect it, partly because the investors are not entitle to exercise political rights reserved to the nationals of the State, such as voting for the authorities that will issue the decisions that affect such investors.[235]

Relying on European Court of Human Rights' decision of *James and Others v UK,*[236] the tribunal accepted that:

> not only must a measure depriving a person of his property pursue, on the facts as well as in principle, a legitimate aim 'in the public interest', but there must also be a reasonable relationship of proportionality between the means employed and the aim sought to be realised . . . . The requisite balance will not be found if the person concerned has had to bear 'an individual and excessive burden' . . . a measure must be both appropriate for achieving its aim and not disproportionate thereto.[237]

On the facts, the tribunal held that there were factors other than the investor's purported non-compliance with the permit's conditions or Mexican environmental protection laws that accounted for the denial of the permit's renewal. These factors included certain political circumstances, namely community pressure to close the landfill. The resolution passed was not proportional to such circumstances nor to the neutralisation of the economic and commercial value of the claimant's investment caused as a result. Interestingly, the resolution was not adopted against the backdrop of the dangers associated with the operation of the landfill (public health, ecological balance, or the environment). To the contrary, the state's concerns were to ensure the relocation of the landfill to a different site far away from Hermosillo's urban centre, and thereby put an end to the political problems, namely opposition to the project by community groups.

In assessing the proportionality of the measure in the light of the purpose pursued, the tribunal did not attribute significance to the technical infringements committed by the investor during the operation of the landfill on which the Resolution was apparently based, but rather

234 ICSID Case No. ARB (AF)/00/2, Award, 29 May 2003.

235 ibid 122.

236 ECtHR Judgment of February 21, 1986, Application No. 8793/79, paras. 19, 20.

237 *Tecmed v Mexico*, ICSID Case No. ARB (AF)/00/2, Award, 29 May 2003, para. 122.

the community pressure faced by the state. In the tribunal's view, the alleged actions of the investor did not constitute

> emergency situations, genuine social crisis or public unrest or urgency, which, due to their severity, could have led the competent authorities to terminate the contractual relationship governing the transport operation or to revoke or deny the renewal of the licenses or permits under which such transport operation was carried out.[238]

In any event, opposition put up by community associations to the landfill did not give rise, in the opinion of the tribunal, to a serious urgent situation, crisis, need, or social emergency that, weighed against the deprivation or neutralisation of the economic or commercial value of the claimant's investment, permitted the Resolution.[239]

In short, the tribunal concluded that the resolution was not proportionate to the alleged violations when such infringements did not pose a present or imminent risk to the ecological balance or to people's health, and the Resolution, without providing for the payment of compensation, led to the neutralisation of the investment's economic and business value and the claimant's return on investment and profitability expectations upon making the investment, and was thus expropriatory.

By contrast, some tribunals have refused to definitively find, or have outrightly rejected, the assertion that a proportionality requirement is part of the assessment of public purpose. In *South American Silver Limited v Bolivia*,[240] for example, the tribunal considered that

> Article 5 of the Treaty does not expressly refer to a proportionality requirement as an element to establish the lawfulness of the expropriation. The Parties also do not address whether the standard for the lawfulness of an expropriation requires the expropriatory measure to be proportionate and, therefore, the Tribunal will not address this issue.[241]

Yet, still, it appears to have gone on to consider proportionality, having regard to the circumstances of the case, finding that first, the public order issue was not a temporary concern, or an issue created by a few illegal miners, or a situation created by a few objectors to the Project, or Bolivia's strategy to gain control of the deposit. Second, the impairment sustained to the claimant's investment was not beyond the amounts invested in the project. And third, it was not clear how other measures, short of the Reversion, could have remedied the conflict in the area. In this context,

> having established the existence of the conflict, as well as its severity and consequences, the tribunal [was] unable to conclude that the measure adopted by Bolivia was unnecessary or *disproportionate* and, much less, to speculate without any evidence on other measures that could have been implemented to resolve the conflict.[242]

It appears from the foregoing that arbitral practice on whether proportionality is to be considered in assessing public purpose is unclear, and arguably in a state of flux. Although some tribunals are increasingly referring to proportionality as a matter of course, it is worth remembering the point made in *South American Silver* that most BITs do not expressly reference proportionality in their guarantee against expropriation, and that, in any event, the inclusion of proportionality in *Tecmed* was based on the tribunal's engagement with

238 ibid 137.
239 ibid 139.
240 PCA Case No. 2013–15, Award, 22 November 2018.
241 ibid 570.
242 ibid 577.

the jurisprudence of the ECHR to which Caribbean countries are not bound. Finally, it is counter-intuitive for proportionality to be considered when examining the public purpose requirement under the legality assessment and again under the assessment of police powers. It is submitted that in the interest of coherence and judicial economy, proportionality should continue to be assessed under the latter, but not under the former, barring an explicit indication of such a requirement in the guarantee against expropriation.

B. Non-Discrimination

The second element of the assessment of legality in expropriation cases is whether the measure in question was discriminatory. To determine whether a measure discriminated against an investor in this context, tribunals apply the three-pronged test formulated in *Saluka v Czech Republic*:[243] 'State conduct is discriminatory, if (i) similar cases are (ii) treated differently (iii) and without reasonable justification'.[244] As to the third element, in *Parkerings v Lithuania*,[245] the tribunal considered that there are situations that may justify differentiated treatment, and these must be assessed having regard to the specific circumstances of each case.[246]

243 UNCITRAL Partial Award, 17 March 2006.

244 ibid 313. Other tribunals (whether dealing with the prohibition of discriminatory treatment, or with national treatment provisions, which prohibit nationality-based discrimination), have applied a similar standard. See, e.g. *Joseph C. Lemire v Ukraine*, ICSID Case No. ARB/06/18, Decision on Jurisdiction and Liability, 21 January 2010, para. 261

> (Discrimination, in the words of pertinent precedents, requires more than different treatment. To amount to discrimination, a case must be treated differently from similar cases without justification; a measure must be 'discriminatory and expose[s] the claimant to sectional or racial prejudice'; or a measure must 'target[ed] [sic] Claimant's investments specifically as foreign investments');

Champion Trading Company and Ameritrade International, Inc. v Arab Republic of Egypt, ICSID Case No. ARB/02/9, Award, 27 October 2006, para. 130 ('The national treatment obligation does not generally prohibit a State from adopting measures that constitute a difference in treatment. The obligation only prohibits a State from taking measures resulting in different treatment in like circumstances'); *Total S.A. v Argentine Republic*, ICSID Case No. ARB/04/01, Decision on Liability of 27 December 2010, para. 344

> (This standard requires, as a rule, a comparison between the treatment of different investments, usually within a given sector, of different national origin or ownership . . . . The purpose is to ascertain whether the protected investments have been treated worse without any justification, specifically because of their foreign nationality. The similarity of the investments compared and of their operations is a precondition for a fruitful comparison.) *Teinver S.A., Transportes de Cercanías S.A. and Autobuses Urbanos del Sur S.A. v Argentine Republic*, ICSID Case No. ARB/09/1, Award, 21 July 2017 ('Discrimination requires differential treatment of Claimants' investment from other similar investments in like circumstances.').

245 ICSID Case No. ARB/05/8, Award, 11 September 2007.

246 ibid, para. 368

> 'Discrimination is to be ascertained by looking at the circumstances of the individual cases. Discrimination involves either issues of law, such as legislation affording different treatments in function of citizenship, or issues of fact where a State unduly treats differently investors who are in similar circumstances. Whether discrimination is objectionable does not in the opinion of this Tribunal depend on subjective requirements such as the bad faith or the malicious intent of the State: at least, Article IV of the Treaty does not include such requirements. However, to violate international law, discrimination must be unreasonable or lacking proportionality, for instance, it must be inapposite

In *Crystallex v Venezuela*,[247] although the tribunal was troubled by repeated and rather derogatory references to 'transnationals' and 'transnational companies' in the President's and the Ministers' statements leading up to the termination of the concession, it was not satisfied that there were conclusive elements in the record which would support the conclusion that the expropriation was carried out in a discriminatory manner. It considered that 'to show discrimination the investor must prove that it was subjected to different treatment in similar circumstances without reasonable justification, typically on the basis of its nationality or similar characteristics'.[248]

Similarly, in *A11Y LTD. v Czech Republic*,[249] the state, which funded assistive aids, decided to pay for the least economically demanding aids which answered the needs of the visually-impaired citizens of the Czech Republic. In turn, the claimant, which offered high-end devices for sale, lost business, and thereby became insolvent. The tribunal concluded that the measure was a bona fide regulatory measure, and that if indeed it created an environment in which the claimant's business of providing high-end products to their clients at a premium became commercially unviable, that did not result in an expropriation. The measure did not target in any way or discriminate against the claimant; it was neutral, applying uniformly to all companies providing aids to different groups of people with health impairments.

By contrast, in *von Pezold v Zimbabwe*,[250] the tribunal found that the (Caucasian) claimants were targeted because of their skin colour and, hence, the taking was accordingly discriminatory, and in breach of the guarantee against expropriation. More pointedly, the state's policy towards black farmers (in contrast to that meted out to white farmers) was not to expropriate their farms, and under the new Constitution, black Zimbabweans were to be compensated for land *and* improvements, whereas white Zimbabweans were only to be compensated for improvements. It, however, noted that, in some cases, (but not here), discriminatory policies may be justified:

> Policies that discriminate in favour of the aboriginal inhabitants of a particular State (affirmative action) may, generally speaking, fall within this category as justifiable. These policies aid in promoting, *inter alia*, the health and well-being, general knowledge, social integration, skills, and commercial know-how of, and added employment and business opportunities for, indigenous persons and their broader communities. Such policies may be reasonably expected to exist until the social and economic indicators of the aboriginal population are brought in line with the corresponding averages of the general population for developed States, or global averages for developing States.[251]

Discrimination was also found in *Olin v Libya*.[252] Here, the question arose as to whether the expropriation order issued by the state for the taking over of the lands on which the investor conducted its dairy and juice business was unlawful by virtue of being discriminatory. In other words, were Olin's domestic competitors, OKBA and Al-Aseel, afforded more

or excessive to achieve an otherwise legitimate objective of the State. An objective justification may justify differentiated treatments of similar cases. It would be necessary, in each case, to evaluate the exact circumstances and the context.

247 ICSID Case No. ARB(AF)/11/2, Award, 4 April 2016.

248 ibid 715.

249 ICSID Case No. UNCT/15/1, Award, 29 June 2018.

250 ICSID Case No. ARB/10/15, Award, 28 July 2015.

251 ibid 652.

252 ICC Case No. 20355/MCP, Award, 25 May 2018.

favourable treatment than Olin, as they were definitively exempted from the expropriation order?

The tribunal considered that, as a matter of principle, discrimination arises where those who are in all material respects the same are treated differently, unless the respondent can prove that such different treatment was justified.[253] On the facts, the tribunal found that although Olin, OKBA, and Al-Aseel operated in the same industrial zone and indeed in the same business sector, namely the daily and juice market, Libya treated Olin less favourably than OKBA and Al-Aseel since the former, but not the latter, did not receive a formal and official expropriation exemption from the expropriation order. The respondent also failed to prove that the difference between the treatment accorded to Olin and the treatment accorded to its national competitors was justified.

Similarly, in *ADC v Hungary,*[254] the tribunal rejected the respondent's claim that not only the claimants, but all foreign investors, were prohibited from operating the Airport. The tribunal held that comparison of different treatments was to be made here between that received by the respondent-appointed operator and that received by foreign investors as a whole. The respondent acted in a discriminatory fashion because its actions treated the claimants less favourably than the respondent-appointed airport operator, without sufficient justification.

Finally, it is worth noting, as explained by the tribunal in *Corn Products v Mexico,*[255] that 'discrimination does not cease to be discrimination, nor to attract the international liability stemming therefrom, because it is undertaken to achieve a laudable goal or because the achievement of that goal can be described as necessary.'[256]

C. Due Process

The standard of due process under international law, and more specifically in the expropriation context,[257] has been summarised in *ADC v Hungary*[258] as requiring:

> an actual and substantive legal procedure for a foreign investor to raise its claims against the depriving actions already taken or about to be taken against it. Some basic legal mechanisms, such as reasonable advance notice, a fair hearing and an unbiased and impartial adjudicator to assess the actions in dispute, are expected to be readily available and accessible to the investor to make such legal procedure meaningful. In general, the legal procedure must be of a nature to grant an affected investor a reasonable chance within a reasonable time to claim its legitimate rights and have its claims heard. If no legal procedure of such nature exists at all, the argument that 'the actions are taken under due process of law' rings hollow.[259]

In *Kardassopolous v Georgia,*[260] the tribunal agreed with the reasoning of the *ADC* tribunal and, in particular, with the proposition that whatever the legal mechanism or procedure

253 ibid 217.
254 ICSID Case No. ARB/03/16, Award, 2 October 2006.
255 ICSID Case No. ARB (AF)/04/1, Decision on Responsibility, 15 January 2008.
256 ibid 142.
257 See generally, Ronald Krotoszynski Jr, 'Expropriatory Intent: Defining the Proper Boundaries of Substantive Due Process and the Takings Clause' (2001) 80 *North Carolina Law Review* 713.
258 ICSID Case No. ARB/03/16, Award, 2 October 2006.
259 ibid 435.
260 ICSID Case No. ARB/05/18, Award, 3 March 2010.

put in place, it 'must be of a nature to grant an affected investor a reasonable chance within a reasonable time to claim its legitimate rights and have its claims heard'.[261] A similar approach was countenanced by co-arbitrator Manuel Conthe (dissenting) in *Guaracachi America, Inc. and Rurelec PLC v Bolivia*,[262] where the tribunal considered that:

an expropriation – as an administrative act infringing upon the rights of an individual – must meet, from a legal point of view, three minimum procedural requirements:

(i) It must be reasoned – i.e. accompanied by a justification of its key features.
(ii) Both the act and its reasons must be formally communicated to the individual.
(iii) The legal procedure in question should allow the individual, after being notified of such reasons, to be heard before the State adopts its final decision.[263]

There is authority to suggest that while due process requires that the foreign investors have timely access to a legal proceeding in the territory of the host state of the investment which allows them to question the legality of the expropriation and/or the amount of the compensation offered, this does not entitle the investor to participate in the making of the sovereign decision to expropriate. In this connection, in *South American Silver Limited v Bolivia*,[264] the tribunal considered:

> Neither the context of the Treaty nor its object and purpose support the Claimant's position that, in any event, only rises to the level of arguing that it should have been invited to the meetings where the expropriation was decided and to participate in the process advanced by COMIBOL to establish compensation. The Treaty does not forbid the Contracting Parties from expropriating. Rather, it imposes certain conditions on an expropriation, which if disregarded will result in the international responsibility of the State. That is, the Treaty preserves the State's sovereign right to expropriate subject to certain specific conditions. The Treaty does not make that State prerogative conditional on the investor's participation in the issuance of the act that formalizes the expropriation, nor does the Claimant explain – aside from a reading of Article 5 that the Tribunal does not share, why the investor's right to specifically establish 'by due process of law' the legality of the investment and the amount of compensation involves a participation in the sovereign exercise of a State prerogative.[265]
>
> Such a result does not arise from the object and purpose of the Treaty, and the Claimant does not allege or substantiate that the effective protection of the investment under the Treaty requires participation of the investor in the sovereign decision to expropriate. Nothing in the Treaty mandates a Contracting Party, as the Claimant argues, to establish 'legal recourse' to call into question the 'legality' of a decision that has not yet been made.[266]

There are several cases which illustrate circumstances in which a breach of the due process requirement will be found to exist. In *Vestey Group Limited v Venezuela*,[267] for example, by introducing and applying the Land Law to Vestey's investment and thereby derogating from the procedural guarantees of the Expropriation Law, Venezuela deprived Vestey not only of the opportunity to have the valuation of its investment reviewed by an independent authority,

261 ibid 396.
262 PCA Case No. 2011–17, Award, 31 January 2014.
263 ibid 5. Dissent of Co-Arbitrator Manuel Conthe.
264 PCA Case No. 2013–15, Award, 22 November 2018.
265 ibid 583.
266 ibid 584.
267 ICSID Case No. ARB/06/4, 15 April 2016.

but also of the right to be compensated altogether. Further, Venezuela failed to comply with the procedural regime of the Land Law itself, for example, by failing to communicate the final recovery decisions to Vestey as required by Article 94 of the Land Law, thereby depriving Vestey of the opportunity to appeal the decisions before a judicial authority. Moreover, Vestey learned of the outcome of its appeal from the interim measures through the ensuing arbitration, which infringed Vestey's right of independent review. In short, then, the limited procedural guarantees afforded the claimant were insufficient to comply with the BIT's due process requirement relative to the guarantee against expropriation.

Meanwhile, in *Olin v Libya*,[268] Article 23 of the Libyan Investment Law provided that a foreign investment could not be expropriated without a law or judicial decision. The tribunal, having examined the expropriation order in question, held that it was neither a law nor a judicial ruling. Rather, it was an administrative resolution. For this reason, the Order was not issued in accordance with due process of law.

Separately, in *Copper Mesa Mining Corporation v Ecuador*,[269] the claimant's mining concessions were terminated after local opposition erupted, in part due to the claimant's apparent failure to obtain a so-called 'social license' to operate the mine. More specifically, the respondent's action came against the backdrop of the investor's alleged failure to carry out local consultation. The investor's subsidiary appealed the termination resolutions to the National Mining Director, the Ministry of Mines, and the Transitional Constitutional Court, but their applications were summarily dismissed in each case. In arbitration proceedings, the claimant contended that, in addition to the failure to pay compensation, the respondent failed to adhere to due process requirements when expropriating its investment. Although the tribunal accepted that it could not dictate what was or was not in the national interests of the respondent, its citizens, or the local population because it was not a regulator, it went on to hold that the resolutions did not respect due process requirements. More pointedly, despite its best efforts, the resolutions were issued without giving to the claimant or the concessionaire any opportunity to comply with the mining mandate, and without affording the claimant any effective remedies under Ecuadorian law to challenge the resolutions.

As a matter of principle, it is worth noting if the relevant IIA does not expressly provide that that the expropriation must be carried out in accordance with domestic law on expropriation, the tribunal will likely interpret and apply the due process requirement without reference to domestic law, but rather by reference to the 'minimum regulatory standard commonly accepted in all States under the rule of law which guarantees the subject that any decision affecting it will be adopted after having gone through a fair and equitable process.'[270]

This principle was articulated in *European Group B.V. v Venezuela*.[271] Here, the claimant was the main producer in the glass containers market in Venezuela. President Chávez made a televised speech announcing the immediate expropriation of the Venezuelan companies owned by the claimant. The next day, the Bolivarian Republic enacted the Expropriation Decree, formalising, on an urgent basis, the forced acquisition of the properties owned by the claimant, including the movable property belonging to or found in their plants; their means

268 ICC Case No. 20355/MCP, Award, 25 May 2018.
269 PCA No. 2012–2, Award, 15 March 2016.
270 *OI European Group v Venezuela*, ICSID Case No. ARB/11/25, 10 March 2015, para. 387.
271 ibid.

of transportation, and other tangible goods belonging to them for the purpose of 'strengthening of the public sector industrial capacity in the manufacture of glass containers for the Venezuelan people'.[272] Then, the next day, the Venezuelan Consumer Protection Agency went to the Valera plant to 'carry out the preventive temporary occupation measure'.[273] One day later, it appointed the management board that it entrusted with the management of the company. Although the Bolivarian Republic had material control and possession of the expropriated assets, the formal transfer of ownership was still pending at the time of the arbitration, because the expropriation procedure was making its way through Venezuelan courts. In fact, even after four years had passed since the plants were expropriated, the state had still not paid the claimant any compensation.

In these circumstances, the tribunal held that the Expropriation Decree reduced the claimant's company to a mere empty shell, stripped of any practical and economic use, and all its assets subjected to a forced acquisition in favour of the state. In its view, the measures taken by the Bolivarian Republic were not simply expropriatory; they also entailed nationalisation – the properties and rights for which the investor was deprived went on to become the assets of the National Executive Branch, thus reinforcing the conviction that the adopted measures were expropriatory.

On the question of due process, the claimant asserted that prior to the expropriation of their plants, the Republic never advised it with respect to the alleged violations of environmental, labour, or free competition legislation, and that they were never given the opportunity to argue their defence. The tribunal, however, refused to find that this was a breach of the due process requirement, noting that international law does not require advance notification of the expropriation to the affected party:

> no general principle of international Law exists which requires the appropriating State to notify the expropriated party in advance of its decision. There are imaginable situations-e.g., the midst of a food crisis or a collapse of financial markets-in which immediacy is essential to achieve the objectives sought in the public interest and in which prior notification would frustrate the operation. For those same reasons, international Law cannot recognize an absolute right to the investor to be heard and make allegations prior to the State executing the expropriation measure or to know the execution plan to be adopted.[274]
>
> The requirements of international Law with respect to due process in the expropriation of property owned by foreigners falls more within a grey area: they do not require ex ante notification, but rather the possibility of being able to resort *ex post* to an independent authority. What is essential is that the decision adopted by the expropriating State can be reviewed subsequently by a legal Authority which does not belong to the Executive Branch.[275]

In any event, under Venezuelan law, this requirement had been satisfied in that legal protection was afforded to the expropriated party, which permitted a judge to review the administrative expropriation action and determine the valuation owed to the expropriated party due to its loss of equity.

Meanwhile, the claimant also argued that due process was not honoured by the respondent, because they did not know, with certainty, which assets the state was forcibly acquiring. The tribunal agreed with the claimant, finding that:

272 ibid 334.
273 ibid 336.
274 ibid 391.
275 ibid 392.

> if the expropriation order, which may have been issued *inaudita parte*, did not clearly and with certainty define which assets are to be expropriated, this would allow the Executive Branch to determine, at its discretion, what set of assets would be expropriated and this would undermine the investor's right to obtain an independent review of the decision.[276]

On the facts, the tribunal found that the definition of the assets expropriated in Article I of the Decree was ambiguous, excessively broad, and left it entirely unclear whether the property expropriated covered the property of one of the claimant's subsidiary, OldY, alone, or whether the company as a whole was being expropriated, including its assets and liabilities. The imprecise language of the Decree prevented the claimant from knowing precisely which of its assets would be expropriated, and as such, violated its right to due process. Further, the decision of the First Administrative Court compounded the error by ordering the seizure of property that was not listed in the Expropriation Decree. Moreover, even though the Expropriation Decree only listed certain property and improvements, the respondent actually expropriated the manufacturing and business activity. The respondent took over not only the property comprising the Los Guayos and Valera Plants, but also the goodwill of OldY and Favianca, the cash deposited into the bank accounts held by OldY and Favianca, and the technology and the know-how used at the glass manufacturing Plants. In short, the respondent failed to clearly identify the property subject to expropriation, the definition of which constitutes a basic guarantee of due process required by international law.

D. Adequate Compensation

The measure of compensation in expropriation cases is one of the most hotly contested issues in international investment law.[277] IIAs typically prescribe the measure of prompt, adequate, and effective compensation, although some, especially those concluded by Latin

276 ibid 395.

277 Oscar Schachter, 'Compensation for Expropriation' (1984) 78 *American Journal of International Law* 121; Charles Cheney Hyde, 'Compensation for Expropriations' (1939) 33 *American Journal of International Law* 108; Steven R Ratner, 'Compensation for Expropriations in a World of Investment Treaties: Beyond the Lawful/unlawful Distinction' (2017) 111 *American Journal of International Law* 7; Muthucumaraswamy Sornarajah, 'Compensation for Expropriation: The Emergence of New Standards' (1979) 13 *Journal of World Trade Law* 108; Pamela B Gann, 'Compensation Standard for Expropriation' (1984) 23 *Columbia Journal of Transnational Law* 615; Björn Hoops, 'Expropriation without Compensation: A Yawning Gap in the Justification of Expropriation?' (2019) 136 *South African Law Journal* 261; Lee A O'Connor, 'The International Law of Expropriation of Foreign-Owned Property: The Compensation Requirement and the Role of the Taking State' (1983) 6 *Loyola of Los Angeles International and Comparative Law Review* 355; Bin Cheng, 'The Rationale of Compensation for Expropriation' (1958) 44 *Transactions of the Grotius Society* 267; Domenico Sorace, 'Compensation for Expropriation' in Antonio Pizzorusso (ed), *Italian Studies in Law: A Review of Legal Problems* (Martinus Nijhoff 1992); David Khachvani, 'Compensation for Unlawful Expropriation: Targeting the Illegality' (2017) 32 *ICSID Review-Foreign Investment Law Journal* 385; Tracy Lee Howard, 'Compensating an Owner to the Full Extent of His Loss: A Reevaluation of Compensable Damages in Louisiana Expropriation Cases' (1990) 51 *Louisiana Law Review* 821; Frank Dawson and Burns H Weston, 'Prompt, Adequate and Effective: A Universal Standard of Compensation' (1961) 30 *Fordham Law Review* 727; Rajesh Babu, 'Standard of Compensation for Expropriation of Foreign Investment' in Julien Chaisse, Leïla Choukroune, and Sufian Jusoh (eds), *Handbook of International Investment Law and Policy* (Springer Singapore 2021).

American countries,[278] sometimes prescribe compensation in accordance with the Calvo doctrine.[279] In respect of the former, whose status as a norm of customary international law is not settled,[280] 'prompt' means that the payment is made (or at least offered) without unreasonable delay post the expropriatory measure. 'Adequate' implies that the payment represents the fair market value of the expropriated investment; that is, how much a willing investor will pay for the investment at prevailing market rates for the asset immediately prior to the expropriatory measure. Finally, 'effective' compensation means that the compensation must be fully realisable and be freely transferable at the prevailing market rate of exchange on the date of expropriation. Several cases illustrate the different circumstances in which the obligation to pay compensation might be deemed to have been breached.

In *Ampal-American Israel Corp. and others v Egypt*,[281] for example, the respondent's decision to remove the claimant's tax-free status was held to have deprived the claimant of a defined and valuable interest that had been validly conferred according to Egyptian law at the time that the investment was made and that had been guaranteed by the state for a defined period. This was accordingly a taking tantamount to expropriation. Given that Article III(1) of the relevant BIT created an obligation on the part of the state to pay compensation for expropriated property, and this was not honoured, the tribunal found that the expropriation in question was unlawful.

Meanwhile, in *Teinver v Argentina,*[282] as a means of improving airline connectivity, Argentina sought to take over the claimants' Airlines. To this end, they entered into an agreement which, in part, stated that the requisite compensation would be determined by agreement of two different valuators appointed by each party, or by a third and neutral valuator in case of disagreement. Argentina rejected the investors' valuation. It also refused to agree on a neutral valuator. It used a different valuation method than that which was agreed, causing the airline to lose substantial value. Argentina argued that it provided symbolic compensation of ARS1 (roughly US$0.06) for the shares in the Airlines (because the investment was allegedly loss-making at the time of expropriation and that, as a result, the shareholders' equity had a negative valuation), which the claimants argued was insufficient compensation for the purposes of the expropriation.

278 The Calvo doctrine, which was reflected in General Assembly resolution 1803 (XVII) of 14 December 1962, on permanent sovereignty over natural resources, appeared again in the Charter of Economic Rights and Duties of States, contained in General Assembly resolution 3281 (XXIX) of 12 December 1974, which provided that disputes over compensation arising from the expropriation of foreign property have to be settled under the domestic law of the nationalising State. The influence of the Calvo doctrine was also to be seen in decision 24 of the Andean Pact.

279 Rudolf Dolzer, Ursula Kriebaum and Christoph Schreuer, *Principles of International Investment Law* (3rd edn, OUP 2022) 4; Zoltán Víg and Tamara Gajinov, 'The Development of Compensation Theories in International Expropriation Law' (2016) 57 *Hungarian Journal of Legal Studies* 447; Keith S Rosenn, 'Expropriation in Argentina and Brazil: Theory and Practice' (1974) 15 *Virginia Journal of International Law* 277; Debra F Guajardo, 'Redefining the Expropriation of a Foreign Direct Investment in Mexico' (2000) 42 *South Texas Law Review* 1309; Tim Gebert, 'The Principles of Just Compensation for International Takings' (1995) 4 *Journal of International Law and Practice* 389; Henry Landau, 'Compensation upon the Taking of an Alien's Property' (1974) 12 *American Business Law Journal* 31.

280 Kellie Travis, 'A Plurilateral Investment Treaty: Marrying Trade and Investment to Re-Establish a Customary International Norm' (2017) 50 *Vanderbilt Journal of Transnational Law* 499.

281 ICSID Case No. ARB/12/11, Decision on Liability and Heads of Loss, 21 February 2017.

282 ICSID Case No. ARB/09/1, Award, 21 July 2017.

The tribunal considered that Article V of the relevant BIT and customary international law both required the respondent to pay prompt, adequate, and effective compensation in respect of the expropriated investment. It countenanced the prevailing view that adequate compensation is the fair market value of the investment immediately before the expropriation was known, i.e. the value of the investment unaffected by the impugned measure. It accepted that

> there are circumstances in which no compensation can be adequate compensation for an expropriation . . . when an investment is loss-making and no longer a going concern (and) the State can demonstrate that the investor did not suffer a financial loss as a result of the taking.[283]

On the facts of the case, however, had the formal expropriation of the Airlines' shares been the first measure taken by the respondent and had the respondent otherwise treated the investment fairly and equitably, it might have been possible that adequate compensation for the shares may have been ARS 1. However, in the circumstances of this case, the tribunal was not persuaded that the respondent paid adequate compensation for taking the claimants' investment. More pointedly, the Agreement provided for an independent, third-party valuation in the event that the parties' respective valuations yielded different results, and the parties could not agree to a value. As such, it was not open to the respondent to unilaterally change the agreed valuation method. In short, in refusing to complete the agreed valuation and instead proceeding to a formal expropriation on a different valuation methodology, the respondent failed to provide adequate compensation for the taking of the claimants' investment.

Similarly, in *Vestey Group Limited v Venezuela*,[284] the tribunal rejected the respondent's claim that its offer to buy the claimant's company over one year prior to the expropriatory act could be considered as an offer of compensation for the subsequent expropriation. In other words, the price offer was not made in the context of compensation for expropriation. Throughout the sales negotiations, the government offered to pay a purchase price, without ever making reference to an expropriation. Moreover, the tribunal was critical of Venezuela's failure to meet with Vestey's representatives or respond to their written communications to advise them upon how payment could be effected. In its view, 'if Venezuela was really prepared to pay compensation, one would have expected it to entertain these requests'.[285]

If a respondent demonstrates that it has always been willing to provide just compensation (e.g. it made certain proposals to the investor), particularly in the context of ongoing negotiations, but it has actually made the payment of compensation as yet, the mere fact of not having received compensation does not render the expropriation unlawful. This principle was articulated in *Venezuela Holdings, B.V., et al. (case formerly known as Mobil Corporation, Venezuela Holdings, B.V., et al.) v Venezuela*.[286] Here, the expropriation of the claimants' investments was the result of laws enacted by the National Assembly and of decisions taken by the President of the Republic of Venezuela, the purpose of which was to create new mixed companies in which the state would own more than 50% of the shares. Negotiations with the oil companies were foreseen to that effect for a period of four months, and nationalisation was contemplated only in case of failure of those negotiations. In the present case, the negotiations failed, whereas the state's negotiations with the likes of Chevron, Total, Statoil, Sinopec, and BP, were successful. The claimants alleged that the respondent did not

283 ibid 1036.
284 ICSID Case No. ARB/06/4, Award, 15 April 2016.
285 ibid 315.
286 ICSID Case No. ARB/07/27, Award, 9 October 2014.

determine, offered, nor paid the compensation required by the Treaty, which was enough to render the expropriation wrongful.

Although the tribunal acknowledged that the claimants did not receive compensation and that Venezuela therefore did not fulfil its obligation to pay compensation in respect of the expropriation, it considered that this did not automatically render the expropriation unlawful. In its view, if an offer of compensation has been made to the investor, the legality of the expropriation will depend on the terms of that offer, which is a fact-sensitive question. On the facts, it was not disputed that negotiations took place, and that Venezuela made proposals during those negotiations. Because there were discussions at the time on the method of valuation of the expropriated interests, on the relevance of the cap provisions referred to by Venezuela, and on the exact amount of the compensation payable to the claimants, the tribunal found that the evidence did not demonstrate that the proposals made by Venezuela were incompatible with the requirement of 'just' compensation under Article 6(c) of the relevant BIT. Accordingly, the claimants failed to establish the unlawfulness of the expropriation.

The principle, then, appears to be that the legality of an expropriation where the state has taken the investment but has failed to pay compensation depends on whether a good faith offer of at least the market value of the investment was made. In this connection, in *Rusoro Mining Ltd. v Venezuela*,[287] a good faith offer for a reasonable amount of compensation was held to have not been made. The circumstances of the case were that President Chávez publicly announced the immediate nationalisation of the gold mining industry in Venezuela. Shortly thereafter, Venezuela adopted the Nationalization Decree which declared all assets and operations of all gold producing companies associated with the mining and exploitation of gold in Venezuela under state control, ordered the transfer of all existing concessions or contracts to mixed companies controlled by the state, decreed the automatic extinction of all existing concessions or contracts if holders did not agree within 90 days to their transfer to mixed companies, and ordered that compensation to investors be equal to the book value of the investment. Negotiations between Rusoro and the Negotiation Commission were suspended as no agreement on compensation could be reached. Although the claimant's mining rights were automatically extinguished, and their mining rights and other assets located in Venezuela were taken over by the Bolivarian Republic, no compensation had been paid.

The tribunal held that in a case such as this where the Nationalization Decree provided for the payment of compensation to investors in the gold sector, but established a cap, which was not foreseen either in the BIT or in domestic Venezuelan law, and in any event the state then submitted an offer for an amount which was significantly below the cap established by the Decree, this failed to fulfil the requirement of adequate compensation. The alleged reason for the reduced offer of compensation, namely the illegality of Rusoro's investment, was dismissed by the tribunal.

It is, thus, prudent for a state which carries out an expropriation to accurately and professionally assess the true value of the expropriated assets and offer compensation commensurate with this valuation. This point was noted in *Guaracachi America, Inc. and Rurelec PLC v Bolivia*,[288] which concerned arbitral proceedings brought for damages allegedly caused by modifications made to the regulatory framework governing the electricity sector, the alleged failure of the Bolivian judiciary to provide justice to the claimants and, ultimately, the nationalisation of the investors' 50.001% stake in their subsidiary, EGSA. The tribunal held Bolivia

287 ICSID Case No. ARB(AF)/12/5, Award, 22 August 2016.
288 UNCITRAL, PCA Case No. 2011–17, Award, 31 January 2014.

did not actually compensate (or intend to compensate) the claimants, as it did not make an accurate assessment of EGSA's value at the time. In fact, it did quite the opposite; the valuation was manifestly inadequate, which necessitated a finding of an unlawful expropriation.

Finally, it is worth remembering that 'the relevant time period for determining whether the compensation paid for the expropriation of an investment is adequate is immediately before the taking or immediately before the taking became known'.[289]

Standard of Compensation in Lawful v Unlawful Expropriation Cases

The Permanent Court of International Justice (PCIJ) in the *Chorzow Factory*[290] case made a distinction between compensation due for lawful expropriation and damages due for unlawful expropriation. It held that, in the case of lawful expropriation, payment of fair compensation, or the just price of what was expropriated at the time of the expropriation is required. By contrast, it considered that in the case of unlawful expropriation, international law provides for *restitutio in integrum* or, if impossible, its monetary equivalent at the time of the judgment.[291]

In recent years, there has been fierce debate over this distinction. On the one hand, the Iran-United States Claims Tribunal in the *Amoco*[292] case observed that although the *Chorzow Factory* case 'is nearly sixty years old, this judgment is widely regarded as the most authoritative exposé of the principles applicable in this field and is still valid today'.[293] It noted further that:

> obviously, the value of an expropriated enterprise does not vary according to the lawfulness or the unlawfulness of the taking . . . . The difference is that, if the taking is lawful the value of the undertaking at the time of the dispossession is the measure and the limit of the compensation, while if it is unlawful, this value is or may be, only a part of the reparation to be paid.[294]

An ICSID tribunal has similarly held that the BIT's standard of compensation applies only to lawful expropriations and that those standards 'cannot be used to determine the issue of damages payable in the case of an unlawful expropriation.'[295]

However, a contrary opinion has also been advanced by some tribunals.[296] In *Burlington Resources Inc. v Republic of Ecuador*,[297] for example, the question arose as to whether the standard of compensation under customary international law (full reparation) was different for expropriations that are unlawful solely as a result of the failure to pay compensation as opposed

289 *Teinver S.A., Transportes de Cercanías S.A. and Autobuses Urbanos del Sur S.A. v Argentine Republic*, ICSID Case No. ARB/09/1, Award, 21 July 2017, para. 1035.

290 Factory at Chorzów (*Germany v Poland*), Merits, 1928 PCIJ (Ser. A) No.17 (13 September 1928).

291 ibid 76.

292 *Amoco International Finance Corporation v Iran Amoco International Finance Corporation v The Government of the Islamic Republic of Iran, National Iranian Oil Company, National Petrochemical Company and Kharg Chemical Company Limited*, IUSCT Case No. 56.

293 ibid 191.

294 ibid 197.

295 *ADC Affiliate Ltd and ADC & ADMC Mgmt Ltd v Hungary*, (ICSID Case No. ARB/03/16), Award of 2 October 2006, para. 481.

296 *CME Czech Republic B.V. (The Netherlands) v The Czech Republic*, UNCITRAL, Award, 14 March 2003; *Wena Hotels Ltd. v Arab Republic of Egypt*, ICSID Case No. ARB/98/4, Award, 8 December 2000; *Metalclad Corp. v United Mexican States*, ICSID Case No. ARB(AF)/97/1 Award, 30 August 2000; *Middle East Cement Shipping and Handling Co. S.A. v Arab Republic of Egypt*, ICSID Case No. ARB/99/6) Award, 12 April 2002.

297 ICSID Case No. ARB/08/5, Decision on Liability, 14 December 2012.

to expropriations that are unlawful on other grounds. Although the tribunal did not definitively pronounce on this question (principally because the expropriation was unlawful not only for failure to pay compensation but also because there was a breach of the FET standard), it did suggest, relying on ILC Article 31 and the *Charzow Factory* case, that the appropriate standard of compensation might be the customary international law standard of full reparation. In its view, where the IIA in question merely describes the conditions under which an expropriation is considered lawful, but does not set out the standard of compensation for expropriations resulting from breaches of the Treaty, it is appropriate to turn to the customary international law standard of compensation in determining the compensation due for an unlawful expropriation.

In *Guaracachi America, Inc. and Rurelec PLC v Bolivia*,[298] the tribunal was more definitive, finding that once the proper valuation method was used and the compensation awarded was the fair market value of the expropriated investment, the 'standard of compensation does not seem to differ whether the expropriation is deemed legal or not'.[299]

It is submitted that a good middle ground between the two conflicting positions on the subject, which should inform future arbitral awards, appears to be the *Phillips Petroleum*[300] case which held that

> the lawful/unlawful taking distinction . . . is relevant only to two possible issues: whether restitution of the property can be awarded and whether compensation can be awarded for increase of the value of the property between the date of the taking and the date of the judicial or arbitral decision awarding compensation.[301]

A similar position was taken in *Bernardus Henricus Funnekotter and others v Zimbabwe*,[302] where it was considered that where the parties did not exclude restitution of the farms expropriated and it was not alleged that there was some increase of the value of those farms between the date of the taking and the date of the present award, there was no basis for distinguishing the computation of damages for lawful expropriation from computation of damages for unlawful expropriation.

VIII. POLICE POWERS

It is now widely accepted that under customary international law, states are exonerated from international responsibility where they adopt general regulations to achieve particular public purpose, provided that such regulations are proportionate, and non-discriminatory, adopted in good faith and adhere to the requirements of due process.[303] Several arbitral tri-

298 UNCITRAL, PCA Case No. 2011–17, Award, 31 January 2014.

299 ibid 433.

300 *Phillips Petroleum Co. Iran v Iran*, Partial Award, Iran-U.S. Cl. Trib., No. 425-39-2 (28 June 1989).

301 ibid 122.

302 ICSID Case No. ARB/05/6, Award, 22 April 2009 111–12.

303 Ben Mostafa, 'The Sole Effects Doctrine, Police Powers and Indirect Expropriation Under International Law' (2008) 15 *Australian International Law Journal* 267; Ranjan and Anand (n 95); Zamir (n 3) 318; Catharine Titi, 'Police Powers Doctrine and International Investment Law' in Andrea Gattini, Attila Tanzi, and Filippo Fontanelli (eds), *General Principles of Law and International Investment Arbitration* (Brill Nijhoff 2018); Utkarsh Mishra, 'State's Power to Regulate: The Use of Police Power Doctrine as a Reason for Non-Payment of Compensation in Cases of Expropriation' (2014) 8 *NUALS Law Journal* 15; Howard Mann and Julie Soloway, 'Untangling the Expropriation and Regulation Relationship: Is There a Way Forward?' (Report to the Ad Hoc Expert Group on Investment Rules and the Department of Foreign Affairs and International Trade, Canada, 31 March 2002); Prabhash Ranjan, 'COVID-19, India and Indirect Expropriation: Is the Police Powers Doctrine a Reliable Defence?' (2020) 13 *Contemporary Asia*

bunals not only recognise this principle, but treat it as indisputable. In *Tecmed v Mexico*,[304] for example, the tribunal stated:

> The principle that the State's exercise of its sovereign power within the framework of its police power may cause economic damage to those subject to its powers as administrator without entitling them to any compensation whatsoever is undisputable.[305]

The police powers doctrine is not, however, an absolute one. As noted by the tribunal in *El Paso v Argentina*,[306] while, as a matter of principle, states that adopt general regulations in the exercise of their police powers are not under a duty to pay compensation, this does not exempt them from liability where they have acted in an intentionally discriminatory way or the interference with the private rights of the investor is disproportionate to the public interest pursued. On the question of proportionality, it is necessary to assess whether the actions or measures in question are proportional to the public interest and to the protection legally granted to investments, taking into account the significance of the impact of the measure.

Over the years, several cases have provided insights into the circumstances in which the police powers doctrine may be invoked. In *Methanex v USA*,[307] for example, the claimant, a Canadian investor and the world's largest producer of methanol, a feedstock for a gasoline additive known as 'MTBE' (methyl tertiary-butyl ether), initiated arbitration proceedings against the USA under the NAFTA arguing that it had suffered losses caused by the State of California's ban on the sale and use of MTBE. California's ban on MTBE was aimed at averting the significant risk to human health or the environment caused by using MTBE in gasoline. Methanex alleged that California intended to benefit the US ethanol industry by banning ethanol's competition, namely methanol and MTBE. Among other things, Methanex claimed that there had been a breach of the guarantee against expropriation.

The tribunal, however, found that there had been no unlawful expropriation, in effect invoking the police powers doctrine. It held:

> . . . as a matter of general international law, a non-discriminatory regulation for a public purpose, which is enacted in accordance with due process and, which affects, *inter alios*, a foreign investor or investment is not deemed expropriatory and compensable unless specific commitments had been given by the regulating government to the then putative foreign investor contemplating investment that the government would refrain from such regulation.[308]

Given the important environmental protection and public health purposes served by the ban on the MTBE, as well as the fact that the ban did not specifically target Methanex, and Methanex had the opportunity to challenge the legality of the ban, the tribunal considered that the USA could successfully invoke the police powers doctrine. The tribunal, however, cautioned that if the USA had given assurances to the investor at the very outset that it would not adopt such a ban but later proceeded to do so, it would likely have found that there was

---

Arbitration Journal 205; Christian Riffel, 'Indirect Expropriation and the Protection of Public Interests' (2022) 71 *International & Comparative Law Quarterly* 945; D Benjamin Barros, 'The Police Power and the Takings Clause' (2003) 58 *University of Miami Law Review* 471; Stephen Olynyk, 'A Balanced Approach to Distinguishing Between Legitimate Regulation and Indirect Expropriation in Investor-State Arbitration' (2012) 15 *International Trade and Business Law Review* 254.

304 ICSID Case No. ARB (AF)/00/2, Award, 29 May 2003.

305 ibid 119.

306 ICSID Case No. ARB/03/15, Award, 31 October 2011.

307 UNCITRAL Award, 3 August 2005.

308 ibid PART IV – CHAPTER D 7.

a breach of the guarantee against expropriation, and thereby disapply the police powers doctrine. In short, however, on the facts, according to the tribunal, 'from the standpoint of international law, the California ban was a lawful regulation and not an expropriation'.[309]

Later cases seemingly suggest that the police powers doctrine is part of customary international law, and that, provided that the regulation in question meets certain minimum requirements (i.e. public purpose, good faith, proportionality, non-discrimination, and due process), the host state will be exempt from liability, notwithstanding the fact that the measure in issue has the effect of eviscerating the investor's asset. In *Saluka v Czech Republic*,[310] for example, the claimant asserted that it had been deprived of the value of its shares in a bank by the Czech Republic's intervention which culminated in its forced administration. Under Section 14 of the Banking Act, banks were obligated to continually maintain payment ability both in Czech currency and in foreign currencies. The investor here, however, continually failed to maintain liquidity both in Czech currency and in foreign currencies and, accordingly, failed to comply with its obligation under Section 14. Against this backdrop, the Czech National Bank decided to subject the claimant to forced administration, which necessitated the present arbitration proceedings, with the investor arguing that it had been subject to an unlawful expropriation. The only issue before the tribunal was whether this alleged deprivation was unlawful. The Czech Republic denied that it had violated Article 5 of the relevant BIT, arguing that its decision to put the investor into forced administration was a permissible regulatory action which cannot be considered as expropriatory.

The tribunal acknowledged that Article 5 of the Treaty did not contain an exception for the exercise of regulatory power. However, it accepted that the concept of 'deprivation', which was found in Article 5 of the BIT, imported the customary international law notion that 'a deprivation can be justified if it results from the exercise of regulatory actions aimed at the maintenance of public order'.[311] The tribunal went on to note that:

> It is now established in international law that States are not liable to pay compensation to a foreign investor when, in the normal exercise of their regulatory powers, they adopt in a non-discriminatory manner bona fide regulations that are aimed at the general welfare.[312]

After considering the provisions of the Harvard Draft Convention on the International Responsibility of States for Injuries to Aliens, the 1967 OECD Draft Convention on the Protection of Foreign Property, and the United States Third Restatement of the Law of Foreign Relations, the *Saluka* tribunal concluded that measures that fall within the police power of States are permissible, non-compensable regulatory actions, though it accepted that the 'so-called police power exception is not absolute'.[313] The Tribunal, having endorsed *Methanex*, then summarised its stance on the nature and status of the police powers doctrine in international law:

> the principle that a State does not commit an expropriation and is thus not liable to pay compensation to a dispossessed alien investor when it adopts general regulations that are 'commonly accepted as within the police power of States' forms part of customary international law today. There is ample case law in support of this proposition.[314]

309 ibid 15.
310 *Saluka v Czech Republic*, UNCITRAL Partial Award. 17 March 2006.
311 ibid 254.
312 ibid 255.
313 ibid 258.
314 ibid 262.

The tribunal, however, recognised that the police powers doctrine remains in a state of flux in international law in that:

> . . . international law has yet to identify in a comprehensive and definitive fashion precisely what regulations are considered 'permissible' and 'commonly accepted' as falling within the police or regulatory power of States and, thus, non-compensable. In other words, it has yet to draw a bright and easily distinguishable line between non-compensable regulations on the one hand and, on the other, measures that have the effect of depriving foreign investors of their investment and are thus unlawful and compensable in international law.[315]
>
> It thus inevitably falls to the adjudicator to determine whether particular conduct by a state 'crosses the line' that separates valid regulatory activity from expropriation. Faced with the question of when, how and at what point an otherwise valid regulation becomes, in fact and effect, an unlawful expropriation, international tribunals must consider the circumstances in which the question arises. The context within which an impugned measure is adopted and applied is critical to the determination of its validity.[316]

On the facts, the tribunal found that the Czech Republic had not 'crossed that line'[317] and did not, therefore, breach Article 5 of the Treaty, since the measures at issue could be justified as 'permissible regulatory actions'.[318] The measures were intended to protect the stability of the Czech Republic's banking system, and were non-discriminatory, and due process was respected. This decision was arrived at 'notwithstanding that the measure had the effect of eviscerating Saluka's investment'.[319]

Meanwhile, in *Marfin v Cyprus*,[320] the investor, which was experiencing financial difficulty at the time, was subject to a reorganisation of its management team, including the removal of two of its directors, and the imposition of a framework (recapitalization) to enable it to increase its liquidity. The investor argued that these measures amounted to a breach of the guarantee against expropriation as they effectively nationalised the company. By contrast, the host state contended that there had been no such breach, and that, in any event, its actions were justified under the police powers doctrine.

The tribunal in *Marfin*, like the tribunal in *Saluka*, agreed with the host state, thereby invoking the police powers doctrine. It accepted that:

> the economic harm consequent to the non-discriminatory application of generally applicable regulations adopted in order to protect the public welfare do not constitute a compensable taking, provided that the measure was taken in good faith, complied with due process and was proportionate to the aim sought to be achieved.[321]

It further explained that:

> While every application of a regulation that causes some economic damage to an investor could be seen as giving rise to a duty to compensate, under customary international law, a distinction exists between the reasonable bona fide exercise of police powers, which does not amount to a compensable taking, and indirect expropriation. The Tribunal thus aligns itself with the long

315 ibid 262.
316 ibid 263.
317 ibid 265.
318 ibid.
319 ibid 276.
320 ICSID Case No. ARB/13/27, Award, 26 July 2018.
321 ibid 826.

> line of arbitral awards finding that the characterization of a measure as expropriatory depends on the nature and purpose of the State's action. In this respect, '[i]t is . . . established in international law that States are not liable to pay compensation to a foreign investor when, in the normal exercise of their regulatory powers, they adopt in a non-discriminatory manner bona fide regulations that are aimed at the general welfare'.[322]

The tribunal in *Marfin* noted that, in addition to the fact that the measure in question had to be adopted for a public purpose and had to be non-discriminatory and respect due process, the measure must be bona fide and proportionate.

After having examined the facts of this case, the tribunal reached the conclusion that the measures challenged by the claimants, either cumulatively or individually, did not constitute a compensable taking. The tribunal was not persuaded that the respondent was motivated by the intent to nationalise the Bank or that it acted in furtherance of a plan to obtain control over the Bank. Rather, the respondent's intention was to prevent the destabilisation of its banking system in light of unfavourable practices on the part of the Bank such as granting loans with balloon payments, taking insufficient collateral, preferential treatment afforded to a number of customers to the detriment of the interests of the Bank, inadequate assessment of borrowers' repayment ability and the low interest charged which created significant pressure on the Bank's liquidity and assets. Even further, the Bank had failed to offer a convincing response to the regulator's concerns.

Against this backdrop, the tribunal held that the removal of two members of the Bank's management team and the imposition of a framework for recapitalizing the Bank's finances served to protect the health and optimal operation of the banking system in Cyprus, the protection of depositors and clients, and, ultimately, the protection of taxpayers. Further, the measures in question were non-discriminatory and were taken in good faith. More particularly, the decision to reorganise the management team was based on clear and compelling evidence.[323] The state did not accordingly err or otherwise act improperly. After weighing the competing interests at stake: on the one hand, the state's legitimate interest to protect the public welfare and, on the other hand, the investor's legitimate interest to continue managing its investment, the tribunal held that the removal of the management team satisfied the condition of proportionality and that the claimants were not made to bear an excessive burden. In fact, the claimants were not deprived of the ownership of their shares in the Bank as they retained their right to have representatives as members of the Board of Directors and their attendant right to vote in the General Shareholders' meeting or to collect dividend, if such were to be distributed. The limitation imposed on their ownership rights was thus proportionate to the aim sought to be achieved, i.e. the protection of depositors against the

322 ibid 828.

323 The following reasons were advanced by the Tribunal (i) management's irrational granting of loans without the use of prudent banking practice during periods of loss of deposits from the group; (ii) the consequent non-compliance of the Bank with the regulatory minimum liquidity levels in euros and foreign currency; (iii) the Bank's reliance on another entity for the amount of €4.6 billion; (iv) management's refusal to acknowledge that the Bank's pre carious condition, while significantly affected by the economic crisis, was also due to managerial failures, in particular its imprudent banking practices and its failure to promptly take remedial measures; (v) the loss of market confidence in management, reflected in the Bank's three notch down grade by Moody's, in contrast to the one-notch downgrade of other Cypriot banks similarly affected by the crisis; (vi) the alarming rate of deposit loss, which was higher than that of other Cypriot banks; (vii) the urgency of reinstating the credibility and the good reputation of the bank and of the depositors' trust towards the group; and (viii) the need to protect depositors' interests.

disorderly bankruptcy and of the taxpayers against the risk of insolvency of the state were the state to be called upon to support guaranteed deposits.

Meanwhile, regarding the Bank's recapitalization, the tribunal equally found that such a measure was a legitimate exercise of Cyprus' regulatory powers and was therefore not expropriatory. There was nothing arbitrary or discriminatory in the Ministry's representation that, before the examination of the Bank's request for support, the Government would require a due diligence of the Bank by category and subcategory of assets, country of activity, and an assessment of possible losses. In fact, such due diligence would have been required in order for the state to understand the financial condition of the Bank and assess the extent of the support that was needed. Further, the tribunal did not find that Cyprus delayed clarifying the terms of its support, which, according to the claimant, the delay then acted as a deterrent to private investors. The tribunal, instead, found that any delays in the Bank's recapitalization with state funds were due to the Bank's efforts to attract private capital.

In short, the recapitalization framework was not expropriatory, but rather represented a legitimate exercise of the state's regulatory powers. The framework was necessary in order for the Bank to be able to continue operating as a going concern. Had this measure not been taken, there might have been a massive deposit flight. The measure was also non-discriminatory and taken in good faith. The law was of general application, and was intended to ensure that Cyprus could rapidly intervene in order to support banks in financial distress. It was not part of any plan to bring the claimant under state control. The tribunal also found that the adoption of the Underwriting Decree ensured the claimants' due process rights; the Bank was consulted in the drafting process of the Underwriting Decree, and its input was reflected in the final draft of the Underwriting Decree. The recapitalization was also held to be proportionate. The measure gave the respondent the tools to intervene in order to support distressed banks and avoid systemic risks to its banking system and economy. In other words, when weighed against the public interest sought to be protected, i.e. the safety and soundness of the financial system, the tribunal considered that the limitations imposed by law were not excessive, so as to effectively deter private investment. For these reasons, the tribunal concluded that the Bank's recapitalization was not expropriatory, but fell within the state's police powers.

A similar outcome was arrived at in *Continental Casualty Company v Argentina.*[324] Here, the claimant alleged that its investment portfolio was primarily in assets denominated in Argentine pesos, which were at the time fully convertible to US dollars at a one-to-one exchange rate. In order to hedge the risk of devaluation, its management decided to invest assets in Argentina in low-risk US denominated assets. As a result of various investment operations, the claimant alleged that it held a portfolio of cash accounts, certificates of deposit, T-bills, Government bonds and Government loans (GGLs) for a US value of \$100,998,000. It further alleged that commencing in December 2001, Argentina enacted a series of decrees and resolutions that destroyed the legal security of its assets and frustrated its ability to hedge against the risk of the devaluation of the peso. The claimant condemned Argentina's restrictions on transfers out of its territory; rescheduling of cash deposits; pesification of US dollar deposits; and default on its debt obligations. It contended that due to these measures, it suffered an absolute loss in value of its assets of US\$46,412,000. In addition, it contended, it is or was unable, due to the bank freeze, to access its investments in Argentina.

324 ICSID Case No. ARB/03/9 Award, 5 September 2008.

The issue before the tribunal was whether Argentina had given a specific commitment to the investor that its assets would be linked to the US dollar, and that it would be immune from any evolution of the currency regime in Argentina. The tribunal held that it could not detect from the evidence presented any such specific commitment. The alleged measures taken by Argentina were held to have fallen within the scope of Argentina's police powers. The tribunal concluded in this connection:

> The fixing of an exchange rate and deciding the mechanism by which the national currency may be exchanged for foreign currency and its conditions, including the possibility of maintaining accounts and deposits denominated in a foreign currency within the country, pertain to the monetary sovereignty of each State. . . . They do not render the State liable for the burden or losses that may be suffered by those affected, provided there is no discrimination or unfairness in their application.[325]

Meanwhile, in *Feldman v Mexico*,[326] which concerned a Mexican government policy designed to limit cigarette resellers, including the claimant, from exporting cigarettes from Mexico to other countries, the tribunal considered that although confiscatory taxation, denial of access to infrastructure or necessary raw materials, and the imposition of unreasonable regulatory regimes, among others, can be considered to be expropriatory actions:

> governments must be free to act in the broader public interest through protection of the environment, new or modified tax regimes, the granting or withdrawal of government subsidies, reductions or increases in tariff levels, imposition of zoning restrictions and the like. Reasonable governmental regulation of this type cannot be achieved if any business that is adversely affected may seek compensation, and it is safe to say that customary international law recognizes this.[327]

Like the tribunal in *Saluka*, the tribunal in *Feldman* acknowledged the great difficulty that adjudicators face in drawing the line between indirect expropriation and general regulation. In this context, it noted that the determination must be made having regard to all the circumstances of the case. Instructively, the tribunal acknowledged the police powers doctrine can be relied upon even where the investor suffers loss:

> not all government regulatory activity that makes it difficult or impossible for an investor to carry out a particular business, change in the law or change in the application of existing laws that makes it uneconomical to continue a particular business, is an expropriation under Article 1110. Governments, in their exercise of regulatory power, frequently change their laws and regulations in response to changing economic circumstances or changing political, economic, or social considerations. Those changes may well make certain activities less profitable or even uneconomic to continue.[328]

Measures that have been adopted to achieve public health goals have also been challenged by foreign investors, and, in turn, host states have sought to rely upon, with variable success, the police powers doctrine. In *Chemtura v Canada*,[329] for example, the investor alleged that Canada's cancellation of its lindane registration was an unlawful expropriation. Lindane is a

325 ibid 278.
326 ICSID Case No. ARB(AF)/99/1, Award, 16 December 2002.
327 ibid 116.
328 ibid 112.
329 UNCITRAL PCA Case No. 2008–012, Award, August 2010.

pesticide which has long been viewed as toxic to human health. In turn, Canada argued that the termination of the lindane registration did not amount to a substantial deprivation, and that, in any event, the measure fell within the police powers doctrine.

On the first question, the tribunal held that the sales from lindane products were a relatively small part of the overall sales of the claimant at all relevant times. Under these circumstances, the interference of the respondent with the claimant's investment was not be deemed to be 'substantial'. More pointedly, the claimant remained operational and its yearly sales, although reduced in 2002, continued an ascending trend between 2003 and 2007 reaching levels comparable to those of 1997 to 1999. Further, the respondent did not interfere with the claimant's management, daily operations, or the payment of dividends. In other words, the claimant remained at all relevant times in control of its investment. In short, the measures did not amount to a substantial deprivation of the claimant's investment.

On the second question, the tribunal noted that even if it had been concluded that there was a substantial deprivation of the claimant's investment, there was still no expropriation because the state's decision to phase out all agricultural applications of lindane was a valid exercise of its police powers to protect public health and the environment. In the tribunal's view, the decision to de-register lindane satisfied the police powers requirements because:

> (i) it was not made in an arbitrary manner since it respected due process and was based on valid science; (ii) it was nondiscriminatory; (iii) it was not excessive; and (iv) it was made in good faith to combat the serious occupational exposure risks posed by lindane.[330]

It is worth noting that the reference to 'excessive' here appears to synonymous with proportionality, since proportionality is defined as a measure not doing more than is necessary to achieve the stated objective.

A similar outcome to the *Chemtura* decision was arrived at in *Philip Morris v Uruguay.*[331] Here, the dispute concerned allegations by the claimants that, through several tobacco-control measures regulating the tobacco industry, the respondent violated the BIT in its treatment of the trademarks associated with cigarettes brands in which the claimants had invested. These measures included the Government's adoption of a single presentation requirement precluding tobacco manufacturers from marketing more than one variant of cigarette per brand family (the 'Single Presentation Requirement' or 'SPR'), and the increase in the size of graphic health warnings appearing on cigarette packages (the '80/80 Regulation'). The SPR required each cigarette brand to have a 'single presentation' and prohibited different packaging or 'variants' for cigarettes sold under a given brand. Until the enactment of the SPR, the claimants sold multiple product varieties under each of its brands (for example, 'Marlboro Red', 'Marlboro Gold', 'Marlboro Blue', and 'Marlboro Green'). As a result of the SPR, the claimants ceased selling all but one of the product variants of each brand that it owns or holds licences to (e.g. only Marlboro Red). The claimants alleged that the measure and lack of variant sales substantially impacted the value of the company. Meanwhile, the 80/80 Regulation imposed an increase in the size of prescribed health warnings of the surface of the front and back of the cigarette packages from 50% to 80%, leaving only 20% of the cigarette pack for trademarks, logos, and other information. According to the claimants, this wrongfully limited its subsidiary's right to use its legally protected trademarks and prevented it from displaying them in their proper form. This, in the claimants'

330 ibid 254.
331 ICSID Case No. ARB/10/7, Award, 8 July 2016.

view, caused a deprivation of their intellectual property rights, further reducing the value of their investment. According to the claimants, these measures constituted, *inter alia*, a breach of the guarantee against expropriation. Uruguay, however, argued that the measures were adopted in compliance with Uruguay's international obligations, including the BIT, for the purpose of protecting public health. According to Uruguay, both regulations were applied in a non-discriminatory manner to all tobacco companies, and they amounted to a reasonable, good faith exercise of Uruguay's sovereign prerogatives. For Uruguay, the SPR was adopted to mitigate the ongoing adverse effects of tobacco promotion, including the claimants' false marketing that certain brand variants were safer than others, even after misleading descriptors such as 'light', 'mild', and 'ultra-light' were banned. Uruguay further argued that the 80/80 Regulation was adopted to increase consumer awareness of the health risks of tobacco consumption and to encourage people, including younger people, to quit or not to take up smoking, while still leaving room on packages for brand names and logos. Thus, for the respondent, the measures could not be considered expropriatory since they were a legitimate exercise of the state's sovereign police power to protect public health.

The tribunal held that the measures adopted by Uruguay were a valid exercise of the state's police powers, with the consequence of defeating the claim of expropriation under Article 5(1) of the BIT. It considered that protecting public health had for a long time been recognised as an essential manifestation of the state's police power, subject to certain conditions:

> in order for a State's action in exercise of regulatory powers not to constitute indirect expropriation, the action has to comply with certain conditions. Among those most commonly mentioned are that the action must be taken bona fide for the purpose of protecting the public welfare, must be non-discriminatory and proportionate.[332]

Having cited, with approval, the 1961 Harvard Draft Convention on the International Responsibility of States for Injury to Aliens, the Third Restatement of the Foreign Relations Law of the United States of 1987, and the OECD Guidelines, the tribunal explained that:

> The principle that the State's reasonable bona fide exercise of police powers in such matters as the maintenance of public order, health, or morality, excludes compensation even when it causes economic damage to an investor and that the measures taken for that purpose should not be considered as expropriatory did not find immediate recognition in investment treaty decisions. But a consistent trend in favor of differentiating the exercise of police powers from indirect expropriation emerged after 2000. During this latter period, a range of investment decisions have contributed to develop the scope, content, and conditions of the State's police powers doctrine, anchoring it in international law. According to a principle recognized by these decisions, whether a measure may be characterized as expropriatory depends on the nature and purpose of the State's action.[333]

The tribunal then cited, with approval, the *Bischoff Case*,[334] *Chemtura v Canada*,[335] the 2004 and 2012 US Model BITs, the 2004 and 2012 Canada Model BITs, the EU-Canada

332 ibid 305.

333 ibid 295.

334 *Bischoff* Case, German-Venezuelan Commission, Decision (1903), 10 UNRIAA 420. The Claims Commission ruled: 'certainly during an epidemic of an infectious disease there can be no liability for the reasonable exercise of police powers'.

335 PCA Case No. 2008–01, Award, 2 August 2010.

Comprehensive Economic and Trade Agreement and the EU-Singapore FTA to buttress its claim that these authorities, 'whether or not introduced *ex abundanti cautela*, reflect the position under general international law'[336] that the police powers doctrine is a legitimate response to a claim of expropriation.

On the facts, the tribunal agreed that the SPR and the 80/80 Regulation were adopted in fulfilment of Uruguay's international legal obligations for the protection of public health, including the WHO Framework Convention on Tobacco Control, and were consistent with the Uruguayan Constitution and its 1934 Organic Law. Further, in the tribunal's view, the measures were both adopted in good faith and were non-discriminatory. They were proportionate to the objective they meant to achieve, evidenced, in part, by their limited adverse impact on the claimants' business. Contrary to the claimants' contention, the tribunal considered that the measures in question were not arbitrary and unnecessary but rather were potentially effective means to protect public health. In fact, the tribunal noted that since the measures were introduced, the incidence of smoking in Uruguay had been declining, notably among young smokers. Against this backdrop, it concluded that the measures were a valid exercise by Uruguay of its police powers for the protection of public health. As such, they could not constitute an expropriation of the claimants' investment.

Separately, and quite controversially, at least one tribunal has held that in circumstances where an IIA has expressly articulated certain exceptions, tribunals should not be minded to, in addition to these exceptions, apply the police powers doctrine. In *Bear Creek Mining Corporation v Republic of Peru*,[337] the claimant decided to mine silver ore deposits located in an area of Peru known as Santa Ana in the Puno department. In accordance with Article 71 of the Peruvian Constitution, to invest in this location, which is within 50 kilometres of the border between Peru and Bolivia, the claimant was obliged to obtain – along with a multitude of other permitting requirements – a 'public necessity' Decree from the Peruvian Council of Ministers. In November 2007, the Council of Ministers proceeded to adopt Supreme Decree 083–2007, declaring the Santa Ana Project to be a 'public necessity'. This authorised the claimant to acquire seven mining rights in the Santa Ana area of Puno. Three years and six months later, in June 2011, the Council of Ministers adopted Supreme Decree 032–2011-EM. This revoked Supreme Decree 083–2007 and the finding of 'public necessity', thereby ending the claimant's right to operate its Santa Ana concessions. In between those two dates – November 2007 and June 2011 – there were protests and considerable social unrest in the Puno department, which the respondent argued were caused in part by the Santa Ana Project.

The tribunal held that the effect of Supreme Decree 032–2011 was to expropriate by indirect means the right of the claimant to operate the Santa Ana concessions, in violation of Article 812 of the FTA. Other and less draconian options were available to the Council of Ministers, including the suspension of Decree 083–2007, rather than revocation. These other options were not explored or assessed properly or even at all.

Peru argued that its decision to revoke the Decree was motivated by the social unrest which ensued from among members of the Indigenous communities who were affected by the mining. In any event, it argued that the Decree was adopted pursuant to Article 2201.1 – the 'Exceptions' clause of the FTA, which, *inter alia*, aimed to preclude from being rendered unlawful measures taken to protect human, animal or plant life or health. This was argument, however, rejected by the tribunal. Interestingly, the tribunal also rejected the host

336 *Philip Morris v Uruguay*, ICSID Case No. ARB/10/7, Award, 8 July 2016, para. 301.
337 ICSID Case No. ARB/14/21, Award, 30 November 2017.

state's reliance on the police powers doctrine, finding that, notwithstanding Canada's submission that 'a State is not required to compensate an investment for any loss sustained by the imposition of a non-discriminatory, regulatory measure designed and applied to protect legitimate public welfare objectives',[338] the express provisions of the FTA on 'Exceptions' automatically precluded the application of the police powers doctrine. The majority concluded that:

> the list is not introduced TA regarding expropriation (Article 812 and Annex 812.1) and regarding exceptions in Article 2201 expressly designated to 'Chapter Eight (Investment)', the interpretation of the FTA must lead to the conclusion that no other exceptions from general international law or otherwise can be considered applicable in this case.
>
> There is, thus, no need to enter into the discussion between the Parties regarding the jurisprudence concerning any police power exception for measures addressed to investments.[339]

It is submitted that the majority's assessment of the non-application of the police powers doctrine in this case was clearly wrong, a view also endorsed by Phillipe Sands QC, who dissented in the *Bear Creek* decision. Indeed, in keeping with the decisions of the Annulment Committees in *CMS*[340] and *Sempra v Argentina*,[341] the operation of a *lex specialis* in a BIT does not have the effect (unless the BIT explicitly provides otherwise) of precluding the operation of secondary rules of international law, even when an exception under the *lex specialis* is not available. In this regard, it is arguable that the police powers doctrine should have been given more careful consideration by the majority in this judgment.

Such appears to be the thinking in the recent case of *Eco Oro v Columbia*,[342] where the question arose as to whether the challenged measures, namely the failure to delimit the Subturban Páramos resulting in Eco Oro losing the opportunity to apply for an approved permit to operate and an environmental licence in relation to that part of the concession which overlapped with the area delimited by resolution as well as the rejection of Eco Oro's application for an environmental licence for an open-cast mining project on environmental grounds, was expropriatory or a legitimate exercise by Columbia of its police powers. Eco Oro argued that its share price had dropped significantly when its open-pit mining application was rejected, which in turn had a devastating economic impact on its concession. The tribunal agreed, finding that Eco Oro suffered a complete deprivation of the potential right to exploit. Without this right to exploit, albeit a right which was dependent upon an approved permit to operate and environmental licence, there was no possibility of exploiting the Angustura Deposit such that the concession became valueless. In short, the exploitation right was lost in totality as a result of the state's conduct. Such loss was 'capable of being considered to be a substantial deprivation, such as to amount to an indirect expropriation'.[343]

However, was the state's conduct was a legitimate exercise of Colombia's police powers pursuant to Annex 811(2)(b) of the of the Columbia-Canada FTA? In other words, were the measures adopted a non-discriminatory series of measures designed and applied to protect

338 ibid 471.

339 ibid 474.

340 ICSID Case No. ARB/01/8, Decision of the ad hoc Committee on the Application for Annulment of the Argentine Republic, 25 September 2007.

341 ICSID Case No. ARB/02/16, 28 September 2007.

342 ICSID Case No. ARB/16/41, Decision on Jurisdiction, Liability and Directions on Quantum, 9 September 2021.

343 ibid 634.

the environment? If the answer to this question was yes, there could be no indirect expropriation, unless 'a rare circumstance' (namely, discrimination and disproportionality) applied.[344] The tribunal considered that Annex 811(2)(b) reflected the more general doctrine of police powers in customary international law, principally because this provision did not expressly exclude the application of general international law. On the facts, the tribunal considered that once it was clear that a Páramo ecosystem overlapped with a significant part of the concession area, it was inevitably challenging for Eco Oro to satisfy the environmental authorities that it could undertake exploitation activities without damaging the Páramo, particularly in circumstances where the precautionary principle had been enshrined in Colombian law.

Turning first to their purpose, the tribunal considered that the measures adopted by the state were for the protection of the environment, and this was in all respects a legitimate one. More particularly, the Páramos have significant environmental importance, recognised at the national and international levels as they provide ecosystem services, the most important of which is water supply (supplying 70% of Colombia's water) and the regulation of the water cycle. The Páramos effectively act like sponges, taking in water from the atmosphere and enabling it to move down to the water tables and so the soil plays a critical role in absorbing and carrying the water. The state's measures sought to protect the Páramos which are under threat from both human intervention and climate change.

Second, the tribunal did not find that the measures were discriminatory. The measures affected all mining concessionaires (65 in total) whose concessions overlapped the Santurbán Páramo, including some locally owned and some owned by foreign companies. There was no evidence of an intention expressly to target Eco Oro, or that Eco Oro was inadvertently targeted. Third, the measures were adopted in good faith. For these reasons, the tribunal concluded that the measures were a legitimate exercise by Colombia of its police powers, and therefore did not constitute an indirect expropriation under Annex 811(2)(a).

Finally, the tribunal considered whether the state's measures were a 'rare circumstance' under Annex 811(2)(b), namely so severe that they cannot reasonably be regarded as having been adopted in good faith. The tribunal noted that the ordinary meaning of the word 'rare' in the context of 'a rare event' is one which seldom occurs, is unusual, uncommon, or exceptional while a 'severe' measure connotes 'something bad or undesirable', 'harsh', 'brutal', 'serious', or 'grave', and the addition of the word 'so' before 'severe' emphasises the extreme nature of the severity contemplated.[345] Accordingly, for the measures to comprise an actionable indirect expropriation, as opposed to a legitimate exercise of a State's police powers, there had to have been a very significant aggravating element or factor in the conduct of the state and not just a bureaucratic muddle or state inefficiency. In the tribunal's view, even before the concession had been signed, both parties had been aware of the significance of the Páramo. As such, the intended purpose of the measures as designed and applied were clearly bona fide.

The tribunal then considered the manner in which the Páramo ecosystem was delimited. Was it proportionate given its purpose? It found that the Páramo required protection, and once damaged, it is uncertain whether or not they can be restored and, if so, the length of time such restoration will take. This was precisely the circumstance in which the precautionary principle, reflected in the preamble to the 1992 Biodiversity Convention and set out in Principle 15 of the Rio Declaration on Environment and Development, was applicable. For this reason, it was not unreasonable for the Transition Zone to have been included when

344 ibid 635.
345 ibid 643.

delimiting the Santurbán Páramo, having regard to the precautionary principle. In short, it was not disproportionate in terms of its purpose of protecting the Páramo ecosystem to include the Transition Zone in the delimited area.

The tribunal also considered whether Colombia's failure to re-delimit the Santurbán Páramo as ordered by the Constitutional Court was proportionate. On balance, the tribunal did not find that including the Transition Zone in the Santurbán Páramo was unreasonable or evidenced a lack of good faith.

Notwithstanding this, however, the tribunal was troubled by the manner in which the delimitation was declared by MinAmbiente. More specifically, the social and economic studies undertaken by MinAmbiente were incomplete. Furthermore, MinAmbiente had not respected the principle of good faith, having failed to provide access to information and not ensured the community's active and deliberative participation. However, in its view, this did not mean the measures adopted by the state were themselves of a sufficiently egregious nature to comprise a lack of bona fides on the part of Colombia. In any event, MinAmbiente's breaches in failing to consult were not directed towards Eco Oro but to the local farmers and miners. Thus, while the execution of the measures was not carried out in compliance with the requirements of domestic law, the tribunal did not find that such non-compliance, in itself, was sufficient to constitute a lack of bona fides on the part of Colombia.

In considering the factors listed in Annex 811(2)(a), the tribunal assessed whether the state's measures interfered with any distinct reasonable investment-backed expectations or, in other words, did the state give specific commitments that it would refrain from the acts complained of? It noted in this connection that, as a matter of principle, a distinct reasonable investment-backed expectation was not the same as a legitimate expectation. In the tribunals view, even the most cursory due diligence by the investor before the concession was granted would have revealed (i) the potential existence of a Páramo ecosystem within the boundaries of the concession; (ii) the Government's commitment and obligation to protect these ecosystems; and (iii) that such protection could be achieved by the imposition of a mining ban. In other words, at the time the concession was entered into, there was already significant understanding and awareness of the importance of protecting the Páramo and events subsequent to the concession being registered, but prior to the FTA coming into force, should further have given rise to an awareness on the part of Eco Oro of the potential for a mining exclusion ban to be imposed over a part of the concession. For this reason, the tribunal did not find that Colombia made any specific commitment, either in the 2001 Mining Code or the concession itself, that there would be no retrospective mining exclusion zone imposed on any part of the concession area. The fact that Eco Oro received support from parts of the government of Colombia at a time when Colombia did not mean that these representations constituted specific commitments not to impose a mining exclusion zone in the area of the concession; rather, they comprised nothing more than general expressions of support for the project. In short, Eco Oro did not have any distinct reasonable investment-backed expectations that exploitation would be permitted in the entirety of the concession area.

Finally, the question arose as to whether the failure of Colombia to respect its obligations to preserve and protect the Páramo in its interactions with Eco Oro rise to the level of a lack of bona fides. While it was clear that there were failings, at times significant failings, on the part of Colombian state organs and officials in the manner in which they sought to comply with their domestic and international obligations with respect to the protection of the Páramo, the tribunal noted that its task under Annex 811(2) was to consider the measures adopted and not to judge Colombia's actions or its failure to act to preserve the Páramo. Here, bona fide non-discriminatory regulatory measures taken to protect the environment, even if they are based on precaution (i.e. in dubio pro ambiente), did not require compensation, even if they affected the value and/or viability of an investment of the investor. In short, 'given the measures were adopted as a part of Colombia's valid and legitimate exercise of its police powers, pursuant to Annex 811(2)(b), under international law, no compensation [was] payable'.[346]

THE ROLE OF INTENT

It is incorrect to say that an act of state must be presumed to be regulatory, absent proof of bad faith. In fact, there is extensive authority for the proposition that the state's intent, or its subjective motives are at most a secondary consideration.[347]

While intent will weigh in favour of showing a measure to be expropriatory, it is not a requirement, because the *effect* of the measure on the investor, not the state's intent, is the critical factor.[348] As Professor Christie[349] has explained, a state may expropriate property where it interferes with it even though the state expressly disclaims such intention. In short, the preponderance of international tribunals, jurists and scholars share the view that states may accomplish expropriations in ways other than by formal decree, often in ways that may seek to cloak expropriative conduct with a veneer of legitimacy.[350]

CONCLUSION

The guarantee against expropriation is a cornerstone of international investment law, prominently featured in regional IIAs across the Caribbean. While these agreements generally cover both direct and indirect forms of expropriation (with the notable exception of the Guyana-Brazil BIT), they do not outright prohibit expropriatory measures. Instead, they establish a framework of conditions for lawful expropriation: public purpose, non-discrimination, due process, and prompt, adequate, and effective compensation.

346 ibid 698.

347 *Tippetts, Abbett, McCarthy, Stratton v TAMS-AFFA Consulting Engineers of Iran, The Government of the Islamic Republic of Iran, Civil Aviations Organization, Plan and Budget Organization, Iranian Air Force, Ministry of Defence, Bank Melli, Bank Sakhteman, Mercantile Bank of Iran and Holland*, Award, 29 June 1984, Iran-U.S. C.T.R. 219, Award No. 141-7-2, paras. 225, 226; *Phillips Petroleum Company Iran v the Islamic Republic of Iran and NIOC*, Award No. 425-39-2, Award, 29 June 1989, 21 Iran-U.S. C.T.R. 79, paras. 97, 98; *Técnicas Medioambientales Tecmed, S.A. v United Mexican States*, ICSID Case No. ARB (AF)/00/2), Award, 29 May 2003; *Occidental Exploration & Production Co. v Republic of Ecuador*, LCIA Case No. UN3467, para. 186; *Metalclad Corporation v The United Mexican States*, ICSID Case No. ARB(AF)/97/1, Award, 30 August 2000, 40 *ILM* 36 (2001), para. 111; and *Pope & Talbot Inc. v The Government of Canada*, Arbitration under Chapter 11 of the North American Free Trade Agreement, Interim Award, 26 June 2000, UNCITRAL (NAFTA), para. 181.

348 *Phillips Petroleum Co Iran v The Islamic Republic of Iran*, 1 Iran-U.S. C.T.R. 487, para. 97: the arbitral tribunal decided that

> [t]he intent of the government is less important than the effects of the measures on the owner, and the form of the measures of control or interference is less important than the reality of their impact . . . . Therefore, the Tribunal need not determine the intent of the Government of Iran . . . .

349 G Christie, 'What Constitutes a Taking Under International Law?' (1962) 33 *BYIL* 307.

350 W Michael Reisman and Robert D Sloane, 'Indirect Expropriation and its Valuation in the BIT Generation' (2004) 74 *BYIL* 115, 121.

This chapter's examination of arbitral jurisprudence reveals that while many aspects of expropriation law have been clarified over time, several critical issues remain contentious and unresolved. Chief among these is the appropriate test for establishing indirect expropriation. This analysis strongly supports the view that tribunals should require evidence of substantial deprivation of the fundamental incidents of ownership (use, enjoyment, control, and management). Mere diminution in an investment's value or profitability, while potentially relevant, should not be sufficient on its own to constitute an indirect expropriation.

The role of proportionality in assessing the public purpose requirement presents another area of ongoing debate. We argue that proportionality should not be considered at the initial stage of determining whether a public purpose exists, as this approach appears to be an unwarranted importation from European human rights jurisprudence. However, proportionality remains a crucial factor when evaluating the applicability of the police powers doctrine as a defence against expropriation claims.

The book's analysis also grapples with the thorny questions of whether partial deprivations or temporary measures can amount to compensable expropriations. While we maintain that, as a general principle, neither should typically qualify as an indirect expropriation, we acknowledge the potential for exceptional circumstances. In rare cases, where the nature, intensity, duration, and impact of a measure on the incidents of ownership are particularly severe, even a partial or temporary interference might rise to the level of an indirect expropriation.

The evolving nature of the police powers doctrine presents both opportunities and challenges for states and investors alike. While its recognition as a principle of customary international law seems increasingly accepted, its precise contours and application remain subject to debate. The analysis in this chapter underscores the need for a careful balancing act between legitimate state regulatory interests and the protection of foreign investments.

As investment arbitration continues to evolve, it is crucial that tribunals strike a careful balance between protecting legitimate investor expectations and preserving states' regulatory space. The framework for analysing expropriation claims must be sufficiently flexible to account for the diverse circumstances in which alleged expropriations occur, while also providing a degree of predictability and consistency for both states and investors. By addressing the unresolved issues identified in this chapter, the international investment law community can work towards a more coherent and equitable approach to expropriation claims, ultimately fostering a more stable and mutually beneficial investment climate.

CHAPTER 5

THE FAIR AND EQUITABLE TREATMENT STANDARD

INTRODUCTION

The Fair and Equitable Treatment (FET) standard is an absolute standard of protection. Because of its absolute nature, it can be violated even where similarly placed domestic investors and third-party investors are treated in the same prejudicial manner as the foreign investor.[1] The FET standard is aimed at 'assuring that the normal law-abiding conduct of the business activity by the foreign investor is not hampered without good reasons by the host government and other authorities'.[2] The standard has a long history,[3] its first citing being in Article 11(2) of the 1948 Havana Charter for an International Trade Organisation,[4] and then again in Article 22 of the Economic Agreement of Bogotá in 1948.[5] In the 1950s, the standard found its way into several US treaties on Friendship, Commerce and Navigation (FCN),[6] and then again in 1959 in Article 1 of the Draft Convention on Investments Abroad,[7] developed under the leadership of Herman Abs, the Director-General of the Deutsche Bank and Lord Shawcross, the UK Attorney General. Since that time, the FET clause has appeared in thousands of international investment agreements with increasing regularity. In fact, it has been described by UNCTAD as the 'most frequently invoked by investors in ISDS cases'.[8] In addition to being the most frequently invoked investor protection standard, it is arguably also the most contentious.[9]

1 Christopher Campbell, 'House of Cards: The Relevance of Legitimate Expectations under Fair and Equitable Treatment Provisions in Investment Treaty Law' (2013) 30(4) *Journal of International Arbitration* 1, 2.

2 *Continental Casualty Company v The Argentine Republic,* ICSID Case No. ARB/03/9, Award, 5 September 2008, para. 254.

3 'Fair and Equitable Treatment Standard in International Investment Law' (OECD Working Papers on International Investment, 2004/03, OECD Publishing, OECD 2004) 3–5.

4 Havana Charter, ITO Charter 1948, UN Doc E/CONF.2/78.

5 Convenio Economico De Bogota Los Estados Americanos Epresentados En La Novena Conferencia Internacional Americana, 2 May 1948.

6 Wolfgang Alschner, 'Americanization of the BIT Universe: The Influence of Friendship, Commerce and Navigation (FCN) Treaties on Modern Investment Treaty Law' (2013) 5 *Goettingen Journal of International Law* 455.

7 For commentary, see Ioana Tudor, *The Fair and Equitable Treatment Standard in the International Law of Foreign Investment* (OUP 2008) 18.

8 UNCTAD, *International Investment Agreements and Their Implications for Tax Measures: What Tax Policymakers Need to Know: A Guide based on UNCTAD's Investment Policy Framework for Sustainable Development* (United Nations 2021) 4.

9 Rudoff Dolzer, 'Fair and Equitable Treatment: A Key Standard in Investment Treaties' (2005) 39 *International Law* 87; Marc Jacob and Stephan W Schill, 'Fair and Equitable Treatment: Content, Practice, Method' in *International Investment Law: A Handbook* (Nomos/CH Beck/Hart 2015); Kenneth J Vandevelde, 'A Unified Theory of Fair and Equitable Treatment' (2010) 43 *New York University Journal of International Law and Politics* 43; Rudolf Dolzer, 'Fair and Equitable Treatment: Today's Contours' (2013) 12 *Santa Clara Journal of International Law* 7; Ioana Tudor, *The Fair and Equitable Treatment Standard in the International Law of Foreign Investment* (OUP 2008); Thomas J Westcott, 'Recent Practice on Fair and Equitable Treatment' (2007) 8(3) *The Journal of World Investment & Trade* 409; Rumana Islam and Ghosh Islam, *Fair and Equitable Treatment (FET) Standard in International Investment Arbitration* (Springer 2018); Kathleen

DOI: 10.4324/9781003734185-5

In the context of the Caribbean, the FET clause finds resonance in nearly all of the international investment agreements that have been concluded to date. Notwithstanding its long and controversial history, however, the FET clauses contained in regional IIAs have been subject to very little judicial consideration, much less academic commentary. In this context, this chapter is an important one as it aims to fill this lacuna by providing a critical assessment of the scope, nature and operation of the FET standard, from a distinctly Caribbean perspective. It begins by examining the various formulations of the FET standard, followed by an assessment of the standard's constituent elements. The central argument advanced by this chapter is that although it is one of the most important standards in extant IIAs, the FET clause, as variously interpreted by arbitral tribunals, is arguably the most invasive investor protection standard that in appropriate cases may have a chilling effect on regulatory autonomy in the region.[10]

I. THE VARIOUS FET FORMULATIONS

There are several different formulations that characterise FET clauses in Caribbean IIAs. These are examined below.

A. The FET Clause That is Linked to Customary International Law/International Minimum Standard

Of the Commonwealth Caribbean Bilateral Investment Treaties concluded to date, only two of these instruments make express mention to the fair and equitable treatment standard linked to customary international law or the minimum standard of treatment. Article 4(1) of the Trinidad and Tobago-Guatemala BIT reads:

Minimum Standard of Treatment

> Each Contracting Party shall accord to investments of investors of the other Contracting Party treatment in accordance with customary international law.[11]

Liddell and Michael Waibel, 'Fair and Equitable Treatment and Judicial Patent Decisions' (2016) 19(1) *Journal of International Economic Law* 145; Barnali Choudhury, 'Evolution or Devolution?: Defining Fair and Equitable Treatment in International Investment Law' (2005) 6(2) *The Journal of World Investment & Trade* 297; Kendra Leite, 'The Fair and Equitable Treatment Standard: A Search for a Better Balance in International Investment Agreements' (2016) 32 *American University International Law Review* 363; Yulia Levashova, 'Fair and Equitable Treatment And Investor's Due Diligence under International Investment Law' (2020) 67(2) *Netherlands International Law Review* 233; Annika Wythes, 'Investor-State Arbitrations: Can the 'Fair and Equitable Treatment' Clause Consider International Human Rights Obligations?' (2010) 23(1) *Leiden Journal of International Law* 241; Christoph Schreurer, 'Fair and Equitable Treatment in Arbitral Practice' (2005) 6 *Journal of World Investment and Trade* 357; Theodore Kill, 'Don't Cross the Streams: Past and Present Overstatement of Customary International Law in Connections with Conventional Fair and Equitable Treatment Obligations' (2007) 106 *Michigan Law Review* 853; Alireza Falsafi, 'International Minimum Standard of Treatment of Foreign Investors' Property: A Contingent Standard' (2006) 30 *Suffolk Transnational Law Review* 317.

10 Jason Haynes, 'The Evolving Nature of the Fair and Equitable Treatment (FET) Standard: Challenging Its Increasing Pervasiveness in Light of Developing Countries' Concerns – The Case for Regulatory Rebalancing' (2013) 14(1) *The Journal of World Investment & Trade* 114.

11 Trinidad and Tobago-Guatemala BIT (2013).

Meanwhile, Article II(2)(a) of the SVG-Taiwan BIT provides:

> Each Contracting Party shall accord investments or returns of investors of the other Contracting Party:
>
> (a) fair and equitable treatment,
>
> in accordance with the principles of customary international law.[12]

Interestingly, although the Trinidad and Tobago-USA BIT speaks to the Contracting Parties being required to afford investments in their territory FET treatment no less 'favorable than that required by international law', paragraph 3 of the letter of submittal which precedes the substantive provisions of the instrument makes it clear that the FET clause is linked to 'customary international law'.[13]

The meaning of the FET clause which is linked to customary international law, or the minimum standard of treatment, is one of the most contentious aspects of international investment law[14] because it affects the intensity of evidence needed to prove the host state's international responsibility. One the one end of the spectrum, several arbitral tribunals have staunchly equated the customary international law standard to the minimum standard of treatment ('MST') articulated in the *Neer Claims*[15] case. The MST provides that:

> the treatment of an alien, in order to constitute an international delinquency, should amount to an outrage, to bad faith, to willful neglect of duty, or to an insufficiency of governmental action so far short of international standards that every reasonable and impartial man would readily recognize its insufficiency.[16]

In *Glamis Gold v United States*,[17] the tribunal, having countenanced the *Neer Claims* standard, advanced the view that the customary international law minimum standard of treatment is 'a minimum standard' and 'is meant to serve as a floor, an absolute bottom, below which conduct is not accepted by the international community.'[18] In its view, this standard 'is not meant to vary from state to state or investor to investor'.[19] The tribunal further noted that the level of scrutiny required under the customary international law minimum standard is

12 Saint Vincent and the Grenadines-Taiwan Province of China BIT (2009). See, also, CARICOM Draft Investment Code:

Article 6: MINIMUM STANDARD OF TREATMENT

1. Each Contracting Party shall accord to investments of CARICOM investors treatment in accordance with the customary international law minimum standard of treatment of foreign nationals, including fair and equitable treatment and full protection and security.
2. The concepts of 'fair and equitable treatment' and 'full protection and security' in paragraph 1 do not require treatment in addition to or beyond that which is required by the customary international law minimum standard of treatment of foreign nationals.

13 Trinidad and Tobago-United States of America BIT (1994).

14 Patrick Dumberry, *Fair and Equitable Treatment: Its Interaction with the Minimum Standard and Its Customary Status* (Brill Research Perspectives in International Investment Law and Arbitration 2017).

15 (*United States v Mexico*) (1926) 4 RIAA 60.

16 Claims Commission, 'United States and Mexico' (1927) 21 *American Journal of International Law*.

17 UNCITRAL Award, 8 June 2009.

18 ibid 615.

19 ibid.

the same as the one articulated in the 1926 *Neer* case, requiring evidence of 'egregious and shocking' conduct. It noted, in this connection, that:

> to violate the customary international law minimum standard of treatment codified in article 1105 of the NAFTA, an act must be sufficiently egregious and shocking – a gross denial of justice, manifest arbitrariness, blatant unfairness, a complete lack of due process, evident discrimination, or a manifest lack of reasons – so as to fall below accepted international standards and constitute a breach of article 1105(1).[20]

Similar sentiments were expressed in *Apotex v United States*[21] which emphasised that, in light of the Contracting Parties' *Notes of Interpretation*, which explicitly require treatment in accordance with the minimum standard of treatment under customary international law, a high threshold of severity and gravity is required in order to conclude that the host state has breached the FET standard under Article 1105.[22] The need for this high threshold was also reiterated in other NATFA cases such as *Waste Management v Mexico (II)*[23] and *Mobil Investments Canada Inc and Murphy Oil Corporation v Canada*,[24] as well as non-NAFTA cases such as *Perenco Ecuador Ltd. v Republic of Ecuador*.[25] In *Perenco*, the tribunal, citing *Waste Management Inc v Mexico, Biwater Gauff (Tanzania) Ltd v United Republic of Tanzania* and *Saluka Investments BV v Czech Republic*, considered that the terms 'arbitrary', 'grossly', 'unfair, unjust or idiosyncratic', and 'manifest' 'imply a search for the "something more" that distinguishes an act in violation of international law from the perceived unfairness occasioned by many governmental actions that do not rise to a breach of international law.'[26]

The high threshold countenanced by the handful of Caribbean BITs referred to above is highly advantageous because it affords these countries a significant margin of appreciation to take appropriate measures to address their developmental and regulatory interests without the prospect of being hauled before tribunals in circumstances where the alleged breach does not reach the required level of outrageousness. By requiring that conduct reach a high level of seriousness, developing Caribbean states, which often take measures to advance certain legitimate public interests that may conflict with foreign investments, are, in principle at least, protected from investors' relentless opposition to every proposed or actual measure that may adversely impact their investment. The high threshold also serves to ensure that the fair and equitable treatment standard is not used by investors from primarily capital-exporting countries as a weapon or 'proverbial big stick' against Caribbean countries. The fear, in this connection, is that wealthy and powerful investors who have the indirect backing of their equally powerful home states may otherwise use a low threshold for a finding of breach of the FET standard to create a *de facto* stabilisation clause that effectively freezes regional governments' ability to adopt meaningful measures to respond to evolving political, social, and economic issues, in circumstances where such measures cannot be properly described as 'arbitrary, grossly, unfair, unjust or idiosyncratic'.

20 ibid 616.
21 ICSID Case No. ARB(AF)/12/1, Award, 25 August 2014.
22 ibid 9.47.
23 ICSID Case No. ARB(AF)/00/3, Award, 30 April 2004.
24 ICSID Case No. ARB(AF)/07/4, Decision on Liability and on Principles of Quantum, 22 May 2012.
25 ICSID Case No. ARB/08/6, Decision on Remaining Issues of Jurisdiction and on Liability, 12 September 2014
26 ibid 559.

That said, there is another school of thought which advocates a low(er) threshold for a finding of a breach of the FET clause that is linked to customary international law. This low(er) threshold was articulated in *Clayton/Bilcon v Canada*[27] in which the tribunal made it clear that the international minimum standard is not limited to conduct by host states that is outrageous or egregious. In the tribunal's view, 'the contemporary minimum international standard involves a more significant measure of protection'.[28]

Other tribunals have been more explicit in countenancing the view that the minimum standard has evolved since the *Neer* Claims award. In *RDC v Guatemala*,[29] for example, the tribunal countenanced previous NAFTA decisions and considered that the minimum standard of treatment is constantly in a process of development such that it is not limited to the *Neer* formulation. This view was affirmed in *Merrill and Ring v Canada*[30] in which the tribunal identified two developmental tracks associated with the FET standard; the first being narrow in nature (i.e. requiring 'outrageous' conduct of some kind), and the second being broader, open and unrestricted, protecting 'against all such acts or behaviour that might infringe a sense of fairness, equity and reasonableness'.[31] Finding that the minimum standard of treatment has evolved in line with the second track, the tribunal concluded that 'fair and equitable treatment has become a part of customary law',[32] though this claim has been resisted by scholars.[33] Meanwhile, the tribunal in *Mesa Power v Canada*[34] went even further by agreeing with the investor's argument that the minimum standard of treatment under customary international law had evolved to such an extent that it may now be considered equivalent to the so-called 'autonomous' fair and equitable treatment (FET) standard found in other IIAs. The tribunal found that the evolution of the customary international standard was evident in state practice and *opinio juris.*

According to the latter taxonomy of cases, given that state practice and *opinio juris* evolve with changing circumstances, the content of the FET clause linked to customary international has arguably evolved since 1926. In this connection, it appears that, though Caribbean host states may not agree or benefit from such an evolutionary approach, it appears from the preponderance of authority that outrageousness may not be required for a finding of a breach of the FET clause linked to customary international law. Rather, such a clause may be violated where the conduct of the state does not reach the high threshold of being 'grossly unfair' or represent a 'manifest failure of natural justice' or otherwise demonstrate a 'complete lack of transparency'. In any event, the preponderance of authority also suggests that bad faith is not a prerequisite for a state's international responsibility to ensue under customary international law.[35]

27 PCA Case No. 2009–04, Award on Jurisdiction and Liability, 17 March 2015.

28 ibid 433.

29 ICSID Case No. ARB/07/23, Award, 29 June 2012.

30 ICSID Case No. UNCT/07/1, Award 31 March 2010.

31 ibid 210.

32 ibid 211.

33 Hussein Haeri, 'A Tale of Two Standards: 'Fair and Equitable Treatment' and the Minimum Standard in International Law' (2011) 27(1) *Arbitration International* 27. Cf. Martins Paparinskis, *The International Minimum Standard and Fair and Equitable Treatment* (OUP 2013).

34 UNCITRAL, PCA Case No. 2012–17.

35 Patrick Dumberry, 'Has the Fair and Equitable Treatment Standard Become a Rule of Customary International Law?' (2017) 8(1) *Journal of International Dispute Settlement* 155.

B. The FET Clause That is Linked to International Law

A small number of Caribbean IIAs specifically link the FET clause to international law proper, without specifically referring to customary international law. By way of example, Article II(2) of the Barbados-Canada BIT reads:

> Each Contracting Party shall accord investments or returns of investors of the other Contracting Party
>
> a. fair and equitable treatment in accordance with principles of international law . . . .[36]

A provision of this nature[37] was considered in *Allard v Barbados*,[38] a case in which the claimant argued that the aforementioned FET clause linked to international law could not be equated to the customary international law minimum standard. He contended that, unlike Article 1105 of the NAFTA, Article II(2)(a) of the Barbados-Canada BIT does not have a heading that refers to a *minimum standard of treatment*. He further argued that the wording of Article II(2)(a) of the BIT is consistent with the wordings of most bilateral investment treaties that contain an autonomous FET standard which protects legitimate expectations. The respondent state, Barbados, however, advanced the argument that the FET standard contained in Article II(2)(a) of the BIT was not a 'bare treaty standard', but rather corresponded to the minimum standard of treatment of aliens under customary international law such that its 'very high threshold' relegated legitimate expectations to a secondary role.

The tribunal, quite regrettably, did not take the opportunity to shed light on the precise contours of the FET clause linked to international law, merely finding that this issue was 'not material for the outcome of the case'.[39] It then went on to, however, note that irrespective of whether the clause operates as an autonomous FET standard or corresponds to the minimum standard, it includes the protection of investors' legitimate expectations.

Other tribunals, like the tribunal in *Tecmed v Mexico*,[40] when addressing the FET clause linked to international law, have adopted the approach that such a clause lends to an autonomous interpretation, and that tribunals should, in this context, take account of principles of international law, including the principle of good faith. Relying on the Partial Award in *S.D Myers v USA*,[41] the tribunal in *Tecmed* suggested that the FET clause linked to international law encapsulates the principles of due process, economic rights, obligations of good faith, and natural justice.[42] It is submitted that *Tecmed's* treatment of the FET clause linked to international law is largely defensible as it implicitly accepts that all sources of international law, including general principles of international law, might provide the normative basis for the FET standard. What the tribunal did not do, however, is underscore that, as customary international law is a source of international law, the FET clause that is linked to international law must necessarily include, though not exclusively, elements of customary

36 Barbados-Canada BIT (1996).

37 See, also, Barbados-Venezuela BIT: Article 2(2); Grenada-USA BIT: Article II: 2; Jamaica-USA BIT: Article II: 2(a); Trinidad and Tobago-Canada BIT: Article 2; Trinidad and Tobago-USA BIT: Article II 3. (a).

38 PCA Case No. 2012–06, Award, 27 June 2016.

39 ibid 192.

40 ICSID Case No. ARB (AF)/00/2, Award, 29 May 2003.

41 UNCITRAL, Award, 13 November 2000.

42 *Tecmed v Mexico,* ICSID Case No. ARB (AF)/00/2 189 citing *S.D. Myers, Inc. v Government of Canada*, Partial Award, November 13, 2000, 29.

international law. Interestingly, the *Tecmed* tribunal intimated that only where the state's conduct can be considered as arbitrary i.e. where it 'shocks, or at least surprises, a sense of juridical propriety' that the state's international responsibility will come into question, a standard of review that is seemingly aligned to customary international law.[43]

Tecmed aside, other tribunals seem to equate the FET standard linked to international law to customary international law as a matter of course. For example, in *Bilcon v Canada*,[44] although the investors advanced an interesting argument that, notwithstanding the NAFTA Commission's *Interpretation Notes*, Article 1105 should be interpreted as referring to *all sources* of international law as enumerated in Article 38(1) of the Statute of the International Court of Justice, including general principles, the tribunal took the view that Article 1105 encapsulates the international minimum standard of treatment. The tribunal accepted, in this context, that mere breaches of domestic law do not violate the international minimum standard.[45] In its view, even when controversial judgments, clear-cut mistakes in following procedures, gathering and stating facts and identifying the applicable substantive rules are present, provided that they are bona fide in nature, the state may escape international responsibility.[46] Conscious that State authorities are faced with competing demands on their administrative resources and there can be delays or limited time, attention, and expertise brought to bear in dealing with issues, the tribunal considered that the 'imprudent exercise of discretion or even outright mistakes do not, as a rule, lead to a breach of the international minimum standard.'[47]

To violate the minimum standard, at least in the NAFTA context, the tribunal noted that the State's conduct must amount to unjust or arbitrary treatment that rises to the level that is unacceptable from the international perspective. This high threshold has the practical effect that acts or omissions constituting a breach must be of a serious nature. In this connection, while the tribunal accepted that the terms 'grossly unfair', 'manifest failure of natural justice' and 'complete lack of transparency' are apt descriptors, there is no requirement in all cases that the challenged conduct reaches the level of shocking or outrageous behaviour since the 'contemporary minimum international standard involves a more significant measure of protection.'[48] Various other NAFTA tribunals have similarly interpreted the FET clause contained in Article 1105 NAFTA.[49]

43 ibid 159.

44 PCA Case No. 2009–04, Award on Jurisdiction and Liability, 17 March 2015.

45 ibid 436.

46 ibid 437.

47 ibid.

48 ibid 433.

49 *Mobil Investments Canada Inc. and Murphy Oil Corporation v Canada*, ICSID Case No. ARB(AF)/07/4, Decision on Liability and on Principles of Quantum, 22 May 2012, paras. 138–153; *Waste Management Inc. v Mexico*, ICSID Case No. ARB(AF)/00/3, Award, 30 April 2004, para. 98; *Mondev International Ltd. v United States of America*, ICSID Case No. ARB(AF)/99/2 Award, 11 October 2002, paras. 119, 126–127; *Cargill Incorporated v United Mexican States*, ICSID Case No. ARB(AF)/05/2) Award, 18 September 2009, paras. 277–278; *ADF Group Inc. v United States of America*, ICSID Case No. ARB(AF)/00/1, Award, 9 January 2003, para. 184; *International Thunderbird Gaming Corporation v The United Mexican States*, (UNCITRAL) Arbitral Award, 26 January 2006, para. 194. This practice is not confined to NAFTA tribunals but has also been adopted by CAFTA tribunals; see *TECO Guatemala Holdings, LLC v Republic of Guatemala*, ICSID Case No. ARB/10/23, Award, 19 December 2013, paras. 454–456; *Railroad Development Corporation v Republic of Guatemala*, ICSID Case No. ARB/07/23, Award, 29 June 2012, paras. 217, 219.

Separately, some tribunals in non-NAFTA cases have adopted an approach similar to that adopted in *Bilcon*. More particularly, in *CMS v Argentina*,[50] the tribunal, when interpreting the FET clause linked to international law, noted that,

> the Treaty standard of fair and equitable treatment and its connection with the required stability and predictability of the business environment, founded on solemn legal and contractual commitments, is not different from the international law minimum standard and its evolution under customary law.[51]

In the Caribbean context, the tribunal in *Michael Anthony Lee-Chin v Dominican Republic*[52] recently equated the FET clause linked to international law with the customary international law standard. Here, a Concession Agreement was entered into between a Jamaican national, who indirectly owned and controlled subsidiary, Lajun Corporation, and the Municipality of Santo Domingo Norte ('ASDN') for the administration and operation of the Duquesa Landfill, in which final disposal of urban solid waste was carried out in the area of the Gran Santo Domingo in the Dominican Republic. As consideration for the performance of services under the Concession Agreement, Lajun was authorised to charge the Municipalities of the Gran Santo Domingo area a tipping fee per tonne of waste. Over time, the claimant alleged that this tipping fee had become insufficient to cover the operating costs of the Duquesa Landfill, and that the respondent had acknowledged that the fee was inadequate both in the amendments to the Concession Agreement and in the settlement agreements executed thereafter.

According to the claimant, just 13 days following his acquisition of Lajun, under the pretext of Lajun's failure to comply with certain environmental regulations, the ASDN notified Lajun of its decision to rescind the Concession Agreement, taking possession of the landfill and ejecting Lajun and their employees from the property. He contended that ASDN and Lajun concluded a settlement agreement whereby the ASDN returned the possession of the land and authorised Lajun to continue with the operation and administration of the landfill, but that subsequently the Ministry of Environment imposed sanctions on Lajun for violations of its environmental permit and Law No. 64–00 of the Environment. The ASDN and Lajun then executed a second settlement agreement pursuant to which the claimant regained control of his property.

Shortly thereafter, on account of Lajun cutting back on its hours of operation which in turn allegedly seriously affected waste collection and public health, ASDN unilaterally terminated the Concession Agreement, notifying Lajun of alleged breaches of its obligations under the Concession Agreement and giving Lajun thirty days to cure them. ASDN then initiated administrative proceedings before the Superior Administrative Court of the Dominican Republic seeking the nullification of the Concession Agreement as well as a request for judicial administration of the Duquesa Landfill. The Superior Administrative Court issued an interim measure whereby it ordered the provisional intervention and administration of the Duquesa Landfill by a commission composed of the Minister of Environmental and Natural Resources, the Minister of Public Health, and the Mayor of the ASDN. The following day, this commission took control of the Duquesa Landfill. Ultimately, the Superior Administrative Court ruled on the Nullification Action filed by the ASDN, declaring the

50 ICSID Case No. ARB/01/8.

51 ibid 284.

52 ICSID Case No. UNCT/18/3, Award, 6 October 2023.

nullification of the Concession Agreement on the basis of violations of Law No. No. 340–06 of Public Procurement. Against this backdrop, the claimant contended that the State's actions were unreasonable and discriminatory, were motivated by political interests only, and violated the State's obligations to afford it fair and equitable treatment without frustrating its legitimate expectations.

The Tribunal was tasked with interpreting Article IV of the Agreement on Reciprocal Promotion and Protection of Investments contained in Annex III of the Agreement Establishing the Free Trade Area between the Caribbean Community ('CARICOM') and the Dominican Republic which provides:

> Each Party shall ensure, at all times, fair and equitable treatment for investments and returns . . . and shall not receive a treatment less favourable than established under international law.[53]

The tribunal considered that this clause ought to be equated with the international minimum standard under customary international law, though it noted that the approach of the *Neer Claims* tribunal requiring a high threshold, including bad faith, is now 'obsolete'.[54] In its view, because investor-state disputes today look very differently from what they were almost a century ago, the minimum standard of conduct expected of the state has evolved. That said, it accepted that this evolution is 'limited by the contemporary requirements of the minimum treatment standard',[55] which while no longer requiring bad faith on the part of the state, nonetheless imposes '(i) the obligation to honour legitimate expectations; (ii) the obligation to act in a non-discriminatory fashion; (iii) the obligation to act transparently; and (iv) the obligation to act consistently'.[56]

It is submitted that while *Bilcon* and related NAFTA cases appear to correctly construe the FET standard linked to international law as equating to the customary international law standard in the light of the NAFTA Interpretation Notes, whether these tribunals' reasoning can be transposed and applied to non-NAFTA cases is a question with which we must contend. Given the fact that, having regard to Article 31 of the VCLT, tribunals must first examine the natural and ordinary meaning of the treaty provision in question, the better approach is that the FET clause linked to international law must necessarily be construed to encapsulate *all* sources of international law, and not be exclusively equated to customary international law, as the tribunal in *Michael Lee-Chin v Dominican Republic* appears to suggest. It is submitted that, the approach countenanced by the tribunal in *Vivendi v Argentina*[57] is a more rational approach to the FET clause linked to international law. Here, the tribunal found that there was no basis for equating the FET clause linked to international law to the international minimum standard, as this interpretation ran counter to the ordinary meaning of the text of Article 3 of the BIT in question. In the tribunal's view:

> First, the reference to principles of international law supports a broader reading that invites consideration of a wider range of international law principles than the minimum standard alone. Second, the wording of Article 3 requires that the fair and equitable treatment conform to the principles of international law, but the requirement for conformity can just as readily set a floor as a ceiling on the Treaty's fair and equitable treatment standard. Third, the language

53 CARICOM-Dominican Republic FTA (1998).

54 *Michael Anthony Lee-Chin v Dominican Republic*, ICSID Case No. UNCT/18/3, Award, 6 October 2023, para. 432.

55 ibid 433.

56 ibid 434.

57 ICSID Case No. ARB/97/3, Award, 21 November 2000.

of the provision suggests that one should also look to contemporary principles of international law, not only to principles from almost a century ago.[58]

The tribunal in *Vivendi* cited with approval the scholarship of Dr F.A. Mann,[59] one of the twentieth century's leading authorities on the interaction between municipal law and public international law, Professor Stephen Vasciannie[60] of Jamaica, and Professor Schreuer,[61] who endorsed the view that 'fair and equitable treatment' envisages conduct which goes beyond the minimum standard. In the tribunal's view, where the fair and equitable treatment standard is invoked, the central issue is not whether the state's conduct was outrageous but rather simply 'whether the actions in question are in all the circumstances fair and equitable or unfair and inequitable'.[62] In other words, in assessing whether the standard has been transgressed, tribunals must determine whether, in all of the circumstances of the particular case, the conduct properly attributable to the state has been fair and equitable, or unfair and inequitable, which is unrelated to whether the respondent has had any deliberate intention or bad faith in adopting the measures in question, albeit that such intention and bad faith can aggravate the situation.

C. The Autonomous FET Clause

The vast majority of Caribbean BITs contain autonomous FET clauses. A typical FET provision of this nature reads similarly to Article 3(1) of the Bahamas-China BIT:

> Investments of investors of each Contracting Party shall all the time be accorded fair and equitable treatment in the territory of the other Contracting Party.

How must such a provision[63] that is unlinked from the minimum standard of treatment or international law be construed? Different tribunals have taken different approaches.

58 ibid 7.4.7.

59 F.A. Mann, 'British Treaties for the Promotion and Protection of Investments' 52 (1981) *British Yearbook of International Law* 241, 244.

60 Stephen Vasciannie, 'The Fair and Equitable Treatment Standard in International Investment Law and Practice' (1999) 70 *British Yearbook of International Law* 99, 144 ('Following Mann, where the fair and equitable treatment standard is invoked, the central question remains simply whether the actions in question are in all of the circumstances fair and equitable or unfair and inequitable.').

61 Christopher Schreuer, 'Fair and Equitable Treatment in Arbitral Practice' (2005) 6(3) *The Journal of World Investment & Trade* 360; See, also, Christopher Schreuer, 'Fair and Equitable Treatment (FET): Interactions with Other Standards' (2007) 4(5) *Transnational Dispute Management* 9–10

> As a matter of textual interpretation, it is inherently implausible that a treaty would use an expression such as 'fair and equitable treatment' to denote a well-known concept such as the 'minimum standard of treatment in customary international law. If the parties to a treaty want to refer to customary international law, it must be presumed that they will refer to it as such rather than using a different expression'.

62 *Vivendi v Argentina*, ICSID Case No. ARB/97/3, Award, 20 August 2007, para. 7.4.9.

63 Antigua-Germany BIT, Article 2(2); Barbados-China BIT, Article 3(1); Belize-China BIT, Article 3(1); Dominica-Germany BIT, Article 2; Guyana-China BIT, Article 2(2); Jamaica-Argentina BIT, Article 3(1); Jamaica-China BIT, Article 3(1); St. Lucia-Germany BIT, Article 2; Trinidad and Tobago-China BIT, Article 3(2); Antigua-UK BIT, Article 2(2); Barbados-Belgium/Luxembourg Cooperation Agreement, Article 2(2); Barbados-Cuba BIT, Article 2(2) Barbados-Germany BIT, Article 2(1); Barbados-Mauritius BIT, Article 4(1); Barbados-Switzerland BIT, Article 3(2); Barbados-UK BIT, Article 2(2); Belize-Cuba BIT, Article 2(2); Belize-El Salvador BIT, Article 3(1); Belize-The Netherlands BIT, Article 3(1);

On the one hand of the spectrum, some tribunals have equated the autonomous FET clause to the customary international law minimum standard. More pointedly, the tribunal in *Siemens v Argentina*,[64] when reviewing the autonomous FET clause, adopted a construction similar to the *Waste Management II* award, finding that conduct that is arbitrary, grossly unfair, unjust, or idiosyncratic, is discriminatory or exposes the claimant to sectional or racial prejudice, or involves a lack of due process leading to an outcome which offends judicial propriety, or a manifest failure of natural justice in judicial proceedings or a complete lack of transparency and candour in an administrative process will give rise to a breach of the FET standard.[65] It further ruled that, because customary international law has evolved since 1927, there is no longer a requirement for bad faith or malicious intent on the part of the host state in order to establish a breach of the FET standard. On the facts, the tribunal considered that the denial of access to the administrative file for purposes of the claimant filing the appeal against Decree 669/01 showed a lack of transparency on the part of Argentina and was therefore a breach of the fair and equitable treatment standard.

Meanwhile, in *Deutsche Bank v Sri Lanka*,[66] although the tribunal, citing Christoph Schreuer, considered that the Contracting Parties ought to be taken to have adopted an autonomous standard, given that it is 'inherently implausible that a treaty would use an expression such as "fair and equitable treatment" to denote a well-known concept such as the minimum standard of treatment in customary international law',[67] it nonetheless came to the conclusion that the actual content of FET standard is not materially different from the content of the minimum standard of treatment under customary international law.[68] In this context, it explained that the constituent elements of the autonomous FET standard include the protection of legitimate and reasonable expectations; good faith (although bad faith on the part of the State is not required for its violation); transparency, consistency, and non-discrimination (not based on unjustifiable distinctions or arbitrary); and judicial propriety (conduct that complies with due process and the right to be heard). A similar approach was adopted in *Biwater Gauff v Tanzania*,[69] in which the tribunal acknowledged the argument that the autonomous FET clause leaves the precise scope of the 'fair and equitable treatment' standard to the determination of the arbitral tribunal, which will have to decide whether in all the circumstances the conduct in issue is fair and equitable or unfair and inequitable',[70] but nonetheless found that 'this is not to say that the general threshold for finding a violation

Belize-UK BIT, Article 2(2); Dominica-UK BIT, Article 2(2); Grenada-UK BIT, Article 2(2); Guyana-Germany BIT, Article 2(1); Guyana-South Korea BIT, Article 2(2); Guyana-Switzerland BIT, Article 1; Guyana-UK BIT, Article 2(2); Haiti-Germany BIT, Article 1; Haiti-UK BIT, Article 2; Jamaica-Egypt BIT, Article 3(1); Jamaica-Germany BIT, Article 2(1); Jamaica-Indonesia BIT, Article III(1); Jamaica-South Korea BIT, Article 3(3); Jamaica-Switzerland BIT, Article 3; Jamaica-The Netherlands BIT, Article 3(1); Jamaica-UK BIT, Article 2; St. Lucia-UK BIT, Article 2(2); Suriname-The Netherlands BIT, Article 3(1); Trinidad and Tobago-Cuba BIT, Article 4(1); Trinidad and Tobago-France BIT, Article 3; Trinidad and Tobago-India BIT, Article 3(2); Trinidad and Tobago-South Korea BIT, Article 2(2); Trinidad and Tobago-Switzerland BIT, Article 4(1); Trinidad and Tobago-Germany BIT, Article 3(1); Trinidad and Tobago-UK BIT, Article 4.

64 ICSID Case No. ARB/02/8, Award, 17 January 2007.

65 ibid 297, 308.

66 ICSID Case No. ARB/09/02, Award 31 October 2012.

67 ibid 418.

68 ibid 419.

69 ICSID Case No. ARB/05/22, Award, 24 July 2008.

70 ibid 595.

of the standard cannot be articulated . . . . This threshold is a high one'.[71] Relying on *Waste Management v Mexico (No. 2),* the tribunal held that conduct that is arbitrary, grossly unfair, unjust or idiosyncratic, is discriminatory and exposes the claimant to sectional or racial prejudice, or involves a lack of due process leading to an outcome which offends judicial propriety, as well as a manifest failure of natural justice in judicial proceedings or a complete lack of transparency and candour in an administrative process would give rise to a state's international responsibility.[72] Although the tribunal here accepted that Article 1105(1) of NAFTA contained a slightly different wording than the UK-Tanzania BIT, it nonetheless ruled that 'the description of the general threshold for violations of this standard is appropriate in the context of Article 2(2) of the BIT'.[73] It then found that the autonomous FET standard is comprised of a number of different components, namely protection of legitimate expectations, good faith, transparency, consistency, and non-discrimination.[74]

On the other side of the spectrum, several tribunals have determined that the autonomous FET standard ought not to be construed as equating to the customary international law standard, as if the parties had intended this to be the case they would have expressly done so. In *Saluka v Czech Republic*,[75] for example, the tribunal explained that:

> Whichever the difference between the customary and the treaty standards may be, this Tribunal has to limit itself to the interpretation of the 'fair and equitable treatment' standard as embodied in Article 3.1 of the Treaty. That Article omits any express reference to the customary minimum standard. The interpretation of Article 3.1 does not therefore share the difficulties that may arise under treaties (such as the NAFTA) which expressly tie the 'fair and equitable treatment' standard to the customary minimum standard. Avoidance of these difficulties may even be regarded as the very purpose of the lack of a reference to an international standard in the Treaty. This clearly points to the autonomous character of a 'fair and equitable treatment' standard such as the one laid down in Article 3.1 of the Treaty.[76]

Similar sentiments have been expressed in *Inmaris Perestroika Sailing Maritime Services GmbH and Others v Ukraine,*[77] a case in which the tribunal noted that:

> There is nothing in the BIT that limits Article 2(1) to the standard required by customary international law. In the absence of such a statement, the Tribunal interprets the language as written, i.e., the government is obligated to accord fair and equitable treatment to foreign investments, and therefore there is no need to establish that the government's actions were in breach of customary international law in order to establish a breach of Article 2(1). Any government act that is unfair or inequitable with respect to a covered investment breaches that obligation. A government act could be unfair or inequitable if it is in breach of specific commitments, if it is undertaken for political reasons or other improper motives, if the investor is not treated in an objective, even-handed, unbiased, and transparent way, or for other reasons.[78]

The tribunal in *Total v Argentina*[79] went even further than the tribunal in *Inmaris* by noting that while the autonomous FET standard would invariably be breached by conduct that is

71 ibid 597.
72 ibid.
73 ibid 599.
74 ibid 602.
75 UNCITRAL Partial Award, 17 March 2006.
76 ibid 294.
77 ICSID Case No. ARB/08/8, Award, 1 March 2012.
78 ibid 265.
79 ICSID Case No. ARB/04/01, Decision on Liability, 27 December 2010.

arbitrary, grossly unfair, unjust, or idiosyncratic, it may also be breached by conduct that does not reach this high threshold if such conduct constitutes a violation of due process and the principle of good faith, which is a rule of general international law.[80] In short, the tribunal was emphatic in its view that the autonomous FET clause, being inherently flexible in nature, invites consideration of 'relevant State practice and judicial or arbitral case law as well as the text of the BIT and other sources of customary or general international law'.[81] In this context, a judgement of what is fair and equitable will not be reached in the abstract; it will depend on the facts of the particular case.

Meanwhile in *Philip Morris v Uruguay*,[82] the tribunal similarly accepted that, in the absence of any additional qualifying language, the reference to FET in Article 3(2) of the Switzerland-Uruguay BIT could not be read as treatment required by the minimum standard of treatment under international law. It noted that, having regard to Articles 31 and 32 of the VCLT, the scope and content of the unqualified FET under Article 3(2) had to be determined by reference to the rules of international law, customary international law being part of such rules, but that the standard is today broader than it was defined in the *Neer* case. In this context, whether a particular treatment is fair and equitable depends on the circumstances of the particular case. In any event, the tribunal implicitly suggested that, in order to identify the following principles as covered by the FET standard, using the constituent elements approach might be the best approach. In this regard, it considered that the constituent elements of the FET clause are transparency and the protection of the investor's legitimate expectations; freedom from coercion and harassment; procedural propriety and due process, and good faith.

It is submitted, from a principled perspective, that the approach countenanced in *Total* and *Philip Morris* best represents the manner in which the autonomous FET clause ought to be construed. The tribunals' view in those cases was essentially that the autonomous FET clause cannot be equated to the customary international law standard, although conduct which can properly be described as arbitrary and idiosyncratic may breach the clause. Indeed, if, as Professor Vasciannie[83] and Professor Muchlinski[84] have explained, Contracting Parties had

80 ibid 110–11.

81 ibid 107.

82 ICSID Case No. ARB/10/7, Award, 8 July 2016.

83 Vasciannie (n 60) 99, 144:

> . . . it is noteworthy that the instances in which States have indicated or implied an equivalence between this standard and the international minimum standard are relatively sparse. Moreover, bearing in mind that the international minimum standard has itself been an issue of controversy between developed and developing States for a considerable period, it is unlikely that a majority of States would have accepted the idea that this standard is fully reflected in the fair and equitable standard without clear discussion. These considerations point ultimately towards the conclusion that the two standards in question are not identical: both standards may overlap significantly with respect to issues such as arbitrary treatment, discrimination and unreasonableness, but the presence of a provision assuring fair and equitable treatment in an investment instrument does not automatically incorporate the international minimum standard for foreign investors. Following Mann, where the fair and equitable standard is invoked, the central issue remains simply whether the actions in question are in all the circumstances fair and equitable or unfair and inequitable.

84 Peter Muchlinski, *Multinational Enterprises and the Law* (2nd edn, OUP 2007) 683:

> It has been suggested that fair and equitable treatment represents a classical international law standard which embodies international minimum standards of treatment. . . . If the intention is to assimilate the two concepts, this should be made explicit in the text. Otherwise, the fair and equitable treatment standard should stand on its own.

intended to treat the autonomous FET clause as synonymous with the minimum standard under customary international law, they would have expressly done so. In the absence of this equivalence, it is submitted that tribunals should not confine themselves to the high threshold for a finding of liability under customary international law, but rather any conduct of the state which, having regard to the circumstances of the case in question, amount to unfairness and inequity, should give rise to a breach of the clause. This does not mean, however, that any and every type of state conduct should give rise to a breach; rather, conduct that does not respect investors' legitimate expectations, is discriminatory, arbitrary or unreasonable, or lacking in due process or not taken in good faith may give rise to a breach of the autonomous FET clause.

D. No FET Clause

Among the IIAs concluded by Caribbean countries, only the Guyana-Brazil and Suriname-Brazil BITs expressly exclude the fair and equitable treatment standard. Article 4(4) of the Guyana-Brazil BIT reads:

> For greater certainty, the standards of fair and equitable treatment and full protection and security shall not be used or raised by either Party to this Agreement as a ground for any dispute settlement procedure in relation to the application or the interpretation of this agreement.[85]

This provision appears to have been included at the insistence of Brazil, in keeping with its recent treaty practice,[86] so as to stem the increasing pervasiveness of the FET standard, its vague and ambiguous normative content, and the unending legitimacy concerns over the divergent manner in which tribunals interpret the clause. Of course, given the traditional importance of the fair and equitable treatment standard, it might very well be argued that the Contracting Parties, in adopting this bold approach, have signalled a new era in respect of the operation of the clause in ways that attempt the rebalance the asymmetrical approach of this aspect of international investment law. This may very well inform future investment treaty practice in the region.

II. CONSTITUENT ELEMENTS

As intimated above, tribunals often analyse particular factual circumstances that arise for their consideration by reference to certain benchmarks, or constituent elements of the FET standard. In this section, we will critically assess the nature, scope, merits, and limitations of the various constituent elements of the FET standard.

A. Legitimate Expectations

The concept of legitimate expectations is not unique to international investment law. In fact, it has long been a corner stone of common law jurisdictions,[87] including the Commonwealth

85 Brazil-Guyana BIT (2018); Brazil-Suriname BIT (2018), signed (not in force).

86 Andreas Buser, 'Recalibrating Policy Space in Bilateral Investment Treaties: Is There a Common B (R) ICS Approach?' in Congyan Cai, Huiping Chen, and Yifei Wang (eds), *The BRICS in the New International Legal Order on Investment* (Brill Nijhoff 2020) 188; Catharine Titi, 'International Investment Law and the Protection of Foreign Investment in Brazil' (2016) 2 *Transnational Dispute Management* 1, 11.

87 See generally, Christopher Forsyth, 'Legitimate Expectations Revisited' (2011) *Judicial Review* 429; Alexander Brown, *A Theory of Legitimate Expectations for Public Administration* (OUP 2017); Soren

Caribbean.[88] The concept appears to be tied to the rule of law; a state should honour the lawful, unambiguous, and unqualified representations which it has made to others who reasonably rely on these representations to their detriment. In the context of international investment law, the concept of legitimate expectations is usually pleaded as a matter of course in arbitration proceedings. In this connection, the tribunals in *Electrabel v Hungary*[89] and *Ulysseas v Ecuador*[90] rightly asserted that the most important function of the FET standard is the protection of investors' reasonable and legitimate expectations.

Despite the increasing pervasiveness of the concept of legitimate expectations in international investment law, it will be incorrect to assume that once a promise or representation is frustrated by the State then liability automatically ensues. In fact, several tribunals, including the Panels in *Mobil & Murphy v Canada*[91] and *Peter Allard v Barbados*,[92] have articulated the cumulative requirements that must necessarily be satisfied by foreign investors, namely (i) the State has given clear and explicit representations that induced the investment; (ii) these representations were, by reference to an objective standard, reasonably relied on by the investor; and (iii) these representations were repudiated by the state in the absence of a significant countervailing interest. These requirements will be addressed in turn.

(i) Specific, Unambiguous, and Unqualified Representation/Assurance

Not every representation that is made by the state would qualify as giving rise to a legitimate expectation.[93] Rather, the purported representation must be specific, unambiguous, and unqualified in nature.[94] In other words, from an objective point of view, there should be no doubt about the nature of the representation; the representation must be precise as to its content and clear as to its form. General, vague, and qualified assurances will likely not reach the required standard of legitimacy.[95] As the tribunal in *Parkerings v Lithuania*[96] has noted in this context, 'not every hope amounts to an expectation under international law'.[97] A similar view was expressed in *Charanne and Construction Investments v Spain*,[98] when

Schønberg, *Legitimate Expectations in Administrative Law* (OUP 2000); Philip Sales, 'Legitimate Expectations' (2006) *Judicial Review* 186; Richard Clayton, 'Legitimate Expectations, Policy, and the Principle of Consistency' (2003) *Cambridge Law Journal* 93.

88 See generally, Calvin Eversley, 'Legitimate Expectation and the Creation of Procedural and Substantive Legal Rights in Commonwealth Caribbean Public Law' (2004) 33 *Common Law World Review* 332; Alicia Elias-Roberts, 'A Comparative Analysis of the UK and Commonwealth Caribbean Approach Towards Legitimate Expectation' (2013) 39 *Commonwealth Law Bulletin* 143.

89 ICSID Case No. ARB/07/19, Award, 25 November 2015, para. 7.75.

90 UNCITRAL Final Award, 12 June 2012, para. 249.

91 ICSID Case No. ARB(AF)/07/4, Decision on Liability and on Principles of Quantum, 22 May 2012, para. 152.

92 PCA Case No. 2012–06, Award, 27 June 2016, para. 183.

93 Michele Potestà, 'Legitimate Expectations in Investment Treaty Law: Understanding the Roots and the Limits of a Controversial Concept' (2013) 28(1) *ICSID Review* 88.

94 Arwel Davies, 'Investment Treaty Interpretation, Fair and Equitable Treatment and Legitimate Expectations' (2018) 15 *Manchester Journal of International Economic Law* 314.

95 Khasan Sayfutdinov, 'Promises and Commitments: The Role of Fair and Equitable Provisions and Local Foreign Direct Investment Law and Regulations in Generating Legitimate Expectations' in Rustamjon Urinboyev (ed), *The Political Economy of Central Asian Law: A Law and Society Analysis* (Springer 2024) 197.

96 ICSID Case No. ARB/05/8, Award, 11 September 2007.

97 ibid 344.

98 SCC Case No. V 062/2012, Award, 21 January 2016.

the tribunal explained that stabilisation provisions provided for in general legislation, or political announcements, like press releases and others, cannot create legitimate expectations because of their inherent vagueness.

One of the most far-reaching expositions on the need for specificity with respect to legitimate expectations was given in *Peter Allard v Barbados*.[99] Here, Allard, a Canadian investor, purchased property in Barbados to develop the Graeme Hall Wildlife Sanctuary. Allard began operating the Sanctuary as an ecological site, but could not proceed with the development of the site because the government had amended the 1986 National Physical Development Plan to reclassify a zone located to the north of the Sanctuary that had been allocated to recreational and agricultural uses under the 1986 Plan into two zones: a 'predominantly residential' zone closest to the Sanctuary, and an 'urban corridor'. Allard also complained that he could not proceed with the Sanctuary because the Sluice Gate, which allowed for the ingress of clean water from the sea, and the egress of contaminated debris from the Sanctuary, was not operational, hence resulting in bacterial contamination of the area. Allard claimed that a failure by Barbados to take environmental protection measures breached the BIT and resulted in the destruction of the value of his investment in the eco-tourism site.

Among other things, Allard contended that the Government of Barbados had breached his legitimate expectations in several ways. First, he argued that the government had given an assurance that it would not amend the 1986 Plan to reclassify the zoning of the area, but had, subsequently, in 2008, proceeded to amend the said Plan. To this, however, the tribunal found that Allard could not point to any specific statement made by Barbados to the effect that the 1986 Plan would not be amended at all or in part.

Second, Allard alleged that, in a letter from the Town and Country Planner, he had received an assurance from the State about the importance of the Graeme Hall Swamp, and the government's purported commitment to grant him planning permission to develop the area. He also contended that representations were made to him to the effect that the State would provide him with certain permits, tax breaks, land leases, and the lease of the Sluice Gate. The tribunal, however, found that the Town and Country Planner had made it clear that he could not address at that stage the Allard's specific investment plan, as it was 'difficult to comment on the proposal as submitted'.[100] Moreover, it was found that the Town and Country Planner did not give any of the assurances related to tax breaks requested by Allard, nor indeed the land leases and the lease of the Sluice Gate.

A further argument raised by Allard was that two reports produced by external consultants hired by the Government of Barbados, which examined the feasibility of, and made recommendations for, appropriate arrangements for operating a proposed Reserve at Graeme Hall as a tourism attraction, and which recommended the establishment of the Sanctuary, gave rise to a legitimate expectation. The tribunal, however, held that the external consultants who were charged with producing a recommendation for the State were not an organ of the State. As such, any representations made by the consultants could not be attributed to Barbados.

Meanwhile, Allard also attempted to rely on a letter from the Permanent Secretary in the Ministry of Physical Development, stating that he 'remain[ed] firmly committed to the

99 PCA Case No. 2012–06, Award, 27 June 2016.
100 ibid 201.

principle that the entire Graeme Hall Swamp must be managed as a single ecological unit',[101] which he argued gave rise to a legitimate expectation. The tribunal, however, considered that the statement made by the Permanent Secretary could not be treated as a specific representation attributable to the Government of Barbados. In the tribunal's view, the Permanent Secretary unequivocally stated that the letter's subject fell 'outside [his] immediate remit',[102] and that, therefore, 'any remarks [he] offer[ed] must simply be construed as general observations'.[103] He also took care to explain that all statements were based on '[his] own view'.[104]

Finally, Allard also claimed that Barbados made specific and direct representations that it undertook to manage the Sluice Gate. Allard's complaint was that Barbados then failed to adequately maintain and operate the Sluice Gate to allow ingress and egress of water from and to the sea, failing, in particular, to operate the Sluice Gate in a way that would allow contaminants to be flushed from and seawater to enter the Sanctuary. The tribunal, however, did not find any implicit undertaking of the State to manage the Sluice Gate as proposed. Barbados did not make specific and direct representations giving rise to any legitimate expectations on the part of Allard regarding the maintenance and operation of the Sluice Gate.

In short, then, it was the tribunal's view that none of the statements relied upon by Allard was amenable to characterisation as a specific representation capable of creating a legitimate expectation that Barbados would take any specific steps with regard to the environmental protection of the Sanctuary. The terms and context of the various statements relied upon by Allard did not suffice to support the expression of an intention to create an obligation for the State.

In *Crystallex v Venezuela*,[105] the tribunal made a clear demarcation between specific assurances from general assurances, finding that the former were capable of being protected under the fair and equitable treatment standard, but not the latter. Here, the claimant, a Canadian mining company, acquired the rights to exploit the gold deposits in the Las Cristinas gold mine in Venezuela. The claimant thereafter entered into a mining operation contract with the Corporación Venezolana de Guayana (CVG), a Venezuelan State corporation and thereby sought the necessary permits to commence operations. Subsequently, the claimant received a letter from Venezuela's Ministry of Environment indicating that the environmental permit would be granted once the company posted a bond. The letter read:

> [The bond] shall guarantee the implementation of the measures proposed in the document presented for the Environmental Impact Evaluation of the project, which have been analyzed and approved by this Office, and are presented as follows [list of measures follows]: . . . .
>
> Once the Bond has been posted, checked, and found to be compliant by this Office, the Authorization for the Affectation of Natural Resources for the execution of the activities associated with the project, 'Construction of Infrastructure and Services and for the Gold Ore Exploration State of the Las Cristinas Project' to be carried out within the jurisdiction of the Autonomous Municipality of Sifontes in Bolivar State, will be handed over.[106]

Although Crystallex posted the bond as required, the Ministry of Environment, nearly a year later, denied the claimant the environmental permit, apparently based on concerns about

101 ibid 173.
102 ibid 186.
103 ibid.
104 ibid.
105 ICSID Case No. ARB(AF)/11/2, Award, 4 April 2016.
106 ibid 561.

the project's impact on the environment and Indigenous peoples. The Mining Operation Contract was terminated three years later at the instance of the respondent government.

In arbitration proceedings under the Canada-Venezuela BIT, the claimant argued, *inter alia*, that its legitimate expectation to the environmental permit was frustrated. In this context, it sought to ground its purported legitimate expectations in a statement made by the Ministry of Mines that the permit was 'well on track';[107] a statement by the President of the Commission of Mines of the National Assembly and the Mayor of Sifontes, expressing their joint support for the commencement of the claimant's Project; and certain statements made by Planning Director in the Ministry of Environment which referred to various environmental aspects of the claimant's project. The tribunal, however, refused to find that a legitimate expectation was created, concluding instead that these were general, vague, equivocal statements that did not 'meet the level of specificity required to create legitimate expectations which, if later frustrated, are relevant for a finding of an FET breach'.[108] However, the tribunal arrived at the opposite conclusion with respect to the letter referred to above which made reference to an evaluation process to be carried out by the Ministry and that the measures proposed by the claimant were 'analysed'. It added that these measures were 'approved' by 'this Office', i.e. the Administrative Office of Permissions, which oversaw the processing of requests for the relevant permits. Finally, the letter stated, in unambiguous terms, that 'once the Bond has been posted, checked, and found to be compliant by this Office, . . . the [Permit] . . . will be handed over'.[109] In the tribunal's view, the use of the indicative mode and the future tense – expressing a fact rather than a possibility or a conjecture – and the structure of the sentence made it clear that the Administration had come to the conclusion that the process of analysis and approval had been completed and that the Office of Permissions was at the time ready to 'hand over' the permit, once the bond formality is cleared. In this connection, in circumstances where the claimant immediately posted the bond and paid the relevant taxes in anticipation of being granted the permit, this letter was deemed by the tribunal to have given rise to a specific assurance that the permit would be granted, which was frustrated by the respondent's failure to honour the expectation that it had created.

It appears that tribunals will find a specific representation capable of giving rise to a legitimate expectation where, notwithstanding that certain assurances are found in a generalised scheme (e.g. legislation), these are later crystallised in an instrument (e.g. investment certificate) made available to the investor upon which the investor reasonably relies. The case of *Micula v Romania*[110] is instructive in this regard. Here, in 1993, Romania entered into an association agreement with the European Community (EC, now European Union – EU). The Agreement included a provision on state aid and required Romania eventually to introduce state aid rules similar to the EC rules on state aid. The Agreement further encouraged Romania to establish and improve a legal framework which favoured and protected investment and to conclude agreements for the promotion and protection of investments. In 1999, in the context of attempting to develop its regional policy, Romania adopted an investment incentive scheme in the form of Emergency Government Ordinance No 24/1998 ('EGO 24'). This scheme afforded incentives for new investors, including customs duties and profit tax exemptions, investing in a disadvantaged region of Romania for a ten-year period, provided

107 ibid 511.
108 ibid 555.
109 ibid 562.
110 ICSID Case No. ARB/05/20, Award, 11 December 2013.

that certain conditions were satisfied.[111] During the early 2000s, the claimants, in reliance on the EGO 24 incentives (which required investments to be maintained for twice the period of the benefits received) invested in a large, highly integrated food production operation in that region as part of a ten-year business plan. However, during the formal accession negotiations between Romania and the EU from 2000 to 2004, the EU informed Romania that various Romanian government schemes, including the EGO 24 scheme, were not in line with the state aid rules. The EU urged Romania to bring its schemes into alignment without delay. The Romanian Government responded by passing a Government Ordinance repealing all but one of the tax incentives provided in EGO 24. The claimants, having been deprived of the previously granted incentives, filed a request for arbitration with ICSID under the terms of the BIT, claiming that the repeal of the EGO 24 incentives was a repeal of its legitimate expectations.

The tribunal ruled in favour of the claimants, ultimately finding that Romania had breached the terms of the BIT by failing to respect the claimants' legitimate expectations and awarded the claimants approximately £70m in compensation in this regard. The tribunal found that the EGO 24 created a general scheme of incentives available to investors who fulfilled certain requirements, which were later 'granted' to qualifying investors through a specific administrative act (the 'PIC'). In other words, the legislation created a generalised entitlement that could be claimed by qualifying investors, but this general entitlement was later crystallised with respect to qualifying investors, like the claimants, through the granting of the PICs, becoming from that moment on a specified entitlement with respect to specified investors. In the tribunal's view, the legislative framework in Romania between the years 1998–2002, together with the PICs, instilled in the claimants a legitimate expectation that they would be entitled to the EGO 24 incentives in substantially the same form as when they received their PICs until 2009. Although the tribunal found that some of the investments made prior to 2000 were not made in reliance on the EGO 24 incentives, it nonetheless considered that a significant part of the claimants' investments (from 2000 to 2004) was made in reliance on the incentives. In this context, the tribunal felt satisfied that the existence of the incentives was one of the reasons for the scale and manner of those investments; the claimants built a large and complex platform to produce food and drink products, and that its profits depended largely on the reduction of their operating costs resulting from the Raw Materials Incentive.

A similar ruling was arrived at it *Rumeli Telekom v Kazakhstan*.[112] Here, a Turkish company won a bid to operate the second mobile telephone network in Kazakhstan. The investment contract concluded between the claimant and the State Committee on Investment obliged the claimant to make investments, to apply advanced technology, and to provide the investment committee with regular and detailed information on the progress of its investment, while the state was obliged to grant the claimant tax and other benefits, including a five-year total exemption from corporate and property tax, and reduced rates for the five

111 The regime required a certain quid pro quo from the investors; investors had to fulfil certain requirements, and undertook certain obligations, namely: (i) create employment; (ii) create new investments; (iii) undergo substantial monitoring to continue receiving their incentives; and (iv) maintain their investments in the disadvantaged area for at least twice the time they benefitted from the incentives. The EGO 24 put investors on notice that, if they planned to benefit from the incentives for the full period they were offered, they had to be prepared to make long-term commitments and investments in the region.

112 ICSID Case No. ARB/05/16, Award, 29 July 2008.

years thereafter. A few years after the conclusion of the contract, however, differences arose between the parties to the agreement, which ultimately culminated with the respondent's decision to unilaterally terminate the investment contract. Before the arbitral tribunal, the claimant argued that the respondent's termination of the contract, which deprived it of the incentives to which it was entitled, amounted to a breach of its legitimate expectations. The tribunal agreed, finding that the respondent's decision to terminate, and not suspend the contract, did not respect the claimant's legitimate expectations, and was also arbitrary, unfair, unjust, and lacking in due process.

Although most tribunals have held that only specific assurances/representations will give rise to legitimate expectations, several other tribunals have taken the approach that general assurances may be sufficient. More specifically, the tribunal in *Murphy Exploration & Production Company International v Ecuador*[113] suggested that an investor may hold legitimate expectations based on an objective assessment of the legal framework, absent specific representations or promises made by the State to the investor. Similarly, in *9REN Holding S.À.R.L., v Spain,*[114] the tribunal proffered that legitimate expectations may arise from 'rules not specifically addressed to a particular investor but which are put in place with a specific arm to induce foreign investments and on which the foreign investor relied on making his investment.'[115] In its view, although a bare regulatory measure addressed to the entire world lies at the weaker end of the spectrum, it may nonetheless give rise to a legitimate expectation.

Similarly, the tribunal in *Masdar Solar & Wind Cooperatief U.A. v Spain,*[116] relied upon *Suez v Argentina*[117] to conclude that where an investor undertakes an investment, a host state, through its laws, regulations, policies, and statements can create certain expectations about the nature of the treatment that it anticipates on the part of the state. In the tribunal's estimation, because these factors influence the investor's initial decisions and afterwards the manner in which the investment is managed, they should properly constitute reasonable and legitimate expectations. In similar vein, in *Glencore International A.G. and C.I. Prodeco S.A. v Colombia,*[118] the tribunal endorsed the view expressed in *Masdar* that legitimate expectations can be created in some cases by the state's general legislative and regulatory framework in that an investor may make an investment in reasonable reliance upon the stability of that framework, so that in certain circumstances reform of the framework may breach the investor's legitimate expectations. It added that state-investor contracts are among the instruments which can generate such representations, assurances, and commitments, albeit it cautioned that not every violation of a contract would trigger a finding of breach of legitimate expectations. It considered that where the investor suffers loss as a result of a breach of 'special significance' or where such breach involves an act of puissance publique, or loss of a secure and stable legal framework, this may give rise to a finding of breach of legitimate expectations.[119]

113 ICSID Case No. ARB/08/4, Award on Jurisdiction, 15 December 2010.
114 ICSID Case No. ARB/15/15, Award, 31 May 2019.
115 ibid 294.
116 ICSID Case No. ARB/14/1, Award, 16 May 2018.
117 ICSID Case No. ARB/03/19, Award, 9 April 2015.
118 ICSID Case No. ARB/16/6, Award, 27 August 2019.
119 ibid 1378.

Meanwhile, in *Cube Infrastructure Fund v Spain*,[120] the tribunal:

> [did] not consider it necessary that a specific commitment be made to each individual claimant in order for a legitimate expectation to arise. At least in the case of a highly-regulated industry, and provided that the representations are sufficiently clear and unequivocal, it is enough that a regulatory regime be established with the overt aim of attracting investments by holding out to potential investors the prospect that the investments will be subject to a set of specific regulatory principles that will, as a matter of deliberate policy, be maintained in force for a finite length of time. Such regimes are plainly intended to create expectations upon which investors will rely; and to the extent that those expectations are objectively reasonable, they give rise to legitimate expectations when investments are in fact made in reliance upon them.[121]

It is submitted that the better approach, at least from a Caribbean perspective, appears to be the sentiments expressed in *Philip Morris v Uruguay*:[122]

> legitimate expectations depend on specific undertakings and representations made by the host State to induce investors to make an investment. Provisions of general legislation applicable to a plurality of persons or of category of persons, do not create legitimate expectations that there will be no change in the law.[123]

In that case, the claimant sought to rely on what they considered 'justifiable expectations' that the respondent would allow them to continue to deploy and capitalize on their brand assets without imposing the 80/80 warning requirement on their products as to the dangers of tobacco use in keeping with their intellectual property rights. The tribunal, however, held that there was no evidence of specific undertakings or representations made to the claimants by Uruguay at the time of their investment or, for that matter, subsequently. Although the Uruguayan legal system provided for the protection of trademarks, the tribunal found that no undertaking or representation could be grounded on these legal rules of general application, which were subject in any case to the state's regulatory power in the public interest. In the tribunal's view, as a manufacturer/distributor of harmful products such as cigarettes, the claimants could have no expectation that new and more onerous regulations would not be imposed. In short, the expectation could only be that regulation of the sale and use of tobacco products would become progressively more stringent.[124]

(ii) Reasonable Reliance

The second requirement for establishing a legitimate expectation is that reliance on the putative expectation must have been objectively reasonable and justified in the circumstances.[125]

120 ICSID Case No. ARB/15/20, Decision on Jurisdiction, Liability and Partial Decision on Quantum, 19 Feb 2019.

121 ibid 388.

122 ICSID Case No. ARB/10/7, Award, 8 July 2016.

123 ibid 426.

124 ibid 430.

125 *Parkerings Lithuania*, ICSID Case No. ARB/05/8, Award, 11 September 2007, para. 333; *Saluka v Czech Republic*, UNCITRAL Partial Award, 17 March 2006, paras. 304 and 309; *Mondev v U.S*, ICSID Case No. ARB(AF)/99/2, Award, 11 October 2002, para. 118; *Waste Management v Mexico*, ICSID Case No. ARB(AF)/00/3, Award, 30 April 2004, paras. 98, 99; *Lauder v Czech Republic*, UNCITRAL Award, 3 September 2001, para. 292.

According to the tribunal in *Duke Energy v Ecuador*,[126] the assessment of the reasonableness of reliance on the expectation must take into account all the relevant circumstances, including not only the facts surrounding the investment, but also the political, socioeconomic, cultural, and historical conditions prevailing in the host State.[127] Reliance on subjective expectations will hardly suffice unless they are objectively reasonable; that is, expectations must arise from the conditions that the state offered the investor, and the latter must have relied upon them when deciding to invest.

In *Peter Allard v Barbados*,[128] the tribunal considered whether the claimant reasonably relied on representations allegedly made by the Government of Barbados. In this connection, the tribunal held that Allard did not make either his initial or later investment decisions in reliance on any representations made by Barbados. In the tribunal's estimation, Allard was a person of philanthropic intentions; he took the decision to invest in 1994, before any of the alleged representations were made, with the exception of the 1986 Plan. Further, in 1994, he made what may be described as an impulsive commitment, followed by an offer to buy the first part of the Sanctuary grounds in February 1995. The evidence showed that there was no confirmation that the taking of any of the investment decisions during this period was predicated upon the receipt by Allard of any relevant assurances from Barbados. In short, Allard moved toward the realisation of his project irrespective, and not in reliance upon, any relevant representations made by Barbados.

The tribunal considered that Allard had purchased the first and second parcels of the Sanctuary, and commenced its development, before even submitting an environmental management plan for approval, and did so against the advice and warnings of Barbadian officials. As to the management and operation of the Sluice Gate, Allard bought all of the Sanctuary land and began the development of the project before the Amended EMP was approved, despite having been of the view that 'correct ecological operation of [the] sluice gate is a necessity to maintain the right saline content of Graeme Hall'.[129] The tribunal accordingly concluded that:

> Allard appears to have been of visionary disposition in respect of this project. Unfortunately, when things go wrong, good intentions do not directly translate to establishing a backstop to shift responsibility under the terms of the BIT to the State.[130]

In the final analysis, the tribunal did not, however, find it necessary to determine whether the claimant's reliance on the purported representations made was reasonable, given its findings above.

An opposite outcome was arrived at in *Micula v Romania*,[131] a case in which the tribunal found that the claimants' expectation that the incentives were compatible with Romanian law was reasonable. More particularly, the tribunal considered that it was reasonable for the claimants to believe that the incentives were legal under Romanian law and would be maintained for the full 10 year period because the Government, through Parliament, did not follow the Competition Council's recommendation to abolish the incentives, and decided

126 ICSID Case No. ARB/04/19, Award, 18 August 2008.
127 ibid 340.
128 PCA Case No. 2012–06, Award, 27 June 2016.
129 ibid 225.
130 ibid 222.
131 ICSID Case No. ARB/05/20, Award, 11 December 2013.

instead to confirm them via new legislation (EGO 75/2000), and immediately afterwards issued the claimants PICs confirming their eligibility for the incentives in question. In this context, it was reasonable for the claimants to believe that the Government considered that such incentives were legitimate and intended to maintain them for the stated period. In short, a significant part of the claimants' investments (from 2000 to 2004) was made in reliance on the incentives. In particular, the tribunal was satisfied that the existence of the incentives was one of the reasons for the scale and manner of those investments; the claimants built a large and complex platform for the production of food and drink products, and that its profits depended largely on the reduction of their operating costs resulting from the Raw Materials Incentive.

As a matter of principle, it should be noted that foreign investors must accept the conditions of the host state as they find them. In this connection, an investor cannot complain if its business suffers economically from laws or practices that were in place at the time of the investment.[132] The investor must conduct its business in a reasonable manner, which includes undertaking due diligence with respect to the regulatory environment in which it operates and the likelihood that it may change or evolve.[133] This means that, if necessary, investors must seek relevant professional advice in assessing the risks inherent in a particular host state.[134] An investor cannot be expected to have failed to exercise due diligence and still be regarded to have reasonably relied upon purported assurances, since BITs 'are not insurance policies against bad business judgments'.[135]

When determining the question of whether an investor reasonably relied upon certain assurances, the investor must anticipate that the law may change, especially if the general legislative climate is in a state of flux.[136] In other words, regulatory change must be anticipated all the more in regulatory environments where there is public and continuous scrutiny of the actions of the state,[137] and in transition or otherwise unstable economies.[138] In short, investors cannot reasonably expect regulatory stability in the absence of a stabilisation clause.

Finally, the sentiments of the tribunal in the recently decided *Michael Lee-Chin v Dominican Republic*[139] case on the question of investors' due diligence in the context of the fair and equitable treatment standard are worth noting:

> the lack of the required due diligence of an investor – irrespective of its approach, namely, financial, technical, environmental or legal – before its investment decision, may affect the legitimacy of its expectations. In other words, an investor can hardly rely on legitimate expectations if it failed to conduct adequate due diligence that could have enabled it to identify certain risks for its investment. The Tribunal should assess credibility – not veracity – of the due diligence conducted.[140]

132 *MTD v Chile*, ICSID Case No. ARB/01/7, Award, 25 May 2004, para. 204.

133 *Parkerings v Lithuania*, ICSID Case No. ARB/05/8, Award, 11 September 2007, para. 333.

134 *Feldman v Mexico*, ICSID Case No. ARB(AF)/99/1, Award, 16 December 2002, paras. 114, 132.

135 *Maffezini v Spain*, ICSID Case No. ARB/97/7, Award, 13 November 2000, para. 64.

136 *Glamis Gold v United States*, UNCITRAL, Award 8 June 2009, para. 767.

137 *Methanex v United States*, UNCITRAL, Award 3 August 2005, Part IV D, 10; *Glamis Gold v United States*, UNCITRAL, Award 8 June 2009; *Chemtura v Canada*, PCA Case No. 2008–01, Award, 2 August 2010.

138 *Olguín v Paraguay*, ICSID Case No. ARB/98/5, para. 65(b); *Generation Ukraine v Ukraine*, ICSID Case No. ARB/00/9, Award, 16 September 2003, para. 20.37; *Parkerings v Lithuania*, ICSID Case No. ARB/05/8, Award, 11 September 2007, paras. 335–338.

139 ICSID Case No. UNCT/18/3, Award, 6 October 2023.

140 ibid 439.

On the facts of the case, the tribunal ruled that the claimant's decision to invest followed proper exercise of due diligence as his investment decision was based on an analysis of technical, financial and environmental considerations, and the applicable legal framework.[141]

(iii) The Respondent State must have Reneged upon the Expectation Created

Once an expectation has been created, whether by express or implicit specific representations or a course of conduct, and reasonably relied upon by the investor, a *prima facie* finding of breach of said expectation will made if the State has reneged upon the assurance given.

In *Tecmed v Mexico,*[142] the claimant, a Spanish company, through its Mexican subsidiaries, had acquired property, buildings, facilities, and other assets relating to a controlled landfill of hazardous industrial waste. A licence was required to operate the landfill, and this was granted initially, subject to it being extended every year. For many years, the licence had been extended, but on one occasion, which was the subject of the arbitration, the respondent rejected Tecmed's request to renew the permit, citing certain minor breaches in the mode of operation of the landfill. The tribunal found that the refusal to renew the licence was largely due to the political circumstances at the time, that is, the change of administration in the municipality in which the landfill was physically located, rather than to legal considerations. The state had reneged on its representations to the investor by refusing to renew the landfill's operating permit, which constituted a breach of the FET standard. This, in the tribunal's view, frustrated the investor's justified expectation of the continuity and duration of the investment, particularly in the light of the fact that the same conditions remained over time. The tribunal then went on to express what has become one of the most cited and arguably controversial dicta in arbitral practice to date:

> The foreign investor expects the host State to act in a consistent manner, free from ambiguity and totally transparently in its relations with the foreign investor, so that it may know beforehand any and all rules and regulations that will govern its investments, as well as the goals of the relevant policies and administrative practices or directives, to be able to plan its investment and comply with such regulations. Any and all State actions conforming to such criteria should relate not only to the guidelines, directives or requirements issued, or the resolutions approved thereunder, but also to the goals underlying such regulations. The foreign investor also expects the host State to act consistently, i.e. without arbitrarily revoking any pre-existing decisions or permits issued by the State that were relied upon by the investor to assume its commitments as well as to plan and launch its commercial and business activities. The investor also expects the State to use the legal instruments that govern the actions of the investor or the investment in conformity with the function usually assigned to such instruments, and not to deprive the investor of its investment without the required compensation. In fact, failure by the host State to comply with such pattern of conduct with respect to the foreign investor or its investments affects the investor's ability to measure the treatment and protection awarded by the host State and to determine whether the actions of the host State conform to the fair and equitable treatment principle.[143]

141 ibid.
142 ICSID Case No. ARB (AF)/00/2, Award, 29 May 2003.
143 ibid 154.

The tribunal's pronouncement in this regard is problematic because it appears to place an impossibility high burden on developing countries and countries in transition to effectively always act consistently with investors' expectations, irrespective of their peculiar circumstances. This standard of exemplary conduct is not only remarkably utopian in the light of the exigencies of public life, but it also imposes a disproportionate and unreasonable burden on the state, inconsistent with the spirit and intent of the FET clause, which is to ensure 'fairness' and 'equity' from the perspective of both the state and the investor. It is no surprise, therefore, that the *Tecmed* formulation has been the subject of significant contestation in the existing literature.[144]

In the Caribbean context, in *Michael Lee-Chin v Dominican Republic*,[145] the state was held to have reneged on its obligations under the Concession Agreement in question. Here, the tribunal found that the state had unlawfully reneged on the expectation that the claimant would be afforded the exclusive right to operate, manage, maintain, and administer the Duquesa Landfill, as well as the exclusive right to receive a tipping fee for all waste deposited at the landfill (these rights were reflected in the Concession Agreement). Further, the state was held to have reneged on the expectation created by ASDN that it would review and revise the tipping fee on a yearly basis (later amended to twice a year) and to liaise with the landfill's users and municipalities so they would accept adjustments to the tipping fee. Although the contractual relationship included the obligation to periodically revise the fees, there was no express obligation to increase the fees. Nonetheless, the tribunal considered that by repeatedly acknowledging that the fees were insufficient, the respondent agreed to be fully committed to taking part in the revision process, but, in fact, failed to do so. In other words, although, as claimed by the respondent, a tariff revision could not always necessarily result in an increase, in the tribunal's view, the 'context' and 'specific variables' of the case necessitated that the revision should inevitably lead to an increase. However, with regard to the claimant's allegation that a legitimate expectation had been created in favour of it having the right to develop a recycling facility and a waste-to-energy plant (WTE), the tribunal held that there was no evidence of any contractual assurance regarding the construction of a recycling facility and a WTE plant that would have generated a legitimate expectation by claimant.

It is submitted that this decision is problematic because it seems to have equated the state's acknowledgement that the fees were insufficient as *an ipso facto* assurance that the fees would be increased. In this respect, the tribunal seems to have treated the putative

144 Michele Potestà, 'Legitimate Expectations in Investment Treaty Law: Understanding the Roots and the Limits of a Controversial Concept' (2013) 28(1) *ICSID Review* 88, 91–92. Zachary Douglas, 'Nothing if Not Critical for Investment Treaty Arbitration: Occidental, Eureko and Methanex' (2006) 27(1) *Arbitration International* 27, 28 (noting that

> [t]he *Tecmed* 'standard' is actually not a standard at all; it is rather a description of perfect public regulation in a perfect world, to which all states should aspire but very few (if any) will ever attain. But in the aftermath of the tribunal's correct finding of liability in *Tecmed*, the quoted obiter dictum in that award, unsupported by any authority, is now frequently cited by tribunals as the only and therefore definitive authority for the requirements of fair and equitable treatment.

In *White Industries Australia Limited v The Republic of India*, UNCITRAL, Final Award, 30 November 2011, para. 10.3.5, the Tribunal referred to the *Tecmed* statement as having been 'subject to what it considers to be valid criticism'.

145 ICSID Case No. UNCT/18/3.

expectation as absolute in these circumstances, in a manner that may not have been contemplated by the parties.

(iv) There must be no Justifiable Countervailing Circumstances

Legitimate expectations are not absolute.[146] In appropriate circumstances, the State can lawfully, and without liability, renege upon these expectations if to do so will achieve a legitimate aim, and the means chosen to achieve that aim are reasonable and proportionate in the circumstances.

In *El Paso v Argentina*,[147] the tribunal accepted that countervailing circumstances may justify a state not honouring its legitimate expectations:

> Firstly, economic stability cannot be a legitimate expectation of any economic actor . . .
>
> Secondly, it is inconceivable that any State would accept that, because it has entered into BITs, it can no longer modify pieces of legislation which might have a negative impact on foreign investors, in order to deal with modified economic conditions and must guarantee absolute legal stability.
>
> In the Tribunal's understanding, FET cannot be designed to ensure the immutability of the legal order, the economic world and the social universe and play the role assumed by stabilisation clauses specifically granted to foreign investors with whom the State has signed investment agreements.
>
> The State has to be able to make the reasonable changes called for by the circumstances and cannot be considered to have accepted a freeze on the evolution of its legal system.
>
> Under a FET clause, a foreign investor can expect that the rules will not be changed without justification of an economic, social or other nature. Conversely, it is unthinkable that a State could make a general commitment to all foreign investors never to change its legislation whatever the circumstances, and it would be unreasonable for an investor to rely on such a freeze.[148]

Similar sentiments were expressed in *AWG v Argentina*,[149] where the tribunal noted that 'in interpreting the meaning of fair and equitable treatment to be accorded to investors, the tribunal must balance the legitimate and reasonable expectations of the claimants with Argentina's right to regulate the provision of a vital public service.'[150] In this connection, as stated in *Paushok v Mongolia*,[151] in the absence of a stabilisation clause, 'investors cannot legitimately expect that the taxation environment which they face at the time of their first

146 Robert Bradshaw, 'Legal Stability and Legitimate Expectations: Does International Investment Law Need a Sense of Proportion?' (2020) 5(1) *European Investment Law and Arbitration Review* 240; Christopher Schreuer, 'Fair and Equitable Treatment in Arbitral Practice' (2005) 6(3) *JWIT* 374: the principle of legitimate expectations is

> not absolute and does not amount to a requirement for the host State to freeze its legal system for the investor's benefit. A general stabilization requirement would go beyond what the investor can legitimately expect.

147 ICSID Case No. ARB/03/15, Award, 31 October 2011.

148 ibid 366–68, 371–72.

149 UNCITRAL, Award, Decision on Liability, 30 July 2010.

150 ibid 236.

151 UNCITRAL, Award, 2 September 2008.

investment will not be substantially altered with the passage of time and the evolution of events'.[152] Further, in *Impregilo v Argentina*,[153] the tribunal accepted that once the changes made to a state's regulatory framework are not unreasonable and arbitrary, 'the legitimate expectations of foreign investors cannot be that the State will never modify the legal framework, especially in times of crisis'.[154]

Finally, in *Michael Lee-Chin v Dominican Republic*,[155] although the tribunal, on the facts, rejected the respondent's argument that environmental considerations justified reneging on the legitimate expectations it had created, it nonetheless accepted that, as a matter of principle:

> the Claimant could not have any legitimate expectation that, if he breached the terms of the Concession Agreement and environmental and health regulations, thereby jeopardizing the health of millions of people and the Dominican environment, the Republic would not take any measures to prevent or attempt to remedy that situation.[156]

B. Transparency

Over the last two decades, Commonwealth Caribbean countries have increasingly shown their affinity for attracting and retaining foreign direct investments by, among other things, operationalising legislative and policy frameworks that are open, fair, and transparent. These frameworks are intended to demonstrate regional governments' political will and liberalised foreign policy, as well as to comply with their transparency obligations under the International Investment Agreements (IIAs) which they have entered into.

A handful of Caribbean IIAs directly address the transparency obligation, separate and apart from transparency as a constituent element of the FET standard. By way of example, Article XV of the *St Vincent and the Grenadines-Taiwan BIT* describes the transparency obligation in the following terms:

> Each Contracting Party shall, to the extent practicable, ensure that its laws, regulations, procedures, and administrative rulings of general application respecting any matter covered by this Agreement are promptly published or otherwise made available in such a manner as to enable the other Contracting Party to become acquainted with them.[157]

This provision establishes a core minimum requirement for the Contracting Parties to the BIT in question to publish relevant legal instruments that touch and concern investments made in their jurisdiction. Of particular relevance, in this context, is the fact that the modifier *to the extent practicable* is used to connote that the transparency obligation invites reasonable steps, having regard to the nuances of the applicable regulatory environment, on the part of the respective Contracting Parties in question.

152 ibid 370.
153 ICSID Case No. ARB/07/17, Award, 21 June 2011.
154 ibid 291.
155 ICSID Case No. UNCT/18/3, Award, 6 October 2023.
156 ibid 438.
157 Saint Vincent and the Grenadines-Taiwan Province of China BIT (2009), signed 17 December 2009, entered into force 1 February 2010.

Other regional IIAs are, however, more prescriptive in respect of their articulation of the transparency obligation both in their preambular and substantive sections. For example, Guyana's BIT with Brazil (2018) provides that:

Preamble

> The Federative Republic of Brazil and the Cooperative Republic of Guyana herein after designated as the 'Parties' or individually as 'Party'),
> Recognizing the importance of fostering a transparent and friendly environment for investments by investors of the Parties.

Article 9

> Each Party shall ensure that its laws, regulations, procedures and general administrative resolutions related to any matter covered by this Agreement, in particular regarding qualification, licensing and certification, are published in the official gazette and, when possible, in electronic format, as to allow interested persons of the other Party to become acquainted with them.
>
> 2. Each Party shall, as provided for in its laws and regulations
>   a) publish any such investment-related measure that it proposes to adopt; and
>   b) provide interested persons and the other Party a reasonable opportunity to comment on such proposed measures.
> 3. Whenever possible, each Party shall disseminate this Agreement to their respective public and private financial agents, responsible for the technical evaluation of risks and the approval of loans, credits, guarantees and related insurances for investment in the territory of the other Party.[158]

This provision is, on the one hand, enabling, while simultaneously, on the other hand, potentially disabling. It is enabling because it demonstrates the Contracting Parties' willingness to meaningfully engage with foreign investors before passing legislative and policy measures that might affect their investment. However, if this requirement is to be treated as an absolute one, such that no departure is permitted, it may potentially have a chilling effect on the host state's ability to act expediently in circumstances where time in respect of the passage of legislative and policy measures is of the essence. The need to consult with foreign investors before taking bona fide and proportionate policy measures may also invite unnecessary confrontations, particularly in respect of the adoption of socially laudable initiatives to which investors might object because of additional burdens that may ensue, such as environmental regulations. It may also mean that the host state may incur unforeseen expenses in circumstances where investors are invited to comment, in the context of meetings held with the state, on multiple iterations of a particular measure.

Notwithstanding this, however, the state's compliance with the transparency obligation may very well demonstrate its desire to subject its policy-making process to reasonable scrutiny, which may, in turn, contribute to improved public and institutional governance; as well as signal its openness to investment, investment protection, investment promotion and facilitation, and cooperation.[159]

158 Guyana-Brazil BIT (2018) (signed but not entered into force).

159 Carl-Sebastian Zoellner, 'Transparency: An Analysis of an Evolving Fundamental Principle in International Economic Law' (2005) 27 *Michigan Journal of International Law* 579; Mohammad Shamsaei and Seyed Ali Hosseiniazad, 'The Role of Transparency in Interpretation of the FET Standard in International Investment Law' (2021) 51(2) *Public Law Studies Quarterly* 797.

In *Metalclad Corporation v Mexico*,[160] the tribunal addressed the transparency obligation contained in Article 102(1) of the then NAFTA Agreement. Here, Mexico had issued a federal permit to Coterin (a local investor) to construct a hazardous waste landfill in that country. Thereafter, Metalclad acquired Coterin, together with its permits, in order to construct and operate the facility. The evidence pointed to the senior officials of the state advising Metalclad that all required permits for the facility had been secured by Coterin. As such, Metalclad commenced construction of the landfill, but the municipality shortly thereafter ordered a halt to construction on account of Metalcald's alleged failure to obtain a municipal construction permit. Metalclad applied for a municipal construction permit and was granted approval and resumed construction of the landfill and saw it through to completion. However, the opening ceremony of the facility was impeded by demonstration over environmental concerns. In fact, 13 months after Metalclad's application for municipal construction permit, the city (municipal) denied it, without giving Metalclad an opportunity to participate in the process. A decree was then issued, preventing the landfill's operation. The constructed landfill was never put into operation, thereby necessitating a claim alleging a breach of the minimum standard of treatment under the NAFTA Agreement, as well as a breach of the transparency obligation. The tribunal held that Metalclad was denied transparency by Mexico because applicable Mexican legislation contained no clear rule as to the requirement for obtaining a municipal construction permit. More than this, there was no established practice or procedure with respect to the manner of handling applications for a municipal construction permit.

In its discussion of the transparency obligation, the tribunal sought to flesh out the normative content of the transparency obligation, finding that:

> The Tribunal understands this to include the idea that all relevant legal requirements for the purpose of initiating, completing and successfully operating investments made, or intended to be made, under the Agreement should be capable of being readily known to all affected investors of another Party. There should be no room for doubt or uncertainty on such matters. Once the authorities of the central government of any Party (whose international responsibility in such matters has been identified in the preceding section) become aware of any scope for misunderstanding or confusion in this connection, it is their duty to ensure that the correct position is promptly determined and clearly stated so that investors can proceed with all appropriate expedition in the confident belief that they are acting in accordance with all relevant laws.[161]

In short, the tribunal concluded that Mexico had failed to ensure a transparent and predictable framework for Metalclad's business planning and investment. That said, it is instructive to note, according to Vandevelde,

> this portion of the award subsequently was set aside by the British Columbia Supreme Court, which held that transparency is not an element of customary international law. Because the NAFTA explicitly provides that the fair and equitable treatment standard is part of customary law, transparency could not be an element of that standard either, according to the court.[162]

Nonetheless, other tribunals, in the context of their examination of the Fair and Equitable Treatment standard, appear to countenance a similar description of the transparency

160 ICSID Case No. ARB(AF)/97/1, Award, 30 August 2000.

161 ibid 76.

162 Kenneth Vandevelde, 'A Unified Theory of Fair and Equitable Treatment' (2010) 43 *New York University Journal of International Law and Politics* 43

obligation. More particularly, in *Frontier Petroleum v Czech Republic*,[163] after linking the protection of investors' legitimate expectations to the concept of transparency, the tribunal ruled that:

> Transparency means that the legal framework for the investor's operations is readily apparent and that any decisions of the host state affecting the investor can be traced to that legal framework.[164]

A similar approach was countenanced in *Minnotte and Lewis v Poland*,[165] in which the tribunal noted that there is 'a general expectation that states will observe basic standards such as reasonable consistency and transparency',[166] implicitly endorsing the earlier ruling in *Tecmed, S.A. v Mexico* that:

> The foreign investor expects the host State to act in a consistent manner, free from ambiguity and totally transparently in its relations with the foreign investor, so that it may know beforehand any and all rules and regulations that will govern its investments, as well as the goals of the relevant policies and administrative practices or directives, to be able to plan its investment and comply with such regulations.
>
> The foreign investor also expects the host State to act consistently, i.e. without arbitrarily revoking any pre-existing decisions or permits issued by the State that were relied upon by the investor to assume its commitments as well as to plan and launch its commercial and business activities.[167]

While, as intimated earlier, there is scope for argumentation that states should take reasonable steps to afford investors a transparent legal framework, it is submitted that the very notion that an investor could expect a legal framework that is 'free from ambiguity and totally transparent' is borderline preposterous. How could a reasonable investor, cognizant of the exigencies of public regulation particularly in developing countries, such as those in the Commonwealth Caribbean, which are more times than not influenced by external shocks and vulnerabilities, reasonably expect a totally transparent legal framework? In this connection, the argument of Douglas that 'the *Tecmed* "standard" is actually not a standard at all; it is rather a description of perfect public regulation in a perfect world, to which all states should aspire but very few (if any) will ever attain'[168] is particularly apt.

Notwithstanding the foregoing, it appears, having regard to the award in *Cargill v Mexico*,[169] that the *Tecmed* approach to transparency cannot be applied to all cases in which the state may have acted inconsistently or lacked transparency in its dealings with foreign investors. Whether the *Tecmed* approach is countenanced very much depends on whether the IIA in question references the minimum standard under customary international law standard or the autonomous FET standard. If it references the latter, it is likely that tribunals will treat transparency as a constituent element of the FET standard, whether or not

163 UNCITRAL, Final Award, 12 November 2010.

164 ibid 285.

165 ICSID Case No. ARB(AF)/10/1, Award, 16 May 2014.

166 ibid 193.

167 ibid 198.

168 Zachary Douglas, 'Nothing if Not Critical for Investment Treaty Arbitration: Occidental, Eureko and Methanex' (2006) 22(1) *Arbitration International* 27, 28.

169 ICSID Case No. ARB(AF)/05/Z, Award, 18 September 2009.

linked to the concept of legitimate expectations. For example, in *Maffezini v Spain,*[170] the tribunal found that Spain demonstrated a lack of transparency, in breach of the FET standard, when it transferred a large sum of money from the investor's private bank account to service a loan, without the investor's permission, after the investor ordered halting of the construction of the chemical plant and dismissal of his employees. Meanwhile, in *Siemens v Argentina,*[171] the tribunal found that Argentina breached the transparency obligation under the FET clause when it denied the investor access to an administrative file containing the details of an important meeting with senior state officials that would have otherwise enabled it to file an appeal against the state's decree that had the effect of terminating a long-term contract for the provision of immigration control, ID and electoral services. A similar result was obtained in *Teinver v Argentina,*[172] a case in which the tribunal found that Argentina breached the transparency obligation under the FET standard by appointing a comptroller over the Airlines, maintaining a Mr. Alak as General Manager of the Airlines coupled with its decision to expropriate the Airlines in question after the claimants rejected its attempt to alter the agreed valuation method in respect of the acquisition of the claimants' Airlines.

While these cases demonstrate a trend whereby tribunals are increasingly filling the normative content of the FET standard by reference to the transparency obligation, this should not be viewed as a ubiquitous development. Rather, some tribunals have staunchly advanced the view that transparency does not form part of customary international law. As such, where an FET clause exists in an IIA that is linked to customary international law or the IIA includes a minimum standard, tribunals will be misplaced to interpret these clauses in a manner that countenances the transparency obligation. This point was forcibly made in the mid-2000s by the tribunal in *Cargill v Mexico,*[173] which explained that:

> the Claimant has not established that a general duty of transparency is included in the customary international law minimum standard of treatment owed to foreign investors per Article 1105's requirement to afford fair and equitable treatment. The principal authority relied on by the Claimant – *Tecmed* – involved the interpretation of a treaty-based autonomous standard for fair and equitable treatment and treated transparency as an element of the 'basic expectations' of an investor rather than as an independent duty under customary international law.[174]

This point was also made, more recently, in *Mercer International Inc. v Canada,*[175] in which the tribunal reiterated that 'the customary international law standard had not yet been shown to embrace a claim to transparency'.[176] Not all tribunals, however, adopt this approach. In *Michael Lee-Chin v Dominican Republic,*[177] for example, the tribunal determined that 'a requirement of a certain degree of transparency has reached the level of customary international law',[178] but did not specifically pronounce on what degree this might be or the magnitude of the state practice and *opinio juris* supporting its position.[179] Similarly, the tribunal

170 ICSID Case No. ARB/97/7, Award, 13 November 2000.
171 ICSID Case No. ARB/02/8, Award, 17 January 2007.
172 ICSID Case No. ARB/09/1, Award, 21 July 2017.
173 ICSID Case No. ARB(AF)/05/Z, Award, 18 September 2009.
174 ibid 294.
175 ICSID Case No. ARB(AF)/12/3, Award, 6 March 2018.
176 ibid 7.77.
177 ICSID Case No. UNCT/18/3, Award, 6 October 2023.
178 ibid 445.
179 The Tribunal, when addressing Article IV of Annex III of the Treaty – a specific provision on transparency, considered that this obligation required states not to prevent the exchange of relevant and available

in the recently decided case *of Eco Oro v Columbia*[180] noted that the 'concepts of non-arbitrariness, transparency and fairness are recognised elements of customary international law within the confines of reasonableness.'[181] This ruling may similarly be challenged on account of the tribunal's failure to meaningfully engage with evidence of state practice and *opinio juris* relative to the crystallisation of transparency as an element of customary international law. Against this backdrop, it is arguable that the approach countenanced in *Waste Management v Mexico*[182] strikes a more defensible balance between the state's right to regulate in ways which may result in some degree of inconsistency and non-transparency, and the investor's right to be a reasonably transparent legal framework. In that case, the tribunal accepted that there may very well be a breach of the minimum standard under customary international law if the state, through its acts or omissions, demonstrates a 'complete lack of transparency and candour in an administrative process'.[183] It is submitted that the use of the modifier, 'complete', effectively introduces a high threshold such that mere technical infringements of the transparency obligation ought not to give rise to the state's liability; only in the most egregious cases where there has been a manifest breach of transparency should the obligation be breached.

This view appears to comport with the ruling in *Al Tamimi v Oman.*[184] Here, Omani Ministries of Finance and Environment issued initial permits to the investor to operate a quarry, a condition for the maintenance of which being that he limited activity in respect of the exploitation of limestone products. Once the investor began operations, the Ministry of Environment issued a number of complaints, warnings and fines because of the investor's alleged taking of material from the Jebel Wasa area, his operation of machinery without the necessary permits, failure to obtain permits for housing, and his uprooting of trees. Ultimately, the state took the decision to terminate the agreement with one of the investor's companies, and to declare the agreement with his other company to be null because of the initial failure to register the company in Oman. As the claimant did still not stop operations, the state issued further warnings, and police arrested Al Tamimi at the request of the Ministry of Environment for the alleged unauthorised operation. Among other things, the investor alleged a breach of the transparency obligation under the FET standard that was linked to customary international law. The tribunal rejected reliance on *Tecmed's* articulation of the transparency obligation, finding instead that the minimum standard 'imposes a higher threshold for breach'.[185] More importantly, for the purposes of this discussion, it also found that while the standard of consistency and transparency provided to the claimant by the respondent as to the permitted scope and location of the quarry project 'certainly left something to be desired',[186]

information. It further considered that the requirement of transparency means that the legal framework for the investor's operations is readily apparent and that any decisions of the host state affecting the investor can be traced to that legal framework. On the facts, the tribunal held that the claimant had failed to successfully argue that there had been a violation as regards publication of laws, judgments, administrative practices, and procedures relating to investment

180 ICSID Case No. ARB/16/41, Decision on Jurisdiction, Liability and Directions on Quantum, 9 September 2021.

181 ibid 752.

182 ICSID Case No. ARB(AF)/00/3, Award, 30 April 2004.

183 ibid 98.

184 ICSID Case No. ARB/11/33, Award, 3 November 2015.

185 ibid 386.

186 ibid 399.

> the Tribunal is not persuaded that this conduct reaches the level of 'manifest arbitrariness' or 'complete lack of transparency and candour' required for a breach of the minimum standard of treatment. . . . It appears to the Tribunal that the Respondent's regulatory failures in this respect arose through mismanagement rather than malice.[187]

It is arguable, therefore, that the transparency obligation must not be deemed as imposing an absolute obligation of perfection, but rather an obligation of reasonableness that properly accounts for the state's development status, *bona fide* regulatory changes in the public interest, external shocks and vulnerabilities which may impact upon the state's ability to act transparently, as well as the extent to which the investor can be said to have itself exercised due diligence. The question of investors' due diligence is increasingly becoming an important one in the context of an international investment regime which has for many decades operated in an asymmetrical, and even hostile, manner against developing countries. Several cases support this proposition.

In *Plama v Bulgaria,*[188] the tribunal lamented the fact that the 'claimant, as the investor, was responsible for doing its due diligence regarding the tax consequences of debt reduction and for taking the necessary measures to deal with them.'[189] In other words, if the state is actively debating or otherwise engaged in a process of consultation about the possible introduction of a measure that may affect investments, it is incumbent upon the investor to participate in that exercise, and to make appropriate representations, where necessary.

The approach of the tribunal in *Methanex v United States*[190] on the question of investors' due diligence is also instructive. Here, the tribunal rejected the claimant's argument that the respondent breached the minimum standard by banning the use of MTBE as a gasoline additive because it was polluting surface water and groundwater, notwithstanding the fact that the ban came about as a result of concerns raised by environmental groups and expert studies. The tribunal noted that the investor should have been aware of the volatile nature of the political economy in which it was entering, and accordingly not expect that the state would never regulate in the interest of the environment. In this connection, it noted:

> Methanex entered a political economy in which it was widely known, if not notorious, that governmental environmental and health protection institutions at the federal and state level, operating under the vigilant eyes of the media, interested corporations, nongovernmental organizations and a politically active electorate, continuously monitored the use and impact of chemical compounds and commonly prohibited or restricted the use of some of those compounds for environmental and/or health reasons. Indeed, the very market for MTBE in the United States was the result of precisely this regulatory process. Methanex appreciated that the process of regulation in the United States involved wide participation of industry groups, non-governmental organizations, academics and other individuals, many of these actors deploying lobbyists. Methanex itself deployed lobbyists. Mr Wright, Methanex's witness, described himself as the government relations officer of the company.[191]

187 ibid.
188 ICSID Case No. ARB/03/24, Award, 27 August 2008.
189 ibid 268.
190 UNCITRAL, Final Award, 3 August 2005.
191 ibid part IV, ch D, 9–10.

Separately, in *Chemtura v Canada*,[192] the tribunal intimated that the more sophisticated and experienced that the investor is, the more likely that they should guard against exposure to risks within the host state,[193] while the tribunal in *Unglaube v Costa Rica*[194] considered that:

> As intelligent and experienced investors, Claimants were, of course, required, as part of their due diligence, to become familiar with Costa Rican law and procedure. The Tribunal understands that the workings of the courts and administrative agencies of Costa Rica surely involve noticeable differences from those with which Claimants may be more familiar. But, because governments are accorded a considerable degree of deference regarding the regulation/administration of matters within their borders, such differences are not significant, insofar as this Tribunal is concerned, unless they involve or condone arbitrariness, discriminatory behavior, lack of due process or other characteristics that shock the conscience, are clearly 'improper or discreditable' or which otherwise blatantly defy logic or elemental fairness.[195]

In short, then, to avert against the argument that international investment law lacks legitimacy because of the lack of determinacy in respect of the transparency obligation, evident from awards such as *Tecmed*, and to avoid having a chilling effect on policy developments, arbitral tribunals are best advised to adopt a balanced approach that countenances a view of transparency akin to the tribunal's in *Unglaube v Costa Rica.*

C. Denial of Justice

The prohibition of denial of justice is another constituent element of the FET standard, and, indeed, the minimum standard under customary international law.[196] It does not arise from a mere error in judicial proceedings,[197] but rather in the most exceptional circumstances when it can properly be said that judicial proceedings are fundamentally unfair and final and binding decisions are outrageously wrong.[198] In the words of the tribunal in *Oestergetel v Slovak Republic,*[199] '[a] denial of justice implies the failure of a national system as a whole to satisfy minimum standards'.[200] A similar view was espoused in *Franck Charles Arif v Moldova*:[201]

> [t]he responsibility of States not to breach the fair and equitable treatment standard through a denial of justice is engaged if and when the judiciary has rendered final and binding decisions after fundamentally unfair and biased proceedings or which misapplied the law in such an egregiously wrong way, that no honest, competent court could have possibly done so.[202]

192 UNCITRAL, Award, 2 August 2010.

193 ibid 149.

194 ICSID Case No. ARB/09/20, Award, 16 May 2012.

195 ibid 258.

196 Martins Paparinskis, *The International Minimum Standard and Fair and Equitable Treatment* (OUP 2013) 190. See, also, Jan Paulsson, *Denial of Justice in International Law* (Vol. 17. CUP 2005).

197 *Robert Azinian, Kenneth Davitian, and Ellen Baca v The United Mexican States*, ICSID Case No. ARB(AF)/97/2, Award dated 1 November 1999, para. 99. Incorrect application of the law does not constitute denial of justice – otherwise aliens would be afforded a new opportunity to appeal, once all local remedies have been exhausted.

198 *Arif v Moldova*, ICSID Case No. ARB/11/23, Award, 8 April 2013.

199 *Oostergetel v Slovakia*, UNCITRAL Award, 23 April 2012.

200 ibid 273.

201 ICSID Case No. ARB/11/23, 8 April 2013.

202 ibid 442.

According to the tribunal in *Lion Mexico v Mexico*,[203] the concept of denial of justice is not a new one. It has existed since the Middle Ages, although scholars like de Visscher famously described denial of justice as 'one of the oldest and one of the worst elucidated [concepts] in international law'.[204] The tribunal considered that 'despite the passage of nearly a century, de Visscher's statement still stands true'.[205]

Because a claim alleging a denial of justice is of the most extraordinary kind, not being merely an appeal,[206] the claimant bears the burden of proffering evidence of egregiously unfair judicial proceedings that result in an outrageous failure of the judicial system. To do this, the claimant is first required to establish that the judicial system of the host state has subjected the foreign investor to treatment that is clearly and manifestly illegal, and, secondly, the investor has exhausted local remedies.[207] While there have, in the past, been some delineation between substantive and procedural denial of justice, most tribunals and scholars now accept denial of justice is essentially procedural in nature.[208]

(i) Manifest Illegality

Several circumstances can give rise to a finding of manifest illegality, and therefore a denial of justice, as surmised by Judge Tanaka in the *Barcelona Traction* case:[209]

> corruption, threats, unwarranted delay, flagrant abuse of judicial procedure, a judgement dictated by the executive or so manifestly unjust that no court which was both competent and honest could have given it.[210]

As a matter of practice, a denial of justice may occur where the investor has been denied access to the courts in circumstances where he has not been notified of hearings[211] and the ensuing case is nonetheless decided upon in his absence[212] or where, although notice is given of an impending hearing, insufficient time has been given for him to physically appear in court.[213]

203 ICSID Case No. ARB(AF)/15/2, Award, 20 September 2021.

204 Charles De Visscher, *Le déni de justice en droit international* (Martinus Nijhoff 1935) 7.

205 *Lion Mexico v Mexico*, ICSID Case No. ARB(AF)/15/2, Award, 20 September 2021, para. 202.

206 *Franck Charles Arif v Moldova*, ICSID Case No. ARB/11/23, Award, 8 April 2013, para. 441: 'International tribunals must refrain from playing the role of ultimate appellate courts'.

207 *OOO Manolium-Processing v Belarus*, PCA Case No. 2018–06, Award, 22 June 2021, para. 535.

208 *Lion Mexico Consolidated v Mexico*, ICSID Case No. ARB(AF)/15/2, Award, 20 September 2021, paras. 218, 219; *Rumeli v Kazakhstan*, ICSID Case No. ARB/05/16, Award, 29 July 2008, para. 653:

> The standard is indeed of a procedural nature. In that sense, a court procedure which does not comply with due process is in breach of the duty. On the other hand, as pointed out by Respondent, the substance of a decision may be relevant in the sense that a breach of the standard can also be found when the decision is so patently arbitrary, unjust or idiosyncratic that it demonstrates bad faith.

209 *Barcelona Traction, Light and Power Company Limited (New Application 1962), Belgium v Spain*, Judgment, Merits, Second Phase, ICJ GL No 50, [1970] ICJ Report 3.

210 ibid Separate Opinion of Judge Tanaka, 156.

211 Case Concerning Elettronica Sicula S.p.A. (ELSI) (*United States of America v Italy*), ICJ Reports 1989, p. 15, Merits, Judgement, 20 July 1989 ['ELSI'] 76.

212 *Al-Bahloul v The Republic of Tajikistan*, SCC Case No. V (064/2008), para. 221.

213 Idler (US-Venezuela Commission) 21 November 1824, 152–53.

Lion v Mexico[214] addressed the failure of the host state to properly notify the investor of the impending proceedings such that the investor was denied a fair hearing. The tribunal considered that:

> In a judicial proceeding, a basic principle of natural justice requires that the defendant, who is being sued, is properly notified of the terms of the claims, and is afforded the opportunity to appear before the Court, to rebut these claims, to make allegations and to present evidence.[215]

The facts of the case were that Lion, a Canadian corporation with corporate domicile in Dallas, Texas, had issued notes and three loans in favour of the debtor, which were secured by three mortgages. The debtor, being unable to make the requisite payments despite multiple extensions of time, came up with an elaborate plan to forge an agreement in which it purported to formalise a settlement in which Lion agreed to cancel the loans, the notes and the mortgages in exchange for a participation in Sr. Cárdenas's companies. The agreement contained a purported address for service which was in Mexico, although Lion was domiciled in Texas. Upon the initiation of cancellation proceedings at which both Lion and the debtor were required to attend, a notice of the proceedings was sent to Lion's purported Mexican address, and, when unsuccessfully delivered, was handed to a person purporting to be the lawyer acting for Lion on another occasion. The notice regarding the proceedings was also placed on the relevant court's notice board. When Lion did not show up to participate in the proceedings, the relevant court proceeded by way of entering a default judgment. This resulted in the cancellation of the mortgages forthwith, at a tremendous loss to Lion. Upon finding out from third parties about the default judgement, and despite multiple requests made subsequently by Lion for the court to correct its earlier judgment, the Mexican judiciary refused to inquire further into the matter, including the authenticity of the forged agreement, and did not entertain an appeal. As such, Lion argued that Mexico had committed a denial of justice.

The tribunal agreed with Lion, finding that Lion was never properly notified[216] that it was being sued in the Cancellation Proceeding, which the debtors had filed before the *Juez de lo Mercantil* in Jalisco, requesting the cancellation of the mortgages. Being unaware of these proceedings, Lion failed to appear before the *Juez* and failed to submit a defence. As a result, the Juez declared Lion *en rebeldía*, and without any further effort to

214 ICSID Case No. ARB(AF)/15/2, Award, 20 September 2021.

215 ibid 397.

216 The tribunal found that the court did not perform close scrutiny of compliance with the service requirement in that Lion should have received international service of the notice of the proceedings. Among other things, due diligence would have revealed that Lion's denomination, 'LP, did not correspond to any incorporation under Mexican law; a certified copy of the Nayarit Mortgage stated that the actual domicile of Lion was the USA; and the mortgages included attachments to the Loans which explicitly stated that Lion's domicile is in the USA. The tribunal described this omission as

> especially shocking, because the Cancellation Proceeding was not a minor case, but rather a complex procedure, which pitched a group of well-known local companies against a US-based corporation, which affected well-known and highly valuable pieces of real estate located within the State of Jalisco and which could result (and indeed resulted) in the cancellation of multi-million USD Mortgages granted in favour of the US creditor. Under these circumstances the Judge should have doublechecked 'de manera exhaustiva' that the respondent had been properly notified.

It noted that the mere 'formalistic notice to appear', posted on the court's notice board, amounted to a lack of effective notification

ascertain whether Lion was aware of the proceedings, issued the Cancellation Judgement in absentia, mandating that the mortgages be forthwith cancelled. In the tribunal's view, the Cancellation Proceeding was procedurally faulty and had devasting consequences, such that Mexico must be held to have denied justice to Lion. The state's denial of justice was further compounded by the fact that the judiciary never corrected this situation, including by way of appeal, despite multiple opportunities to do so at Lion's request. In the tribunal's estimation, the absence of proper notice of the proceedings, coupled with Lion having been denied the right to appeal the default judgment and having also been denied the opportunity to present evidence in defence of its case, constituted 'improper and egregious procedural conduct',[217] which 'did not meet the basic international accepted standards of administration of justice and due process, and which shocks or surprises the sense of judicial propriety',[218] The ruling in *Lion* supports the view of other tribunals that denial of the right of the investor to marshal evidence[219] or wilful disregard of such evidence when proffered to the court[220] or unreasonable impediments to initiating an appeal may amount to a denial of justice under international law.

Having obtained a favourable decision, if the investor is prevented from enforcing it in the host State, this may amount to a denial of justice. In addition, clearly arbitrary decisions that lack proper motivation, have no justification or are contrary to all legal logic, and which exceed a mere judicial error, may also amount to a denial of justice.[221] Moreover, decisions rendered by tribunals that lack independence or impartiality, and whose decisions are impaired by external interferences may give rise to a finding of denial of justice.[222] It is important to note, however, that a claim for denial of justice must rest on the specific treatment meted out by the courts of the host state to the investor, rather than on the general assessment of the host state's judicial system. In other words, it is not sufficient for a claimant to base its claims on general allegations regarding the judicial system of the host state, if it is unable to prove that it has suffered a denial of justice on the facts of the case. Thus, in *Oostergetel*,[223] the claimants sought to support a denial of justice claim by offering general reports of corruption in Slovak courts. The tribunal, however, held that such general reports were not sufficient to ground a denial of justice claim. In the tribunal's assessment:

> mere suggestions of illegitimate conduct, general allegations of corruption and shortcomings of a judicial system do not constitute evidence of a treaty breach or a violation of international law. . . .
>
> While such general reports are to be taken very seriously as a matter of policy, they cannot substitute for evidence of a treaty breach in a specific instance. . . . Mere insinuations cannot meet the burden of proof which rests on the Claimants.[224]

217 ibid 508.

218 ibid.

219 *OOO Manolium-Processing v Belarus*, PCA Case No. 2018–06, Award, 22 June 2021.

220 Joseph F. Rihani, American Mexican Claims Commission, Decision No. 27-C (1942), 1948 AM. MEX. CLAIMS REP. 254.

221 Elettronica Sicula SpA (ELSI) (*United States of America v Spain*), 1970 ICJ REP. 3, 76.

222 *The Loewen Group, Inc. and Raymond L. Loewen v United States of America*, ICSID Case No. ARB(AF)/98/3, Award, 26 June, paras. 135–137. See, also, *Manolium v Belarus,* PCA Case No. 2018–06, Award, 22 June 2021, para. 562: 'a denial of justice may arise where a court simply follows political directions and does not therefore apply its independent judgment to resolve the case in issue'.

223 *Oostergetel v The Slovak Republic*, UNCITRAL, Award, 23 April 2012.

224 ibid 302–3.

A different outcome was, however, arrived at in *Chevron and TexPet v Ecuador.*[225] Here, TexPet (with Texaco) made an investment in the form of an oil concession in the Oriente, Ecuador, beginning in 1964. This investment was, however, subsequently acquired by Chevron when it merged with Texaco and acquired TexPet, as Texaco's subsidiary in 2001. Ecuador had agreed, between 1995–1998, on the extent of the responsibility of TexPet, Texaco and subsequently Chevron for clean-up operations and on the extent of their residual liability for environmental harm in the concession area. In breach of that agreement, however, Ecuador facilitated legal proceedings by the Lago Agrio Plaintiffs in the form of the Lago Agrio Litigation against Chevron. The claimant argued that such proceedings were, however, subject to procedural fraud and judicial misconduct by judges of the Lago Agrio Court. In particular, as alleged by the claimant, the Lago Agrio Judgment was 'ghostwritten' by representatives of the Lago Agrio Plaintiffs in collusion with the presiding judge of the Lago Agrio Court. The claimant further alleged that the Lago Agrio Appellate Court, the Cassation Court and the Constitutional Court left such fraud, misconduct and corruption unremedied. The claimant, in arbitration proceedings, alleged that Ecuador had committed a denial of justice.

The tribunal began its lengthy and methodical assessment of the complex issues raised by, first, explaining that a denial of justice under customary international law necessarily will entail a breach of the FET standard in Article II(3)(a) of the USA-Ecuador BIT. Accordingly, it found that denial of justice under the FET standard should be understood, where appropriate, as referring also to denial of justice under customary international law. On the facts, the tribunal found that the claimant had made out its case that Judge Zambrano had acted 'grossly improper[ly]' by engaging in 'ghostwriting' of the Lago Agrio Judgment in collusion with certain of the Lago Agrio Plaintiffs' representatives. It considered this type of conduct to be 'the very gravest concerns as to judicial propriety'[226] and was especially concerned that the Lago Agrio Appellate Court, Cassation and Constitutional Courts left the Lago Agrio Judgment materially unremedied. Citing *ELSI*, the Chevron tribunal concluded that the Lago Agrio Judgment was 'clearly improper and discreditable',[227] with the result that the claimant's investments were subjected to unfair and inequitable treatment. There was a denial of justice, in short, because Ecuador's 'national system as a whole to satisfy minimum standards required under international law'.[228]

Additional requirements as preconditions for obtaining justice which are obviously unnecessary or impossible to satisfy or in breach of a fundamental right may amount to a denial of justice. In *Dan Cake v Hungary*,[229] for example, the tribunal found a denial of justice on this ground. Here, under Hungarian law, the claimant's enterprise that was in liquidation, was entitled to convene a composition hearing in order to seek an agreement with its creditors. Instead of following the established procedure, the Metropolitan Court of Budapest ordered the claimant to submit seven documents which were not required by law, and which the claimant was unable to provide. The tribunal considered that requiring the production of these additional documents was unnecessary in that it prejudged and denied the claimant's right to seek an agreement with its creditors. In this context, and in light of

225 PCA Case No. 2009–23, Second Partial Award, 30 August 2018.
226 ibid 8.59.
227 ibid 8.60.
228 ibid.
229 ICSID Case No. ARB/12/9, Decision on Jurisdiction and Liability, 24 August 2015.

the fact that there was no appeal from the court's order, the tribunal found that the court's conduct '[did] shock a sense of judicial propriety',[230] and that thus the claimant had been denied justice.

Separately, tribunals have held that a lack of due process leading to an outcome which offends a sense of judicial propriety may also give rise to a denial of justice. *Loewen v USA*[231] is instructive in this regard. Here, a Canadian funeral home conglomerate challenged a Mississippi State Court jury award of US$100 million in compensatory damages and US$400 million in punitive damages on claims against it in respect of allegations of fraud and other violations of Mississippi anti-trust law. The claimant argued that, apart from the egregious damages decision by the Mississippi State Court, it was also harmed by the wrongful and unfair application of the civil procedure rules which required it to post US$625 million to stay execution of the judgment pending appeal. The tribunal intimated that it would have been prepared to find a breach of natural justice in respect of the Mississippi court proceedings, which it described as wrong in the 'strongest terms' as it was 'unfair . . . towards the foreign investor',[232] it was ultimately decided that the claimant had failed to exhaust all available local remedies when it decided to reach a settlement rather than pursue its case before the US Supreme Court, and that Loewen's claims were dismissed for lack of standing, due to claimant's buyout by a company of the host state (which led to the claimant losing its status as a foreign investor under the NAFTA).

The failure to allow an investor who has a substantial interest in the proceedings the right to intervene in said proceedings may amount to a denial of justice. The case of *Flughafen v Venezuela*[233] is instructive in this regard. Here, the claimant, a consortium, and the respondent state had entered into a strategic alliance contract in which the former would administer, control and operate the Santiago Mariño Airport. After the claimant took over the Airport, however, the Governor elect initiated several proceedings to invalidate or revoke the concession. This resulted in the Airport being taken over by the state by force. The claimant, in response, regained control through court injunctions, but later, the state enacted Decree 806, effectively taking over the Airport and terminated the contract for reasons of public interest, recognising the investors' right to compensation. The investors asked the Supreme Court to invalidate Decree 806, claiming that it was unconstitutional and illegal. Interestingly, two years later, the Supreme Court issued an order remanding the cases to a lower administrative court, and, without allowing interventions from the claimant, handed the Airport over to the federal administration. Parliament then passed a law confirming the Supreme Court's decision. The claimant argued that this amounted to a denial of justice.

The tribunal characterised the Supreme Tribunal's decision, which remanded the proceedings back to the lower court and handed the Airport over to the federal administration, as giving rise to no reasonable expectation that the pending appeals could restore the investors as administrators of the Airport. In this context, the majority of the tribunal held that the Supreme Tribunal's decision consisted of a denial of justice. Accordingly, the Supreme Tribunal's decision was held to have been procedurally flawed, as it was delivered in the absence of a petition by the claimant, and the government, by extension, and without giving them – either the investors deprived of their right of managing the Airport or the federal

230 ibid 145–46.
231 ICSID Case No. ARB(AF)/98/3, Award, 26 June 2003.
232 ibid 241.
233 ICSID Case No. ARB/10/19, Award, 18 November 2014.

government charged with running it – an opportunity to intervene. Furthermore, the tribunal affirmed that the decision lacked proper grounds and reasoning, in that it failed to refer to supporting law. In essence, the Supreme Tribunal's decision had the objective of consolidating the policy of centralizing in the National Executive Power the authority over airports and was therefore unlawful.

An undue delay can give rise to a finding of a denial of justice. Indeed, international tribunals, from as early as the *Fabiani*[234] case, have agreed that 'justice delayed is justice denied'.[235] While all tribunals agree that undue delay amounts to a denial of due process,[236] there is some disagreement as to what constitutes unreasonable delay. In this context, it is to be borne in mind that there is no abstract manner of determining whether a particular period constitutes reasonable delay. Rather, each case must be decided in the context of the specific facts raised.[237]

The leading arbitral award on the question of undue delay is *Chevron I*.[238] Here, under the 1973 Agreement between the parties, TexPet was entitled to explore and exploit oil reserves in certain regions of Ecuador, and TexPet was required to provide a percentage of its crude oil production to the Government to help meet Ecuadorian domestic consumption needs. The Government of Ecuador was entitled to set the price at which it would purchase oil from TexPet for Ecuadorian domestic consumption needs, referred to as the 'Domestic Market Price'. The Government consistently set the Domestic Market Price well below the prevailing international market price. Once TexPet satisfied its obligation to contribute oil for Ecuador's domestic consumption at the low Domestic Market Price, TexPet was entitled to receive prevailing international prices for the remainder of its oil. Specifically, once it satisfied its obligation to contribute its share of oil for domestic consumption, TexPet was free to export its remaining oil internationally. The sole exception to TexPet's important right to export was the Government's right to purchase TexPet's oil for refining and export, but if the Government made such a request for oil that it would not use to satisfy domestic consumption, the Government was obligated to pay TexPet the prevailing international price for oil. Chevron alleged that the Ecuadorian Government breached the Agreements and related Ecuadorian laws by requiring TexPet to contribute substantially more oil than it was obligated to provide at the reduced Domestic Market Price. Ecuador then exported this additional contribution by TexPet, either directly or as refined derivative oil products, but it did not pay TexPet the international market price that it was contractually required to pay. TexPet accordingly commenced lawsuits in Ecuador seeking the difference in price between

234 *Antoine Fabiani* Case, 31 July 1905 Volume X 83–139.

235 Hussein Haeri and Ruzin Dagli, 'Fairness and the Final Word: State Responsibility for Court Action in Investment Arbitration' (2016) 2 *Turkish Commercial Law Review* 3.

236 Al-Bahloul Tajikistan, SCC Case No. V (064/2008), para. 221; *Oostergetel v The Slovak Republic*, UNCITRAL, Award 23 April 2012, paras. 73–77.

237 *Lion Mexico Consolidated v Mexico*, ICSID Case No. ARB(AF)/15/2, Award, 20 September 2021, para. 241. Citing *Pey Casado Chile (I)*, ICSID Case No. ARB/98/2, Award, 8 May 2008, para. 659, in which it was held that a period of seven years without rendering a first instance decision by local courts amounted to a denial of justice. Meanwhile, the tribunal also cited El *Oro Mining and Railway Co.* (p. 191, [9]), in which the Great Britain and Mexico Claims Commission found that the passage of nine years without a hearing in its case for compensation for having provided materials to the government, constituted a denial of justice. This is to be contrasted with *Oostergetel v Slovakia* (paras. 208, 290), in which it was held that the length of local proceedings of two years was not a breach of the international minimum standard.

238 *Chevron-Texaco v Ecuador*, UNCITRAL, Partial Award on the Merits, 30 March 2010.

the reduced Domestic Market Price that it received and the international market price at the time, or a return of the barrels overcontributed. In fact, between 1991 and 1993, TexPet filed seven breach-of-contract cases against the Ecuadorian Government in Ecuadorian courts in which it claimed more than US$ 553 million in damages, which included interest to that point in time. However, even after 13 years had elapsed, there was no finality to the cases that had been initiated by Chevron. Chevron accordingly claimed, in arbitral proceedings, that there had been a denial of justice.

The tribunal began its assessment by reiterating that a state may be guilty of a denial of justice in respect of an undue delay. It, however, explained that such a finding is not automatic, as much depends on the circumstances of the case:

> some of the factors that may be considered are the complexity of the case, the behaviour of the litigants involved, the significance of the interests at stake in the case, and the behaviour of the Courts themselves.[239]

On the facts, the tribunal considered that the cases initiated by Chevron having been pending for at least 13 years at the time of the arbitration was a 'significant period', but that the 'specific amount of delay alone [does not] result in an automatic breach of Article II(7) of the BIT'.[240] In this context, the tribunal sought to consider, first, the complexity of the case. Having reviewed the facts of the case carefully, the tribunal considered that although the cases in question involved very significant sums of money, they were 'in essence straightforward contractual disputes'.[241] More pointedly, the tribunal considered the cases to be of 'average complexity due to the submission of expert reports and laborious calculations required for the assessment of damages';[242] they were, however, not 'so complex as to justify many years of delay in deciding them'.[243]

With respect to the claimants' behaviour, the tribunal found that the claimants pursued their cases to the point of being ready for a decision and sent numerous and continuous requests for a judgment. In the tribunal's assessment, there was no evidence that any of the claimants' actions actively and significantly contributed to the delays.[244] While the claimants were chided for filing recusals in respect of two of the seven cases, the tribunal felt that these were pursued and resolved in under a year in 1993–1994 and could not, therefore, explain or justify the later delays.

The tribunal also considered the nature of the delay, pointing in particular to the 'apparent unwillingness of the Ecuadorian courts to allow the cases to proceed'.[245] In the tribunal's view, the very existence of long delays, even after official acknowledgements by the courts that they were ready to decide the cases, was a decisive factor demonstrating that the delays experienced by TexPet were sufficient to breach the BIT.

The tribunal also considered the question of whether the generalised backlog in the Ecuadorian courts could explain or excuse the delays in question. To this the tribunal explained that:

239 ibid VIII:B 19.
240 ibid 253.
241 ibid 254.
242 ibid.
243 ibid.
244 ibid 255.
245 ibid 262.

> Court congestion and backlogs are relevant factors to be considered in determining the period of delay that is reasonable in the circumstances. Court congestion, however, cannot be an absolute defense. The question of whether effective means have been provided to the Claimants for the assertion of their claims and enforcement of their rights is ultimately to be measured against an objective, international standard. To the extent that generalized court congestion could alone produce the persistent and long delays of the kind observed here, it would evidence a systemic problem with the design and operation of the Ecuadorian judicial system and would breach Article II(7) according to the systemic standard advocated by the Respondent itself.[246]

The tribunal then went on to consider the contours of acceptable backlogs in the court system. It noted, in this connection, that court congestion must be temporary and must be promptly and effectively addressed by the host state if this encumbrance is to act as a defence to a claim of denial of justice. In other words,

> the State must have previously been in compliance with and must return to compliance with the international standard within a short amount of time from when the backlogs arise.[247]

The panel acknowledged that backlogs will not provide an excuse when measures taken to relieve the backlog are hollow or ineffective.[248] Having weighed the relevant facts in issue, the tribunal noted that despite the evidence of judicial reform in Ecuador aimed at increasing the clearance rate of cases in Ecuadorian courts, the delays with which the claimants were afflicted were too long to be excused. In other words, the fact that the backlog applied from the filing of the claimants' cases in the early 1990s and continued unabated through the end of that decade meant that the backlogs could not be considered temporary enough to provide justification for otherwise undue delay.[249]

A final interesting observation made by the tribunal was that once delay has become unreasonable and a breach of the BIT has been completed, a decision issued after that date cannot affect the liability of the state for the undue delay. However, it may very well affect the questions of causation and damages that flow from that breach.[250]

Ultimately, the tribunal concluded that the Ecuadorian courts failed to act with reasonable dispatch. More pointedly, the prolonged periods of complete inactivity on the part of the Ecuadorian courts in relation to which no reasonable explanations were provided strongly suggested that there was a denial of justice.

Extenuating circumstances in the host country may, according to the tribunal in *Toto v Lebanon,*[251] exonerate a state that would otherwise be liable for its courts' undue delay. In this case, an Italian company was awarded a contract to construct part of a highway between Beirut and Damascus. In August 2001, Toto filed two claims before the Lebanese Administrative Court seeking indemnification for unforeseen works it had to carry out because the nature of the soil did not meet the specifications set out in the contract and because the design specified in the contract had been substantially changed. By March 2007, however, the court had still not decided the claims. Against this backdrop, Toto initiated

246 ibid 263.
247 ibid 264.
248 ibid.
249 ibid 265.
250 ibid 273.
251 ICSID Case No. ARB/07/12, Award, 7 June 2012.

arbitration proceedings under the Italy–Lebanon BIT, arguing that the delay was a denial of justice which breached Lebanon's obligation to provide FET treatment.

The tribunal in *Toto* countenanced factors apposite in assessing whether there is a denial of justice in respect of a delay, as outlined earlier in *Chevron*, finding that:

> There is not, under international law, a specific measure by which lapses of time may be condemned as excessive: the lapse is to be considered on a case-by-case basis, taking into account (i) the complexity of the matter; (ii) the need for celerity of decision; and (iii) the diligence of claimant in prosecuting its case.[252]

On the facts of the case, although the tribunal found that there was indeed a very long delay between the closing of the debates in the two proceedings before the *Conseil d'Etat* in 2002 and the request by the *Conseil d'Etat* for submission of documents on 16 January 2008, this in itself, however, did not constitute a breach of Article 3.1 of the Treaty.[253] In arriving at this conclusion, the tribunal paid particular attention to the fact that, in February 2005, Lebanon's former Prime Minister, Rafic Hariri, was assassinated. This was followed by several terrorist bombings and assassinations that disrupted normal life in Lebanon. Moreover, in the summer of 2006, a destructive war took place between Lebanon and Israel. Further, in Mid-2007 there was severe internal fighting between the organisation Fatah al-Islam and the Lebanese Army. Then, in May 2008, another internal armed conflict exploded following a 17-month-long political crisis. In the tribunal's view, 'these circumstances undoubtedly were not conductive to the functioning of Lebanon's judicial system and affected the proper functioning of Lebanese courts between 2002 and 2008.'[254] As such, the tribunal declined to find that there was a denial of justice.

While the *Toto* decision appears to countenance a proportionality analysis in which the prevailing circumstances, including resources of the host state, are considered in making the assessment as to whether undue delay amounts to a denial of justice, arbitrator Jan Paulsson in *Pantechniki v Albania*[255] appears to suggest, albeit *obiter*, that a State's international responsibility does not bear any proportion to its resources:

> Should a poor country be held accountable to a minimum standard which it could attain only at great sacrifice while a rich country would have little difficulty in doing so? No such proportionality factor has been generally accepted with respect to denial of justice. Two reasons appear salient. The first is that international responsibility does not relate to physical infrastructure; states are not liable for denial of justice because they cannot afford to put at the public's disposal spacious buildings or computerized information banks. What matters is rather the human factor of obedience to the rule of law. Foreigners who enter a poor country are not entitled to assume that they will be given things like verbatim transcripts of all judicial proceedings – but they are entitled to decision-making which is neither xenophobic nor arbitrary. The second is that a relativist standard would be none at all. International courts or tribunals would have to make ad hoc assessments based on their evaluation of the capacity of each state at a given moment of its development. International law would thus provide no incentive for a state to improve. It would in fact operate to the opposite effect: a state which devoted more resources to its judiciary would run the risk of graduating into a more exacting category.[256]

252 These factors were affirmed in *Lion Mexico Consolidated L.P. v United Mexican States*, ICSID Case No. ARB(AF)/15/2, Award, 20 September 2021, para. 244.

253 ibid Decision on Jurisdiction, 11 September 2009, para. 165.

254 ibid.

255 ICSID Case No. ARB/07/21, Award, 30 July 2009.

256 ibid 76.

While Paulsson's argument that investors must be protected against xenophobic and arbitrary decision-making processes makes good sense, we are concerned that he appears to treat infrastructural resource constraints as being completely isolated from human resource constraints when the reality is that in many developing countries these factors are intimately connected, and in many cases adversely impact on the capacity of the state to deliver justice in a timely fashion. Furthermore, holding all states to the same standard, regardless of their resources and historical context, including the enduring effects of colonialism in many developing countries, creates an unfair burden on developing countries to put in place a judicial system that resembles their western counterparts. It also dilutes investors' responsibility to take appropriate cognizance of the state's judicial system when investing.

High Threshold

There is a presumption that municipal courts have acted properly unless the claimant proves otherwise.[257] In fact, most tribunals have declined to find a denial of justice to date. This is because, as intimated above, tribunals do not consider themselves to be appellate courts. In this context, a claimant alleging denial of justice will only succeed if there is evidence of 'a willful disregard of due process of law, . . . which shocks, or at least surprises, a sense of judicial propriety'.[258] In this connection, the tribunal in *Mondev* was emphatic in noting that:

> the word 'surprises' does not occur in isolation. The test is not whether a particular result is surprising, but whether the shock or surprise occasioned to an impartial tribunal leads, on reflection, to justified concerns as to the judicial propriety of the outcome, bearing in mind on the one hand that international tribunals are not courts of appeal, and on the other hand that Chapter 11 of NAFTA (like other treaties for the protection of investments) is intended to provide a real measure of protection. In the end the question is whether, at an international level and having regard to generally accepted standards of the administration of justice, a tribunal can conclude in the light of all the available facts that the impugned decision was clearly improper and discreditable, with the result that the investment has been subjected to unfair and inequitable treatment. This is admittedly a somewhat open-ended standard, but it may be that in practice no more precise formula can be offered to cover the range of possibilities.[259]

It means, therefore, that mere errors/procedural irregularities are insufficient to constitute a denial of justice under the fair and equitable treatment standard. Indeed, tribunals have held that the fact that different domestic courts on the same plane arrive at different outcomes with respect to the same issue is not indicative of there being a denial of

257 *Chevron II v Ecuador,* PCA Case No. 2009–23, First Partial Award on Track I, 17 September 2013, para. 8.35; *Lion v Mexico*, ICSID Case No. ARB(AF)/15/2, ICSID Case No. ARB(AF)/15/2, para. 369.

258 *Monde v United States of America*, ICSID Case No. ARB(AF)/99/2, Award, 11 October 2002, para. 127. This case concerned a failed investment in the USA by a Canadian construction company and involved a claim that the local authorities prevented the claimant from exercising an option to purchase a certain parcel of land. When the claimant filed a case before US courts, the jury found against the local authorities, a decision which was later overturned on appeal. The claimant then failed to obtain a judgment in its favour from the Massachusetts Supreme Court and the US Supreme Court rejected the case by not granting certiorari. According to the claimant, the Massachusetts Supreme Court deviated from its previous rulings to the extent that it had in effect applied 'a new rule'. The tribunal did not find that denial of justice had occurred as, in any common law jurisdiction, one may and should expect 'new' judge-made law and the decisions taken by the US courts were not 'extreme cases' that would amount to a denial of justice.

259 ibid.

justice, unless the decisions can be said to have been shocking and serious. Decisions merely appearing unusual or even surprising are not sufficient, according to the tribunal in *Philip Morris v Uruguay.*[260] In that case, the claimant had challenged the so-called '80/80 Regulation'[261] which obliged tobacco companies to increase the size of graphic health warnings appearing on cigarette packages through two separate actions, one before the SCJ (constitutional proceedings) and the other before the TCA (administrative proceedings). Both courts arrived at the conclusion that the regulation was legal but proffered different interpretations of the regulation and reasonings for their respective decisions. The claimants, feeling aggrieved by the different outcomes in both cases, argued that there had been a denial of justice. The tribunal, however, found that the claimants were able to have their day in court, and that the courts in question gave properly reasoned decisions. Although the tribunal found that the failure of the TCA to follow the Supreme Court's interpretation of the regulation to be unusual, and even surprising, it did not consider this to be shocking and serious enough to constitute a denial of justice. In this connection, the tribunal considered that 'outright conflicts within national legal systems may be regrettable but they are not unheard of'.[262]

It further noted that the high standard required for establishing a denial of justice claim in international law means that it was not enough for there to be an erroneous decision or an incompetent judicial procedure, since arbitral tribunals are not courts of appeal. On the facts, there was 'no clear evidence of an outrageous failure of the judicial system'[263] or a demonstration of 'systemic injustice' or that the impugned decisions were 'clearly improper and discreditable'.[264] It, however, cautioned that, in some cases, grave procedural errors may result in a denial of justice, depending on the circumstances of the case.

Several other cases also take the view that if a court renders a decision which a reasonably competent court could arrive at, there will be no denial of justice. Thus, in *Azinian v Mexico,*[265] the mere fact that the State Administrative Tribunal and its Superior Chamber, and a Mexican federal circuit court, all refused to countenance the claimant's claim that the government's annulment of the concession did not constitute wrongful repudiation of the concession did not amount to a denial of justice, as this decision was within the range of responses that a reasonably competent court could arrive at. Similarly, in *Iberdrola v Guatemala,*[266] the tribunal refused to find a denial of justice in circumstances where the national courts upheld the state's decision to review and fix the rate of the claimant's electricity distribution for a five-year period.

Bad Faith and Malicious Intent not Required

The tribunal in *Mondev v USA*[267] held that the threshold for establishing treatment in violation of denial of justice does not require subjective elements on the part of the host state such as bad faith:

260 ICSID Case No. ARB/10/7, Award, 8 July 2016.

261 ibid. This required that tobacco companies place warnings as to the danger of nicotine on 80% of every packet that they marketed.

262 ibid 529.

263 ibid 500.

264 ibid.

265 ICSID Case No. ARB (AF)/97/2, Award, 1 November 1999.

266 ICSID Case No. ARB/09/5, Award, 17 August 2012.

267 ICSID Case No. ARB(AF)/99/2, Award, 11 October 2002.

> To the modern eye, what is unfair or inequitable need not equate with the outrageous or the egregious. In particular, a State may treat a foreign investment unfairly and inequitably without necessarily acting in bad faith [. . .][268]

Loewen v USA[269] also endorsed the *Mondev* view that under contemporary international customary law, bad faith or malicious intent is not required for a denial of justice:

> Neither state practice, the decisions of international tribunals nor the opinion of commentators support the view that bad faith or malicious intention is an essential element of unfair and inequitable treatment or denial of justice amounting to a breach of international justice.[270]

(ii) *Exhaustion of Local Remedies*

A necessary precondition that arbitral tribunals will consider when assessing claims alleging denial of justice in respect of the fair and equitable treatment standard is whether the investor has exhausted all domestic recourses available against the allegedly illegal decision. If the investor can still challenge the impugned court decision, it cannot be said that it has experienced a denial of justice.[271] Tribunals' position on the exhaustion of local remedies was summed up in *Chevron II*[272] as follows:

> In the Tribunal's view, it is well settled that a claimant asserting a claim for denial of justice committed by a State's judicial system must satisfy, whether as a matter of jurisdiction or admissibility, a requirement as to the exhaustion of local remedies or, as now better expressed, a substantive rule of judicial finality. Even the grossest misconduct by a lower court or manifest unfairness in its procedures is not by itself sufficient to amount to a denial of justice by a State, unless the judicial remedies that exist in that State either do not correct the deficiencies in the lower court's judgment (once exhausted by the foreign national) or are such that none affords to the foreign national any reasonable prospect of correcting those deficiencies in a timely, fair and effective manner.[273]

Meanwhile, in *Marfin et al. v Cyprus,*[274] an international investment holding company incorporated in Greece owned Cyprus Popular Bank, the second largest bank in Cyprus. Cyprus, through a series of public measures, acquired the Bank and took over its management in 2012 in an effort to mitigate the country's exposure to defaulting Greek debt. A Cypriot Nicosia court issued a worldwide freezing order on the claimant's funds. The respondent also recapitalized the Bank with €1.8 billion. The question arose as to whether the claimants exhausted local remedies before proceeding to international arbitration. The tribunal held that they had not. More pointedly, the tribunal noted that other remedies were available, namely they could have requested an award of damages from the Cypriot courts to compensate them for the business and reputational harm allegedly suffered on account of the enforcement proceedings commenced abroad. In the tribunal's view, the claimants could not raise a claim that a judicial act constitutes a breach of international law, without first

268 ibid 116.
269 ICSID Case No. ARB(AF)/98/3, Award, 26 June 2003.
270 ibid 132.
271 ibid 151.
272 PCA Case No. 2009–23, Second Partial Award on Track II, 30 August 2018.
273 ibid 7.117.
274 ICSID Case No. ARB/13/27, Award, 26 July 2018.

proceeding through the judicial system that it purported to challenge, and thereby allowing the system an opportunity to correct itself. It explained, in this connection, that exhaustion of local remedies 'is not, in the case of a denial of justice claim, a mere pre-condition to arbitration, but a constituent element of the delict'.[275]

Suffice it to say, the exception to the general rule that local remedies must be exhausted is that the investor is not required to exhaust local remedies when access to the courts is being denied, when decisions are affected by undue delays or when further recourse would be futile.[276] In this context, the tribunal in *Apotex v United States*[277] ruled that:

> [U]nder established principles, the question whether the failure to obtain judicial finality may be excused for 'obvious futility' turns on the unavailability of relief by a higher judicial authority, not on measuring the likelihood that the higher judicial authority would have granted the desired relief.[278]

Meanwhile, the tribunal in *Marfin v Cyprus*[279] explained that:

> what is required is 'an actual unavailability of recourse, or recourse that is proven to be manifestly ineffective – which, in turn, requires more than one side simply proffering its best estimate or prediction as to its likely prospects of success, if available recourse had been pursued'.[280]

The futility exception was countenanced in *Lion v Mexico.*[281] Here, after Lion had been deprived by an idiosyncratic decision of the *Juez de lo Mercantil* of the opportunity to file an ordinary appeal against the Cancellation Judgement (issued by the same Juez de lo Mercantil), it sought to pursue proceedings before the Amparo. However, it had spent almost three years seeking to advance the case but with little success. The Amparo proceedings had little prospect of success, since Lion was prohibited from presenting evidence to prove the alleged forgery. In addition, even if Lion were successful, the effect of the Amparo would be limited to a declaration that the Cancellation Judgement had been improperly rendered. A new procedure before the Juez de lo Mercantil would then be required to annul the Cancellation Judgement, a process that would at least require a further three years for the Cancellation Judgment to be overturned. Against this backdrop, the tribunal found that Lion effectively exhausted all reasonable and available remedies, and that, in this connection,

275 ibid 1272.

276 *Loewen v USA*, ICSID Case No. ARB(AF)/98/3, Award, 26 June 2003, paras. 166–70; Case Concerning Barcelona Traction, Light, and Power Company, Ltd [1970] ICJ 1, Judge Tanaka's Separate Opinion, 5 February 1970, 144–45; Finnish shipowners against Great Britain in respect of the use of certain Finnish Vessels during the war (Finland, Great Britain), R.I.A.A, Vol. III, 1479–550, Award, 9 May 1934, 1503–5; Certain Norwegian Loans (*France v Norway*), ICJ Reports 1957, Separate Opinion of Judge Lauterpacht, 6 July 1957, 34, 39; *Abaclat and Others (Case formerly known as Giovanna a Beccara and Others) v The Argentine Republic*, ICSID Case No. ARB/07/5, Decision on Jurisdiction and Admissibility, 4 August 2011, paras. 582–584 and 587–588, 590; *Ambiente Ufficio S.p.A. and Others (Case formerly known as Giordano Alpi and Others) v The Argentine Republic*, ICSID Case No. ARB/08/9, Decision on Jurisdiction and Admissibility, 8 February 2013, paras. 599–611, 620; V. Freeman Alwyin, *International Responsibility of States for Denial of Justice* (Kraus Reprint Co. 1970), 423–34; C Amerasinghe, *Local remedies in International Law* (2nd edn, CUP 2004) 204–12.

277 ICSID Case No. ARB(AF)/12/1, Award, 25 August 2014.

278 ibid 276.

279 ICSID Case No. ARB/13/27, Award, 26 July 2018.

280 ibid 1275.

281 ICSID Case No. ARB(AF)/15/2, Award, 20 September 2021.

Lion was excused from continuing the Amparo proceeding in light of its obvious futility in the sense of its lack of any reasonable prospect of reversing the cancellation of the mortgages.

Meanwhile, in *Chevron I*,[282] the tribunal considered the burden of proof in these proceedings. In this context, it noted that the respondent state is required to prove that local remedies are available, while the burden of proof will be on the claimant to show that such remedies are ineffective and futile. In that case, the 'hearing in stands' and 'written closing arguments', purported remedies to advance the pending cases, were not shown to be able to result in the prompt issuance of a decision in respect of the pending cases. Similarly, the claimant pursuing monetary and disciplinary sanctions against individual judges would not have expedited the judgment. Against this backdrop, the tribunal found that exhausting local remedies was a futile exercise.

By contrast, in *Corona Materials v Dominican Republic*,[283] the tribunal considered that the claimant had not established that the remedies in question would have been futile. Here, the state refused to favourably respond to an application for an environmental licence in respect of a proposed Concession Agreement. Corona submitted a request for reconsideration to which it received no formal response. After the Dominican Republic explained that the deadline to seek reconsideration had expired, Corona initiated arbitration against the Dominican Republic alleging a denial of justice. The tribunal, however, ruled that the challenged measure was an administrative act at the level of a first-instance decision-maker, which could not be regarded as a systemic failure of the state's justice system. In this context, the tribunal concluded that Corona had failed to prove that taking a further step in the domestic legal system of the Dominican Republic would have been futile.

D. Prohibition of Arbitrary, Unreasonable and Discriminatory Treatment

Another important constituent element of the FET standard is that of the prohibition against arbitrary, unreasonable, and discriminatory treatment. According to the International Court of Justice (ECJ) in *Elettronica Sicula S.p.A. (ELSI)*:[284]

> Arbitrariness is not so much something opposed to a rule of law, as something opposed to the rule of law . . . . It is a willful disregard of due process of law, an act which shocks, or at least surprises, a sense of juridical propriety.[285]

The tribunal in *Siemens v Argentina*[286] endorsed the approach countenanced in *ELSI*, finding that the ordinary meaning of 'arbitrary' is that of 'derived from mere opinion', 'capricious', 'unrestrained', and 'despotic'.[287] It further explained that arbitrary conduct is conduct that is fundamentally antithetical to the rule of law, that is, conduct which demonstrates a wilful disregard of the law.[288] It also countenanced the view that bad faith is not an indispensable

282 *Chevron-Texaco v Ecuador*, UNCITRAL, Partial Award on the Merits, March 30, 2010.

283 ICSID Case No. ARB(AF)/14/3, Award, 31 May 2016.

284 *United States v Italy*, Judgment, Merits, ICJ GL No 76, [1989] ICJ Reports 15.

285 ibid 128.

286 ICSID Case No. ARB/02/8, Award, 17 January 2007.

287 ibid 318.

288 ibid.

aspect of arbitrariness.[289] On the facts of *Siemens,* the tribunal found that Argentina's permanent suspension of two identification systems (DNM and RPN) operated by the claimant on the basis that the claimant had not obtained authorisation to start operating these subsystems was arbitrary. In the tribunal's view, the permanent suspension of the systems was not based on reason, and that, in any event, if there were errors in the identification systems that needed correction, the claimant could easily have corrected them. However, the claimant was denied the opportunity to correct the errors in question by virtue of the permanent suspension of the systems.

Over the years, tribunals have sought to fill the normative content of the obligation against arbitrary treatment. In this connection, authoritative guidance on the indicia of arbitrary measures, initially formulated by Professor Christoph Schreuer when acting as an expert, were espoused in *EDF (Services) Limited v Romania*:[290]

a. a measure that inflicts damage on the investor without serving any apparent legitimate purpose;
b. a measure that is not based on legal standards but on discretion, prejudice, or personal preference;
c. a measure taken for reasons that are different from those put forward by the decision-maker; and
d. a measure taken in willful disregard of due process and proper procedure.[291]

These have been cited with approval in subsequent cases.[292]

What is immediately discernible from the foregoing indicia is that the prohibition against arbitrary treatment is intended to capture egregious conduct committed by the host state.[293] Mere errors of judgments or mistakes that affect the investment that arise in the context of the state weighing social and economic factors may not result in a finding of arbitrariness. This principle was articulated in *Cargill v Mexico.*[294] In that case, the claimant undertook to sell high fructose corn syrup (HFCS) in Mexico. However, Mexico imposed a tax on soft drinks containing HFCS, coupled with a decision to issue an import permit to the claimant that would have otherwise enabled it to import HFCS from the United States. As a result of Mexico's actions in this regard, the claimant was forced to import HFCS without a permit, and thus was obliged to pay the higher MFN tariffs. The claimant argued that Mexico's

289 ibid.

290 ICSID Case No. ARB/05/13, Award, 8 October 2009.

291 ibid 303.

292 *Teinver v Argentina*, ICSID Case No. ARB/09/1, Award, 21 July 2017; *Glencore v Colombia*, ICSID Case No. ARB/16/6, Award, 27 August 2019; *Global Telecom v Canada*, ICSID Case No. ARB/16/16, Award, 27 March 2020.

293 Jacob Stone, 'Arbitrariness, the Fair and Equitable Treatment Standard, and the International Law of Investment' (2012) 25(1) *Leiden Journal of International Law* 77

> arbitrariness – has rarely been the focus of scholarly works and, thus, its scope and meaning are difficult to ascertain. When examined in the context of international investment disputes, however, one may conclude that, while its scope and meaning may vary, arbitrariness is indeed a legitimate basis for claim under the fair and equitable treatment standard. The thresholds for demonstrating arbitrariness, however, are decidedly and consistently high.

294 ICSID Case No. ARB(AF)/05/2, Award, 18 September 2009.

conduct was manifestly unjust in that it was arbitrary in nature. The tribunal agreed, finding that the requirement for an import permit represented an intentional targeting of the claimant's investment that was designated to deprive the claimant of the permit. This was not simply a case of poor administration; this was manifestly unjust conduct that was akin to an act in bad faith.

The tribunal, in its *obiter*, went on to clarify that, even the unlawfulness of a municipal law does not necessarily mean that the act is unlawful under international law, but that much depends on the gravity of the state's conduct. In this connection, the tribunal agreed:

> . . . with the view expressed in *S.D. Myers* that a tribunal, in assessing whether an action of a State is arbitrary, need recognize that governments 'make many potentially controversial choices' and, in doing so, may 'appear to have made mistakes, to have misjudged the facts, proceeded on the basis of a misguided economic or sociological theory, placed too much emphasis on some social values over others and adopted solutions that are ultimately ineffective or counterproductive'. Therefore, an actionable finding of arbitrariness must not be based simply on a tribunal's determination that a domestic agency or legislature incorrectly weighed the various factors, made legitimate compromises between disputing constituencies, or applied social or economic reasoning in a manner that the tribunal criticizes. The Tribunal thus finds that arbitrariness may lead to a violation of a State's duties under Article 1105, but only when the State's actions move beyond a merely inconsistent or questionable application of administrative or legal policy or procedure to the point where the action constitutes an unexpected and shocking repudiation of a policy's very purpose and goals, or otherwise grossly subverts a domestic law or policy for an ulterior motive.[295]

The high threshold for a finding of arbitrariness that was countenanced in *Cargill v Mexico* appears to have been satisfied in *Biwater Gauff v Tanzania*.[296] Here, the claimant, through City Water, entered into a 10-year contract with the government for the provision of water and sewerage services in Tanzania. During this period, the foreign investor was entitled to receive certain VAT exemptions. However, a disagreement arose between the parties, and the relevant Minister sought to terminate the contract and unilaterally withdraw the VAT exemptions. City Water objected to the government's conduct, which resulted in their senior management being deported. Representatives of the state then seized the company's assets, installed a new management and took over City Water's business. The tribunal held that these acts, which were executed with the assistance of its police force, went well beyond the ambit of normal contractual behaviour. In fact, these acts were unreasonable and arbitrary, and unjustified by any public purpose, there being no emergency at the time.

A similar outcome was arrived at in *Rompetrol v Romania*,[297] a case which arose out of investigations commenced by the National Anti-Corruption Office of Romania (PNA) relating to the privatisation of Petromidia, shortly after the sale of its controlling shares to the claimant. The investigating file was transferred from the PNA to the General Prosecutor's Office (GPO) which had jurisdiction for investigating alleged economic crimes. GPO thereafter opened an investigation into Rompetrol conduct, and Mr. Patriciu, who was a 100% shareholder in Rompetrol, was arrested, detained and threatened with the prospect of imprisonment. The claimant asserted that these investigations were oppressive and in breach of, *inter alia*, the prohibition against arbitrary and unreasonable conduct. The tribunal agreed,

295 ibid 292–93.

296 ICSID Case No. ARB/05/22, Award, 24 July 2008.

297 ICSID Case No. ARB/06/3, Award, 6 May 2013.

finding the prosecutorial staff showed hostility towards Mr. Patriciu, and a determination to succeed in nailing criminal charges on him, even though he had disclosed the company's engagement in swap transactions in respect of the Privatization Contract. It considered that the procedural irregularities in the instigation of criminal proceedings against Mr. Patriciu, including his unreasonable arrest and detention, evidenced arbitrary treatment in breach of the FET standard. The tribunal, however, cautioned that future tribunals should be mindful that this conclusion was arrived at based on the facts of the case in question, and should not be taken to mean that in all cases where criminal investigations are commenced against investors this would constitute arbitrary treatment. In this context, it noted:

> the Tribunal wishes to make it plain that it would not regard any breach, or indeed any series of breaches, of procedural safeguards provided by national or international law in the context of a criminal investigation or prosecution as giving rise to the breach of an obligation of fair and equitable treatment. All will depend on the nature and strength of the evidence in the particular case, on the impact of the events complained about on the protected investor or investment, and on the severity and persistence of any breaches that can be duly proved, as well as on whatever justification the respondent State may offer for the course of events. The Tribunal's finding is based entirely on the facts of the present case.[298]

Meanwhile in *Eco Oro v Columbia*,[299] the claimant, a Canadian mining company, invested in the Municipality of California, Columbia. It was granted a concession that allowed it to explore the designated area for deposits of precious metals and associated minerals, which it did, at great expense, for a number of years. While it was able to obtain authorisation to explore for the precious metals on multiple occasions, its applications for an environmental licence that would have enabled it to engage in construction and mounting and, subsequently, the exploitation phases, were repeatedly refused by the competent national authorities. This refusal was principally because of a law that prohibited mining activities in the Páramos region, which are high-mountain ecosystems that play a central role in maintaining biodiversity, premised on a unique capacity to absorb and restore water. The Santurbán Páramo provides water to around 2.5 million people in 68 surrounding municipalities. The law, however, made limited exceptions for mining activities carried out in the reservation areas by companies that were already engaged in mining at the time of the law's enactment.

These exceptions were challenged in the Columbian Constitutional Court, which ruled that they were unconstitutional. It also ruled that the relevant competent authorities should delimit the Santurbán Páramo. The relevant authorities then engaged in a lengthy process of trying to delimit the Santurbán Páramo over the course of many years. However, despite multiple requests by the claimant, the coordinates associated with the delimitation were not forthcoming. When they were finally announced, the delimitation entailed a 54.7% overlap with the area granted to Eco Oro under the concession. This delimitation was not, however, the finalized coordinates. Notwithstanding multiple requests for the final coordinates so that the claimant could have certainty about what mining activities were permitted within the area, these were never provided. As such, Eco Oro brought a claim under the FTA concluded between Canada and Columbia alleging, among other things, arbitrary and discriminatory treatment in breach of the fair and equitable treatment standard.

298 ibid 279.

299 ICSID Case No. ARB/16/41, Decision on Jurisdiction, Liability and Directions on Quantum, 9 September 2021.

The tribunal agreed with Eco Oro, finding that Columbia had failed to comply with its legal obligations to delimit the Santurbán Páramo pursuant to the provisions of Colombian law. It considered that this failure to lawfully and finally delimit the Santurbán Páramo in breach of the Constitutional Court's judgement amounted to a wilful neglect of Colombia's statutory duty and caused harm to Eco Oro as no environmental licences could be issued for mining projects in the vicinity of the Santurbán Páramo until the new delimitation had been completed. Colombia's refusal to allow Eco Oro a concomitant extension of time to submit its Construction and Works Plan (PTO), in circumstances where the Páramo boundary had not been finally determined, meant that Eco Oro had no certainty as to where the Páramo overlapped with the Angostura Deposit, if at all. In the tribunal's view, this conduct was arbitrary and disproportionate, and inflicted damage on Eco Oro without serving any apparent purpose. In short, then, the majority of the tribunal found that Colombia's actions with respect to the delimitation of the Santurbán Páramo were grossly inconsistent and gave rise to considerable confusion and uncertainty as to (i) what activities could and could not be undertaken within the Páramo as then currently delimited; (ii) what the final boundaries would comprise; and (iii) when the final delimitation would be announced.[300]

Although the discussion above has almost exclusively addressed the question of arbitrariness, it is important to note that the FET clause has also been interpreted by various tribunals as also prohibiting unreasonable conduct on the part of the host state. According to the tribunal in *Plama v Bulgaria*,[301] the prohibition of unreasonable treatment and arbitrary treatment overlap. In this context, unreasonableness means conduct which is 'not founded in reason or fact but on caprice, prejudice or personal preference.'[302] Meanwhile, the tribunal in *Saluka v Czech Republic*[303] noted that

> the standard of 'reasonableness' has no different meaning in this context than in the context of the 'fair and equitable treatment' standard with which it is associated; and the same is true with regard to the standard of 'non-discrimination'. The standard of 'reasonableness' therefore requires, in this context as well, a showing that the State's conduct bears a reasonable relationship to some rational policy.[304]

Some regional BITs specifically identify unreasonable conduct as giving rise to a breach of the treaty, separate and apart from the FET clause.[305] By way of example, Article V of the Agreement on Reciprocal Promotion and Protection of Investments contained in Annex III

300 For general critique of this case, see Hou-Chih Kuo and Jeffrey Lo, 'Runaway Tribunal? An Assessment of the Eco Oro Tribunal's Opinion on the General Exceptions' (2022) 15 *Contemporary Asia Arbitration Journal* 143; Güneş Ünüvar, 'A Tale of Policy Carve-Outs and General Exceptions: *Eco Oro v Colombia* as a Case Study' (2023) 14(4) *Journal of International Dispute Settlement* 517; Robert Garden, '*Eco Oro v Colombia*: The Brave New World of Environmental Exceptions' (2023) 38(1) *ICSID Review-Foreign Investment Law Journal* 17.

301 ICSID Case No. ARB/03/24, Award, 27 August 2008.

302 ibid 184.

303 UNCITRAL Partial Award, 17 March 2006.

304 ibid 460.

305 Dominican Republic-Korea BIT, Article 2(3); Dominican Republic-Finland BIT, Article 2(3); Barbados-Venezuela BIT, Article 2(2); Barbados-Germany BIT, Article 2(2); Barbados-Belgium-Luxembourg Agreement, Article 2(3); Antigua and Barbuda-Germany BIT, Article 2(3); Trinidad and Tobago-South Korea BIT, Article 2(2); Haiti-USA BIT, Article II:4; Guyana-South Korea BIT, Article 2(3); Grenada-USA BIT, Article II:2.

of the Agreement Establishing the Free Trade Area between the Caribbean Community ('CARICOM') and the Dominican Republic provides that:

> Each Party shall comply with its commitments regarding investment and shall, in no way, impair, through the adoption of arbitrary and discriminatory measures, the management, development, maintenance, utilisation, usufruct, acquisition, expansion or transfer of said investments.[306]

In *Michael Lee-Chin v Dominican Republic*,[307] the tribunal was asked to interpret this provision. It began by determining whether the impugned conduct amounted to arbitrary *and* discriminatory treatment, and second, whether such conduct impairs the management, development, maintenance, utilisation, usufruct, acquisition, expansion or transfer of said investments. On the first point, the tribunal considered that, unlike the FET prohibition whereby arbitrary *or* discriminatory treatment may suffice for the purposes of state liability, in respect of this provision (Article V) only conduct that meets the threshold of arbitrary *and* discriminatory treatment will suffice. On the facts, although the tribunal held that the series of inconsistent declarations to which the claimant was subject demonstrated the respondent's changing attitudes throughout the investment, and were therefore arbitrary (and a breach of this constituent element of the FET), such conduct did not breach Article V because it was not proved to also be discriminatory.

Meanwhile, the tribunal in *Swisslion v Macedonia*,[308] when interpreting Article 4(1) of the Macedonia-Switzerland BIT (prohibition of impairment of investments by arbitrary and unreasonable measures), noted that this provision was duplicative of the FET standard. The tribunal further considered that 'the claimed breach of Article 4(1) adds little to the Claimant's case and would not in any event increase the measure of damages'.[309]

On the question of discrimination, the tribunal in *Saluka v Czech Republic*[310] considered that the prohibition of discrimination requires that

> any differential treatment of a foreign investor must not be based on unreasonable distinctions and demands, and must be justified by showing that it bears a reasonable relationship to rational policies not motivated by a preference for other investments over the foreign-owned investment.[311]

A similar view was countenanced in *Plama v Bulgaria*,[312] a case in which the tribunal considered that discrimination:

> corresponds to the negative formulation of the principle of equality of treatment. It entails like persons being treated in a different manner in similar circumstances without reasonable or justifiable grounds.[313]

Finally, it is important to remember that, as noted by the tribunal in *CMS v Argentina*,[314] discriminatory treatment requires less favourable treatment of the foreign investor vis-à-viz

306 CARICOM-Dominican Republic FTA (1998).
307 ICSID Case No. UNCT/18/3, Award, 6 October 2023.
308 ICSID Case No. ARB/09/16, Award, 6 July 2012.
309 ibid 329.
310 UNCITRAL Partial Award, 17 March 2006.
311 ibid 307.
312 ICSID Case No. ARB/03/24, Award, 27 August 2008.
313 ibid 184.
314 ICSID Case No. ARB/01/8, Award, 12 May 2005.

domestic investors who are *similarly placed* or in like circumstances.[315] In this connection, in *Michael Lee-Chin v Dominican Republic*,[316] the tribunal did not find any evidence of Lajun being treated less favourably than other similarly placed investors in the waste disposal sector.

E. Stability

The tribunal in *Plama v Bulgaria*[317] noted that the question of whether stability, that is the purported obligation of host states to provide a stable, secure and predictable legal and regulatory framework, forms part of the FET clause is 'a controversial area'.[318] It is controversial because, on the one hand, investors often insist, even in the absence of a stabilisation clause, that the host state should not make any changes to its legal framework subsequent to their admission, while, on the other hand, host states are adamant that they retain their sovereign right to make necessary changes that may be in the public interest.[319]

Over the years, tribunals have increasingly had to grapple with this tension. While some tribunals, including those in *LG&E v Argentina*[320] *and Plama v Bulgaria,*[321] have considered that stability is an 'emerging standard of fair and equitable treatment in international law', other tribunals have staunchly maintained that the stability obligation has crystallised as an important aspect of the FET standard. This latter view was countenanced by the tribunal in *CMS v Argentina*,[322] which noted that stability is an 'essential element of fair and equitable treatment'[323] and that 'fair and equitable treatment is inseparable from stability and predictability',[324] and *Photovoltaik v Czech Republic*,[325] which considered that stability 'forms part of the FET standard'.[326]

In *CMS v Argentina*,[327] at the time of a serious economic crisis in Argentina in the late 1990s, Argentina first suspended, and then permanently terminated, both the claimant's right to calculate tariffs in US dollars and its right to make inflation adjustments. The peso was devalued with the effective rate being 3.6 peso for one dollar, whereas the respective tariffs were redenominated at a rate of one peso to the dollar. This led to a great decrease in TGN's profits and to the loss of value of the claimant as a company. The claimant argued, among other things, that there had been a breach of the stability obligation under the relevant FET standard. The tribunal agreed with the claimant, finding that the relevant measures 'entirely transform[ed] and alter[ed] the legal and business environment under which the investment was decided and made'.[328] Meanwhile, while some tribunals ground the stability

315 ibid 293.
316 ICSID Case No. UNCT/18/3, Award, 6 October 2023.
317 ICSID Case No. ARB/03/24, Award, 27 August 2008.
318 ibid 175.
319 Federico Ortino, 'The Obligation of Regulatory Stability in the Fair and Equitable Treatment Standard: How Far Have We Come?' (2018) 21(4) *Journal of International Economic Law* 845.
320 ICSID Case No. ARB/02/1, Decision on Liability, 3 October 2006, para. 125.
321 *Plama v Bulgaria*, ICSID Case No. ARB/03/24, Award, 27 August 2008, para. 177.
322 ICSID Case No. ARB/01/8, Award, 12 May 2005.
323 ibid 274.
324 ibid 276.
325 PCA Case No. 2014–21, Award, 15 May 2019.
326 ibid 483.
327 ICSID Case No. ARB/01/8, Award, 12 May 2005.
328 ibid 275.

obligation in the express FET standard, others, like the tribunals in *OEPC v Ecuador*[329] and *LG&E v Argentina*,[330] ground the stability obligation both in the FET clause and the preamble of the relevant BITs in question.

Interestingly, some tribunals have treated the stability obligation in absolute terms, seemingly from which no derogation is permitted. For example, in *OEPC v Ecuador,*[331] the tribunal found that the failure of the Ecuadorian Government to continue its practice of reimbursing VAT to the claimant in respect of purchases required for its exploitation activities under the contract for oil production breached the stability obligation. The tribunal was especially concerned that the tax law in issue was changed without providing any clarity about its meaning and extent, and that, in any event, the practice and regulations in respect of this matter were also inconsistent with such changes. Noting that it was inconsequential whether Ecuador had acted with good faith, the tribunal considered that its principal concern was whether the legal and business framework met the requirements of stability and predictability under international law. In finding against Ecuador, the tribunal described the stability obligation in absolute terms:

> there is certainly an obligation not to alter the legal and business environment in which the investment has been made. In this case it is the latter question that triggers a treatment that is not fair and equitable.[332]

In other cases, however, tribunals, while recognising the existence of the stability obligation as a constituent element of the FET standard, have nonetheless been sure to caution that this obligation is not absolute, and that, absent a stabilisation clause, the host state can make necessary changes to its legal and regulatory framework, once these changes are not arbitrary and/or discriminatory. The case of *Micula v Romania*[333] is instructive in this regard. In that case, the tribunal opined that:

> the fair and equitable treatment obligation is not an unqualified guarantee that regulations will never change. Investors must expect that the legislation will change from time to time, absent a stabilization clause or other specific assurances giving rise to a legitimate expectation of stabilization. The BIT's protection of the stability of the legal and business environment cannot be interpreted as the equivalent of a stabilization clause. In the Tribunal's view, the correct position is that the state may always change its legislation, being aware and thus taking into consideration that: (i) an investor's legitimate expectations must be protected; (ii) the state's conduct must be substantively proper (e.g., not arbitrary or discriminatory); and (iii) the state's conduct must be procedurally proper (e.g., in compliance with due process and fair administration). If a change in legislation fails to meet these requirements, while the legislation may be validly amended as a matter of domestic law, the state may incur international liability.[334]

The sensible approach adopted in *Micula* appears to find support among other arbitral tribunals. Thus, for example, in *Mobil v Canada*,[335] the tribunal considered that:

> This applicable standard does not require a State to maintain a stable legal and business environment for investments, if this is intended to suggest that the rules governing an investment

329 ICSID Case No. ARB/06/11, Award, 5 October 2012.
330 ICSID Case No. ARB/02/1, Decision on Liability, 3 October 2006.
331 ICSID Case No. ARB/06/11, Award, 5 October 2012.
332 ibid 191.
333 ICSID Case No. ARB/05/20, Award, 11 December 2013.
334 ibid 529.
335 ICSID Case No. ARB(AF)/07/4, Award, 20 February 2015.

> are not permitted to change, whether to a significant or modest extent. Article 1105 may protect an investor from changes that give rise to an unstable legal and business environment, but only if those changes may be characterized as arbitrary or grossly unfair or discriminatory, or otherwise inconsistent with the customary international law standard. In a complex international and domestic environment, there is nothing in Article 1105 to prevent a public authority from changing the regulatory environment to take account of new policies and needs, even if some of those changes may have far-reaching consequences and effects, and even if they impose significant additional burdens on an investor. Article 1105 is not, and was never intended to amount to, a guarantee against regulatory change, or to reflect a requirement that an investor is entitled to expect no material changes to the regulatory framework within which an investment is made. Governments change, policies changes and rules change. These are facts of life with which investors and all legal and natural persons have to live with. What the foreign investor is entitled to under Article 1105 is that any changes are consistent with the requirements of customary international law on fair and equitable treatment. Those standards are set at, as we have noted above, at a level which protects against egregious behaviour.[336]

Investors have a due diligence duty to ensure that they factor into their decision-making any foreseeable risks associated with the legal environment in which they are investing. If the jurisdiction in which they are investing is unstable, they cannot reasonably expect a stable environment. The tribunal in *Parkerings v Lithuania*,[337] in this context, held that:

> In the view of the Tribunal, Claimant . . . was without doubt aware that the business environment . . . were not certain. In fact, it would have been foolish for a foreign investor in Lithuania to believe, at that time, that it would proceeding on stable legal ground, as considerable changes in the Lithuanian political regime and economy were undergoing.[338]
>
> . . .
>
> In principle, an investor has a right to a certain stability and predictability of the legal environment. The investor will have a right of protection of its legitimate expectations provided it exercised due diligence and that its legitimate expectations were reasonable in light of the circumstances. Consequently, an investor must anticipate that the circumstances could change, and thus structure its investment to adapt to the potential changes of legal environment.[339]
>
> . . .
>
> In 1998, at the time of the Agreement, the political environment in Lithuania was characteristic of a country in transition from its past being part of the Soviet Union to candidate for the European Union membership. Thus, legislative changes, far from being unpredictable, were in fact to be regarded as likely. As any businessman would, Claimant was aware of the risk that changes of laws would probably occur after the conclusion of the Agreement. The circumstances surrounding the decision to invest in Lithuania were certainly not an indication of stability of the legal environment. Therefore, in such a situation, no expectation that the laws would remain unchanged was legitimate.[340]

It seems, then, that irrespective of whether stability is an essential or emerging element of the FET standard, host states do not guarantee investors absolute stability. Indeed, absolute stability will in practice have a chilling effect on host states' willingness and ability to enact much-needed regulatory and legislative changes, which may result in stagnated

336 ibid 153.
337 ICSID Case No. ARB/05/8, Award, 11 September 2007.
338 ibid 306.
339 ibid 333.
340 Ibis 335.

economic development. It may also have implications for citizens of host states who may be deprived of the opportunity to benefit from policy initiatives which, while not contemplated by foreign investors, are nonetheless *bona fide* and proportionate and designed to advance the interests of citizens. This point was countenanced in *Photovoltaik v Czech Republic,*[341] which concerned the respondent state having introduced a solar levy on electricity produced from solar radiation as well as the repeal of certain tax measures previously afforded companies in the photovoltaic industry, such as tax holidays. The tribunal, in finding that these measures did not constitute a breach of the stability obligation, considered that 'the requirement of stability is not absolute and must not be interpreted overly broadly.'[342] It then went on to explain that the obligation:

> does not in all circumstances affect the state's inherent right to exercise its sovereign power to respond to changing circumstances, for example with revisions in its legislation or legal system. As aptly put by the Tribunal in *Total*, in words with which the Tribunal is in full agreement, 'changes to general legislation, in the absence of specific stabilization promises to the foreign investor, reflect a legitimate exercise of the host state's governmental powers that are not prevented by a BIT's fair and equitable treatment standard'.[343]

The tribunal in *Photovoltaik* considered the implications of countenancing a broad description of the stability obligation. In this connection, it noted that the mere use of the word stability does not:

> signal an undertaking by the Respondent, much less a specific undertaking to this Claimant, that there would be no changes whatsoever to the legal framework created by the Act on Promotion – in particular in the event of radically changed circumstances (such as the solar boom in 2009–2010, which fundamentally changed the financial soundness of the support regime). On any view, this would have been a far-reaching undertaking, with potentially extreme consequences for the Respondent and its citizens.[344]

In short, the tribunal concluded that the disputed changes introduced by the respondent to the incentive regime were part of the exercise of the respondent's sovereign right to regulate tariffs – in particular in the context of the solar boom and its substantial adverse consequences. As such, these changes were not held to have violated the respondent's obligation to provide a stable and predictable legal framework for foreign investment.

In view of the sentiments expressed above regarding the non-absolute nature of the stability obligation, can it also be said that the development status of a country could be a deciding factor in the determination of whether changes made by the host state breach this obligation? One tribunal, *Mamidoil v Albania,*[345] appears to suggest that this is the case. In *Mamidoil*, the tribunal noted that:

> [a]n investor may have been entitled to rely on Albania's efforts to live up to its obligations under international treaties, but that investor was not entitled to believe that these efforts would generate the same results of stability as in Great Britain, USA or Japan.[346]

341 PCA Case No. 2014–21, Award, 15 May 2019.
342 ibid 484.
343 ibid.
344 ibid 486.
345 ICSID Case No. ARB/11/24, Award, 30 March 2015.
346 ibid 626.

It is submitted that *Mamidoil's* sentiments augur well, if countenanced by other tribunals, for developing countries like those in the Caribbean who have often expressed their dissatisfaction with the manner in which the stability obligation has been interpreted as devoid of consideration of their development status. The *Mamidoil* approach strong suggests that these countries may be insulated from liability in circumstances where they pursue policy objectives that may perhaps give rise to some instability, whereas these same measures may give rise to a breach of the stability obligation in more developed countries.

On a final note, the recent case of *Eco Oro v Columbia*[347] seems to have added another interesting dimension to the debate regarding the stability obligation. Here, the tribunal appears to reject stability as a standalone obligation in circumstances where no stabilisation clause exists:

> . . . Eco Oro was entitled to expect that Colombia would treat its investment in an even-handed and just manner to ensure a predictable business environment and foster the promotion of foreign investment but that, in doing so, it would ensure the enhancement and enforcement of environmental laws and regulations, such that neither investment protection nor environmental protection takes precedence.[348]
>
> This does not mean that Colombia was under an obligation to guarantee that the domestic regulatory environment would remain stable. The Tribunal has found that Concession 3452 did not contain a stability clause and it accepts that a State cannot be rigidly bound to those rules and regulations in force at the time the investment is made. Whilst Mobil Investments was an arbitration under NAFTA, the Tribunal agrees with the principle that Article 805 cannot act as a restraint upon Colombia's legitimate ability to regulate matters within its borders. The Tribunal further understands it is inevitable that, in exercising its police powers, a State will find itself at times having to make difficult and potentially controversial choices, particularly when considering issues of environmental protection and public health.[349]

Whether other tribunals countenance the narrow approach adopted in *Eco Oro* is left to be seen. Interestingly, in the recent *Michael Lee-Chin v Dominican Republic*[350] award, the tribunal, while accepting that the FET standard demands that the state act in a transparent manner, noted that this must be 'distinguished from the separate issue of the stability of the legal framework'.[351] Based on this pronouncement, as well as the fact that it identified early in its award only four constituent elements of the FET standard (legitimate expectations, freedom from arbitrary or discriminatory treatment, transparency, and consistency), one could assume that the tribunal here does not consider stability as a separate constitutive element of the FET standard. Interestingly, although the Tribunal appears to disavow a stability obligation, it considered that an obligation to act consistently is a constitutive element of the FET standard. In its view, although

> a State may change its position on a specific policy and thus legislate or adopt decisions as the executive branch in a manner that may not be in line with its preceding behavior, . . . those deviations should not violate the other constituent elements of the standard applicable.[352]

347 ICSID Case No. ARB/16/41, Decision on Jurisdiction, Liability and Directions on Quantum, 9 September 2021.

348 ibid 748.

349 ibid 751.

350 ICSID Case No. UNCT/18/3, Award, 6 October 2023.

351 ibid 446.

352 ibid 442.

On the facts, it found that the respondent engaged in a series of contradictory actions which, on the one hand, sought to reassure the claimant regarding the successful operation of his investment, and, on the other hand evinced an intention to terminate this operation. This inconsistency, in the tribunal's view, amounted to a violation of the FET standard, 'not because it represents a change of the State's position per se, but because it is a change of position against the constituent elements of the FET standard as a whole'.[353] It then cautioned that:

> a State is entitled to change its position on a foreign investment-related matter, to the extent that such change does not violate the applicable FET standard overall. Otherwise, the change of State position does bear consequences. What the State cannot do – or rather what it cannot do without violating its duty to provide FET – is to certify that the investment meets all applicable requirements and, at the same time, terminate the concession while arguing otherwise.[354]

It is submitted that the tribunal, relying on the obligation of consistency, appears to have brought in a requirement of stability as a constituent element of the FET standard through the back door without fully substantiating the extent to which this requirement has attained the status of customary international law, which is cause for concern. Indeed, given that both scholars[355] and UNCTAD[356] have to date taken issue with the inclusion of consistency as a constituent element of the FET standard, the tribunal should have done more to evidence the place of this requirement in international law.

A REQUIREMENT OF PROPORTIONALITY?

As illustrated above, tribunals are often called upon to balance the competing rights of investors, on the one hand, and the countervailing interests of the state, on the other.[357] This is inherently a difficult exercise given that tribunals in the normal course of things wish to afford host states the requisite margin of appreciation to take necessary steps to advance their public interest, while simultaneously trying to protect the investor against treatment that is disproportionate. Although most tribunals engage in this balancing exercise in the

353 ibid 443.

354 ibid.

355 Kenneth Vandevelde, *Bilateral Investment Treaties: History, Policy, and Interpretation* (OUP 2010) 198. See, also, Jason Haynes, 'The Evolving Nature of the Fair and Equitable Treatment (FET) Standard: Challenging Its Increasing Pervasiveness in Light of Developing Countries' Concerns – The Case for Regulatory Rebalancing' (2013) 14(1) *The Journal of World Investment & Trade* 114.

356 UNCTAD, 'Fair and Equitable Treatment', (UNCTAD Series on Issues in International Investment Agreements II (United Nations 2013) 63: 'A number of possible elements, such as transparency or consistency, have generated concern and criticism. So far, they may not be said to have materialized into the content of fair and equitable treatment with a sufficient degree of support'.

357 See generally, Benedict Kingsbury and Stephan Schill, 'Public Law Concepts to Balance Investors' Rights with State Regulatory Actions in the Public Interest – The Concept of Proportionality' in Stephan W. Schill (ed), *International Investment Law and Comparative Public Law* (OUP 2010) 75; David Schneiderman, 'Global Constitutionalism and Its Legitimacy Problems: Human Rights, Proportionality, and International Investment Law' (2018) 12(2) *The Law & Ethics of Human Rights* 251; Caroline E Foster, 'Why Due Regard is More Appropriate than Proportionality Testing in International Investment Law' (2022) 23(3) *The Journal of World Investment & Trade* 388; Gebhard Bücheler, *Proportionality in Investor-state Arbitration* (OUP 2015).

context of alleged violations of the FET standard by reference to the notion of reasonableness, other tribunals are increasingly relying on the principle of proportionality, which is particularly utilised in human rights and administrative law proceedings.[358] Proportionality requires that the means chosen to achieve the aims in question are rationally connected, and that the state does only that which is necessary to achieve those aims. Measures which place a disproportionate burden on the investor may, therefore, fall afoul of the proportionality requirement.

The first notable reference to proportionality in the context of the fair and equitable treatment appeared in *MTD v Chile*.[359] Here, the tribunal, citing Judge Schwebel, explained that:

> 'fair and equitable treatment' is a broad and widely-accepted standard encompassing such fundamental standards as good faith, due process, non-discrimination, and proportionality.[360]

While, over the years, proportionality analyses have permeated conversations around expropriation, the same cannot be said of the fair and equitable treatment standard. Instead, arbitral tribunals, when deciding FET claims, have simply been prepared to adopt, wholeheartedly and without serious interrogation, the sentiments countenanced in *Tecmed v Mexico,*[361] a case in which the tribunal noted that it:

> will consider, in order to determine if they are to be characterized as expropriatory, whether such actions or measures are proportional to the public interest presumably protected thereby and to the protection legally granted to investments, taking into account that the significance of such impact has a key role upon deciding the proportionality. Although the analysis starts at the due deference owing to the State when defining the issues that affect its public policy or the interests of society as a whole, as well as the actions that will be implemented to protect such values, such situation does not prevent the Arbitral Tribunal, without thereby questioning such due deference, from examining the actions of the State in light of Article 5(1) of the Agreement to determine whether such measures are reasonable with respect to their goals, the deprivation of economic rights and the legitimate expectations of who suffered such deprivation. There must be a reasonable relationship of proportionality between the charge or weight imposed to the foreign investor and the aim sought to be realized by any expropriatory measure.[362]

Tecmed concerned the commission of certain minor licensing infringements in respect of their operation of a landfill in Mexico. Certain community groups were opposed to the operation and existence of the landfill, which dealt with hazardous waste, and when Tecmed applied for the renewal of its licence in 1998, the relevant government body refused to renew the licence, citing the alleged infringements. The tribunal concluded that the responsible regulatory agency was predominantly influenced and/or motivated by socio-political factors beyond the alleged licence violations (concerning storage of impermissible types of waste, or storage of excess waste). The tribunal held that the manner of operation of the

358 Paul Craig, 'Proportionality and Judicial Review: A UK Historical Perspective' in S Vogenauer and S Weatherill (eds), *General Principles of Law: European and Comparative Perspectives* (OUP 2016); Grainne De Burca, 'Proportionality and Wednesbury unreasonableness: the influence of European legal concepts on UK law' (1997) 3 *European Public Law* 561; Anne Davies and JR Williams, 'Proportionality in English Law' in *The Judge and the Proportionate Use of Discretion* (Routledge 2015).

359 ICSID Case No. ARB/01/7, Award, 25 May 2004.

360 ibid 109.

361 ICSID Case No. ARB (AF)/00/2, Award, 29 May 2003.

362 ibid 122.

landfill never compromised the ecological balance, the protection of the environment or the health of local people (as alleged by certain pressure groups), and that all the infringements allegedly committed were either remediable or remediated or subject to minor penalties. Against this backdrop, although the licence and applicable regulations *prima facie* permitted a refusal to renew the licence in the case of such violations, the state's response in this connection was not proportionate.

Apart from *Tecmed*, another 'go to' point of reference for most tribunals is that of *Azurix v Argentina,*[363] a case which considered that:

> a measure depriving a person of his property [must] pursue, on the facts as well as in principle, a legitimate aim 'in the public interest', and bear 'a reasonable relationship of proportionality between the means employed and the aim sought to be realized'. This proportionality will not be found if the person concerned bears 'an individual and excessive burden' . . . 'such a measure must be both appropriate for achieving its aim and not disproportionate thereto'.[364]

Similarly, in *EDF v Romania,*[365] the tribunal discussed proportionality, albeit in connection with an alleged expropriation, finding that:

> in addition to a legitimate aim in the public interest there must be 'a reasonable relationship of proportionality between the means employed and the aim sought to be realized'; that proportionality would be lacking if the person involved 'bears an individual and excessive burden'.[366]

Meanwhile, in *LG&E v Argentina,*[367] the tribunal, when addressing proportionality in the context of expropriation, similarly noted that:

> With respect to the power of the State to adopt its policies, it can generally be said that the State has the right to adopt measures having a social or general welfare purpose. In such a case, the measure must be accepted without any imposition of liability, except in cases where the State's action is obviously disproportionate to the need being addressed. The proportionality to be used when making use of this right was recognized in *Tecmed*, which observed that 'whether such actions or measures are proportional to the public interest presumably protected thereby and the protection legally granted to investments, taking into account that the significance of such impact, has a key role upon deciding the proportionality'.[368]

Regrettably, apart from the foregoing references to key cases that address proportionality in the context of expropriation, most tribunals have, by and large, not engaged in any serious or critical analysis of proportionality in the specific context of the fair and equitable treatment standard. One of the few exceptions, in this connection, however, is *Electrabel v Hungary.*[369] Here, following the conclusion of a Power Purchase Agreement (PPA), Electrabel invested substantial funds in Dunamenti as shareholders. However, after Hungary acceded to the European Union in 2004, the European Commission conducted a formal investigation into unlawful state aid provided by Hungary under the PPA. The European Commission ultimately issued a final decision that effectively resulted in Hungary having to terminate the

363 ICSID Case No. ARB/01/12, Award, 14 July 2006.
364 ibid 311.
365 ICSID Case No. ARB/05/13, Award, 8 October 2009.
366 ibid 293.
367 ICSID Case No. ARB/02/1, Decision on Liability, 3 October 2006.
368 ibid 195.
369 ICSID Case No. ARB/07/19, Award, 25 November 2015.

PPA. In so doing, however, Hungary, instead of providing no compensation to Dunamenti while receiving a cash payment from Dunamenti in the amount of 125 billion HUF, decided to provide compensation in the sum of 125 billion HUF (i.e. 85% of Dunamenti's eligible stranded costs as approved by the Commission), by setting them off against the 125 billion HUF it was entitled to receive as State aid. Dunamenti, dissatisfied with this outcome, challenged Hungary's decision as being a breach of the fair and equitable treatment standard.

The tribunal found in favour of Hungary, concluding that although Hungary had the possibility of receiving 125 billion HUF in cash, it forewent this possibility in order to compensate Dunamenti for 85% of its eligible stranded costs. In this context, although Dunamenti did not receive compensation for 100% of its eligible stranded costs, Hungary's exercise of its discretion was nonetheless reasonable and proportionate. In the tribunal's view, in keeping with the test for proportionality discussed in *Tecmed* and related cases, Hungary pursued a legitimate aim, and its conduct bore a reasonable relationship to that aim.

The *Electrabel* tribunal, citing with approval the case of *AES v Hungary*,[370] explained the nature of the proportionality analysis in respect of alleged breaches of the FET standard:

> A rational policy is taken by a state following a logical (good sense) explanation and with the aim of addressing a public interest matter. Nevertheless, a rational policy is not enough to justify all the measures taken by a state in its name. A challenged measure must also be reasonable. That is, there needs to be an appropriate correlation between the state's public policy objective and the measure adopted to achieve it. This has to do with the nature of the measure and the way it is implemented. In the Tribunal's view, this includes the requirement that the impact of the measure on the investor be proportional to the policy objective sought. The relevance of the proportionality of the measure has been increasingly addressed by investment tribunals and other international tribunals, including the ECtHR. The test for proportionality has been developed from certain municipal administrative laws, and requires the measure to be suitable to achieve a legitimate policy objective, necessary for that objective, and not excessive considering the relative weight of each interest involved.[371]

In the tribunal's view, once a measure satisfies the proportionality test, a state has a wide scope of discretion to determine the exact contours of the measure. This means that when approached with allegations regarding alleged breaches of the FET standard, tribunals must engage in a 'balancing or weighing exercise so as to ensure that the effects of the intended measure remain proportionate in regard to the affected rights and interests'.[372] In this connection, the tribunal further explained that:

> Provided that there is an appropriate correlation between the policy sought by the State and the measure, the decision by a State may be reasonable under the ECT's FET standard even if others can disagree with that decision. A State can thus be mistaken without being unreasonable. It is therefore no proof of unreasonableness, by itself, that other States have taken different decisions in regard to net stranded costs, as advocated by Electrabel, particularly in regard to Poland and Portugal. Moreover, the Tribunal is not convinced that the position of these two States was materially similar to Hungary so as to provide any useful benchmark of reasonableness in regard to Hungary in the present case.[373]

370 ICSID Case No. ARB/07/22, 23 September 2010.
371 *Electrabel v Hungary*, ICSID Case No. ARB/07/19, Award, 25 November 2015, para. 179.
372 ibid 180.
373 ibid.

The tribunal, having ruled in favour of Hungary, concluded, quite instructively, that:

> There is no balancing exercise if the scale is pre-determined to tip completely towards the investor. Whether the Tribunal, acting in Hungary's shoes, would have come to a different figure from Hungary is not the right question under the ECT's FET standard. The Tribunal is not a court of appeal. Rather, the question is whether Hungary, at the relevant time, acting in good faith, could have arrived at that figure in a rational manner under the ECT's FET standard . . . .[374]

Another important case that furthers our understanding of proportionality in the context of the fair and equitable treatment standard is that of *Occidental v Ecuador*.[375] Here, contrary to the terms of a Participation Contract entered into between Occidental and Ecuador regarding the exploitation of hydrocarbons in the Ecuadorian Amazon region, Occidental concluded a farmout agreement with a Canadian company (AEC) in which AEC acquired a 40% economic interest in the region in return for certain capital contributions. The transfer, however, violated both the Participation Contract and Ecuadorian law, which required ministerial approval. Against this backdrop, Ecuador issued a decree (Caducidad Decree) terminating with immediate effect its Participation Contract with Oxy and seized all of its property. In ensuing arbitration proceedings, Occidental argued that, although it was in breach of the Participation Contract and Ecuadorian law, the response of the government was disproportionate and therefore a breach of the fair and equitable treatment standard. Ecuador, on the other hand, argued that the question of proportionality did not arise in circumstances where the sanction imposed (termination of the contract) was one specifically agreed upon by the parties in the Participation Contract.

On the question of proportionality, the tribunal, relying on WTO jurisprudence, jurisprudence from the European Court on Human Rights (ECtHR) and European Court of Justice (ECJ), and arbitral awards, found that 'there is a principle of proportionality which requires that administrative measures must not be any more drastic than is necessary for achieving the desired end.'[376] The tribunal in *Occidental* cited with approval the decisions of *MTD*, *LG&E*, *Tecmed*, and *Azurix*, in grounding its view that 'the obligation for fair and equitable treatment has on several occasions been interpreted to import an obligation of proportionality'.[377] The tribunal then boldly asserted that, it had:

> no doubt that the principle of proportionality is applicable as a matter of general international law, and has been applied in many ICSID arbitrations in the past.[378]

In assessing whether the principle of proportionality was satisfied on the facts of the instant case, the tribunal considered that:

> The argument is not that the State must prove harm, but that any penalty the State chooses to impose must bear a proportionate relationship to the violation which is being addressed and its consequences. This is neither more nor less than what is encapsulated in the Respondent's own constitutional rules about proportionality. In cases where the administration wishes to impose a severe penalty, then it appears to the Tribunal that the State must be able to demonstrate (i) that sufficiently serious harm was caused by the offender; and/or (ii) that there had been a flagrant or persistent breach of the relevant contract/law, sufficient to warrant the sanction

374 ibid 219.
375 ICSID Case No. ARB/06/11, Award, 5 October 2012.
376 ibid 403.
377 ibid 403.
378 ibid 427.

imposed; and/or (iii) that for reasons of deterrence and good governance it is appropriate that a significant penalty be imposed, even though the harm suffered in the particular instance may not have been serious. The potential justification predicated on deterrence explains why, for example, it may be proportionate to give a heavy fine for speeding even where no accident occurred and where, plainly, the State suffered no direct 'harm' from the driver's breach of the law. The potential for harm, and the need to deter others from acting in the same way, justifies the imposition of a penalty even though no identifiable harm was caused in the particular instance.[379]

In the tribunal's view, the proportionality test is 'one of overall judgment, balancing the interests of the State against those of the individual, to assess whether the particular sanction is a proportionate response in the particular circumstances'.[380]

Interestingly, the tribunal appeared to suggest that states cannot contract out the requirement of proportionality.[381] To the extent, therefore, that a state is exercising discretion, it must, as a minimum, act proportionately in those circumstances. Thus:

> The fact that a contractor agrees that caducidad may be a remedy in certain situations does not mean that the contractor has waived its right to have such a remedy imposed proportionately, or otherwise imposed in accordance with all relevant laws. That is particularly so when, as in the present case, the parties agree that the contract is to be governed by a system of law (Ecuadorian law) which expressly requires the principle of proportionality to be observed. There is nothing in the Participation Contract to indicate an intention to 'contract out' of proportionality or any other legal principles of general application.[382]

In short, Ecuador could have achieved the objective of sanctioning the investor for breach of the Participation Contract by other, less stringent means, including a variation of the provision requiring the contractor to enter into a new contract with more favourable terms for the respondent, payment of a transfer fee (US$11.8 million), a sum by way of compensation for any damage suffered, or penalty sums charged at a higher level than that initially agreed upon. In other words, the test of proportionality was not satisfied by the respondent state:

> Tribunal does not necessarily disagree with the reasoning that the Respondent could justifiably have wished to re-emphasize the importance of adherence to its regulatory regime. But the overriding principle of proportionality requires that any such administrative goal must be balanced against the Claimants' own interests and against the true nature and effect of the conduct being censured. The Tribunal finds that the price paid by the Claimants – total loss of an investment worth many hundreds of millions of dollars – was out of proportion to the wrongdoing alleged against OEPC, and similarly out of proportion to the importance and effectiveness of the 'deterrence message' which the Respondent might have wished to send to the wider oil and gas community.[383]

Against the backdrop of *Electrabel* and *Occidental*, it seems clear that, increasingly, tribunals are becoming attuned to the need to engage in a robust proportionality analysis when seeking to balance the rights of investors as against the countervailing interests of states. From a Caribbean perspective, this is not an objectionable approach.

379 ibid 416.
380 ibid 417.
381 ibid 422.
382 ibid 422.
383 ibid 450.

CONCLUSION

The Fair and Equitable Treatment (FET) standard has emerged as a cornerstone of international investment law, evolving from a simple treaty provision to a complex and frequently invoked standard of protection. As we have explored in this chapter, its interpretation and application have significant implications for Caribbean nations navigating the intricate landscape of international investment agreements.

The journey through various FET formulations reveals a standard that defies simple categorisation. From its linkage to customary international law to its existence as an autonomous standard, the FET clause wears many hats, each with its own set of expectations and obligations. This diversity presents both challenges and opportunities for Caribbean states as they negotiate and interpret their investment treaties.

As arbitral tribunals have grappled with FET claims, they have sketched out a constellation of constituent elements – legitimate expectations, transparency, denial of justice, and the prohibition of arbitrary treatment. Yet, the boundaries of these elements remain fluid, their definitions constantly refined through the lens of arbitral practice. This ongoing evolution keeps the FET standard dynamic but also introduces an element of uncertainty that Caribbean nations must navigate carefully.

Perhaps one of the most contentious aspects of the FET standard is the notion of stability. While investors crave a stable and predictable environment, states, particularly developing ones, require flexibility to address evolving societal needs. The emerging consensus that the stability obligation is not absolute offers a glimmer of hope for Caribbean countries seeking to balance investor protections with their right to regulate in the public interest. This nuanced approach acknowledges that while dramatic, arbitrary changes may breach the FET standard, reasonable and proportionate regulatory adjustments fall within a state's sovereign prerogative. Indeed, the principle of proportionality is gaining ground as a valuable tool in FET analysis. By weighing investor rights against state interests, this approach offers a more balanced framework for addressing FET claims. For Caribbean nations, often caught between the need to attract foreign investment and the imperative to preserve policy space, this trend towards proportionality could prove particularly significant.

Encouragingly, some tribunals are beginning to factor in the development status of host states when assessing FET obligations. Cases like *Mamidoil v Albania* suggest a growing recognition that the expectations of stability and predictability must be tempered by the realities of investing in developing economies. If this trend continues and gains wider acceptance, it could provide Caribbean countries with greater leeway in implementing necessary policy changes without running afoul of their FET obligations.

Caribbean states face a complex but not insurmountable challenge in navigating the FET landscape. The broad and sometimes ambiguous nature of the standard undoubtedly creates potential pitfalls. However, the evolving jurisprudence also offers opportunities for more balanced interpretations that account for the unique circumstances of developing states. To effectively manage these dynamics, Caribbean nations would do well to approach their engagement with the FET standard strategically. This might involve carefully crafting FET clauses in future agreements to clarify their intended scope and relationship to customary international law. It could also mean developing consistent state practice and articulating clear positions on FET interpretations that align with their development needs and regulatory priorities.

Moreover, proactive engagement in international forums, like the ongoing UNCITRAL Working Group reform process, could help shape the evolution of FET jurisprudence in a manner more conducive to their interests. By contributing to the global dialogue on investment protection, Caribbean states can work towards an interpretation of the FET standard that provides meaningful safeguards for investors while preserving necessary policy space for sustainable economic development.

In sum, then, while the FET standard will likely remain a central pillar of international investment protection, its precise contours are far from set in stone. For Caribbean nations, this fluidity presents both risks and opportunities. By staying informed, engaged, and strategic in their approach, these countries can work towards an interpretation of FET that balances the legitimate interests of foreign investors with their own developmental imperatives. In doing so, they can strive to create an investment climate that is truly fair and equitable for all stakeholders involved.

CHAPTER 6

FULL PROTECTION AND SECURITY, UMBRELLA CLAUSES, AND OTHER STANDARDS OF PROTECTION

INTRODUCTION

In the high-stakes world of international investment, the relationship between foreign investors and host states is a delicate one, fraught with potential missteps and misunderstandings. At the heart of this intricate relationship lie several key promises that host states make to entice and protect foreign capital: full protection and security, free transfer of funds, the sanctity of contractual obligations, and freedom from burdensome performance requirements. These seemingly straightforward guarantees, however, are anything but simple in practice. Imagine a Canadian mining company investing millions in Guyana, only to find its assets threatened by civil unrest. Does the host state's obligation to provide 'full protection and security' extend to hiring private security forces to guard the mine? Or picture a British investor in Jamaica, suddenly unable to repatriate profits due to new currency controls. Has the host state breached its promise of free transfer of funds, or is this a justified response to an economic crisis? These scenarios are not mere academic exercises. They represent real conflicts that have erupted into high-profile legal battles, albeit in other contexts, shaping the landscape of international investment law. This chapter seeks to unravel the complexities of these key protections, exploring how tribunals have interpreted them and the far-reaching consequences of their decisions. From the controversial 'umbrella clause' that can elevate a simple contract dispute to an international treaty violation, to the delicate balance between a state's right to regulate and an investor's right to operate free from excessive requirements, this chapter examines the intricate web of rights and obligations that governs the modern global economy.

I. FULL PROTECTION AND SECURITY

The obligation to afford investors full protection and security is often found alongside the fair and equitable treatment standard in IIAs. Traditionally, the FPS standard has been used to hold states accountable where emanations of the state engage in conduct that physically harm investors' investment or where they fail to take appropriate steps to respond with due diligence to third parties' prejudicial conduct that harm an investor's investment.[1] The clause is found in the vast majority of regional IIAs, although, in practice, it is not invoked by litigants in arbitral proceedings as frequently as the FET clause.[2]

1 Christoph Schreuer, 'Full Protection and Security' (2010) 1(2) *Journal of International Dispute Settlement* 353.

2 Mahnaz Malik, 'The Full Protection and Security Standard Comes of Age: Yet another Challenge for States in Investment Treaty Arbitration?' (2012) *International Institute for Sustainable Development* 1: 'The full protection and security standard has maintained a low profile in international investment law circles in comparison with its more controversial sibling, the fair and equitable treatment provision.'

DOI: 10.4324/9781003734185-6

A. Various Formulations

In the Caribbean context, most IIAs make explicit reference to the FPS standard, alongside the FET clause. For example, Article 2(2) of the St Lucia-UK BIT (1983) provides:

> Investments of nationals or companies of either Contracting Party all times be accorded fair and equitable treatment and shall enjoy protection and security in the territory of the other Contracting Party.[3]

Other IIAs, like Article III(I) of the Jamaica-Indonesia BIT (1999), adopt more limiting language, providing only for '*physical* protection and security':

> Each Contracting Party shall accord investments adequate physical protection and security.[4]

Meanwhile, at least one regional IIA does not mention physical protection, but instead provides for *legal* protection and security – Article 3(2) of the Jamaica-Argentina BIT (1994) reads:

> Each Contracting Party, once it has admitted investments in its territory by investors of the other Contracting Party shall grant full legal protection to such investments and shall accord them treatment which is no less favourable than that accorded to investments by its own investors or by investors of third States.

The question as to whether international law obliges states to offer physical security, as opposed to legal security, is considered in greater detail later in this chapter, but it suffices here to note that the FPS clause, although it typically appears alongside the FET clause in most IIAs, is different in normative content from the latter.[5] Whereas the FET clause covers a range of conduct that may impair an investor's investment, such as a lack of transparency and breach of an investor's legitimate expectations, the FPS clause, at least according to some tribunals, is primarily concerned with the question of whether the state has exercised due diligence with respect to the protection of the investor's physical investment. In this connection, the tribunal in *Ulysseas, Inc. v Ecuador*[6] explained:

3 See, also, Antigua-UK BIT Article 2(2); Barbados-Belgium/Luxembourg Cooperation Agreement Article 2(2); Barbados-Cuba BIT Article 2(2); Barbados-UK BIT Article 2(2); Belize-UK BIT Article 2(2); Grenada-UK BIT Article 2(2); Guyana-China BIT Article 2(2); Guyana-South Korea BIT Article 2(2); Guyana-UK BIT Article 2(2); Haiti-UK BIT Article 2; Haiti-USA BIT Article II(4); Jamaica-South Korea BIT Article 3(3); Jamaica-Switzerland BIT Article 3; Jamaica-UK BIT Article 2; Trinidad and Tobago-China BIT Article 3(2); Trinidad and Tobago-Cuba BIT Article 4(1); Trinidad and Tobago-India BIT Article 3(2); Trinidad and Tobago-South Korea BIT Article 2(2); Trinidad and Tobago-Switzerland BIT Article 4(1); Trinidad and Tobago-Germany BIT Article 3(1); Trinidad and Tobago-UK BIT Article 4.

4 See, also, Jamaica-Indonesia BIT Article III(I); Suriname-The Netherlands BIT Article 3(1).

5 *Franck Charles Arif v Moldova*, ICSID Case No. ARB/11/23, Award, 8 April 2013, para. 505:

> The Tribunal is not persuaded by Claimant's argument that if a State breaches the FET standard, it is *ipso facto* also in breach of the FPS standard. The standard of FPS is clearly addressed in a separate article in the BIT.

Electrabel S.A. v Republic of Hungary, ICSID Case No. ARB/07/19, Award, 25 November 2015, para. 7.83: 'In the Tribunal's view, given that there are two distinct standards under the ECT, they must have, by application of the legal principle of "effet utile", a different scope and role'.

6 UNCITRAL, Final Award, 12 June 2012.

> Full protection and security is a standard of treatment other than fair and equitable treatment, as made manifest by the separate reference made to the two standards by Article II (3)(a) of the BIT. This standard imposes an obligation of vigilance and care by the State under international law comprising a duty of due diligence for the prevention of wrongful injuries inflicted by third parties to persons [. . .][7]

Separately, at least one regional IIA contains an autonomous FPS clause – Article 2 of the Trinidad-Canada BIT (1995):

> Each Contracting Party shall accord investments or returns of investors of the other Contracting Party:
>
> b. full protection and security.

Meanwhile, only one regional IIA links the FPS clause to customary international law:

> Article II(2) of the SVG-Taiwan BIT (2009):
>
> Each Contracting Party shall accord investments or returns of investors of the other Contracting Party:
>
> (b) full protection and security, in accordance with the principles of customary international law.

In arbitral practice, some tribunals have emphasised that where the FPS clause is used alongside the FET standard, it automatically imports the international minimum standard of treatment under customary international law.[8] By contrast, other tribunals have maintained that if the FPS clause is included without any qualifications, then it is to be treated as an autonomous or unqualified FPS clause and interpreted as such. In *Cystallex v Venezuela*,[9] for example, the tribunal noted that '"full protection and security" is a distinct treaty standard whose content is not to be equated to the minimum standard of treatment',[10] while in *Frontier Petroleum Services Ltd v The Czech Republic*,[11] the tribunal considered that:

> On the basis of the wording of Article III(1) of the BIT, 'full protection and security' and general international law appear as two discrete standards. By contrast, the fair and equitable treatment clause of Article III(1) is supplemented by the words 'in accordance with principles of international law'. Whatever the exact meaning of this reference, the fact that it does not qualify the full protection and security standard is an argument against the latter standard being regarded as equivalent to customary international law.[12]

Although, indeed, the natural and ordinary meaning of the words used in the BIT should be respected, in accordance with Article 31 of the VCLT, it might very well be that this is largely inconsequential as arbitral practice demonstrates that, whatever the phraseology of the FPS clause, tribunals interpret the obligation as imposing a due diligence obligation,

7 ibid 272.
8 *Mondev v USA*, ICSID Case No. ARB(AF)/99/2. Award, 11 October 2002; *CMS Gas Transmission Company v The Republic of Argentina*, ICSID Case No. ARB/01/8, Award, 12 May 2005.
9 ICSID Case No. ARB(AF)/11/2, Award, 4 April 2016.
10 ibid 632.
11 Final Award, 12 November 2010.
12 ibid 268.

and nothing more. Indeed, the tribunal in *Deutsche Bank v Sri Lanka*,[13] articulated that 'the full protection and security standard only involves a best efforts obligation, a duty of "due diligence"',[14] a view also countenanced in *Peter Allard v Barbados*,[15] a Caribbean case in which the tribunal considered that 'the obligation is limited to reasonable action, and a host State is not required to take any specific steps that an investor asks of it'.[16] In other words, as explained by the tribunal in *Tulip Real Estate and Development v Turkey*:[17]

> the FPS standard does not impose on the State a 'strict liability' obligation. In other words, the State cannot insure or guarantee the full protection and security of an investment. The question of whether the State has failed to ensure FPS is one of fact and degree, responsive to the circumstances of the particular case.[18]

This due diligence duty, which is discussed in greater detail below, according to the tribunal in *Mamidoil v Albania*,[19] 'does not oblige the State to prevent each and every injury',[20] but is instead primarily aimed at 'prevent[ing] harassment and injuries to investors'.[21]

In determining whether the host state has accorded the appropriate level of diligence, international tribunals have historically taken several factors into account, including:

a) whether the facts at issue were either publicly known, or had been brought to the attention of the authorities;[22]
b) whether the host state conducted investigations in response to complaints by the foreign investor;[23]
c) whether the host state took adequate steps to apprehend the wrongdoer, or otherwise adequately enforce a penalty;[24] and
d) whether the standard of police protection for foreign nationals was less than what is provided generally for a State's own nationals.[25] This factor may not be determinative on its own, however, as even where a state acts in a lackluster fashion in responding to harms

13 ICSID Case No. ARB/09/02, Award, 31 October 2012.
14 ibid 537.
15 PCA Case No. 2012–06, Award, 27 June 2016.
16 ibid 244.
17 ICSID Case No. ARB/11/28, Award, 10 March 2014.
18 ibid 430.
19 ICSID Case No. ARB/11/24, Award, 30 March 2015.
20 ibid 821.
21 ibid.
22 *Mexico City Bombardment Cases, British-Mexican Claims Commission* (1930) 5 RIAA 80; *George Adams Kennedy (U.S.A.) v United Mexican States, US-Mexico Claims Commission* (1927) 4 RIAA 194.
23 *Too v Greater Modesto Insurance Associates and the United States of America*, US-Iran Claims Tribunal, Award No. 460-880-2 (29 December 1989).
24 *Fransico Mullén (United Mexican States) v United States of America*, US-Mexico Claims Commission (1927) 4 RIAA 173; *Thomas H. Youmans (U.S.A.) v United Mexican States*, 4 RIAA 110 (23 November 1926); *S.J. Stallings (U.S.A.) v United Mexican States*, 4 RIAA 478 (22 April 1929); *Richard A. Newman (U.S.A.) v United Mexican States*, 4 RIAA 518 (6 May 1929); *Sarah Ann Gorham (U.S.A.) v United Mexican States*, 4 RIAA 640 (24 October 1930); *Norman T. Connolly and Myrtle H. Connolly (U.S.A.) v United Mexican States*, 4 RIAA 387 (15 October 1928); *Lillian Greenlaw Sewell, In Her Own Right and As Guardian of Vernon Monroe Greenlaw, a Minor (U.S.A.) v United Mexican States*, 4 RIAA 626 (24 October 1930).
25 *Too v Greater Modesto Insurance Associates and the United States of America*, US-Iran Claims Tribunal, Award No. 460-880-2 (29 December 1989), para. 22.

committed against domestic investors, this does not *per se* excuse the state from reasonably responding to prevent harm to the investor's assets.

When determining what is 'reasonable' in respect of the full protection and security standard, tribunals must engage in a case-by-case, fact-specific evaluation. The essential considerations for tribunals are in this regard: (i) what type of protection was necessary (objective test); and (ii) whether the actions of the host state, viewed against the backdrop of what was objectively necessary, were reasonable in the circumstances (subjective test).

Whether the state has taken reasonable measures is not determined in abstract. Much depends on the circumstances of the case in question, including the resources at the relevant state's disposal, its level of development and overall socio-political stability. In this context, the sentiments expressed in *Pantechniki v Albania*[26] are instructive. Here, the sole arbitrator, Jan Paulsson, considered that:

> . . . an evaluation of what is 'reasonable under the circumstances' must include the host State's level of development and resources:
>
> Although the host state is required to exercise an objective minimum standard of due diligence, the standard of due diligence is that of a host state in the circumstances and with the resources of the state in question. This suggests that due diligence is a modified objective standard – the host state must exercise the level of due diligence of a host state in its particular circumstances.[27]

When a state has less capacity to act or greater instability, the due diligence standard appears to be less demanding, as noted by the tribunal in *Mamidoil v Albania*:[28]

> In practice, tribunals will likely consider the state's level of development and stability as relevant circumstance in determining whether there has been due diligence. An investor investing in an area with endemic civil strife and poor governance cannot have the same expectation of physical security as one investing in London, New York, or Tokyo.[29]

In *Pantechniki*, arbitrator Paulsson rejected the investor's FPS claim because Albania could not reasonably intervene to stop the looting of the investor's property; the scale of the social unrest precluded any action, rendering the authorities powerless.

B. Key Cases on the Application of the FPS Clause

There is a burgeoning corpus of jurisprudence on the application of the FPS standard. The first and most authoritative case[30] on FPS is *Asian Agricultural Products (AAPL) v Sri*

26 ICSID Case No. ARB/07/21, Award, 30 July 2009.

27 ibid 81.

28 ICSID Case No. ARB/11/24, Award, 30 March 2015.

29 ibid 624.

30 For comments and critique of the case, see Stephen Vasciannie, 'Bilateral Investment Treaties and Civil Strife: The AAPL/Sri Lanka Arbitration' (1992) 39 *Netherlands International Law Review* 332; Noel Dias, 'Responsibility of States in Respect of the Aliens' Property: Arbitral Award in *AAPL v Republic of Sri Lanka*' (1998) 10 *Sri Lanka Journal of International Law* 289; Chittharanjan Amerasinghe, 'The Prawn Farm (AAPL) Arbitration' (1992) 4 *Sri Lanka Journal of International Law* 155; Muthucumaraswamy Sornarajah, 'ICSID Involvement in Asian Foreign Investment Disputes: The AMCO and AAPL Cases' in Ko Swan Sik and others (eds), *Asian Yearbook of International Law* (Vol. 4, Brill Nijhoff 1994); Dilini

Lanka.[31] Here, AAPL, a Hong Kong corporation, established a joint venture in Sri Lanka – Serendib Seafoods Ltd – to cultivate and export shrimp to Japan. Its principal facility had come under the control of Tamil insurgents during a major insurrection. During the counter-insurgency operation conducted by the Sri Lankan Security Forces, Serendib's farm was destroyed, and several of the claimant's employees were killed. AAPL relied on the 1980 Sri Lanka-UK BIT (which was extended to Hong Kong) arguing, *inter alia*, a breach of the full protection and security standard under Article 2 of the BIT.

The tribunal ruled that the full protection and security standard in Article 2(2) of the Sri Lanka-UK BIT did not impose strict liability on the host state. The tribunal rejected the claimant's argument that this provision created an absolute obligation or guarantee against any damage. Instead, the tribunal found that the standard required the host state to exercise due diligence in protecting the investment, in line with customary international law. The tribunal stated that the addition of words like 'full' or 'constant' to 'protection and security' could indicate a higher standard of due diligence than the minimum standard under customary international law, but did not transform the nature of the obligation into one of strict liability. The tribunal emphasised that the state is not an insurer or guarantor of the foreign investment's security.

A claim as to breach of the FPS standard can be made out by an investor even if the state has also failed to protect other similarly placed investors, including local investors. The case of *AMT v Zaire*[32] is instructive in this regard. Here, AMT, a US company, held a 94% share in SINZA, in Zaire (now DRC). SINZA was engaged in production and sale of automotive and dry cell batteries, as well as in the importation and resale of consumer goods and foodstuffs. Members of the Zairian armed forces destroyed property located in the industrial complex. Among other things, they also broke into the stores owned by SINZA and destroyed, damaged, and carried away all the finished goods and almost all the raw materials and objects of value found on the premises. When the commercial complex was later reopened, it was destroyed for the second time a year later. In this connection, AMT contended that Zaire had failed to respect its general obligation to afford protection and security of its investment. The respondent, on the other hand, opposed AMT's claim for compensation, arguing that other victims of looting (domestic businesses and other foreign investors) had not been compensated for similar losses and thus were not treated more favourably than AMT.

The tribunal held that Zaire had 'manifestly failed' to comply with the standard of full protection and security.[33] More pointedly, Zaire had not taken any precautionary measure that would serve to ensure the protection and security of AMT's investment. In the tribunal's estimation, the fact that the host state had also failed to protect other investors was irrelevant. The failure of Zaire to take all measures necessary to ensure the full enjoyment

---

Pathirana, 'An Overview of Sri Lanka's Bilateral Investment Treaties: Status Quo and Some Insights into Future Modifications' (2017) 7 *Asian Journal of International Law* 287; Surya Sharma, 'Interpretation of Bilateral Investment Treaties: The Case of *Asian Agricultural Products Ltd (AAPL) v Republic of Sri Lanka*' (1992) 1 *Asia Pacific Law Review* 123; Niroshika Liyana Muhandiram, 'Investor-State Arbitration in ICSID and Sri Lanka: A Critical Appraisal' (2022) 2 *KDU Law Journal* 77; Amazu A Asouzu and Vikram Raghavan, 'The Legal Framework for Arbitration in Sri Lanka Past and Present' (2000) 17 *Journal of International Arbitration* 1; Niroshika Liyana Muhandiram, 'The Formulation and Determination of Expropriation Clauses in BITs of Sri Lanka: Gaps and Prospects' (2023) 31 *Asia Pacific Law Review* 146.

31 ICSID Case No. ARB/87/3, Award, 27 June 1990.

32 ICSID Case No. ARB/93/1, Award, 21 February 1997.

33 ibid 6.10.

of protection and security of the claimant's investment put Zaire afoul of its due diligence obligation under the FPS standard.[34]

Meanwhile, in *Wena Hotels v Egypt*,[35] the claimant, a British company, entered into two long-term agreements with the Egyptian Hotels Company ('EHC') which was wholly owned by the Egyptian Government. Under these agreements, the claimant sought to lease and develop two hotels for 25 years. The agreements provided that EHC would not interfere in the management and/or operation of the hotels or interfere with the enjoyment of the leases by Wena. However, shortly after entering into the agreements, disputes arose. Among other things, Wena was alleged to have received the hotels in a condition below that stipulated in the agreements and, accordingly, withheld part of the rent. In response, Egypt claimed that Wena had failed to pay the rent, which resulted in EHC taking possession of both hotels by force. Later, the Chief Prosecutor of Egypt ruled that the seizure of the hotels had been illegal, and the hotels were returned to Wena, but in a damaged state. Subsequently, due to Egypt's Ministry of Tourism interference with operating licences for the hotels, Wena was ultimately prevented from operating the hotels again.

The tribunal considered that, having regard to all the circumstances of the case, Egypt had failed to accord Wena full protection and security, in violation of the UK-Egypt BIT. More pointedly, Egypt was aware of EHC's intentions to seize the hotels and took no actions to prevent EHC from doing so. Egypt never imposed substantial sanctions on EHC/senior officials, suggesting Egypt's approval of EHC's actions. The tribunal usefully articulated several factors in its determination as to whether there had been a breach of the diligence standard:

- the delay on the part of the authorities to go to the investment to investigate;
- the failure to take any immediate act of protection;
- the delay in returning the investment to the investor;
- the damage to, and deterioration of, the investment;
- the failure of the host state to provide compensation; and
- the lack of serious punishment of the perpetrators.[36]

34 For commentary on the case, see Charles Chatterjee, 'Arbitration between American Manufacturing & Trading Inc. and the Republic of Zaire-When Challenges to the Jurisdiction of an ICSID Tribunal Are Not Valid' (1999) 16 *Journal of International Arbitration* 37; José Gustavo Prieto Munoz, 'Foreign Investment and Armed Conflicts in International Law: The Responsibility of States In Recent Struggles' in Maurizio Arcari and Louis Balmond (eds), *The Use of Force in International Relations: Issues of International and European Law* (Editoriale Scientifica 2018); Facundo Pérez-Aznar, 'Investment Protection in Exceptional Situations: Compensation-for-Losses Clauses in IIAs' (2017) 32 *ICSID Review-Foreign Investment Law Journal* 696; Rumana Islam, 'Current Arbitral Practice Relating to Political and Socio-political Circumstances in Host Developing Countries and Countries in Transition: FET Standard in Context' in *The Fair and Equitable Treatment (FET) Standard in International Investment Arbitration: Developing Countries in Context* (Springer 2018); Jure Zrilič, 'International Investment Law in the Context of Jus Post Bellum: Are Investment Treaties Likely to Facilitate or Hinder the Transition to Peace?' (2015) 16 *Journal of World Investment & Trade* 604; Kathryn Greenman, 'Protecting Foreign Investments in Revolution and Civil War: Critiquing the Contemporary Arbitral Practice' (2021) 9 *London Review of International Law* 293; Christoph Schreuer, 'War and Peace in International Investment Law' in Katia Fach Gómez, Anastasios Gourgourinis and Catharine Titi (eds), *International Investment Law and the Law of Armed Conflict* (Springer 2019).

35 ICSID Case No. ARB/98/4, Award, 8 December 2000.

36 ibid 84–85.

UNCTAD, commenting on the *AAPL*, *AMT* and *Wena* cases, has noted that:

> while not an obligation of result, an obligation of good faith efforts to protect the foreign-owned property has been established by these recent cases, without special regard for the resources available to do so. This has been referred to as a standard of 'due diligence' on the part of the host country. As a result, this standard should be understood as being very much a 'living' one. It places a clear premium on political stability, and the obligation of host countries to ensure that any instability does not have negative effects on foreign investors, even above the ability to protect domestic investors.[37]

In similar vein to *Wena Hotels*,[38] the decision of *Eureko B.V. v Republic of Poland*[39] makes it clear that if harassment is 'repeated and sustained, it may be that the responsibility of the [Host State] would be incurred by a failure to prevent them'.[40]

Not only is the conduct of state agencies and personnel that adversely impact investors' property a breach of the FPS standard, but also where the state fails to take reasonable steps to prevent third parties from causing harm to investors. In *von Pezold and Others v Zimbabwe*,[41] for example, the claimants, foreign owners of several estates, including a tobacco plant, a pole treatment plant and two factories, and a mixed plantation, growing coffee, bananas, maize, macadamia nuts, avocados, and timber for the production of transmission poles, alleged that the respondent breached the FPS standard by its police playing a passive role in addressing the Settlers/War Veterans' activity and the active involvement of government officials and agents in supporting and providing resources for invaders on the estates. The case arose out of a long history of racialised tensions, beginning during the period of colonial rule, when land in Rhodesia, as it then was, was subdivided into white areas, or white commercial farms, and tribal trust lands where those native to the land were forced to live. The result of Rhodesian-era land policies and colonial oppression was nothing short of devastating on the Indigenous population and gave rise to a violent and persistent struggle for liberation. Following Zimbabwe's independence and the election of Robert Mugabe as President in 1980, the land policies of the Rhodesian era which favoured the white minority population were reversed and replaced with land policies favouring the black Indigenous population.

More particularly, in February 2000, a new draft constitution was put to a referendum to the people of Zimbabwe, which would have permitted the Government to compulsorily acquire land without compensation but this was rejected. Following the rejection of the draft constitution, the first invasions of white-owned farms began in Masvingo Province,

37 UNCTAD Series on International Investment Policies for Development, *Investor-State Disputes Arising from Investment Treaties: A Review* (UNCTAD 2005) 40–41.

38 For commentary on the case, see Julie Maupin, 'The Awards in *Wena Hotels Limited v Arab Republic of Egypt*' in Guillermo Aguilar Alvarez and W Michael Reisman (eds), *The Reasons Requirement in International Investment Arbitration* (Brill Nijhoff 2008); Andrés Rigo Sureda, 'Chapter Six. Introduction to Investor-state Arbitration. A Case Study: *Wena Hotels Limited (Wena) v Arab Republic of Egypt*' in Christophe Paulussen and others (eds), *The Legal Practice in International Law and European Community Law* (Brill Nijhoff 2007); Assaduzzaman, 'State Liability for the Conduct of Its Entities in International Investment Arbitration' (2012) 5 *International Journal of Private Law* 276; John Riggs, 'Investment Protection in Colombia: Can Investors Rely on the Full Protection and Security Clause?' (2014) 7 *Journal of World Energy Law and Business* 264.

39 UNCITRAL, Partial Award, 19 August 2005.

40 ibid 237.

41 ICSID Case No. ARB/10/15, Award, 28 July 2015.

near the capital of Harare, and gradually spread across the country. The invasions were accompanied by a racial rhetoric that was overwhelmingly anti-white. Several judgments by the Zimbabwean courts recorded that, during 2000, the police took little or no action in respect of the acts of the invaders, despite multiple court orders declaring the invasions to be unlawful and directing the police to ensure that the invaders vacate the farms. Moreover, various public servants, including the Army, were found to have actively supported, encouraged, transported and financed the Settlers/War Veterans. Against this backdrop, the investor argued that, *inter alia*, there had been a breach of the FPS standard by the respondent.

The tribunal found that the respondent had breached the FPS standard in relation to the failure of police to protect the claimants' properties from occupation or to remove Settlers/War Veterans.[42] The tribunal also found that the respondent breached the standard in relation to the non-responsiveness of police to various violent incidents that occurred. In the tribunal's estimation, the exception in the BITs for situations of war, revolution, etc. did not apply in the present case. The respondent's further defences that the police were overwhelmed, or that intervention would have required disproportional force, were deemed by the tribunal to be unconvincing.[43]

A similar outcome was arrived at in *Ampal-American Israel Corp. and Others v Egypt*.[44] Here, in the wake of the Arab Spring Revolution, armed militant groups took advantage of the political instability, security deterioration and general lawlessness that ensued in the North Sinai to perpetrate attacks on the Trans-Sinai Pipeline. The claimants argued that Egypt failed to take reasonable precautionary, preventive, and remedial measures to ensure the physical security of its pipeline network from attacks by saboteurs between February 2011, which corresponded to the beginning of the Arab Spring Revolution, and April 2012, which corresponded to the termination of the General Sale and Purchase Agreement (GSPA) that had earlier been concluded between the Egyptian General Petroleum Corporation and the claimants. They contended that the pipeline was attacked thirteen times over this period by saboteurs who were intent on preventing the flow of gas from being supplied from Egypt to Israel. These attacks, in their view, caused damage that prevented them from supplying gas for substantial periods over 2011 and early 2012, in breach of the FPS standard.

The tribunal began its assessment by accepting that the first attack on 5 February 2011 could not have been prevented by the respondent and could not therefore amount to a breach of the full protection and security standard, since '. . . it seems difficult to maintain that a government incurs international responsibility for failure to plan for unprecedented trouble of unprecedented magnitude in unprecedented places'.[45] However, the tribunal considered that the thirteen attacks that were perpetrated on the Trans-Sinai Pipeline breached the standard of full protection and security under the Treaty. In the tribunal's view, a certain pattern emerged from the facts: an attack was perpetrated, to which the state reacted months later and then adopted some measures to heighten the security of the pipeline, but those measures were seldom implemented, and another attack then happened, and so on. In this

42 For commentary, see Thomas Leary, 'Non-Disputing Parties and Human Rights in Investor-State Arbitration: *Bernhard von Pezold and Others v Republic of Zimbabwe*, ICSID Case No. ARB/10/15, Final Award, 28 July 2015' (2017) 18(5–6) *The Journal of World Investment & Trade* 1062.

43 For a critique of the decision, see Ntina Tzouvala, 'Full Protection and Security (for Racial Capitalism)' (2022) 25(2) *Journal of International Economic Law* 224.

44 ICSID Case No. Arb/12/11, Decision on Liability and Heads of Loss, 21 February 2017.

45 ibid 244 citing Sole Arbitrator Paulsson in *Pantechniki v Albania*, ICSID Case No. ARB/07/21, Award, 30 July 2009.

regard, the tribunal concluded that the state's security forces in the Northern Sinai had failed to take any steps to stop saboteurs from damaging the lifeline of the claimants' investment, whether preventive or reactive. As the attack was unfolding, the claimants' personnel made contact with an Egyptian Army patrol and asked them to stop saboteurs from laying explosives on the pipeline at a facility just 1.5 kilometres away from where the patrol was stationed. The Egyptian security forces, however, refused to mobilize an appropriate response. Some 40 minutes later, the explosives were detonated, and gas supply to the claimant was cut-off for almost three months thereafter.

The tribunal considered that the first four attacks had been carried out on the facilities between February and July 2011. In its view, these four first attacks should have been seen as a warning to the Egyptian State that further attacks might be carried out if security measures were not implemented. Regrettably, notwithstanding this warning, Egyptian authorities failed to take any concrete steps to protect the claimants' investment from damage in reaction to third-party attacks on the upstream pipeline system, as of the date of attack (12 July 2011), which constituted a breach of the obligation of due diligence that Egypt was required to exercise in ensuring the full protection and security of the claimants' investment.

There is, however, an increasing number of cases in which tribunals have refused to find a breach of the FPS standard, primarily on account of claimants failing to establish, on a balance of probabilities, the lack of due diligence on the part of a host state. One of the earliest cases decided in this vein, albeit by the International Court of Justice and not an arbitral tribunal, was *Elettronica Sicula S.p.A. (ELSI) (United States of America v Italy)*.[46] Here, having run into financial difficulties, the management of ELSI took the view that one of the reasons for its lack of success was that it had trained and had employed an excessively large labour force. Against this backdrop, it decided to suspend 168 workers, with limited pay by ELSI for a period not exceeding six weeks. After a training programme during which the workers were paid by the Sicilian Government, it was contemplated that ELSI would endeavour to reemploy the suspended employees. The necessary additional business to make this possible was not forthcoming, and the suspended employees were dismissed. In consequence, a number of random strikes occurred, as well as occupation of the plant by disgruntled employees.

The USA, espousing the claim on behalf of its national, ELSI, argued that Italy had breached Article V(1) of the Friendship, Commerce and Navigation (FCN) Treaty which provided for 'the most constant protection and security' for nationals of each High Contracting Party, both for their persons and property. The USA contended that the workers' occupation had the tacit approval of local authorities, who made no effort to prevent or to end it, or otherwise to protect the premises. To this occupation the United States attributed injurious consequences, namely a deterioration of the plant and related material and equipment, and secondly that it impeded the efforts of the trustee in bankruptcy to dispose of the plant.

The tribunal, in finding against the investor, concluded that:

> The reference in Article V to the provision of 'constant protection and security' cannot be construed as the giving of a warranty that property shall never in any circumstances be occupied or disturbed. The dismissal of some 800 workers could not reasonably be expected to pass without some protest. Indeed, the management of ELSI seems to have been very much aware that the closure of the plant and dismissal of the workforce could not be expected to pass without disturbance; as is apparent from the removal of the company's books and 'quite a lot of

46 [1989] ICJ Reports 15, Judgment of 20 July 1989.

> inventory' to Milan. In any event, considering that it is not established that any deterioration in the plant and machinery was due to the presence of the workers, and that the authorities were able not merely to protect the plant but even in some measure to continue production, the protection provided by the authorities could not be regarded as falling below 'the full protection and security required by international law'; or indeed as less than the national or third-State standards. The mere fact that the occupation was referred to by the Court of Appeal of Palermo as unlawful does not, in the Chamber's view, necessarily mean that the protection afforded fell short of the national standard to which the FCN Treaty refers. The essential question is whether the local law, either in its terms or its application, has treated United States nationals less well than Italian nationals. This, in the opinion of the Chamber, has not been shown. The Chamber must, therefore, reject the charge of any violation of Article V, paragraphs 1 and 3.[47]

Subsequent cases adopt a similar approach to *ELSI*, including the leading Caribbean ISDS case on this issue, *Peter Allard v Barbados.*[48] Here, Allard, a Canadian investor, claimed that there was physical interference with his property, the Graeme Hall Nature Sanctuary, through the unlawful trespassing of pollutants. In this connection, he contended that Barbados denied full protection and security to his investment by failing to take reasonable care to protect the Sanctuary. In particular, he was of the view that Barbados had failed to adequately manage the Sluice Gate and enforce its environmental laws, such as the Marine Pollution Control Act.

The tribunal found that while Barbados was aware of the potential environmental importance of the Sluice Gate and the possible presence of contaminants in both the natural runoff to the Sanctuary and in any emergency discharge from the South Coast Sewage Plant, Barbados did indeed take reasonable steps to protect it. More pointedly, Barbadian officials implemented procedures to prevent environmental damage to the Sanctuary both on their own initiative and in response to the claimant's complaints. By way of example, Barbados established the Graeme Hall Stewardship Committee which sought to address the issues related to effective management of the Graeme Hall ecosystem and undertook to develop a Master Plan for the long-term preservation of the Graeme Hall Swamp. In addition, the committee operationalised immediate steps to ameliorate the environmental problems, including, *inter alia*, sewage management, use of adjacent lands, drainage, and the Sluice Gate. The committee also addressed the interaction between the Sanctuary and the South Coast Sewage. In this regard, when the Sluice Gate became inoperable, the committee coordinated the action of the responsible ministries to ensure drainage of the Graeme Hall Swamp by other means. More than this, the Government collected data in terms of water levels and water quality and carried out relevant studies to ascertain the hydrology of the site and the interaction between the swamp and the seas. Having regard to the foregoing, the tribunal ruled that Barbados' approach in addressing the Sluice Gate and general pollution issues at the Sanctuary as part of its governance of the entire area did not fall short of what was appropriate and sufficient for the purposes of the due diligence obligation under Article II(2)(b) of the Barbados-Canada BIT.

Further afield, in *Noble Ventures, Inc. v Romania*,[49] the tribunal rejected the American investor's claim that the respondent had breached the FPS standard. Here, Noble Ventures, a firm which offered business consulting services for steel companies in Romania, contested a

47 ibid 108.

48 PCA Case No. 2012–06, Award, 27 June 2016.

49 ICSID Case No. ARB/01/11, Award, 12 October 2005.

privatisation agreement concerning the acquisition, management, operation and disposition of a substantial steel mill and other assets. At the time of the privatisation, more than ten years had elapsed since the end of the Communist regime in Romania. Being still in a period of transition at the time of the conclusion of the Privatisation Agreement, the Romanian Government strongly supported the privatisation process of State-owned enterprises. For this purpose, they created a public institution (SOF) with legal personality, which was in charge of negotiating privatisation agreements with investors.

Six months after the privatisation took place, political control changed to an opposition party. The change of government resulted in the replacement of SOF by the Authority for the Privatization and Management of the State Ownership (APAPS). A local union initiated a demonstration with the goal of forcing the government to cancel the privatisation contract due to Noble Ventures' failure to make an increase in capital in a so-called 'CSR' facility. The counsellor to the Prime Minister made a statement to the press that the privatisation was dishonourable and that SOF officials should be investigated over their role in the sale of the CSR facility. His actions encouraged local citizens to engage in labour unrest. The claimant argued that local police refused to take adequate measures to protect Noble Ventures from unlawful activity on its premises. Their view was that, during the period of unrest, Noble Ventures made ongoing reports to the local Prefect, personally and to the Office of the Prime Minister, but little was done to protect its investment, thereby giving rise to a breach of the full protection and security standard. They further alleged that, as a result of unlawful strikes and occupations, Noble Ventures' premises were repeatedly occupied, its files and cash accounts were pilfered, facilities and equipment were sabotaged, and members of its management were confined and, in some cases, beaten.

The respondent, by contrast, argued that there was no failure to provide full protection and security. More pointedly, they argued that requests for protection by the claimant were never directly addressed to the respondent; the claimant also failed to provide sufficient evidence that acts occurred could give rise to an obligation to protect; and that the workers' demonstrations, which were caused by the claimant's failure to pay their wages, were conducted in an orderly manner and after notice had been given to the Prefect's office. The tribunal agreed with the respondent, finding that, even assuming that the claimant's allegations were factual, it was difficult to identify any specific failure by the respondent to exercise due diligence in protecting the claimant. In any event, none of the respondent's alleged failures were sufficiently grave to be regarded as a violation. It was not established that non-compliance with the obligation prejudiced the claimant to a material degree. In short, the tribunal concluded that the claimant had failed to prove that its alleged injuries and losses could have been prevented had the respondent exercised due diligence.

C. 'Physical' v 'Legal' Protection and Security

One of the longest running debates in international investment law centres around the question of whether the FPS standard offers only physical protection to investors or extends to legal protection and security.[50] In some Caribbean BITs, like Article 2(2) of the St Lucia-UK

50 George Foster, 'Recovering Protection and Security: The Treaty Standard's Obscure Origins, Forgotten Meaning, and Key Current Significance' (2012) 45 *Vanderbilt Journal of Transnational Law* 1095; Nartnirun Junngam, 'The Full Protection and Security Standard in International Investment Law: What and Who Is Investment Fully Protected and Secured From' (2018) 7 *American University Business Law*

BIT (1983), protection and security is mentioned, while in other BITs, like Article III(I) of the Jamaica-Indonesia BIT (1999), only 'physical protection and security' is used. Yet still, in other BITs, like Article 3(2) of the Jamaica-Argentina BIT (1994), 'full legal protection' is used.

It is submitted, as a matter of principled treaty interpretation, that in accordance with Article 31 of the VCLT, the ordinary and natural meaning of words in the relevant BIT must be respected.[51] It means, therefore, that where 'physical protection and security' is referred to, the word 'physical' qualifies and implicitly limits the other words such that the clause should be interpreted by tribunals as only referring to *physical* protection, and not *legal* protection and security. By the same token, if the provision refers only to 'legal protection',[52] then it should be interpreted as such, thereby, in principle, excluding physical protection, though one might argue that customary international law due diligence standards on physical protection would nonetheless apply. Meanwhile, where 'full protection and security' is used, ordinary rules of treaty interpretation demand that it be interpreted widely to include both physical and legal protection and security, although an argument can be made that legal security might already be covered by one or more of the constituent elements of the FET standard.

One of the earliest cases[53] to address the possibility that the FPS standard includes not just a physical element but also a legal element was *Azurix v Argentina*.[54] Here, a US corporation took part in the privatisation of water services in Argentina. It was granted a 30-year concession for the distribution of potable water, and the disposal of sewerage. A new regulatory authority ('ORAB') was established to oversee and regulate the concession. OAB issued a resolution precluding Azurix from billing amounts in excess of those billed prior to the granting of the concession. In fact, it froze the water rates that consumers were required to pay. Azurix alleged that this was contrary to the information provided to the bidders at the time of the tender and that this decision was politically motivated. Interestingly, because the Province did not complete certain infrastructural repairs before Azurix took over the water concession, there was an algae outbreak, and provincial health authorities warned customers that they should boil tap water. This warning incited public panic and encouraged

---

Review 1; Sebastián Mantilla Blanco and Sebastián Mantilla Blanco, '"Protection and Security" Clauses in Investment Treaties: A Typology' in Sebastián Mantilla Blanco (ed), *Full Protection and Security in International Investment Law* (Spring 2019) 495; Sébastien Manciaux, 'The Full Protection and Security Standard in Investment Law: A Specific Obligation?' in Katia Fach Gómez, Anastasios Gourgourinis and Catharine Titi (eds), *International Investment Law and the Law of Armed Conflict* (Springer 2019) 217. For discussion of the FPS to digital assets, see David Collins, 'Applying the Full Protection and Security Standard of International Investment Law to Digital Assets' (2011) 12(2) *The Journal of World Investment & Trade* 225.

51 *Total v Argentina*, ICSID Case No. ARB/04/01, Decision on Liability, 27 December 2010, para (applying a plain reading of the terms of the BIT, in accordance with Vienna Convention Article 31).

52 In *Siemens v The Argentine Republic*, ICSID Case No. ARB/02/8, Award, 17 January 2007, the applicable clause in the Argentina-Germany BIT (1991) expressly provided for 'legal security'.

53 See, also, cases that held that full protection and security extends beyond physical security: *Renée Rose Levy de Levi v Republic of Peru*, ICSID Case No. ARB/10/17, Award, 26 February 2014, para. 406; *Vivendi II v Argentina*, ICSID Case No. ARB/97/3, Award of August 20, 2007, para. 7.4.15; *Frontier Petroleum v Czech Republic*, UNCITRAL, Final Award, 12 November 2010, para. 263: '[I]t is apparent that the duty of protection and security extends to providing a legal framework that offers legal protection to investors – including both substantive provisions to protect investments and appropriate procedures that enable investors to vindicate their rights.'

54 ICSID Case No. ARB/01/12, Award, 14 July 2006.

consumers to refuse to pay their water bills following the incident. The investor, having suffered harm, argued that there was a breach of the FPS standard.

The tribunal held that the politicization of the tariff regime (freezing charges) because of concerns with forthcoming elections and repeated calls of the Provincial governor and other officials for non-payment of bills by customers amounted to a breach of the FPS standard. In its view, Argentina did not afford the investor the stability of a secure investment environment (legal security). Having regard to the factual circumstances of the case, the tribunal was persuaded that:

> full protection and security was [to be] understood to go beyond protection and security ensured by the police. It is not only a matter of physical security; the stability afforded by a secure investment environment is as important from an investor's point of view. The Tribunal is aware that in recent free trade agreements signed by the United States, for instance, with Uruguay, full protection and security is understood to be limited to the level of police protection required under customary international law. However, when the terms 'protection and security' are qualified by 'full' and no other adjective or explanation, they extend, in their ordinary meaning, the content of this standard beyond physical security.[55]

The subsequent case of *Biwater Gauff v Tanzania*[56] cited *Azurix* with approval, concluding that:

> when the terms 'protection' and 'security' are qualified by 'full', the content of the standard may extend to matters other than physical security. It implies a State's guarantee of stability in a secure environment, both physical, commercial and legal. It would in the Arbitral Tribunal's view be unduly artificial to confine the notion of 'full security' only to one aspect of security, particularly in light of the use of this term in a BIT, directed at the protection of commercial and financial investments.[57]

In this connection, the tribunal was prepared to adhere to

> the *Azurix* holding that when the terms 'protection' and 'security' are qualified by 'full', the content of the standard may extend to matters other than physical security. It implies a State's guarantee of stability in a secure environment, both physical, commercial and legal. It would in the Arbitral Tribunal's view be unduly artificial to confine the notion of 'full security' only to one aspect of security, particularly in light of the use of this term in a BIT, directed at the protection of commercial and financial investments. The Arbitral Tribunal also does not consider that the 'full security' standard is limited to a State's failure to prevent actions by third parties, but also extends to actions by organs and representatives of the State itself. That is also implied by the term 'full', as well as the purposes of the BIT and the *Wena* and *AMT* awards . . . .[58]

Having regard to the foregoing, the tribunal found that even if no force was used in removing the management from the offices or in the seizure of City Water's premises, these acts were unnecessary and abusive and amounted to a violation by the respondent of its obligation to ensure full protection and security to its investors. However, these acts were not shown to have caused any quantifiable financial or commercial loss to the investor.

Meanwhile, in *Rusoro Mining Limited v Venezuela*,[59] the tribunal, in acknowledging that the FPS standard was not limited to physical security, found that Venezuela had failed to

55 ibid 408.
56 ICSID Case No. ARB/05/22, Award, 24 July 2008.
57 ibid 729.
58 ibid.
59 ICSID Case No. ARB(AF)/12/5, Award, 22 August 2016.

ensure FPS to Rusoro's investment by imposing a range of measures. These included limitations on the exportation of gold; relaxing the rules on exportation applicable to public companies while reaffirming the limitations for private companies; shutting-down the Swap Market; and denying Rusoro access to foreign currency in the post-nationalisation phase. The tribunal considered that even if the Treaty were found to guarantee only physical security, Rusoro would still benefit from FPS, pursuant to the Treaty's MFN clause, because Venezuela guaranteed 'full protection and legal security' to third-State nationals under the Uruguay-Venezuela BIT.

A similar outcome was arrived at in *National Grid v Argentina*,[60] a case in which the tribunal held that measures dismantling Argentina's regulatory framework violated the full protection and security standard of the applicable investment treaty. Here, as a response to the Argentinean financial crisis, the government enacted a series of legal reforms that resulted in the claimant losing its right to calculate public utility tariffs in dollars and adjust those tariffs on the basis of international price indices; the conversion of public service tariffs into Argentine pesos at the rate of one peso to one US dollar and their freezing at that rate; as well as the fact that the claimant, as an electricity transmission and public utility company, could not suspend or modify compliance with their obligations under their concessions and licences. In arriving at the conclusion that there was a breach of the FPS standard, the tribunal reasoned that 'the phrase "protection and constant security" as related to the subject matter of the Treaty [did] not carry with it the implication that this protection is inherently limited to protection and security of physical assets'.[61]

Separately, in *CME Czech Republic v Czech Republic,*[62] the tribunal considered a case in which private actors colluded with government agencies to oust a foreign investor from a broadcasting joint venture. In these circumstances, it was held that the government's actions and inactions were aimed at removing the security and legal protection of the claimant's investment and were thus in breach of its obligation to provide full protection and security.

Some tribunals have interpreted the FPS clause to include an obligation on the part of the host state to ensure the proper functioning of its judicial system and make available adequate remedies at the domestic level to resolve complaints made by investors. In *Frontier Petroleum Services Ltd v Czech Republic*,[63] for example, the tribunal considered that:

> where the acts of the host state's judiciary are at stake, 'full protection and security' means that the state is under an obligation to make a functioning system of courts and legal remedies available to the investor. On the other hand, not every failure to obtain redress is a violation of the principle of full protection and security. Even a decision that in the eyes of an outside observer, such as an international tribunal, is 'wrong' would not automatically lead to state responsibility as long as the courts have acted in good faith and have reached decisions that are reasonably tenable. In particular, the fact that protection could have been more effective, procedurally or substantively, does not automatically mean that the full protection and security standard has been violated.[64]

A similar approach was adopted in *Ronald Lauder v Czech Republic*.[65] Here, the tribunal noted that while the state as not obliged to intervene in a dispute between two companies

60 UNCITRAL Award, 3 November 2008.
61 ibid 189.
62 UNCITRAL Award, 14 March 2003.
63 UNCITRAL Award, 12 November 2010.
64 ibid 273.
65 UNCITRAL Award, 3 September 2001.

over the nature of their legal relationships, its duty 'under the treaty was to keep its judicial system available for the Claimant and any entities he controls to bring their claims, and for such claims to be properly examined and decided in accordance with domestic and international law'.[66]

In the same vein, in *Parkerings v Lithuania,*[67] the tribunal analysed the host state's duty under the full protection and security clause to make its judicial system available in the following terms:

> The Respondent's duty under the Treaty was, first, to keep its judicial system available for the Claimant to bring its contractual claims and, second, that the claims would be properly examined in accordance with domestic and international law by an impartial and fair court. There is no evidence – not even an allegation – that the Respondent has violated this obligation. The Claimant had the opportunity to raise the violation of the Agreement and to ask for reparation before the Lithuanian Courts. The Claimant failed to show that it was prevented to do so. As a result, the Arbitral Tribunal considers that the Respondent did not violate its obligation of protection and security under Article III of the BIT.[68]

While, having regard to the foregoing, it might be assumed, on face value at least, that there is widespread agreement regarding the coverage of legal protection and security by the FPS standard, there is a growing corpus of case law which strongly suggests the contrary might be the case.[69] The leading case on this point is *Saluka v The Czech Republic*,[70] a case in which the tribunal found that the obligation to grant full security does not address all kinds of impairment, but only those which affect the physical integrity of the investment against the use of force.

Obiter statements in other cases have similarly adopted the approach that full protection and security does not extend to legal protection and security. For example, in *Liman Caspian Oil BV and NCL Dutch Investment BV v Kazakhstan*,[71] the tribunal considered that the FPS standard 'does not extend to any contractual rights [as its] purpose is rather to protect the integrity of an investment against interference by the use of force and particularly physical damage'.[72] In the same vein, the tribunal in *Crystallex v Venezuela*[73] concluded that:

66 ibid 314.

67 ICSID Case No. ARB/05/8, Award, 11 September 2007.

68 ibid 360.

69 *BG Group Plc. v Republic of Argentina*, UNCITRAL, Award, 24 December 2007, paras. 323–28 (supporting a 'traditional' interpretation of the standard limited to 'situations where the physical security of the investor or its investment is compromised' and finding it 'inappropriate to depart from the originally understood standard'); *AWG Group Ltd. v Argentine Republic*, UNCITRAL, Decision on Liability, 30 July 2010, paras. 174–77 (declining to 'depart from the historical interpretation traditionally employed by courts and tribunals and [to] expand that concept to cover non-physical actions and injuries'). *Sempra Energy International v Argentine Republic*, ICSID Case No. ARB/02/16, Award, 28 September 2007, para. 323; *AWG Group Ltd. v Argentine Republic*, UNCITRAL, Decision on Liability, 30 July 2010, para. 174 ('an overly extensive interpretation of the full protection and security standard may result in an overlap with the other standards of investment protection, which is neither necessary nor desirable'); *Oxus Gold v The Republic of Uzbekistan*, Final Award, 17 December 2015 (the claimant failed to substantiate and establish how the alleged failure to duly fulfil its contractual duties towards them amounted to a breach by the State of its 'duty of vigilance or due diligence' towards the claimant. Because the claimant had not raised any claim based on the use of force, the matter did not fall under the scope of the FPS standard).

70 UNCITRAL Partial Award, 17 March 2006.

71 ICSID Case No. ARB/07/14, Award, 22 June 2010.

72 ibid 289.

73 ICSID Case No. ARB(AF)/11/2, Award, 4 April 2016.

> [the FPS] standard only extends to the duty of the host state to grant physical protection and security. Such interpretation best accords with the ordinary meaning of the terms 'protection' and 'security'.
>
> The Tribunal is of the view that the more 'traditional' interpretation better accords with the ordinary meaning of the terms. Furthermore, as rightly observed by a number of previous decisions, a more extensive reading of the 'full protection and security' standard would result in an overlap with other treaty standards, notably FET, which in the Tribunal's mind would not comport with the 'effet utile' principle of interpretation. The Tribunal is thus unconvinced that it should depart from an interpretation of the 'full protection and security' standard limited to physical security.[74]

Similar sentiments were expressed in *Enron v Argentina*,[75] a case in which the tribunal rejected 'the argument made in general about a possible lack of protection and security in the broader ambit of the legal and political system' because such argument was 'not proven or even adequately developed.'[76] It, however, cautioned that that it

> cannot exclude as a matter of principle that there might be cases where a broader interpretation could be justified, but then it becomes difficult to distinguish such situation from one resulting in the breach of fair and equitable treatment, and even from some form of expropriation.[77]

In the final analysis, given the divergent approaches countenanced by different tribunals, it is submitted that the most logical and defensible approach is that tribunals should give the natural and ordinary meaning to words contained in the FPS clause. If the provision reads 'full protection and security', the qualification 'full' should be treated as referring to both physical and legal protection; if 'protection and security' is used, it should be taken to refer to 'physical protection'; if 'physical protection' is used, it should properly be construed as such, and not extend to legal protection; and if 'legal protection' is used, it should be interpreted as such, with the caveat that customary international law also implies observance of physical protection and security.

D. The Application of the MFN Clause in Respect of the FPS Standard

While, in the majority of cases, the FPS clause is explicitly provided for in the relevant BIT, and tribunals, therefore, have to simply decide whether the state failed to take due diligence steps to protect the investor in question, there are some cases in which investors seek to rely upon the MFN clause to import an FPS clause from a BIT concluded by the host state with a third country into the relevant BIT (base treaty) in question. For example, in *Rusoro Mining Limited v Venezuela*,[78] the tribunal considered that, pursuant to the Canada-Venezuela BIT's MFN clause, it could import an FPS provision because Venezuela guaranteed 'full protection and legal security' to third-State nationals as contained in another BIT. A similar position was obtained in *Hesham Talaat M. Al-Warraq v Indonesia*,[79] and *Rumeli v Kazakhstan*.[80]

74 ibid 634.
75 ICSID Case No. ARB/01/3, Award, 22 May 2007.
76 ibid 287.
77 ibid 286.
78 ICSID Case No. ARB(AF)/12/5, Award, 22 August 2016.
79 UNCITRAL, Final Award, 15 December 2014, para. 630 (importing full protection and security provision from UK-Indonesia BIT).
80 ICSID Case No. ARB/05/16, Award, 29 July 2008, para. 575 (importing full protection and security provision from UK-Kazakhstan BIT).

However, in *Crystallex v Venezuela*,[81] the tribunal declined to import a more favourable full protection and security provision from the Belarus-Venezuela BIT, and in *Impregilo SpA v Argentine Republic*,[82] the tribunal equally declined to import a more favourable full protection and security provision from the Argentina-US BIT into the Italy-Argentina BIT because, having found a breach of the FET standard, it was unnecessary to examine whether there had also been a failure to ensure full protection and security.

For Caribbean countries, often parties to multiple BITs with varying levels of investor protection, this inconsistency in arbitral practice creates both opportunities and risks. The divergent approaches highlight a critical juncture in international investment law, where the interplay between MFN and FPS clauses remains unsettled.

Moving forward, a more consistent approach may be necessary. Tribunals could first evaluate the scope of the MFN clause in question. If broadly drafted to encompass various BIT provisions, including FPS, tribunals might reasonably allow the importation of more favourable FPS standards from third-party BITs. However, this approach is not without its drawbacks.

The primary concern is the potential for 'treaty shopping', where investors might circumvent carefully negotiated BIT provisions. This is particularly problematic when a BIT limited to physical protection could be expanded to include legal protection or broader 'full protection and security' through MFN importation. For Caribbean nations, often seeking to balance investor protection with policy flexibility, this unpredictability in treaty interpretation could have significant implications for their investment climates and regulatory autonomy.

In short, as Caribbean countries continue to engage with international investment agreements, they must carefully consider the potential interactions between MFN and FPS clauses. The ongoing flux in this area of law underscores the need for precise treaty drafting and a thorough understanding of the potential ramifications of broad MFN clauses in the context of investor protection standards.

E. Summary

The FPS standard stands as a cornerstone of international investment law, particularly relevant to Caribbean nations as they navigate the complex waters of foreign investment. This principle, woven into the fabric of numerous bilateral investment treaties (BITs), places a significant responsibility on host states to safeguard foreign investments within their borders. In the foregoing sections, we unveiled a landscape marked by ebbs and flows. The language of FPS clauses differs from one treaty to another, sometimes explicitly mentioning 'physical' protection, other times referencing 'legal' security, and oftentimes employing the broader term 'full protection and security'. This diversity in wording has led to a rich tapestry of legal interpretations and debates.

At its core, the FPS standard embodies a principle of due diligence rather than strict liability. Host states are expected to take reasonable measures to protect investments, with tribunals considering the state's resources, level of development, and other contextual circumstances when assessing compliance. This nuanced approach recognises the varying capacities of different nations to provide security.

81 ICSID Case No. ARB(AF)/11/2, Award, 4 April 2016, para. 632.
82 ICSID Case No. ARB/07/17, Award, 21 June 2011, para. 334.

One of the most contentious aspects of FPS interpretation revolves around its scope. Does it extend beyond physical security to encompass legal and regulatory protection? Arbitral tribunals have grappled with this question, reaching divergent conclusions. Some favour a broad interpretation that includes legal security, while others adhere to a more traditional view limiting FPS to physical protection.

As has been noted, several landmark cases have shaped our understanding of FPS. *The AAPL v Sri Lanka* case set an early precedent, emphasising the importance of context in assessing a state's protective measures. *Wena Hotels v Egypt* further refined the concept, outlining factors for determining whether a state has met its FPS obligations. In the Caribbean context, *Peter Allard v Barbados* demonstrated how a state's reasonable efforts to address environmental concerns could satisfy the FPS standard.

Adding another layer of complexity, some investors have attempted to leverage MFN clauses to import more favourable FPS provisions from other treaties. This strategy has met with mixed success, highlighting the interconnected nature of treaty provisions and the potential for unexpected interpretations. For Caribbean nations, often parties to multiple BITs, the evolving interpretation of FPS clauses carries significant implications. These countries must balance the need to attract foreign investment with the preservation of policy flexibility and regulatory space. The ongoing debates surrounding FPS underscore the importance of careful treaty drafting and a comprehensive understanding of potential arbitral interpretations.

II. THE UMBRELLA CLAUSE

The umbrella clause is arguably one of the most controversial standards of protection in international investment law.[83] This is because, depending on the approach adopted by the

83 *Continental v Argentina*, ICSID Case No. ARB/03/9, Award, 5 September 2008, para. 296:

> The Tribunal is conscious that the interpretation of umbrella clauses, such as the one found in Art. II (2)(c) of the BIT, remains controversial and that there is a lack of consistency in the practice of investment arbitral tribunals on the matter.

For commentary and critique, see Anthony C Sinclair, 'The origins of the umbrella clause in the international law of investment protection' (2004) 20(4) *Arbitration International* 411; Stephan W Schill, 'Enabling Private Ordering: Function, Scope and Effect of Umbrella Clauses in International Investment Treaties' (2009) 18 *Minnesota Journal of International Law* 1; Jarrod Wong, 'Umbrella Clauses in Bilateral Investment Treaties: Of Breaches of Contract, Treaty Violations, and the Divide Between Developing and Developed Countries in Foreign Investment Disputes' (2006) 14 *George Mason Law Review* 135; Katia Yannaca-Small, 'Interpretation of the Umbrella Clause in Investment Agreements' (OECD working papers on international investment, 2006) 03; Thomas W Wälde, 'The "Umbrella" Clause in Investment Arbitration: A Comment on Original Intentions and Recent Cases' (2005) 6(2) *Journal of World Investment & Trade* 183; Katherine Jonckheere, 'Practical Implications from an Expansive Interpretation of Umbrella Clauses in International Investment Law' (2014) 11 *South Carolina Journal of International Law & Business* 143; Jonathan B Potts, 'Stabilizing the Role of Umbrella Clauses in Bilateral Investment Treaties: Intent, Reliance, and Internationalization' (2010) 51 *Virginia Journal of International Law* 1005; Kartika Paramita, 'Much in Little: The Umbrella Clause that Changes the International Investment Protection Standard' (2020) 6(1) *Hasanuddin Law Review* 25; Gregorio Salatino, 'Overview of Umbrella Clauses' (2012) 13 *Business Law International* 51; Elisabeth Meurling and Bart Volders, 'Umbrella Clauses in International Investment Litigation' (2007) 2 *European Public-Private Partnership Law Review* 80; Zachary Douglas, 'The Umbrella Clause Revisited' (2023) 38(2) *ICSID Review-Foreign Investment Law Journal* 472; Katherine Jonckheere, 'Practical Implications from an Expansive Interpretation of Umbrella Clauses in International Investment Law' (2015) 11(2) *South Carolina Journal of International Law and*

tribunal in question, there could be a blurring of the lines between ordinary contractual breaches and treaty breaches.

In principle, states are obliged under international law to observe their undertakings. This is part of the duty of good faith and the principle of *pacta sunt servanda*. This is the essence of an umbrella clause, which first appeared in 1959 in the context of the *Ab-Shawcross Draft Convention on Investments Abroad*.[84] The umbrella clause in that instrument stipulated that:

> [e]ach Party shall at all times ensure the observance of any undertakings which it may have given in relation to investments made by nationals of any other Party.[85]

This provision's purpose was intended to ensure that a state's unilateral violation of a concession contract that relates to foreign investment would be deemed to constitute an international wrong.[86] In this connection, Sinclair has argued that:

Business 5; Omolade Adeyemi Oniyinde and Tosin Ezekiel Ayo, 'The Protection of Energy Investments under Umbrella Clauses in Bilateral Investment Treaties: A Myth or a Reality' (2017) 61 *Journal of Law, Policy and Globalization* 161; Adkham Rajabov, 'Application Of The Umbrella Article Rule In Bilateral Investment Agreements International Practice' (2021) 3(12) *American Journal of Political Science Law and Criminology* 68; Kamal Ghobadi, 'Analysis of Legal Effects of Umbrella Clauses on Bilateral Foreign Investment Treaties' (n.d.) 8 *Public International Law* 246; Lee Carroll, 'What Place Does an Umbrella Clause Have in the New Generation of Bilateral Investment Treaties?' (2023) 40(2) *Journal of International Arbitration*; Heikki Marjosola, 'Public/Private Conflict in Investment Treaty Arbitration–a Study on Umbrella Clauses' (2009) 3(1) *Helsinki Law Review* 103; Hee-Moon Jo, 'Interpretation of the Umbrella Clause in Investment Treaties' (2009) 19 *Journal of Arbitration Studies* 95; Tang Sisi, 'The Endangered Umbrella Clause: To Save It or to Leave It' (2019) 9 *Journal of WTO and China* 92; Alperen Afşin Gözlügöl, 'The Effects of Umbrella Clauses: Their Relevance in Interpretation and in Practice' (2020) 21(4) *Journal of World Investment & Trade* 558; Krithika Radhakrishnan and Ritwik Mukherjee, 'Umbrella Clauses in International Investment Arbitration: Adopting a Narrow or Broad Interpretation for Mutual Protection of Investors and Host States' (2014) 4 *NLIU Law Review* 386; Tarcisio Gazzini and Attila Tanzi, 'Handle with care: Umbrella clauses and MFN treatment in investment arbitration' (2013) 14(6) *Journal of World Investment & Trade* 978; Jaemin Lee, 'Putting a Square Peg into a Round Hole? Assessment of the "Umbrella Clause" from the Perspective of Public International Law' (2015) 14(2) *Chinese Journal of International Law* 341; J O Voss, 'The Umbrella Clause' in *The Impact of Investment Treaties on Contracts between Host States and Foreign Investors* (Brill Nijhoff 2011); Taida Begic Sarkinovic, 'Umbrella Clauses and Their Policy Implications' (2011) 24 *Hague Yearbook of International Law* 313; Tavakkol Habibzadeh and Afifeh Gholami, 'The Role of Umbrella Clause in Settlement of Foreign Investor and Host State Disputes in the Light of ICSID Arbitral Jurisprudence' (2018) 35(59) *International Law Review* 85; Aslı Bayata Canyaş, 'How to Interpret Umbrella Clauses in Bilateral Investment Treaties: Different Perspectives and Solutions' (2023) 9(4) *International Journal of Public Law and Policy* 418–28; Bjørn Kunoy, 'Singing in the Rain: Developments in the Interpretation of Umbrella Clauses' (2006) 7(2) *Journal of World Investment & Trade* 275; Elnur Karimov, 'Umbrella Clauses within Energy Charter Treaty' (2018) 4 *Baku State University Law Review* 80; Leonardo Carpentieri, 'Contractual Claims Versus Treaty Claims in Investor-State Disputes: Do Umbrella Clauses Have a Future?' in *Commercial Contract Law and Arbitration* (Routledge); Raúl Pereira de Souza Fleury, 'Umbrella Clauses: A Trend Towards Its Elimination' (2015) 31(4) *Arbitration International* 679; Shotaro Hamamoto, 'Parties to the "Obligations" in the Obligations Observance ("Umbrella") Clause' (2015) 30(2) *ICSID Review-Foreign Investment Law Journal* 449.

84 H Abs and H Shawcross, 'Draft Convention on Investments Abroad' (1960) *Journal of Pubic Law* 115. See, also, Georg Schwarzenberger, 'The Abs-Shawcross Draft Convention on Investments Abroad: A Critical Commentary' (1960) 9 *Journal of Pubic Law* 147.

85 ibid Article II, 1959.

86 Anthony Sinclair, 'The Origins of the Umbrella Clause in the International Law of Investment Protection' (2004) 20(4) *Arbitration International* 411.

> The purpose of the clause is to dispel whatever doubts may possibly exist as to whether a unilateral violation of a concession contract is an international wrong . . . . [It thus] served two purposes: it involved an undertaking that the state would not interfere with contractual arrangements made with foreign investors and crucially, when coupled with compulsory dispute settlement provisions, it would create a remedy for breach of that obligation in international law where one did not exist in municipal law.[87]

In the same year, 1959, the umbrella clause made its way into the first-known BIT between Germany and Pakistan.[88] It read as follows:

> [e]ither Party shall observe any other obligation it may have entered into with regard to investments by nationals or companies of the other Party.[89]

The next citing of the umbrella clause was in 1967, when the Organization for Economic Cooperation and Development (OECD) recommended to its member states a draft Convention on the Protection of Foreign Property[90] as both a model for their bilateral investment treaties and as a general statement of international law rules applicable to foreign investment. Article 2 of that instrument, under the heading, 'Observance and Undertakings', stipulated similar language to the abovementioned Germany-Pakistan BIT. Commenting on the effect of this provision, Elihu Lauterpacht argued that the umbrella clause 'puts [investor-State contracts] on a special plane in that breach of them becomes immediately a breach of convention'.[91] Sinclair, in reflecting on the preparatory work for the OECD Draft, similarly explained that:

> There is no suggestion in the preparatory work for the OECD Draft (or the Abs-Shawcross Draft) or the commentaries thereon, that the undertakings referred to in the umbrella clause should be limited only to other international obligations. To limit the scope of the umbrella clause only to a host state's other obligations arising in international law would add nothing to the existing state of international law. The consistent understanding of commentators and drafters alike is that while the umbrella clause probably did cover international obligations, the focus of the umbrella clause was contractual obligations and unilateral commitments accepted by the host state with regard to foreign property.[92]

Apart from the Germany-Pakistan BIT, other early Model BITs drafted by both France and the United States adopted the umbrella clause using the same terminology as did the OECD's Draft Convention. Kenneth Vandevelde, who participated in the preparation of the US Model BIT and in the negotiation of several US BITs, explains that, pursuant to an umbrella clause:

> a party's breach of an investment agreement with an investor becomes a breach of the BIT, for which the investor or its state may seek a remedy under the investor-to-state or state-to-state

87 ibid 420.

88 Treaty for the Promotion and Protection of Investments, with Protocol and Exchange of Notes (Germany–Pakistan) (signed 25 November 1959, entry into force 28 April 1962) 457 UNTS 23.

89 ibid Article 7.

90 OECD, Resolution of the Council on the Draft Convention on the Protection of Foreign Property, OECD/LEGAL/0084.

91 Elihu Lauterpacht, 'Drafting of Conventions for the Protection of Investment' (1962) 3 *International and Comparative Law Quarterly* 218, 229.

92 Sinclair (n 86) 411, 428.

> disputes procedures. In effect this clause authorizes use of the BIT's disputes procedures to enforce investment agreements between the investor and the host state.[93]

More recently, the United Nations Conference on Trade and Development (UNCTAD) has noted that the existence of an umbrella clause in a BIT means that 'violations of commitments regarding investment by the host country would be redressable through the dispute settlement procedures of a BIT'.[94] In the same vein, the United Nations Centre on Transnational Corporations likewise concluded that an umbrella clause

> makes the respect of such contracts [between the host State and the investor] . . . an obligation under the treaty. Thus, the breach of such a contract by the host State would engage its responsibility under the agreement and – unless direct dispute settlement procedures come into play – entitle the home State to exercise diplomatic protection of the investor.[95]

In the Caribbean context, several regional IIAs contain umbrella clauses[96] in terms similar to Article 10(2) of the Belize-El Salvador BIT (2001):

> Each Party shall observe any obligation it may have *entered into* with regard to investments of investors of the other Party.

Only one regional BIT adopts a slightly different wording, namely Article 10(2) of the Guyana-Switzerland BIT (2005):

> Each Contracting Party shall observe any obligation it has *assumed* with regard to investments in its territory by investors of the other Contracting Party.

A. Constituent Elements of the Cause of Action

(i) There Must be an Obligation

An investor wishing to establish that a state has breached the umbrella clause must first prove that the state owes an obligation toward it. According to the tribunal in *JSW Solar v Czech*

93 Kenneth Vandevelde, *United States Investment Treaties: Policy and Practice* (Kluwer 1992). See, also, Wong (n 83) 135, 143 (noting that the purpose of the umbrella clause

> is to create an inter-state obligation to observe investment agreements that investors may enforce when the BIT confers a direct right of recourse to arbitration. More specifically, the history of the umbrella clause makes clear that it was designed to allow for any breach of a relevant investment contract to be resolved under the treaty in an international forum.)

94 UNCTAD, *Bilateral Investment Treaties in the Mid-1990s* (UNCTAD 1998) 56.

95 United Nations Centre on Transnational Corporations, *Bilateral Investment Treaties* (UNCTC 1988) 39.

96 Antigua and Barbuda-UK BIT, Article 2(2); Barbados-Belgium-Luxembourg Agreement, Article 2(4); Barbados-Cuba BIT, Article 2(2); Barbados-Switzerland BIT, Article 11; Barbados-Venezuela BIT, Article 2(2); Barbados-China BIT, Article 10(2); Belize-El Salvador BIT, Article 10(2); Belize-The Netherlands BIT, Article 3(4); Dominica-UK BIT, Article 2(2); Grenada-UK BIT, Article 2(2); Grenada-US BIT, Article II(2); Guyana-Switzerland BIT, Article 10(2); Jamaica-The Netherlands BIT, Article 3(4); Jamaica-USA BIT, Article II(2)(c); St Lucia-UK BIT, Article 2(2); Trinidad and Tobago-Germany BIT, Article 3(3); Trinidad and Tobago-Switzerland BIT, Article 10(2); Trinidad and Tobago-UK BIT, Article 4.

Republic,[97] for the umbrella clause to 'come into operation, the Contracting Party must first be obliged to do something. If there is no obligation, *a fortiori*, there can be no breach.'[98] On the facts of that case, the claimant had not established that there was any firm, unconditional undertaking, whether contractual or not, to provide state aid. The tribunal noted that an obligation to provide aid would have required the establishment of a clear, unconditional commitment which would specify its essential terms, including the amount of aid, the date to be provided and so on. However, no such obligation was proven by the claimant here. In its view, an encouragement by the state to an investor to apply for aid or an expectation by an investor that aid would be provided was not sufficient by itself to constitute an obligation to provide aid.

Meanwhile, in *Burlington Resources v Ecuador*,[99] the tribunal articulated the following test when interpreting whether an obligation is owed:

> The word 'obligation' is thus the operative term of the umbrella clause. The BIT does not define 'obligation'. The Parties agree – and rightly so – that the clause refers to legal obligations. This is of little assistance, however, to resolve the question of privity. To answer this question, the Tribunal relies primarily on two elements which in its view inform the ordinary meaning of 'obligation'. First, in its ordinary meaning, the obligation of one subject is generally seen in correlation with the right of another. Or, differently worded, someone's breach of an obligation corresponds to the breach of another's right. An obligation entails a party bound by it and another one benefiting from it, in other words, entails an obligor and an obligee. Second, an obligation does not exist in a vacuum. It is subject to a governing law. Although the notion of obligation is used in an international BIT, the court or tribunal interpreting the BIT may have to look to municipal law to give it content. This is not peculiar to 'obligation'; it applies to other notions found in investment treaties, e.g. nationality, property, exhaustion of local remedies to name just these. In this case, the PSCs are governed by Ecuadorian law. It is that law that defines the content of the obligation including the scope of and the parties to the undertaking, i.e. the obligor and the oblige.[100]

Tribunals have, in general, taken the view that the obligation being relied upon by the investor must be specific,[101] and not general in nature. For example, the tribunal in *WNC Factoring*

97 PCA Case No. 2014–03, Award, 11 October 2017.

98 ibid 464.

99 ICSID Case No. ARB/08/5, Decision on Liability, 14 December 2012.

100 ibid 214.

101 *Micula v Romania*, ICSID Case No. ARB/05/20, Award 11 December 2013, para. 415. The tribunal agreed with the tribunal in *Eureko v Poland* that the term '"any" obligations is capacious; it means not only obligations of a certain type, but "any" – that is to say, all – obligations entered into with regard to investments of investors of the other Contracting Party'. The obligation must be specific. Thus, the umbrella clause in this BIT covers obligations of any nature, regardless of their source, provided that they are indeed "obligations" entered into with a particular investor 'with regard to his or her investment'. On the facts, however, there was no obligation under Romanian law to maintain the claimed tax and related incentives through 1 April 2009 with respect to the claimants, such that there was no violation of the BIT's umbrella clause. See, also, e.g. FA Mann, 'British Treaties for the Promotion and Protection of Investments' (1981) 52 *British Yearbook of International Law* 246 (explaining that an umbrella clause

> only covers an obligation arising from a particular commitment either of the Contracting Parties may have entered into. . . . What is assumed is that the State has entered into a particular commitment which imposes obligations. Such obligations may arise from contract with the State or from the terms of the licence granted by it. It may be express or implied, it may be in writing or oral. But it must be clearly ascertainable as an obligation of the State itself arising from its own commitments. No difficulty occurs where the contract is made with the State itself – and the term may fairly be said to comprise its instrumentalities, even if they are separate legal entities, as well as companies of which it is the sole shareholder. But where the contract

Ltd v Czech Republic[102] concluded that:

> the requisite elements of an undertaking to be observed under international law are a specific, clear, and direct commitment from a State to an identified beneficiary. It is not sufficient, for example, that there be a general policy, a generic statement of principle, a general legal principle, or a municipal law of universal application (which would not include a law specifically identified to provide foreign investment with protections or a law formalizing a concession agreement).[103]

Similarly, in *Baywa v Spain*,[104] the tribunal considered that:

> the umbrella clause in the last sentence of Article 10.1 of the ECT only applies to obligations specifically entered into by the host State with the investor or the investment. The paradigm case is an obligation under an investment contract duly entered into. By contrast, the Tribunal does not accept that obligations arising under the general law, including legislation, of the host State, fall within the scope of the clause. When enacting legislation, the State establishes binding rules of conduct, but it does not make specific promises to each person entitled to claim under the law, nor does it enter into obligations to specific investors or their investments even when these entities are numbered among the beneficiaries of the law. A general law is not a promise.[105]

Other tribunals,[106] including the tribunal in *Oxus Gold v Uzbekistan*,[107] have suggested that obligations contained in the Laws on Foreign Investments are general obligations not

is made with a private person, then the provision only applies if and in so far as an obligation of the State arising from its own particular commitment (as opposed to existing general legislation) may be discerned. Thus, if the law of the land provides that the State is liable for the torts of its servants this is not an 'obligation arising from a particular commitment' the State may have entered into and may be changed, though in certain circumstances this may become subject to the provisions about expropriation.).

102 PCA Case No. 2014–34, Award, 22 February 2017.

103 ibid 322.

104 ICSID Case No. ARB/15/16 Decision on Jurisdiction, Liability and Directions on Quantum, 2 December 2019.

105 ibid 442.

106 *Philip Morris v Uruguay,* ICSID Case No. ARB/10/7, Award, 8 July 2016, para. 480. Proceeding from the proposition that the treaty's umbrella clause in Article 11 would protect contractual commitments made by the state, but not general obligations imposed by the law of the host state, the tribunal concluded: Uruguay entered into no commitment 'with respect to the investment' by granting a trademark. It did not actively agree to be bound by any obligation or course of conduct; it simply allowed the investor to access the same domestic IP system available to anyone eligible to register a trademark.

As a result, the investor's claim failed. On the other end of the spectrum, however, some tribunals have adopted the approach that the umbrella clause covers obligations arising from the state's legal framework. This view finds resonance in *LG&E v Argentina,* ICSID Case No. ARB/02/1, Decision on Liability, 3 October 2006, a case in which the claimant alleged that the respondent had breached the umbrella clause by failing to comply with the provisions of its Gas Law relating to the regulation of its tariff scheme. The tribunal found that Argentina's abrogation of the guarantees under the statutory framework, namely calculation of the tariffs in dollars before conversion to pesos, semi-annual tariff adjustments and no price controls without indemnification, violated its obligations under the umbrella clause. In the tribunal's view, Argentina made these specific obligations to foreign investors, such as LG&E, by enacting the Gas Law and other regulations, and then advertising these guarantees in the Offering Memorandum to induce the entry of foreign capital to fund the privatisation programme in its public service sector. These laws and regulations, according to the tribunal, became obligations within the meaning of the umbrella clause, by virtue of targeting foreign investors and applying specifically to their investments.

107 UNCITRAL, Award, 17 December 2015.

specifically entered into with investors such that they may not trigger a host state's liability under the umbrella clause. The tribunal in *El Paso v Argentina*[108] similarly noted that the umbrella clause only protects specific consensual obligations and not general obligations imposed by municipal law.

The restrictive approach countenanced by these tribunals to the question of whether obligations contained in foreign investment laws are covered by the umbrella clause has not received uncontroversial acceptance, however. In fact, in *Khan Resources v Mongolia*,[109] the tribunal considered the umbrella clause under the Energy Charter Treaty, which requires Contracting States to observe 'any obligations' entered into with a covered investor/investment, covered statutory obligations of the host state, and, more specifically, Mongolia's obligations laid down in its Foreign Investment Law. Without in-depth analysis, however, the tribunal simply held that 'a breach by Mongolia of any provision of the Foreign Investment Law would constitute a breach' of the ECT's umbrella clause.[110] Having found that Mongolia's actions breached the Foreign Investment Law, the tribunal ruled that the same conduct breached the ECT's umbrella clause.

It is submitted that the *Khan Resources* liberal approach is not defensible principally because the obligations included in a state's foreign investment laws are oftentimes couched in a high degree of generality, and only become specific to the investor or 'perfected' when the state subsequently agrees, whether expressly or impliedly, to accord the investor the obligations stipulated in the applicable foreign investment law. This is akin to the view taken in *Micula v Romania*,[111] a case in which the tribunal considered that EGO 24 created a general scheme of incentives available to investors who fulfilled certain requirements, which were later 'granted' to qualifying investors through a specific administrative Act (the PIC). In other words, the legislation created a generalised entitlement that could be claimed by qualifying investors, but this general entitlement later crystallised with respect to qualifying investors through the granting of the PICs, becoming from that moment on a specific entitlement with respect to specific investors. In short, the granting of the PIC was the moment at which a particular relationship between the Government and the investor was 'perfected': an investor could benefit from the privileges offered by the legislative framework only after having applied for a PIC, proved it fulfilled the requirements and received a favourable decision from the government in the form of a PIC. Only thereafter did the investor have the actual entitlement to the incentives, and only after that moment did it have the obligations established under EGO 24.

(ii) The Obligation must be owed to a Specific Investor

The Annulment Committee in *CMS v Argentina*[112] acknowledged that one of the necessary preconditions for establishing a breach of the umbrella clause is that the investor must prove that the obligation in issue was owed to it. In this connection, the Annulment Committee explained:

108 ICSID Case No. ARB/03/15, Award, 31 October 2011.

109 UNCITRAL Award, 2 March 2015.

110 ibid 295.

111 ICSID Case No. ARB/05/20, Award, 11 December 2013.

112 ICSID Case No. ARB/01/8, Decision of the ad hoc Committee on the Application for Annulment of the Argentine Republic, 25 September 2007.

> In speaking of 'any obligation it may have entered into with regard to investments', it seems clear that Article II(2)(c) is concerned with consensual obligations arising independently of the BIT itself (i.e. under the law of the host state or possibly under international law): Further they must be specific obligations concerning the investment. They do not cover general requirements imposed by the law of the host state. *Consensual obligations are not entered into erga omnes but with regard to particular persons.* Similarly, *the performance of such obligations or requirements occurs with regard to, and as between, obligor and oblige.*[113] (emphasis added)

A similar view was adopted in *Mobil v Argentina,*[114] a case in which the tribunal agreed with Argentina that the applicable umbrella clause concerned consensual obligations which were not entered into *erga omnes*, but regarding particular persons; these were specific obligations concerning the investment.

(iii) Obligation must have been owed by the State: Privity

Although there is no consensus on this requirement,[115] the dominant view appears to be that in respect of contractual obligations owed to investors by host states, only parties entitled to enforce these obligations under the proper law of the contract may sue. This necessarily invites consideration of the contractual principle of privity, particularly in relation to parent companies which, as investors, claim that their subsidiaries operating in the host state have suffered prejudice as a result of the state's failure to comply with some obligation owed to them.

This issue was considered in *WNC Factoring Ltd v Czech Republic.*[116] Here, the tribunal noted that under international law, merely because a state may owe an obligation to observe an undertaking given to a company does not mean that the state also owes that same obligation to observe the undertaking to that company's shareholders, unless there are specific transfer provisions, such as in agreements to extend the benefit of the undertaking to shareholders, affiliates, heirs or assignees.

Meanwhile, in *Azurix v Argentina,*[117] the tribunal considered whether it had jurisdiction under the umbrella clause in the US-Argentina BIT to consider obligations arising from a concession agreement concluded between the claimant's subsidiary and the Provence of Buenos Aires. In this connection, it noted:

> none of the contractual claims as such refer to a contract between the parties to these proceedings; neither the Province [of Buenos Aires] nor ABA are parties to them. While Azurix may submit a claim under the BIT for breaches by Argentina, there is no undertaking to be honored by Argentina to Azurix other than the obligations under the BIT.[118]

113 ibid 95.

114 ICSID Case No. ARB/04/16, Award, 25 February 2016).

115 Fleury de Souza and Raúl Pereira, 'Treaty-protected Investment Agreements: Of Umbrella Clauses and Privity of Contract' (2016) 23(2) *Willamette Journal of International Law and Dispute Resolution* 319. See, also, Jan Paulsson, 'Arbitration without Privity' (1995) 10 *ICSID-Investment Law Journal* 232.

116 PCA Case No. 2014–34, Award, 22 February 2017.

117 ICSID Case No. ARB/01/12, Award, 14 July 2006.

118 ibid 384.

A similar outcome was arrived at in *Oxus Gold v Uzbeldstan*,[119] in relation to an alleged breach of a contract concluded between Goskomgeology, a State Committee of Uzbekistan, and Marakand, a subsidiary of Oxus.

Regrettably, this area remains in a state of flux since the decision of *Continental v Argentina*,[120] a case in which the tribunal asserted:

> provided that these obligations have been entered 'with regard' to investments, they may have been entered with persons or entities other than foreign investors themselves, so that *an undertaking by the host State with a subsidiary such as CNA is not in principle excluded*.[121] (emphasis added)

Similarly, in *Michael Lee-Chin v Dominican Republic*,[122] the tribunal was tasked with interpreting Article V of the CARICOM-Dominica Republic FTA, which provided that 'each Party shall comply with its commitments regarding investment'. The claimant, a Jamaican national, alleged that the respondent breached the umbrella clause by failing to make adjustments to the tipping fees charged by Lajun for its waste disposal services. In his estimation, the Concession Agreement (as well as its amendments) required the ASDN to review and update Lajun's tipping fees from time to time, and that pursuant to the Second Amendment to the Concession Agreement, the ASDN agreed to increase the frequency with which it would review and modify the tipping fees received by Lajun from once a year to twice a year. Furthermore, the Concession Agreement and its amendments required that the ASDN employ its best efforts to assist Lajun in negotiating the tipping fees to be paid by the other municipalities of the state. The respondent, on the other hand, contended that the umbrella clause contained in Article V of Annex III was not applicable in this case because there was no contractual relationship between the claimant and respondent. In this case, argued the respondent, the Concession Agreement was entered into with a municipality, ASDN, not with the respondent, and it contained obligations undertaken exclusively by the ASDN and governed by Dominican law. In short, it was the respondent's view that contractual obligations entered into with a public entity other than the state could not be automatically attributed to the state.

The tribunal considered that although no contractual relationship between the claimant and the respondent existed, but rather one between the claimant and the ASDN and other municipalities, the conduct of organs other than the state (like the ASDN and municipalities in this case) was in principle attributable to the state in certain circumstances, as recognised by the ILC Draft Articles.

Relying on the *Strabag v Libya*[123] award, the tribunal in *Michael Lee-Chin* considered that where the language of the applicable umbrella clause does not evidence any limits, the state will be bound in circumstances where it contracts with an investor for public works, but thereafter breaches its commitments to the investor. On the facts of *Michael Lee-Chin*, the tribunal held that the municipalities' breach of their commitment was, at least partially, the consequence of a public policy decision made by the central government with respect

119 UNCITRAL, Award, 17 December 2015.
120 ICSID Case No. ARB/03/9, Award, 5 September 2008.
121 ibid 297.
122 ICSID Case No. UNCT/18/3, Award, 6 October 2023.
123 ICSID Case No. ARB(AF)/15/1, Award, 29 June 2020.

to budgetary allocations, hence rejecting the respondent's first objection related to the non-application of the umbrella clause due to a lack of privity.

A second argument raised by the respondent was that the Concession Agreement itself contained a dispute settlement clause, and that this should accordingly prevent the tribunal from exercising jurisdiction over the umbrella clause. In the tribunal's view, however, the presence of such a clause does not automatically nor necessarily result in a state being able to avoid its international obligations:

> In the Tribunal's view, once the umbrella clause is deemed applicable, the contractual dispute settlement clauses are irrelevant to the claims covered by the umbrella clause, as these are Treaty-based claims and therefore fall within the Tribunal's jurisdiction. But, even if this were not the understanding (as seems to be the case in the argument advanced by Respondent), the exclusivity of the contractual clause — which is very commonly found in this type of contract — would, in the Tribunal's opinion, be only one of the factors to be taken into account, in conjunction with others, of no lesser relevance. These include, in general, the availability of the exclusive forum designated in the agreement, the potential for parallel proceedings, the use of available resources by the State, its general attitude towards the investment and the investor, as well as the nature of the contractual obligations in question.[124]
>
> In the case at hand, in the Tribunal's opinion, the last two factors mentioned would be particularly relevant. Indeed, it is clear to the Tribunal that the obligations undertaken by Respondent through the Concession Agreement and its amendments refer to matters closely connected with essential public policies, instead of complying with the obligation to review and update the tipping fees that it itself acknowledged through various means to be inadequate, Respondent sent contradictory messages throughout the duration of the investment.[125]

Against this backdrop, the tribunal considered that the contractual obligations in issue were covered by the umbrella clause of the Treaty, and these obligations were breached. More pointedly, (i) the lack of revision and modification of the tipping fees, and (ii) the constant obstruction of the operation and management of the landfill in violation of the exclusive right to manage, administer, maintain, and operate the Duquesa Landfill were held to have been contractual provisions whose violations were elevated to treaty breaches.

It is submitted that the tribunal was correct in finding that the absence of direct contractual privity between the state and the investor did not automatically prevent the application of the umbrella clause, and that, in this connection, tribunals should examine whether the state entity with which the investor contracted was exercising quintessential government or policy powers. That said, we are concerned by the slight treatment afforded the exclusive jurisdiction clause included in the Concession Contract. It is submitted that greater weight should have been afforded this clause, as it evidenced the parties' intention to have ensuing disputes resolved through processes other than international arbitration. The parties in question were in relatively equal bargaining positions, and the claimant, having taken due diligence steps, should have accounted for the implications of this exclusive jurisdiction clause; were a BIT not in place, would the investor not have had to utilise the options agreed to in the exclusive jurisdiction clause? Our further concern is that the FTA, having been concluded by states parties years before the Concession Contract, lacks the specificity

124 *Michael Anthony Lee-Chin v Dominican Republic*, ICSID Case No. UNCT/18/3, Award, 6 October 2023, para. 513.

125 ibid 514.

compared to as it were the *lex specialis* that was the Concession Contract; had the parties wished for international arbitration to be pursued, they should have provided for this or at least referenced the relevant concession contract.

(iv) The Obligation must have been with Regard to Investments

In *Continental v Argentina*,[126] the tribunal asserted that the investor cannot seek to invoke any and every obligation purportedly owed by the host state as the basis for a claim under the umbrella clause. Rather, the investor must show a causal link between the obligation in question and their investments. In the tribunal's view:

> the covered obligations must have been entered 'with regard to' investments. Thus, they must concern one or more investments and, moreover, must address them with some degree of specificity. They are not limited to obligations based on a contract. Finally, provided that these obligations have been entered 'with regard' to investments, they may have been entered with persons or entities other than foreign investors themselves, so that an undertaking by the host State with a subsidiary such as CNA is not in principle excluded.[127]

(v) Breach

The obligation owed by the state to the investor must have been breached, referred to in international law as *puissance publique.* In this connection, the tribunal in *Impregilo v Pakistan*[128] explored the nature of breaches that would engage the state's international responsibility in the following terms:

> In fact, the State or its emanation, may have behaved as an ordinary contracting party having a difference of approach, in fact or in law, with the investor. In order that the alleged breach of contract may constitute a violation of the BIT, it must be the result of behaviour going beyond that which an ordinary contracting party could adopt. Only the State in the exercise of its sovereign authority ('puissance publique'), and not as a contracting party, may breach the obligations assumed under the BIT. In other words, the investment protection treaty only provides a remedy to the investor where the investor proves that the alleged damages were a consequence of the behaviour of the Host State acting in breach of the obligations it had assumed under the treaty.[129]

The case of *Garanti Koza v Turkmenistan*[130] illustrates the circumstances in which a breach of the umbrella clause may occur. Here, Turkmenistan's insistence on Smeta invoicing effectively forced Garanti Koza to choose between submitting accurate invoices, and consequently accepting less compensation than it had bargained for or manipulating its invoices in order to receive the full compensation that the state had agreed to pay. The tribunal considered that using governmental power to put an investor in such a situation was fundamentally unfair; the state's behaviour represented a failure by Turkmenistan to observe the obligations owed to Garanti Koza undertaken in the context of the contract between the parties, in breach of the umbrella clause under the BIT in question.

126 ICSID Case No. ARB/03/9, Award, 5 September 2008.
127 ibid 297.
128 ICSID Case No. ARB/03/3, Decision on Jurisdiction, 22 April 2005.
129 ibid 260.
130 ICSID Case No. ARB/11/20, Award, 19 December 2016.

An investor must show that it is actually the state that has breached the relevant obligation in question. This may be accomplished through a showing of direct causation or through attribution of liability. Thus, in *Tulip Real Estate v Turkey*,[131] the tribunal concluded that the conduct of Emlak, a Turkish real estate investment trust, in unilaterally terminating the contract for a mixed-use residential and commercial real estate development project in Istanbul in which the claimant held interests, was not attributable to the state under Article 5 of the ILC Articles, since none of the conduct in question amounted to the exercise of governmental (i.e. sovereign) power. In the tribunal's view, the conduct was not carried out under the instructions, direction or control of the state in pursuit of a sovereign purpose.

Meanwhile, in *Alpha Projektholding GMBH v Ukraine*,[132] the events giving rise to the claim arose out of a series of commercial arrangements involving the claimant, the Hotel Dnipro, and other parties regarding the reconstruction and renovation of several floors of the Hotel. The claimant argued that the temporary suspension of payments under the agreements regarding the reconstruction and renovation of floors 11–12; the transformation of the Hotel from a State-owned enterprise into a state-owned open joint stock company; the transfer of management of the Hotel to the State Administration of Affairs; and the cessation of payments to the claimant amounted to a breach of the umbrella clause. The tribunal, however, held that the contracts were between the claimant and the Hotel, not between the claimant and the respondent. The tribunal further concluded that the Hotel was not acting as an organ of the state when it entered into the contracts. Consequently, the respondent assumed no contractual obligations with respect to claimant, and thus did not violate Article 8(2) of the applicable BIT.

EFFECT OF BREACH

Yet another area of contention in respect of the application of the umbrella clause is its effect. Does it elevate/transform contractual breaches into treaty breaches? Does it apply only when the state is acting in its sovereign capacity or when it is acting both in its sovereign and contractual capacity? Different tribunals take very different approaches on this question.

On the one hand, the tribunal in *SGS v Paraguay*[133] noted that there was nothing in Article 11 of the Paraguay-Switzerland BIT that stated or implied that a government would only fail to observe its commitments if it abuses its sovereign authority. Accordingly, it considered that if the respondent failed to observe any of its contractual commitments, it would be in breach of Article 11 and no further examination of whether the respondent's actions were properly characterised as 'sovereign' or 'commercial' in nature was necessary.

Meanwhile, in *Noble Ventures v Romania*,[134] the tribunal held that Article II(2)(c) of the US-Romania BIT had the effect of 'transform[ing] contractual undertakings into international law obligations and accordingly a breach of the BIT'.[135] After analysing the plain language and purpose of the umbrella clause, as well as arbitral precedent, the tribunal concluded that:

131 ICSID Case No. ARB/11/28, Award, 10 March 2014.
132 ICSID Case No. ARB/07/16, Award, 8 November 2010.
133 ICSID Case No. ARB/07/29, Award, 10 February 2012.
134 ICSID Case No. ARB/01/11, Award, 12 October 2005.
135 ibid 46.

> An umbrella clause is usually seen as transforming municipal law obligations into obligations directly cognizable in international law . . .
>
> [T]wo States may include in a bilateral investment treaty a provision to the effect that, in the interest of achieving the objects and goals of the treaty, the host State may incur international responsibility by reason of a breach of its contractual obligations towards the private investor of the other Party, the breach of contract being thus 'internationalized', i.e., assimilated to a breach of the treaty. In such a case, an international tribunal will be bound to seek to give useful effect to the provision that the parties have adopted.[136]

Similarly, the *LG&E v Argentina,*[137] tribunal held that the umbrella clause requires host states to comply with their contractual and legal obligations while providing foreign investors with an international remedy for the resolution of such disputes:

> an 'umbrella clause' is a general provision included in a fairly large number of bilateral treaties that creates a requirement for the host State to meet its obligations towards foreign investors, including those that derive from a contract. Hence such obligations receive extra protection by virtue of their consideration under the bilateral treaty.[138]

Several other tribunals have confirmed that the umbrella clause refers not only to statutory, but contractual obligations,[139] and, in this connection, may elevate a breach of a contractual obligation into a breach of a treaty.

On the other hand, however, other tribunals have taken the view that there is a clear delineation between the state acting in its sovereign capacity and it acting in its contractual capacity, and that umbrella clauses do not elevate contractual breaches to treaty breaches. The leading case on this point is *SGS v Pakistan.*[140] Here, the tribunal, having examined the umbrella clause contained in the Switzerland–Pakistan BIT, rejected SGS's claim that the clause had the effect of entitling the investor to, notwithstanding the existence of a valid contractual forum selection clause, 'elevate' its contract claims to claims grounded on the BIT, thereby allowing it to bring such contract claims to the ICSID tribunal. It noted that to read umbrella provisions as suggested by SGS – i.e. to be 'so far-reaching in scope, and so automatic and unqualified and sweeping in their operation, [and] so burdensome in their potential impact upon a Contracting Party' – there should be 'clear and convincing evidence' that that was what the parties had intended.[141] Because SGS had adduced no such evidence of intent, its asserted interpretation of the umbrella clause failed. That said, the

136 ibid 53.

137 ICSID Case No. ARB/02/1, Decision on Liability, 3 October 2006.

138 ibid 170.

139 *Al-Bahloul v Tajikistan* SCC Case No. V (064/2008), Award, 8 June 2010 confirmed that the umbrella clause in the ECT 'is broadly stated, referring as it does to "any obligation" and, as such, by the ordinary meaning of the words, includes both statutory and contractual obligations'. In *Plama v Bulgaria,* ICSID Case No. ARB/03/24, Award, 27 August 2008 the tribunal analysed the ordinary meaning of the term 'any obligation' in the last sentence of Article 10(1) of the ECT and concluded that its wide ambit encompassed 'any obligation regardless of its nature, i.e. whether it be contractual or statutory'. In *Khan Resources v Mongolia,* UNCITRAL Award, 2 March 2015, the tribunal held that a breach by Mongolia of any provision of its Foreign Investment Law would constitute a breach of the ECT's umbrella clause. The tribunal concluded that Mongolia had breached its Foreign Investment Law and was therefore 'liable towards the Investor through operation of the umbrella clause'.

140 ICSID Case No. ARB/01/13, Decision of the Tribunal on Objections to Jurisdiction, 6 August 2003.

141 ibid 167.

tribunal appeared to leave open the door to the possibility of a treaty provision elevating contractual breaches to treaty breaches, noting that 'Article 11 of the BIT would have to be considerably more specifically worded before it can reasonably be read in the extraordinarily expansive manner submitted by the Claimant'.[142]

Meanwhile, the tribunal in *Hamester v Ghana*,[143] concurring with the approach taken in *Impregilo v Pakistan*, found that contracts concluded between an investor and a legal entity separate from the respondent state (in *Impregilo*, the Pakistan Water and Power Development Authority) do not fall within the scope of an umbrella clause. The tribunal explained that 'the consequence of an automatic and wholesale elevation of any and all contract claims into treaty claims risks undermining the distinction between national legal orders and international law'[144] and 'this is not a result that is in line with the general purpose of the ICSID/BIT mechanism for the international protection of foreign investments'.[145]

It is submitted that where an unqualified umbrella clause – 'any obligations' – is used, the natural and ordinary meaning of the words must be given effect to. In this connection, it accords with the natural and ordinary meaning to interpret such a provision as applying to not just commitments entered into by the state in its sovereign capacity, but also commitments entered into by it in its contractual capacity once these have been assumed in relation to the investment, and provided that the obligation in question is specific. It means, therefore, that where commitments are breached, whatever their source, their elevation to breaches of the state's international obligations should fortify the jurisdiction of tribunals to hear the relevant claims. This view accords with the sentiments expressed by the tribunal in *SGS v Philippines*,[146] when it considered the following matters in relation to the interpretation of umbrella clauses: first, a legal obligation (including, but not limited to, contractual commitments) must have been assumed vis-à-vis the specific investment (not as a matter of the application of some legal obligation of a general character, such as general municipal legislative or administrative or other unilateral measures of a Contracting Party);[147] and, second, 'non-binding domestic blandishments' are not converted into binding international obligations;[148] that is, questions of contract law are not converted into questions of treaty law. In other words, the umbrella clause does not address the scope of the commitments entered into with regard to specific investments, but the *performance* of these obligations, once they are ascertained.[149] It means therefore that while the umbrella clause applies to commitments or obligations arising under contracts entered into by the host state, a basic obligation on the state to pay what is due under a contract, which is an obligation assumed with regard to the specific investment (the performance of services an agreement) does not mean that the determination of how much money the state is obliged to pay becomes a treaty matter. The *extent* of the obligation is still governed by the contract, and it can only be determined by reference to the terms of the contract, whereas the fact of *performance* of the obligation may be elevated to a treaty matter.

142 ibid 171.
143 ICSID Case No. ARB/07/24, Award, 18 June 2010.
144 ibid 349.
145 ibid.
146 ICSID Case No. ARB/02/6, Decision of the Tribunal on Objections to Jurisdiction, 29 January 2004.
147 ibid 121.
148 ibid 126.
149 ibid 127.

This view also appears to be consistent with leading scholars in the field. For example, Professor Prosper Weil has argued that:

> [A]n 'umbrella treaty' between the contracting State and the State of the [investor] . . . turns the obligation to perform [a] contract into an international obligation of the contracting State vis-à-vis the State of the other contracting party. The intervention of the umbrella treaty transforms the contractual obligations thereby ensuring . . . 'the inviolability of the contract under threat of violating the treaty'; any non-performance of the contract, even if it is legal under the national law of the contracting State, gives rise to the international liability of the latter vis-à-vis the State of the other contracting party.[150]

Meanwhile, Professor Christoph Schreuer has explained that, pursuant to umbrella clauses, contractual violations may become treaty violations:

> [Umbrella clauses] have been added to some BITs to provide additional protection to investors beyond the traditional international standards. They are often referred to as umbrella clauses because they put contractual commitments under the BIT's protective umbrella. They add the compliance with investment contracts, or other undertakings of the host State, to the BIT's substantive standards. In this way, a violation of such a contract becomes a violation of the BIT.[151]

Dolzer and Stevens similarly explain that umbrella clauses protect foreign investors against simple breaches of contract:

> [Umbrella clauses] seek to ensure that each Party to the treaty will respect specific undertakings towards nationals of the other Party. The provision is of particular importance because it protects the investor's contractual rights against any interference which might be caused by either a simple breach of contract . . . .[152]

Other commentators have noted that the umbrella clause would be devoid of all meaning if 'mere' breaches of contract were not actionable under it:

> Denying any effects of an umbrella clause on breaches of contractual obligations by the host state would mean the degradation of the clause to an empty phrase. If one took the view that in a BIT arbitration the tribunal is not allowed to take 'mere' breaches of contract into consideration, even if the BIT contains an umbrella clause, one would deprive the umbrella clause of any meaning . . . If a state has promised in a treaty – without reservation – to observe all obligations it has assumed towards investors of the other state, it appears difficult to argue that

150 Wong (n 83) 135, 147 (citing Stanimir Alexandrov, 'Breaches of Contract and Breaches of Treaty: The Jurisdiction of Treaty-based Arbitration Tribunals to Decide Breach of Contract Claims in *SGS v Pakistan* and *SGS v Philippines*' (2004) 5(4) *The Journal of World Investment & Trade* 566, 567 (quoting Prosper Weil, 'Problèmes relatifs aux contrats passés entre un Etat et un particulier' (1969) 128 *Recueil des cours/ Académie de Droit International de La Haye* 97, 130). See, also, Mann (n 101) 241, 246; JP Gaffney and JL Loftis, 'The "Effective Ordinary Meaning" of BITs and the Jurisdiction of Treaty-based Tribunals to Hear Contract Claims' (2007) 8(1) *Journal of World Investment and Trade* 5, 17 (citing E. Gaillard, 'Investment Treaty Arbitration and Jurisdiction over Contract Claims – The SGS Cases Considered' in Todd Weiler (ed), *International Investment Law and Arbitration: Leading Cases from the ICSID, NAFTA, Bilateral Treaties and Customary International Law* (Cameron May 2005).

151 Christoph Schreuer, 'Travelling the BIT Route: Of Waiting Periods, Umbrella Clauses and Forks in the Road' (2004) 5(2) *The Journal of World Investment & Trade* 245, 250.

152 R Dolzer and M Stevens, *Bilateral Investment Treaties* (Kluwer 1995) 81–82; See, also, Gaffney and Loftis (n 150) 5, 17 (citing GS Tawil, 'The Distinction Between Contract Claims and Treaty Claims: An Overview' paper presented at the 11th ICCA Congress, Montreal, Canada 2006) 53).

> the failure to comply with these contractual obligations would not automatically constitute a breach of the promise given in the BIT.[153]

Against the backdrop of the foregoing, if Caribbean governments are particularly concerned to limit the application of umbrella clauses, they must consider reforming their legal framework to omit said clauses, or issue joint interpretative notes that restrict the application of these clauses.

IMPORTING UMBRELLA CLAUSES VIA MFN CLAUSES

One of the most controversial aspects of extant arbitral practice relative to the umbrella clause is the extent to which an investor can utilise the MFN clause contained in a BIT concluded by its home country with the host country to import an umbrella clause found in another BIT(s) concluded by the host country and a third country where such clause is absent from the former BIT. Some tribunals adopt the approach that, to the extent that the wording of the MFN clause is clear or at least silent on its application to substantive investor protection standards found in BITs concluded between the host state and third countries, they are permitted to rely on the MFN clause to import the umbrella clause. By way of example, in *EDFI and Others v Argentine Republic*,[154] the tribunal allowed the claimants to rely on the MFN clause contained in the extant BIT to invoke the umbrella clause found in Article 10(2) of the Argentina-Luxembourg BIT and Article 7(2) of the Argentina-Germany BIT so as to challenge the state's alleged failure to respect explicit undertakings found in concession agreements. The tribunal considered that 'to ignore the MFN clause in this case would permit more favorable treatment to investors protected under third countries, which is exactly what the MFN Clause is intended to prevent.'[155]

On the other end of the spectrum, however, the tribunal in *İçkale İnşaat Limited Şirketi v Turkmenistan*[156] arrived at the opposite conclusion by applying an arguably dubious approach to interpretation. In this case, the tribunal, in rejecting the purported invocation of the MFN clause to import the umbrella clause contained in treaties concluded between the host state and third countries, ruled that:

> The terms 'treatment accorded in similar situations' therefore suggest that the MFN treatment obligation requires a comparison of the factual situation of the investments of the investors of the home State and that of the investments of the investors of third States, for the purpose of determining whether the treatment accorded to investors of the home State can be said to be less favorable than that accorded to investments of the investors of any third State. It follows that, given the limitation of the scope of application of the MFN clause to 'similar situations', it cannot be read, in good faith, to refer to standards of investment protection included in other investment treaties between a State party and a third State. The standards of protection included in other investment treaties create legal rights for the investors concerned, which may be more favorable in the sense of being additional to the standards included in the basic treaty, but such differences between applicable legal standards cannot be said to amount to 'treatment

153 H Schramke, 'The Interpretation of Umbrella Clauses in Bilateral Investment Treaties' (2007) 4 *Transnational Dispute Management* 1, 21–22.

154 ICSID Case No. ARB/03/2, Award, 11 June 2012.

155 ibid 932.

156 ICSID Case No. ARB/10/24, Award, 8 March 2016.

> accorded in similar situations', without effectively denying any meaning to the terms 'similar situations'. Investors cannot be said to be in a 'similar situation' merely because they have invested in a particular State; indeed, if the terms 'in similar situations' were to be read to coincide with the territorial scope of application of the treaty, they would not be given any meaning and would effectively become redundant as there would be no difference between the clause 'treatment no less favourable than that accorded in similar situations . . . to investments of investors of any third country' and 'treatment no less favourable than that accorded . . . to investments of investors of any third country'.[157]

It is submitted that the *İçkale İnşaat Limited Şirketi* tribunal's is misplaced, as it places the proverbial chicken before the eggs. More pointedly, the question of whether the MFN clause is capable of invoking the umbrella clause from other BITs is not one, at least at the initial stage, which is concerned with whether or not the investments and investors are in factually similar situations, but rather, first, whether the MFN clause is drafted broadly enough to encompass the substantive provision sought to be relied upon, i.e. the umbrella clause. If, for example, the MFN clause refers to treatment of investments, and imposes no delimitation in respect of its application such that it may be applied to the FET, FPS, or umbrella clause for that matter, tribunals would not be wrong to import the umbrella clause from the third-country BIT, and only then engage in the assessment as to whether or not the investments/investors are in like circumstances, and whether, in that light, the foreign investment/investor was treated less favourably compared to the third county investment/investor. In other words, the tribunal in *İçkale İnşaat Limited Şirketi* conflated the invocation of the umbrella clause via the MFN clause with the subsequent determination of whether the umbrella clause, having been imported, was breached.

SUMMARY

In the complex landscape of international investment law, few provisions have stirred as much debate as the enigmatic 'umbrella clause'. Born out of a desire to provide foreign investors with an extra layer of protection, these clauses have become a double-edged sword, simultaneously praised for their protective power and criticised for their potential to upset the delicate balance between investor rights and state sovereignty.

At their core, umbrella clauses aim to elevate a host state's obligations to an investor – be they contractual or otherwise – to the lofty heights of international treaty commitments. It is a seemingly simple concept with far-reaching implications. Imagine a world where a state's every promise to an investor, no matter how small, could potentially trigger international arbitration. This is the world that umbrella clauses have created, and it is a world that has left legal scholars, arbitrators, and policymakers grappling with tough questions.

The controversy surrounding these clauses runs deep. Some see them as a necessary safeguard in a world where investors often find themselves at the mercy of capricious state actions. Others view them as a Trojan horse, allowing savvy investors to bypass domestic courts and potentially undermine a state's ability to regulate in the public interest.

This divide is reflected in the wildly divergent interpretations of umbrella clauses by investment tribunals. Some tribunals have embraced a broad interpretation, effectively transforming any breach of a state's obligations to an investor into a treaty violation. Others

157 ibid 329.

have taken a more cautious approach, limiting the clause's application to cases where a state has clearly overstepped its sovereign bounds.

The debate does not end there. Questions of privity have further muddied the waters. Can a parent company claim a breach of an umbrella clause for wrongs done to its subsidiary? Some tribunals say yes, others no. The plot thickens when we consider the interaction between umbrella clauses and MFN provisions. Can an investor use an MFN clause to import a more favourable umbrella clause from another treaty? It's a legal puzzle that continues to perplex.

For states, the stakes are high. A broadly interpreted umbrella clause could significantly expand their liability, potentially chilling their ability to implement new regulations or respond to changing public needs. It is no wonder that some states are reconsidering their approach to these clauses, with some opting to omit them entirely from new treaties or issuing interpretative notes to clarify their intended scope.

III. THE FREE TRANSFER PROVISION (FTP)

Although rarely subject to critical examination in the existing literature,[158] nearly all Caribbean IIAs include express provisions on the free transfer of payments in connection with investments.[159] For example, Article 5 of the Antigua and Barbuda-Germany BIT (1998) provides:

> Each Contracting State shall guarantee to investors of the other Contracting State the free transfer of payments in connection with an investment, in particular

158 Marcin Menkes, 'Monetary Transfer Provisions and the Rule of Law from the International Investment Law Perspective' (2024) 8(1) *European Investment Law and Arbitration Review Online* 36: 'Despite their crucial importance for the realisation of foreign investment, and interpretation difficulties, they have not attracted much doctrinal attention to date'.

159 Antigua and Barbuda-UK BIT: Article 6; Barbados-Belgium-Luxembourg Economic Union Agreement; Barbados-Canada BIT: Article IX; Barbados-China BIT: Article 6; Barbados-Cuba BIT: Article 6; Barbados-Germany BIT: Article 5; Barbados-Mauritius BIT: Article 7; Barbados-Switzerland BIT: Article 4; Barbados-UK BIT: Article 6; Barbados-Venezuela BIT: Article 6; Belize-China BIT: Article 6; Belize-Cuba BIT: Article 6; Belize-El Salvador BIT: Article 6; Belize-Netherlands BIT: Article 5; Belize-UK BIT: Article 6; Dominica-Germany BIT: Article 5; Dominica-UK BIT: Article 7; Germany-Haiti BIT: Article 4; Grenada-UK BIT: Article 6; Grenada-USA BIT: Article IV; Guyana-Brazil BIT: Article 10; Guyana-China BIT: Article 6; Guyana-Germany BIT: Article 5; Guyana-South Korea BIT: Article 6; Guyana-Switzerland BIT: Article 5; Guyana-UK BIT: Article 6; Jamaica-Argentina BIT: Article 5; Jamaica-China BIT: Article 5; Jamaica-Egypt BIT: Article 6; Jamaica-Germany BIT: Article 5; Jamaica-Indonesia BIT: Article VI; Jamaica-South Korea BIT: Article 6; Jamaica-Switzerland BIT: Article 4; Jamaica-Netherlands BIT: Article 5; Jamaica-UK BIT: Article 7; Jamaica-USA BIT: Article IV; St Lucia-Germany BIT: Article 5; St Lucia-UK BIT: Article 6; SVG-Germany BIT: Article 5; SVG-Taiwan BIT: Article VII; Trinidad and Tobago-Canada BIT: Article IX; Trinidad and Tobago-China BIT: Article 7; Trinidad and Tobago-Cuba BIT: Article 8; Trinidad and Tobago-France BIT: Article 6; Trinidad and Tobago-Germany BIT: Article 7; Trinidad and Tobago-Guatemala BIT: Article 9; Trinidad and Tobago-India BIT: Article 7; Trinidad and Tobago-Korea BIT: Article 6; Trinidad and Tobago-Switzerland BIT: Article 5; Trinidad and Tobago-UK BIT: Article 8; Trinidad and Tobago-USA BIT: Article V. Note: most of these agreements allow for some restrictions on transfers in exceptional circumstances, like balance of payments difficulties. For example: the Jamaica-Indonesia BIT allows transfers to be phased over three years in periods of exceptional balance of payments difficulties; the Jamaica-Netherlands BIT allows Jamaica to limit transfers in cases of exceptional balance of payments difficulties, but guarantees a minimum transfer of 33 1/3% per year; the Jamaica-UK BIT guarantees a minimum transfer of 20% per year in cases of balance of payments difficulties.

(a) the principal and additional amounts to maintain or increase the investment;
(b) the returns;
(c) the repayment of loans;
(d) the proceeds from the liquidation or the sale of the whole or any· part of the investment;
(e) the compensation provided for in Article 4.

According to the tribunal in *Biwater Gauff v Tanzania*,[160] a provision of this nature is:

> not a guarantee that investors will have funds to transfer. It rather guarantees that if investors have funds, they will be able to transfer them, subject to the conditions stated in Article 6. The free transfer principle is aimed at measures that would restrict the possibility to transfer, such as currency control restrictions or other measures taken by the host State which effectively imprison the investors' funds, typically in the host State of the investment.[161]

Although there are slight variations in the wording used in the different regional IIAs that have been concluded to date, most IIAs contain the general guarantee with regard to the free transfer of investments and returns, followed by an itemized listing of what constitute investments and returns, which is then followed by exceptions carved out by the Contracting Parties. For example, Article 6 of the Guyana-South Korea BIT is instructive in this regard. It reads as follows:

1. Each Contracting Party shall guarantee to investors of the other Contracting Party the free transfer of their investments and returns. Such transfers shall include, in particular, though not exclusively:
   (a) net profit, capital gains, dividends, interest, royalties, fees and any other current income accruing from investments;
   (b) proceeds accruing from the sale or the total or partial liquidation of investments;
   (c) funds in repayment of loans related to investments;
   (d) earnings of nationals of the other Contracting Party who are allowed to work in connection with investments in its territory;
   (e) additional funds necessary for the maintenance or development of the existing investments;
   (f) amounts spent for the management of the investment in the territory of the other Contracting Party or a third State; and
   (g) compensation pursuant to Articles 4 and 5.
2. All transfers under this Agreement shall be made in a freely convertible currency, without undue restriction and delay, at the market exchange rate which is effective for the current transactions or determined in accordance with the official rate of exchange in force on the date of transfers.
3. Notwithstanding paragraphs 1 and 2 above, a Contracting Party may delay or prevent a transfer through the equitable, nondiscriminatory and good faith application of laws relating to:
   (a) bankruptcy, insolvency or other legal proceedings to protect the rights of creditors;
   (b) issuing, trading or dealing in securities;
   (c) criminal or administrative violations;
   (d) reports of transfer of currency or other monetary instruments; or

160 ICSID Case No. ARB/05/22, Award, 24 July 2008. Here, the tribunal rejected the allegation that Tanzania had breached its obligation under Article 6 of the applicable UK-Tanzania BIT preventing BGT from transferring its investment and returns by having sold its shares in City Water and by preventing it from transferring returns because no dividends were forthcoming. The tribunal, however, disagreed, finding that there were no funds to transfer in the first place, and that, in any event, no restrictions that imprisoned the transfer of funds were shown to exist on the facts.

161 ibid 735.

(e) ensuring the satisfaction of judgments in adjudicatory proceedings.

A provision of this nature is not an absolute restriction on the state's right to adopt monetary policies that may require certain authorisations before a transfer can be effected,[162] nor is it intended to convert subject matter that are neither funds or returns into funds or returns. The case of *Rusoro Mining Limited v Venezuela*[163] is instructive in this regard. Here, Rusoro, after having indirectly acquired 58 mining concessions and contracts to explore and produce gold in Venezuela, was subject to various restrictions, including a limitation in the exportation of gold. Rusoro argued that the measures in question effectively imprisoned its returns in Venezuela, forcing it to repatriate to Venezuela the totality of the proceeds from each export sale, for conversion at an exchange rate, and that other measures compelled it to sell most of its gold in Venezuela. In its view, since gold fell within the definition of 'returns', this represented a breach of the BIT's provision on free transfer. It further argued that the abolition of the Swap Market in 2010, and the obligation to sell the foreign currency obtained from the gold exports at the distorted official exchange rate, represented a breach. The tribunal, however, held that the gold produced by Rusoro could not be considered for the purposes of the BIT as 'returns'. Gold, in its view, was a commodity, not a currency. In this connection, it could only become a currency if it is minted and becomes legal tender by government, which did not happen in this case. Rusoro's subsidiaries mined the gold to sell it as a commodity to unrelated third parties, not to distribute it to their shareholder in lieu of dividends. The claimant's gold, in this context, was no more a return than is a car produced by a foreign investor in its car factory in Venezuela.

The second issue raised was the compatibility with the BIT's provision on free transfer of various measures, including Venezuela's imposition of a stringent exchange control mechanism, in which residents in Venezuela had to acquire foreign currency via an administrative authorisation, and had to sell a high percentage of foreign currency earned to the Central Bank of Venezuela, and in which the Official Exchange rate was established by fiat of the Central Bank. In the tribunal's view, once the investor was able to transfer funds related to its investments and returns without delay, in a convertible currency and at the rate of exchange prevailing at the date of transfer, Venezuela complied with its obligation under the BIT. It noted that the BIT's provision on free transfer did not:

> impose restrictions on the manner in which Contracting States decide to regulate their exchange control regime. States have the choice of abolishing all exchange control restrictions, of establishing certain limits or of submitting all foreign currency transactions to administrative control.[164]

On the facts, it accepted that each of the measures taken by Venezuela was a policy decision, which the country was empowered to adopt in the exercise of its monetary sovereignty, and which was compatible with the guarantees offered to protected investors under the BIT. Venezuela's decisions could only give rise to a breach of Article VIII if Rusoro was able to prove that it had requested foreign currency in connection with an investment or a return,

162 *VJ v Poland*, ICSID Case No. ARB(AF)/11/3, Award, 24 November 2015. The tribunal held that the requirement by the tax authorities of Poland that the expenses towards the claimant's management fees would be admitted as legitimate deductions only if proper supporting documentation was produced could not be regarded as a clog on the right to free transfer of funds. There was, accordingly, no breach of the applicable BIT in question.

163 ICSID Case No. ARB(AF)/12/5, Award, 22 August 2016.

164 ibid 577.

and that the authorisation had not been granted as required by the BIT (without delay, in a convertible currency and at the rate of exchange prevailing at the date of transfer) – which Rusoro did not allege.

A state will not breach the provision on the free transfer of investments and returns in circumstances where the investor knew of certain regulations, for example, requesting authorisation from the Central Bank to transfer its fund, but does not follow these regulations. This issue arose for consideration in *Metalpar v Argentina*.[165] Here, the claimant argued they had asked BankBoston of Buenos Aires to transfer US$200,000, which corresponded to a distribution of dividends, and had also asked BankBoston to advise them on the procedure to be followed to perform such an operation. They added that, in a telephone conversation, BankBoston indicated that they should refer to the legislation in force [meaning the Presidential Decree No. 1570/2001], which they alleged banned those transfers. In reality, however, the Presidential Decree did not ban transfers; rather the Central Bank of Argentina had to give authorisation. Argentina explained that it always permitted international transfers and, only in the most difficult moment of the crisis, it required the prior approval of the Central Bank for those transfers.

The tribunal agreed with Argentina, concluding that the investor, who knew the regulations on this matter well, did not comply with the established procedure, which consisted of requesting authorisation from the Central Bank, not BankBoston, and that Argentina did not accordingly breach Article 5(b) of the BIT, which guaranteed the transfer of funds abroad. In its view, even if it were concluded that the events were the result of incorrect advice provided by BankBoston to the claimants, the consequences of that error could not be charged to Argentina either.

Von Pezold and Others v Zimbabwe[166] is one of only a handful of cases in which an investor has succeeded in a claim alleging a breach of a BIT's free transfer guarantee. Here, the claimants contended that the respondent breached Article 5 of the German-Zimbabwe BIT, which provided that the respondent must guarantee to investors free transfer in connection with an investment, including the transfer of 'returns' on investment and the 'repayment of loans'. The tribunal considered that the respondent breached this provision by refusing to release foreign currency to allow the Forrester Estate to repay the Loans to Elisabeth in 2001. The BIT's free transfer provision was also breached between 2004 and 2008 when the respondent forced the claimants to be paid for tobacco in Zimbabwean dollars, and between 2003 and 2009 when it forced the claimants to exchange US currency for Zimbabwean dollars. In the tribunal's view, the respondent's failure to release US dollars earned by the claimants through the sale of tobacco also breached this standard.

What is clear from the foregoing is that the free transfer provision is an undoubtedly important one for investors, as it guarantees them the ability to enjoy the fruits of their labour, even if that means said fruits are transferred out of the jurisdiction. While a state is not precluded from adopting a monetary policy in this connection, such policy must be consistent with the requirements of the BIT in question and should not arbitrarily restrict the investor's right to transfer payments in connection with their investment out of the jurisdiction.

165 ICSID Case No. ARB/03/5, Award on the Merits, 6 June 2008.
166 ICSID Case No. ARB/10/15, Award, 28 July 2015.

SUMMARY

One of the stand-out provisions of every IIA is the guarantee of free transfer of payments, which offers a proverbial lifeline for investors. This seemingly straightforward concept is in fact yet another complex aspect of the relationship between investors and host states.

Imagine you are an investor who has poured millions into a foreign country, only to find your profits trapped behind an impenetrable wall of regulations. This nightmare scenario is precisely what the free transfer provision aims to prevent. It is not about guaranteeing that investors will have funds to transfer; rather, it ensures that when they do have funds, they can move them freely, unimpeded by the host state's whims.

But like all things in international law, the devil is in the details. These provisions typically start with a broad guarantee, followed by a meticulous list of what constitutes 'investments' and 'returns'. Think of it as a financial buffet: net profits, capital gains, dividends, royalties, and more are all on the menu. Even the proceeds from liquidating your investment are covered, offering an escape hatch if things go south.

Yet, this is not a blank check for investors. States, wary of potential abuse, have carved out exceptions. Bankruptcy proceedings, securities regulations, criminal investigations – these can all put a temporary hold on transfers. It is a delicate balance between investor protection and state sovereignty.

The interpretation of these provisions has led to some fascinating legal acrobatics. Take the case of *Rusoro Mining in Venezuela*. When Venezuela restricted gold exports, Rusoro cried foul, claiming it violated the free transfer provision. But the arbitrators didn't agree. Gold, they ruled, was a commodity, not a currency. An investor cannot transfer what isn't a 'return' in the first place. This case highlights a crucial point: free transfer provisions do not strip states of their monetary sovereignty. Venezuela's stringent exchange control mechanism, while frustrating for investors, was not inherently a violation. As long as investors could eventually transfer their funds without undue delay and at a fair exchange rate, the state was in the clear.

But states are not given carte blanche either. In von Pezold, when the government forced investors to accept payment in rapidly devaluing Zimbabwean dollars instead of US currency, arbitrators saw red. This wasn't just inconvenient; it was a clear violation of the free transfer guarantee.

The message is clear: while states retain the right to regulate their economies, they cannot use this power to trap investor funds or significantly devalue them through arbitrary currency controls. It is a fine line, one that continues to be tested in arbitrations around the world.

For investors, these provisions are more than just legal jargon – they're a vital assurance that the fruits of their labour would not be locked away in a foreign land. For states, they represent a commitment to fair play in the global economic arena, even as they try to maintain control over their financial systems.

IV. THE GUARANTEE AGAINST PERFORMANCE REQUIREMENTS

Performance requirements appear infrequently in Caribbean investment agreements, hence they have generally not subject to been subject to much scrutiny.[167] However, they can be found in a few agreements to which the United States is state party, namely the Grenada-USA BIT,[168] the Jamaica-USA BIT[169] and the Trinidad and Tobago-USA BIT. Article VI of the latter provides as follows:

> 1. Neither Party shall mandate or enforce, as a condition for the establishment, acquisition, expansion, management, conduct or operation of a covered investment, any requirement (including any commitment or undertaking in connection with the receipt of a governmental permission or authorization):
>   (a) to achieve a particular level or percentage of local content, or to purchase, use or otherwise give a preference to products or services of domestic origin or from any domestic source;
>   (b) to limit imports by the investment of products or services in relation to a particular volume or value of production, exports or foreign exchange earnings;
>   (c) to export a particular type, level or percentage of products or services, either generally or to a specific market region;
>   (d) to limit sales by the investment of products or services in the Party's territory in relation to a particular volume or value of production, exports or foreign exchange earnings;
>   (e) to transfer technology, a production process or other proprietary knowledge to a national or company in the Party's territory, except pursuant to an order, commitment or undertaking that is enforced by a court, administrative tribunal or competition authority to remedy an alleged or adjudicated violation of competition laws; or
>   (f) to carry out a particular type, level or percentage of research and development in the Party's territory.
>
> 2. Nothing in paragraph 1 shall preclude a Party from providing benefits and incentives conditioned upon such requirements.

This provision bears some resemblance to NAFTA Article 1106, which (prior to the coming effect of the United States-Mexico-Canada Agreement [USMCA]) provided that:

167 Cf. Jason Haynes and Antonius Hippolyte, 'The Covid-19 pandemic and the potential for investor-state claims: a Caribbean perspective' (2021) 21(2) *Oxford University Commonwealth Law Journal* 212. Further afield, see David Collins, 'Performance Requirement Prohibitions in International Investment Law' in Julien Chaisse, Leïla Choukroune, and Sufian Jusoh (eds), *Handbook of International Investment Law and Policy* (Springer 2021) 357; Suzy Nikièma, 'Performance Requirements in Investment Treaties' (IISD Best Practices Series 30, 2014); Tania Voon and Dean Merriman, 'Incoming: How International Investment Law Constrains Foreign Investment Screening' (2022) 24(1) *The Journal of World Investment & Trade* 75; Timothy Meyer and Tae Jung Park, 'Renegotiating International Investment Law' (2018) 21(3) *Journal of International Economic Law* 655.

168 Grenada-USA BIT Article II(5): Neither Party shall impose performance requirements as a condition of establishment, expansion, or maintenance of investments, which require or enforce commitments to export goods produced, or which specify that goods or services must be purchased locally, or which impose any other similar requirements.

169 Jamaica-USA BIT Article II(5): Neither Party shall impose performance requirements as a condition of establishment, expansion or maintenance of investments, which require or enforce commitments to export goods produced, or which specify that goods or services must be purchased locally, or which impose any other similar requirements, provided, however, that nothing in this paragraph shall preclude a Party from providing benefits and incentives to investments which export a proportion of the goods produced.

1. No Party may impose or enforce any of the following requirements, or enforce any commitment or undertaking, in connection with the establishment, acquisition, expansion, management, conduct or operation of an investment of an investor of a Party or of a non-Party in its territory:
   (a) to export a given level or percentage of goods or services;
   (b) to achieve a given level or percentage of domestic content;
   (c) to purchase, use or accord a preference to goods produced or services provided in its territory, or to purchase goods or services from persons in its territory;
   (d) to relate in any way the volume or value of imports to the volume or value of exports or to the amount of foreign exchange inflows associated with such investment;
   (e) to restrict sales of goods or services in its territory that such investment produces or provides by relating such sales in any way to the volume or value of its exports or foreign exchange earnings;
   (f) to transfer technology, a production process or other proprietary knowledge to a person in its territory, except when the requirement is imposed or the commitment or undertaking is enforced by a court, administrative tribunal or competition authority to remedy an alleged violation of competition laws or to act in a manner not inconsistent with other provisions of this Agreement; or
   (g) to act as the exclusive supplier of the goods it produces or services it provides to a specific region or world market.
2. A measure that requires an investment to use a technology to meet generally applicable health, safety or environmental requirements shall not be construed to be inconsistent with paragraph 1(f). For greater certainty, Articles 1102 and 1103 apply to the measure.
3. No Party may condition the receipt or continued receipt of an advantage, in connection with an investment in its territory of an investor of a Party or of a non-Party, on compliance with any of the following requirements:
   (a) to achieve a given level or percentage of domestic content;
   (b) to purchase, use or accord a preference to goods produced in its territory, or to purchase goods from producers in its territory;
   (c) to relate in any way the volume or value of imports to the volume or value of exports or to the amount of foreign exchange inflows associated with such investment; or
   (d) to restrict sales of goods or services in its territory that such investment produces or provides by relating such sales in any way to the volume or value of its exports or foreign exchange earnings.
4. Nothing in paragraph 3 shall be construed to prevent a Party from conditioning the receipt or continued receipt of an advantage, in connection with an investment in its territory of an investor of a Party or of a non-Party, on compliance with a requirement to locate production, provide a service, train or employ workers, construct or expand particular facilities, or carry out research and development, in its territory.
5. Paragraphs 1 and 3 do not apply to any requirement other than the requirements set out in those paragraphs.
6. Provided that such measures are not applied in an arbitrary or unjustifiable manner, or do not constitute a disguised restriction on international trade or investment, nothing in paragraph 1(b) or (c) or 3(a) or (b) shall be construed to prevent any Party from adopting or maintaining measures, including environmental measures:
   (a) necessary to secure compliance with laws and regulations that are not inconsistent with the provisions of this Agreement;
   (b) necessary to protect human, animal or plant life or health; or
   (c) necessary for the conservation of living or non-living exhaustible natural resources.

Tribunals, particularly in the NAFTA context, have been especially cautious when interpreting Article 1106, generally favouring a strict interpretation of performance requirements. Tribunals typically begin by asking (i) whether the measures in issue constitute performance requirements and (ii) if answered in the affirmative, whether the state violated the relevant article of the IIA on performance requirements. In respect of (i), the tribunal in *Cargill v Poland*[170] defined performance requirements as:

> stipulations, imposed on investors, requiring them to meet certain specified goals with respect to their operations in the host country. Export requirements and restrictions on sales of goods and services in the territories where they are produced or provided fall within this category.[171]

In *Cargill v Poland*, the claimant sought to diversify its sweetener production in Poland, with a focus on the domestic market, which led it to invest in the production and marketing of isoglucose. At the time when Cargill decided to invest in isoglucose production in Poland, there were no quota restrictions on its production or sale. However, after the passing of the 2001 Sugar Law and the EU Commission Regulation No. 1464/95, Cargill was required to export outside Poland or outside the European Union any amount of production that exceeded a particular quota ('C volume levels'), creating thereby, in Cargill's view, performance requirements. It contended that these performance requirements were inadmissible under Article 11:4 of the Poland-United States Business and Economic Relations Treaty since they conditioned Cargill's investment expansion and maintenance. In other words, Cargill considered that it could only use and benefit from its full isoglucose capacity only if it exported output above the quota level. This, in its view, implied that any use of the capacity above the quota level was subject to the export requirement. On the other hand, Poland alleged that Cargill's claim was without merit, because the national and EU export requirements did not condition the expansion or maintenance of Cargill's investment. In other words, the quotas were not inadmissible performance requirements as producers were not required to export the products exceeding quotas, although it could choose to do so. In any event, Poland argued that the provision regulating 'C' volume production of isoglucose was adopted at a time when Cargill had already completed the expansion of its investments. It further argued that Cargill had not proven that it produced quantities of isoglucose in excess of the A and B quotas levels, so the regulation regarding C volume production did not even apply to it.

The tribunal held that the C volume levels constituted performance requirements as the Sugar Law required that production exceeding the A and B quotas 'must be exported' outside Poland. Where a producer did not manage to fulfil the obligation to export all C volume products, the remaining product was subject to financial sanctions. In the tribunal's view, in these circumstances, exportation was a performance requirement; in requiring the export of volume C level, Poland set a condition on the activities of Cargill in Poland. Poland's argument that because the measure applied equally to isoglucose and sugar it should not be characterised as a performance requirement was not accepted by the tribunal. In the tribunal's view, comparison of the two products in question was not required in the context of the assessment of performance requirements because, as a matter of principle, 'performance requirements are not to be determined by comparing the positions of two companies, unlike national treatment'.[172]

On the question of whether there had been a breach of the guarantee against performance requirements, the Tribunal considered that Article 11:4 of the Treaty sought to prohibit the imposition of performance requirements which required exporting goods produced

170 ibid ICSID Case No. ARB(AF)/04/2, Award, 29 February 2008.
171 ibid 541.
172 ibid 546.

locally, provided it was made 'as a condition of establishment, expansion or maintenance of investments'. In respect of 'establishment' and 'maintenance', the Tribunal found that no quotas and consequently no performance requirements were imposed when the claimant established its investment and while it maintained its investment in Poland. The Tribunal then had to examine whether the quota imposed hindered the expansion of the investment. Interestingly, the claimant's claim did not relate to quotas A and B, but to volume C production. Whereas quotas A and B limited Cargill's possible expansion on the Polish market, the same did not apply to volume C level. Had Cargill intended to expand, it could have done so, notwithstanding quotas A and B, by producing for export. Therefore, the Tribunal refused to find that volume C level had the same effect as a maximum production quota.

The tribunal also rejected the claimant's argument that export was not an alternative due to high costs of storing, transportation, and import tariffs, which worsened after Poland's EU accession, when the export markets of countries close to Poland were no longer available. In this connection, the tribunal held that notwithstanding these practical and financial impediments, Cargill took a commercial decision not to export more of its production. In this context, Cargill failed to convince the tribunal that its decision not to expand into foreign markets was due to the imposition of the volume C level. Against this backdrop, it was concluded that there was no breach of the guarantee against performance requirements as the volume C level was not imposed as a condition of the 'expansion' of its investment.

Meanwhile, in the context of NAFTA, in *Cargill v Mexico*,[173] the respondent imposed a tax on soft drink bottlers (including, but not specifically, the claimant) who used high fructose corn syrup (HFCS). The tax was avoided by domestic investors because they primarily produced soft drinks from domestically cultivated sugar cane. The claimant argued that this was a performance requirement in violation of NAFTA Article 1106(3) because it conditioned the receipt of a tax advantage – or rather the avoidance of the tax – on the use by soft drink bottlers of domestically produced cane sugar. This, the claimant asserted, accorded a preference to goods produced in Mexico, and was therefore a performance requirement within the meaning of Article 1106(3)(b), which provided:

> 3. No Party may condition the receipt or continued receipt of an advantage, *in connection with an investment* in its territory of an investor of a Party or of a non-Party, on compliance with any of the following requirements:
> (a) to achieve a given level or percentage of domestic content;
> (b) to purchase, use or accord a preference to goods produced in its territory, or to purchase goods from producers in its territory.

The respondent retorted, arguing that, for Article 1106(3) to apply, the advantage on which the use of domestic goods was conditioned had to be 'in connection with' an investment of the investor. According to the respondent, the claimant had to demonstrate that the conditioned tax advantage was imposed 'in connection with' its investment in Mexico. However, the respondent claimed that the tax measure was not in connection with Cargill's investment in its subsidiary, Cargill de Mexico.

The tribunal summarised the issue raised as concerned with whether the tax on soft drinks containing HFCS could be said to be a measure 'in connection with' an investment relating to the business of supplying HFCS to the soft drink industry. In other words, did

173 ICSID Case No. ARB(AF)/05/2, Award, 18 September 2009.

the tax condition an advantage 'in connection with' Cargill's investment in Mexico, Cargill de Mexico?

The tribunal refused to equate 'in connection with' with 'directly affected by'. In its view, the dictionary meaning of 'connection' is 'an association or relationship' and the phrase 'in connection with' is defined as 'together with' or 'in conjunction with'.[174] In this context, it had to determine, on the facts, what degree of relationship or conjunction was necessary between the requirements on which the advantage was conditioned and the investment in order to fall within Article 1106(3). In its estimation, the performance requirement in question was integrally related to the investment. The objective of the tax was to put pressure on the United States by restricting, if not eliminating, the opportunities for the sale of HFCS in Mexico. In effect, by its very design, the performance requirement – conditioning the receipt of a tax advantage on the use by soft drink bottlers of domestically produced cane sugar – was 'in connection with' the operation of an investment that supplied HFCS to the soft drink bottling industry. In other words, absent the objective of targeting the supply of HFCS in Mexico in order to bring pressure on the United States, there would have been no tax. Accordingly, the respondent was held to have breached Article 1106(3).

A similar factual scenario arose in *Archer Daniels Midland Company and Tate & Lyle Ingredients Americas, Inc. v Mexico*,[175] where the claimant contended that the tax imposed by the respondent on producers of HFCS was an impermissible performance requirement in breach of Article 1106 of NAFTA because it conferred advantages 'in connection with an investment', i.e. exemption from the tax on Mexican bottlers who used domestic cane sugar. In the claimants' view, the advantages conferred on Mexican investors had a direct impact on the claimants' investment in HFCS production and distribution facilities, causing it substantial loss/damage in violation of Article 1106. The respondent did not deny that the tax provided advantages to bottlers of beverages sweetened exclusively with cane sugar but argued that the advantage was not provided 'in connection with an investment' within the meaning of Article 1106(3). In short, the essence of the parties' dispute related to whether Article 1106(3) was intended to reach performance requirements connected with all investments in a party's territory, i.e. Mexico or it simply referred to performance requirements imposed directly on investors of the other member states.

The tribunal considered that Article 1106(3) prohibited member states from imposing performance requirements on any investor from the NAFTA region, including the respondent's own investors. In its view, the respondent conferred advantages upon the cane sugar industry in Mexico by levying a 20% on soft drinks and syrups that used any sweetener other than cane sugar, such as HFCS, exempting from the tax soft drinks and syrups sweetened exclusively with cane sugar. In this regard, the Mexican legislature conferred an advantage – the tax exemption – conditioned upon the use of cane sugar instead of any other sweetener, placing the claimants at a competitive disadvantage vis-à-vis sugar producers in Mexico. In other words, notwithstanding the fact that the tax conferred advantages on the sugar industry generally, without distinguishing between domestic and foreign investors in the sugar industry, the reality was that the sugar industry in Mexico was essentially domestic; consumption of non-Mexican cane sugar during the period the tax was in force was non-existent. In short, the tribunal concluded that both the structure of the Mexican sugar industry and the underlying intent of the tax conferred advantages on the sugar industry in

174 ibid 315.
175 ICSID Case No. ARB (AF)/04/5, Award, 21 November 2007.

Mexico. These advantages – consisting of an exemption from the tax – were provided in connection with the claimants' investment in Mexico because they had a detrimental effect on the profitability of the investment. As these advantages were conditioned on the exclusive use of cane sugar – which the tribunal believed was essentially domestic – and discriminated against the HFCS industry in which claimants had made their investment, the tax was an inconsistent performance requirement in breach of Article 1106(3) of the NAFTA.

Notwithstanding the foregoing arbitral awards that appear to impugn the imposition of performance requirements, there have been several arguments which respondent states have successfully raised in defence of an allegation that the measures they have adopted have amounted to a performance requirement. The first is that the claimant has misconstrued the nature of the measure in question such that the case is not a performance requirement case at all. For example, in *S.D. Myers, Inc. v Canada*,[176] the claimant alleged that the Interim Order adopted by the Canadian government effectively forced it, as a condition of operating in Canada, to carry out a major part of its proposed business, the physical disposal of PCB waste, in Canada. It contended that this was a performance requirement because it required PCB disposal operators to accord preference to Canadian goods and services and to achieve a given level of domestic content, contrary to the state's obligations under Article 1106 NAFTA. In other words, the claimant contended that the export ban effectively required it to consume goods and services in Canada. On the other hand, Canada argued that the Interim Order neither imposed nor enforced a prohibited performance requirement as there was no requirement to buy Canadian goods or services or to achieve a certain level of Canadian content.

The tribunal held that the only part of the definition contained in Article 1106 that might apply to the current situation was 'conduct or operation of an investment', as subparagraph (b) clearly did not apply and, neither did subparagraph (c). Looking at the substance and effect of the Interim Order, as well as the literal wording of Article 1106, the majority of the tribunal considered that no 'requirements' were imposed on the claimant that fell within Article 1106. In other words, contrary to the claimant's argument that the effect of the Interim Order was to require it to undertake all of its operations in Canada, by a majority, the tribunal concluded that this was not a 'performance requirements' case.

Another defence, albeit a controversial one, that an investor has been able to successfully raise is that the measure in question, though on the face of it a performance requirement, is nonetheless 'saved' or justified because it is compatible with, or advances, the object and purpose of the relevant IIA in question. This was the finding in *Joseph Charles Lemire v Ukraine*.[177] Here, Ukraine passed a law which provided that 'music produced in Ukraine shall constitute at least 50% of general broadcasting time of each . . . radio organization'. This requirement applied to all broadcasters in Ukraine, not only to the claimant's radio station. The implementation of this new requirement was not immediate, but gradual. The claimant's basic criticism of the new Ukrainian music requirement was that there were too few Ukrainian musical hits, and since its formula was 100% hits, it had to continuously replay the same few Ukrainian hits. In the claimant's opinion, the 50% Ukrainian music requirement violated Article II.6 of the BIT, which read

176 UNCITRAL, Partial Award, 13 November 2000.

177 ICSID Case No. ARB/06/18, Decision on Jurisdiction and Liability, 28 March 2011.

> Neither Party shall impose performance requirements as condition of, establishment, expansion or maintenance of investments, which require or enforce commitments to export goods produced, or which specify that goods or services must be purchased locally, or which impose any other similar requirements.

According to the claimant, the high level of the local source requirement and its abrupt incorporation caused it to lose significant advertising revenue.

The tribunal explained that Article II.6 had to be interpreted in accordance with the ordinary meaning to be given to the terms of the treaty in their context and in the light of its object and purpose. When interpreting the BIT, which prohibited local law that specify that 'goods or services . . . must be purchased locally', the tribunal considered that the 50% Ukrainian music requirement did not fall foul of this rule; the law did not specify that radio stations had to purchase any goods or services locally, but rather that a certain percentage of the music broadcast should be authored, composed or produced by Ukrainian artists. In any event, when Article II.6 was interpreted in the light of the object and purpose of the BIT, which aimed to 'promote greater economic cooperation' between the USA and Ukraine (Preamble II) and to avoid the imposition of local content requirements as a means of protecting local industries against competing imports, it was clear that the underlying reasons for the 50% Ukrainian music requirement were not to protect local industries and restrict imports, but rather to promote Ukraine's cultural inheritance, a purpose which was compatible with Article II.6 of the BIT. The tribunal concluded that, as a sovereign state, Ukraine had the inherent right to regulate its affairs and adopt laws in order to protect the common good of its people. The promotion of domestic music, according to the tribunal, validly reflected the state's policy to preserve and strengthen cultural inheritance and national identity.

Although a measure adopted by a respondent state may have conferred an advantage to the state, it will not automatically be held to be an unlawful performance requirement, unless the claimant is able to establish that the measure in question amounted to a requirement for establishing, acquiring, expanding, managing, conducting, or operating their business in the host state. This was the basis on which the case of *Pope & Talbot Inc. v Canada*[178] was decided. Here, the investor argued that Canada regulated its activity in a manner that violated NAFTA Article 1106(1)(a) because the Export Control Regime (ECR) required it to export a given level of goods that was lower than that which it would have exported if it were not forced to pay export fees on exports above its fee-free allocation. It further argued that the Regime violated the guarantee against performance requirements because it penalised softwood lumber producers for under-utilisation of export quotas under the so-called 'use it or lose it' provisions. These provisions allegedly created a *de facto* requirement to export up to quota levels. Canada retorted, arguing that the aim of the ECR was to raise foreign exchange earnings and increase employment in the export sector.

The tribunal held that the granting and maintaining of the fee-free (EB) and/or lower fee (LFB) quotas to exporters under the provisions of the ECR was an 'advantage' within the meaning of Article 1106(3). However, the investor was held to have not made out a valid claim under Article 1106(1)(a), because the Regime did not 'impose or enforce . . . requirements'. Rather, it was a tariff-rate export restraint regime fixing only the level up to which covered products could be exported fee-free, then at a lower fee up to a given higher

178 UNCITRAL Partial Award, 26 June 2000.

level, and thereafter in unlimited quantities at a higher fee (UFB). The Regime functioned based on the allocation of EB and/or LFB quotas to specific exporters, and, where applicable, the payment by the exporter to Canada of export fees, which were later remitted by Canada to the respective covered provinces. In the tribunal's view, while the Regime deterred increased exports to the US, that deterrence was not a 'requirement' for 'establishing, acquiring, expanding, managing, conducting, or operating' foreign-owned business in Canada. Separately, regarding Articles 1106(1)(e) and 1106(3)(d), it was held that the Export Control Regime imposed no restrictions or limitations on domestic sales of softwood lumber. Hence, the investor's claim was dismissed.

Some tribunals have taken the position that the measure in question, to constitute a performance requirement, must be directly and specifically connected to exports. In other words, under NAFTA Article 1106, the measure in question must not merely have an indirect effect on exports. In *Merrill and Ring Forestry L.P. v Canada,*[179] the claimant complained that the requirement to advertise for the export of logs from remote areas in a minimum volume of 2,800 m3 and a maximum volume of 15,000 m3 contravened Article 1106(1)(a) NAFTA because it restricted the level of the investor's export of logs. In the claimant's view, as this was a precondition for export approval, any advertisement of logs outside those levels could not be exported. The claimant also complained that the requirement to cut, sort and scale its logs in accordance with the specifications of the Coast Domestic Market End Use Sort Description constituted an obligation to produce certain types of goods in contravention of Article 1106(1)(c), in that a preference was accorded to goods which met the requirements of the domestic market. Finally, the claimant contended that the requirement to hire services in Canada for the purposes of cutting, sorting and scaling logs or retrieving logs that were broken loose was also a performance requirement. In the claimant's view, these requirements impacted the way it managed its investments in Canada. In sum, the claimant's argument was that Article 1106(1) had to be read in the light of the object and purpose of the treaty as a whole, with particular reference to the objective of eliminating barriers to trade, and that the alleged performance requirements imposed did not further this objective.

The respondent, on the other hand, argued that none of the measures complained of involved the imposition or enforcement of a 'requirement, commitment or undertaking', and thus did not meet the ordinary meaning of Article 1106. Its view was that there were no requirements in the regime to increase or limit log exports, and thus producers were free to sell logs in both the domestic and international markets. They further argued that the advertisement of a minimum volume of logs concerned only the advertising of logs and had no bearing on the level of goods exported. In fact, Canada pointed out that the claimant did not export almost 20% of the logs for which it had obtained an export permit. In its view, the measure was designed to prevent the advertisement of small volumes in remote areas to discourage offers by processors. Further, the respondent contended that the maximum volume complained of had no connection with exports and did not restrict the investor's capacity to export as many logs as were authorised. In other words, the claimant was free to sell as many logs as it wished in the domestic market, and it was in no way constrained from so doing because of a performance requirement.

On the investor's second argument, the respondent retorted that the use of the metric system in the scaling of logs was simply an application of the measurement system applied in Canada and had no connection with the manufacture or sale of logs. In its view, neither

179 ICSID Case No. UNCT/07/1, Award, 31 March 2010.

the use of this system nor the recovery of logs compelled the claimant to purchase services from persons in Canada, and the claimant was free to hire workers from outside Canada. In other words, to hire such services in Canada was purely a business decision.

The tribunal considered that the objective of NAFTA Article 1106 was to prohibit performance requirements designed to oblige an investor to export more than it otherwise would have exported. On the question of the requirement related to the advertisement of goods as a step in the process of obtaining an export permit, the tribunal held that this could not be seen as a restriction on exports themselves, which could be undertaken at any level which had been authorised. Indeed, the claimant had every right to export an aggregated amount of logs by adding up the various permits obtained within the period of authorisation. In respect to the investor's complaint about the requirement to cut, sort and scale its logs in accordance with the specifications of the Coast Domestic Market End Use Sort Description, while the tribunal accepted that this requirement related to the manner in which goods were to be shipped to the domestic market, it was not a performance requirement designed to restrict or enhance exports. Further, scaling in accordance with the metric system was held to be a measure which related to the measurement system in use throughout Canada, and it was rather unusual to expect Canada to apply different systems of measurement to different ends.

While the tribunal accepted the requirement in question might have had an incidentally adverse effect to the extent that it might wish to cut, sort, and scale its logs as required by its customers in foreign markets, this did not appear to be the kind of prohibited performance requirement banned by Article 1106, which needed to be directly and specifically connected to exports. In other words, the provision did not capture other requirements which merely had some indirect effect on exports. That said, the tribunal cautioned that it was conceivable that, in certain circumstances, incidental effects, when aggregated may be seen to constitute something more than an incidental effect may be a performance requirement, even though each measure, when considered individually, does not result in the breach of a specific performance requirement.

In sum, then, the tribunal concluded that the claimant was free to sell as many logs as it wished in the domestic market, and this was in no way restricted by the minimum and maximum volumes required for advertising in connection with an export permit. Thus, the measures complained of did not lend themselves to inclusion in the closed list of performance requirements laid down under Article 1106.

It is worth noting that Article 1108(8) NAFTA created exemptions in respect of the application of Article 1106 NAFTA. Article 1108(8) NAFTA read:

> The provisions of:
>
> a. Article 1106(1)(a), (b) and (c), and (3)(a) and (b) do not apply to qualification requirements for goods or services with respect to export promotion and foreign aid programs;
> b. Article 1106(1)(b), (c), (f) and (g), and (3)(a) and (b) do not apply to procurement by a Party or a state enterprise; and
> c. Article 1106(3)(a) and (b) do not apply to requirements imposed by an importing Party relating to the content of goods necessary to qualify for preferential tariffs or preferential quotas.

The scope of Article 1108(8) NAFTA was considered in *Mobil Investments Canada Inc. and Murphy Oil Corporation v Canada (I)*.[180] Here, the claimants argued that the respondent's imposition of the 2004 Guidelines requiring investors to spend a fixed percentage of project

180 ICSID Case No. ARB(AF)/07/4, Award, 20 February 2015.

revenues on research and development (R&D), and the enforcement of this requirement by a Board, constituted a prohibited performance requirement, in violation of Article 1106(1) NAFTA. They asserted that the 2004 Guidelines compelled their project operators to spend several million more dollars per year on R&D activities under their revised Benefits Plans than they would otherwise be required to spend by reference to Benefits Plans in previous Guidelines. As a result, the claimants argued that the Board substituted its own development objectives for the business judgment of investors, thereby distorting investment flows in favour of the Province. In short, the claimants alleged that the requirement to spend on R&D, pursuant to the 2004 Guidelines, constituted an impermissible performance requirement within the meaning of Article 1106(1)(c) NAFTA.

The respondent retorted that Article 1106(1)(c) NAFTA did not prohibit requirements regarding R&D. Its position was that this provision did not encompass R&D performance requirements because such performance requirements had to be distinguished from the requirement to purchase local goods or services. It further contented that even if R&D requirements could fall within the scope of Article 1106, the 2004 Guidelines did not necessarily compel the purchase, use or accordance of a preference to local goods or services. Further or alternatively, the respondent argued that the 2004 Guidelines fell within the scope of Canada's Annex I Reservation to Article 1106, and, in particular, that the 2004 Guidelines were adopted 'under the authority of and consistent with' the Accord Acts and were therefore compatible with NAFTA (paragraph 2(f)(ii) of Annex 1 of the NAFTA).

The tribunal assessed the proper scope and interpretation of Article 1106, and in particular, whether the R&D requirements under the 2004 Guidelines (and the application thereof) constituted 'services' within the meaning of Article 1106; and, second, whether the 2004 Guidelines compelled spending on R&D such that they constituted a 'requirement' to 'purchase, use, accord a preference to goods produced or services provided in its territory, or to purchase goods or services from persons in its territory'.

In the tribunal's view, in respect of Article 1106(1), which prohibits the imposition of certain listed performance requirements in connection with the establishment, acquisition, expansion, management, conduct or operation of an investment, the 2004 Guidelines purported to impose conditions on the claimants with respect to their management, conduct or operation in the Province. Although the text of Article 1106 did not refer specifically to R&D as such, the tribunal was not convinced that the absence of such express reference necessarily meant that the terms were to be interpreted to the effect that 'services' did not include R&D. In other words, the ordinary meaning of the term 'services' was broad enough to encompass R&D. Thus, on its face, the term 'services' covered a broad range of economic activities, and R&D could be seen as mainstream forms of service sector activity. Against this backdrop, there was nothing inherent in the term 'services' in Article 1106(1) that necessarily excluded R&D; R&D fell into the broad definitional category of 'economic activity'.

The tribunal acknowledged that this dispute was significantly different from other cases that involved NAFTA performance requirements because, in the present case, the 2004 Guidelines were not only imposing incidental effects with respect to the purchase, use or accordance of a preference to local goods or services. On the facts, the 2004 Guidelines were designed to ensure that expenditures for R&D services occurred in the Province, thereby implying a legal requirement for the purposes of Article 1106. It was clear, in the view of the tribunal, that such spending on R&D in the Province was a central feature of the 2004 Guidelines, and not an ancillary objective or consequence.

The tribunal then addressed the structure and operation of Article 1108 (the exemption). In this context, Canada argued that it had included the Accord Acts provisions on R&D in its Article 1108 exemptions, and the tribunal should thus attach weight to that decision for the purposes of an evaluation under Article 1106. In other words, Canada listed the Accord Acts' requirement that Benefits Plans include R&D expenditures as one such measure in Annex I to the NAFTA. In the final analysis, the tribunal concluded the inclusion of the Accord Acts and their provisions governing R&D meant that the R&D requirements of the Accord Acts constituted a prohibited performance requirement, but these were saved by Article 1108 which excluded the application of Article 1106 to 'procurement by a Party'.

The exception for 'procurement' contained under Article 1108 was considered in *ADF Group Inc. v United States of America.*[181] This case concerned the procurement of steel components to a highway interchange construction project in Northern Virginia, where the claimant, a Canadian company, challenged the 'Buy America' clause that applied to the fabrication of steel. More specifically, the respondent implemented the 'Buy America' provisions of the Clean Water Act which the claimant argued violated Article 1106(1)(b) by imposing a 100% domestic (United States) content requirement, and Article 1106(1)(c) by requiring preference to be given to United States-produced steel materials and products, if the claimant was to provide fabricated steel products to federal-aid highway projects.

The claimant challenged the granting of federal-aid funds to the Virginia Department of Transportation (VDOT) to enable the latter to construct the Springfield Interchange Project. The claimant contended that it was obliged to purchase only US steel and either to fabricate that steel in the US itself, or to subcontract the fabrication to US steel fabricators rather than to its Canadian parent. For the claimant, these measures constituted performance requirements relating to or connected with the 'management, conduct or operation' of its investment within the meaning of the chapeau of Article 1106 since those measures 'directly impact[ed] its daily activities, operations, and sales'.

The United States admitted that the 'Buy America' provisions of the Clean Water Act were inconsistent with the requirements of Article 1106 but argued that it was 'saved' under Article 1108(1) and the US Schedule to Annex I, which permits a Party to derogate from the performance requirement obligation when making grants and subsidies or for 'procurement by a Party'. More particularly, the respondent argued that the Commonwealth of Virginia, in purchasing steel and services from Shirley (which in turn contracted with the investor), was engaged in 'procurement'. Virginia, being one of the States of the United States, there was procurement by a 'governmental unit of the United States'. For the respondent, the purchase of steel and services by a governmental unit of the United States was plainly 'procurement by a Party' within the meaning of Article 1108. The respondent stressed that, by virtue of the Buy America provision, every steel fabricator in the United States – whether of US or Canadian or Mexican or other nationality – faced precisely the same constraints that ADF International faced; none could subcontract work to fabricators outside the United States and use the resulting steel products in a federal-aid highway project like the Springfield Interchange Project.

The tribunal considered that, in respect of NAFTA Article 1106, the measures taken by the respondent appeared to be requirements of 'local content' and other performance requirements. In other words, the measures constituted a requirement of domestic content within the sense of Article 1106(1)(b), and a requirement to accord preference to goods produced or services provided in the US for the purposes of Article 1106(1)(a).

181 ICSID Case No. ARB (AF)/00/1, Award, 9 January 2003.

In the tribunal's view, what was excluded from the scope of 'procurement' was governmental assistance to a public entity or agency engaged in procurement, especially assistance in the form of financing or funding of the procurement activity by providing grants, loans, equity infusions, guarantees, and fiscal incentives. In other words, the government entity or agency providing or arranging for funds for the purchase of goods, supplies, or materials used or to be used in the construction of a government project was not itself thereby engaged in procurement. On this basis, the construction of the Springfield Interchange Project constituted or involved governmental procurement for purposes of Article 1001(5). Because the Virginia Department of Transportation (VDOT) was designated as 'Owner' of the Springfield Interchange Project, notwithstanding the fact that the US Federal Government did provide federal funds for the construction of the Project, this did not result in the US Federal Government, or any agency thereof, being itself engaged in 'procurement'. As a matter of principle, the tribunal concluded that 'an "existing non-conforming measure" of a "Party" saved by Article 1108(1) may not only be a federal government measure but also a state or provincial government measure and even a measure of a local government'.[182]

The tribunal's ruling can be summarised as follows:

> Firstly, by virtue of Article 1108(7)(a) and (8)(b), the provisions of Articles 1102, 1103, 1106 and 1107 are not applicable in respect of procurement by a Party, whether the procurement is carried out by an office or entity of the U.S. Federal Government or by an office or entity of the Commonwealth of Virginia. In other words, the exclusionary effect of Article 1108(7)(a) and (8)(b) operates on both federal and state governmental procurement. Secondly, by granting Federal-aid funds to the VDOT to enable the latter to construct the Springfield Interchange Project, the FHWA of the U.S. Department of Transportation did not constitute itself as the procuring entity in that Project, and did not itself engage in procurement. Thirdly, the procurement carried out by the Commonwealth of Virginia through its VDOT in the Springfield Interchange Project was not subject to the restraints imposed in NAFTA Chapter 10 because the Commonwealth of Virginia is not listed in a U.S. Schedule which has yet to be negotiated and attached to Annex 1001.1a-3; nor has VDOT voluntarily subjected itself to the restraints of Chapter 10.[183]

In other words, the tribunal concluded that the claimant had not shown that the US measures in question were inconsistent with the requirements of NAFTA Article 1106.

SUMMARY

Provisions against the imposition of performance requirements, often buried deep within the text of investment treaties, represent a delicate balancing act between a nation's desire to attract foreign investment and its need to ensure that such investment contributes meaningfully to the local economy. Imagine a foreign investor eager to tap into a new market. They have the capital, the expertise, and the vision. After they have set up shop, they are told that they must export a certain percentage of their goods, use local content, or transfer their cutting-edge technology. These may very well constitute performance requirements. While relatively rare in Caribbean investment agreements, these provisions have taken centre stage in treaties involving economic powerhouses like the United States. They are designed to

182 ibid 165.
183 ibid 170.

prevent host states from imposing conditions that could distort investment flows or unfairly advantage domestic industries. But as with many aspects of international law, the devil is in the details.

Take the case of *Cargill v Poland*, which concerned sweeteners and quotas. Cargill, a global agricultural giant, found itself caught in a sticky situation when Poland imposed export requirements on isoglucose production. The tribunal's task? To determine whether these quotas constituted performance requirements. Their verdict? Yes, but with a twist. While the quotas were indeed performance requirements, they were not imposed as a condition for Cargill's investment expansion. A narrow escape for Poland, but a bitter pill for Cargill to swallow.

But it is not just about exports. In *Cargill v Mexico*, a tax on soft drinks became a battleground for performance requirements. The tax, designed to favour domestically produced cane sugar over imported high fructose corn syrup, was seen as an indirect way of forcing companies to 'buy local'. The tribunal in this case had to grapple with the thorny question of whether an advantage conferred on one industry could be considered a performance requirement for another. Their conclusion? A resounding yes, highlighting the far-reaching implications of these provisions. Yet, not all measures that seem like performance requirements actually are. In *SD Myers v Canada*, a ban on PCB waste exports was challenged as a *de facto* requirement to use Canadian goods and services. The tribunal, however, saw through this argument, reminding us that not every regulation that affects business operations qualifies as a performance requirement. Perhaps most intriguingly, some tribunals have shown a willingness to consider the broader context and purpose of these measures. In *Lemir v Ukraine*, a requirement for radio stations to play a certain percentage of Ukrainian music was challenged as a performance requirement. The tribunal's response? A nuanced recognition that promoting cultural heritage could be a valid reason for such a measure, even if it affected foreign investors.

A few key lessons emerge from extant arbitral practice. First, the specificity of the measure matters. Vague or indirect effects on investment may not rise to the level of a performance requirement. Second, the intent behind the measure is crucial. Is it designed to protect local industries, or does it serve a broader public policy goal? And, finally, the precise wording of the treaty provision is paramount. A single phrase can make the difference between a permissible regulation and a treaty violation. For states, particularly those in the Caribbean looking to refine their investment agreements, the message is clear: tread carefully. Performance requirements can be a powerful tool for ensuring that foreign investment contributes to local development. But they must be crafted with precision and implemented with care. As for investors, the take-away is equally important: due diligence is key. Understanding not just the letter of the law, but its interpretation and application, can mean the difference between a successful venture and a costly legal battle. In the end, performance requirements remain a contentious yet fascinating aspect of international investment law. They represent the ongoing struggle to balance the interests of foreign investors with the development goals of host states. As global economic dynamics continue to evolve, so too will the interpretation and application of these crucial provisions.

CONCLUSION

This chapter has argued that the obligations of full protection and security, free transfer provisions, umbrella clauses, and performance requirements are far from static requirements in international investment law. Rather, they form a dynamic and complex web of obligations that continue to evolve through interpretation and application by arbitral tribunals. The full protection and security standard, once limited to physical protection, has in some cases expanded to encompass legal and economic security, reflecting the changing nature of threats to foreign investments in our increasingly interconnected world. Meanwhile, free transfer provisions have been tested by economic crises, forcing tribunals to balance investor rights against states' need to manage their economy in turbulent times. Perhaps most controversial of all, however, is the umbrella clause which has sparked intense debate over its potential to elevate contractual disputes to the realm of international law, challenging traditional boundaries between the domestic and international legal spheres. Performance requirements, too, have proven to be a battlefield where state sovereignty clashes with investor protections, as evidenced by the nuanced interpretations in cases like *Cargill v Poland* and *Archer Daniels Midland v Mexico.* What emerges from this analysis is a picture of international investment law as a field in constant flux, shaped by the push and pull between investor protection and state sovereignty. As global economic patterns shift and new challenges emerge – from climate change to technological disruption – these legal standards will undoubtedly face fresh tests and interpretations.

Key questions, however, remain: how will tribunals balance the expanding notion of full protection and security against a state's limited resources? can the controversy surrounding umbrella clauses be resolved, or will divergent interpretations persist? As states grapple with pressing policy objectives, how will the limits of permissible performance requirements be defined? One thing is certain: the interplay between these legal standards will continue to shape the landscape of international investment, influencing the flow of capital across borders and the economic destinies of nations. As practitioners, scholars, and policymakers navigate this complex terrain, they must remain attuned to the delicate balance these provisions seek to strike – fostering a climate conducive to foreign investment while preserving the legitimate regulatory space of sovereign states.

CHAPTER 7

THE MERITS AND RELATED MATTERS

INTRODUCTION

This chapter examines the substantive aspects of investment arbitration that come into play once jurisdictional and admissibility requirements have been satisfied. After establishing jurisdiction, tribunals must address the merits of an investor's claims, applying the governing law to determine whether the host state has breached its treaty obligations. The merits phase involves careful consideration of multiple legal sources, depending on the scope of the applicable law – national investment laws, international investment agreements, customary international law, and general principles of international law – within the specific factual context of each dispute.

The chapter begins by exploring the range of remedies available when state responsibility has been established, with particular emphasis on restitution and monetary compensation. It also analyses the various valuation methodologies employed by tribunals, from the widely used, but hotly disputed, Discounted Cash Flow (DCF) method to alternative methods such as replacement value, book value, and investment cost. The chapter then turns to the potential defences host states may invoke to excuse non-performance of their obligations, including *force majeure*, contributory fault, and security exceptions contained in investment treaties and customary international law. The chapter also addresses the growing importance of public interest considerations – particularly human rights, environmental protection and corporate social responsibility – in investment arbitration, examining how tribunals have balanced these concerns against investor protections. Finally, the chapter examines procedural aspects that follow merits determinations, including annulment, enforcement of awards, and the allocation of costs. Throughout, the chapter highlights relevant Caribbean case examples to demonstrate how these principles operate in practice.

I. THE MERITS STAGE

Once a tribunal has established jurisdiction over a case and deemed that the issues raised by the claim are admissible, the matter proceeds to the merits hearing,[1] where the tribunal examines whether the claimant has established, on a balance of probabilities, that there has been a breach occasioned by the respondent's state's conduct.[2] In circumstances where

1 CL Jean Ho Lim and Martins Paparinskis, *International Investment Law and Arbitration: Commentary, Awards and Other Materials* (2nd edn, CUP 2021) 276.

2 Note that this raises the question of attribution. According to Article 2 of the ILC Articles: [t]here is an internationally wrongful act of a State when conduct consisting of an action or omission: (a) is attributable to the State under international law; and (b) constitutes a breach of an international obligation of the State. In short, a state can only be held responsible for conduct which is attributable to it under international law, and which is not in conformity with what is required of it under the provisions of the BIT. Some tribunals have expressed the view that 'the issue of attribution relates both to the Tribunal's jurisdiction and to the merits of [the] dispute' (*Tulip Real Estate and Development Netherlands v Republic of Turkey*, ICSID Case No. ARB/11/28, Award, 10 March 2014, para. 276). Another tribunal took the view that '[t]he question whether the issue of attribution

DOI: 10.4324/9781003734185-7

the tribunal has made findings at the jurisdictional hearing, these findings do not, however, strictly bind the tribunal hearing the merits of the dispute, as noted by the tribunal in *Tidewater v Venezuela*:[3]

> However, it is axiomatic that no findings of fact made by an international tribunal in the context of a jurisdictional challenge can bind it in its subsequent determination of the merits of the dispute. On the contrary, an arbitral tribunal must, for the purpose of its jurisdictional determination, presume the facts that found the claim on the merits as alleged by the claimant to be true (unless they are plainly without any foundation). In that sense, its determination may be said to be *prima facie*. In the application of those presumed facts to the legal question of jurisdiction before it, the tribunal must objectively characterise those facts in order to determine finally whether they fall within or outside the scope of the Parties' consent. In making this determination, the tribunal may not simply adopt the claimant's characterisation without examination. In this way, a tribunal whose jurisdiction is contested strikes the balance between avoiding pre-judging the merits, on the one hand, and objectively determining the question of jurisdiction on the other. This is the consistent jurisprudence of the International Court of Justice,164 and of ICSID tribunals.
>
> It follows therefore that the Tribunal approaches the determination of Respondent's substantive liability to Claimants, if any, entirely afresh and on the basis of the evidentiary record presented to it in the written and oral phase on the merits.[4]

At the hearing, the tribunal considers the facts and arguments raised and decides the case in the light of the governing law.[5] Parties can choose a specific law to govern their arbitration agreement, but in the absence of such a choice, the law of the seat of arbitration (where the arbitration takes place) is often applied.[6]

---

is, in a given case, one of jurisdiction or of merits is not . . . susceptible of a clear-cut answer'. (*Gustav F.W. Hamester GmbH & Co KG v Republic of Ghana*, ICSID Case No. ARB/07/24, Award, 18 June 2010, para. 140). In *Venezuela SRL v Venezuela*, PCA Case No. 2013-34, Partial Award, the tribunal dealt with the question of attribution as part of the merits of the dispute. Meanwhile, in *F-W Oil Interests, Inc v The Republic of Trinidad and Tobago*, ICSID Case No. ARB/01/14, Award, 3 March 2006, paras. 204, 207), the tribunal noted:

> although there must be serious doubt as to whether either Trinmar or Petrotrin constituted organs of the State of Trinidad and Tobago, it is by no means to be excluded that, for some of their individual activity at least, either of those two bodies might, in the particular circumstances established in evidence in this arbitration, have been acting sufficiently within the overall aegis of public authority as to engage the responsibility of the State for international law purposes. The possibility is given particular meaning by the general nature of the activity in question in this arbitration, namely the winning of a sovereign natural resource of undeniably major significance to the entire economy of the country. It would, self-evidently, be necessary to show, in addition to the attributability of their conduct in this sense, that it also gave rise in substance to a breach of the international obligations of the State . . . . It follows from the above that in the factual circumstances of the present arbitration, if the necessary 'investment' had been present, the Tribunal – even while declining to accept either the Respondent's denial of State liability of any kind, or the Claimant's tendency to treat conduct at all three levels within Trinidad and Tobago as an undifferentiated lump – would have been prepared to find, on the facts, that the various admitted interventions by Trinidad & Tobago Government Ministers into the part-commercial/part-statal operations of Petrotrin and Trinmar were quite sufficient to raise serious issues as to answerable breaches of the BIT in relation to FWO.

3 ICSID Case No. ARB/10/5, Award, 13 March 2015, paras. 84–85.

4 ibid 85.

5 Borzu Sabahi et al., *Investor-State Arbitration* (2nd edn, Oxford Law Pro 2019) 112–226. See, also, Hege Elisabeth Kjos, *Applicable Law in Investor-State Arbitration* (OUP 2013).

6 Yannick Radi, *Rules and Practices of International Investment and Arbitration* (CUP 2020) 269.

A. Remedies

Some Caribbean IIAs[7] identify remedies that are available in the event of a breach by a state of its treaty obligations. For example, Article 17 of the Belize-Austria BIT provides:

> (1) Arbitration awards, which may include an award of interest, shall be final and binding upon the parties to the dispute and may provide the following forms of relief:
> (a) a declaration that the Contracting Party has failed to comply with its obligations under this Agreement;
> (b) pecuniary compensation, which shall include interest from the time the loss or damage was incurred until time of payment;
> (c) restitution in kind in appropriate cases, provided that the Contracting Party may pay pecuniary compensation in lieu thereof where restitution is not practicable; and
> (d) with the agreement of the parties to the dispute, any other form of relief.
> (2) Each Contracting Party shall make provision for the effective enforcement of awards made pursuant to this Article and shall carry out without delay any such award issued in a proceeding to which it is party.

Most Caribbean IIAs are, however, silent on the question of remedies. This does not, however, preclude tribunals from making an award consisting of appropriate remedies. Indeed, where a tribunal finds that there has been a breach in respect of which loss is sustained by the investor, it has competence to award appropriate remedies.[8] More pointedly, the Permanent Court of International Justice clarified in its 1928 judgment in *Chorzów Factory*[9] that:

> The essential principle contained in the actual notion of an illegal act – a principle which seems to be established by international practice and in particular by the decisions of arbitral tribunals – is that reparation must, as far as possible, wipe out all the consequences of the illegal act and re-establish the situation which would, in all probability, have existed if that act had not been committed. Restitution in kind, or, if this is not possible, payment of a sum corresponding to the value which a restitution in kind would bear; the award, if need be, of damages for loss sustained which would not covered by restitution in kind or payment in place of it.[10]

The aforementioned remedies are considered in further detail hereafter.

(i) Restitution

Restitution, according to Article 35 of the International Law Commission's (ILC) Draft Articles,[11] requires a state responsible for an internationally wrongful act to re-establish the situation which existed before the wrongful act was committed, provided, and to the extent, that restitution: (i) is not materially impossible; (ii) does not involve a burden out of all

7 For example, Trinidad and Tobago-Guatemala BIT Article 11(4).

8 *Biwater Gauff v Tanzania*, ICSID Case No. ARB/05/22, Award 24 July 2008. The tribunal explained that the requirement of causation requires a sufficient link between the wrongful act and the loss/damage in question. The loss/suffered must also not be too remote.

9 (*Germany v Poland*) (Merits) (1928) PCIJ Rep Series A No 17.

10 ibid 125.

11 International Law Commission, *Draft Articles on Responsibility of States for Internationally Wrongful Acts* in *Report of the International Law Commission on the work of its fifty-third session* (23 April–1 June and 2 July–10 August 2001) UN Doc A/56/10, chp IV.

proportion to the benefit deriving from restitution instead of compensation. In practice, restitution is a rarely sought remedy. In one of the few cases in which restitution was ordered, *Franck Charles Arif v Moldova*,[12] the claimant argued that restitution would require the respondent to enable it to open and operate his duty-free store at Chisinau International Airport without undue interruption. This would have required all relevant licences and authorisations to be (re)issued by the respondent and its organs to Le Bridge, as well as a new lease agreement, at identical or essentially similar terms as the former Airport Lease agreement, leasing out the exact same premises at the Airport to Le Bridge for the same duration (and preferential renewal rights), which would start to run at the date of the actual opening of the Airport store. The claimant, however, contested that the reality was that the respondent was unwilling or unable to extend a firm offer of restitution, backed by adequate guarantees and so insisted on reparation in the form of damages. In response, the respondent in its letters requested time to consider the form restitution might take in relation to the Airport store.

The tribunal considered that restitution was an appropriate remedy in this case. It held:

> The Tribunal notes that the general position in international law is that the injured State may elect between the available forms of reparation and may prefer compensation to restitution. On the other hand, restitution is more consistent with the objectives of bilateral investment treaties, as it preserves both the investment and the relationship between the investor and the Host State.[13]
>
> The Tribunal considers restitution to be the preferable remedy, but as in the present case Respondent has not been able to confirm that restitution is possible, and the Tribunal cannot supervise any restitutionary remedy, the best course is to order restitution and compensation as alternatives, with the remedy of compensation suspended for a period of ninety days. This provides Respondent with the opportunity, in light of the findings of this award, to formulate and propose to Claimant the exact mechanism of restitution. If restitution is not possible, or the terms of restitution proposed by Respondent are not satisfactory to Claimant then the damages awarded will satisfy the violation of Claimant's right to fair and equitable treatment. This solution provides a final opportunity to preserve the investment, while also preserving Claimant's right to damages if a satisfactory restitutionary solution cannot be found.[14]

In most cases, however, restitution is neither sought nor is possible given the exigency of the circumstances in question. In such cases, an award of compensation is appropriate.

(ii) Compensation

Compensation (including interest) is a monetary award of damages that seeks to remedy the loss sustained by the investor.[15] If no loss is sustained, there will be no basis for an award of compensation.[16] The purpose of compensation is to make the injured party whole. In

12 ICSID Case No. ARB/11/23, Award, 8 April 2013.

13 ibid 570.

14 ibid 571.

15 Hrefried Wöss, Adriana San Román Rivera, Pablo Spiller, and Santiago Dellepiane, *Damages in International Arbitration under Complex Long-term Contracts* (OUP 2014) 186; *Opinion in the Lusitania Cases* (1923) 7 *Reports of International Arbitral Awards* 32.

16 *Philip Morris Brands Sàrl, Philip Morris Products S.A. and Abal Hermanos S.A. v Oriental Republic of Uruguay*, ICSID Case No. ARB/10/7, Award, 8 July 2016, para. 192.

most Caribbean IIAs, the precise measure of compensation prescribed is that of the 'Hull formula' principally in the context of the guarantee against expropriation,[17] though the same formula is typically applied in non-expropriation cases.[18]

For example, Article III of the Jamaica-USA BIT provides:

> 1. Investments shall not be expropriated or nationalized either directly or indirectly through measures tantamount to expropriation or nationalization ('expropriation') except for a public purpose; in a non-discriminatory manner; upon payment of prompt, adequate and effective compensation; and in accordance with due process of law and the general principles of treatment provided for in Article II(2). Compensation shall be equivalent to the fair market value of the expropriated investment immediately before the expropriatory action was taken or was made known by the authorities, whichever is earlier; be paid without delay; include interest at a commercially reasonable rate from the date of expropriation; be fully realizable; and be freely transferable at the prevailing market rate of exchange on the date of expropriation. The determination of fair market value shall not reflect any change in the value of the investment attributable to the expropriatory or to public knowledge of the expropriatory action before it was taken or made known by the authorities.

Although Latin American countries have generally advocated for the *Calvo* formula[19] as the basis for calculating damages in respect of which the law of the host state decides the measure of compensation, this has not gained traction globally.[20] In fact, most arbitral tribunals have insisted on the *Hull* formula,[21] which requires the provision of prompt, adequate and effective compensation in case of a breach. Compensation must be paid as soon as possible after the harmful action has occurred; any delays that occur will result in the imposition of accrued interest. Meanwhile, 'adequacy' of compensation is normally defined by reference to the market; that is, what someone is willing to pay for it on the market at the time the damaging treaty violation(s) occurred, such as the moment just before a decree expropriating the assets was issued. Finally, compensation for the harms suffered must be in a recognisable and usable currency that is transferable to the investor's own currency.

In *Michael Lee-Chin v Dominican Republic*,[22] on the basis of the respondent's violation of the FET standard by failing to revise the tipping fees – as provided for in the Concession Agreement – US$17,133,000 was awarded in damages by the tribunal. The tribunal then applied the Discount Cash Flow method (DFC),[23] finding that, in addition to the other applicable discounts on the amounts actually collected by Lajun, the percentage attributable

17 See full listing of Caribbean expropriation provisions in Chapter 4 of this book.

18 *CMS v Argentina*, ICSID Case No. ARB/01/8, Award, 12 May 2005.

19 In respect of the *Calvo* formula, tribunals can consider the quality of the investor's goods and services; the extent of the profits already made by the investor; and the extent of the investor's contributions to the host state's economy.

20 Shuo Feng and Wei Shen, 'Calvo Is Back! Changing Sovereignty and Evolutionary Investment Law in a Leaving and Return of the State Paradigm' (2020) 13 *Journal of East Asia and International Law* 307; Omar E García-Bolívar, 'Sovereignty vs. Investment Protection: Back to Calvo?' (2009) 24(2) *ICSID Review Foreign Investment Law Journal* 464.

21 Kaj Hobér, 'Compensation', in Katia Fach Gómez and Catharine Titi (eds), *The Award in International Investment Arbitration* (OUP 2024) 41.

22 ICSID Case No. UNCT/18/3, Award, 6 October 2023.

23 The DCF method is usually applied where a large investment had been made up front, and the investor is seeking to recoup money based on the likely level of return. It equates to future cash flows minus costs.

to taxes, the net amount of damages attributable to the respondent for failing to adjust the tipping fees in the period 2013–2017 was US$5,422,898; that is, US$17,133,000 (but-for cash flows) minus the following amounts: US$8,000,000 (sanitary investment), US$2,005,730 (taxes), and US$1,044,277 (actual cash flows). However, only 90% of this amount was ultimately awarded, which was the claimant's ownership interest, that is, US$4,880,609.

A similar approach was countenanced in *Dunkeld v Belize*.[24] Here, the tribunal addressed a dispute concerning Belize's 2009 expropriation of Dunkeld's 71.2% interest in Belize Telemedia Limited. Central to the valuation was the disputed Accommodation Agreement between Belize and Telemedia, which provided tax benefits, import duty exemptions, and VoIP service restrictions. The tribunal determined that this agreement was valid through apparent authority principles and included its value in calculating damages, albeit with a 5% supplemental discount reflecting its status as an un-arbitrated contingent claim. The tribunal adopted the respondent's DCF approach based on Telemedia's 2009–2010 business plan, finding the claimant's 'bottom-up' market-based projections were excessively speculative. However, the tribunal modified the Government's calculations to use only economic data available on the valuation date and rejected the inclusion of potential synergies absent evidence of specific telecommunications buyers who would pay for such synergies. The tribunal determined Telemedia's value at BZ$5.65 per share (considerably higher than the Government's BZ$1.44 valuation but lower than Dunkeld's BZ$10.23 claim), with Dunkeld's interest worth US$96,935,233. The tribunal awarded pre-award interest at 8.34% compounded quarterly, totalling US$72,017,410, plus the costs of related proceedings and post-award interest at the same rate.

The speculative nature of damages, often resulting in crippling compensation,[25] particularly in circumstances in which the DCF method is applied, has provoked considerable contestation among states and scholars.[26] Indeed, in *Dunkeld*,[27] the tribunal warned against speculative damages, noting 'the effect of [too many] projections is to increase the degree of

24 PCA Case No. 2010–13, Award, 28 June 2016.

25 The so-called *Yukos* claimants brought three ISDS cases (*Hulley Enterprises Ltd. (Cyprus) v Russian Federation* (PCA Case No. AA 226), *Yukos Universal Ltd. (Isle of Man) v Russian Federation* (PCA Case No. AA 227), *and Veteran Petroleum Ltd. (Cyprus) v Russian* Federation (PCA Case No. AA 228, Award, 18 July 2014)) and parallel proceedings before the ECtHR. The ISDS tribunals and the ECtHR applied the same compensation standard of 'full reparation' to the same set of facts. The ISDS cases collectively awarded approximately US$50 billion in damages against the Russian Federation. UNCTAD reports that

> whereas tribunals ordered on average payment of USD 68 million between 2000 and 2009, this number nearly quadrupled to over USD 250 million in the past decade. This does not include the interest due on the principal amounts awarded, which can be substantial.

https://unctad.org/system/files/official-document/diaepcbinf2024d3_en.pdf.

26 Jonathan Bonnitcha, José Manuel Álvarez-Zárate, Martin Menkes, Josef Ostřanský, and Yanwen Zhang, 'The Assessment and Calculation of Damages in Treaty-based ISDS' (Academic Forum on ISDS Concept Paper 2025/1, 28 February 2025); Toni Marzal, 'Critique of Valuation in the Calculation of Damages in ISDS: Between Law, Finance and Politics' in Isabel Feichtner and Geoff Gordon (eds), *Constitutions of Value: Law, Governance, and Political Ecology* (Routledge 2023) 181–98; Anastasia Fomenko, 'Assessment of Damages and Compensation in the Context of Proposals to Reform the Investor-State Dispute Settlement System' (2023) 1(2) *HSE University Journal of International Law* 72–92.

27 PCA Case No. 2010–13, Award, 28 June 2016.

uncertainty in the claimant's calculations beyond what the Tribunal considers reasonable'. Similarly, in *Franck Charles Arif v Moldova*,[28] the tribunal considered that:

> . . . the DCF methodology is not appropriate for a business that never operated and where a satisfactory basis for its projected revenues has not been demonstrated. Use of a DCF methodology in these circumstances gives an excessively speculative outcome.[29] ibid para 241.

Given the highly disputed nature of the DCF method,[30] and its inappropriateness in certain cases (e.g. where the investor has not commenced its operations), other valuation methods have been employed by different tribunals. For example, the replacement value method,[31] which involves an award reflecting the cost of replacing the damaged or lost investment, was applied in *Grenada Private Power v Grenada*.[32] At issue here was the valuation of GRENLEC shares following a 'Repurchase Event' triggered by Grenada's 2016 electricity sector restructuring. The disputed valuation relied on the 'Second Schedule' formula from the 1994 Electricity Supply Act, which incorporated replacement cost as a fundamental component. The Second Schedule valuation specified that GRENLEC's assets should be valued based on the 'replacement cost on site' of fixed assets, including buildings, plant, works, and fixtures. This replacement cost approach diverged from more common discounted cash flow methods, focusing instead on what it would cost to replace physical assets at the valuation date rather than their future earning potential. That said, several contested aspects of the replacement valuation emerged during the arbitration. The tribunal determined that replacement cost properly includes customs and import duties, even when such duties were never actually paid due to tax exemptions, because replacement at the valuation date would necessitate paying these duties. The treatment of assets allegedly destroyed by Hurricane Ivan was disputed, with the tribunal accepting the claimants' methodology that attributed EC$17.4 million to replacement of destroyed assets rather than repairs. Depreciation methodology was another point of contention, with the tribunal rejecting the 5% depreciation rate for computer equipment as unreasonable, instead supporting a 20% rate that better reflected computers' shorter useful life. Interestingly, the experts' applications of the replacement value method produced significantly different valuations: EC$361,882,000 from the claimants' experts versus EC$276,239,000 from the respondent's. After making its own adjustments for issues like the Hurricane Insurance Reserve and customer contributions to line extensions, the tribunal arrived at a final valuation of EC$337,711,000. The tribunal ultimately held that the replacement value approach specified in the Second Schedule was a valid contractual methodology that should be enforced despite the respondent's arguments that it produced an excessive valuation compared to fair market value.

Separately, in other cases, such as *Rusoro Mining Ltd RUSORO v Venezuela*,[33] the book value method was applied. The net difference between a firm's entire assets and liabilities

28 ICSID Case No. ARB/11/23, Award, 8 April 2013.
29 ibid 576.
30 Bonnitcha et al. (n 26).
31 Mark Bezant and David Rogers, 'Asset-Based Approach and Other Valuation Methodologies' in John A. Tenor (eds), *The Guide to Damages in International Arbitration* (2nd edn, Law Business Research Ltd 2017) 219–20.
32 ICSID Case No. ARB/17/13, Award, 29 March 2020.
33 ICSID Case No. ARB(AF)/12/5, Award, 22 August 2016.

is the book value of that investment.[34] Book value represents the total worth of an investor's assets that shareholders would get if the company were to be liquidated.[35] The book value of an asset equals its carrying value on the balance sheet.[36] Meanwhile, the liquidation value is appropriate in those cases in which the investment is in the process of being liquidated.[37] The liquidation value is arrived at by estimating the value of the investor's individual assets if they were sold during liquidation proceedings, minus costs.[38] The respondent asked that the tribunal apply this method in *Tidewater v Venezuela,*[39] but the tribunal ultimately refused to do so, finding that it was not appropriate to determine the fair market value by reference to the liquidation value of the assets of the SEMARCA Enterprise, as this method would likely only be appropriate, as the World Bank Guidelines point out, where the enterprise was not a proven going concern. Finally, some tribunals, such as *Mobil v Venezuela*,[40] make an award of damages on the basis of the cost of the investment; that is, the amount the investor spent setting up their business.[41] This, however, does not take account of projected profits in circumstances where the investment was in its developmental stage.

(A) Moral Damages

Article 31 of the ILC Draft Articles intimates that moral damages may be appropriate in certain cases where an internationally wrongful act for which the state is responsible has been established. While, in the investment context, moral damages are not intended to punish the wrongdoer nor make an example of them in order to deter future wrongdoing,[42] it nonetheless is important in vindicating the harms suffered as a result of egregious behaviour on the part of the respondent that that causes physical injuries or distress or which amount to harassment to the investor or loss of business reputation.[43]

An amount of US$1,000,000 in moral damages, including for loss of reputation, was awarded to the investor in *Desert Line v Yemen*[44] in circumstances where Yemeni armed forces, along with members of the local council and local tribes, confronted and threatened Desert Line's personnel by open firing with automatic weapons and removing the claimant's equipment. The tribunal considered that:

> Even if investment treaties primarily aim at protecting property and economic values, they do not exclude, as such, that a party may, in exceptional circumstances, ask for compensation for moral damages. It is generally accepted in most legal systems that moral damages may also be recovered besides pure economic damages. There are indeed no reasons to exclude them. The Arbitral Tribunal knows that it is difficult, if not impossible, to substantiate a prejudice of the

34 Jonathan Bonnitcha, Malcolm Langford, José M Alvarez-Zárate, and Daniel Behn, 'Damages and ISDS Reform: Between Procedure and Substance' (2023) 14(2) *Journal of International Dispute Settlement* 244.

35 ibid.

36 ibid.

37 Irmgard Marboe, *Calculation of Compensation and Damages in International Investment Law* (OUP 2009) 287–93.

38 ibid 206.

39 ICSID Case No. ARB/10/5, Award, 13 March 2015, para. 165.

40 ICSID Case No. ARB/07/27, Award, 9 October 2014.

41 ibid 136.

42 Stephen Jagusch and Thomas Sebastian, 'Moral Damages in Investment Arbitration: Punitive Damages in Compensatory Clothing?' (2013) 29 *Arbitration International* 59.

43 *Joseph Charles Lemire v Ukraine*, ICSID Case No. ARB/06/18, Award, 28 March 2011, para. 333.

44 ICSID Case No. ARB/05/17, Award, 6 February 2008.

> kind ascertained in the present award. Still, as it was held in the Lusitania cases, non-material damages may be 'very real, and the mere fact that they are difficult to measure or estimate by monetary standards makes them none the less real and affords no reason why the injured person should not be compensated'.[45]

However, an award of moral damages is an exceptional remedy, and a claim for same has generally been rejected by tribunals. For example, in *Michael Lee-Chin v Dominican Republic*,[46] the claimant requested moral damages estimated at US$5,000,000 for what he considered to be a defamation campaign against him carried out by the state through the media, and discriminatory intimidation tactics that the state allegedly employed against Mr. Adrian Christopher Lee-Chin by seeking his criminal prosecution. According to the claimant, these actions caused not only severe damage to his reputation but also significant emotional trauma to both him and his family members. The tribunal, however, rejected this claim, finding that the arguments were unconvincing in the light of the fact that the threshold for an award of moral damages is particularly high. It held:

> The threshold for awarding compensation for moral damages is particularly high. It is not enough to claim alleged suffering or harm to a person's reputation for moral damages to arise. On the contrary, such damages must be convincingly proven, including proof of the causal link between the party causing the damage and the victim. It should be noted that, as has been pointed out, the most important aspect of the alleged facts do not even refer directly to Claimant but to his son. The evidence submitted by Claimant to support his request has been anything but persuasive.
>
> In contrast, Respondent has submitted several precedents in which other arbitral tribunals refer to the 'exceptional circumstances' that must be present for moral damages to arise, providing some examples of such circumstances. Claimant has fallen far short of this threshold, which the Tribunal considers to be appropriate. Moreover, Claimant did not even make a proper case regarding the Tribunal's jurisdiction to award moral damages under the specific applicable regulatory framework.[47]

Similarly, in *Lemire v Ukraine*,[48] the tribunal denied the investor's claim for moral damages in circumstances where the respondent rejected a long string of applications for new radio frequencies. Although that the tribunal acknowledged that the recurring rejections of applications probably had a negative impact on his entrepreneurial image, this was not enough: the main question was whether the injury inflicted was substantial. On the facts, the claimant did not allege, and the tribunal did not find any indication, that the National Council tried to intimidate Gala Radio through its inspections. Additionally, the two warnings issued by the National Council were annulled by court decisions. There was no evidence that Ukraine had orchestrated a cat-and-mouse game of some kind. Therefore, the claimant's situation prior to the inspections had been reestablished and, thus, no lasting prejudice was caused. Further, while the National Council's initial decision that Gala Radio's renewal of licence should be charged at the new increased fee rate was incorrect, and the claimant may have suffered some degree of stress or anxiety until the mistake was corrected, in the end he had paid the renewal fee at the correct lower rates. Finally, although the tribunal acknowledged that the claimant was mistreated by the regulator, the National Council, and had sympathy

45 ibid 289.
46 ICSID Case No. UNCT/18/3, Award, 6 October 2023.
47 ibid 575–76.
48 *Lemire v Ukraine*, ICSID Case No. ARB/06/18, Award, 28 March 2011.

and understanding for the stress and anxiety which he must have felt at certain times during his long fight in the defence of his rights, the moral aspects of his injuries were already compensated for by the award of a significant amount of economic compensation. In short, the extraordinary threshold required for the recognition of separate and additional moral damages was not met in this case:

> as a general rule, moral damages are not available to a party injured by the wrongful acts of a State, but that moral damages can be awarded in exceptional cases, provided that – the State's actions imply physical threat, illegal detention or other analogous situations in which the ill-treatment contravenes the norms according to which civilized nations are expected to act; – the State's actions cause a deterioration of health, stress, anxiety, other mental suffering such as humiliation, shame and degradation, or loss of reputation, credit and social position; and – both cause and effect are grave or substantial.[49]

A similar finding was arrived at in *OL European Group B.V. v Venezuela,*[50] a case in which the tribunal rejected the claimant's request for moral damages in circumstances where the investor claimed that its bottle-making plants were nationalised during Chávez's administration. In the tribunal's view, the investor did not appropriately describe the relevant facts in their statements of claim and other materials. More particularly, the investor could not demonstrate that Venezuela's officials harassed or threatened their employees to continue working in the plants, and nor could they demonstrate that Venezuela's officials were physically aggressive or threatening when dealing with the companies.

(B) Reduction of Damages

The amount awarded in damages may be reduced on account of a failure by the claimant to mitigate their loss, as well as where it is shown that the claimant has contributed to the losses it has sustained. These are addressed in turn below.

(1) Mitigation

Damages may be reduced on account of a failure to mitigate on the part of the claimant in question.[51] Although IIAs do not generally mention a duty to mitigate, the duty is one widely recognised as a general principle of international law, as noted by the tribunal in *Middle East Shipping & Handling Co. v Arab Republic of Egypt.*[52] There, the tribunal held that, in respect of restrictions imposed on the claimant's shipment of grey cement,

> an investor who has been subjected to a revocation of the essential license for its investment activity, three years earlier, has good reason to decide that, after that experience, it shall not continue with the investment activity, after the activity is again permitted.[53]

In *Dunkeld v Belize,*[54] the respondent argued that Dunkeld was barred from recovering damages because it had failed to mitigate damages largely due to its failure to make use of a

49 ibid 333.

50 ICSID Case No. ARB/11/25, Award, 10 March 2015.

51 Decision taken by the Governing Council of the United Nations Compensation Commission during the resumed Fourth Session at the 23rd meeting (6 March 1992) UN Doc S/AC.26/1992/9, para. 6.

52 7 ICSID Rep 173, 205 (Award) (12 April 2002).

53 ibid 169.

54 PCA Case No. 2010–13, Award, 28 June 2016.

fair and independent mechanism to mitigate its alleged damages through the local compensation process. As a matter of principle, the tribunal considered that:

> recourse to local remedies is not strictly linked to the mitigation of losses, such that any duty to mitigate should require the exhaustion of local remedies or require a party to prefer a local remedy to one that may be available to it through international arbitration. Nevertheless, it may be the case that local administrative procedures may offer a remedy that appears more rapid or certain than that of an international claim, such that a party would be derelict in failing to attempt the local process.[55]

The tribunal further explained that:

> The duty to make reasonable use of available administrative procedures to reduce losses certainly does not imply that a potential Claimant must forego the option of pursing international remedies or must agree to whatever compensation is offered at the local level.[56]

On the facts, given that the Registered Owners pursued local compensation without a successful result, and the respondent did not identify any other steps that the claimant could reasonably have taken to mitigate its losses, the claimant was found not to have failed in its duty to mitigate.

Finally, it is important to note that investors are required to exercise due diligence when making their investment, failing which a tribunal may evaluate such conduct in determining the threshold of violation, which is unrelated to the question of mitigation. For example, in *Biwater v Tanzania*,[57] the tribunal held that 'countervailing factors such as the responsibility of foreign investors, both in terms of prior due diligence as well as subsequent conduct' must be taken into account to determine the threshold of violation. Legitimate expectations are limited when 'an investor itself takes on risks in entering a particular investment environment'.[58] Similarly, in *Lemire v Ukraine*,[59] the tribunal insisted that it had to take 'the investor's conduct in the host country' and in particular its 'duty to perform an investigation before effecting the investment' into consideration,[60] not as an element for the mitigation of damages but for the evaluation of the state's conduct.

(2) Contributory Fault

Contributory fault will be dealt with in greater detail in the subsequent section on 'defences'. For the purposes of this discussion, however, it is important to note that damages awarded may be reduced on account of the fault of the claimant, including its contribution to the injury by wilful or negligent actions or omissions.[61] In this regard, the tribunal in *MTD v*

55 ibid 197.

56 ibid 199.

57 ICSID Case No. ARB/05/22, Award, 24 July 2008.

58 ibid 601.

59 *Lemire v Ukraine*, ICSID Case No. ARB/06/18, Award, 28 March 2011.

60 *Joseph Charles Lemire v Ukraine*, ICSID Case No. ARB/06/18, Decision on Jurisdiction and Liability, 14 January 2010, para. 285.

61 *Quiborax S.A., Non-Metallic Minerals S.A. v Plurinational State of Bolivia*, ICSID Case No. ARB/06/2, Award, 16 September 2015, paras. 327, 328; *Ioan Micula, Viorel Micula et al. v Romania*, ICSID Case No. ARB/05/20, Final Award 11 December 2013, [917]; *Biwater Gauff (Tanzania) Limited v United Republic of Tanzania*, ICSID Case No. ARB/05/22, Award 24 July 2008, para. 776.

Chile[62] reduced the damages awarded by 50%, while in *Occidental v Ecuador,*[63] damages were reduced by 25% on account of the respective claimants' contributory fault.

Compensation due to war, armed conflict etc

Some IIAs[64] make provision for the award of compensation in the case of injury sustained in the context of exigencies, including armed conflict. For example, Article 4(2) Jamaica-Argentina BIT provides:

> Investors of either Contracting Party who suffer losses of their investments in the territory of the other Contracting Party due to war or other armed conflict, a state of national emergency, revolt, insurrection or riot shall be accorded with respect to restitution, indemnification, compensation or other settlement, a treatment which is no less favourable than that accorded to its own investors on to investors of any third State.

It is important to note that such provision does not provide for an automatic right to damages *per se* but provides for compensation that is no less favourable that than awarded to domestic and third state investors. According to Schreuer, these clauses do not create a substantive right to restitution but merely assert that once compensation is provided by the state, it should make available similar compensation to foreign and third-party investors who are similarly placed.[65] The dissenting opinion of Samuel K.B. Asante in *AAPL v Sri Lanka*[66] is instructive in this regard:

> it is my view that it is fundamentally erroneous to construe Article 4(1) in such a manner as to impose a substantive liability to pay compensation. This provision does not prescribe a substantive obligation on the part of the host State to pay compensation where foreign investments sustain losses by reason of war or other armed conflict, revolution, a state of national emergency, revolt or other civil disturbance. It merely requires that, in these situations, the foreign investor be accorded national treatment or most-favoured-nation treatment with respect to compensation, restitution, indemnity or other settlement. The words 'shall be accorded treatment as regards restitution, indemnification, compensation or other settlement, no less favourable than that which the latter Contracting Party accords to its own nationals or companies or to nationals of any third state' mean that no issue of paying compensation arises unless it has been established to the Tribunal that the host State has provided or undertaken to provide 'restitution, indemnification, compensation or other settlement' for its own nationals or companies or the nationals or companies of a third State. In other words, the foreign investor does not derive any benefit from Article 4(1) unless some right or privilege has been explicitly granted by the host State to its nationals or companies or to the nationals or companies of a third State in similar circumstances. With regard to national treatment, such a right or privilege will be assured by an explicit provision of domestic law or other domestic measure. The most-favoured-nation treatment clause, on the other hand, will be triggered into operation by the conclusion of a treaty or the adoption of a specific policy or measure by the host State granting a right or privilege or concession to the nationals or companies of a third State with respect to compensation or other forms of settlement.[67]

62 *MTD Equity Sdn. Bhd. and MTD Chile S.A. v Republic of Chile*, ICSID Case No. ARB/01/7, Award, 25 May 2004, para. 243.

63 *Occidental Petroleum Corporation and Occidental Exploration and Production Company v The Republic of Ecuador*, ICSID Case No. ARB/06/11, Award, 5 October 2012, para. 687.

64 For example, Barbados-Cuba BIT Article 4(1); Barbados-Mauritius BIT Article 6(1); Barbados-UK BIT Article 4(1); Trinidad and Tobago-China BIT Article 5.

65 Christoph Schreuer, 'The Protection of Investments in Armed Conflicts' (2012) TDM 1.

66 ICSID/ARB/87/3, Award, 27 June 1990.

67 ibid Dissenting Opinion of Samuel K.B. Asante, 586.

Meanwhile, in *CMS v Argentina*,[68] the tribunal reaffirmed that the 'plain meaning of the Article is to provide a floor treatment for the investor in the context of the measures adopted in respect of the losses suffered in the emergency, not different from that applied to nationals or other foreign investors. The Article does not derogate from the Treaty rights but rather ensures that any measures directed at offsetting or minimising losses will be applied in a discriminatory manner.'[69]

B. Defences

Faced with an investor-state arbitration claim, the respondent may invoke one or more relevant defences, depending on the nature of the facts in question. The defences typically invoked by host states as respondents in arbitration proceedings are considered hereafter.

(i) Force Majeure

Unforeseen events which make it materially impossible for a state to perform its international investment obligations may provide the basis for a tribunal to excuse the non-performance of such obligations by the state.[70] However, several cumulative conditions must be met, as articulated by Article 23 of the ILC Draft Articles:

1. The wrongfulness of an act of a State not in conformity with an international obligation of that State is precluded if the act is due to *force majeure*, that is the occurrence of an irresistible force or of an unforeseen event, beyond the control of the State, making it materially impossible in the circumstances to perform the obligation.
2. Paragraph 1 does not apply if:
   (a) The situation of *force majeure* is due, either alone or in combination with other factors, to the conduct of the State invoking it; or
   (b) The State has assumed the risk of that situation occurring.

Force majeure is only applicable in the event of an unforeseen event or events not of an easily foreseeable kind,[71] potentially including earthquakes, droughts, wars, revolutions, mob violence, economic crises or pandemics. A difficulty in performance is not, however, an adequate defence, nor is a circumstance rendering performance more difficult or burdensome. In addition, the state is responsible for the conduct of all public authorities within its territory and is under a due diligence obligation to take reasonable steps to prevent third parties from engaging in acts that would lead to an unforeseen event. In this connection, the state may not invoke *force majeure* if it is responsible for the situation nor when it has assumed the risk of the event occurring. If successfully invoked, the plea of *force majeure* is a valid excuse for the non-performance of a contractual obligation in international law.

68 *CMS v Argentina*, ICSID Case No. ARB/01/8, Award, 12 May 2005.
69 ibid 375.
70 Lu Wang and Wenhua Shan, 'Force Majeure and Investment Arbitration' (2022) 37(1–2) *ICSID Review* 138–59.
71 Federica Paddeu, *Justification and Excuse in International Law: Concept and Theory of General Defences* (CUP 2018) 285–333.

These principles were applied in *Aucoven v Venezuela*,[72] a case in which the tribunal addressed a dispute arising from a 30-year concession agreement for the construction, maintenance, and operation of an alternate bridge on the highway connecting Caracas and the seaport. The concession's financial structure depended critically on toll revenue, with planned increases necessary to fund the project and compensate Aucoven, the concessionaire. When the time came for the first toll increase, Venezuela's Ministry of Infrastructure refused to implement it, citing public resistance. This resistance was not insignificant; the announcement of planned toll increases sparked major protests from trucking companies and officials of the State of Vargas. The Ministry ultimately requested that Aucoven refrain from collecting any tolls until further notice. Despite this setback, Aucoven began operating the highway system without collecting tolls. Despite Aucoven's numerous requests for Venezuela to adjust the tolls according to their agreement, the toll rates remained at their initial level. This failure to raise tolls made it impossible to fund the construction costs as planned. Faced with this situation, Aucoven terminated the Concession Agreement and initiated arbitration proceedings against Venezuela. In its defence, Venezuela sought to rely on *force majeure* to excuse its non-performance of the Concession Agreement. This raised the central issue of whether the protests and related events satisfied the conditions required for a successful *force majeure* claim.

The tribunal analysed three key elements of *force majeure*: unforeseeability, impossibility, and attributability. Regarding unforeseeability, the tribunal noted that approximately ten years before these events, Venezuela had experienced the tragic events of the 1989 Caracazo – a violent popular protest triggered by increases in transportation prices. The tribunal reasoned that Venezuelan officials negotiating the agreement could not reasonably have ignored that the contractual mechanism of toll rate increases could potentially lead to violent popular protests similar to those of 1989. Venezuela appeared to acknowledge, or at least not deny, that some public resistance was foreseeable. The tribunal concluded that if popular protest could be foreseen, then the possibility of very violent protest could not be ruled out. Given the well-known tragic precedent of the Caracazo and the similar impact of contractual toll increases on the population, Venezuela failed to convince the tribunal that the possibility of civil unrest could not have been foreseen at the time of negotiating the Concession Agreement. For lack of unforeseeability alone, Venezuela's non-performance could not be excused on the grounds of *force majeure*.

Although not decisive for the outcome, the tribunal also addressed the conditions of impossibility and attributability for the sake of completeness. Regarding impossibility, the tribunal noted that it was not necessary for the *force majeure* event to be irresistible; it sufficed that, by all reasonable judgment, the event impeded the state from normal performance of the contract. While the civil protest was not irresistible in the sense that it could not have been mastered by the use of force, the tribunal was inclined to find that, considering the events of 1989 and the risk of repetition, the impossibility requirement appeared to have been met. On the question of attributability, the tribunal examined whether the 1997 civil unrest was attributable to Venezuela. The evidence showed that the protest had the full support of the local government of the State of Vargas. Although some local officials tried to quell the protests, the local government's support for the protest was clear. The extent to which such support was causal for the protests, or their seriousness was not readily apparent from the evidence, but given the finding on unforeseeability, the tribunal did not need to make a final judgment on this issue. Ultimately, the tribunal determined that Venezuela's breach of its

72 ICSID Case No. ARB/00/5, Award, 23 September 2003.

contractual obligation to raise the tolls was not excused by *force majeure*. The key factor in this determination was that the protests, given Venezuela's history with the Caracazo, were foreseeable at the time the parties had entered into the Concession Agreement.

(ii) Contributory Fault

For the defence of contributory fault to arise, the respondent must establish that, on the basis of the totality of the evidence, there is a causal link between the act or omission of the claimant, and the respondent's unlawful conduct.[73] Article 39 of the International Law Commission's Articles on the Responsibility of States for Internationally Wrongful Acts deals with the situation where damage has been caused by an internationally wrongful act of a state, which is accordingly responsible for the damage, but where the injured investor has materially contributed to the damage by some wilful or negligent act or omission. It is not any contribution by the injured party to the damage, however, which it has suffered which will trigger a finding of contributory fault. The contribution must be material and significant. In this connection, tribunals have a wide margin of discretion in apportioning fault.[74]

In *MTD Equity Sdn. Bhd. and MTD Chile S.A. v Republic of Chile*,[75] a Malaysian company invested in a planned residential development project in Pirque, Chile after receiving approval from Chile's Foreign Investment Committee, but was later denied the necessary zoning change by Chile's Department of Housing and Urban Development. The tribunal found a breach of the FET standard, but reduced the amount of damages ultimately awarded by 50% on account of the fact that the claimants, at the time of their contract with a Mr. Fontaine (as a partner), had made decisions that increased their risks in the transaction. More particularly, they had accepted to pay a price for the land without appropriate legal protection. Given that Chile had no say in Mr. Fontaine's selection nor were the financial difficulties of Mr. Fontaine attributable to Chile, the claimants, who had known all along about Mr. Fontaine's financial difficulties, had to bear the risk inherent in Mr. Fontaine's offer, and thus a reduction of damages by 50% was appropriate. Ultimately, the tribunal concluded that:

> a wise investor would not have paid full price up-front for land valued on the assumption of the realisation of the Project; he would at least have staged future payments to project progress, including the issuance of the required development permits.[76]

The operation of the defence of contributory fault was also evident in *Occidental Petroleum Corporation and Occidental Exploration and Production Company v The Republic of Ecuador*.[77] Here, OEPC agreed to a contractual framework with Ecuador that explicitly authorised Caducidad (declaration of termination) if a violation were to occur. The claimant sold a 40% interest to another entity (AEC) without obtaining the required government

73 Jean-Michel Marcoux and Andrea K. Bjorklund, 'Foreign Investors' Responsibilities and Contributory Fault in Investment Arbitration' (2020) 69(4) *International and Comparative Law Quarterly* 877–905.

74 *MTD Equity Sdn. Bhd. and MTD Chile S.A. v Republic of Chile*, (ICSID Case No. ARB/01/7), Decision on Annulment of 21 March 2007, para. 101.

75 ICSID Case No. ARB/01/7.

76 ibid 242.

77 ICSID Case No. ARB/06/1.

authorisation, resulting in Ecuador terminating the Participation Contract. The tribunal found that the issuance of the Caducidad Decree was a disproportionate sanction and a measure tantamount to expropriation of the claimants' substantial investment in Ecuador. The claimants' damages were, however, reduced by 25% because of the claimant's imprudence and negligence (although they did not act in bad faith) in obtaining the ministerial authorisation as required by Ecuadorian law. In the tribunal's view, if the claimant had sought the Minister's consent, in all likelihood it would have obtained it and it was probable that the respondent would not have declared Caducidad. In other words, without the violation of the law by the claimant, the Caducidad may not have happened. The claimant's fault prevented the respondent from exercising, in a formal way, its sovereign right to vet and approve AEC as the transferee of those rights and to vet any other unknown investor to which AEC could eventually transfer its rights. In this connection, the unlawful act of OEPC contributed to its injury in a material and significant way. As such, the claimants were awarded the amount of US$1,769,625,000 (US one billion, seven hundred sixty-nine million, six hundred twenty-five thousand dollars), one of the largest arbitral awards to date, though this was reduced by 25%.

Meanwhile, in *Yukos Universal Ltd v Russia,*[78] a tribunal established under the Energy Charter Treaty awarded over US$50 billion in damages (the largest arbitration award at that time) to Yukos shareholders after finding that Russia had expropriated Yukos Oil Company through a series of targeted tax assessments, enforcement actions, and forced sales of assets that the tribunal determined were politically motivated rather than legitimate tax collection measures. However, damages were reduced by 25% on account of the claimants' tax avoidance arrangements in some of the low-tax regions, which, because of its abusive nature, contributed to their injury in a material and significant way.

Finally, in some cases, respondent states have raised the question of the 'clean hands' doctrine,[79] arguing that, separately from the contributory fault defence, this doctrine can serve as a basis for the reduction of damages awarded. However, tribunals have generally treated the clean hands doctrine and contributory fault as synonymous. In *Copper Mesa Mining Corporation v Republic of Ecuador*,[80] for example, a foreign investor, by its local agents, (notwithstanding illegal provocations by local residents in the form of road-blocks, violence, arson and other impediments) resorted to recruiting and using armed men, firing guns and spraying mace at civilians, not as an accidental or isolated incident but as part of premeditated, disguised and well-funded plan to take the law into its own hands. In finding that the claimant's conduct against members of the Indigenous community was a 'sustained act of folly . . . [that] was bound to fail and to make the situation far worse for the Claimant',[81] the tribunal held that contributory fault had been established. On the evidence, the tribunal preferred to base its decision on the claimant's negligence, rather than the wilful conduct of its Canadian senior management, noting that if it were based on the latter's own wilful

78 *Yukos Universal Limited v The Russian Federation*, PCA Case No. AA 22, Final Award, 18 July 2014, para. 1634.

79 Igor Hron, '(Un)Clean Hands in International Investment Arbitration: Some Cleaning Required?' in Radovan Malachta and Patrik Provaznik (eds) *Cofola International: International and National Arbitration – Challenges and trends of present and future* (Masaryk University Press 2021) 213; Patrick Dumberry, 'The Clean Hands Doctrine as a General Principle of International Law' (2020) 21 *Journal of World Investment & Trade* 489.

80 PCA No. 2012–2, 15 March 2016.

81 ibid 6.99.

conduct as the claimant's alter ego, the result would be much graver for the claimant's case. On the relationship between contributory fault and the clean hands doctrine, the tribunal concluded:

> . . . the general approach taken in all these decisions, whether treated as causation, contributory fault (based on wilful or negligent act or omission) or unclean hands, is materially the same, deriving from a consistent line of international legal materials. The Tribunal decides to apply that general approach in this case.[82]

In this connection, given that the claimant's injury was caused both by the respondent's unlawful expropriation and by the claimant's own contributory negligent acts and omissions and unclean hands, the tribunal reduced the amount of damages awarded by 30%.

(iii) Self-Judging Non-Precluded Measures Clauses

Some Caribbean IIAs[83] provide self-judging defences, essentially providing that a host state may adopt, maintain and enforce measures which 'it considers' appropriate to ensure its essential security interests. For example, Article XVI(3) of the SVG-Taiwan BIT provides:

> 3. Nothing in this Agreement shall be construed to prevent a Contracting Party from adopting, maintaining or enforcing any measure that *it considers* appropriate to ensure that investment activity in its territory is undertaken in a manner in compliance with its essential security and sensitive to environmental concerns.[84]

A provision of this nature was recently interpreted by the tribunal in *Seda v Columbia*,[85] which concerned the seizure of the investor's real estate by the state, pursuant to money laundering legislation, because of close connections between drug cartels who allegedly laundered money through property acquisitions. The tribunal was asked to interpret Article 22.2(b) 'ESI Provision' of the United States-Colombia Trade Promotion Agreement (TPA), which read as follows:

> Article 22.2: Essential Security Nothing in this Agreement shall be construed: (a) to require a Party to furnish or allow access to any information the disclosure of which it determines to be contrary to its essential security interests; or
>
> (b) to preclude a Party from applying measures that it considers necessary for the fulfilment of its obligations with respect to the maintenance or restoration of international peace or security, or the protection of its own essential security interests.
>
> [Footnote 2: For greater certainty, if a Party invokes Article 22.2 in an arbitral proceeding initiated under Chapter Ten (Investment) or Chapter Twenty-One (Dispute Settlement), the tribunal or panel hearing the matter shall find that the exception applies.]

82 ibid 6.97.

83 Barbados-Canada BIT Article 17; Trinidad and Tobago-Canada BIT Article 17; Trinidad and Tobago-Taiwan BIT Article 16; Guyana-Brazil BIT Article 17; Suriname-Brazil BIT Article 17.

84 See, also, Trinidad and Tobago-Taiwan BIT Article XVI 3.

85 *Angel Samuel Seda and others v Republic of Colombia*, ICSID Case No. ARB/19/6, Award, 27 June 2024.

Because of the significance of the tribunal's ruling in this case, and the ongoing scholarly concerns around the fact that this area is in a state of flux,[86] its discussion of the various issues raised in the case are detailed below.

(A) Timing of Invocation

First, the tribunal held that Article 22.2(b) of the TPA did not contain any reference to a point in time at which it had to be invoked. In this regard, the respondent did not need to identify its essential security interest as such in connection with implementing the measures against the claimants. In contrast to denial of benefits clauses which are, by definition, forward-looking, in that they allow a state to prevent abuses of substantive treaty protections and forum shopping, an essential security exception is, on the other hand, necessarily invoked in a specific case and only after an essential security concern is implicated.

(B) Justiciability

Second, the tribunal addressed the difficult question as to whether the ESI Provision was non-justiciable, i.e. as soon as it was invoked, whether the tribunal could not conduct any further inquiry into its invocation or the effects thereof and had to dismiss the case. In the tribunal's view, this approach was unstable because it would require the tribunal to stop short of assessing its jurisdiction to hear the case, let alone the merits of the claimant's claims and associated damages. In short, even if the ESI Provision was non-justiciable, the tribunal considered that it could only determine this to be the case through interpreting Article 22.2(b) of the TPA. In arriving at the conclusion that it was not deprived of the ability to subject such invocation to legal assessment, the tribunal contrasted the TPA (which did not contain 'nonjusticiable' language) to other instruments, which contained non-justiciable language, for example, the Singapore-India Comprehensive Economic Cooperation Agreement, which provides in Article 6.12(4):

> This Article shall be interpreted in accordance with the understanding of the Parties on non-justiciability of security exceptions as set out in their exchange of letters, which shall form an integral part of this Agreement.

Similarly, in 2009, Columbia itself signed a Joint Interpretative Declaration with the Republic of India regarding the Agreement for Promotion and Protection of Investments Between India and Colombia, where it explicitly provided:

> Where the Contracting Party asserts as a defence that the measure alleged to be a breach of its obligations under this Agreement is for the protection of its 'essential security interests' . . . as set out in Article 13, any decision of such Contracting Party taken on such security considerations shall be non-justiciable in that *it shall not be open to any arbitral tribunal to review the merits of any such decision*, even where the arbitral proceedings concern an assessment of any claim for damages and/or compensation, or an adjudication of any other issues referred to the tribunal.

86 Michael Waibel, 'Two worlds of necessity in ICSID arbitration: CMS and LG&E' (2007) 20(3) *Leiden Journal of International Law* 637. See, also, Jonathan Bellish, 'In Principle but Not in Practice: The Expansion of Essential State Interests in the Doctrine of Necessity under Customary International Law' (2012) 41 *Denver Journal of International Law and Policy* 127.

In short, while acknowledging Contracting States' sovereign power to define the scope of an exception to an international law obligation in the treaty they conclude, the ESI Provision, if interpreted as a non-justiciable exception, would have been an omnipotent tool at the state's disposal, which could have potentially undermined legal certainty and predictability for the investors, who were not a Contracting Party to the TPA but nonetheless protected thereunder.[87] In short, the tribunal considered that Article 22.2(b) of the TPA as well as footnote 2 thereto fell short of the express language exempting the measures taken under the ESI Provision from any review by a tribunal upon invocation. Article 22.2(b) was thus not a non-justiciable provision.

(C) KOMPETENZ-KOMPETENZ

Third, Article 22.2(b) did not operate to exclude the tribunal's jurisdiction. More pointedly, while the tribunal could defer to the state on the question of whether the measures enacted were 'necessary' to further the declared security interest, this did not translate into depriving the tribunal of its *Kompetenz-Kompetenz* entirely.

(D) SELF-JUDGING

Fourth, the tribunal proceeded to interpret the phrase 'Nothing in [the TPA] shall be construed . . . to preclude a Party from applying measures that it considers necessary'. As a preliminary point, it recalled that this formulation of the essential security clause could be traced back to the ICJ judgements in *Military and Paramilitary Activities in and against Nicaragua*[88] and *Oil Platforms*.[89] It accepted that because Article 22.2(b) of the TPA explicitly stated that 'it', i.e. referring to the Contracting State applying the measures, 'considers' necessary, there was no doubt that this provision was self-judging, affording a margin of deference a *fortiori* to a state invoking said exception.[90]

87 See, also, *Continental Casualty Company v Argentina*, ICSID Case No. ARB/03/9, Decision on the Application for Partial Annulment, and the Application for Partial Annulment, 16 September 2011 (an Argentina award spared by an ad hoc committee) noted:

> Although a provision such as Art. XI, as earlier indicated, involves naturally a margin of appreciation by a party invoking it, caution must be exercised in allowing a party unilaterally to escape from its treaty obligations in the absence of clear textual or contextual indications. This is especially so if the party invoking the allegedly self-judging nature of the exemption can thereby remove the issue, and hence the claim of a treaty breach by the investor against the host state, from arbitral review. This would conflict in principle with the agreement of the parties to have disputes under the BIT settled compulsorily by arbitration, both between an investor and the host State or between the Contracting Parties, as the case may be.

88 Military and Paramilitary Activities in and against Nicaragua (*Nicaragua v United States of America*), concerning Jurisdiction and Admissibility, is 1984 ICJ Reports 392.

89 Oil Platforms (*Iran v United States*, Judgment), merits, ICJ GL No 90, [2003] ICJ Reports 161.

90 Stephan Schill and Robyn Briese, '"If the State Considers": Self-Judging Clauses in International Dispute Settlement' (2009) 13 *Max Planck Yearbook of United Nations Law* 67:

> At the most general level, self-judging clauses have the function of allowing a state to enter into international cooperation on the basis of binding international obligations, while at the same time retaining the power to escape from such obligations in certain circumstances, most frequently if the state determines that it would harm its sovereignty, security, public policy, or more generally, its essential interests. It constitutes a safety valve for reconciling international cooperation and for state's occasional preference for unilateralism within cooperative regimes.

(E) 'The Protection of its Own Essential Security Interests'

Given that the peace and security obligations were not invoked by the respondent in the present case, the tribunal focused on 'essential security interests'. Because the TPA itself did not define the Contracting State's 'own essential security interests', the tribunal, applying the ordinary meaning of these terms, found that essential security interests carried at least two defining qualities: (i) they had to be of higher importance than just any interest – vital and going to the core of the state's main functions, and (ii) they had to be related to the matters of security, i.e. protection from threats. In the tribunal's view, not only are states' essential security interests no longer understood to be limited to the sphere of military threats and territorial integrity, but it is the state itself which can best identify the scope of its own essential security interests. On the facts, given that the essential security interests of a state are an expression of its sovereignty, and the open-ended approach taken by the state parties to the TPA, a broad margin of appreciation was held to have been afforded Contracting States in identifying their essential security interest. For this reason, the tribunal noted the limitations to its mandate and scope of inquiry. However, although the ordinary meaning of the ESI Provision suggested that it was for the state to determine the scope of its 'own essential security interests', such determination had to be restrained by the requirement of good faith.

On the facts, the tribunal held that the interests invoked by the respondent 'to fight against organized crime, money laundering, and drug trafficking, thus ultimately protecting its population from the threats of paramilitary and marginalized groups that have been ravaging the country for years' – directly related to public safety, national security, and socioeconomic stability of Columbia and therefore constituted essential security interests. Given how seriously the policies aimed at combatting organised crime and drug trafficking were to the respondent, the tribunal consequently did not consider that there was any doubt that it could be invoked in good faith as an essential security interest by the respondent. There was no evidence that the respondent identified its essential security interest for the purposes in bad faith.

(F) The Nexus Requirement

Sixth, the tribunal considered the implications of the 'nexus between the measures and the ESI'. In other words, given that the ESI Provision used the language 'for', the nexus between the measures the state considered necessary and the goal it pursued had to be established. More particularly, the tribunal considered that the measures had to be connected in some form to the underlying essential security interest. In its view, the plausibility standard (i.e. whether measures were not implausible as measures protective of these interests – they could not be so remote from, or unrelated to the interest to be protected) was the appropriate benchmark against which to evaluate the nexus between the measures adopted by the state and the essential security interest sought to be protected under Article 22.2(b) of the TPA. In the tribunal's view, such an approach thereby required a 'light-touch' good faith review – not too restrictive as to infringe on the explicit self-judging language of the ESI Provision. The tribunal also considered that the other tests invoked by the parties (i.e. *bona fide* connection, rational connection, prima facie standard) would lead to a very similar, if not identical, scope of review.

On the facts, having regard to the plausibility analysis for determining the connection between the contested measures and the essential security interest invoked by the respondent, it was held that there was no need for the respondent to establish that the measures enacted by the respondent were the main avenue for combatting organised crime, let alone the sole instrument. It was sufficient here that the measures could serve such purpose on their face, i.e. were not 'so remote from, or unrelated to' the stated objective as to render the connection implausible. The fact that a different measure taken or not taken by a state could be more plausibly connected with the declared essential security interest was not a relevant consideration. Furthermore, because the exception allowed the state a measure of discretion in identifying essential security concerns and addressing them, the tribunal could not instruct the respondent on how to conduct the large-scale, evolving criminal investigation that it conducted. Moreover, it was plausible that Asset Forfeiture Proceedings under the Asset Forfeiture Law involving the claimants' assets – related to other asset forfeiture and criminal proceedings – were connected to the interest of combatting drug trafficking. In other words, had the contested measures been entirely disconnected from the law enforcement actions in fighting organised crime – geographically, temporarily, and in scope of people involved – the tribunal noted that it would have been hard-pressed to see the nexus. However, having been briefed extensively on the status of the criminal investigations, the tribunal found it plausible that the measures the respondent took were connected to its stated essential security interest.

(G) Nature of the Review

The tribunal's ruling did not, however, stop there; it proceeded to examine the nature of the review a tribunal should apply in cases involving the self-judging exception. It found that the ESI Provision was a self-judging exception to the TPA, which allowed the respondent to invoke an interest that it judged to be critical for its security as a justification for the measures – which would otherwise be in violation of the substantive provisions of the TPA. In this connection, the ESI Provision had to take precedence over the substantive and procedural rights of the investors contained in the TPA. Consistent with the ad hoc committees' views in *CMS v Argentina*[91] and *Sempra v Argentina*,[92] the tribunal interpreted Article 22.2(b) as a derogation from the treaty-based obligations of the respondent, essentially an exception to the scope of the treaty. In other words, it was not simply an affirmative defence against liability, in that it did not presuppose that an act was committed that was incompatible with the state's international obligations and was therefore 'wrongful'. Instead, it precluded the measures from being incompatible with the Treaty in the first place. In short, once invoked, the tribunal's inquiry stops short of establishing wrongfulness of the respondent's actions (if any) – let alone awarding any compensation.

(H) Standard of Review

Finally, on the question of the standard of review, the tribunal noted that it had a limited mandate in light of the self-judging nature of the ESI Provision. More particularly, the tribunal could only engage in a 'good faith review',[93] drawing on the ICJ's jurisprudence to the effect that 'where a State possesses a discretionary power under a treaty, such a power must

91 ICSID Case No. ARB/01/8, Decision of the ad hoc Committee on the Application for Annulment of the Argentine Republic, 25 September 2007.

92 ICSID Case No. ARB/02/16, Award, 28 September 2007.

93 With its finding that the US-Argentina BIT provision in question was not self-judging, the tribunal in *LG&E v Argentina*, ICSID Case No. ARB/02/1, Award, 25 July 2007 remarked, in obiter, that: 'Were the Tribunal to conclude that the provision is self-judging, Argentina's determination would be subject

be exercised reasonably and in good faith'.[94] In *Djibouti v France*,[95] for example, the ICJ subjected to a good faith review France's discretionary power to refuse to provide mutual assistance in criminal matters under the corresponding convention in circumstances it considered that execution of the request was likely to prejudice its essential interests.[96]

Although the ESI Provision was held to be self-judging, the tribunal did not agree with the proposition that it was solely for the state parties to the TPA to ensure that the provision was invoked in good faith and, ultimately, that the other state party was the judge of the proper invocation of the ESI Provision. In its view, tribunal could (and did) conduct a limited review as to whether the respondent invoked the ESI Provision in good faith. In this connection, it found that a measure was adopted by the respondent (the Asset Forfeiture Proceedings commenced in 2016); such measure was necessary in the light of the plausible nexus between drug trafficking and money and the public interest. Having, therefore, concluded that the ESI Provision was invoked in good faith, the tribunal ruled that the measures enacted by the respondent against the claimants were placed outside of the scope of the Treaty such that the tribunal had no mandate to review further objections to its jurisdiction and the merits of the case. In fact, the tribunal refused to consider further objections to its jurisdiction raised by the respondent or the merits of the claimants' claims.

To summarise, self-judging precluded measures clauses, while affording states significant deference in determining their essential security interests, are not entirely non-justiciable and remain subject to limited judicial review. The standard applied is a 'good faith review' with a 'plausibility test' – meaning tribunals will examine whether the state's invocation of essential security interests was made in good faith and whether there is a plausible nexus between the measures taken and the security interest claimed. Crucially, once properly invoked, these clauses operate as derogations from treaty obligations rather than mere affirmative defences, precluding the measures from being incompatible with the treaty in the first place and stopping any inquiry into wrongfulness or compensation.

(iv) Non-Self-Judging Precluded Measures Clauses

Several Caribbean IIAs[97] contain non-self-judging non-precluded measures clauses. For example, Article XIV(1) of the Trinidad and Tobago-USA BIT provides:

---

to a good faith review anyway . . .'. Similarly, the tribunal in *Continental v Argentina*, ICSID Case No. ARB/03/9, 5 September 2008 referred to a good faith review in a hypothetical:

> if Art. XI granted unfettered discretion to a party to invoke it, in good faith, in order to exempt a particular measure which the investor claims has breached its treaty rights from any scrutiny by a tribunal, then that tribunal would be prevented from entering further into the merits, after having recognized that an economic crisis such as the one experienced by Argentina in 2001–2002 qualified under Art. XI.

94 Rights of Nationals of the United States of America in Morocco (*France v United States of America*), Judgment, ICJ Reports 1952, p. 212; Certain Questions of Mutual Assistance in Criminal Matters (*Djibouti v France*), Judgment, ICJ Reports 2008, 229, para. 145.

95 Certain Questions of Mutual Assistance in Criminal Matters (*Djibouti v France*), Judgment, [2008] ICJ Reports 177, 4 June 2008.

96 ibid 145.

97 Trinidad and Tobago-USA BIT Article 14; Jamaica-USA BIT Article 10; Haiti-USA BIT Article 10; Grenada-USA BIT Article 10; Barbados-Mauritius BIT Article 11; Trinidad and Tobago-India BIT Article 12; Guyana-Brazil BIT Article 13; Suriname-Brazil Article 13.

1. This Treaty shall not preclude a Party from applying measures necessary for the fulfilment of its obligations with respect to the maintenance or restoration of international peace or security, or the protection of its own essential security interests.[98]

A variation of this clause (reference to 'circumstances of extreme emergency') can be found in the now terminated Trinidad and Tobago-India BIT (Article 12(2)), which read:

> (2) Notwithstanding paragraph (1) of this Article nothing in this Agreement precludes the host Contracting Party from taking action for the protection of its essential security interests or in circumstances of extreme emergency, in accordance with its laws normally and reasonably applied on a non-discriminatory basis.

In interpreting essential security clauses of this nature, investment tribunals have generally called for clear indications of the self-judging character of the provision in question,[99] the absence of which will be indicative of its non-self-judging character. For example, the tribunal in the *Deutsche Telekom v India*[100] interpreted Article 12 of the Germany-India BIT, which reads, 'Nothing in this Agreement shall prevent either Contracting Party from applying prohibitions or restrictions to the extent necessary for the protection of its essential security interests', as a non-self-judging clause, and rightly so. Clear indications in the text of the treaty would have been required in order to infer that such a provision was self-judging, given its scope and potential for abuse.

Despite not being self-judging, as noted by the *Deutsche Telekom* tribunal, such a provision does offer some deference to the host state in its determination of the necessity of the measures taken:

> In that review, the Tribunal will undoubtedly recognize a margin of deference to the host state's determination of necessity, given the state's proximity to the situation, expertise and competence. Thus, the Tribunal would not review de novo the state's determination nor adopt a standard of necessity requiring the state to prove that the measure was the 'only way' to achieve the stated purpose. On the other hand, the deference owed to the state cannot be unlimited, as otherwise unreasonable invocations of Article 12 would render the substantive protections contained in the Treaty wholly nugatory.[101]

Although a degree of deference is owed to a state's assessment, such deference is not, however, unlimited. Indeed, the limits of essential security interests cannot be stretched beyond their natural meaning. For the tribunal in *Deutsche Telekom*, the natural meaning

98 See, also, Trinidad and Tobago-USA BIT (1994) Article XIV(1); SVG-Taiwan BIT Article IX(1); Jamaica-USA BIT Article X(1); Grenada-USA BIT Article X(1); Barbados-Mauritius BIT Article 11(2); Trinidad and Tobago-India BIT Article 12(1); Guyana-Brazil BIT Article 13(1) Guyana-Brazil BIT Article 13.

99 *CMS Gas Transmission Company v Argentine Republic*, ICSID Case No. ARB/01/8, Award, 12 May 2005, para. 370: 'The Tribunal is convinced that when States intend to create for themselves a right to determine unilaterally the legitimacy of extraordinary measures importing non-compliance with obligations assumed in a treaty, they do so expressly'. *Deutsche Telekom AG v The Republic of India*, PCA Case No. 2014–10, Interim Award, 13 December 2017, paras. 225, 231. A similar interpretation was given by investment tribunals to Article XI of the US-Argentina BIT: *Continental Casualty Company v Argentine Republic*, ICSID Case No. ARB/03/9, Award, 5 September 2008, para. 188; *Enron Creditors Recovery Corporation (formerly Enron Corporation) and Ponderosa Assets, L.P. v Argentine Republic*, ICSID Case No. ARB/01/3, Award, 22 May 2007, para. 335.

100 PCA Case No. 2014–10, Interim Award, 13 December 2017, para. 225.

101 ibid 238.

of the treaty terms required the presence of interests concerned with security (as opposed to other public or societal interests) that were 'essential', i.e. that went to the core (the 'essence') of state security. Since the defence excluded all the obligations of the Treaty, including the obligation to provide compensation for a lawful taking, it had to protect something of higher value than any 'public interest'. In other words, 'essential security interests' are of higher importance than just any interest. It accordingly includes matters which threaten the political or economic survival of a state, the maintenance of conditions in which its essential services can function, the keeping of its internal peace, the survival of part of its population,[102] protection of the environment,[103] and economic security and stability.[104] In any case, it is the state itself which can best identify the scope of its own essential security interests.[105]

For the defence to come into play, a measure amounting to a prohibition or restriction must not simply be 'related to' essential security interests but indeed must be 'necessary

102 Documents of the Thirty-Second Session, Yearbook of the International Law Commission, U.N. Doc. A/CN.4/SER.A/1980/Add.1 (Part 1) cited in OECD, *Essential Security Interests under International Investment Law in International Investment Perspectives: Freedom of Investment in a Changing World* (OECD 2007) 100. In the Commentaries to the 2001 Draft Articles on State Responsibility, the examples cited by the Commission include 'safeguarding the environment, preserving the very existence of the State and its people in time of public emergency, or ensuring the safety of a civilian population'. International Law Commission Draft Articles on Responsibility of States for Internationally Wrongful Acts with Commentaries, 2001, 83, para. 14.

103 See, e.g. *Gabčíkovo-Nagymaros Project (Hungary v Slovakia)*, International Court of Justice, Judgment, 25 September 1997 cited in OECD (n 102) 100.

104 *Continental Casualty Company v Argentine Republic*, ICSID Case No. ARB/03/9, Award, 5 September 2008, para. 175:

> As to 'essential security interests', it is necessary to recall that international law is not blind to the requirement that States should be able to exercise their sovereignty in the interest of their population free from internal as well as external threats to their security and the maintenance of a peaceful domestic order. It is well known that the concept of international security of States in the Post World War II international order was intended to cover not only political and military security but also the economic security of States and of their population.

CMS v Argentina, para. 360; *LG&E Energy Corp., LG&E Capital Corp. and LG&E International Inc. v Argentine Republic*, ICSID Case No. ARB/02/1, Decision on Liability, 3 October 2006, para. 238:

> The Tribunal rejects the notion that Article XI is only applicable in circumstances amounting to military action and war. Certainly, the conditions in Argentina in December 2001 called for immediate, decisive action to restore civil order and stop the economic decline. To conclude that such a severe economic crisis could not constitute an essential security interest is to diminish the havoc that the economy can wreak on the lives of an entire population and the ability of the Government to lead. When a State's economic foundation is under siege, the severity of the problem can equal that of any military invasion.

105 *CC/Devas (Mauritius) Ltd., Devas Employees Mauritius Private Limited, and Telcom Devas Mauritius Limited v Republic of India*, PCA Case No. 2013–09, Award on Jurisdiction and Merits, 25 July 2016, para. 245:

> An arbitral tribunal may not sit in judgment on national security matters as on any other factual dispute arising between an investor and a State. National security issues relate to the existential core of a State. An investor who wishes to challenge a state decision in that respect faces a heavy burden of proof, such as bad faith, absence of authority or application to measures that do not relate to essential security interests.

See, also, Schill and Briese (n 90) 77, 78.

for the protection' of such interests.[106] Whether a measure is 'necessary' or imposed 'to the extent necessary' is subject to review by the tribunal, as the clause is not self-judging. In this context, a tribunal will afford a margin of deference to the host state's determination of necessity, given the state's proximity to the situation, expertise and competence. It would not review *de novo* the state's determination nor adopt a standard of necessity requiring the state to prove that the measure was the 'only way' to achieve the stated purpose. On the other hand, the deference owed to the state is not unlimited, as otherwise unreasonable invocations of the defence would render the substantive protections contained in the Treaty wholly nugatory. To assess the necessity of the measures to safeguard the state's essential security interests, then, the tribunal will determine whether the measure was principally aimed at protecting the essential security interests at stake and was objectively required to achieve that protection, taking into account whether the state had reasonable alternatives, less in conflict or more compliant with its international obligations.

A treaty-based non-self-judging national security defence – Article XVII(2) of the CARICOM-Dominican Republic FTA – was subject to interpretation by the tribunal in *Michael Lee-Chin v Dominican Republic*.[107] This provision reads as follows:

> This Agreement shall not preclude the application by either Party of measures necessary for the protection of its own national security interest.

The respondent's central argument was that the measures it adopted (in particular, the passage of the Environmental and Health Emergency Declaration, the request for termination and afterwards nullification of the Concession Agreement, the request for interim measures, the judicial intervention of the Duquesa Landfill and the subsequent resolution ordering its technical closing) were necessary to protect the Republic's own national security interests, since absent said measures, the Republic would have reached the point of a serious health and environmental crisis in Gran Santo Domingo, and both the health and the environment would have been put at greater risk. More pointedly, the respondent contended that the unsanitary state of the landfill caused air and water pollution due to the actions and omissions of the claimant, including the blockage of trucks and waste accumulation at the entrance of the Duquesa Landfill caused by the closings that took place as a result of the reduction in the Duquesa Landfill's hours of operation and Lajun's unilateral decision to

106 Under WTO jurisprudence, 'necessary' invokes a more stringent requirement, akin to the measure being 'indispensable', than 'relating to'. See Appellate Body Report, Korea-Beef Report of the Appellate Body. WT/DS161/AB/R WT/DS169/AB/R, para. 164:

> In sum, determination of whether a measure, which is not 'indispensable', may nevertheless be 'necessary' within the contemplation of Article XX(d), involves in every case a process of weighing and balancing a series of factors which prominently include the contribution made by the compliance measure to the enforcement of the law or regulation at issue, the importance of the common interests or values protected by that law or regulation, and the accompanying impact of the law or regulation on imports or exports.

The Appellate Body considered that the para. 166: 'weighing and balancing' process was, 'comprehended in the determination of whether a WTO-consistent alternative measure which the Member concerned could "reasonably be expected to employ" is available, or whether a less WTO-inconsistent measure is "reasonably available"'. See, also, Brazil – Measures Affecting Imports of Retreaded Tyres WT/DS332/AB/R (Report No AB-2007-4) dated 3 December 2007, para. 150 to be necessary, the measure must be apt to make a material contribution to the achievement of its objective.

107 ICSID Case No. UNCT/18/3, Award, 6 October 2023.

prevent access for the disposal of solid waste originating from many of the municipalities. As a consequence, the respondent argued that serious health problems were caused in Gran Santo Domingo.

The tribunal accepted that the protection of the environment is a priority in all human activities,[108] and that, therefore, 'environmental measures may be necessary, in certain circumstances, to ensure national security interests.'[109] It further accepted that the state, in this connection, has a 'broad margin of appreciation'[110] and that it should be afforded 'great deference',[111] though measures adopted by the state are not absolutely immune from the tribunal's scrutiny.[112] The tribunal then considered the necessity defence under customary international law, but found that, in the circumstances of this case, it would not 'directly'[113] apply said defence, though it noted that it would 'not rule out taking into account considerations similar to those applying the standard under customary international law.'[114]

On the facts, the tribunal held that the respondent failed to prove that the situation in question, despite posing a 'very serious health and environmental situation that called for urgent measures',[115] constituted a 'state of emergency associated with the impairment of national security'.[116] It further considered that

> as deplorable as the health situation may be at a given time and taking into consideration the risks it entails for health and the environment, this case is a matter of whether that situation constituted an 'emergency' and whether that characterization can be likened to a situation affecting 'national security' within the specific applicable legal framework.[117]

While the tribunal cannot be faulted for treating serious environmental issues as being concerned with a state's essential security interests, it is the majority's ruling that the situation in question must rise to the level of a 'state of emergency' that is deeply problematic. Such a restrictive approach, requiring a state of emergency as indispensable to invoking Article XVII(2), is neither supported by the text of the applicable provision, nor extant jurisprudence.[118] Indeed, while arguably a situation that gives rise to a state of emergency would more easily, from an evidentiary perspective, satisfy the high threshold of 'essential' or

108 ibid 238.
109 ibid.
110 ibid 245.
111 ibid.
112 ibid.
113 ibid 246.
114 ibid.
115 ibid 248.
116 ibid.
117 ibid 250.
118 In none of the Argentinian cases did the tribunals suggest that the declaration of a state of emergency was decisive: *CMS Gas Transmission Company v Argentine Republic*, (Award) ICSID Case No. ARB/01/8, IIC 65 (2005), Award, 12 May 2005; *Enron Corporation and Ponderosa Assets, LP v Argentine Republic*, (Award) ICSID Case No. ARB/01/3, IIC 292 (2007), Award, 22 May 2007; *Sempra Energy International v Argentine Republic*, (Award) ICSID Case No. ARB/02/16, IIC 304 (2007), Award, 28 September 2007; *LG&E Energy Corp, LG&E Capital Corp, and LG&E International, Inc v Argentine Republic*, (Decision on Liability) ICSID Case No. ARB/02/1, IIC 152 (2006), Award 3 October 2006; *Continental Casualty Company v Argentine Republic*, (Award) ICSID Case No. ARB/03/9, IIC 336 (2008), Award, 5 September 2008; *Total SA v Argentine Republic*, (Decision on Liability) ICSID Case No. ARB/04/1, IIC 484 (2010), Award, 27 December 2010.

'national security' interests, this cannot be required as a matter of course. In this connection, it appears that the majority obfuscated the 'national security interests' exception with Article X of the FTA, which provides for compensation, on a basis no less favourable than that accorded to third state investors, for losses owing to, *inter alia*, 'a state of national emergency'.

On a related point, the majority could also be faulted for treating as decisive the respondent's apparent failure to declare a 'security exception' pursuant to the provisions of the Dominican Republic's Constitution. On this basis, it noted that it could 'only conclude that the issue was not perceived as an exceptional matter of national interest warranting the intervention of the highest State authorities'.[119] It is submitted that the majority, in so treating the state's non-declaration as *ipso facto* decisive, privileges form over substance, thereby effectively minimising,[120] by its own admission, objective evidence of 'the deplorable conditions in which the landfill was found due to the accumulation of waste and the inability to adequately treat it',[121] as well as the fact that 'the health situation [was] caused by the lack of trash collection and its subsequent accumulation'.[122]

In is arguable that the recently decided case of *Seda v Columbia*[123] represents a more principled approach, though of course its insights must be treated with caution since the tribunal there was dealing with a self-judging non-precluded measures clause. In that case, the tribunal considered that the interest being protected must be 'of higher importance than just any interest – vital and going to the core of the State's main functions, and it must be related to the matters of security, i.e., protection from threats',[124] but did not at any point suggest that it must be so high as to amount to a state of emergency or that it must be formally declared as such. In this context, the majority's ruling in *Michael Lee-Chin* does not appear comport the ruling in *Seda*, nor indeed with its very own pronouncement that the state must be afforded 'great deference', and that 'national security issues are obviously crucial for States and that they are certainly in a privileged position to assess these interests'.[125] Interestingly, in *Seda*, the tribunal considered that 'essential security interests of a State are an expression of its sovereignty, so the Tribunal is especially conscious of the associated limitations to its mandate and scope of inquiry'.[126]

Separately, the majority in *Michael Lee-Chin* considered that although a situation involving a serious health and environmental crisis was occurring, it had 'not been proven that such a crisis had a national scope or impact'.[127] It held that the situation invoked as a reason for the declaration was confined to a limited portion of the national territory and to a populated area, which, although relatively large, was also limited. In its view, 'a national emergency has to affect the general population to such an extent that it takes on such importance that the entire nation must respond, allocate resources, take impact measures, or be

119 *Michael Lee-Chin v Dominican Republic*, ICSID Case No. UNCT/18/3, Award, 6 October 2023, para. 260.
120 ibid *Dissenting Opinion of Professor Marcelo Kohen*, para. 45. Interestingly, in his dissent, Professor Marcelo Kohen noted that 'the declaration of a state of emergency (or whatever it may be called under the different constitutions) is not the only way in which States can face situations concerning their national security'.
121 *Michael Lee Chin v Dominican Republic Award*, ICSID Case No. UNCT/18/3, 6 October 2023, para. 249.
122 ibid.
123 ICSID Case No. ARB/19/6, Award, 27 June 2024.
124 ibid 642.
125 *Michael Lee-Chin v Dominican Republic*, ICSID Case No. UNCT/18/3, Award, 6 October 2023, para. 262.
126 *Seda v Republic of Colombia*, ICSID Case No. ARB/19/6, Award, 27 June 2024, para. 644.
127 *Michael Lee-Chin v Dominican Republic*, ICSID Case No. UNCT/18/3, Award, 6 October 2023, para. 251.

prepared to absorb the consequences of such an emergency'.[128] Although the majority conceded that, in some circumstances a serious local crisis may have 'a considerable — and even inescapable — national repercussion',[129] it did not find that that such was the situation in the instant case.

It is submitted that, in accordance with the *Gabčíkovo-Nagymaros Project* case,[130] a crisis need not have national scope or impact to give rise to the essential security exception. Rather, a 'grave danger to . . . the ecological preservation of all or *some* of [the] territory [of a State]'[131] might be sufficient. With this mind, it is arguable that the majority in *Michael Lee-Chin*, in finding that the respondent had not proven that the crisis had national scope or impact, failed to fully account for the objective circumstances existing in a large and important part of a small island developing state. More pointedly, the majority arguably failed to give adequate weight to the fact that the non-operation of Lajun in the discharge and disposal of waste in the Duquesa Landfill affected trash collection of thousands of households, resulting in the piling up of a large amount of trash in all of Gran Santo Domingo. It also did not pay adequate attention to objective evidence detailing the fact that there had been several fires which threatened the safety of neighbouring areas, and which had put the health of the said neighbouring areas at risk due to the potential development of acute respiratory infections. In fact, over four million people (out of a total population of 11.2 million) were *directly* affected by pollution on a daily basis and countless others *indirectly* affected, given that the landfill managed almost half of the country's solid waste. In this connection, it is unsurprising that Professor Kohen, in his dissent, chided the majority for ignoring the 'fact that the situation concerns the capital of the Republic, where more than forty per cent of the total population of the country lives, and that Duquesa was the only landfill in such area'.[132]

The final issue considered by the tribunal in *Michael Lee-Chin* was whether there was a nexus between the measures taken by the state and its national security interests. In its view, the respondent had failed to establish why the situation had reached the point where the nation's national security interests were at risk. More pointedly, the Environmental and Health Emergency Declaration adopted by the Ministry of Environment and the Ministry of Public Health was not, in its view, shown to have responded to a situation that could be linked to national security. In short, although the state had genuine environmental concerns, more than the existence of these concerns was required. In particular, in addition to invoking and proving the temporary unhealthy situation and the potential risks that could derive from it, [the] respondent should have furnished a coherent explanation as to how that situation and those risks affected its 'national security interests'.[133] This approach appears to be correct, as in contradiction to the self-judging clause in *Seda v Columbia*, more than a plausible explanation was needed by the respondent in *Lee-Chin* to establish that the measures taken were necessary to protect its national security interests. In other words, it was rightly not sufficient for to respondent to establish that the measures were not so remote from, or unrelated to, the interest to be protected. A coherent explanation was required.

128 ibid 254.

129 ibid 255.

130 *Hungary v Slovakia*, ICJ, Judgment dated September 25, 1997, ICJ Reports, 7 (1997).

131 ibid 53.

132 ibid *Dissenting Opinion of Professor Marcelo Kohen* in *Michael Lee-Chin v Dominican Republic*, ICSID Case No. UNCT/18/3, Award, 6 October 2023, para. 46.

133 ibid 265.

In the final analysis, however, although the majority in *Michael Lee-Chin* abided by its caution to not '*directly* apply the conditions applicable to the standard under customary law',[134] it is arguable that it *indirectly* applied the stringent conditions of the customary international necessity defence in a manner that was not contemplated by the FTA, and which cannot be justified as a matter of principle. It is, therefore, unsurprising that Professor Kohen, in his dissent, cautioned that the 'the Final Award confuses the protection of national security interests and the state of necessity'[135] by 'equat[ing] or compar[ing] in a misguided fashion the situations of national emergency set forth by law or a treaty with the state of necessity, a circumstance precluding wrongfulness, which is a different legal notion in International Law'.[136]

Where the BIT non-self-judging defence is successfully invoked by the state, as noted by the *CMS v Argentina*[137] ad hoc committee, 'the substantive obligations under the Treaty do not apply', and 'there could be no possibility of compensation being payable during that period'.[138] It is not simply an excuse which is only relevant once it has been decided that there has otherwise been a breach of those substantive obligations. In other words, as stated by the ad hoc committee in *Sempra*,[139] where the BIT non-self-judging defence applies, the taking of such necessary for essential security interests measures is not incompatible with the State's international obligations and is not therefore 'wrongful'.[140]

(v) Customary International Law Defence of Necessity

Where a BIT necessity defence exists, the *CMS v Argentina*[141] ad hoc Annulment Committee noted that the tribunal is under an obligation to consider first whether there has been a breach of the BIT and whether such a breach was excluded by the BIT necessity defence. Only if it is concluded that there is conduct not in conformity with the Treaty would it have to consider whether the state's responsibility could be precluded in whole or in part under customary international law. The customary international law defence of necessity may also be relied upon if the BIT in question does not contain an essential/national security interests clause.

Under Article 25 of ILC's Draft Articles:

> 1. Necessity may not be invoked by a State as a ground for precluding the wrongfulness of an act not in conformity with an international obligation of that State unless the act:
>   (a) is the only way for the State to safeguard an essential interest against a grave and imminent peril; and
>   (b) does not seriously impair an essential interest of the State or States towards which the obligation exists, or of the international community as a whole.

134 *Michael Lee-Chin v Dominican Republic*, ICSID Case No. UNCT/18/3, Award, 6 October 2023, para. 246.
135 ibid *Dissenting Opinion of Professor Marcelo Kohen*, para. 44.
136 ibid 4.
137 *CMS v Argentina*, Decision of the ad hoc Committee on the Application for Annulment of the Argentine Republic, ICSID Case No. ARB/01/8, 25 September 2007.
138 ibid 146.
139 ICSID Case No. ARB/02/16, Decision on the Argentine Republic's Application for Annulment of the Award, 29 June 2010.
140 ibid 204.
141 *CMS v Argentina*, Decision of the ad hoc Committee on the Application for Annulment of the Argentine Republic, ICSID Case No. ARB/01/8, 25 September 2007, paras. 133–135.

2. In any case, necessity may not be invoked by a State as a ground for precluding wrongfulness if:
   (a) the international obligation in question excludes the possibility of invoking necessity; or
   (b) the State has contributed to the situation of necessity.

All of the aforementioned requirements must be met cumulatively, and the state raising the plea has the burden of proving that all of those requirements have been satisfied.[142]

Regrettably, the customary international law necessity defence was erroneously applied by a number of tribunals in the wake of the Argentinian financial crisis.[143] *Enron v Argentina*,[144] *CMS v Argentina*,[145] and *Sempra Energy International v Argentina*[146] for example, arose out of measures taken by Argentina in the wake of the 2001 financial crisis to address the economic fallout associated therewith, namely revoking previously promised concessions and guarantees with respect to the calculation of tariffs. Notwithstanding the fact that economic indicators had reached 'catastrophic proportions', the respective tribunals nonetheless insisted that there were other ways available to stabilise Argentina's economy, although the arbitrators did not specifically indicate the nature and content of those alternative measures. Indeed, in these cases, there was a precipitate decline in the gross domestic product, a widespread decline in stock prices and in the value of assets located in Argentina, and a widespread decline in capital outflows resulting in the banking system's loss of 25% of its total deposits. Further, unemployment had reached nearly 25 per cent, nearly half of the population was living in poverty. Many Argentinians could not afford access to basic food or healthcare, and there was widespread fear among the population that the government would seize bank deposits. To prevent the bankruptcy of the banking system, an emergency law was passed. There followed a succession of presidents over the period of 20 December 2001 to 1 January 2002. Yet still, the tribunals in the aforementioned cases ignored the approach countenanced in *LG&E v Argentina*,[147] instead resorting to the requirements of the state of necessity defence under customary international law, even though Article XI of the 1991 Argentina-United States of America BIT provided

142 Articles on Responsibility of States for Internationally Wrongful Acts annexed to UNGA Res 56/83 (12 December 2001) UN Doc A/RES/56/83, para. 331.

143 August Reinisch, 'The Argentinian Crisis Arbitrations' in Hélène Ruiz Fabri and Edoardo Stoppioni (eds), *International Investment Law An Analysis of the Major Decisions* (Hart Publishing 2022) 119–34; Antoine Martin, 'Investment Disputes after Argentina's Economic Crisis: Interpreting BIT Non-precluded Measures and the Doctrine of Necessity under Customary International Law' (2012) 29(1) *Journal of International Arbitration* 49–70.

144 *Enron Corporation and Ponderosa Assets, L.P. v Argentine Republic*, ICSID Case No. ARB/01/3, Decision on the Application for Annulment of the Argentine Republic, 30 July 2010, para. 333:

> The Tribunal notes that the Treaty does not define what is to be understood by essential security interest . . . . The specific meaning of these concepts and the conditions for their application must be searched for elsewhere. . . . The situation is more complex in respect of security interests because there is no specific guidance to this effect under the Treaty. This is what makes necessary to rely on the requirements of state of necessity under customary international law, as outlined above in connection with their expression in Article 25 of the Articles on State Responsibility, so as to evaluate whether such requirements have been met in this case.

145 ICSID Case No. ARB/01/8, Award, 12 May 2005, para. 373.

146 ICSID Case No. ARB/02/16, Award, 28 September 2007, para. 375.

147 ICSID Case No. ARB/02/1, Award, 25 July 2007.

> This Treaty shall not preclude the application by either Party of measures necessary for the maintenance of public order, the fulfilment of its obligations with respect to the maintenance or restoration of international peace or security, or the protection of its own essential security interests.

Here, in incorporating the stringent requirements of the plea of necessity under customary international law into the BIT's essential security exception, the tribunals effectively conflated two distinct legal norms, despite the *lex specialis* nature of the treaty-based provision.

Thankfully, the *CMS v Argentina*, *Enron v Argentina*, and *Sempra v Argentina* awards were subsequently annulled by ICSID ad hoc committees on the basis of, *inter alia*, of the erroneous convergence of the legal standards. In *CMS v Argentina*,[148] in particular, the ad hoc committee, consisting of Mr. Nabil Elaraby, Judge James Crawford, and Judge Gilbert Guillaume as chair, elaborated on the difference between the pleas of necessity under customary international law and a treaty-based essential security exception:

> . . . Article XI specifies the conditions under which the Treaty may be applied, whereas Article 25 [of the ILC's Articles on State Responsibility] is drafted in a negative way: it excludes the application of the state of necessity on the merits, unless certain stringent conditions are met. Moreover, Article XI is a threshold requirement: if it applies, the substantive obligations under the Treaty do not apply. By contrast, Article 25 is an excuse which is only relevant once it has been decided that there has otherwise been a breach of those substantive obligations.[149]
>
> . . . In other terms the requirements under Article XI are not the same as those under customary international law as codified by Article 25 . . . .[150]

The ad hoc committee in *Sempra*,[151] which also placed its focus on the differences in the operation of the essential security interest exception and the defence of necessity, noted:

> More importantly, Article 25 is concerned with the invocation by a State Party of necessity 'as a ground for precluding the wrongfulness of an act not in conformity with an international obligation of that State'. Article 25 presupposes that an act has been committed that is incompatible with the State's international obligations and is therefore 'wrongful'. Article XI, on the other hand, provides that 'This Treaty shall not preclude' certain measures so that, where Article XI applies, the taking of such measures is not incompatible with the State's international obligations and is not therefore 'wrongful'.[152]

In other words, the requirements under Article 25 of the ILC Articles are stricter than those the BIT necessity defence.[153] In this connection, the possibility exists, according to the ad hoc committee in *Sempra*, 'that a state could meet the requirements of a treaty exception

148 *CMS Gas Transmission Company v The Argentine Republic*, ICSID Case No. ARB/01/8, Decision of the ad hoc Committee on Argentina's Application for Annulment, 25 September 2007.

149 ibid 129.

150 ibid 130.

151 *Sempra Energy International v Argentine Republic*, ICSID Case No. ARB/02/16, Decision on the Argentine Republic's Application for Annulment of the Award, 29 June 2010.

152 ibid 200.

153 Peter Tomka, 'Defenses Based on Necessity under Customary International Law and on Emergency Clauses in Bilateral Investment Treaties' in Kinnear et al. (eds), *Building International Investment Law: The First 50 Years of ICSID* (ICSID 2016) 493 ('nowhere does a clause such as Article XI provide that such a measure must be the only one available, nor that a State should not have contributed to the occurrence of the emergency').

clause and therefore be exempt from liability under an investment treaty without satisfying the state of emergency requirements envisioned by Article 25'.[154]

Against this backdrop, if the necessity defence under customary international law – which imposes a high threshold, namely 'a situation of necessity', and is not self-judging,[155] is successfully invoked, this constitutes an affirmative defence against liability. Effectively, its successful invocation presupposes that an act has been committed that is incompatible with the state's international obligations and is therefore 'wrongful', but it does not preclude the measures from being incompatible with the treaty in the first place.

It is important to note, having regard to what the ad hoc committees in *Enron*, and *Sempra* intimated in their rulings, that the preclusion under a BIT's essential security defence and the state of necessity under customary international law differ as to their effects. If the latter obtains, Article 27 of the ILC Articles applies, which provides that 'The invocation of a circumstance precluding wrongfulness . . . is without prejudice to . . . [t]he question of compensation for any material loss caused by the act in question'. If, however, the treaty's essential security defence is found to apply, no compensation is payable since such provision excludes the operation of the substantive provisions of the BIT.

One of the few cases in which the customary international law necessity defence was successfully invoked was *LG&E v Argentina*.[156] Here, the tribunal accepted that protecting the population's health and preserving their access to drinking water was an essential security interest. It also found that the government's actions were not such as to amount to a contribution to the state of necessity of such a nature and importance that would preclude the respondent from invoking the defence. On the facts, it was not shown that the government's acts were such that they either were directed towards the financial crisis resulting in the emergency situation that the country experienced in early 2002, or at least of such a nature that the government must have known that such crisis and emergency must have been the outcome of its economic and financial policy. In the tribunal's view, economic policies evaluated as wrong as they allegedly were in the 1990s in Argentina were not of a kind that they could lead to a crisis and emergency of such a magnitude as it blew up in the second half of 2001. In short, there was no link of causality between such conduct in respect of Argentina's economy and the outbreak of the crisis.

On the question of whether Argentina could claim a state of necessity exception when it allegedly had available other means that would have permitted it to avoid a violation of its obligations under international law, the tribunal held that, given the emergency measures and the state of necessity associated with them (extreme economic, institutional and social disturbances suffered by the country and its population) were events of nation-wide importance, the respondent had made more than a *prima facie* showing that the emergency measures taken were the only ones available to it at the time. In other words, the emergency measures were justified by the fact that no other reasonably available remedy existed. However, the tribunal cautioned that such argument supporting the state of necessity defence disappears as soon as alternative measures become available and are no longer in breach of the state's international obligations. Ultimately, the tribunal concluded that there existed a situation of state of necessity as sufficient support for the emergency measures which were promulgated in January 2002.

154 Jeswald Salacuse, *The Law of Investment Treaties* (OUP 2010) 384–85 ('normal principles of treaty interpretation require that the exception clause be read on its own terms and that the state of necessity defence not be unjustifiably incorporated into the treaty').

155 The State concerned is not the sole judge of whether those conditions have been met.

156 ICSID Case No. ARB/02/1 Decision on Liability, 3 October 2006, para. 259.

By contrast, in *Unión Fenosa v Egypt,*[157] which concerned the alleged suspension of gas supplies by an Egyptian State-owned enterprise to the claimant's liquefied natural gas plant in contravention of the gas purchase agreement in the context of the Arab Spring, the tribunal refused to find that Egypt was justified by the necessity defence under customary international law. It considered that, in light of the fact that the claimant's interests were disproportionately affected, the respondent's conduct was not the only way to safeguard its essential interests. Accordingly, Egypt was held to have breached the FET standard by disrupting gas supplies to the claimant.

In short, then, though a high threshold to satisfy, the successful invocation of the defence of necessity excuses a wrongful act of a state where that state has breached an obligation.[158]

(vi) Public Interest Considerations

Foreign direct investment raises several public interest considerations, particularly in developing countries.[159] From human rights abuses, including labour rights violations, to environmental degradation, imprudent foreign investors have often engaged in a range of activities which threaten the well-being and broader societal interests of host countries.[160] How should host countries respond to these issues? How does international investment law regulate such issues? These matters are considered hereafter.

(A) Human Rights

Multinational corporations have, particularly in recent years, been increasingly castigated for failing to comply with myriad human rights standards, including respect for the life, liberty, private and family life, dignity, and equality of nationals residing in the host state.[161] Unfortunately, however, most IIAs do not include explicit binding human rights obligations, and international consensus on the scope of application of international human rights law to investment disputes remains hotly contested.[162] Relatedly, a treaty on business and human rights remains elusive, and the UN Guiding Principles on Business and Human Rights merely restates international law,[163] which arguably imposes a negative (but not a positive)

157 ICSID Case No. ARB/14/4, 31 August 2018.

158 August Reinisch, 'Necessity in International Investment Arbitration – An Unnecessary Split of Opinions in Recent ICSID Cases?' (2007) 8(2) *The Journal of World Investment & Trade* 191.

159 Tim Büthe and Helen Milner, 'The Politics of Foreign Direct Investment into Developing Countries: Increasing FDI through International Trade Agreements?' (2008) 52(4) *American Journal of Political Science* 741–62; Tobias Rommel, 'Local Economic Consequences of Foreign Direct Investment in Democracies and Autocracies' (2025) 69(2) *International Studies Quarterly*.

160 Belengar Francis Maïnkade, 'Corporate Human Rights Obligations of Investors in Recent Investment Agreements: The Progressive Hardening Process of CSR Clauses' (2023) 9(4) *Heliyon* 1–19.

161 Brian Berkey, 'Exploitation, Human Rights and Corporate Obligations' (2025) 9(3) *Business and Human Rights Journal* 361–80.

162 Crina Baltag, Riddhi Joshi, and Kabir Duggal, 'Recent Trends in Investment Arbitration on the Right to Regulate, Environment, Health and Corporate Social Responsibility: Too Much or Too Little?' (2023) 38(2) *ICSID Review-Foreign Investment Law Journal* 381–421; Raymond Yang Gao, 'Bridging Separate Worlds – Application of Human Rights Law in Investment Treaty Arbitration' (2021) 42(1) *Northwestern Journal of International Law & Business* 1.

163 Peter Muchlinski, 'The Impact of the UN Guiding Principles on Business Attitudes to Observing Human Rights' (2021) 6(2) *Special Issue: BHR Landscape after 10 years of the UNGPs: An Assessment Business and Human Rights Journal* 212–26.

duty on corporations to refrain from committing human rights violations.[164] Although there is some momentum in countries within Europe in particular regarding the adoption of legislation requiring human rights due diligence on the part of multinational corporations,[165] these obligations largely remain at the level of domestic law, and may not, unless the applicable law clause in the relevant IIA allows for it, be invoked as a matter of course. In short, the current position on investor human rights is asymmetrical in nature; this is not by coincidence, however, as the designers of the system intended for investors to play by their own rules, according to Perrone.[166]

In the Caribbean context, only one IIA refers explicitly to investors' human rights obligations: Article 15(2) of the Guyana-Brazil BIT, which provides:

> 2. The investors and their investment shall endeavour to comply with the following voluntary principles and standards for a responsible business conduct and consistent with the laws adopted by the Host State:
>   b) Respect the internationally recognised human rights of those involved in the investors' activities;
>   e) Refrain from seeking or accepting exemptions that are not established in the legal or regulatory framework relating to human rights, environment, health, security, work, tax system, financial incentives, or other issues.

There are several unique features of this provision. First, it points out that the principles and standards, including human rights standards, mentioned therein are 'voluntary', and thus not mandatory. Second, and, in any event, it does not impose any positive human rights obligations; rather, the obligation is couched in negative terms, namely to 'respect' human rights, and to 'refrain' from an approach which results in exemptions being granted in respect of the adherence to human rights standards.

That said, in practice, tribunals sometimes resort to human rights courts' jurisprudence in a variety of contexts. For example, tribunals may resort to human rights as an interpretive aid, as in *Mondev International Ltd. v United States of America*.[167] Here, the tribunal noted that decisions from the European Court on Human Rights (ECtHR) on the 'right to a court' (access to a court by a third-country national) 'provide guidance by analogy as to the possible scope of NAFTA's guarantee of "treatment in accordance with international law, including fair and equitable treatment and full protection and security"'.[168] Similarly, in *Tulip Real Estate Investment and Development Netherlands B.V. v Republic of Turkey*,[169] the annulment committee explained that:

> Provisions in human rights instruments dealing with the right to a fair trial and any judicial practice thereto are relevant to the interpretation of the concept of a fundamental rule of

164 ibid.

165 Jernej Letnar Černič, 'The Human Rights Due Diligence Standard-Setting in the European Union: Bridging the Gap Between Ambition and Reality' (2022), 10 *Global Business Law Review* 1; Surya Deva, 'Mandatory Human Rights Due Diligence Laws in Europe: A Mirage for Rightsholders?' (2023) 36(2) *Leiden Journal of International Law* 389–414.

166 Nicolás M. Perrone, 'Bridging the Gap between Foreign Investor Rights and Obligations: Towards Reimagining the International Law on Foreign Investment' 7(3) Special Issue: *Business and Human Rights Journal* 375–96.

167 ICSID Case No. ARB(AF)/99/2, Award, 11 October 2002.

168 ibid 144.

169 ICSID Case No. ARB/11/28 (Decision on Annulment), 30 December 2015.

> procedure as used in Article 52(1)(d) of the ICSID Convention. This is not to add obligations extraneous to the ICSID Convention. Rather, resort to authorities stemming from the field of human rights for this purpose is a legitimate method of treaty interpretation.[170]

At other times, tribunals refer to human rights to reaffirm the centrality of peremptory norms of international law in their application to investment arbitration. For example, in *Phoenix Action, Ltd. v The Czech Republic*,[171] the tribunal cautioned that 'nobody would suggest that ICSID protection should be granted to investments made in violation of the most fundamental rules of protection of human rights, like investments made in pursuance of torture or genocide or in support of slavery or trafficking of human organs.'[172] Similarly, the tribunal in *Urbaser v Argentina*[173] affirmed that *jus cogens* norms (e.g. prohibitions against genocide or slave trading) 'must certainly prevail over any contrary provision of the BIT, as per the express statement in Article 53 of the Vienna Convention'.[174]

Yet, still, on other occasions, arbitral tribunals refer to international human rights instruments and courts and tribunals as a means of confirming that a general principle of international law arises in favour of a foreign investor. For example, in *Hesham Warraq v Republic of Indonesia*,[175] the tribunal referred extensively to the Universal Declaration on Human Rights, International Covenant on Civil and Political Rights, and the jurisprudence of the Human Rights Committee, Inter-American Court on Human Rights and European Court of Human Rights to ground the claimant's right to a fair trial, in particular, the presumption of innocence.

(1) Human Rights Counterclaims

Counterclaims are contemplated by Article 46 of the ICSID Convention in the following terms:

> Except as the parties otherwise agree, the Tribunal shall, if requested by a party, determine any incidental or additional claims or counterclaims arising directly out of the subject-matter of the dispute provided that they are within the scope of the consent of the parties and are otherwise within the jurisdiction of the Centre.[176]

In the absence of an express reference to human rights (as is the case in most Caribbean IIAs), can tribunals nonetheless interpret and apply international human rights obligations? Much will depend on whether the IIA in question expressly or implicitly allows for the institution of counterclaims, and whether the applicable law in this connection imposes substantive human rights obligations (whether arising from the BIT itself, domestic law, customary international law, or general international law) binding on foreign investors.[177] The applicable law clause of the Belize-Austria BIT (Article 16), for example, reads as follows:

170 ibid 92.

171 ICSID/ARB/06/5, Award, 15 April 2009.

172 ibid 78.

173 *Urbaser S.A. and Consorcio de Aguas Bilbao Bizkaia, Bilbao Biskaia Ur Partzuergoa v The Argentine Republic*, ICSID Case No. ARB/07/26, Award, 8 December 2016.

174 ibid 1203.

175 UNCITRAL, Award, 15 December 2014.

176 Convention on the Settlement of Investment Disputes between States and Nationals of Other States (entered into force 14 October 1966) 575 UNTS 159 (ICSID Convention) Article 46.

177 Eric De Brabandere, 'Human Rights Counterclaims in Investment Treaty Arbitration' (2017) 50(2) Rev BDI 591.

(1) A tribunal established under this Part shall decide the dispute in accordance with this Agreement and applicable rules and principles of international law.
(2) Issues in dispute under Article 9 shall be decided, absent other agreement, in accordance with the law of the Contracting Party, party to the dispute, the law governing the authorization or agreement and such rules of international law as may be applicable.

The dispute resolution clauses of some Caribbean IIAs are arguably permissible of counterclaims because of their reference to 'either party'.[178] For example, Article 9(3) of the India-Trinidad and Tobago BIT provides:

> Should the Parties fail to agree on a dispute settlement procedure provided under paragraph (2) of this Article or where a dispute is referred to conciliation, but conciliation proceedings are terminated other than by signing of a settlement agreement, the dispute may be referred to international arbitration. Where the dispute is referred to international arbitration, either party may submit the dispute to:
>
> (a) the International Centre for the Settlement of Investment Disputes if both the Contracting Party of the Investor and the other Contracting Party are parties to the Convention on the Settlement of Investment Disputes between States and nationals of other States, 1965 and the investor consents in writing to submit the dispute to the Centre; or
> (b) the Additional Facility for the Administration of Conciliation, Arbitration and Fact-finding proceedings, if both parties to the dispute so agree; or
> (c) an ad hoc arbitral tribunal in accordance with the Arbitration Rules of the United Nations Commission on International Trade Law, 1976.

Such a clause in principle allows for the institution of counterclaims since it refers to either party, including the respondent host state, being able to initiate proceedings.

By contrast, some dispute resolution clauses are couched in much stricter language (limiting submission of the claim to the 'investor'),[179] thereby arguably precluding counterclaims. For example, Article XI(2) of the St Vincent and the Grenadines-Taiwan BIT provides:

> If a dispute has not been settled amicably within a period of six months from the date on which it was initiated, it may be submitted *by the investor* to arbitration in accordance with Article XII. For the purposes of this paragraph, a dispute is considered to be *initiated when the investor* of one Contracting Party has delivered notice in writing to the other Contracting Party alleging that the latter Contracting Party is in breach of this Agreement, and that the investor has incurred loss or damage by reason of, or arising out of, that breach.

178 See Trinidad and Tobago-India BIT Article 9(3); Jamaica-Egypt BIT Article 8(2); Grenada-USA BIT Article 6(3)(a); Jamaica-USA BUT Article 6(3)(b).

179 Barbados-Venezuela BIT Article 8; Belgium-Luxembourg-Barbados Agreement Article 8(3); Barbados-Mauritius BIT Article 10(2); Barbados-China BIT Article 9(2); Guyana-China BIT Article 9(4); Trinidad and Tobago-China BIT Article 10(2); Belize-China BIT Article 7(1); Belize-El Salvador BIT Article 7(1); Barbados-Cuba BIT Article 8(1); Trinidad and Tobago-Cuba BIT Article 10(2); Barbados-Germany BIT Article 11(2); Antigua-Germany BIT Article 11(2); Antigua-UK BIT Article 8(1); Belize-UK BIT Article 8(1); Dominica-UK BIT Article 8(1); Grenada-UK BIT Article 8(1); St Lucia-UK BIT Article 8(1); Trinidad and Tobago-UK BIT Article 10(1); Barbados-Canada BIT Article 13(4); Trinidad and Tobago-Canada BIT Article 13(4); SVG-Taiwan BIT Article 12(1); SVG-Taiwan BIT Article 11(2); Trinidad and Tobago-Guatemala BIT Article 10(3); Grenada-USA BIT Article 6(3)(a); Jamaica-USA BIT Article 6(3)(a); Trinidad and Tobago-USA BIT Article 9(3)(a); Guyana-South Korea BIT Article 8(3); Trinidad and Tobago-South Korea BIT Article 8(3); Jamaica-South Korea BIT Article 8(3); Guyana-Switzerland BIT Article 8(2); Trinidad and Tobago-Switzerland BIT Article 8(2); Jamaica-Switzerland BIT Article 9(2); St Lucia-Germany BIT Article 10(2).

The jurisdiction of the tribunal in respect of a human rights counterclaim was considered in *Urbaser v Argentina*,[180] a case which concerned the termination of the claimant's concession contact in the context of the Argentine financial crisis, and the respondent's attendant counterclaim that the claimant failed to fulfil its international human rights obligation to supply water to the citizens of Argentina. Article X of the Argentina-Spain BIT provided:

> 1. Disputes arising between one of the Parties and an investor of the other Party relating to investments within the meaning of this Agreement shall, as far as possible, be settled amicably between the parties to the dispute.
> 2. If a dispute within the meaning of paragraph 1 cannot be settled within six months; counting from the date on which one of the parties to the dispute initiated it, it shall be referred, at the request of one of them, to the competent courts of the Party in whose territory the investment was made.
>
> Article VII(1): Where a matter is governed by this Agreement and also by another international agreement to which both Parties are a party or by general international law, the Parties and their investors shall be subject to whichever terms are more favorable.

This provision, according to the *Urbaser* tribunal, was completely neutral as to the identity of the claimant or respondent in an investment dispute arising 'between the parties'. It did not indicate that a state party could not sue an investor in relation to a dispute concerning an investment. Article X(2) further stated that when no settlement had been reached within six months from the date 'on which one of the parties to the dispute' instigated it, 'it shall, at the request of either party', be submitted to the competent tribunals of the host state – again without making any distinction depending on whether the investor or the host state may be 'one of the parties' or 'either party'. This view was confirmed by Article X(3), which stated that in certain circumstances the dispute may be submitted to an international arbitral tribunal 'at the request of either party to the dispute'. In this connection, either the investor or the host state could be a party submitting a dispute in connection with an investment to arbitration. In the tribunal's view, when both parties are entitled to lodge a claim; it could not be that, in acting first, one party could prevent the other from raising its claim.

With respect to the second requirement for invoking a counterclaim, namely, a factual link between the two claims, the tribunal found that, on the facts, this link was manifest. Both the principal claim and the claim opposed to it were based on the same investment, or the alleged lack of sufficient investment, in relation to the same concession. The legal connection was also established to the extent the counterclaim was not alleged as a matter based on domestic law only; the respondent had argued that the claimants' failure to provide the necessary investments caused a violation of the fundamental right for access to water, which was the very purpose of the investment agreed upon in the Regulatory Framework and the Concession Contract and embodied in the protection scheme of the BIT. Against this backdrop, the tribunal explained that once seized with such a claim, it had to assume its competence, provided that the respondent submitted a claim-based *prima facie* on a dispute relating to an investment covered by the BIT and to facts that if established as alleged could constitute violations of rights and obligations that were within the scope of the arbitration agreement governed by Article X. This being affirmed by the tribunal, the claimants' objections in this respect were dealt with as relating to the examination of the merits of the counterclaim.

180 ICSID Case No. ARB/07/26, Award, 8 December 2016, paras. 1182–1221.

In assessing the merits of the counterclaim, the tribunal had to confront, first, the claimants' principled objection that the asymmetric nature of the BIT meant that the Treaty did not provide for any right of the host state and, correspondingly, did not impose any obligation upon the investor. The tribunal, however, noted that there was no provision stating that the host state would not have any right under the BIT.

The next step was for the tribunal to assess the law applicable, having regard to Article X(5) of the BIT. Such decision had to be made 'on the basis of this Agreement', the host state's domestic law, or the general principles of international law. This provision made it clear that a source of international law that was external to the BIT could provide more favourable rights that were granted on the basis of Article VII(1) of this BIT and therefore subject to be claimed, if needed be, through the dispute resolution mechanism provided in Article X. The claimant's contention, however, was that because the right to water is a duty to be borne by the state, an investor, as a private entity, could never bear this obligation. While the tribunal noted the traditional position that corporations, by nature, are not able to be subjects of international law and therefore not capable of holding obligations as if they are participants in the state-to-state relations governed by international law, it considered that this principle has lost its impact and relevance today, evidenced by the fact that investors are entitled to invoke rights resulting from international law, and the UN Guiding Principles on Business and Human Rights, which include commitments to comply with human rights in host states. In the light of these recent developments, the tribunal noted that:

> it can no longer be admitted that companies operating internationally are immune from becoming subjects of international law. On the other hand, even though several initiatives undertaken at the international scene are seriously targeting corporations human rights conduct, they are not, on their own, sufficient to oblige corporations to put their policies in line with human rights law.[181]

Having cited extensively the 1948 Universal Declaration of Human Rights, the 1966 International Covenant on Economic, Social and Cultural Rights, and the International Labor Office's Tripartite Declaration of Principles concerning Multilateral Enterprises and Social Policy (of 1977, as amended in 2006), the tribunal noted that 'the human right for everyone's dignity and its right for adequate housing and living conditions are complemented by an obligation on all parties, public and private parties, not to engage in activity aimed at destroying such rights'.[182] After construing the applicable BIT in harmony with other rules of international law of which it formed part, including those relating to human rights, the tribunal explained that the state had an obligation to afford safe and clean drinking water and sewage services. However, in the same breath, nothing in the BIT extended or transferred to the concessionaire an obligation to perform services complying with the residents' human right to access to water and sewage services. In other words, 'the human right to water entails an obligation of compliance on the part of the State, but it does not contain an obligation for performance on part of any company providing the contractually required service'.[183]

181 ibid 1195.
182 ibid 1199.
183 ibid 1208.

In short, while the tribunal accepted that foreign investors have *negative* human rights obligations (not to infringe human rights), the investor's purported obligation to ensure the population's access to water (a positive obligation) was held to not be based on international law:

> While it is thus correct to state that the State's obligation is based on its obligation to enforce the human right to water of all individuals under its jurisdiction, this is not the case for the investors who pursue, it is true, the same goal, but on the basis of the Concession and not under an obligation derived from the human right to water. Indeed, the enforcement of the human right to water represents an obligation to perform. Such obligation is imposed upon States. It cannot be imposed on any company knowledgeable in the field of provision of water and sanitation services. In order to have such an obligation to perform applicable to a particular investor, a contract or similar legal relationship of civil and commercial law is required. In such a case, the investor's obligation to perform has as its source domestic law; it does not find its legal ground in general international law. The situation would be different in case an obligation to abstain, like a prohibition to commit acts violating human rights would be at stake. Such an obligation can be of immediate application, not only upon States, but equally to individuals and other private parties. This is not a matter for concern in the instant case.[184]

In light of the foregoing, the tribunal concluded that the respondent did not establish any legal ground to claim damages as a consequence of an alleged violation of the human right to water. In other words, there was a lack of a legal ground *based on international law* that would entitle the state to raise a claim for delivery of water and sewage services directed against a company or any other private party. For this reason, the respondent's counterclaim failed. This decision has provoked significant contestation from among scholars.[185]

As intimated earlier, most Caribbean BITs[186] seemingly restrict counterclaims through their wording, either expressly allowing the investor to institute arbitral proceedings, or using language such as 'disputes . . . concerning an obligation of the latter'. For example, Article 8(1) of the Antigua and Barbuda-United Kingdom BIT provides:

> (1) Disputes between a national or company of one Contracting Party and the other Contracting Party concerning an obligation of the latter under this Agreement in relation to an investment of the former which have not been amicably settled shall after a period of three months from written notification of a claim be submitted to international arbitration if either party to the dispute so wishes.

On the basis of the language 'disputes . . . concerning an obligation of the latter', the tribunal in *Spyridon Roussalis v Romania*[187] considered that there was no consent to counterclaims

184 ibid 1210.

185 Edward Guntrip, 'Private Actors, Public Goods and Responsibility for the Right to Water in International Investment Law: An Analysis of *Urbaser v Argentina*' (2018) 1(1) *Brill Open Law* 37–60; Simon Burger, '*Urbaser v Argentina* Arbitration' (2020) *Max Planck Encyclopaedias of International Law*; Yulia Levashova, 'The Right of Access to Water in the Context of Investment Disputes in Argentina: Urbaser and Beyond' (2020) 16(2) *Utrecht Law Review* 110–24.

186 Antigua-UK BIT Article 8(1); Barbados-Cuba BIT Article 8(1); Belize-Cuba BIT Article 8(1); Grenada-UK BIT Article 8(1); Dominica-UK BIT Article 8(1); St Lucia-UK BIT Article 8(1); Belize-UK BIT Article 8(1); Trinidad and Tobago-UK BIT Article 10(1); Trinidad and Tobago-Germany BIT Article 13(1); Trinidad and Tobago-Cuba BIT Article 10(1); Barbados-Canada BIT Article 13(1); Trinidad and Tobago-Canada BIT Article 13(1); SVG-Taiwan BIT Article 11(1); Guyana-China BIT Article 9(1); Trinidad and Tobago-China BIT Article 10(1); Barbados-China BIT Article 9(1); Grenada-USA BIT Article 6(1); Jamaica-USA BIT Article 6(1); Trinidad and Tobago-USA BIT Article 9(1).

187 ICSID Case No. ARB/06/1, Award, 7 December 2011.

flowing from this restrictive provision, which only spoke to the obligation of the respondent host state. The tribunal reiterated that 'the investor's consent to the BIT's arbitration clause can only exist in relation to counterclaims if such counterclaims come within the consent of the host State as expressed in the BIT'.[188] The tribunal, moreover, considered that where, as in this case, the relevant BIT imposes no obligations on investors, only on Contracting States, or where the BIT does specify that the applicable law is the BIT itself, counterclaims fall outside the tribunal's jurisdiction.

In the final analysis, it is submitted that, in the light of the above, a counterclaim would only succeed if the consent offered by the BIT's dispute resolution clause is broad enough to cover the initiation of the counterclaim by the respondent; there is a close connection between the original claim and the counterclaim; and there is a legal basis for asserting a particular human right, and it has been established, on the merits, that that human right has been breached by the foreign investor. Because, as recalled by *Urbaser*, corporations are not generally bound by international human rights law,[189] in particular positive obligations, and only to a limited extent in any event bound by negative obligations, it is very likely that only a handful of human rights counterclaims would ever succeed in practice.

(B) The Environment

In recent years, the protection of the environment has taken centre stage, particularly at the United Nations, especially in the light of the International Court of Justice's (ICJ) recent advisory opinion on climate change,[190] the passage of the Paris Agreement,[191] and the UN's adoption of the resolution on the right to a healthy environment.[192] Despite international consensus that global temperatures are rising, which have serious implications for vulnerable small island developing nations, including those in the Caribbean, foreign investors in many parts of the world continue to engage in activities that circumvent international and domestic environmental laws and policies.[193] From the failure to conduct environmental impact assessment, to failing to deal with the environmental externalities of mining, foreign

188 ibid 866.

189 John Ruggie, Final Report on 'Guiding Principles on Business and Human Rights: Implementing the United Nations "Protect, Respect and Remedy" Framework' (A/HRC/17/31, 21 March 2011). According to these non-binding principles, business enterprises should respect human rights, a negative obligation (No. 11). This responsibility refers to internationally recognized human rights (No. 12). It requires that business enterprises: (i) Avoid causing or contributing to adverse human rights impacts through their own activities and address such impacts when they occur; (ii) Seek to prevent or mitigate adverse human rights impacts that are directly linked to their operations, products or services by their business relationships, even if they have not contributed to those impacts. (No. 13) In all contexts, business enterprises should: (i) Comply with all applicable laws and respect internationally recognized human rights, wherever they operate; (ii) Seek ways to honour the principles of internationally recognized human rights when faced with conflicting requirements; (iii) Treat the risk of causing or contributing to gross human rights abuses as a legal compliance issue wherever they operate. (No. 23).

190 ICJ, Legal Consequences of the Obligations of States under International Law to Protect the Climate System from Anthropogenic Emissions, Advisory Opinion, July 23, 2025.

191 Paris Agreement to the United Nations Framework Convention on Climate Change, 12 December 2015, T.I.A.S. No. 16–1104.

192 UN General Assembly Resolution 76/300 on July 28, 2022.

193 Antonius Hippolyte and Jason Haynes, 'Asymmetrical Approaches to Environmental Regulation in the Caribbean: A Critique of the Region's Foreign Investment Landscape' (2024) 21(2) *Haynes Manchester Journal of International Economic Law* 122.

investors have been implicated in serious environmental disasters.[194] Yet, still, international investment law has been largely protective of foreign investors. For example, in *S.D. Myers, Inc. v Government of Canada*,[195] the NAFTA tribunal rejected Canada's contention that the ban on the export of PCB waste to the US was driven by environmental concerns. In the tribunal's view, Canada could have better served the objective of ensuring a safe environment if it had kept the Canadian border open but put in place safeguards.

However, there have been cases where tribunals have rendered awards that are arguably more protective of the environment. For example, the United States' jurisdictional challenge was upheld in *Methanex Corporation v United States of America*[196] in connection with Article 1101(1) of NAFTA. The tribunal held that Methanex failed to establish, on a balance of probabilities, that in adopting the challenged measures (the California ban of MTBE on methanol) California intended to harm foreign methanol producers, including Methanex. The tribunal was not satisfied that a malign pretext underlined California's measures, but rather, the measures were necessary to protect the environmental interests of the citizens of California. More specifically, faced with widespread and potentially serious MTBE contamination of its water resources, California had ordered a careful assessment of the problem and thereafter responded reasonably to independent findings that large volumes of the state's ground and surface water had become polluted by MTBE and that preventative measures were called for. The evidential record, in the tribunal's view, did not establish ill will towards Methanex or methanol. Indeed, the weight of evidence contradicted entirely one of Methanex's core assertions that the US measures constituted nothing more than a politically corrupt sham designed by the Governor to protect the domestic ethanol industry and to harm foreign producers of methanol (and Methanex) or benefit domestic ethanol producers. For this reason, in the context of Article 1101(1) of NAFTA, there was no legally significant connection between the US measures, Methanex and its investments, in that the US measures did not 'relate to' Methanex or its investments. Accordingly, the USA succeeded on its jurisdictional challenge under Article 1101; the tribunal accordingly lacked jurisdiction to determine Methanex's substantive claims alleged under NAFTA Articles 1102, 1105, and 1110.

In the Caribbean context, some IIAs[197] only refer to the environment in their preambles. For example, the preamble of the Trinidad and Tobago-Switzerland BIT provides:

> Convinced that these objectives can be achieved without relaxing health, safety and environmental measures of general application.

A provision of this nature does not impose substantive obligations[198] but nonetheless is useful to the extent that it can assist tribunals as an interpretive guide when assessing substantive

194 David Boyd, *Paying Polluters: The Catastrophic Consequences of Investor-State Dispute Settlement for Climate and Environment Action and Human Rights* (Special Rapporteur on the human right to a clean, healthy and sustainable environment, A/78/168, 13 July 2023).

195 UNCITRAL Partial Award, 13 November 2000.

196 UNCITRAL Final Award of the Tribunal on Jurisdiction and Merits, 3 August 2005.

197 Trinidad and Tobago-USA BIT Preamble; Trinidad and Tobago-Cuba BIT Preamble; Trinidad and Tobago-China BIT Preamble; Trinidad and Tobago-South Korea BIT Preamble; Trinidad and Tobago-India BIT Preamble; Trinidad and Tobago-Switzerland BIT Preamble; Suriname-The Netherlands BIT Preamble; Guyana-China BIT Preamble.

198 In *Bayindir v Pakistan* (Decision on Jurisdiction), 14 November 2005, para. 230 the tribunal expressed that, in the absence of a specific provision in the Treaty, it was doubtful that the sole text of the preamble would provide a sufficient basis for a self-standing FET obligation. At the merits, the tribunal considered that para. 155 the preambular language 'is of little assistance as it does not establish any operative obligation'.

provisions. Indeed, in accordance with Article 31 of the VCLT, it is arguable that in making a determination as to the meaning of a provision, the preamble may be referred to as part of the context,[199] and, indeed, object and purpose of the BIT in question.[200]

Separately, very few Caribbean IIAs contain specific environmental clauses.[201] One such clause can be found in Article XVII of the Trinidad and Tobago-Canada BIT, which provides:

> 1. This Agreement shall apply to any investment made by an investor of one Contracting Party in the territory of the other Contracting Party before or after the entry into force of this Agreement.
> 2. Nothing in this Agreement shall be construed to prevent a Contracting Party from adopting, maintaining or enforcing any measure otherwise consistent with this Agreement that it considers appropriate to ensure that investment activity in its territory is undertaken in a manner sensitive to environmental concerns.
> 3. Provided that such measures are not applied in an arbitrary or unjustifiable manner, or do not constitute a disguised restriction on international trade or investment, nothing in this Agreement shall be construed to prevent a Contracting Party from adopting or maintaining measures, including environmental measures:
>   a. necessary to ensure compliance with laws and regulations that are not inconsistent with the provisions of this Agreement;
>   b. necessary to protect human, animal, or plant life or health; or
>   c. relating to the conservation of living or non-living exhaustible natural resources.

The interpretation to be ascribed to a provision of this nature was considered in *Infinito Gold Ltd. v Costa Rica.*[202] Here, a majority of the tribunal found that the respondent breached its FET obligation through the 2011 Legislative Mining Ban and, as an ancillary act, the 2012 MINAET Resolution (to the extent that it implemented that Ban), which had the effect of depriving Industrias Infinito of the opportunity to apply for a new exploitation concession. That said, the tribunal proceeded to address the respondent's argument that the environmental exception in Section III(1) of Annex I of the BIT exempted Costa Rica from liability. Annex I, Section III(1) of the Costa Rica-Canada BIT provided:

> Nothing in this Agreement shall be construed to prevent a Contracting Party from adopting, maintaining or enforcing any measure *otherwise consistent* with this Agreement that it considers appropriate to ensure that investment activity in its territory is undertaken in a manner sensitive to environmental concerns.

The tribunal considered that reference in the BIT to 'any measure otherwise consistent with this Agreement' made it clear that measures meant 'to ensure that investment activity . . . is undertaken in a manner sensitive to environmental concerns' must also be consistent with the investment protections set forth in the BIT. The terms 'otherwise consistent with this

199 ibid at the merits, the tribunal noted para. 155

> even though it does not establish an operative obligation, the preamble is relevant for the interpretation of the MFN clause in its context and in the light of the Treaty's object and purpose pursuant to Article 31(1) of the VCLT.

200 See *Ero Oro v Columbia*, ICSID Case No. ARB/16/41, Award, 15 July 2024, paras. 828, 829.

201 Belize-El Salvador BIT Article 3(5); Trinidad and Tobago-Guatemala Article 2(2); Trinidad and Tobago-Canada BIT Article 17(2); Trinidad and Tobago-Taiwan BIT Article 16(3).

202 ICSID Case No. ARB/14/5, Award, 3 June 2021.

Agreement' also applied to measures that were 'maintain[ed]' or 'enforc[ed]', and not only to measures that were 'adopted'. Consequently, in accordance with its ordinary meaning, Annex I, Section III(1) did not exempt an environmental measure from the substantive provisions of the BIT, regardless of whether that measure was a new measure that was 'adopted' or whether it was a measure that 'maintained' or 'enforced' an earlier measure. The tribunal concluded that, interpreted in accordance with the VCLT, Annex I, Section III(1) was not a carve-out from the BIT's protections, but rather a reaffirmation of the state's right to regulate. In other words, a provision of this nature does not exempt a state from liability for the adoption of environmental measures. Rather, it protects the host state's legitimate regulatory space and reserves a margin of discretion in environmental matters. However, while the provision confirms the state's right to sanction violations of its environmental laws in a manner that does not otherwise breach its obligations under the treaty, it does not operate as a defence where those measures are in breach of the treaty. In short, this provision is not a defence to substantive breaches of the BIT, which is in contradistinction to other provisions which, for example, enable Contracting Parties to adopt or maintain 'reasonable measures for prudential reasons' related to financial market protection and regulation or which exempts 'investments in cultural industries' from the provisions of the BIT. Because these latter provisions do not contain the 'otherwise consistent' language, they cannot be construed as exception or exemption from the BIT protections for environmental measures. On the facts, the tribunal found that Annex I, Section III(1) of the Costa Rica-Canada BIT did not exempt the respondent from liability for breaches of the substantive protections granted by the BIT. Accordingly, it could not exempt the respondent for its breaches of its FET obligation.

A similar outcome was arrived at in *Adel A Hamadi Al Tamimi v. Sultanate of Oman.*[203] Here, Article 10.10 of the United States-Oman Free Trade Agreement provided:

> Nothing in this Chapter shall be construed to prevent a Party from adopting, maintaining, or enforcing any measure *otherwise consistent* with this Chapter that it considers appropriate to ensure that investment activity in its territory is undertaken in a manner sensitive to environmental concerns.

In that case, the tribunal found that fines imposed by the government for repeated and serious breaches of environmental regulations were issued in furtherance of its right to regulate and supervise compliance with Oman's environmental laws. More particularly, the tribunal considered that Oman had the right to sanction violations of its environmental laws in a manner that did not otherwise breach its obligations under the treaty. On the facts, there was nothing *per se* unlawful (in domestic or international law) in the domestic authorities forming the view that the claimant was engaged in unlawful activities and requesting a public prosecutor to file misdemeanour charges. Nor was there anything *prima facie* unlawful about the request for police intervention upon discovering that Al Tamimi continued to flout Oman's environmental regulations. In the tribunal's view, this was precisely the kind of environmental regulatory enforcement that the parties sought to protect through the inclusion of Article 10.10. Arguably, had the tribunal found that the measures breached the treaty, Article 10.10 would not have operated as a defence. In short, then, the tribunal considered that while states enjoyed a 'margin of discretion' in relation to the enforcement of their environmental laws, 'even an express provision such as Article 10.10 will not protect a State

203 ICSID Case No. ARB/11/33, Award, 3 November 2015.

from liability for measures that are carried out in bad faith, or in violation of the expected standards of basic fairness or due process'.[204] On the facts, however, there was no evidence that the authorities acted against Al Tamimi in bad faith, or for an ulterior purpose, or in a procedurally unfair manner. For this reason, the defence applied.

Commentators[205] agree that provisions with such wording – a requirement that environmental measures be 'otherwise consistent' with the investment treaty – 'undermines the effectiveness of that shield'.[206] Nikièma opines that the scope of these provisions is 'extremely limited', and that, despite the fact that most of them are entitled 'general exceptions', 'they do not really do much to narrow States' potential liability . . . . Rather, they merely recognize and affirm the State's sovereign right to regulate . . . .'[207] It means, therefore, that once the state has acted inconsistently with one of the substantive investor protection standards, it loses its ability to rely on the defence.[208]

Notwithstanding the foregoing, however, some Caribbean IIAs[209] contain environmental exceptions drafted in less restrictive terms. For example, Article 17 of the Guyana-Brazil BIT provides:

> 1. Nothing in this Agreement shall be construed to prevent a Party from adopting, maintaining or enforcing any measure it deems appropriate to ensure that investment activity in its territory is undertaken in a manner according to labor, environmental and health legislation of that Party, provided that this measure is not applied in a manner which would constitute a means of arbitrary or unjustifiable discrimination or a disguised restriction.

A provision of this nature was subject to interpretation in *Eco Oro Minerals Corp. v Republic of Colombia.*[210] Article 2201(3) of the Canada-Columbia FTA provided:

> (3) For the purposes of Chapter Eight (Investment), subject to the requirement that such measures are not applied in a manner that constitute arbitrary or unjustifiable discrimination between investment or between investors, or a disguised restriction on international trade or investment, nothing in this Agreement shall be construed to prevent a Party from *adopting or enforcing measures necessary*:
> (a) To protect human, animal or plant life or health, which the Parties understand to include *environmental measures* necessary to protect human, animal or plant life and health;
> (b) To ensure compliance with laws and regulations that are *not inconsistent with this Agreement*; or
> (c) For the conservation of living or non-living exhaustible natural resources.

204 ibid 445.

205 Todd Weiler, 'A First Look at the Interim Merits Award in *S.D. Myers, Inc. v Canada*: It Is Possible to Balance Legitimate Environmental Concerns with Investment Protection' (2001) 24(2) *Hastings International and Comparative Law Review* 173, 182

206 Lise Johnson and Lisa Sachs, 'International Investment Agreements, 2011–2012: A Review of Trends and New Approaches' in Andrea Bjorklund (ed), *Yearbook on International Investment Law & Policy 2012–2013* (OUP 2014) 235.

207 Suzy Nikièma, *Best Practices: Indirect Expropriation* (International Institute for Sustainable Development 2012) 9

208 ibid.

209 Suriname-Brazil BIT Article 17; SVG-Taiwan BIT Article 16; Trinidad and Tobago-Taiwan BUT Article 16; Barbados-Canada BIT Article 17; Trinidad and Tobago-Canada BIT Article 17; Belize-El Salvador BIT Article 3; Trinidad and Tobago-Guatemala BIT Article 2.

210 ICSID Case No. ARB/16/41, Award, 15 July 2024.

The tribunal rejected Canada's non-disputing party submission, which had argued that if the measure in question met the requirements of Article 2201(3), then there was no violation of the Agreement and no state liability, and so payment of compensation was not required. While the tribunal accepted that the state could not be prohibited from adopting or enforcing an environmental measure in accordance with Article 2201(3), it refused to accept Canada's statement that in such circumstances payment of compensation was not required. In its view, in the absence of an express provision to this effect, and in the light of the fact that the FTA was equally supportive of investment protection, there was nothing in Article 2201(3) permitting environmental action to be taken without the payment of compensation.

Several scholars argue that the tribunal appears to have adopted a flawed reading of the provision[211] when it ruled that while a state may adopt or enforce a measure pursuant to environmental objectives in Article 2201(3) without finding itself in breach of the FTA, this did not prevent an investor claiming that such a measure entitles it to the payment of compensation. The question arises in this connection – if there is no breach, how can an obligation to pay compensation arise? A better approach is that if the measures are not arbitrary or unjustifiably discriminatory between investment or between investors or were not a disguised restriction on trade and were taken to protect the environment, no liability arises on the part of the state, and therefore no compensation is payable. That said, the tribunal again appears to have fallen into error when it considered that

> Colombia also provided no justification as to why it is necessary for the protection of the environment not to offer compensation to an investor for any loss suffered as a result of measures taken by Colombia to protect the environment, nor explained how such a construction would support the protection of investment in addition to the protection of the environment.[212]

Such an approach is misplaced, in that the tribunal arguably asked the wrong question; the question that it should have asked, in accordance with the plain reading of the provision, was whether the environmental measures were necessary in the circumstances, not whether they were necessary for the protection of the environment not to offer compensation. Nonetheless, the tribunal sought to justify its position by quoting Article 27(b) of the ILC Draft Articles, which provides:

> The invocation of a circumstance precluding wrongfulness in accordance with this chapter is without prejudice to: . . .
>
> (b) the question of compensation for any material loss caused by the act in question.

The tribunal's analysis in this connection is supported by the award in *Bear Creek Mining Corporation v Republic of Peru*,[213] which considered an identical provision. In that case, the tribunal held that the exception in Article 2201 of the relevant treaty did not offer any waiver from the obligation in Article 812 to compensate for the expropriation. Like the tribunal in *Eco Oro*, the tribunal considered that 'the Respondent has also failed to explain why it was

211 See Robert Garden, '*Eco Oro v Colombia*: The Brave New World of Environmental Exceptions' (2023) 38(1) *ICSID Review-Foreign Investment Law Journal* 17; Güneş Ünüvar, 'A Tale of Policy Carve-Outs and General Exceptions: *Eco Oro v Colombia* as a Case Study' (2023) 14(4) *Journal of International Dispute Settlement* 517; Laura Létourneau, 'In Need of a Paradigm Shift: Reimagining *Eco Oro v Colombia* in Light of New Treaty Language' (2022) 23(5) *The Journal of World Investment & Trade* 915.

212 ibid 832.

213 ICSID Case No. ARB/14/21, Award, 30 November 2017.

necessary for the protection of human life not to offer compensation to Claimant for the derogation of Supreme Decree 083'.[214]

Finally, it is noteworthy that Guyana's recent BIT with Brazil provides a uniquely worded provision (Article 17(2)), which does not appear in most other IIAs, namely:

> 2. The Parties recognize that it is inappropriate to encourage investment by lowering the standards of their labour and environmental legislation or measures of health. Therefore, each Party guarantees it shall not amend or repeal, nor offer the amendment or repeal of such legislation to encourage the establishment, maintenance or expansion of an investment in its territory, to the extent that such amendment or repeal involves decreasing heir labour, environmental or health standards. If a Party considers that another Party has offered such an encouragement, the Parties shall address the issue through consultations.

Such a provision is binding on the Contracting States, requiring them not to modify their legal framework to attract or maintain investments in a manner that is inconsistent with their environmental standards. A similar provision appears in Article 17.2.1 of the US-Oman BIT. In *Adel A Hamadi Al Tamimi v Sultanate of Oman*,[215] the tribunal considered that:

> The very existence of Chapter 17 exemplifies the importance attached by the US and Oman to the enforcement of their respective environmental laws. The State Parties intended to reserve a significant margin of discretion to themselves in the application and enforcement of their respective environmental laws – indeed, Article 17.2.1 compels each State to ensure the effective enforcement of environmental laws.[216]

The obvious limitation of the provision, however, is that it does not directly impose environmental obligations on investors, as it is essentially directed at states.

(1) Environmental Counterclaims

Counterclaims are an extremely useful tool to hold investors accountable for violations of environmental norms.[217] Beyond accountability, the admission of counterclaims has several practical advantages on procedural economy and efficiency, for the benefit of both the host state and the foreign investor, as Professor Reisman highlighted in *Spyridon Roussalis v Romania*:[218]

> It is important to bear in mind that such counterclaim jurisdiction is not only a concession to the State Party: Article 46 works to the benefit of both respondent state and investor. In rejecting ICSID jurisdiction over counterclaims, a neutral tribunal – which was, in fact, selected by the claimant – perforce directs the respondent State to pursue its claims in its own courts where the very investor who had sought a forum outside the state apparatus is now constrained to become the defendant. (And if an adverse judgment ensues, that erstwhile defendant might well transform to claimant again, bringing another BIT claim.) Aside from duplication and inefficiency, the sorts of transaction costs which counterclaim and set-off procedures work to

214 ibid 477.

215 ICSID Case No. ARB/11/33, Award, 3 November 2015.

216 ibid 389.

217 Tomoko Ishikawa, *Corporate Environmental Responsibility in Investor-State Dispute Settlement: The Unexhausted Potential of Current Mechanisms* (CUP 2022) 57–86.

218 ICSID Case No. ARB/06/1, 7 December 2011.

> avoid, it is an ironic, if not absurd, outcome, at odds, in my view, with the objectives of international investment law.[219]

The availability, however, of counterclaims in environmental cases is not automatic. Indeed, as noted by the tribunal in *Spyridon Roussalis v Romania*,[220] the first issue which the tribunal has to determine is whether the parties consented to have the state's counterclaims arbitrated. Under the system created by the ICSID Convention, consent by both parties is an indispensable condition for the exercise of the Centre's jurisdiction. The Convention only requires that consent be in writing, leaving the parties otherwise free to choose the manner in which to express their consent. Whether it is so must be determined in the first place by reference to the dispute resolution clause contained in the BIT. The investor's consent to the BIT's arbitration clause can only exist in relation to counterclaims if such counterclaims come within the consent of the host state as expressed in the BIT.[221]

Some Caribbean dispute settlement clauses appear to implicitly contemplate counterclaims. For example, Article 9 Jamaica-Indonesia BIT provides:

> 1. Any dispute which arises within the terms of this Agreement concerning an investment between an investor of one Contracting Party and the other Contracting Party shall, if possible, be settled amicably.
> 2. If the dispute cannot be settled within six months following the date on which the dispute has been raised by either party, it may be submitted to:
>   (i) the judicial procedures provided by the Contracting Party in whose territory the investment was made; or
>   (ii) international arbitration according to the provisions of Paragraph 3.
> 3. Where a dispute has been raised by an investor and the parties disagree as to the choice of (i) or (ii) the opinion of the investor shall prevail.

Such a provision appears broad enough to encompass counterclaims as it simply says that the dispute 'may be submitted to', without specifying by whom. Though subsection 3 then goes on to mention the circumstance where the dispute is raised by an investor, this does not appear, in light of the open-textured nature of subsection 2, to suggest that only the investor can initiate proceedings.

By contrast, other IIAs appear to foreclose the availability of counterclaims. For example, Article 7 of the Belize-China BIT provides:

> 1. Disputes between an investor of either Party and the other Party concerning an obligation of the latter under this Agreement in relation to an investment of the former which have not been amicably settled shall, after a period of three months from written notification of a claim, be submitted to international arbitration if the investor concerned so wishes.

Second, the BIT must impose obligations on investors, and not only on Contracting States. In circumstances where the BIT specifies that the applicable law is the BIT itself, counterclaims fall outside the tribunal's jurisdiction. Indeed, in order to extend the competence of a tribunal to a state's counterclaim, 'the arbitration agreement should refer to disputes that

219 ibid Declaration 28 November 2011.
220 ICSID Case No. ARB/06/1, Award, 7 December 2011, paras. 860–877.
221 ibid.

can also be brought under domestic law [or international law] for counterclaims to be within the tribunal's jurisdiction'.[222]

Practical insights into the treatment of environmental counterclaims by arbitral tribunals were offered in *David Aven and Others v Republic of Costa Rica*.[223] On the issue of consent, the tribunal considered that the language of Article 10.15 and 10.16 of DR-CAFTA was in principle wide enough to encompass counterclaims and that Article 10.16 did not imply that it applied only to disputes in which it was an investor which initiated claims. The tribunal then found that investors had the obligation, not only under domestic law but also under Section A of Chapter 10 of DR-CAFTA, to abide by and comply with the environmental domestic laws and regulations, including the measures adopted by the host state to protect human, animal, or plant life or health. In this regard, no investor could ignore or breach such measures; in fact, its breach was a violation of both domestic and international law, so the perpetrator could not be exempt from liability for the damage caused. While acknowledging that most international investment tribunals have not recognised jurisdiction over the counterclaims in the absence of an explicit agreement between the parties to submit the counterclaim to the arbitral tribunal, the tribunal acknowledged that some tribunals have asserted their jurisdiction over counterclaims, in particular the tribunals of *Urbaser v Argentina*[224] and *Burlington v Ecuador*,[225] both within the framework of the ICSID Convention and of two BITs (Spain-Argentina and USA-Ecuador, respectively). In this light, it considered that environmental law is integrated in many ways into international law, including DR-CAFTA, and although the enforcement of environmental law is primarily left to states, a foreign investor could be subject to international law obligations in this field, particularly in the light of Articles 10.9.3, 10.11, and 17 of DR-CAFTA. Having found that 'it can no longer be admitted that investors operating internationally are immune from becoming subjects of international law',[226] the tribunal felt persuaded that 'there are no substantive reasons to exempt foreign investor of the scope of claims for breaching obligations under Article 10 Section A DR-CAFTA, particularly in the field of environmental law'.[227]

Although the tribunal refused to declare the respondent's counterclaim inadmissible and thereby accepted *prima facie* jurisdiction over the counterclaim filed by the respondent, two issues prevented it from examining the merits of the counterclaim. First, the language of Article 10.9.3.c and 10.11 sought to ensure that the respondent retain a significant margin of appreciation in respect of environmental measures in its jurisdiction, but they did not – in and of themselves – impose any affirmative obligation upon investors. In other words, like the *Urbaser* decision, only negative obligations were imposed, but not positive obligations,

222 Pierre Lalive and Laura Halonen, 'On the Availability of Counterclaims in Investment Treaty Arbitration' (2011) *Czech Yearbook of International Law* 141.

223 ICSID Case No. UNCT/15/3, Award, 18 September 2018.

224 Urbaser S.A. and Consorcio de Aguas Bilbao Bizkaia, *Bilbao Biskaia Ur Partzuergoa v The Argentine Republic*, ICSID Case No. ARB/07/26, Award, 8 December 2016.

225 *Burlington Resources Inc. v Republic of Ecuador*, ICSID Case No. ARB/08/5, Decision on Liability, 14 December 2012.

226 *Urbaser v Argentina*, ICSID Case No. ARB/07/2, Award, 8 December 2016, para. 1195.

227 *David Aven and Others v Republic of Costa Rica*, ICSID Case No. UNCT/15/3, Final Award, 18 September 2018, para. 739.

on investors. Nor did they provide that any violation of state-enacted environmental regulations would amount to a breach of the Treaty which could be the basis of a counterclaim. Furthermore, the counterclaim here was subject to the UNCITRAL Arbitration Rules, whose Article 21 establishes that 'the provisions of article 20, paragraphs 2 to 4, shall apply to a counterclaim . . .'. In turn, Article 20(2) reads as follows:

> 2. The statement of claim shall include the following particulars:
>   (a) The names and contact details of the parties;
>   (b) A statement of the facts supporting the claim;
>   (c) The points at issue;
>   (d) The relief or remedy sought;
>   (e) The legal grounds or arguments supporting the claim. . . .
>
> 4. The statement of claim should, as far as possible, be accompanied by all documents and other evidence relied upon by the claimant, or contains references to them.

The tribunal considered that a counterclaim is a separate claim, autonomous with respect to the respondent's statement of defence, although it is usual that materially it is a part of that statement. As such, the counterclaim must satisfy by itself the requirements of Articles 20.2 and 20.4 of the UNCITRAL Arbitration Rules, in the same way that the main claim does. In the tribunal's view, on the facts here, Costa Rica did not meet such requirements. More particularly, in its Counter-Memorial (statement of defence under Article 21 of the UNCITRAL Arbitration Rules) as well as in its Rejoinder, Costa Rica only made a general reference to environmental damage in the Las Olas Project site attributed to the claimants' activity. There was no precise statement of the facts supporting the claims but rather a reference to expert reports attached to those pleadings. There was no specification of the relief sought but in very general terms and the quantification was much approximated, based only on the personal experience of an expert rather than any accurate method of valuation. Moreover, the evidence that Costa Rica had mentioned was diluted in its statement of defence, without specifying clearly and precisely the facts to be proved within the counterclaim, particularly the evidence that the claimants were the perpetrators of all the environmental damage sustained. For these reasons, the tribunal concluded that the counterclaim filed by the respondent did not meet the requirements of Articles 21 and 20 of the UNCITRAL Arbitration Rules.

Separately, in *Burlington Resources Inc. v Republic of Ecuador*,[228] the issue of jurisdiction was not at the stake, because the parties had reached an agreement where they 'expressed their agreement and consent that this arbitration is the 'appropriate forum for the final resolution of the Counterclaims arising out of the investments made by Burlington Resources and its affiliates in Blocks 7 and 21, so as to ensure maximum judicial economy and consistency'.[229] Consequently, the investor (Burlington) did not challenge the tribunal's jurisdiction to decide the counterclaims. Having regard to Article 46 of ICSID Convention, and the fact that consent of the parties was explicit and unambiguous in this case, this award is not generally useful where there is no consent expressed in similar terms.

228 ICSID Case No. ARB/08/5, Decision on Liability, 14 December 2012 (formerly *Burlington Resources Inc. and others v Republic of Ecuador and Empresa Estatal Petróleos del Ecuador* (PetroEcuador).
229 ibid Decision on Ecuador's Counterclaims 7 February 2017, para. 60.

(c) Corporate Social Responsibility

Provisions on corporate social responsibility are rarely found in IIAs globally,[230] and the Caribbean is not exception in this regard, largely because most of these agreements are older generation treaties. The exception to this, however, is Article 15 of the Guyana-Brazil BIT, which provides:

> 1. Investors and their investment shall strive to achieve the highest possible level of contribution to the sustainable development of the Host State and the local community, through the adoption of a high degree of socially responsible practices, based on the voluntary principles and standards set out in this Article.
> 2. The investors and their investment shall endeavour to comply with the following voluntary principles and standards for a responsible business conduct and consistent with the laws
>
>   adopted by the Host State:
>
>   a) Contribute to the economic, social and environmental progress, aiming at achieving sustainable development;
>   b) Respect the internationally recognized human rights of those involved in the investors' activities;
>   c) Encourage local capacity building through dose cooperation with the local community;
>   d) Encourage the creation of human capital, especially by creating employment opportunities and offering professional training to workers;
>   e) Refrain from seeking or accepting exemptions that are not established in the legal or regulatory framework relating to human rights, environment, health, security, work, tax system, financial incentives, or other issues;
>   f) Support and advocate for good corporate governance principles, and develop and apply good practices of corporate governance;
>   g) Develop and implement effective self-regulatory practices and management systems that foster a relationship of mutual trust between the companies and the societies in which its operations are conducted;
>   h) Promote the knowledge of and the adherence to, by workers, the corporate policy, through appropriate dissemination of this policy, including programs for professional training;
>   i) Refrain from discriminatory or disciplinary action against employees who submit grave reports to the board or, whenever appropriate, to the competent public authorities, about practices that violate the law or corporate policy;
>   j) Encourage, whenever possible, business associates, including service providers and outsources, to apply the principles of business conduct consistent with the principles provided for in this Article; and
>   k) Refrain from any undue interference in local political activities.

Terms such as 'strive to' and 'voluntary principle' suggest that the provision is drafted in hortatory language, and that therefore, while investors' compliance with these principles is desirable, such compliance is not entirely mandatory and certainly is not justiciable. In fact, Article 25 of the BIT confirms that Article 15 'may not be subject to arbitration'. In this regard, the practical value of Article 15 is necessarily limited.

230 Jason Haynes, 'Charting the Path Towards Sustainability: A Critique of Guyana's Recent Investment Treaty Practice' (2023) *University of the West Indies St Augustine Law Journal* 65.

In *Grenada Private Power Limited and WRB Enterprises, Inc. v Grenada*,[231] the respondent considered the claimants to have been poor corporate citizens. Grenada argued that the claimants sought at all times to maximise their return on investment with little regard for meeting GRENLEC's capital investment needs or the well-being of the island economy (including, in particular, the claimants' persistent failure to develop Grenada's ample renewable energy resources). However, the tribunal rejected this argument as a basis for their alleged violation of the Agreement, finding that:

> In the Tribunal's view, it has no authority to judge whether or not in the period 1994 to 2016, the Claimants caused GRENLEC to behave as a good 'corporate citizen' of Grenada. The task of the Tribunal is to determine whether the complex contractual arrangements between the Parties have been complied with and, if not, what remedy should be awarded.[232]

The tribunal later went on to note that:

> GRENLEC under the guidance of WRB may have fallen short of what might be expected of a good corporate citizen, but the root of the problem is the decision of the NDC Government in 1994 to create the regulatory framework which the NNP Government now considers 'toothless' and the 1994 failure to set performance standards for renewable energy which, with the benefit of hindsight, would have promoted its development.[233]

In short, then, while it is sensible that Guyana's BIT with Brazil reaffirms a self-regulating business model that integrates social and environmental concerns into a company's operations and interactions with stakeholders, its utility is necessarily limited by its hortatory and voluntary nature.

C. Annulment

Once an award is rendered, appeals are not allowed in arbitral proceedings.[234] Instead, at least in the context of ICSID proceedings, annulments are possible, pursuant to Article 52 (1) of the ICSID Convention, which provides:

> Either party may request annulment of the award by an application in writing addressed to the Secretary-General on one or more of the following grounds:
> (a) that the Tribunal was not properly constituted;
> (b) that the Tribunal has manifestly exceeded its powers;
> (c) that there was corruption on the part of a member of the Tribunal;
> (d) that there has been a serious departure from a fundamental rule of procedure; or
> (e) that the award has failed to state the reasons on which it is based.
>
> (2) The application shall be made within 120 days after the date on which the award was rendered except that when annulment is requested on the ground of corruption such application shall be made within 120 days after discovery of the corruption and in any event within three years after the date on which the award was rendered.
>
> (3) On receipt of the request the Chairman shall forthwith appoint from the Panel of Arbitrators an ad hoc Committee of three persons. None of the members of the Committee shall have been a member of the Tribunal which rendered the award, shall be of the same nationality as any such member, shall be a national of the State party to the dispute or of

231 ICSID Case No. ARB/17/13, Award, 29 March 2020.
232 ibid 8.
233 ibid 140.
234 Antonio Parra, *ICSID: An Introduction to the Convention and Centre* (Oxford Law Pro 2020) 87.

the State whose national is a party to the dispute, shall have been designated to the Panel of Arbitrators by either of those States, or shall have acted as a conciliator in the same dispute. The Committee shall have the authority to annul the award or any part thereof on any of the grounds set forth in paragraph (1).

(4) The provisions of Articles 41–45, 48, 49, 53 and 54, and of Chapters VI and VII shall apply mutatis mutandis to proceedings before the Committee.

(5) The Committee may, if it considers that the circumstances so require, stay enforcement of the award pending its decision. If the applicant requests a stay of enforcement of the award in his application, enforcement shall be stayed provisionally until the Committee rules on such request.

(6) If the award is annulled the dispute shall, at the request of either party, be submitted to a new Tribunal constituted in accordance with Section 2 of this Chapter.

Annulment proceedings are about reviewing the integrity of an arbitration.[235] It is an exceptional remedy available only in extraordinary cases of gross departures from basic principles.[236] Article 52 provides limited grounds for annulment. In practice, the annulment stage is not one where facts that were not before the tribunal can be introduced.[237] At the same time, the arguments raised on annulment are those that relate to the grounds for annulment, which themselves need not have been raised in the original arbitration. An applicant cannot be inhibited from raising arguments in annulment proceedings relating to the interpretation or application of Article 52 that best support its position. In this connection, the ad hoc committee noted in *Sempra v Argentina*[238] that although new arguments or evidence on the merits are irrelevant for the annulment process, and therefore not admissible, it cannot be excluded, however, that evidence, particularly expert evidence, may exceptionally be accepted in annulment proceedings insofar it is specifically relevant for the annulment grounds listed in Article 52(1) of the Convention. It went on to note that it is standard practice for applicants seeking annulment to invoke more than one ground for annulment. The committee's task is to gauge the circumstances invoked in support of each ground independently. The fact that a particular set of facts may have a bearing on more than one ground of annulment does not, as such, render any error alleged in support of anyone of those grounds of annulment any the more manifest.

Once an ad hoc committee has concluded that there is one instance of manifest excess of powers (or any other ground for annulment), which warrants annulment of the Award in its entirety, this will be the end of the ad hoc committee's examination. Since annulment of an award in its entirety necessarily leads to the loss of the *res judicata* effect of all matters adjudicated by the tribunal, it is unnecessary for a tribunal to consider whether there are other grounds – whether in respect of the same matter or other matters – that may also lead to annulment. On the other hand, an ad hoc committee will need to proceed differently where it decides not to annul the Award or decides to annul the Award only in part. In those instances, it will be necessary for the ad hoc committee to examine all of the grounds invoked by the applicant in support of its application.

235 Steffen Hindelang and Julia Nassl, 'Annulment and Set- Aside' in Katia Fach Gómez and Catharine Titi (eds) *The Award in International Investment Arbitration* (Oxford Law Pro 2024) 414.

236 Tannaz Koohpaie et al., 'Annulment of International Arbitration Awards in the Light of Foreign Investment Law' (2022) 12(4) *International Journal of Political Science* 71–87.

237 *RSM Production Corporation v Saint Lucia*, ICSID Case No. ARB/12/10, Decision on Annulment, 29 April 2019, para. 151.

238 *Sempra Energy International v Argentine Republic*, ICSID Case No. ARB/02/16, Decision on the Argentine Republic's Application for Annulment of the Award, 29 June 2010, para. 74.

In *RSM v St Lucia,*[239] the committee examined several grounds for annulment. Regarding *improper constitution* under Article 52(1)(a), RSM challenged an arbitrator's impartiality based on comments made about third-party funders. The committee held that evocative language alone does not demonstrate bias, finding no basis to conclude the tribunal was improperly constituted. The committee also noted that decisions on arbitrator challenges are not themselves subject to annulment, though they may be considered when determining whether a tribunal was properly constituted.

The *manifest excess of powers*[240] ground in Article 52(1)(b) has generated considerable jurisprudence. In *RSM v St Lucia,* for example, the committee addressed whether a tribunal's 'ordering' rather than 'recommending' provisional measures (in this case, security for costs) constituted such excess. Despite Article 47's ICSID use of 'recommend', the committee found no manifest excess, reasoning that consequences can flow from non-compliance with recommendations and that using 'order' rather than 'recommend' cannot itself constitute excess of power. Similarly, the committee upheld the tribunal's order for security for costs, finding that Article 47 does not exclude contingent rights. However, the committee in *RSM*[241] did find manifest excess where the tribunal dismissed certain claims 'with prejudice'. While the committee upheld the tribunal's power to discontinue proceedings for non-compliance with provisional measures orders, it found no basis in the ICSID Convention for dismissing cases on the merits without hearing arguments. This resulted in a partial annulment, preserving the discontinuation but removing the prejudicial effect.

The manifestness requirement for the ground of excess of powers has been interpreted as requiring something 'plain', 'clear', or 'obvious'. The *Sempra* committee favoured a two-step approach: first determining whether excess exists and then assessing whether it is manifest. The committee found that the tribunal's failure to apply Article XI was manifest from a simple reading of the award, particularly its statement that 'there is no need to undertake a further judicial review under Article XI'. In contrast, the *CMS v Argentina* committee, while acknowledging the tribunal gave an erroneous interpretation to Article XI of the Argentina-United States BIT (by applying the requirements of the customary international law defence of necessity) and failed to properly examine whether its conditions were fulfilled, ultimately declined annulment. The committee reasoned that despite applying Article XI 'cryptically and defectively',[242] the tribunal had nonetheless applied it, thus no manifest excess of powers

239 *RSM Production Corporation v Saint Lucia*, ICSID Case No. ARB/12/10, Decision on Annulment, 29 April 2019.

240 The applicable test for a manifest excess of powers is to determine whether (i) there is an excess of powers; and (ii) whether the excess is 'manifest'. A failure to apply the proper law or a failure to apply the law chosen by the parties may amount to an excess of powers. An excess of power must be 'manifest'; in other words, it must be plain, evident, obvious and clear to warrant annulment. As stated by the Wena annulment committee at paragraph 25: 'The excess of power must be self-evident rather than the product of elaborate interpretations one way or the other. When the latter happens the excess of power is no longer manifest'. The annulment proceeding is not an appeal and therefore, is not a mechanism to correct alleged errors of fact or law that a tribunal may have committed. Annulment under the ICSID Convention is a limited remedy destined to ensure the fundamental fairness of the arbitration proceeding.

241 *RSM Production Corporation v Saint Lucia*, ICSID Case No. ARB/12/10, Decision on Annulment, 29 April 2019, paras. 196–201.

242 *CMS v Argentina*, ICSID Case No. ARB/01/8, Decision of the ad hoc Committee on the Application for Annulment of the Argentine Republic, 25 September 2007, para. 136.

existed. This illustrates the fine line committees must draw between erroneous application (not annullable) and failure to apply (potentially annullable).

The distinction between *manifest errors of law*[243] and *failure to apply the law*[244] proved crucial in *Sempra v Argentina.* The committee confirmed that while erroneous application of law does not constitute grounds for annulment, failure to apply the applicable law may amount to manifest excess of powers. This principle was applied to the tribunal's treatment of Article XI of the BIT, where the committee found the tribunal had failed to apply Article XI as the primary applicable law, instead subordinating it to customary international law requirements. In *Sempra*, the committee determined that the tribunal's equation of Article XI of the BIT with customary international law state of necessity under Article 25 of the ILC Articles constituted a fundamental error. The committee reasoned that Article XI operates as a treaty-based exception that precludes wrongfulness, while Article 25 addresses justification for breach of international obligations – two conceptually distinct situations. The tribunal's failure to apply Article XI as the primary norm, instead requiring it to meet customary law requirements, constituted manifest excess of powers warranting total annulment.

Regarding *failure to state reasons*[245] under Article 52(1)(e), the *Sempra* committee articulated the standard as requiring 'reasonably comprehensible and consistent' reasoning

243 A serious error of law is not in itself a ground for annulment under Article 52(1) of the ICSID Convention. However, a serious error of law may, in certain exceptional circumstances, constitute a manifest excess of powers (and therefore be annullable on that ground). Several ad hoc committees have dealt with this issue and opined, for instance, that incorrect application of law might constitute a manifest excess of powers if 'it amounts to effective disregard of the applicable law'. See for example, *Amco Asia Corporation and others v Republic of Indonesia*, (ICSID Case No. ARB/81/1) (Amco II), Decision on Annulment of 3 December 1992. Similar statements have been made by other ad hoc committees, e.g. the MTD Annulment Committee, which stated that annulment may be a consequence of the purported application of the relevant law, while in fact applying quite a different law (*MTD Equity Sdn Bhd. & MTD Chile S.A. v Chile*, (ICSID Case No. ARB/01/7), Annulment Decision of 21 March 2007, para. 47).

244 *Daimler Financial Services AG v Argentine Repu*blic, ICSID Case No. ARB/05/1, para. 189:

> When an allegation is made that there was a manifest excess of powers for failure to apply the applicable law, it is not the role of an ad hoc committee to verify whether the interpretation of the law by the tribunal was correct, or whether it correctly ascertained the facts or whether it correctly appreciated the evidence. These are issues relevant to an appeal, but not for annulment proceedings in view of the limited grounds provided for under the ICSID Convention.

It further clarified, para. 189:

> what the Committee can do is to determine whether the Tribunal correctly identified the applicable law and endeavoured to apply it. As to the latter, there is a distinction between endeavouring to apply the correct law and correctly applying the law. While the former may provide a ground for annulment the latter is outside the scope of authority of an ad hoc annulment committee.

245 The ad hoc committee, in the *MINE v Guinea*, ICSID Case No. ARB/84/4, Decision of the Ad hoc Annulment Committee, 22 December 1989, paras. 5.08–5.09:

> The Committee is of the opinion that the requirement that an award has to be motivated implies that it must enable the reader to follow the reasoning of the Tribunal on points of fact and law. It implies that, and only that. The adequacy of the reasoning is not an appropriate standard of review under paragraph (1)(e), because it almost inevitably draws an ad hoc Committee into an examination of the substance of the tribunal's decision, in disregard of the exclusion of the remedy of appeal by Article 53 of the Convention. . . . In the Committee's view, the requirement to state reasons is satisfied as

demonstrating 'a logical and discernible line of thinking'.[246] While finding the tribunal had provided detailed reasoning on the defence of necessity under customary international law, the committee held this did not cure the fundamental failure to apply the correct legal framework.

Finally, the *serious departure from a fundamental rule of procedure*[247] ground under Article 52(1)(d) was examined in *RSM v St Lucia* regarding the arbitrator challenge. The committee found that even taking account of all considerations, no basis existed for concluding the arbitrator's alleged lack of impartiality constituted such a departure.

> long as the award enables one to follow how the tribunal proceeded from Point A to Point B and eventually to its conclusion, even if it made an error of fact or of law. This minimum requirement is in particular not satisfied by either contradictory or frivolous reasons.

Meanwhile, regarding contradictory reasons, the ad hoc committee in *Daimler Financial Services AG v Argentine Republic*, ICSID Case No. ARB/05/1, Decision on Annulment, 7 January 2015, para. 77:

> Two tests must be satisfied before an ad hoc committee can annul an award based on contradictory reasons. First, the reasons must be genuinely contradictory in that they cancel each other out so as to amount to no reasons at all. Second, the point with regard to which these reasons are given is necessary for the tribunal's decision. It went on to hold that at, para. 79: The standard for annulment under Article 52(1)(e) of the ICSID Convention is, therefore, high. It does not permit an ad hoc committee to second guess the reasoning of the tribunal and that imposes on the applicant the burden of proving that the reasoning of the tribunal on a point that is essential for the outcome of the case was either absent, unintelligible, contradictory or frivolous. In order to succeed the Applicant must discharge this burden.

246 ICSID Case No. ARB/02/16, Decision on the Argentine Republic's Application for Annulment of the Award, 29 June 2010, para. 167.

247 *Daimler Financial Services AG v Argentine Republic*, ICSID Case No. ARB/05/1, Decision on Annulment, 7 January 2015, paras. 262–265:

> The Committee considers that under Article 52(1)(d) of the ICSID Convention, a departure from a procedural rule justifies annulment of the award provided that (i) the given departure is serious; and (ii) the rule in question is fundamental. A departure is serious if it deprives a party of the protection afforded by the said rule.

In the words of the *Maritime International Nominees Establishment v Republic of* Guinea (II), ICSID Case No. ARB/84/4, Decision of the Ad hoc Annulment Committee, 22 December 1989, the Annulment Committee noted:

> 5.05 A first comment on this provision concerns the term 'serious'. In order to constitute a ground for annulment the departure from a 'fundamental rule of procedure' must be serious. The Committee considers that this establishes both quantitative and qualitative criteria: the departure must be substantial and be such as to deprive a party of the benefit or protection which the rule was intended to provide. . . . . In other words, for a violation of the procedural rule to be serious, such violation 'must have caused the Tribunal to reach a result substantially different from what it would have awarded had the rule been observed'. . . . With respect to the rules of procedure that are to be considered fundamental, the Committee considers that they are the rules of natural justice i.e., rules concerned with the essential fairness of the proceeding.

Meanwhile, as pointed out by the *CDC Group plc v Republic of Seychelles*, ICSID Case No. ARB/02/14, Decision on Annulment, 29 June 2005, Annulment Committee:

> A departure is serious where it is substantial and [is] such as to deprive the party of the benefit or protection which the rule was intended to provide. . . . As for what rules of procedure are fundamental, the drafters of the Convention refrained from attempting to enumerate them, but the consensus seems to be that only rules of natural justice.

These cases demonstrate that annulment committees maintain a high threshold for intervention, consistently distinguishing their limited review function from appellate reconsideration. The manifest excess of powers ground has emerged as the most successful basis for annulment, particularly where tribunals fail to apply the applicable law entirely, rather than merely misapplying it. The requirement that any excess be 'manifest' serves as an additional safeguard, ensuring annulment remains an exceptional remedy reserved for clear departures from fundamental principles rather than mere disagreements with tribunals' reasoning or conclusions.

D. Compliance, Recognition and Enforcement

The ICSID Convention[248] establishes a comprehensive and self-contained legal framework for investor-state arbitration, with provisions addressing post-award remedies and the recognition and enforcement of awards.[249] The final and binding nature of ICSID awards and their enforcement provisions represent key features distinguishing the Convention from other arbitration regimes. Article 53(1) of the ICSID Convention provides that awards 'shall be binding on the parties and shall not be subject to any appeal or to any other remedy except those provided for in this Convention. Each party shall abide by and comply with the terms of the award'.[250] This obligation encompasses both pecuniary and non-pecuniary obligations and applies to all disputing parties.[251] The drafters of the Convention expected voluntary compliance, considering it unlikely that states would not observe their obligations under an award.[252] This expectation has been largely validated in practice, with ICSID research demonstrating that award debtors voluntarily comply with or reach post-award settlements in 66% of damages awards.[253]

Article 54(1) requires each member state to 'recognize an award rendered pursuant to this Convention as binding and enforce the pecuniary obligations imposed by that award within its territories as if it were a final judgment of a court in that State'.[254] Significantly, the Convention provides no grounds for refusing recognition and enforcement, requiring only that parties furnish a copy of the award certified by the Secretary-General.[255] This simplified procedure contrasts markedly with the New York Convention regime. As the UK High Court observed in *Unión Fenosa Gas SA v Arab Republic of Egypt*,[256] the ICSID Convention differs significantly from the New York Convention in providing no substantive grounds for refusing enforcement.[257] Indeed, the drafters deliberately rejected incorporating

248 The ICSID Convention distinguishes between *compliance* (the immediate treaty obligation to voluntarily abide by an award under Article 53), *recognition* (a domestic court's formal acknowledgement of the award's authenticity and binding force), *enforcement* (the judicial process of compelling payment of pecuniary obligations as if the award were a final domestic judgment under Article 54), and *execution* (the actual seizure of assets to satisfy the award, governed by domestic law and subject to sovereign immunity under Articles 54(3) and 55).

249 ICSID, 'Background Paper on Compliance with and Enforcement of ICSID Awards' (June 2024), para. 2.

250 Convention on the Settlement of Investment Disputes between States and Nationals of Other States (adopted 18 March 1965, entered into force 14 October 1966) 575 UNTS 159, Article 53(1)

251 ICSID, 'Background Paper on Compliance with and Enforcement of ICSID Awards' (June 2024), para. 87.

252 ibid 53.

253 ibid 28.

254 ICSID Convention, Article 54(1).

255 ibid Article 54(2).

256 *Unión Fenosa Gas SA v Arab Republic of Egypt* [2020] EWHC 1718 (Comm), para. 66.

257 ibid 67.

grounds for refusal similar to those in the New York Convention, including public policy exceptions, voting against their inclusion after extensive discussion.[258] This creates what Bermann describes as a system where

> if Contracting States foreswore the right to reject ICSID awards not only on such fundamental grounds as those embodied in the New York Convention, but also on grounds of public policy standing alone, it is difficult to see on what substantive grounds they are nevertheless privileged to reject them.[259]

Domestic courts have consistently recognised their limited role in ICSID award enforcement. Courts are restricted to verifying the award's authenticity and cannot review its merits or the tribunal's jurisdiction.[260] Indeed, as the Swiss Federal Supreme Court held in *OperaFund Eco-Invest*,[261] 'apart from the verification of the authenticity of the award, no control at all should be allowed'.[262]

The Convention distinguishes between immunity from jurisdiction and immunity from execution. Courts have consistently held that states waive immunity from jurisdiction by joining the ICSID Convention.[263] However, Article 55 preserves domestic laws on immunity from execution, meaning sovereign assets may remain immune from execution despite successful enforcement. In this connection, recent challenges to ICSID award enforcement have emerged in the context of intra-EU arbitrations following CJEU decisions in *Achmea* and *Komstroy*.[264] Courts have reached divergent conclusions, with some EU Member State courts denying enforcement while non-EU courts have granted it.[265] Despite these challenges, however, the ICSID Convention's enforcement regime remains highly effective, with satisfaction obtained in 97% of damages awards where outcomes are known.[266] The system's self-contained nature, simplified enforcement procedures, and limited grounds for challenge continue to provide confidence in the dispute resolution process.

Awards rendered under UNCITRAL Rules, Permanent Court of Arbitration (PCA) administration, or other arbitral rules in investment disputes follow different enforcement pathways. These awards typically rely on the New York Convention on the Recognition and Enforcement of Foreign Arbitral Awards 1958,[267] provided the seat is in a Convention state and the enforcing state is a party. Article III of the New York Convention requires recognition and enforcement of foreign awards in accordance with the enforcing state's procedural rules, with conditions no more onerous than for domestic awards. Meanwhile, Article V provides limited grounds for refusing enforcement, including incapacity, procedural irregularities, excess of authority, non-arbitrability, and public policy violations. Unlike ICSID awards, non-ICSID investment awards remain subject to review at the seat of

258 ICSID, *Background Paper on Compliance with and Enforcement of ICSID Awards* (ICSID, June 2024) 64–73.

259 George Bermann, 'Understanding ICSID Article 54' (2020) 35 *ICSID Rev–FILJ* 311, 341.

260 See, e.g. *Mobil Cerro Negro Ltd v Bolivarian Republic of Venezuela*, SDNY, 13 February 2015, para. 102.

261 *OperaFund Eco-Invest SICAV PLC v Kingdom of Spain*, Swiss Federal Supreme Court, 17 March 2023.

262 ibid 3.2.2.

263 See, e.g. *Antin Infrastructure Services Luxembourg Sàrl v Kingdom of Spain* [2023] HCA 11, para. 75.

264 *Slowakische Republik v Achmea BV*, CJEU, C-284/16, 6 March 2018; *Republic of Moldova v Komstroy LLC*, CJEU, C-741/19, Award, 2 September 2021.

265 See, e.g. Nacka District Court (Sweden), 23 January 2019 (denying enforcement); *Antin Infrastructure Services Luxembourg Sàrl v Kingdom of Spain* [2023] EWHC 1226 (Comm) (granting enforcement).

266 ICSID, 'Background Paper on Compliance with and Enforcement of ICSID Awards' (June 2024), para. 29.

267 Convention on the Recognition and Enforcement of Foreign Arbitral Awards (New York, 10 June 1958) 330 UNTS 3 (entered into force 7 June 1959).

arbitration through set-aside proceedings.[268] A successful set-aside may provide grounds for enforcement refusal under Article V(1)(e) of the New York Convention, though some jurisdictions have enforced annulled awards in exceptional circumstances.[269]

E. Costs

The allocation of costs in international investment arbitration reveals distinct approaches under the ICSID Convention and UNCITRAL Rules, with tribunals exercising considerable discretion in their application despite different starting presumptions.[270] Under Article 61(2) of the ICSID Convention, tribunals have broad authority to assess and allocate costs, though the Convention provides no specific guidance on how this discretion should be exercised. The provision simply states that tribunals shall decide 'how and by whom' the costs shall be paid. This contrasts with the UNCITRAL Rules, which in Article 40(1) establish a presumption that 'costs of arbitration shall in principle be borne by the unsuccessful party', while still permitting tribunals to apportion costs differently if reasonable under the circumstances.

The ICSID tribunal in *RSM v Grenada*[271] demonstrated the flexibility inherent in Article 61(2) by adopting an issue-based approach rather than the traditional 'costs follow the event' principle. Finding that both parties had failed on significant issues – the claimant on its substantive damages claim and the respondent on jurisdictional challenges and counterclaims – the tribunal ordered each party to bear its own costs. Interestingly, the tribunal in *Michael Lee-Chin v Dominican Republic*[272] exercised its Article 61(2) discretion by focusing on parties' conduct throughout the proceedings. Despite the respondent's success on jurisdictional objections and the claimant's failure to prove essential parts of its case, the tribunal found both parties had engaged in similar procedural behaviour and neither had acted improperly. This analysis led to each party bearing its own costs and splitting arbitration expenses equally.

In contrast, the PCA tribunal applying UNCITRAL Rules in *Dunkeld v Belize*[273] interpreted Article 40(1)'s presumption in the light of the case's unique circumstances. Despite the rule's preference for costs following the event, the tribunal determined that a settlement agreement benefiting both parties meant neither could be characterised as 'unsuccessful'. This led to equal apportionment of arbitration costs, with each party bearing its own legal fees. Meanwhile, the UNCITRAL tribunal in *Peter Allard v Barbados*[274] engaged more directly with Article 40's presumption, acknowledging that under the 'costs follow the event' principle, the respondent should prevail having succeeded on all merit's issues. However, the tribunal distinguished between cost categories and invoked proportionality principles. While awarding the respondent its arbitration costs and witness expenses, the

268 Kateryna Bondar, 'Annulment of ICSID and Non-ICSID Investment Awards: Differences in the Extent of Review' (2015) 32(6) *Journal of International Arbitration* 621.

269 Crina Baltag, 'Article V (1)(e) of the New York Convention: To Enforce or Not to Enforce Set Aside Arbitral Awards?' (2022) 39(3) *Journal of International Arbitration* 297.

270 Nicolò Minella, 'The Conundrum of Costs Allocation in International Investment Arbitrations: A Proposed Practical Solution to Enhance Predictability of Costs Decisions' (2024) 40(4) *Arbitration International* 473.

271 ICSID Case No. ARB/05/14

272 ICSID Case No. UNCT/18/3, Final Award, 6 October 2023.

273 PCA Case No. 2010–13, Award, 28 June 2016.

274 PCA Case No. 2012–06, Award, 27 June 2016

tribunal capped recoverable legal fees at less than half the claimed amount, reasoning that deep pockets alone cannot justify full reimbursement of all expenditures.

These cases demonstrate that while UNCITRAL Rules provide a clearer starting presumption than the ICSID Convention, tribunals under both systems ultimately exercise substantial discretion. The UNCITRAL presumption of costs following the event serves more as a guideline than a rigid rule, with tribunals readily departing from it when circumstances warrant.[275] Meanwhile, ICSID tribunals have developed their own approaches drawing from international arbitration practice, including issue-based analysis and proportionality considerations. The jurisprudence reveals that tribunals increasingly favour nuanced assessments over mechanical application of any single principle, considering factors such as relative success on different issues, reasonableness of positions taken, procedural conduct, and proportionality between costs incurred and amounts at stake. This convergence in practice suggests that despite textual differences between the ICSID Convention and UNCITRAL Rules, tribunals under both frameworks share a common understanding that cost allocation should serve broader objectives of fairness and procedural integrity in international investment arbitration.

CONCLUSION

This chapter has made it clear that when tribunals find treaty breaches, they must craft appropriate remedies that balance full reparation principles against practical realities. While compensation remains the predominant form of relief, applying valuation methodologies like DCF often involves significant discretion and can lead to widely divergent outcomes, as demonstrated in cases like *Dunkeld v Belize* and *Grenada Private Power v Grenada.*

State defences represent another area of evolving jurisprudence, with *force majeure*, contributory fault, and security exceptions serving as important counterbalances to investor claims. Non-self-judging security provisions, as interpreted in *Michael Lee-Chin v Dominican Republic*, require proportionality and good faith, while self-judging provisions like those analysed in *Seda v Colombia* afford states greater deference but remain subject to limited good faith review. Meanwhile, tribunals have increasingly confronted tensions between investment protection and broader public interest concerns. Though most Caribbean IIAs lack explicit human rights and environmental obligations for investors, tribunals have developed nuanced approaches to counterclaims and interpretive principles that accommodate these considerations without undermining the treaty framework.

The post-award phase brings its own challenges, with the limited annulment grounds under Article 52 of the ICSID Convention serving as an important safeguard for award finality. The contrasting enforcement regimes for ICSID and non-ICSID awards highlight the trade-offs between automatic recognition and sovereign immunity protections. Finally, tribunal discretion in cost allocation – whether operating under ICSID's flexible approach or UNCITRAL's 'costs follow the event' presumption – emphasises the importance of procedural conduct and proportionality considerations.

275 Matthew Hodgson and Alastair Campbell, 'The allocation of costs in investment treaty arbitration' in Matthew Hodgson and Alastair Campbell (eds), *Contemporary and Emerging Issues on the Law of Damages and Valuation in International Investment Arbitration* (Brill Nijhoff 2018) 398–427.

CHAPTER 8

REFORM OF INTERNATIONAL INVESTMENT LAW

INTRODUCTION

While, compared to their Latin American counterparts,[1] Caribbean states have not appeared regularly as respondents in arbitral proceedings, a growing number of arbitral proceedings have been initiated against these countries, many of which have been successful, in recent years. These proceedings have raised a range of questions, including what qualifies as an 'investment' for the purposes of Investor-State Dispute Settlement (ISDS) proceedings;[2] whether indirect investors[3] or 'shell companies'[4] qualify for protection under applicable international investment agreements (IIAs); the extent to which an investor may be denied protection for breaching the legality requirement;[5] whether there is basis for finding indirect expropriation,[6] a breach of the Fair and Equitable Treatment (FET) standard,[7] and a breach of the full protection and security standard;[8] and the circumstances in which the essential security interests exception may be invoked.[9] Questions relating to security for cost[10] and third-party funding[11] have also been raised by some of these cases.

Although, emanating from some of these cases, there has been increasing recognition that the international investment regime is inherently asymmetrical[12] and arguably even colonial in nature,[13] and that the primarily older generation IIAs to which Caribbean states are parties expose them to the real risk of being sued for significant amounts in compensation, and, in that connection, regulatory chill, very little work has been done by Caribbean countries to reform their investment treaty regime.[14] Not only have the substantive elements of their investment treaty regimes largely escaped the attention of policy makers, but so too the procedural dimensions of their investment landscape. While some developing countries

1 Gonzalo Ruiz Diaz, 'Who Wins in International Investment Arbitration Disputes? Evidence from Latin American and Caribbean Countries' Cases Under ICSID' (2021) *Institutions and Economies* 81.
2 *RSM Corporation v Grenada*, ICSID Case No. ARB/05/14, Award, 13 March 2009.
3 *Michael Lee-Chin v Dominican Republic,* ICSID Case No. UNCT/18/3, Partial Award on Jurisdiction, 15 July 2020.
4 *Gambrinus Corp. v Bolivarian Republic of Venezuela*, ICSID Case No. ARB/11/31, Award, 15 June 2015.
5 *Peter Allard v Barbados*, PCA Case No. 2012–06, Award on Jurisdiction, 13 June 2014.
6 *British Caribbean Bank Ltd. v Belize*, PCA Case No. 2010–18, Award, 19 December 2014.
7 *Michael Lee-Chin v Dominican Republic,* ICSID Case No. UNCT/18/3, Award, 6 October 2023.
8 *Peter Allard v Barbados*, PCA Case No. 2012–06, Award, 27 June 2016.
9 *Michael Lee-Chin v Dominican Republic,* ICSID Case No. UNCT/18/3, Award, 6 October 2023.
10 *RSM Corporation v St Lucia,* ICSID Case No. ARB/12/10, Decision on Annulment, 29 April 2019.
11 ibid.
12 Milcar Jeff Dorce, 'The Experience of Caribbean States with International Investment Arbitration: Unsettling Travels down a Slippery Slope' (2022) 60 *Canadian Yearbook of International Law* 94.
13 Jason Haynes and Antonius Hippolyte, 'The Coloniality of International Investment Law in the Commonwealth Caribbean' (2023) 72(1) *International & Comparative Law Quarterly* 105.
14 Only Guyana has in recent years negotiated a newer generation BIT – Guyanai-Brazil BIT. See Jason Haynes, 'Charting the Path Towards Sustainability: A Critique of Guyana's Recent Investment Treaty Practice' (2023) 1(1) *The UWI St. Augustine Law Journal* 65.

DOI: 10.4324/9781003734185-8

in Latin America[15] and Africa[16] have appreciated the importance of addressing the procedural issues that threaten the legitimacy of international investment law, Caribbean states have been largely disengaged in this connection.

The chapter proceeds as follows: *Part I* examines the *Advisory Centre on International Investment Dispute Resolution*, arguing that while this represents a crucial step toward addressing the capacity and resource asymmetries that plague small island developing states, important concerns remain about fee structures for non-members and the need for genuine Caribbean representation rather than token 'Latin America and Caribbean' groupings. *Part II* then analyses the *Multilateral Instrument on ISDS Reform*, contending that Caribbean states' historical experience with asymmetrically imposed international agreements necessitates an opt-in rather than opt-out approach to the Protocols. The analysis demonstrates how CARICOM's existing but dormant expertise in investment law reform could be leveraged to overcome institutional inertia through regional participation. *Part III* evaluates the *Draft Statute of a Standing Mechanism*, arguing that while the proposed permanent tribunal system addresses long-standing concerns about inconsistency and lack of diversity in arbitral decision-making, critical gaps remain regarding the composition of the Selection Committee and the potential benefits of implementing a binding precedent system, particularly given the success of such approaches in institutions like the Caribbean Court of Justice. *Part IV* provides a detailed analysis of the *Draft Provisions on Procedural and Cross-Cutting Issues*, which the author identifies as potentially the most significant instrument for Caribbean interests. This section systematically examines how provisions on security for costs, counterclaims, third-party funding, denial of benefits, shareholder claims, and the right to regulate could address specific vulnerabilities experienced by Caribbean states in cases like *RSM v Saint Lucia* and *Michael Lee-Chin v Dominican Republic.*

Part V shifts focus to *substantive law reforms*, presenting a comprehensive roadmap for modernising Caribbean IIAs through more precise definitions of 'investment' and 'investor', reformed treatment standards, and enhanced public interest protections. Drawing extensively on the innovative Guyana-Brazil BIT and the draft CARICOM template, this section argues for a fundamental rebalancing that preserves regulatory space while maintaining meaningful investor protections.

The chapter advances three interconnected arguments: first, that Caribbean states' limited engagement with UNCITRAL reform efforts represents a missed opportunity given their acute vulnerability to asymmetrical arbitral awards; second, that the proposed reforms, while welcome, require careful adaptation to address Caribbean-specific concerns about institutional capacity and historical experiences with imposed international obligations; and third, that comprehensive reform of both procedural and substantive aspects of international investment law is essential to prevent regulatory chill and ensure these small island developing states can pursue legitimate public policy objectives without fear of crippling compensation awards.

15 Mélida Hodgson, 'Reform and Adaptation: The Experience of the Americas with International Investment Law' (2020) 21(1) *The Journal of World Investment & Trade* 140.

16 Olabisi Akinkugbe, 'Africanization and the Reform of International Investment Law' (2021) 53 *Case Western Reserve Journal of International Law* 7; Hamed El-Kady and Mustaqeem De Gama, 'The Reform of the International Investment Regime: An African Perspective' (2019) 34(2) *ICSID Review-Foreign Investment Law Journal* 482.

I. UNCITRAL'S PROCEDURAL REFORM PROCESS

To date, since the commencement of UNCITRAL Working Group III's mandate, only Jamaica, from among the English-speaking Caribbean countries, has attempted to strategically engage with the ongoing reform efforts.[17] Indeed, while there have been at least two sessions held to educate Caribbean policy makers about the issues that are being discussed by the Working Group, including one co-hosted by the Organisation of Eastern Caribbean States (OECS) in November 2024,[18] chaired by Shane Spelliscy,[19] there has not been consistent engagement by Commonwealth Caribbean countries with these issues, which ironically are of paramount concern to small island developing states who are at the greatest risk of regulatory chill.[20]

Despite these challenges, however, through my participation in these forums which have attempted to engage attorneys general and their delegates from several Caribbean countries, including Eastern Caribbean states, I have been able to identify some of the main areas of concern which Caribbean countries have in connection with the ongoing reform efforts. In this context, drawing on extant Caribbean IIAs, arbitral awards, and the discussions with policy makers in the region, this chapter attempts to provide a critical assessment of some of the main concerns that have been raised by Caribbean states in connection with the ongoing reform efforts of the Working Group. It argues that while many of the reforms proposed are welcome, some important concerns remain unresolved, or not explicitly addressed, thereby warranting further engagement.

A. The Statute of the Advisory Centre on International Investment Dispute Resolution

For many years, small island developing states, including those in the Caribbean, have agitated for a mechanism that would assist them in understanding and navigating the complexities of investor-state dispute resolution.[21] Many of these countries not only lack local expertise in international investment law and dispute resolution, but many also do not have the fiscal capacity to employ expensive consultants to assist in them in understanding their rights and obligations under international investment law, and, more practically, in defending

17 'Jamaica: Comments on UNCITRAL Draft guidelines on prevention and mitigation of international investment disputes' (submission by Jamaica to the 47th session of UNCITRAL Working Group III, 22–26 January 2024, Vienna, Austria).

18 The session was co-hosted by the Organisation of Eastern Caribbean States (OECS), the Organization for the Harmonization of Business Law in the Caribbean (OHADAC) and the University of the West Indies (UWI) Shridath Ramphal Trade Centre on 19 and 20 November 2024.

19 United Nations Commission on International Trade Law, 'Report of Working Group III (Investor-State Dispute Settlement Reform) on the work of its thirty-fourth session (Vienna, 27 November–1 December 2017)' (1 December 2017) A/CN.9/930/Rev.1. Shane Spelliscy (Canada), having obtained twenty-four votes and consequently the required majority in the first ballot, was elected as the Chairperson of Working Group III.

20 Tim Hagemann, 'The North-South Divide of Regulatory Chill: A Comparative Analysis of the Impact of Investor-State Dispute Settlement on Policy Makers in Developed and Developing Countries' (2022) 35 *New York International Law Review* 27.

21 Antonius Hippolyte, 'Foreign Investment Law and Developing Countries' in Markus Krajewski and Rhea Hoffmann (eds), *Research Handbook on Foreign Direct Investment* (Edward Elgar Publishing 2019) 72.

claims brought against them.[22] For this reason, the proposed Advisory Centre[23] represents an important step in recalibrating these asymmetries. The Centre, which is envisaged to play a leading role in advising states on matters pertaining to dispute prevention, as well as providing training, holding seminars and conferences, and exchanging information on best practices,[24] will no doubt improve the technical and institutional capacity of small island developing states, including Caribbean states, to respond to the challenges of this dynamic area of international legal practice. In a practical sense, the Centre's envisaged 'hand-holding' role, from offering a preliminary assessment of the case, to the selection of mediators and arbitrators, to the preparation of statements, pleadings and active representation before tribunals,[25] places the Centre in a unique position to significantly benefit not only Annex 1 countries, but also Annex 2 countries, many of whom will likely be Caribbean-based. The fact that the fees to be charged to members for use of the services offered by the Centre will reflect the global positionality of states, with lesser developed states, paying less,[26] is a prudent move which heeds the call for equity in international investment law.

Relatedly, it is noteworthy that the Centre's services may be offered to states who are not formal members of the Centre.[27] While access to such services is not automatic, the prospect of accessing these services is hugely important because Caribbean governments may not, at least immediately, join the Centre as members, either because they do not fully appreciate the implications of ISDS claims, and the high costs associated with potentially defending such claims, or simply because of institutional lethargy. Being able to nonetheless access the Centre's services in these circumstances affords these countries the opportunity to benefit from the Centre's expertise, but also to 'test run' the Centre in order to evaluate its efficacy before making a firm commitment to be members. However, there is a real concern among Caribbean countries that given that the fees to be charged by the Centre in such circumstances could potentially be higher than those charged to Annex III members,[28] such fees could be prohibitive and thereby place these countries at an acute disadvantage. This is a matter which the Executive Director of the Advisory Centre, when appointed, should remain cognisant of.

Separately, while it is to be appreciated that members of the Executive Committee will be appointed having regard to, *inter alia*, geographic diversity and gender balance,[29] Caribbean countries are wary of the traditional institutional practice of lumping 'Latin America and the Caribbean' together as a matter of administrative convenience but where there is limited actual representation from the 'Caribbean'. In this regard, the Governing Committee must endeavour to ensure that 'geographic diversity' does not serve to amplify voices from Latin America only, while silencing Caribbean voices.

22 Kevin Gallacher and Elen Shrestha, 'Investment Treaty Arbitration and Developing Countries: A Re-Appraisal' (2011) 12(6) *The Journal of World Investment & Trade* 919.
23 UNCITRAL, 'Possible Reform of Investor-State Dispute Settlement (ISDS): Draft Provisions on the Establishment of an Advisory Centre on International Investment Law' A/CN.9/WG.III/WP.230.
24 ibid Article 6.
25 ibid Article 7.
26 ibid Article 8(3)(b).
27 ibid Article 7(4).
28 ibid Article 8(3)(b).
29 ibid Article 5(3)(c).

B. The Multilateral Instrument on ISDS Reform

For many years, Caribbean scholars have challenged the asymmetrical nature of international investment law, and the incoherence and inconsistency that often characterise extant arbitral jurisprudence.[30] More generally, concerns have been expressed about the independence and impartiality of adjudicators,[31] as well as more general concerns regarding the legitimacy of the dispute settlement system.[32] It is, therefore, heartening to note that at its 43rd session in September 2022, the Working Group requested the Secretariat to prepare a draft of the multilateral instrument on ISDS reform,[33] with the aim of achieving coherence in the application of the reform elements being developed by the Working Group, while also being sufficiently flexible to accommodate future developments.[34] Given ongoing concerns about the narrowing of states' regulatory margin of appreciation occasioned,[35] in part, by judicial activism by some arbitrators,[36] it is useful that the multilateral instrument centres the public interest of states, recognising, in particular, their right to regulate at the very outset in its preamble.[37]

In contemporary international legal practice, Caribbean countries have been staunchly opposed to international mechanisms that appear to be coercive in nature, given their prior experience with asymmetrically imposed international agreements over the last four decades.[38] In this regard, while Caribbean countries may very much welcome the Protocols which collectively address a wide range of their concerns, they may very well not be inclined to have the Protocols automatically apply to them, with the option to opt out through a reservation.[39] Rather, given that their engagement with the reform process may be limited to matters that most affect or potentially affect their interests (namely the draft provisions on cross-cutting issues), they may be more inclined to countenance a system whereby they choose, without the prospect of quasi-unilaterally imposed obligations, which Protocols should apply to them. That said, it appears prudent to require that states, including Caribbean states, make a provisional indication of the Protocols that they may wish to join

30 See for example, Jason Haynes, 'The Contribution of Caribbean ISDS Jurisprudence to International Investment Law's Ongoing Legitimacy Project' (2021) 18 *Manchester Journal of International Economic Law* 205; Jason Haynes and Antonius Hippolyte, 'The Covid-19 PANDEMIC and the Potential for Investor-State Claims: A Caribbean Perspective' (2021) 21(2) *Oxford University Commonwealth Law Journal* 212.

31 Chiara Giorgetti, et al., 'Independence and Impartiality of Adjudicators in Investment Dispute Settlement: Assessing Challenges and Reform Options' (2020) 21(2) *The Journal of World Investment & Trade* 441.

32 Susan Franck, 'The Legitimacy Crisis in Investment Treaty Arbitration: Privatizing Public International Law through Inconsistent Decisions' (2004) 73 *Fordham Law Review* 1521.

33 A/CN.9/1124, para. 88.

34 ibid 79.

35 Stephan Schill, 'Deference in Investment Treaty Arbitration: Re-Conceptualizing the Standard of Review' (2012) 3(3) *Journal of International Dispute Settlement* 577–607.

36 Fuad Zarbiyev, 'Judicial Activism in International Law – A Conceptual Framework for Analysis' (2012) 3(2) *Journal of International Dispute Settlement* 247.

37 UNCITRAL, 'Draft Multilateral Instrument on ISDS reform' (49th Session, Vienna, 23–27 September 2024) A/CN.9/WG.III/WP.246, Preamble.

38 Laurence Helfer, 'Overlegalizing Human Rights: International Relations Theory and the Commonwealth Caribbean Backlash against Human Rights Regimes' (2002) *Columbia Law Review* 1832.

39 Article 2 Draft multilateral instrument on ISDS reform provides a list of options, with the Protocols' automatic application being one.

when signing the Convention.[40] In this way, they may subsequently seek to honour the moral commitment made to adopt the Protocols, albeit on their own time.

While it is acknowledged that the multilateral instrument imposes no substantive obligations arising from becoming a party to the Convention, it is submitted that, in contradistinction to Article 3 of the current draft, Caribbean states may prefer the option of adopting the Protocols even where they are not parties to the Convention. This is because Caribbean nations have traditionally been hesitant to adopting multiple, even if related, instruments due to limited institutional and resource capacity, and, in some cases, simply institutional inertia. However, because the Protocols are meant to supplement the multilateral instrument, it might be more in keeping with international comity for states to first become members of the Convention before becoming parties to the Protocols. This is certainly the approach taken in other contexts, for example, the UN Convention on Transnational Organised Crime,[41] and its related Trafficking, Smuggling and Firearms Protocols.

(i) CARICOM's Participation

The Caribbean Community (CARICOM) has been conferred limited competence under the Revised Treaty of Chaguaramas[42] in respect of trading and investment matters.[43] In fact, CARICOM, nearly 15 years ago, drafted a Code for Investment Chapters in External Trade Agreements, which unfortunately has not yet come into effect, but which nonetheless seeks to address many of the problematic features of ISDS. In this connection, the prospect of regional economic integration organisations, like CARICOM, being able to sign, ratify or accede to the Convention[44] is a welcome development, which may address some of the institutional inertia which currently exists on the part of individual Caribbean states when engaging with the ISDS reform process. Indeed, given CARICOM's limited competence in this area,[45] member states can leverage the organisation's expertise and its extant work in the field by participating as a block in the work of the Conference of the Parties.

40 ibid.

41 United Nations Convention against Transnational Organized Crime (adopted 15 November 2000, entered into force 29 September 2003) 2225 UNTS 209. Article 37. Relation with protocols 1. This Convention may be supplemented by one or more protocols. 2. In order to become a Party to a protocol, a State or a regional economic integration organization must also be a Party to this Convention. 3. A State Party to this Convention is not bound by a protocol unless it becomes a Party to the protocol in accordance with the provisions thereof.

42 Revised Treaty of Chaguaramas Establishing the Caribbean Community Including the CARICOM Single Market and Economy (signed 5 July 2001, entered into force 1 January 2006).

43 ibid Article 14(2).

44 Article 4 Draft multilateral instrument on ISDS reform.

45 See David Berry, *Caribbean Integration Law* (OUP 2014); see, also, Jason Haynes, 'The Transplantation of the European Principle of "State Liability" in Caribbean Community (Caricom) Law: A Normative Assessment' (2014) 14(1) *Oxford University Commonwealth Law Journal* 73; Jason Haynes, 'Revisiting the Locus Standi of Private Applicants in Judicial Review Proceedings under CARICOM and EU Law: A Comparative Perspective' (2015) 41(1) *Commonwealth Law Bulletin* 59; Jason Haynes, 'Mapping the Path of the Teleological Approach: A Normative Analysis of the Caribbean Court of Justice's (CCJ) Primary Approach to Treaty Interpretation' (2013) 39(3) *Commonwealth Law Bulletin* 573.

(ii) *Entry into Force*

Logically speaking, given that the draft Protocols are supplementary to the draft Convention, it makes good sense for the Protocols to only enter into force after, and not before, the Convention enters into force.[46] However, it is likely that in circumstances where multiple states are more inclined to deal with the issues raised by a particular Protocol, e.g. the Protocol on cross-cutting issues, but less inclined to engage with the Convention or the other protocols more generally, the coming into force for that Protocol may be unreasonably stalled by its entry into force being contingent on the Convention first entering into force. In this circumstance, it is worth considering the possibility of a Protocol being able to come into effect even before the Convention comes into force, particularly given that the Convention does not *per se* impose any substantive obligations. Admittedly, however, given that this is not typically the case with regard to other international instruments, there is an understandable degree of unease among Caribbean states to supporting such an unusual approach.

(iii) *Notification of Existing Treaties*

In the interest of transparency, and to respect the autonomy of small island developing states, it makes good sense that states will likely be obliged to submit to the Secretariat a list of investment treaties to which each protocol would apply.[47] This allows these countries the freedom to clearly indicate how the Protocol(s) would modify their extant investment treaties, as listed in the notification, as well as become preview to other states' notifications. That this information would be publicly available is consistent with the ethos of transparency which the reform process is meant to ensure.

However, it is worth noting that the investment treaties that are notified would only be deemed to have been modified by the respective Protocol(s) when all parties to that those treaties include those treaties in their notification(s) to the Secretariat.[48] In circumstances where all of the parties do not issue such a notification, it makes good sense that while the notification issued represents an offer, such offer is to be construed as merely unilateral in nature, and only becomes perfected when the other party(s) to the investment agreement accepts that offer by issuing a reciprocal notification. Surely, an objection to the offer, through inaction or an express indication in the notification of such objection, should mean that the Protocol does not apply to the unilaterally notified investment treaties.

Notwithstanding the foregoing, two points of contention must be sensibly addressed. First, should a state party only be able to accept the offer made by the other party by becoming a party to the Convention and thereby listing the treaty in their notification? From a Caribbean perspective, given the institutional and capacity constraints which confront many of these countries, as well as their general inertia when it comes to ratifying conventions, it might be prudent for these countries to be able to accept an offer made by another state through a mechanism outside of the Convention. This will enable these countries to engage with the Protocols in particular disputes on an ad hoc basis without having to fully commit, unless they wish to, to first signing the Convention and thereby becoming states parties.

46 Article 5 Draft multilateral instrument on ISDS reform.

47 ibid Article 6.

48 ibid Article 7.

Second, a question also arises as to whether the notification made by a state (e.g. Barbados) should be understood broadly as constituting an offer to an investor raising a claim under an investment agreement (with, say, the UK) such that the investor may accept that offer and agree to apply one of the Protocols to the ensuing proceedings. It is submitted that given the much criticised power asymmetry[49] which characterises the extant investment framework which privileges investors by allowing them to institute claims through accepting a standing offer contained in dispute settlement clauses in BITs, in the context of the proposed Convention, as a means of rebalancing this asymmetry, the application of the Protocol should require the consent of both states as a precondition to the application of the Protocol to the proceedings.

Despite these concerns, however, it is certainly welcome that once an investment treaty listed in the notifications of both countries contains provisions on aspects covered by the respective investment agreements which are incompatible with the Protocol, the latter will prevail.[50] This will ensure that the provisions of Protocols aimed at redressing the asymmetries between small island developing states as respondents and powerful investors (e.g. the right to regulate in the public interest, and denial of benefits) can trump the provisions of (notified) older generation treaties which are out of sync with contemporary regulatory realities. It also reflects the contemporary will of the state, whose positionality may have evolved overtime in the light of greater understanding of the dynamics of the international investment regime.

(iv) Non-Application of MFN

The Most-Favoured-Nation (MFN) clause's application to procedural aspects of investment dispute resolution has generated considerable consternation to date,[51] with many small island developing states arguing that their consent to particular dispute resolution processes expressed in certain investment treaties is being actively eviscerated by investors who surreptitiously seek to invoke more favourable dispute resolution processes not envisaged by states parties. To this end, it is a welcome addition to the proposed multilateral instrument that disputing parties would not be able to invoke an MFN provision to seek to apply or avoid the application of the Protocols.[52] Practically, this means, for example, that if Grenada has modified its investment treaties to incorporate the procedural reform in Protocol C, a national of the UK, a state which has not incorporated the procedural reform, may not invoke the MFN clause to apply the procedural reforms. Further, if Grenada and the UK have both included Protocol C in their notification indicating that the Standing Mechanism would have exclusive jurisdiction over claims arising from the investment treaty between Grenada and the UK, a national of the UK cannot invoke the MFN clause to argue that it wishes to pursue arbitration against Grenada using another dispute settlement mechanism based on another treaty concluded by Grenada. This reigns in investors' ability to 'forum

49 Nicolás Perrone, *Investment Treaties and The Legal Imagination: How Foreign Investors Play by Their Own Rules* (OUP 2021).

50 Article 7(5) Draft multilateral instrument on ISDS reform.

51 Zachary Douglas, 'The MFN Clause in Investment Arbitration: Treaty Interpretation off the Rails' (2011) 2(1) *Journal of International Dispute Settlement* 97.

52 Article 7(7) Draft multilateral instrument on ISDS reform.

shop', and better reflects the will of states in restricting the MFN's application to substantive, and not procedural, treaty obligations.

C. Draft Statute of a Standing Mechanism for the Resolution of International Investment Disputes

For many years, small island developing states, including those in the Caribbean, and critical scholars, have contested various aspects of international regime for the settlement of investment disputes. Among other things, there are concerns about significant inconsistency[53] between awards rendered involving the same investment instrument by different arbitral bodies, which is in part due to the lack of a system of *de jure stare decisis*.[54] There have also been concerns about the lack of diversity among arbitrators,[55] there being very few women,[56] and, indeed, very few arbitrators from small island developing states,[57] hearing claims. Questions about the independence and impartiality of arbitrators[58] have also been raised in the light of the practice of some arbitrators 'double-hatting'[59] and rendering decisions that appear to support the party that has appointed them.[60]

Against this backdrop, it is certainly a welcome development that the UNCITRAL Working Group has proposed the establishment of a standing mechanism to adjudicate upon investment disputes. The Standing Mechanism, which is proposed to compromise a Dispute Tribunal[61] and an Appeal Tribunal,[62] is founded on three important principles: (i) independence from undue external influence (including from parties, and donors),[63] (ii) excellence (high moral character, high reputation for fairness and integrity and competence in international law)[64] and (iii) diversity (in particular, equal gender representation, equitable geographic distribution, and representation of the principal legal systems of the world).[65] That the Judges (not ad hoc arbitrators) appointed to the mechanism will be required to adhere to the UNCITRAL Code of Conduct for Judges in International Dispute Resolution, the

53 Julian Arato, Chester Brown and Federico Ortino, 'Parsing and Managing Inconsistency in Investor-State Dispute Settlement' (2020) 21(2) *The Journal of World Investment & Trade* 336.

54 Patrick Norton, 'The Role of Precedent in the Development of International Investment Law' (2018) 33(1) *ICSID Review-Foreign Investment Law Journal* 280.

55 Andrea Bjorklund, et al., 'The Diversity Deficit in International Investment Arbitration' (2020) 21(2) *The Journal of World Investment & Trade* 410.

56 Ksenia Polonskaya, 'Diversity in the Investor-State Arbitration: Intersectionality Must Be a Part of the Conversation' (2018) 19(1) *Melbourne Journal of International Law* 259.

57 Richard Chen, 'The Substantive Value of Diversity in Investment Treaty Arbitration' (2020) 61 *Virginia Journal of International Law* 431.

58 Chiara Giorgetti et al., 'Independence and Impartiality of Adjudicators in Investment Dispute Settlement: Assessing Challenges and Reform Options' (2020) 21(2) *The Journal of World Investment & Trade* 441.

59 Joshua Tayar, 'Safeguarding the Institutional Impartiality of Arbitration in the Face of "Double-Hatting"' (2018) 5 *McGill Journal of Dispute Resolution* 104.

60 Szilárd Gáspár-Szilágyi and Laura Létourneau-Tremblay, 'A Question of Impartiality: Who are the Dissenting Arbitrators in Investment Treaty Arbitration?' in Freya Baetens (ed), *Identity and Diversity on the International Bench: Who Is the Judge?* (OUP 2021) chapter 15.

61 Article 14 Draft statute of a standing mechanism for the resolution of international investment disputes.

62 ibid Article 18.

63 ibid Article 2(2).

64 ibid Article 7(1).

65 ibid Article 8(1).

UNCITRAL Rules of Transparency in Treaty-based Investor-State Arbitration,[66] and be paid an annual salary,[67] and be required to treat parties equally in proceedings, giving them a reasonable opportunity to present their case,[68] offers great promise in terms of the mechanism's commitment to independence and impartiality.

Notwithstanding the foregoing, however, from small island developing states' perspective, concerns arise with respect to the draft Standing Mechanism. First, while various aspects of the proposed mechanism demonstrate a tangible ethos of diversity, there is nothing requiring that the Selection Committee, which is charged with reviewing and verifying whether candidates nominated meet the qualifications and requirements stipulated under the Protocol,[69] and thereby recommending same to the Conference, is diverse in its composition. It is important, however, that the Selection Committee be as diverse as possible (not limited to gender, but also geographically and professional background) as final appointments will necessarily be made on the basis of its recommendations. More pointedly, there is a risk that while the Selection Committee may, for example, present a list of suitable candidates to the Conference that reflect gender equality and geographic diversity, if all of its members have been Ivy League educated or hold certain epistemic positions (e.g. investor-friendly), this may influence the profile of candidates whom they recommend. To democratise the process and thereby ensure the widest range of profiles and backgrounds for recommended candidates, it is important that the Selection Committee itself exemplifies an ethos of diversity in its own composition.

Second, it is concerning that the proposed standing mechanism, while giving Contracting Parties the power to appoint judges,[70] at the same time elides Contracting Parties ability to remove said judges in case of non-compliance with the Protocol or for failure to perform their duties, vesting it instead in members of the respective Tribunal.[71] Given the permanency of their removal from office, and the need to ensure proper oversight and accountability, as well as avoiding the prospect of certain members of panels being targeted for removal by other panel members for holding intractably opposing epistemic positions, it is prudent that any decision on removal be made by the body that appoints them in the first place, the Conference.

Third, while acknowledging the importance of the Dispute Tribunal and Appeal Tribunal being able to judge their own competence,[72] and their jurisdiction only extending to international disputes which the parties to the dispute have consented to in writing[73] (e.g. by providing a list of instruments to which it is a party or legislation governing foreign investment which it has enacted), it is of some concern that the awards rendered are binding only on the parties to the dispute in question.[74] More particularly, while it is appreciated that, in accordance with Article 59 of the ICJ statute,[75] precedent is not generally binding in a

66 ibid Article 22(4).
67 ibid Article 12(5).
68 ibid Article 22(2).
69 ibid Article 10.
70 ibid Article 4(2).
71 ibid Article 13(1).
72 ibid Article 17(1); Article 21(1).
73 ibid Article 14(1).
74 ibid Article 25(2); Article 34(1).
75 Statute of the International Court of Justice (adopted 26 June 1945, entered into force 24 October 1945) 33 UNTS 993.

de jure sense in international law, the realities of contemporary investment treaty practice beg the question as to whether a system of binding precedent should be instituted. In fact, small island developing states have been at the forefront of criticising the markedly inconsistent arbitral awards often rendered by different tribunals on similar factual or legal bases, which have contributed to the ongoing legitimacy crisis afflicting international investment law.[76] To this end, and to ensure consistency (though not uniformity) of awards, stability of the system, and ultimately predictability, it is at least worth considering whether a *de jure* system of precedent should be adopted, ideally by both the Dispute Tribunal and Appeal Tribunal, but at the very least by the latter. While, admittedly, it is anomalous for international tribunals to be bound by a system of *de jure stare decisis*, some tribunals, such as the Caribbean Court of Justice in its original jurisdiction,[77] adopt such an approach with a great degree of success.[78]

Despite the foregoing issues, however, there are several positive aspects of the proposed Standing mechanism. For example, the fact that organisations can nominate candidates for appointment as judges[79] means that regional organisations and academic institutions which are aware of excellent candidates could make appropriate recommendations. Importantly, the requirement that Contracting Parties seeking to nominate candidates will be required to broadly consult representatives of government, judiciary and other bodies, civil society, bar associations, business associations, academic and other relevant organisations,[80] places the mechanism in a good position to attract the highest calibre of candidates possible. Separately, the fact that panels may provide guidance to disputing parties on the potential benefits of mediation as a means of resolving the dispute at any stage of the proceedings is particularly welcomed by Caribbean countries, as it responds to the concerns of Jamaica, for example, which has asserted in its submission to the Working Group:

> mediation can prove very effective in preventing Investor-State arbitration disputes. Mediatory-based processes are indeed often relied on for the early identification of differences between parties to a transaction or a project, and they provide with efficient tools to overcome them.[81]

Finally, the fact that the grounds of appeal are extensive (covering matters such as corruption on the part of a member of the tribunal or a decision in conflict with international public policy) and outlined with some degree with specificity[82] provides a good opportunity for the Appellate Tribunal to correct errors that would threaten the integrity and overall

76 Jason Haynes, 'The Contribution of Caribbean ISDS Jurisprudence to International Investment Law's Ongoing Legitimacy Project' (2021) 18 *Manchester Journal of International Economic Law* 205.

77 Article 221 Revised Treaty of Chaguaramas Establishing the Caribbean Community Including the CARICOM Single Market and Economy (signed 5 July 2001, entered into force 1 January 2006): 'Judgments of the Court shall constitute legally binding precedents for parties in proceedings before the Court unless such judgments have been revised in accordance with Article 219'.

78 Jason Haynes, 'The Emergence of a Doctrine of *de jure* Horizontal Stare Decisis at the Caribbean Court of Justice: Fragmentation or Pluralism of International Law?' (2014) 5(3) *Journal of International Dispute Settlement* 498.

79 Article 9(2) Draft statute of a standing mechanism for the resolution of international investment disputes.

80 ibid Article 9(1).

81 'Jamaica: Comments on UNCITRAL Draft guidelines on prevention and mitigation of international investment disputes' (submission by Jamaica to the 47th session of UNCITRAL Working Group III, 22–26 January 2024, Vienna, Austria).

82 Article 29 Draft statute of a standing mechanism for the resolution of international investment disputes.

legitimacy of the Standing Mechanism. It also opens up the possibility of the Appellate Tribunal broadly interpreting 'international public policy' to include human rights and environmental considerations, thereby addressing the ongoing concern that arbitral awards have not always been consistent with evolving international public policy considerations,[83] a hugely important point of contention in an age of climate change.

D. Draft Provisions on Procedural and Cross-Cutting Issues

The Draft Provisions on Procedural and Cross-Cutting Issues[84] is, from a Caribbean perspective, perhaps the most important of the Protocols. These provisions address a range of issues that have for many years been a proverbial thorn in the sides of small island developing states, including the prohibitive cost and lengthy duration of arbitral proceedings. The key provisions of the Protocol, discussed in turn below, aim to streamline arbitral proceedings by enhancing procedural efficiency.

(i) Security for Costs

There is considerable uncertainty in extant arbitral practice as to whether Article 47 of the ICSID Convention,[85] which empowers tribunals to 'recommend' provisional measures, affords tribunals the power to 'order' security for costs. While it is acknowledged that an order for security for costs is sometimes (in exceptional circumstances) necessary to preserve the integrity of the proceedings (against frivolous claims that would be costly for respondent states to defend, and ensure that the claimant honours any costs award made in favour of the respondent upon the conclusion of the proceedings), the question of whether arbitral tribunals should make such an order, and in what circumstances, has given rise to considerable contestation.[86] In the Caribbean case of *RSM v St Lucia*,[87] for example, an American company that was granted a gas exploration licence but which was prevented from completing its explorations because of a boundary dispute with neighbouring islands, sought to institute proceedings against St Lucia alleging a breach of the Agreement in question. However, in three separate earlier proceedings against another Caribbean state, Grenada, RSM was delinquent in honouring the financial obligations associated therewith, including the full cost of an annulment tribunal which had been constituted by ICSID. Accordingly, in these proceedings, St Lucia sought an order for security for costs.

The respondent, both in its response to St Lucia's request for security for cost, and the subsequent annulment proceedings,[88] argued that Article 47 of the ICSID Convention,

83 Jean-Michel Marcoux, 'Transnational Public Policy as a Vehicle to Impose Human Rights Obligations in International Investment Arbitration' (2020) 21(6) *JWIT* 809.

84 UNCITRAL, 'Draft provisions on procedural and cross-cutting issues' (49th Session, Vienna, 23–27 September 2024) A/CN.9/WG.III/WP.244.

85 Convention on the Settlement of Investment Disputes Between States and Nationals of Other States (opened for signature 18 March 1965, entered into force 14 October 1966) 575 UNTS 159.

86 Christine Sim, 'Security for Costs in Investor-State Arbitration' (2017) 33(3) *Arbitration International* 427.

87 *RSM Production Corporation v Saint Lucia*, ICSID Case No. ARB/12/10, Decision on Saint Lucia's Request for Security for Costs with Assenting and Dissenting Reasons, 13 August 2014.

88 *RSM Production Corporation v Saint Lucia*, ICSID Case No. ARB/12/10, Decision on Annulment, 29 April 2019.

unlike Article 25 of the London Court of International Arbitration (LCIA) Rules, does not explicitly provide for security for costs, and, in any event, even if it were allowed, such could only be 'recommended' but not 'ordered'. The original tribunal considered that it had authority to issue measures to preserve a party's right, including security for costs.[89] It noted that despite reference to 'recommend' in the ICSID Rules, the distinction between the two was merely theoretical rather than practical.[90] It accepted that while provisional measures, including security for costs, do not have binding effect, tribunals can draw negative inferences from non-compliance with such measures.[91] On the facts, the tribunal considered that there was a need to protect St Lucia's asserted right to claim reimbursement of the costs it would incur in the course of the arbitration in the event it prevailed on the merits (by dismissal of the claim) and the Tribunal granted a claim for reimbursement of costs. Further, the exceptional circumstances of the case meant that there was some urgency for security for costs leaving no room for waiting for the final award. In particular, in earlier proceedings against Grenada, RSM was dilatory in honouring advance payments and actual costs incurred before discontinuance of the annulment proceedings; it failed to reimburse Grenada's cost advances in respect of the Treaty Proceedings; and, in respect of (undisclosed) third-party funding it received, in the absence of security for costs being offered, it was doubtful whether the third party would assume responsibility for honouring such an award.[92] These circumstances showed a consistent procedural history of not honouring its obligations, which brought this case into the 'exceptional' category of cases justifying the award of security for costs. The Annulment Tribunal agreed with the original tribunal, holding that no manifest error was demonstrated in the original Tribunal's order for security for costs.[93]

Against this backdrop, it is certainly a welcome development that the draft Protocol explicitly, rather than implicitly, makes provision for security for costs.[94] It makes good sense also that, in making an 'order' (as opposed to a recommendation) for security for costs, tribunals are obliged to consider all relevant circumstances, including the party's (i) ability to comply with an adverse decision on costs; (ii) willingness to comply with an adverse decision on costs; (iii) the effect that providing security for costs may have on that disputing party's ability to pursue its claim [or counterclaim]; (iv) the conduct of the disputing parties; and (v) the existence of third-party funding to support that disputing party in pursuing its claim or counterclaim.[95] Such an approach will not only resolve unnecessary contestation over the legitimacy of an order for security for costs but will provide an enabling environment for better compliance by disputing parties while ensuring transparency on the part of disputing parties with respect the identity of third-party funders.

89 *RSM Production Corporation v Saint Lucia*, ICSID Case No. ARB/12/10, Decision on Saint Lucia's Request for Security for Costs with Assenting and Dissenting Reasons, 13 August 2014, para 65
90 ibid 50.
91 ibid.
92 ibid 78.
93 *RSM Production Corporation v Saint Lucia*, ICSID Case No. ARB/12/10, Decision on Annulment, 29 April 2019 77.
94 Article 5 Draft Provisions on Procedural and Cross-cutting Issues.
95 ibid Article 5(4).

(ii) Counterclaims

To date, there has been only one Caribbean ISDS award in which a counterclaim has been initiated by a respondent state – *RSM Corporation v Grenada,*[96] albeit unsuccessfully. In that case, Grenada alleged multiple forms of misrepresentation by RSM, including false claims about RSM's independent financial resources, misleading statements about commencement time for obligations under the Agreement, misrepresentations regarding farmout intentions, and fraudulent claims about expertise in maritime boundary negotiations. Grenada also sought EC$391,860.00 as compensation for fishermen damaged by RSM's unauthorised research and US$1,000 in nominal damages for RSM's failure to submit a timely application for an exploration licence. However, while accepting that it had jurisdiction over the counterclaim, the tribunal ruled that Grenada failed to establish its factual case on all counts of alleged misrepresentation. More particularly, the tribunal found that RSM made no clear representation about single-handedly financing the Agreement, no unlawful misrepresentation regarding commencement time, no clear representation about farm-outs, and while Mr. Grynberg's (the Managing Director) claims about negotiation expertise were false, they were not fraudulent nor material enough to induce Grenada's acceptance of the Agreement. Consequently, all of Grenada's counterclaims failed.

Notwithstanding the fact that the tribunal here exercised jurisdiction over the counterclaim, it is arguable that, given that none of the extant Caribbean IIAs contain explicit reference to counterclaims and given the highly contested positions on their availability in arbitral practice,[97] future tribunals may decide that counterclaims are not envisaged. To this end, it is noteworthy that the draft provisions include a clause on counterclaims,[98] providing that a counterclaim may be heard with an original claim where it arises directly out of the subject matter of the claim; or in connection with the factual and legal basis of the claim; or where the claimant has failed to comply with its obligations under the Agreement, domestic law, any relevant investment contract or any other instrument binding on the claimant. The latter of these non-cumulative conditions is especially important from a small island developing state's perspective as it enables tribunals to exercise jurisdiction and thereby hear counterclaims brought by developing countries in circumstances where investors have committed material breaches of not only international law (including international public policy – such as breaches of international human rights and environmental law norms), but also domestic law. This thus ensures accountability on the part of investors, thereby contributing to rebalancing the historical asymmetry that has characterised the treatment of counterclaims by tribunals. This, coupled with the fact that once the respondent has consented to the submission of a claim by the claimant, the claimant by necessity also consent to the submission of the counterclaim by the respondent, would likely reduce uncertainty on the permissibility of counterclaims, promote fairness and procedural efficiency, avoid multiple proceedings in different forums involving the same disputing parties, and ultimately ensure

96 *RSM Production Corporation v Grenada*, ICSID Case No. ARB/05/14, Award, 13 March 2009.

97 See for example, Arnaud De Nanteuil, 'Counterclaims in Investment Arbitration: Old Questions, New Answers?' (2018) 17(2) *The Law & Practice of International Courts and Tribunals* 374; Anne Hoffmann, 'Counterclaims in Investment Arbitration' (2013) 28(2) *ICSID Review* 438; Xuan Shao, 'Environmental and Human Rights Counterclaims in International Investment Arbitration: At the Crossroads of Domestic and International Law' (2021) 24(1) *Journal of International Economic Law* 157.

98 Article 10 Draft Provisions on Procedural and Cross-cutting Issues.

a fair balance between the disputing parties in ISDS. However, it must be remembered that the success of counterclaims remains dependent on whether the respondent can link the investor's behaviour to a breach of a legal obligation. Given that investors, after *Urbaser v Argentina*,[99] are arguably only bound by negative international human rights obligations, and not positive obligations as such, it might be that the use of counterclaims against investors is of limited import, unless the IIA allows for counterclaims to also be based on an investor's breach of domestic human rights, labour or environmental laws.

(iii) Third-Party Funding

Third-party funding of investors' claims before arbitral tribunals has grown exponentially in recent years.[100] While, in some cases, third-party funding represents a legitimate site of recourse for investors who may have evidently strong claims but do not have the necessary financial resources to support the initiation of legal proceedings, there is growing concern among scholars,[101] and, indeed, small island developing states, that these arrangements are not always disclosed,[102] and that in some circumstances they may give rise to conflicts of interest.[103] In fact, in *RSM v St Lucia*,[104] one of the reasons for the tribunal finding exceptional circumstances justifying an order for security for costs was the claimant's undisclosed third-party funding arrangements, which prevented the tribunal from ascertaining the willingness of the third-party funder to pay any costs award that might be made. Interestingly, RSM had argued that Dr Griffith, one of the arbitrators, showed bias against third-party funding and funded claimants like RSM when he used pejorative terms such as 'mercantile adventurers' and linked third-party funding with 'gambling' in his Assenting Opinion on security for costs.[105] RSM claimed these views were 'negative and radical in tone' and demonstrated a lack of impartiality.[106] However, the tribunal considered that Dr Griffith's evocative language merely emphasised an important point rather than evidencing bias. The Annulment Committee found no basis to conclude that Dr Griffith lacked the necessary impartiality required by Article 14(1) of the ICSID Convention, noting that his concern was legitimate – that third-party funders are not subject to the arbitral tribunal's jurisdiction and therefore not legally bound to comply with adverse cost orders.[107] The committee determined that even with evocative language, Dr Griffith's views did not constitute grounds for finding the

99 ICSID Case No. ARB/07/26, Award, 8 December 2016.

100 Eric De Brabandere and Julia Lepeltak, 'Third-party Funding in International Investment Arbitration' (2012) 27(2) *ICSID Review* 379; Jean-Christophe Honlet, 'Recent Decisions on Third-Party Funding in Investment Arbitration' (2015) 30(3) *ICSID Review-Foreign Investment Law Journal* 699.

101 Sarah Moseley, 'Disclosing Third-Party Funding in International Investment Arbitration' (2018) 97 *Texas Law Review* 1181.

102 Gary Shaw, 'Third-Party Funding in Investment Arbitration: How Non-Disclosure Can Cause Harm for the Sake of Profit' (2017) 33(1) *Arbitration International* 109.

103 Valentina Frignati, 'Ethical Implications of Third-Party Funding in International Arbitration' (2016) 32(3) *Arbitration International* 505.

104 *RSM Production Corporation v Saint Lucia*, ICSID Case No. ARB/12/10, Decision on Annulment, 29 April 2019 180.

105 ibid 163.

106 ibid.

107 ibid 165.

tribunal was improperly constituted or that there had been a substantial departure from a fundamental rule of procedure.

In light of legitimate concerns around the transparency of ISDS in the context of the growing influence of third-party funding, it is notable that the draft provisions are permissive of third-party funding, though subject to the conditions that a disputing party in receipt of third-party funding must disclose to the Tribunal and the other disputing party, *inter alia*, the name and address (including of the beneficial owner) of the third-party funder, coupled with potential disclosure of information regarding the terms of the funding arrangement and whether the funder agrees to cover any adverse cost award.[108] Importantly, to avoid conflicts of interest, tribunals may also require the disputing party to disclose whether the third-party funder has any right to control or influence the management of the claim or the proceedings or to terminate the funding arrangement.[109] The obligation of disclosure is envisaged to be a continuing one, from the date of submission of the claim, through to any subsequent changes to the funding arrangements.[110]

Significantly, tribunals may limit third-party funding, albeit in exceptional circumstances, namely when the expected return to the third-party funder exceeds a reasonable amount, or when the number of cases that the third-party funder funds against the respondent Contracting Party with regard to the same measure exceeds a reasonable number.[111] To show the seriousness with which the principle of transparency is taken in this connection, and to encourage disputing parties to be transparent, tribunals may suspend the proceedings, or terminate the funding agreement and return any funding received or terminate proceedings if the disputing party fails to comply with their disclosure obligations.[112] Short of termination of proceedings, however, it is envisaged that in these circumstances, tribunals may order security for costs, or at the very least take the fact of non-disclosure into account when allocating costs.[113]

(iv) Denial of Benefits

The Caribbean has often been described as an offshore financial heaven,[114] affording companies the privilege of being able to be incorporated even where they do not carry any or any significant business activities in these jurisdictions.[115] Regrettably, very few Caribbean IIAs contain denial of benefits provisions.[116] In this regard, there is a real risk that foreign companies which are incorporated in these jurisdictions but which do not carry on significant business activities there may benefit from the protections afforded by these IIAs. This point

108 Article 12 Draft Provisions on Procedural and Cross-cutting Issues.
109 ibid Article 12(3)(c).
110 ibid Article 12(5).
111 ibid Article 12(6)(a)-(b).
112 ibid Article 12(8).
113 ibid Article 12(7)(a)–(c).
114 Oral Williams, Esther Suss, and Chandima Mendis, 'Offshore Financial Centres in the Caribbean: Prospects in a New Environment' (2005) 28(8) *World Economy* 1173.
115 Ola Tucker, 'Understanding the Risks and Challenges of Shell Companies in Managing AML Compliance' (2020) 3(4) *Journal of Financial Compliance* 340.
116 Trinidad and Tobago-USA BIT Article XII; Jamaica-USA BIT Article 1(2); Jamaica-Egypt BIT Article 2(1); Grenada-USA BIT Article 1(2).

was raised by the respondent in *Gambrinus v Venezuela*,[117] a case in which the claimant had set up a shell company in Barbados while operating in Venezuela in order to benefit from the protections of the Barbados-Venezuela BIT. Although the tribunal ultimately held that Gambrinus did not have an investment in Venezuela, it seemed willing (but did not rule on this with any degree of finality) to find that the claimant could benefit from the protections afforded by the BIT by virtue of merely being incorporated under Barbados law, even without carrying on substantial business activities in Barbados. That investors could, in principle, not carry on significant business activities in their home country, or otherwise engage in serious conduct that undermines the integrity of the international investment regime and still be able to access ISDS has given rise to considerable contestation.[118]

In this connection, it is a welcome addition to the draft Protocol that provision is made for Contracting Parties to deny investors the benefits of IIAs in circumstances where they carry out no substantial business activities in their home state; or where the host state adopts or maintains measures with respect to a non-Contracting Party or a person of the non-Contracting Party that prohibit transactions with the enterprise or that would be violated or circumvented if the benefits of the Agreement were accorded to the enterprise or to its investment.[119] It is also commendable that a Contracting Party may deny benefits to an investor from the other Contracting Party where, *inter alia*, the investor receives third-party funding but does not disclose same; or the investment was made in violation of the host country's laws and regulations; or the investment was procured through corruption, fraud or deceitful conduct; or where the claim would otherwise constitute a misuse of the Agreement and its objectives.[120] That said, in the light of recent jurisprudence which suggest non-retroactivity,[121] it needs to be more clearly and explicitly indicated whether a host state may still be able to rely upon the denial of benefits clause after arbitration proceedings have been commenced by the investor.

(v) Shareholder Claims

In recent years, there has been significant contestation over whether shareholders, as distinct from corporations, can bring claims for reflective loss; that is, loss in share value occasioned by third-party harm to the firm in question.[122] On the one hand, there is an argument that allowing reflective loss in ISDS proceedings may result in double recovery and parallel

117 *Gambrinus Corp. v Bolivarian Republic of Venezuela*, ICSID Case No. ARB/11/31, Award, 15 June 2015.

118 Lindsay Gastrell and Paul-Jean Le Cannu, 'Procedural Requirements of "Denial-of-Benefits" Clauses in Investment Treaties: A Review of Arbitral Decisions' (2015) 30(1) *ICSID Review-Foreign Investment Law Journal* 78; Loukas Mistelis and Crina Baltag, 'Denial of Benefits Clause' in *Max Planck Encyclopedia of International Procedural Law* (OUP 2019).

119 Article 17(1)(a)-(b) Draft Provisions on Procedural and Cross-cutting Issues.

120 ibid Article 17(2).

121 The majority of cases support the view that retroactive application of the denial of benefits clause is not permissible: *Bridgestone v Panama*, (ICSID Case No. ARB/16/34), Decision on Expedited Objections, 13 December 2017, para. 287; *Masdar v Spain*, ICSID Case No. ARB/14/1, Award, 16 May 2018; *Liman Caspian v Kazakhstan*, (ICSID Case No. ARB/07/14); *Stati & Ascom v Kazakhstan*, SCC Case No. V 116/2010, 19 December 2013; *Ampal-American and others v Egypt* Decision on Jurisdiction, 1 February 2016. cf *Pac Rim Cayman v El Salvador*, ICSID Case No. ARB/09/12, Award, 14 October 2016.

122 David Gaukrodger, 'Investment Treaties as Corporate Law: Shareholder Claims and Issues of Consistency' (2013) *OECD Working Papers on International Investment* 2013/03 http://dx.doi.org/10.1787/5k3w9t44mt0v-en.

proceedings, which in turn can lengthen proceedings and lead to unnecessary costs.[123] There is also the related fundamental argument that as a matter corporate law, because of the principle of separate legal personality, shareholders should not be able to obfuscate the corporate form by claiming for loss occasioned by third-party harms caused to the firm. On the other hand, there is an argument that recovering reflective losses is appropriate where the local entity may not be able to access ISDS because the underlying treaty's nationality rules prevent it from asserting a claim as an investor, though it has suffered loss. It also arguably protects the foreign owner of an investment in circumstances where the investment is made out of necessity through a local company, but they are unable to vindicate their own rights because of, for example, the total expropriation of the local company.[124]

These contending concerns were raised in the context of the recently decided *Michael Lee-Chin v Dominican Republic*[125] case. This case involved a Jamaican national who owned a Panamanian company, which in turn invested in another Panamanian company, which in turn invested in a locally incorporated Dominican firm, Lajun Corporation, in the waste disposal industry. The respondent alleged that, under the Treaty, the claimant was not entitled to claim for indirect damages (reflective loss), i.e. damages allegedly sustained by the company where he indirectly held shares but for which he had not sustained direct injury as a shareholder in Lajun. The respondent further submitted that international law recognises that a company is a legal entity distinct from its shareholders, and that the assets of a company belong to that company, and that accordingly, any harm suffered by Lajun's shareholders as a result of the alleged harm to Lajun would be, by definition, indirect damages. The claimant asserted that his claim was one of reflective loss, and that there was *jurisprudence constante* and global consensus on permitting shareholders to recover for their reflective losses. The claimant further contended that he was claiming on his own behalf for the loss in value of his investments in the Dominican Republic purportedly arising from the alleged violation by the Republic of several obligations set out in the Treaty. The Tribunal ultimately held that this case was not concerned with a situation in which a shareholder was claiming for indirect loss, but rather the claimant here was claiming on his own behalf for direct loss in value of his investments [as opposed to the value of the shareholding or distribution of dividends to shareholders] in the Republic arising from the alleged violation by the Republic of several obligations set out in the Treaty. Unsatisfied by the Tribunal's ruling on this matter within the context of the jurisdiction proceedings, the respondent repeated its claim regarding reflective loss at the merits phase, though this was ultimately rejected by the Tribunal in its final award.[126]

In the light of uncertainty occasioned by the lack of specificity among IIAs on the question of recovery of reflective loss, it is apposite that the draft Protocol contains express provisions on shareholder claims. The Protocol, while not outrightly prohibiting shareholder claims, makes it clear that a shareholder may only submit a claim on its own behalf for direct loss or damage incurred as a result of a breach of the relevant Agreement.[127] The alleged loss

123 Julian Arato, Kathleen Claussen, Jaemin Lee, and Giovanni Zarra, 'Reforming Shareholder Claims in Investor-State Dispute Settlement' (2023) 42(2) *Journal of International Dispute Settlement* 242.

124 ibid.

125 *Michael Anthony Lee-Chin v Dominican Republic*, ICSID Case No. UNCT/18/3 (Partial Award on Jurisdiction).

126 *Michael Anthony Lee-Chin v Dominican Republic*, ICSID Case No. UNCT/18/3, Final Award, 6 October 2023.

127 Article 18(1) Draft Provisions on Procedural and Cross-cutting Issues.

referred to here is separate and distinct from any alleged loss or damage to the enterprise in which the shareholder holds shares.[128] More pointedly, under the Protocol, direct loss or damage would not include diminution in the value of the shareholding or in the distribution of dividends to the shareholder as a result of loss or damage incurred by the enterprise.[129] Further, the loss of an opportunity to conduct business activities carried out or expected to be carried out by the enterprise would not constitute direct loss or damage.[130]

Notwithstanding the foregoing, however, the draft Protocol envisages some circumstances where a shareholder who owns or controls a firm established in the host state may submit a claim against the host state in question, namely, where all the assets of that enterprise are directly or wholly expropriated by the host state; or where the enterprise sought a remedy in the host state to redress its loss or damage but has been subject to treatment which amounts to be a denial of justice under customary international law.[131] This flexibility is necessary to ensure a system that is fair to both states and shareholders.

Practically speaking, when submitting a claim, specific guidance is given by the draft Protocol on what needs to be set out. First, the shareholder must provide evidence of their alleged ownership or control of the enterprise; a statement that the enterprise and itself will not initiate any other adjudicatory dispute resolution proceeding with respect to the same subject matter or the measure alleged to constitute a breach of the Agreement; and a statement that the enterprise and itself have withdrawn from or discontinued such adjudicatory dispute resolution proceedings.[132] Importantly, when the Tribunal makes an award in favour of the shareholder in these circumstances, the award, whether it be monetary damages and applicable interest or restitution of property, will be for the enterprise and not the shareholder.[133]

It is submitted that these provisions will bring needed clarity to this contested area of international investment law, creating a more stable legal framework. However, further clarification may be required for key terms like 'shareholder', 'enterprise', 'own', and 'control'. Specifically, the legal status remains unclear for shareholders who technically 'own' an enterprise in circumstances where over 50% of equity interests are beneficially owned by them, or for shareholders who 'control' an enterprise through powers such as appointing most directors or legally directing its actions.

(vi) Right to Regulate

Very few Caribbean IIAs contain express provisions on the right to regulate.[134] In those IIAs that do contain such a provision, the language of 'essential security interests' or 'nationality security interests' is used. The only Caribbean case to date to have interpreted a provision of

128 ibid.
129 ibid.
130 ibid.
131 ibid Article 18(2).
132 ibid Article 18(3).
133 ibid Article 18(4).
134 Trinidad and Tobago-USA BIT (1994) Article XIV(1); SVG-Taiwan BIT Article IX(1); Jamaica-USA BIT Article X(1); Grenada-USA BIT Article X(1); Barbados-Mauritius BIT Article 11(2); Trinidad and Tobago-India BIT Article 12(1); Guyana-Brazil BIT Article 13(1).

this nature is *Michael Lee-Chin v Dominican Republic*.[135] Here, the tribunal was asked to interpret and apply Article XVII(2) of the CARICOM-Dominican Republic FTA, which provides:

> This Agreement shall not preclude the application by either Party of measures necessary for the protection of its own national security interest.

In the light of the challenges with interpreting and applying the national security exception as exemplified in *Lee-Chin*, and, indeed, other cases involving developing countries, as well as the real threat of regulatory chill in this connection, it is certainly welcome that the draft Protocol expressly affords Contracting States the right to regulate.[136] More pointedly, under the draft Protocol, the right to regulate is self-judging; states may adopt, maintain and enforce any measure which *they consider appropriate* to ensure investments are made in a manner sensitive to the protection of a range of public interests, including public health, safety, human rights, essential security interests, the environment, and the promotion and protection of cultural diversity.[137] This provision affords states a high degree of deference and is intended to ensure that tribunals interpret and apply the state's obligations under the relevant Agreement, in the light, *inter alia*, of the state's international commitments, such as the Paris Agreement on Climate Change.

(vii) Other Positive Additions

Aside from the foregoing draft provisions, the draft Protocol contains several other important provisions. For example, in the light of recurrent allegations about crippling compensation awarded in several investment cases to date,[138] largely based on the Discount Cash Flow (DCF) method, and the threat of regulatory chill in this connection, the draft Protocol provides extensive guidance on the assessment and award of damages and compensation. More particularly, it allows for the award of monetary damages and applicable interest at a reasonable rate, with the important caveat that such damages must reflect only loss or damage incurred by reason of, or arising out of, a breach of the Agreement, thereby precluding the award of damages for speculative losses.[139] Importantly, when making an award of damages, tribunals would be obliged to consider a range of factors, including any contributory fault of the claimant (whether deliberate or negligent); failure by the claimant to make all reasonable efforts to mitigate loss or damage; repeal or modification of the measure alleged to constitute a breach of the Agreement; and any other compensation received by or awarded to the claimant.[140] That tribunals will be obliged to take these matters into consideration ensures that any award of damages made is not only fair to investors having regard to the nature and extent of the alleged breach, but properly reflects the particular circumstances of each case, including the conduct of investors.[141] Relatedly, the fact that the draft Protocol

135 ICSID Case No. UNCT/18/3, Final Award, 6 October 2023.

136 Article 19 Draft Provisions on Procedural and Cross-cutting Issues.

137 ibid.

138 Martins Paparinskis, 'Crippling Compensation in the International Law Commission and Investor-State Arbitration' (2022) 37(1) *ICSID Review-Foreign Investment Law Journal* 289.

139 Article 20(3) Draft Provisions on Procedural and Cross-cutting Issues.

140 ibid.

141 Jason Haynes, 'The Evolving Nature of the Fair and Equitable Treatment (FET) Standard: Challenging its Increasing Pervasiveness in Light of Developing Countries' Concerns – The Case for Regulatory Rebalancing' (2013) 14(1) *The Journal of World Investment & Trade* 114.

also precludes the award of punitive damages[142] is an important safeguard against crippling compensation. That said, though express provision is made for restitution of property, or failing this, an award of damages (and applicable interest) representing the fair market value of the property immediately before an expropriation has taken place,[143] it is regrettable that the draft Protocol in its current iteration does not expressly indicate whether moral damages[144] are permissible. This is concerning not only because recent arbitral practice shows an increasing willingness by tribunals to award moral damages for aggravated breaches on the part of the state,[145] but also because there is a real risk that, under the guise of moral damages, tribunals may surreptitiously award damages akin in magnitude to punitive damages. If, indeed, moral damages are allowable, there is also need for the Protocol to specify whether they may be awarded to states which have suffered non-pecuniary harms as a result of investors' conduct.[146]

Finally, it is commendable that the draft Protocol makes it clear that where joint interpretations are issued by states parties to an agreement, they are binding on tribunals, and that tribunals should accordingly ensure that their decisions and awards are consistent with these joint interpretations.[147] It is also useful that the draft Protocol allows tribunals, after consulting with the disputing parties, to invite and receive submissions from non-disputing treaty parties,[148] which will no doubt help to bring perspectives, particular knowledge and insights to the proceedings that are different from that of the disputing parties.

Nonetheless, it is commendable that the draft Protocol places a premium on settling disputes amicably through consultation, negotiation, mediation and other similar means,[149] and, separately, that it imposes a limitation period for initiating proceedings of three years since the investor first acquired, or should have first acquired, knowledge of the alleged breach of the Agreement and knowledge that it has incurred loss or damage to institute a claim.[150] It is submitted that, collectively, these important additions to the draft Protocol will work together to achieve increased stability and predictability in ISDS proceedings.

II. REFORM OF SUBSTANTIVE ASPECTS OF INTERNATIONAL INVESTMENT LAW

The international investment law regime stands at a critical juncture. With over 2,500 old-generation BITs still in force, the vast majority of which were concluded before 2012, there is an urgent need for comprehensive reform to address the tensions between investor

142 Article 20(4) Draft Provisions on Procedural and Cross-cutting Issues.

143 ibid Article 20(1).

144 Moral damages seek to remedy various forms of non-material harm, including damages to personality and reputation, physical health and well-being, as well as loss of business credit, reputation, good will and opportunities.

145 Lars Markert and Elisa Freiburg, 'Moral Damages in International Investment Disputes – On the Search for a Legal Basis and Guiding Principles' (2013) 14(1) *The Journal of World Investment & Trade* 13.

146 Matthew Parish, Annalise Newlson, and Charles Rosenberg, 'Awarding Moral Damages to Respondent States in Investment Arbitration' (2011) 29 *Berkeley Journal of International Law* 225.

147 Article 21 UNCITRAL, 'Additional Provisions on Procedural and Cross-Cutting Issues' (50th Session, Vienna, 20–24 January 2024) A/CN.9/WG.III/WP.248.

148 ibid Article 22.

149 Article 13 Draft Provisions on Procedural and Cross-cutting Issues.

150 ibid Article 16.

protection and states' regulatory autonomy. This challenge is particularly acute for developing countries, including small island developing states in the Caribbean, which face significant vulnerabilities from poorly drafted investment agreements. By virtue of their small island developing status and relatively volatile economic position, they are among the most vulnerable countries in the world to external shocks, including arbitral awards that could run into the billions.

The need for reform of substantive standards of protection is underscored by arbitral practice, as discussed in Chapters 2–7 of this book. This book has argued that various tribunals have countenanced expansive interpretations of vague treaty provisions, including the FET standard, sometimes constraining legitimate regulatory measures. This has led to what some scholars term as 'regulatory chill',[151] where governments may refrain from adopting necessary public interest measures for fear of triggering costly arbitration proceedings.

Against this backdrop, the analysis that follows examines the options available for reforming substantive aspects of investor protection. Drawing on recent treaty practice and UNCTAD's IIA Reform Accelerator, as well as innovative approaches in agreements like the Brazil-Guyana BIT, this analysis provides a roadmap for creating more balanced investment agreements that protect investors while preserving essential regulatory space.

A. Definition of 'Investment'

Most of the old-generation Caribbean IIAs contain a broad definition of 'investment'. This non-exhaustive definition grants protection to all types of assets. In this connection, economic transactions not contemplated by the parties or assets whose contribution to the host state's economic development is questionable may be covered, such as government bonds[152] and sales contracts.[153] It is suggested that Caribbean IIAs be reformed to specifically exclude certain types of assets from the definition of 'investment'. For example, portfolio investments should be explicitly excluded,[154] as well as debt issued by a Party or loans granted to a Party,[155] claims to money arising solely from commercial contracts for the sale of goods and services,[156] any order or judgment entered in a judicial or administrative action,[157] and costs incurred before the establishment of the investment, including costs for licences, permissions or permits.[158] The latter, in particular, has particular relevance in the Caribbean context, as evidenced by the claimant's allegation in *Allard v Barbados*[159] that he made his initial investment decisions in reliance on representations made by Barbados, a claim ultimately rejected by the tribunal.[160]

151 Kyla Tienhaara, 'Regulatory Chill in a Warming World: The Threat to Climate Policy Posed by Investor-State Dispute Settlement' (2018) 7(2) *Transnational Environmental Law* 229.

152 See for example, *Abaclat v Argentina*, ICSID Case No. ARB/07/5, Decision on Jurisdiction and Admissibility, 4 August 2011.

153 *Petrobart Limited v Kyrgyz Republic*, SCC Case No. 126/2003, Award, 29 March 2005.

154 Brazil-India BIT (2020), Article 2.4.1(iv).

155 Brazil-India BIT (2020), Article 2.4.1(ii).

156 Brazil-India BIT (2020), Article 2.4.1(v).

157 Brazil-India BIT (2020), Article 2.4.1(i).

158 Brazil-India BIT (2020), Article 2.4.1(iii).

159 PCA Case No. 2012–06, Award on Jurisdiction, 13 June 2014.

160 ibid 220. The tribunal described his alleged initial investment as an 'impulsive commitment'.

Article 3 of the Draft CARICOM Template for Investment Chapters in External Trade Agreements is instructive in this regard. After listing a number of matters covered by the term 'investment', it then goes on to state that:

> investment does not mean,
> (x) claims to money that arise solely from
> a. commercial contracts for the sale of goods or services by a national or enterprise in the territory of a Party to an enterprise in the territory of the other Party, or
> b. the extension of credit in connection with a commercial transaction, such as trade financing, other than a loan covered by subparagraph (iv); and
> c. any other claims to money, that do not involve the kinds of interests set out in sub-paragraphs (i) through (ix).

Guyana's approach under Article 3 of its BIT with Brazil is even more extensive in its exclusions:

> For the purposes of this Agreement and for greater certainty, 'Investment' does not include:
>
> i) An order or judgment issued as a result of a lawsuit or an administrative process;
> ii) Debt securities issued by a Party or loans granted from a Party to the other Party, bonds, debentures, loans or other debt instruments of a State-owned enterprise of a Party that is considered to be public debt under the legislation of that Party;
> iii) Portfolio investments, i.e. those that do not allow the investor to exert a significant degree of influence in the management of the enterprise or in another enterprise;
> iv) Claims to money that arise solely from commercial contracts for the sale of goods or services by an investor in the territory of a Party to a national or an enterprise in the territory of another Party, or the extension of credit in connection with a commercial transaction, or any other claims to money that do not involve the kind of interests set out in sub-paragraphs (a)–(e) above; and
> v) Claims deriving from any expenses or other financial obligations incurred by the investor prior to the establishment of the investment, including in order to comply with the regulations for the admission of foreign capital or other specific limits or conditions, according to the legislation on the admission of investments of the Host Party.

As noted by UNCTAD, such an approach has the added value of ensuring the predictability and consistency of the international investment system, thereby lowering costs and enhancing the attainment of sustainable development objectives.[161]

Another approach which Caribbean states may wish to consider is tailoring their definition of 'investment' to target assets conducive to sustainable development by granting protection only to investments that bring concrete benefits to the host country, for example, through long-term capital commitment and employment generation. Article 3 of the CARICOM Draft is non-exhaustive in its identification of these characteristics, evidenced by reference to the term 'including':

> provided that an investment must have the characteristics of an investment, including such characteristics as the commitment of capital or other resources, the expectation of gain or profit, and the assumption of risk.

While, evidently, it might have been useful, *ex abundanti cautela*, for the CARICOM Draft to have expressly mentioned sustainable economic development, in similar vein to Article 1

161 UNCTAD, *International Investment Agreements Reform Accelerator* (IIA Reform Accelerator) (UNCTAD 2020) 11.

of the Morocco-Nigeria BIT (2016), a prudent tribunal might be inclined to interpret Article 3 in a manner consistent with a requirement for such contribution. This approach will bring much-needed clarity and predictability by averting against the line of jurisprudence, including *RSM v Grenada*,[162] which seem to reject or at least is apathetic to the application of all of the *Salini* criteria, including contribution to the host state's development.

Finally, Caribbean states may wish to explicitly make the recognition and protection of investments contingent upon their compliance with the host state's laws. In this context, serious breaches of domestic laws at the admissions phase, such as corruption or fraud, could provide the basis for a tribunal to deny jurisdiction, and avert against the *Bear Creek*[163] tribunal's unwillingness to impute a requirement for compliance with the host state's laws. Article 3(1)(3) of Guyana's BIT with Brazil mentions the legality requirement as part of the definition of 'investment' and is thus instructive:

> Investment means any kind of asset invested by investors of one Party, established or acquired in the territory of the latter Party, that allows, directly or indirectly, the investor to exercise control of the shareholding, or with a significant degree of influence over the management of the production of goods or provision of services in the territory of the other Party, *in accordance with the laws and regulations of each Party*, including but not limited to:
>
> . . .

While the aforementioned reform options are not fool proof against tribunals' erroneous interpretations, if implemented, they at least represent a serious attempt by Caribbean states to recalibrate the asymmetrical nature of the international investment regime.

B. Definition of 'Investor'

Many Caribbean IIAs contain broad definitions of 'investor'. This has resulted in unanticipated or unintended coverage of certain persons (in particular, legal persons). For example, in many Caribbean IIAs, the nationality of a legal entity is solely to be determined on the basis of its place of incorporation, which creates opportunities for treaty shopping or free-riding by investors not conceived to be beneficiaries. Indeed, as cases like *Gambrinus v Venezuela*[164] demonstrate, third-country and host-country investors often channel their investments through 'mailbox' companies established in the territory of a party in order to obtain treaty protection. To avert these challenges, a reformed IIA may add a requirement that a company must have its seat in the home state and carry out real economic activities there. For example, Article 3(1)(1) of the Guyana-Brazil BIT provides:

> 1.1 Enterprise means:
>
> a) Any entity *constituted or organized* under applicable law of any of the Parties, carrying out *substantial business activities* in the territories of the Parties, whether or not for profit, whether privately owned or State -owned, including any corporation, trust, partnership, sole proprietorship or a joint venture.

Caribbean states may also wish to include a denial of benefits clause that would allow states to deny protection to 'mailbox' companies or 'special purpose entities' that have no

162 ICSID Case No. ARB/05/14, Final Award, 13 March 2009.
163 ICSID Case No. ARB/14/21, Final Award, 30 November 2017.
164 ICSID Case No. ARB/11/31, Award, 15 June 2015.

substantial business activities in the home state. For example, Article 20 the CARICOM Draft provides:

> A Party may deny the benefits of this Chapter to an investor of the other Party that is an enterprise of such Party and to investments of that investor if investors of a non-Party own or control the enterprise and the enterprise has no substantial business activities in the territory of the Party under whose law it is constituted or organized.

It may also be necessary for states to clarity that the denial of benefits clause applies retrospectively, such that it can be invoked even after arbitral proceedings have commenced.

Finally, it may be necessary, as Article 35 of India's Model BIT does, to include an anti-circumvention clause for investors/investments that have been obtained or restructured for the primary purpose of submitting an ISDS claim after a dispute arose or was foreseeable to arise.

C. National Treatment Standard

As discussed in Chapter 2, the national treatment standard, which prohibits less favourable treatment of foreign investors/investments vis-à-vis domestic investors/investments, has given rise to serious contestation over the meaning of being 'in like circumstances'. While some tribunals have limited the assessment of likeness to only businesses operating in the same sector, others, like *Occidental v Ecuador*,[165] have adopted a cross-sector approach, thereby treating investors operating in different sectors as being alike, even where there is no competitive relationship between the parties. Against this backdrop, it is recommended that Caribbean IIAs be amended to include specific criteria for comparison, and to make clear that distinctions on the basis of legitimate public welfare or regulatory objectives may render investors/investments not alike. Article 5(4) and (5) of the Guyana-Brazil BIT is instructive in this regard:

> 4. For greater certainty, whether treatment is accorded in 'like circumstances' depends on the totality of the circumstances, including whether the relevant treatment distinguishes between investors or investments on the basis of legitimate public interest objectives.
> 5. For greater certainty, this Article shall not be construed to require any Party to compensate for any inherent competitive disadvantages which result from the foreign character of the investor or investments.

While these provisions go a long way in ensuring clarity and consistency of interpretation, CARICOM's Draft is even more extensive and thus a better model for reform. Article 4(3) of the latter instrument provides:

> For greater certainty,
>
> a. a determination of whether an investor or an investment are in like circumstances for the purposes of this Article shall be based on an assessment of all the circumstances related to the investor or the investment, including:
> (i) the effects of the investment on
> A. third persons;
> B. the community;

165 London Court of International Arbitration (UNCITRAL Award 1 July 2004).

C. the environment, including effects that relate to the cumulative impact of all investments within a jurisdiction;
(ii) the business sector in which the investor operates;
(iii) the goal of the alleged discriminatory measure; and
(iv) the regulations that apply to investments or investors.

b. a measure of a Party that treats investors of the other Party or their investments less favourably than its own investors or their investments is not inconsistent with this Article if it is applied by the Party in pursuit of a legitimate public purpose, including the protection of health, safety, the environment, labour rights and the elimination of bribery and corruption, and it bears a reasonable connection to the purpose.

States may also wish to carve out reservations in respect of the national treatment standard, for example, for particularly sensitive sectors. For example, Article 6(6)(d) of the CARICOM Draft provides that the national treatment standard 'shall not apply to: any measure that a Party adopts or maintains with respect to sectors, sub-sectors or activities as set out in its Schedule in Annex x'. Such an approach establishes a fair middle ground between full policy freedom on the one hand, and a rigid guarantee of non-discrimination on the other.

D. Most-Favoured Nation Treatment Standard

The MFN clause, which aims to protect foreign investors/investments from discrimination vis-à-vis third-country foreign investors, has given rise to contestation over the meaning and implications of investors being in 'like circumstances'. As such, it might be instructive for Caribbean states to countenance the approach adopted by Article 5(3) of the CARICOM Draft, which provides:

3. For greater certainty,
a. a determination of whether an investor or an investment are in like circumstances for the purposes of this Article shall be based on an assessment of all the circumstances related to the investor or the investment, including:
(i) the effects of the investment on
A. third persons;
B. the community;
C. the environment, including effects that relate to the cumulative impact of all investments within a jurisdiction;
(ii) the business sector in which the investor operates;
(iii) the goal of the alleged discriminatory measure; and
(iv) the regulations that apply to investments or investors.
b. a measure of a Party that treats investors of the other Party or their investments less favourably than investors of a non-Party and their investments is not inconsistent with this Article if it is applied by the Party in pursuit of a legitimate public purpose, including the protection of health, safety, the environment, labour rights and the elimination of bribery and corruption, and it bears a reasonable connection to the purpose.

Caribbean states may also wish to exempt specific policy areas or measures and sensitive economic sectors from the scope of the application of the most-favoured-nation treatment standard. For example, Article 5(4) of the CARICOM Draft provides:

This Article shall not apply to:

(a) treatment by a Party pursuant to a regional economic integration arrangement creating an internal market;
(b) treatment by a Party pursuant to any international agreement or arrangement relating wholly or mainly to taxation;
(c) procedural, institutional or dispute settlement provisions of other international investment agreements.

The latter provision is particularly instructive as it effectively precludes the multilateralisation of certain benefits granted by a treaty party, in this case more favourable dispute settlement provisions. While this provision goes a long way to bring clarity to this unsettled area of law, it is submitted that if states are keen to ensure that investors do not use the MFN clause as a basis for importing consent to ICSID from another treaty where no such (automatic) consent to ICSID exists in the base treaty, they should, *ex abundanti cautela*, make this explicitly clear in their reformed IIA. Relatedly, in the light of ongoing contentions regarding the true meaning of 'reserving' the right to impose reservations, Caribbean states are encouraged to include language to the effect that the application of exceptions to the MFN treatment obligation does not require prior notification on their part.

E. Fair and Equitable Treatment Standard

The FET standard is arguable one of, if not the most important, standards of investor protection in contemporary investment treaty practice. Despite its importance, however, it has been variously interpreted by tribunals in a manner that is often vague, inconsistent and in some cases even outrightly hostile to host states regulatory interests.[166] In this regard, there are several reform options are suggested. First, Caribbean states may replace their unqualified FET clauses with an exhaustive list of specific obligations. For example, Article 4 of the Guyana-Brazil BIT provides:

1. Based on the applicable rules of international law as recognized by each of the Parties and their respective national law, no Party shall subject investors of the other Party and their investments to measures which constitute:
   i) Denial of access to justice in any judicial or administrative proceedings;
   ii) Breach of due process;
   iii) Targeted discrimination, such as gender, race, religious or political beliefs;
   iv) Manifestly abusive treatment, such as coercion, duress and harassment; or
   v) Discrimination against investments of investors of the other Party in ensuring the enforcement of the law and the provision of public security.

Because this provision is exhaustively drafted, this could help avoid unanticipated and far-reaching interpretations by tribunals. That said, given the ubiquitous and pervasive nature of tribunals' use and misuse of the doctrine of legitimate expectations as a constituent element of the FET standard, it is suggested that Caribbean states include precise language in

166 Ioana Tudor, *The Fair and Equitable Treatment Standard in The International Law of Foreign Investment* (OUP 2008) 35.

their reformed IIAs regarding the nature and scope of legitimate expectations. For example, Article 6(2) of the CARICOM Draft provides:

> In the absence of a specific commitment by a Party to investors of the other Party and their investments not to modify certain laws or regulations, the obligations in paragraph 1 of this Article shall not be construed as limiting the exercise of that Party's power to regulate in the public interest.

Furthermore, Caribbean countries will need to expressly indicate the standard of review in respect of the application of the FET standard. It is suggested that given the high threshold of the minimum standard of treatment linked to the *Neer Claims* case,[167] namely evidence of behaviour that is arbitrary, grossly unfair, or idiosyncratic, or involves a lack of due process, Caribbean states should adopt treaty language to this effect.

A final option that Caribbean states may want to carefully consider is the wholesale omission of the FET clause, such as contained in Article 4(4) of the Guyana-Brazil BIT, which provides:

> For greater certainty, the standards of fair and equitable treatment and full protection and security shall not be used or raised by either Party to this Agreement as a ground for any dispute settlement procedure in relation to the application or the interpretation of this Agreement.

On the one hand, such an approach reduces the state's exposure to investor claims, given that the FET standard is the most litigated investor protection standard. However, it is worth noting that such an approach may be perceived by investors as reducing the protective value of investment agreements and thus serve as a disincentive to them investing.

F. Full Protection and Security

Although the full protection and security standard has not been invoked with as much frequency in arbitral proceedings as the fair and equitable treatment standard, it nonetheless raises important doctrinal issues in practice which could benefit from reform aimed at providing clarification and thereby improving legal certainty. For example, Caribbean states may want to link the application of the full protection and security standard to customary international law,[168] and thereby require evidence of a failure of due diligence that rises to the level of being arbitrary, grossly unfair, or idiosyncratic. More fundamentally, however, urgent clarification is needed about the scope of the full protection and security standard, and, in particular, the extent to which it only covers physical protection or extends also to legal security, as some tribunals seem to suggest.[169] In this connection, language limiting the standard to physical or 'police' security[170] could exclude legal security, provide certainty and thus limit tribunals' ability to engage in expansive interpretations of the standard. At the extreme end of the spectrum, Caribbean states may also consider omitting the standard altogether, as Article 4(4) of the Guyana-Brazil BIT has done:

167 (*United States v Mexico*) (1926) 4 RIAA 60.

168 Morocco-Nigeria BIT (2016), Article 7.2.

169 See for example, *Azurix v Argentina*, ICSID Case No. ARB/01/12, Award, 14 July 2006; *Enron v Argentina*, ICSID Case No. ARB/01/3, Award, 22 May 2007; *Biwater Gauff v Tanzania*, ICSID Case No. ARB/05/22, Award, 24 July 2008.

170 Morocco-Nigeria BIT (2016), Article 7.2(b).

> For greater certainty, the standards of fair and equitable treatment and full protection and security shall not be used or raised by either Party to this Agreement as a ground for any dispute settlement procedure in relation to the application or the interpretation of this Agreement.

That said, such a restrictive approach may be perceived by investors as reducing the protective value of investment agreements and thus serve as a disincentive to them investing.

G. Expropriation

While direct expropriations are no longer common today, claims of indirect expropriation have been raised with a significant degree of frequency in contemporary investor-state arbitral practice. First, there is tremendous contestation as to what precisely constitutes an indirect taking, as well as the determination of the dividing line between expropriations and legitimate public policymaking,[171] such as for environmental, social or health regulations. To avoid undue constraints on their prerogative to regulate in the public interest, Caribbean states should consider reforming their IIAs to set out general criteria for state acts that may (or may not) be considered an indirect expropriation. For example, Article 12(6) of the CARICOM Draft usefully provides:

> Proof that an action or series of actions by a Party has an adverse effect on the economic value of an investment of an investor of the other Party or interferes with the investment-backed expectations of the investor does not *ipso facto* establish that an expropriation has occurred. The determination of whether an action or series of actions constitutes an indirect expropriation requires a case-by-case, fact-based enquiry considering factors such as the character of the government action and the purpose of this action. Non-discriminatory measures by a Party that are designed and applied to achieve legitimate public welfare objectives, such as public health, safety, the protection and promotion of internationally and domestically recognized labour rights, and the protection of the environment, do not constitute indirect expropriations.

While this does not exclude liability risks altogether, it allows for better balancing of investor and state interests. That said, another option that Caribbean states might want to consider is to explicitly exclude indirect expropriations from treaty coverage, such as what Article 7(6) of the Guyana-Brazil BIT has done:

> For avoidance of doubt, this Article only provides for direct expropriation, where an investment is nationalized or otherwise directly expropriated through formal transfer of title or ownership rights, and does not cover indirect expropriation.

However, it is worth noting that adopting such a restrictive approach may be perceived as considerably reducing the protective value of the agreement as it would leave investors unprotected from certain types of expropriations such as 'creeping' or 'disguised' takings.

H. Public Interest Considerations

In recent years, it has not only become evident that states should be afforded appropriate regulatory space to adopt measures to protect their public interests, but also that investors who

171 Christian Riffel, 'Indirect Expropriation and the Protection of Public Interests' (2022) 71(4) *International & Comparative Law Quarterly* 945.

sometimes commit human rights, environmental and related breaches often escape liability.[172] In this context, it is recommended that Caribbean states, first, explicitly include public interest exceptions that are self-judging, and which specify that the required link or 'nexus' between the measure and the alleged policy objective pursued is a low threshold. More particularly, instead of providing that the measure must be 'necessary' to achieve the policy objective (high threshold), the IIA could require that the measure be 'designed' to achieve or 'related' to the policy objective (lower threshold). For example, Article 13 of the Guyana-Brazil BIT provides that:

1. Nothing in this Agreement shall be construed to prevent a Party from adopting or maintaining measures *aimed at* preserving its national security or public order, or to apply the provisions of their criminal laws or comply with its obligations regarding the maintenance of international peace and security in accordance with the provisions of the United Nations Charter and other relevant international agreements to which the Parties are members.

Relatedly, Caribbean states may also consider placing certain specified obligations on foreign investors in respect of which, in circumstances where there is a failure to comply, the state may initiate a counterclaim. For example, Article 16 of the CARICOM Draft provides:

1. Investors of a Party shall make their investments in the other Party in accordance with the laws and regulations of the other Party.
2. Investors of a Party and their investments shall not offer, promise or give any undue pecuniary or other advantage, whether directly or through intermediaries, to any public official of the other Party or member of his or her family or business associates or other person in close proximity to the official, for that person or for a third party, in order that the official or third party act or refrain from acting in relation to the performance of official duties, or in order to achieve any favour in relation to a proposed investment or any licences, permits, contracts or other rights in relation to an investment.
3. In relation to their activities in the other Party, investors of a Party and their investments shall act in accordance with core labour standards as required by the International Labour Organization (ILO) Declaration on Fundamental Principles and Rights at Work, 1998, to which the Parties are parties.4
4. Investors of a Party shall not manage or operate their investments in the other Party in a manner that circumvents international environmental or labour obligations arising from agreements to which the Parties are parties.
5. In relation to their activities in the other Party, investors of a Party and their investments shall maintain, where appropriate as determined by domestic laws and regulations, local community liaison processes, especially in projects involving extensive natural resource-based activities.
6. The Parties shall cooperate and take, within their respective territories, such measures as may be necessary, *inter alia*, through domestic legislation, to ensure that:
   (a) investors and their investments be forbidden from, and held liable for, the acts referred to in paragraph 1;
   (b) investors and their investments comply with the standards set out in paragraphs 2, 3 and 4.
7. A Party may initiate a counterclaim against an investor of the other Party or its investment before a tribunal established pursuant to Section C of this Chapter at the instance of the investor for an injury suffered by the Party or persons of the Party resulting from a breach of paragraphs 1, 2, 3, 4 or 5.

172 Jason Haynes, 'The Confluence of National and International Law in Response to Multinational Corporations' Commission of Modern Slavery: *Nevsun Resources Ltd. v Araya*' (2022) 8(4) *Journal of Human Trafficking* 441.

Such an approach addresses the concern, as articulated by scholars such as Perrone[173] that, at present, international investment law is asymmetrical in that it generally imposes obligations on states, without commensurate obligations, particularly of a human rights or environmental nature, being directly binding on foreign investors.

CONCLUSION

This chapter has made it clear that the UNCITRAL reform process represents a critical juncture for Caribbean states to fundamentally reshape their relationship with the international investment law regime. Indeed, it notes that while Caribbean nations have historically been marginal participants in investment arbitration compared to their Latin American counterparts, their recent experiences in cases such as *RSM v Saint Lucia*, *Michael Lee-Chin v Dominican Republic*, and *Peter Allard v Barbados* underscore both their acute vulnerability to asymmetrical arbitral outcomes and the urgent necessity for comprehensive reform engagement. In this context, the proposed reforms collectively address the structural deficiencies that have rendered the current system inherently biased against small island developing states. The Advisory Centre's capacity-building mandate directly responds to the expertise and resource gaps that have left Caribbean states inadequately equipped to defend against sophisticated investor claims. However, the Centre's governance structure must ensure meaningful Caribbean representation beyond tokenistic 'Latin America and Caribbean' classifications that historically have marginalized Caribbean voices in international institutional frameworks.

Meanwhile, the multilateral instrument's protocol-based architecture offers Caribbean states unprecedented flexibility to selectively adopt reforms aligned with their specific priorities and institutional capacities. Given Caribbean nations' well-documented wariness of multilateral instruments that impose obligations through opt-out mechanisms – a legacy of decades of asymmetrical international agreements – the chapter supports an opt-in approach that respects state sovereignty while enabling progressive reform adoption. CARICOM's dormant but sophisticated Code for Investment Chapters provides a ready foundation for coordinated regional engagement that could overcome individual member states' institutional lethargy. Relatedly, the Standing Mechanism's permanent tribunal structure addresses the most pernicious aspects of the current ad hoc system: the lack of consistent jurisprudence, limited arbitrator diversity, and questionable independence arising from appointment dynamics and 'double-hatting' practices. While the proposed diversity requirements represent significant progress, the chapter identifies critical gaps in Selection Committee composition that could perpetuate existing biases. The absence of binding precedent, while consistent with general international law principles, may perpetuate the jurisprudential inconsistency that has particularly disadvantaged developing states. That said, the Caribbean Court of Justice's successful implementation of *stare decisis* in its original jurisdiction demonstrates the viability of binding precedent in international tribunals.

Separately, the procedural and cross cutting provisions constitute the reform package's most immediately relevant components for Caribbean interests. These provisions directly address the specific challenges Caribbean states have encountered: from third-party funding

173 Nicolás Perrone, 'Bridging the Gap Between Foreign Investor Rights and Obligations: Towards Reimagining the International Law on Foreign Investment' (2022) 7(3) *Business and Human Rights Journal* 375.

transparency issues in *RSM v Saint Lucia* to denial of benefits questions in *Gambrinus v Venezuela*. The enhanced security for costs framework, expanded counterclaim jurisdiction, and strengthened right to regulate provisions promise to rebalance the investor-state relationship in favour of legitimate regulatory objectives. However, procedural reforms cannot remedy the fundamental asymmetries embedded in substantive investment law standards. The comprehensive reform roadmap presented demonstrates that Caribbean states must simultaneously pursue bilateral and regional treaty reform to modernise their investment agreements. The innovative approaches in the Guyana-Brazil BIT and draft CARICOM template provide tested frameworks for achieving this balance.

Ultimately, this chapter concludes that Caribbean states face a historic opportunity to transform international investment law from a colonial-era relic that constrains regulatory autonomy into a balanced framework that protects both investor rights and state sovereignty. This transformation requires active, strategic engagement with the UNCITRAL process, coordinated regional action through CARICOM, and comprehensive bilateral treaty reform. The alternative – continued passive disengagement – risks perpetuating a system that fundamentally disadvantages small island developing states precisely when climate change and sustainable development imperatives demand maximum regulatory flexibility. The legal and policy foundations for reform exist; what remains is the political will to implement them.

CHAPTER 9

CONCLUSION

The aim of this book is to provide a critical and incisive analysis of the international investment law regime applicable to the Commonwealth Caribbean, though the work has wider implications for the non-English speaking islands of the Caribbean, and, indeed, small island developing states. Its writing was inspired by the relative dearth of Caribbean-centric academic literature on international investment law, despite the fact that region boasts significant FDI inflows, and a burgeoning web of investment agreements and arbitral awards.

This book began by situating international investment law within the context of the Commonwealth Caribbean, addressing a critical gap in scholarship by examining how the international investment regime operates within Commonwealth Caribbean small island developing states. It traced the evolution of international investment law from its colonial origins through Friendship, Commerce and Navigation treaties to the modern BIT system, demonstrating how Caribbean countries were integrated into this system during the 1980s–1990s through 'imposed bilateralism', characterised by asymmetric power relations and coercive negotiation processes. The region has collectively negotiated over 75 international investment agreements across four decades, with 47 currently in force, creating an extensive legal framework comprising BITs, free trade agreements with investment chapters, and domestic investment legislation designed to attract foreign direct investment.

The book' introductory pages critically examined both the purported advantages and significant disadvantages of foreign direct investment, challenging the orthodox narrative that FDI automatically generates developmental benefits. While proponents argue that FDI provides technology transfer, employment creation, infrastructure development, and productivity enhancement, the arguments presented revealed a more complex picture marked by excessive investment incentives, profit expatriation, environmental degradation, and the usurpation of sovereign functions. The book also exposed fundamental structural defects in international investment law, including the asymmetrical nature of investor-state dispute settlement that creates a 'one-way street' favouring investors, the absence of binding investor obligations, institutionalised unpredictability through vague standards like fair and equitable treatment, and regulatory chill that constrains democratic governance. Drawing on scholarship identifying colonial continuities and racial capitalist dynamics, the introductory analysis argued that the current regime perpetuates historical patterns of exploitation and subordination, necessitating fundamental reform to restore policy space for legitimate public interest regulation while establishing meaningful obligations for investors corresponding to their extensive protections.

The book thereafter provided a comprehensive examination of jurisdiction and admissibility requirements in Caribbean investment arbitration, focusing on the evolution from diplomatic protection to investor-state dispute settlement (ISDS) mechanisms. The book centred on the four traditional jurisdictional criteria under Article 25 of the ICSID Convention and Caribbean IIAs: *ratione materiae* (qualifying investments), *ratione personae* (eligible investors), *ratione temporis* (temporal scope), and *ratione voluntatis* (consent to arbitration). The book demonstrated that Caribbean IIAs typically adopt broadly permissive approaches to investment definitions, using 'every kind of asset' formulations, while tribunals have applied the *Salini* criteria requiring contribution of capital, duration, regularity of profit, risk assumption, and contribution to host state development. Key Caribbean cases like *F-W*

DOI: 10.4324/9781003734185-9

Oil v Trinidad and Tobago, *Michael Lee-Chin v Dominican Republic*, and *RSM Production v Grenada* were relied upon to illustrate how tribunals determine qualifying investments and handle complex issues such as indirect investments and pre-contractual arrangements. The book revealed ongoing tensions between investor protection and state sovereignty, particularly regarding corporate nationality determination and procedural requirements. While most Caribbean BITs employ simple incorporation tests for determining corporate nationality, cases like *Gambrinus v Venezuela* and *Blue Bank v Venezuela* demonstrate divergent tribunal approaches to 'shell companies' and beneficial ownership questions. The book's analysis of admissibility requirements, including the legality requirement for investments made 'in accordance with host state laws', and the abuse of process doctrine, revealed how tribunals balance investor access to arbitration against preventing manipulation of the system. Cases such as *Peter Allard v Barbados* and *Metal-Tech v Uzbekistan* were used to illustrate the framework tribunals use to assess investor illegality, focusing on the significance of obligations breached, seriousness of conduct, and proportionality of consequences, while the abuse of process jurisprudence addresses concerns about corporate restructuring timing and multiple proceedings for the same economic harm.

The book then proceeded to examine the principle of non-discrimination in international investment law through detailed analysis of national treatment and most-favoured-nation standards as they apply to Caribbean states. The book's analysis revealed significant jurisprudential inconsistencies in determining 'like circumstances', with tribunals adopting varying methodologies ranging from narrow same-sector tests to broader cross-industry comparisons, as demonstrated in cases like *Occidental v Ecuador* where the tribunal's expansive interpretation potentially undermines states' ability to implement sector-specific regulatory measures. The book advanced the argument that these fragmented approaches create particular challenges for Caribbean states seeking to implement targeted economic policies for development diversification, as inconsistent interpretations of 'less favourable treatment' and justification defences leave governments uncertain about the boundaries of their regulatory autonomy. That said, the book's most significant contribution on the question of non-discrimination lies in its analysis of the contentious procedural use of MFN clauses to import more advantageous dispute settlement provisions from third-party treaties. The detailed examination of the jurisprudential divide between the liberal *Maffezini* approach, which permits such procedural importation based on broad treaty language, and the restrictive *Plama* line, which requires explicit consent for dispute settlement modifications, revealed a fundamental schism in investment arbitration. The book argues that this uncertainty disproportionately affects Caribbean states with limited geopolitical power, as the procedural application of MFN clauses can transform carefully negotiated dispute settlement arrangements into unpredictable arbitral forums selected through investor treaty shopping, ultimately undermining the principle that state consent forms the cornerstone of international arbitration.

The book then segued into a comprehensive examination of the guarantee against expropriation. It began by evaluating the distinction between direct and indirect expropriation and the conditions under which states may lawfully expropriate foreign property. The book's analysis shed important light on the evolving jurisprudential approaches to determining when regulatory measures cross the line from legitimate state action to compensable indirect expropriation, advocating for a framework that focuses on substantial deprivation of the incidents of ownership rather than mere diminution in investment value. The book also explores the police powers doctrine as a defence to expropriation claims, examining how states can balance their sovereign regulatory authority with investor protection obligations under international investment agreements. The book advances the argument that while expropriation is not *per se* prohibited under international law, it must satisfy four cumulative conditions in order to be conceived as lawful: public purpose, non-discrimination, due process, and prompt, adequate and effective compensation. Through extensive analysis of arbitral jurisprudence, the book explains that tribunals should require evidence of substantial interference with fundamental ownership rights (use, enjoyment, control, and management) rather than accepting mere loss of value as sufficient for indirect expropriation claims. The book further contends that proportionality should be assessed under the police powers doctrine rather than at the initial stage of determining public purpose and emphasises that the police powers doctrine serves as a crucial mechanism for protecting legitimate regulatory measures adopted in good faith for public welfare, provided they are non-discriminatory and proportionate to their stated objectives.

The book also examined the FET standard, tracing its evolution from early treaty provisions in FCN treaties to its current status as the most frequently invoked investor protection standard. The analysis revealed the existence of various formulations of the FET standard across Caribbean investment agreements, ranging from clauses explicitly linked to customary international law (requiring high thresholds of 'egregious and shocking' conduct) to autonomous FET clauses that operate independently of international minimum standards. The analysis also systematically explores the constituent elements that tribunals have developed to assess FET violations, including legitimate expectations (requiring specific, unambiguous state representations that are reasonably relied upon), transparency obligations, denial of justice claims, and prohibitions against arbitrary, unreasonable, and discriminatory treatment. The core argument raised centred on the tension between investor protection and state regulatory sovereignty, particularly for developing Caribbean nations. While acknowledging the importance of FET protections, the analysis demonstrated how expansive tribunal interpretations – exemplified by cases like *Tecmed v Mexico* – can create impossibly high standards for state conduct that effectively freeze regulatory capacity. The book accordingly advocates for more balanced approaches that recognise states' legitimate right to regulate in the public interest, supporting emerging trends toward proportionality analysis and consideration of development status in FET assessments.

Thereafter, the book proceeded to examine four important but often underexplored standards of protection in international investment law: full protection and security (FPS), free transfer provisions, umbrella clauses, and performance requirements. The book's analysis revealed how these provisions have evolved from relatively straightforward guarantees into complex legal instruments that blur traditional boundaries between contractual and treaty obligations, with tribunals reaching divergent interpretations that create significant uncertainty for both investors and host states. The book argued that while these standards serve essential protective functions, their inconsistent application, particularly regarding whether FPS extends beyond physical to legal security, how umbrella clauses can transform contractual breaches into treaty violations, and the scope of permissible performance requirements, reflects the ongoing tension between investor protection and state sovereignty in the modern global economy. The book demonstrated through an extensive analysis of case law that arbitral tribunals have struggled to establish consistent approaches to these provisions. With respect to the FPS standard, for example, tribunals are divided over whether protection encompasses only physical security or extends to legal and economic stability, with some adopting broad interpretations while others maintain restrictive views limited to due diligence obligations. Meanwhile, the discussion on the umbrella clause revealed the reality that tribunals disagree fundamentally on whether these clauses elevate ordinary contractual breaches to treaty violations or require state action in a sovereign capacity. Similarly, performance requirements have generated nuanced jurisprudence that attempts to balance legitimate regulatory space with prohibitions on measures that distort investment flows, while free transfer provisions have been tested by economic crises that force tribunals to weigh investor rights against states' monetary sovereignty.

The book went on to examine the merits phase of investment arbitration, analysing how tribunals determine treaty breaches and craft appropriate remedies once jurisdictional requirements are satisfied. In this connection, the book explores the range of remedies at tribunals' disposal, with compensation being the predominant form of relief, though the application of valuation methodologies like discounted cash flow often involves significant discretion and can lead to widely divergent outcomes, as demonstrated in cases such as *Dunkeld v Belize* and *Grenada Private Power v Grenada.* It also addresses state defences, including *force majeure*, contributory fault, and essential security exceptions, examining how these mechanisms can excuse non-performance of treaty obligations, with particular attention to the distinction between self-judging and non-self-judging security provisions as interpreted in cases like *Seda v Colombia* and *Michael Lee-Chin v Dominican Republic.* The book further analysed the growing tension between investment protection and public interest considerations, particularly human rights, environmental protection, and corporate social responsibility. While most Caribbean IIAs lack explicit binding obligations for investors in these areas, the book demonstrated how tribunals have developed nuanced approaches to counterclaims through interpretive principles that accommodate broader societal concerns without undermining the investment treaty framework. The book also examines post-award matters, including the limited annulment grounds under Article 52 of the ICSID Convention, enforcement mechanisms distinguishing ICSID from non-ICSID awards, and cost allocation principles, highlighting how tribunal discretion operates across different procedural frameworks to balance fairness considerations with the finality of arbitral proceedings.

The final substantive chapter provided a comprehensive analysis of the UNCITRAL Working Group III reform process for international investment law, specifically examining its implications for Caribbean small island developing states. The book argued that while Caribbean nations have historically been marginal participants in investment arbitration compared to Latin American counterparts, their recent experiences in cases such as *RSM v Saint Lucia*, *Michael Lee-Chin v Dominican Republic*, and *Peter Allard v Barbados* demonstrate their acute vulnerability to asymmetrical arbitral outcomes and highlight the urgent need for comprehensive reform engagement. The book systematically evaluated four key reform initiatives: the Advisory Centre on International Investment Dispute Resolution (which addresses capacity and resource asymmetries but raises concerns about fee structures and genuine Caribbean representation), the Multilateral Instrument on ISDS Reform (where I advocate for an opt-in rather than opt-out approach given Caribbean states' historical wariness of imposed international agreements), the Draft Statute of a Standing Mechanism (which addresses inconsistency and lack of diversity in arbitral decision-making but has gaps regarding Selection Committee composition), and the Draft Provisions on Procedural and Cross-Cutting Issues (identified as potentially the most significant for Caribbean interests, covering security for costs, counterclaims, third-party funding, denial of benefits, shareholder claims, and the right to regulate). The book advanced three interconnected arguments: first, that Caribbean states' limited engagement with UNCITRAL reform efforts represents a missed opportunity given their acute vulnerability to asymmetrical arbitral awards; second, that the proposed reforms, while welcome, require careful adaptation to address Caribbean-specific concerns about institutional capacity and historical experiences with imposed international obligations; and third, that comprehensive reform of both procedural and substantive aspects of international investment law is essential to prevent regulatory chill and ensure these small island developing states can pursue legitimate public policy objectives without fear of crippling compensation awards. The chapter then concluded with a detailed examination of substantive law reforms, presenting a roadmap for modernising Caribbean international investment agreements through more precise definitions of 'investment' and 'investor', reformed treatment standards, and enhanced public interest protections, drawing extensively on innovative approaches in agreements like the Guyana-Brazil BIT and the draft CARICOM template to achieve a fundamental rebalancing that preserves regulatory space while maintaining meaningful investor protections.

This book represents the culmination of five years of intensive research, which, among other things, involved significant engagement with Caribbean IIAs, arbitral jurisprudence, colleagues, and students. It is hoped that it informs, educates, facilitate reforms, and inspires a new generation of Caribbean thinkers in the burgeoning and exciting field of international investment law.

APPENDIX: CARIBBEAN BITs

TOTAL BITs: 70

- Signed (not yet in force): 21
- In force: 47
- Terminated: 2

TABLE A.1 All BITs by Country (Signed + In Force)

Country	*Signed*	*In Force*	*Terminated*	*Total*
Antigua and Barbuda	0	3	0	3
Bahamas	2	0	0	2
Barbados	3	8	1	12
Belize	3	5	0	8
Dominica	1	2	0	3
Grenada	0	2	0	2
Guyana	4	5	0	9
Jamaica	6	11	0	17
Saint Kitts and Nevis	1	0	0	1
Saint Lucia	0	2	0	2
Saint Vincent and the Grenadines	1	2	0	3
Trinidad and Tobago	1	13	1	15

TABLE A.2 Signed BITs Only (21 total)

Country	*Partner Country*	*Date Signed*
Bahamas	Haiti	29/07/2014
Bahamas	China	04/09/2009
Barbados	United Arab Emirates	04/12/2023
Barbados	BLEU (Belgium-Luxembourg)	29/05/2009
Barbados	Ghana	22/04/2008
Belize	Italy	23/11/2005
Belize	El Salvador	04/12/2001
Belize	Taiwan Province of China	16/01/1999
Dominica	United Arab Emirates	21/01/2020
Guyana	Brazil	13/12/2018
Guyana	Kuwait	17/01/2010
Guyana	Indonesia	30/01/2008
Guyana	Cuba	22/10/1999
Jamaica	Kuwait	01/04/2013
Jamaica	Nigeria	05/08/2002
Jamaica	Indonesia	10/02/1999

(*Continued*)

DOI: 10.4324/9781003734185-10

TABLE A.2 (Continued)

Country	*Partner Country*	*Date Signed*
Jamaica	Zimbabwe	10/02/1999
Jamaica	Egypt	10/02/1999
Jamaica	Cuba	31/05/1997
Saint Kitts and Nevis	United Arab Emirates	24/11/2016
Saint Vincent and the Grenadines	United Arab Emirates	25/11/2018
Trinidad and Tobago	Ghana	24/09/2024

TABLE A.3 In Force BITs Only (47 total)

Country	*Partner Country*	*Entry into Force Date*
Antigua and Barbuda	United Arab Emirates	24/02/2022
Antigua and Barbuda	Germany	28/02/2001
Antigua and Barbuda	United Kingdom	12/06/1987
Barbados	Mauritius	28/06/2005
Barbados	China	01/10/1999
Barbados	Canada	17/01/1997
Barbados	Cuba	13/08/1998
Barbados	Switzerland	22/12/1995
Barbados	Germany	11/05/2002
Barbados	Venezuela	31/10/1995
Barbados	United Kingdom	07/04/1993
Belize	United Arab Emirates	24/10/2017
Belize	Netherlands	01/10/2004
Belize	Austria	01/02/2002
Belize	Cuba	16/04/1999
Belize	United Kingdom	30/04/1982
Dominica	United Kingdom	23/01/1987
Dominica	Germany	11/05/1986
Grenada	United Kingdom	25/02/1988
Grenada	United States	03/03/1989
Guyana	Korea, Republic of	20/08/2006
Guyana	Switzerland	02/05/2018
Guyana	China	26/10/2004
Guyana	Germany	09/03/1994
Guyana	United Kingdom	11/04/1990
Jamaica	Korea, Republic of	05/11/2007
Jamaica	Spain	25/11/2002
Jamaica	China	01/04/1996
Jamaica	Argentina	01/12/1995
Jamaica	United States	07/03/1997
Jamaica	Italy	09/11/1995
Jamaica	France	15/09/1994
Jamaica	Germany	29/05/1996
Jamaica	Netherlands	01/08/1992
Jamaica	Switzerland	21/11/1991
Jamaica	United Kingdom	14/05/1987
Saint Lucia	Germany	22/07/1987
Saint Lucia	United Kingdom	18/01/1983

(*Continued*)

TABLE A.3 (Continued)

Country	*Partner Country*	*Entry into Force Date*
Saint Vincent and the Grenadines	Taiwan Province of China	01/02/2010
Saint Vincent and the Grenadines	Germany	08/01/1989
Trinidad and Tobago	Guatemala	23/06/2016
Trinidad and Tobago	Switzerland	04/07/2012
Trinidad and Tobago	Mexico	16/09/2007
Trinidad and Tobago	Germany	17/04/2010
Trinidad and Tobago	Korea, Republic of	27/11/2003
Trinidad and Tobago	China	07/12/2004
Trinidad and Tobago	Spain	17/09/2004
Trinidad and Tobago	Cuba	07/01/2000
Trinidad and Tobago	Canada	08/07/1996
Trinidad and Tobago	United States	26/12/1996
Trinidad and Tobago	France	16/05/1996
Trinidad and Tobago	United Kingdom	08/10/1993

Note: There are also 2 terminated BITs:

- Barbados-Italy BIT (1995) – Terminated
- India-Trinidad and Tobago BIT (2007) – Terminated

INDEX